CAREER INFORMATION, CAREER COUNSELING, AND CAREER DEVELOPMENT

Tenth Edition

CAREER INFORMATION, CAREER COUNSELING, AND CAREER DEVELOPMENT

Duane Brown, Professor Emeritus

University of North Carolina, Chapel Hill

Boston   Columbus   Indianapolis   New York   San Francisco   Upper Saddle   River
Amsterdam   Cape Town   Dubai   London   Madrid   Milan   Munich   Paris   Montreal   Toronto
Delhi   Mexico City   Sao Paulo   Sydney   Hong Kong   Seoul   Singapore   Taipei   Tokyo

Vice President and Editor in Chief: Jeffery W. Johnston
Senior Acquisitions Editor: Meredith D. Fossel
Editorial Assistant: Nancy Holstein
Marketing Director: Margaret Waples
Senior Marketing Manager: Christopher Barry
Marketing Manager: Chris Barry
Managing Editor: Pamela D. Bennett
Senior Project Manager: Mary M. Irvin
Senior Operations Specialist: Laura Messerly
Senior Art Director: Jayne Conte
Cover Designer: Karen Salzbach
Cover Art: Fotolia
Full-Service Project Management: Chitra Ganesan/PreMediaGlobal
Composition: PreMediaGlobal
Printer/Binder: Courier/Westford
Cover Printer: Lehigh-Pheonix Color Corp
Text Font: 10/12 Times

Every effort has been made to provide accurate and current Internet information in this book. However, the Internet and information posted on it are constantly changing, so it is inevitable that some of the Internet addresses listed in this textbook will change.

Library of Congress Cataloging-in-Publication Data
Brown, Duane.
 Career Information, Career Counseling, and Career Development / Duane Brown.—10th ed.
  p. cm.
 Rev. ed. of: Career information, career counseling, and career development. 9th ed. 2007.
 Includes index.
 ISBN-13: 978-0-13-705194-6
 ISBN-10: 0-13-705194-8
 1. Vocational guidance. 2. Vocational guidance—Bibliography. 3. Vocational guidance—Information services.
4. Information storage and retrieval systems—Vocational guidance. I. Brown, Duane. Career information, career counseling, and career development. II. Title.

HF5381.B67583   2012
658.3'124—dc22

                                                                                    2010040665

10 9 8 7 6 5 4 3 2 1

www.pearsonhighered.com

ISBN 10:   0-13-705194-8
ISBN 13: 978-0-13-705194-6

To Lee E. Isaacson

*The first to show me the importance of career development
and helping people make career decisions*

BRIEF CONTENTS

PART I Foundations of Career Development Practice 1

Chapter 1 Introduction to the Global Economy, Social Justice, and Career Development 2

Chapter 2 Trait-and-Factor and Developmental Theories of Career Choice and Development and Their Applications 24

Chapter 3 Learning Theory-Based, Postmodern, Socioeconomic, and Decision-Making Theories and Their Applications 59

Chapter 4 Ethical and Legal Guidelines and the Competencies Needed for Career Development Practice 80

PART II Career Counseling, Assessment, and Information Dissemination 95

Chapter 5 A Values-Based, Multicultural Approach to Career Counseling and Advocacy 96

Chapter 6 Clients with Special Needs 117

Chapter 7 Assessment in Career Counseling and Development 142

Chapter 8 Using Information to Facilitate Career Development 178

Chapter 9 Virtual and Brick and Mortar Career Exploration Centers: Design and Implementation 192

PART III Facilitating Action Taking 211

Chapter 10 Preparing for Work 212

Chapter 11 Facilitating the Global Job Search: Employability Skills and Placement Services 234

PART IV Managing Career Development Programs in Private and Public Domains 255

Chapter 12 Designing and Implementing Comprehensive K–12 Career Development Programs Within the Framework of the ASCA National Model 256

Chapter 13 Career Development in Postsecondary Educational Institutions 292

Chapter 14 Career Counselors in Private Practice: Counseling, Coaching, and Consulting 313

Chapter 15   Career Development Programming in Business
Organizations   330

Chapter 16   Program Evaluation and Evidence-Based Practice   349

PART V   Trends and Issues: Looking Ahead   361

Chapter 17   Trends in the Labor Market and the Factors
That Shape Them   362

Chapter 18   Trends and Issues in Career Information, the Job Search,
Career Development, and Career Development
Programming   373

CONTENTS

Preface   xviii

Part I   Foundations of Career Development Practice   1

Chapter 1   INTRODUCTION TO THE GLOBAL ECONOMY, SOCIAL JUSTICE, AND CAREER DEVELOPMENT   2

Things to Remember   2

What Factors Led to Globalization?   4

The Unflattened Worker and Social Justice   5

   Social Justice in the United States   5

Is a New Model for Career Development Practice Needed?   7

History of Vocational Guidance and Career Development   9

The Need for Career Development Services   13

The Language of Career Development   13

   Defining Position, Job, Occupation, Career, and Career Development   14

   Career Interventions Defined   15

Organizations and Publications   17

Why People Work   17

   The Future of Work   18

The Goals of This Book   20

   Summary   21   •   Chapter Quiz   21   •   References   22

Chapter 2   TRAIT-AND-FACTOR AND DEVELOPMENTAL THEORIES OF CAREER CHOICE AND DEVELOPMENT AND THEIR APPLICATIONS   24

Things to Remember   24

The Purposes and Evaluation of Theory   25

   A History of Career Development Theorizing   27

Introduction to the Theories   29

Trait-and-Factor Theories   30

   Holland's Theory of Vocational Choice   30

   Theory of Work Adjustment (TWA)   34

A Values-Based Theory of Occupational Choice   37

   Variables That Influence Career Choice and Satisfaction   37

   Propositions of Brown's Values-Based Theory   40

Developmental Theories   41

Super's Life Span, Life Space Theory   42

Gottfredson's Theory of Circumscription and Compromise   49

Summary   53   •   Chapter Quiz   53   •   References   54

Chapter 3   LEARNING THEORY–BASED, POSTMODERN, SOCIOECONOMIC, AND DECISION-MAKING THEORIES AND THEIR APPLICATIONS   59

Things to Remember   59

Theories Based in Learning Theory   60

Krumboltz's Social Learning Theory   60

A Social Cognitive Perspective   62

A Career Information–Processing Model of Career Choice   64

Postmodern Theories   66

A Contextualist Theory of Career   66

Complexity, Chaos, and Nonlinear Dynamics: A Chaos Theory of Career Development and Spirituality   67

Postmodern Career Counseling   69

A Second Approach to Postmodern Career Counseling: Solution-Focused Brief Career Counseling   71

Socioeconomic Theories   73

Status Attainment Theory   73

Dual Labor Market Theory   73

Race, Gender, and Career   73

Theories of Decision Making   74

Status and Use of Decision-Making Theories   75

Summary   77   •   Chapter Quiz   77   •   References   77

Chapter 4   ETHICAL AND LEGAL GUIDELINES AND COMPETENCIES NEEDED FOR CAREER DEVELOPMENT PRACTICE   80

Things to Remember   80

Ethical Principles   81

Principle 1: Above All, Do No Harm (Section A.4.a)   82

Principle 2: Be Competent (Sections C.2.a, b, c, d, and f)   82

Principle 3: Respect Clients' Rights to Choose Their Own Directions (Section A.4.b)   83

Principle 4: Honor Your Responsibilities (Section C)   83

Principle 5: Make Accurate Public Statements (Section C.3)   84

Principle 6: Respect Counselors and Practitioners from Other Professions (Section D)   84

Principle 7: Advocate for Clients in Need (Section A.6.a)   85

Legal Issues and Career Counseling   86

The Competencies Needed by Career Counselors   87

NCDA Competencies and Performance Indicators   87

Credentialing Career Development Practitioners   91

Summary   92   •   Chapter Quiz   92   •   References   93

Part II   Career Counseling, Assessment, and Information Dissemination   95

Chapter 5   A VALUES-BASED, MULTICULTURAL APPROACH TO CAREER COUNSELING AND ADVOCACY   96

Things to Remember   96

Career Counseling Defined   97

Foundation of the Values-Based Approach   98

Values-Based Multicultural Career Counseling (VBMCC)   99

Step 1: Assessing Cultural Variables   99

Step 2: Communication Style and Establishing the Relationship   100

Step 3: Facilitating the Decision-Making Process   103

Step 4: The Identification of Career Issues (Assessment)   103

Steps 5 and 6: The Establishment of Culturally Appropriate Goals and the Selection of Culturally Appropriate Interventions   106

Step 7: The Implementation and Evaluation of the Interventions Used   107

Step 8: Advocacy   107

Some Specifics for Different Minority Groups   108

African Americans   109

Hispanic Americans   109

Asian Americans   110

American Indians   110

Application of VBMCC to Group Career Counseling   111

Developing Your Own Theory   112

Summary   113   •   Chapter Quiz   114   •   References   114

Chapter 6   CLIENTS WITH SPECIAL NEEDS   117

Things to Remember   117

Individuals with Disabilities   118

Career Counseling for Individuals with Disabilities   120

Career Counseling for Individuals with Mental Illness   122

Women in the Workforce   123

Career Counseling for Women   123

Displaced Workers   124

Career Counseling for Displaced Workers   125

The Economically Disadvantaged   125

Career Counseling for the Economically Disadvantaged   127

Gay, Lesbian, Bisexual, and Transgender Individuals   128

Counseling Gay, Lesbian, Bisexual, and Transgendered Clients   129

Atypical Time of Entrance to the Labor Force   129

Former Military Personnel   129

Ex-Offenders   131

Midlife Job Changers   132

Voluntary Changers   133

Older Workers   134

Career Counseling for Older Workers   135

Summary   137   •   Additional Resources   138
•   Chapter Quiz   138   •   References   138

**Chapter 7 ASSESSMENT IN CAREER COUNSELING
AND DEVELOPMENT   142**

Things to Remember   **142**

Personal-Psychological Characteristics   143

Aptitude   143

Interests   143

Personality   144

Values   144

The Marriage Between Tests and Career Counseling   145

**Clinical, Quantitative, and Qualitative Approaches
to Assessment   146**

Quantitative Assessment   146

Qualitative Assessment and Constructivist Theory   148

Quantitative and Objective Assessment Devices   151

Selecting Assessment Devices   168

Technical Qualities   168

Gender and Cultural Bias   169

Other Issues   171

Interpreting Test and Inventory Results   171

Summary   173   •   Chapter Quiz   173   •   References   173

Chapter 8 USING INFORMATION TO FACILITATE CAREER DEVELOPMENT 178

Things to Remember 178

Occupational and Labor Market Information 179

Two Important Sources of Information 180

The Occupational Information Network (O*NET) 180

The Occupational Outlook Handbook 183

Other Types of Occupational Information 184

Children's Materials 188

Educational Information 189

Summary 190 • Chapter Quiz 190 • References 191

Chapter 9 VIRTUAL AND BRICK AND MORTAR CAREER EXPLORATION CENTERS: DESIGN AND IMPLEMENTATION 192

Things to Remember 192

Establishing a CEC 193

Basic Criteria for Locating and Designing a CEC 194

Basic Technological Competencies 195

Should CACGS Be Included in the CEC? 197

What Are Some Frequently Used CACGS? 199

Other CACGS 204

Present Status of CACGS 204

The ASVAB Career Exploration Program 205

Using the Internet to Provide Career Counseling and Assessment 205

Career Assessment Devices Online 207

Summary 207 • Chapter Quiz 208 • References 208

Part III Facilitating Action Taking 211

Chapter 10 PREPARING FOR WORK 212

Things to Remember 212

Training Time 213

High School and Preparation for Work 214

Vocational Education 214

Work Experience Programs 215

Academies 217

Outside the Classroom—No Diploma Required 217

On-the-Job Training   218

Job Training Partnership Act as Amended by STWOA of 1994   218

The Job Corps   219

**Outside the Classroom—High School Diploma Preferred
or Required 220**

Apprenticeship Programs   220

Military Training   222

Postsecondary Schools: Associate's Degrees or Certificates 224

Trade, Vocational, and Technical Schools   224

Community Colleges and Junior Colleges   226

Colleges and Universities 227

Admissions Requirements   227

Financial Aid   229

Factors to Consider When Choosing a College   230

Gaining Admission to College: An Application Strategy   230

Accreditation   231

Continuing Education Needed   231

Summary   232   •   *Chapter Quiz*   •   *References   233*

**Chapter 11 FACILITATING THE GLOBAL JOB SEARCH:
EMPLOYABILITY SKILLS AND PLACEMENT
SERVICES 234**

Things to Remember   234

The Job Search 234

Employability Skills 235

Job Seekers with Disabilities and Those with
Criminal Records   237

Executing the Job Search 237

Step 1: Taking an Inventory of Self and Skills   237

Step 2: Investigating the Job Market   238

Step 3: Developing Employability Skills   239

Job Placement Services 245

Public Employment Services   246

Private Employment Agencies   247

Secondary and Postsecondary School Placement Services   248

Online Job Placement Centers   250

Outplacement Services   251

Summary   252   •   *Chapter Quiz   253*   •   *References   253*

Part IV   Managing Career Development Programs in Private and Public Domains   255

Chapter 12   DESIGNING AND IMPLEMENTING COMPREHENSIVE K–12 CAREER DEVELOPMENT PROGRAMS WITHIN THE FRAMEWORK OF THE ASCA NATIONAL MODEL   256

Things to Remember   256

Historical Background   257

The ASCA Model and Career Development   258

The Process of Program Development   264

Gaining Administrative Support   264

Establishing Preconditions   264

Forming a Planning Committee   265

Conducting a Needs Assessment   265

Writing Goals and Objectives and Establishing Criteria for Success   266

Designing the Career Development Program   269

Addressing the Issue: Program Implementation   271

Budgeting   271

Selecting a Management System   271

Planning and Implementing the Guidance Curriculum   272

Planning and Implementing Individual Student Planning   274

Assessment   277

The End Product   278

Planning and Implementing Responsive Services   278

Planning and Implementing Evaluation and Accountability: Some General Considerations   280

Program Planning Tips: Elementary School   282

Program Planning Tips: Middle School   283

Careers Classes   285

Involving Parents   285

Program Planning Tips: High School   286

Targeting High School Students with Special Needs   286

Involving Community Resources in the Program   288

Summary   289   •   Chapter Quiz   289   •   References   290

Chapter 13   CAREER DEVELOPMENT IN POSTSECONDARY EDUCATIONAL INSTITUTIONS   292

Things to Remember   292

The Students   294

The Institutions   295

Career Development Programs   296

Career Resource Centers   296

Developing the Program   297

An In-Depth Look at Career Program Activities   301

Brief Activity: Web Sites   301

Brief Activity: Advising   302

Brief Activity: Major Fairs   303

Brief Activity: Career Courses   303

Brief Activity: Workshops and Seminars   304

Brief Activity: Self-Directed Activities   304

Brief Activity: Information Dispensation   305

Individualized Case-Managed Activities Internships   305

Consultation   305

Career Counseling   305

Peer Counseling Programs   307

Program Evaluation   308

Summary   309   •   Chapter Quiz   310   •   References   310

Chapter 14   CAREER COUNSELORS IN PRIVATE PRACTICE: COUNSELING, COACHING, AND CONSULTING   313

Things to Remember   313

Qualifications for Private Practice   314

Guidelines for Consumers   314

Credentials   314

Fees   315

Promises   315

Ethics   315

Career Coaching   315

Establishing a Private Practice   317

Types of Services   318

Location of the Office   319

Image   319

Marketing the Service   321

Budgeting   323

Fees   325

Billing   327

Other Business Details   327

Summary   328   •   Chapter Quiz   328   •   References   329

Chapter 15 CAREER DEVELOPMENT PROGRAMMING IN BUSINESS ORGANIZATIONS 330

Things to Remember 330

Programming for Career Development 332

A Brief History 332

Rationale 333

Initiating the Program 334

Early Steps 334

Needs Assessment 335

Designing the Program 338

The Essential Components 339

Integration with HRD 344

Program Implementation 344

Benefits 345

Summary *346* • Chapter Quiz *346* • References *347*

Chapter 16 PROGRAM EVALUATION AND EVIDENCE-BASED PRACTICE 349

Things to Remember 349

Levels of Questions 350

Evaluation Designs 351

Pre-Experimental Designs 351

Quasi-Experimental and Experimental Evaluation Designs 352

Descriptive Designs 353

The Process of Survey Research 354

Qualitative Evaluation Strategies 356

Which Approach to Evaluation? 357

Summary *358* • Chapter Quiz *359* • References *359*

Part V Trends and Issues: Looking Ahead 361

Chapter 17 RENDS IN THE LABOR MARKET AND THE FACTORS THAT SHAPE THEM 362

Things to Remember 362

Causes of Long-Term Trends 364

Technology 364

The Global Economy 365

Other Economic Factors 366

Population Factors 366

The Size of Government 368

Causes of Short-Term Trends 368

The Occupational World Through 2018 369

Projections for the Future 369

Practical Implications 370

Sources of Information on Change and Structure 371

Summary 371 • *Chapter Quiz 371* • *References 372*

Chapter 18 TRENDS AND ISSUES IN CAREER INFORMATION, THE JOB SEARCH, CAREER DEVELOPMENT, AND CAREER DEVELOPMENT PROGRAMMING 373

Things to Remember 373

Trends: Career Information 375

Trends: The Job Hunt 376

Trends: Career Assessment 377

Trends: Career Counseling 377

Trends: Career Development Programming 379

Summary 380 • *Chapter Quiz 381* • *References 381*

Name Index 385

Subject Index 391

PREFACE

The tenth edition of *Career Information, Career Counseling, and Career Development* incorporates many changes, including the addition of some pedagogical aids, an emphasis on the global economy, new discussions of the impact of changes in the global economy on the labor market in the United States, and the increasing importance of technology—especially the Internet. With regard to the Internet I discuss how it can be used to provide free career services, high-quality occupational materials and assessment devices. In 2010, the Department of Labor began to incorporate the Interest Profiler into O*NET, and my prediction is that other inventories will be integrated into the O*NET system in the near future. O*NET will provide a platform for establishing an inexpensive source of assessment data and occupational information once the Interest Profiler is integrated into the system.

NEW TO THIS EDITION

- Three pedagogical aids have been added to each chapter. Chapters begin with an advance organizer called Things to Remember, a list of key points that follow in the text. A Student Learning Exercise within each chapter incorporates major points being discussed. Each chapter concludes with a ten-item true-false quiz.
- Chapter 1 illustrates the impact of the global economy on workers in the United States and throughout the world, ands it also shows that economic success is the key to social justice and that career development specialists can help clients of all types find the key that opens the door to good jobs and economic success.
- Chapter 1 sets the stage for the remainder of Part I, **Foundations of Career Development Practice**. One of the major objectives of this section is to promote the idea that there is nothing as practical as a good theory by illustrating how each of the major theories can be applied.
- Part II, **Career Counseling, Assessment, and Information Dissemination**, addresses the major interventions used by career counselors. The primary objective of this section is to provide a comprehensive model of career counseling, in Chapter 5, that can be used with all client groups, including minority groups, and to supplement that model with additional material in the remaining chapters.
- Part III, **Facilitating Action Taking**, examines issues associated with preparing for work on the job, in postsecondary institutions, and in apprenticeship programs. The final step in the action-taking process, becoming employed either in this country or abroad, is also addressed.
- Part IV, **Managing Career Development Programs in Private and Public Domains**, generally addresses the issue of developing career development programs in public schools, postsecondary institutions, businesses, and community private practices.
- Chapter 16, Program Evaluation and Evidence-Based Practice, is new to this edition. It focuses on the stands recently taken by the American School Counselor Association (ASCA), the American Psychological Association (APA), and the American Counseling Association (ACA) regarding the importance of accountability and evidence-based practice.

- Part V, **Trends and Issues: Looking Ahead**, addresses labor market projections made by the Bureau of Labor Statistics through 2018 as well as my prognostications about changes in career development programming and practice during the same period.
- Council for the Accreditation of Counseling and Related Educational Programs (CACREP) standards are listed and correlated to the chapters where they are met (see inside front cover).

FEATURES RETAINED FROM PREVIOUS EDITIONS

Multiculturalism in career counseling and development has been one of the highlights of this text for many years. That emphasis is continued and strengthened, as is the focus on the poor and disenfranchised and client groups such as offenders, veterans, and workers who are displaced because of the restructuring of the overall labor market. Discrimination is still a major problem in the workplace. Until recently, career development specialists have not had the tools and ethical mandates to address this issue. Advocacy is that tool, and recent changes in the ethical standards of the ACA provide the ethical mandate for advocacy. Career counselors also need to prepare their clients to become advocates for themselves. Women; racial and ethnic minorities; and gay, lesbian, bisexual, and transgender clients should be prepared to deal with discrimination. Moreover, career development specialists should be prepared to become advocates to reduce the incidence of discrimination in the workplace. In my view, we need to return to the roots of the career development movement. The founders of the movement knew that without advocacy and high-quality career development programs, school dropouts, newly arrived immigrants, and people displaced by the restructuring of the occupational structure had little chance of succeeding in the emerging industrial economy.

Several other features have been retained in this edition:

- A focus on meeting all of the career development standards established by the Council for the Accreditation of Counseling and Related Educational Programs (CACREP) necessary for program accreditation.
- Bloch's chaos theory.
- Sections on the application of all career development theories to racial and ethnic minorities.
- Strategies for helping workers who are disabled, displaced, older, or late entry, and others who do not fit the pattern of the high school or college student who goes to school and then to work.
- A discussion regarding the use of the Armed Services Vocational Aptitude Battery (ASVAB), which can be used to help students in high school and postsecondary institutions.
- An illustration of how the ASCA National Model can be used to design a career development program that is fully integrated into the school counseling program.
- Cutting-edge insight into the use of technology to foster career development.
- Explanations of the factors that influence labor market forces and what it will be like in the future.

AUDIENCE

This book is intended to help those who are now engaged, or who expect to be engaged, in facilitating the career development process. It is written expressly with school counselors, rehabilitation counselors, counseling psychologists, employment counselors, placement officers, and career counselors in mind. However, teachers, media specialists, social workers, and others who are influential in the career development process can benefit from the contents of the book.

APPROACH

Like the previous editions of this book, the tenth edition includes both theory and practical applications. The theoretical background is included as one means of helping the reader understand why certain practical approaches may be useful and why work is an important aspect of people's lives. The practical tools allow the reader to gain specific knowledge and skills needed to assist with career development problems. The practical applications also help the reader understand how to design and deliver career development programs in various settings.

ACKNOWLEDGMENTS

I would like to thank the following reviewers for their comments and insights: Larry Buzas, Western Michigan University; Aaron Jackson, Brigham Young University; Varunee Faii Sangganjanavanich, Texas A&M University; and David Scott, Clemson University.

I would also like to thank my wife, Sandra, who has encouraged and supported me throughout my career.

D. B.

Career Information, Career Counseling, and Career Development

PART

I

Foundations of Career Development Practice

1

Introduction to the Global Economy, Social Justice, and Career Development

Things to Remember

- The global economy and its implications for employment in the United States
- The factors that flattened the world economy
- The language of career development

- The reasons why careers and career development are important in the fight for social justice
- The major events in the history of career development

In 2005 Thomas Friedman, a Pulitzer Prize-winning columnist for the *New York Times*, declared in his book about the global economy that the world is flat. His book was not an attempt to turn the clock back to pre-Columbian times when it was widely believed that sailing ships that ventured too far out to sea would fall off the end of the flat earth to their destruction. Rather it was Friedman's attempt to explain how the economy, once made up largely of discrete local economies, had merged into a global economy. Earlier Joseph Stiglitz (2002, 2003), a Nobel Prize winner in economics who acknowledged that globalization of the world's economies was in full swing, defended the impact of the global economy against what he termed its discontents and laid out some of the problems with the economic changes that were occurring and are likely to continue to occur regardless of the barriers that politicians and others erect to protect local economies. The bottom line for both Stiglitz and Friedman is that the global economy is a reality, and for better, and sometimes for worse, it is here to stay.

Today few scholars or knowledgeable laypeople need proof of the existence of the global economy. The interconnectedness of the major economies of the world is a reality, and the economic recession that began in 2008 and continues at this time provides a grim reminder of its presence. In January 2008 the unemployment rate in the United States stood at 4.9 percent. It had risen to 7.2 percent by December of that year and now stands at over 10 percent (BLS, 2009a,d).

Because the United States has the world's largest economy and consumers in this country purchase a large portion of goods and services produced in other countries, the unemployment rates in other countries throughout the world began to rise as the overall purchasing power of U.S. consumers declined. This situation was exacerbated by high levels of credit card debt, the inability of home owners to make mortgage payments, and the high level of foreclosures by lending institutions.

The unemployment rate in the European Union (EU) stood at a collective 9.2 percent in September 2009, led by Spain at 19.3 percent and Ireland at 13.0 percent. Other EU countries had substantially lower unemployment rates. Austria (4.8 percent), Denmark (6.4 percent), and Germany (7.6 percent) were countries that had the lowest unemployment rates (OpenMarket.org, 2009). Russia's economy, which is closely tied to the price of petroleum, had fared a bit better than the average EU country in that its unemployment rate stood at about 6.4 percent. Nevertheless, if the demand for and thus the price of oil continues to decline, it is expected that the unemployment rate in Russia might rise dramatically. Reports form China, which has the world's most carefully managed economy and is the major exporter of goods to the United States, indicate that the urban unemployment in August 2009 stood at 4.2 percent (Yingzi, 2009). However, millions of migrant Chinese workers who travel to cities to find jobs have become discouraged and returned to their villages in rural China, and their numbers are probably not reflected in the unemployment rate, according to a National Public Radio report by Lim (2009). Some estimates of the unemployment rates among the Chinese migrant workers run as high as 15 percent or 20 million workers. The latest available data form Japan, another major U.S. trading partner, places its unemployment rate at 5.3 percent (TradingEconomics, 2009). In an interconnected economic world, when a country with one of the major economies suffers, other countries suffer as well, typically in the form of higher unemployment.

The global economy has given us new vocabulary and a new reality about the labor market. Words and phrases such as offshoring, workforce restructuring, outsourcing, insourcing, home sourcing, in-forming, and of course all of the words, phrases, and ideas associated with the Internet have been incorporated into our day-to-day conversations. Words such as offshoring and outsourcing in particular make it clear that jobs that once were protected by a country's borders, and in some instances by protective tariffs, are now offered on a competitive basis to workers around the world.

Placing jobs and entire industries offshore—that is, in other countries—was initiated decades ago by business leaders in industries such as textiles, furniture, and steel. They saw this as a way to increase profits because of lower wages and fewer government regulations and environmental protection requirements in those countries. Labor cost differences have received the greatest attention and blame for offshoring and outsourcing, perhaps because data regarding the relative labor costs in the United States and other countries are readily available (BLS, 2009b). In 2007 the average comparative compensation (wages plus fringe benefits) costs for U.S. production workers was $24.59. Several countries had higher costs including Canada, Australia, and many European countries. Spain, Portugal, Hungary, the Czech Republic, and Greece were the exceptions. All Asian countries for which data were available had labor costs that were lower than the United States for the same period, some dramatically lower. Sri Lanka's average compensation for production workers was 61 cents per hour followed in ascending order by the Philippines ($1.10), Hong Kong ($5.78), Taiwan, ($6.58), Israel ($13.91), Republic of Korea ($16.02), and Japan ($19.75) (BLS 2009b). Data about wages in China may be harder to collect and perhaps that is the reason they are not included in the Bureau of Labor Statistics (BLS) international database. However, a 2005 report estimated that the average net monthly wages for Chinese manufacturing workers was $134 (World Salaries, 2005). It is also worth noting that the average workweek for these workers is six days.

As mentioned earlier, the most frequently cited basis for outsourcing is the differential between U.S. wages and those in other countries. Wage differential is also one of the reasons for insourcing—the placement of jobs in the United States by businesses in other countries. Hyundai, Kia, Toyota, Honda, Mercedes Benz, Nissan, BMW and other auto manufacturers now assemble many of their cars in the United States, primarily but not exclusively in "right to work states" such as North Carolina, South Carolina, Alabama, and Tennessee that prohibit the establishment of "closed shops"—unionized labor forces that preclude workers from employment in a workplace unless they join the union. Another reason why foreign businesses place a part of their operation in the United States is the size of the U.S. market. Since World War II the United States has been the world's largest economy and its citizens, relative to people in many other countries, generally have a great deal of money at their disposal once necessities such as food and housing are accounted for. Although it is assumed by many that the U.S. economy is losing the outsourcing-insourcing battle for jobs, accurate statistics are difficult to find. What can be assumed is that in the flattened world described by Friedman (2005), U.S. workers will increasingly find themselves looking for jobs outside of this country, and they need to prepare for that eventuality.

WHAT FACTORS LED TO GLOBALIZATION?

Friedman (2005) identified a number of economic "flatteners" beginning with the fall of the Berlin wall which opened up the economies of Eastern Europe and the former Soviet Union. He also lists the Internet, which first came into commercial use in the United States in the 1990s. Friedman points out that almost as quickly as the Internet became a commercial force a digital divide developed between richer and poorer countries, and the advent of outsourcing and off-shoring became a flattening force.

Although it is difficult to disagree with the "flattening forces" identified by Friedman, it seems that the competitive drive of the free market system (the profit motive), treaties such as the North American Free Trade Agreement (NAFTA) which reduced trade barriers among the United States, Canada and Mexico, and the decision by China to move from an economy rooted in communism to one that encouraged entrepreneurship and the accumulation of wealth were also major factors in the development of the global economy. To be sure, computers, ingenious software, and the Internet became basic tools in the globalization process, but it was the failure of communism as an economic system, the realization that the free market system was the engine of wealth and job production, and the realization that technology could accommodate a variety of businesses that flattened the earth.

NAFTA, the development of the European Union, and U.S. and Chinese trade agreements are all factors that are aimed at increasing economic productivity by easing the flow of goods and services among countries and reducing the cost of products sold at home. The emergence of NAFTA revealed that a new occupational classification system was needed in order to compare the economic relationships among the United States, Canada, and Mexico. The North American Industry Classification System (NAICS) was developed jointly by the U.S. Economic Classification Policy Committee (ECPC), Statistics Canada, and Mexico's Instituto Nacional de Estadistica y Geografia. This system provides the three countries with a basis for collecting comparative economic data and thus monitoring the impact of NAFTA.

STUDENT LEARNING EXERCISE 1.1

Fill in the blanks in the following statement:

1. Friedman seems to think that the primary "flatteners" of the world's economy were (1) _____ ; (2) _____ ; (3) _____. Brown (the author of this book) believes that Friedman may have overlooked a very important factor in his list, which is _____.

THE UNFLATTENED WORKER AND SOCIAL JUSTICE

Who are the beneficiaries of the global economy? Names like Bill Gates who cofounded Microsoft, Steve Jobs who founded Apple, and Michael Dell who developed Dell Computers come immediately to mind along with some relatively faceless billionaires such as Larry Page and Sergey Brin, the founders of Google. The fact is that many of us have been the beneficiaries of globalization because of the access to global markets that can produce goods and services at costs less than they can be produced in the United States. However, Stiglitz (2002) suggests that the African, Asian, and South American poor cannot be listed among those who have been helped by globalization and suggests that globalization may have exacerbated their plight in some instances. It has certainly been the case that some of the developed countries have exploited workers in poorer countries and added to the pollution of the environment as well.

At all meetings of the International Monetary Fund (IMF), World Bank, and the G20, an organization made up of countries with the world's twenty largest economies, large groups of protesters demand social justice for the poor and protection of the global environment, as well as the elimination of the IMF and World Bank. According to Greenwell (2009), some of these protesters believe that, with the consent of the G 20 countries, the IMF and World Bank have supported policies that are harmful to impoverished people in Africa and elsewhere. Writing about some of the failed policies of the IMF and the World Bank, Stiglitz (2002) seemed to be in agreement with the protestor's charges, but his remedies are far less dramatic than scrapping the IMF and World Bank. According to Stiglitz, stable governments and stable financial systems are prerequisites to reform that benefit the entire citizenry. Friedman (2005) offers some additional ideas when he discusses why the flattening process has bypassed millions. In order to take advantage of the opportunities presented by the global economy, people need to have governments that provide an infrastructure that includes education, health care, and a social network that helps them weather personal disasters such as loss of jobs.

Social Justice in the United States

In his famous "I have a dream" speech, Martin Luther King Jr. envisioned the United States as a place that would be free from racism and discrimination and where there would be equal opportunity for all. Civil rights legislation has brought about many of the changes he envisioned, but certain aspects of the society he hoped would develop are missing, including economic equity.

The early advocates for career development were concerned about oppression and social justice, including economic equity, as are career development practitioners today. In fact, economic equity is at the forefront of the debate about social justice. At the moment the debate is focused on the best method of providing health care for the uninsured millions in this country. Health care is an important part of the social structure needed by individuals who are able to take advantage in a global economy. Hopefully, once the health care issue is settled, the debate will focus on two related issues: improving education and eliminating the digital divide. Our educational system fails nearly 30 percent of students who leave school before graduation and countless others who graduate (Alliance for Excellence in Education, 2009). Because they do not have computers or cannot afford Internet service, they are ill prepared to take advantage of the opportunities in countries other than their own.

Social justice cannot be fully realized unless people have meaningful jobs. It is not enough to have legislation that precludes discrimination in the workplace when the opportunity to prepare for and enter those jobs is missing. Wage differentials between men and women and white and minority workers illustrate clearly that economic equity is an unrealized dream.

The case for social justice for people who have been harmed or marginalized by the global economy has already been joined. Although many improvements are needed in the social safety nets provided in the United States, the vast majority of citizens in this country should be in a position to take advantage of the economic changes that are occurring. However, career development practitioners should not assume that need for advocacy for the poor and marginalized is past. Consider the following:

- The unemployment rate for minorities lags behind that of whites. In July 2009, the U.S. Bureau of Labor Statistic (BLS) reported that the unemployment rate for white workers was 8.7 percent, whereas the rate for African American and Hispanic American workers was 15 percent and 12 percent, respectively (BLS, 2009a).
- In 2003, the median family income for white families was $43,318. The median for African American was $30,000, whereas for Hispanic Americans it was $33,000 (U.S. Census Bureau, 2005).
- Not surprisingly the percentage of white families living in poverty (10.5 percent) was substantially lower than the percentages for African American (24.7 percent) and Hispanic (21.8 percent) families (U.S. Census Bureau, 2005).
- The median income for men who worked full time was $40,668 as compared to $30,724 for women (U.S. Census Bureau, 2005). Melamed (1995, 1996) suggests that this discrepancy is a result of three factors: career choice, unequal time spent on the job, and discrimination. It seems likely that initial career choices and discrimination account for some of the discrepancies among white workers and Hispanic and African American workers.
- Based on workforce data gathered in 2000, participation rates for workers with disabilities ages 20 to 64 was 38 percent as opposed to approximately 80 percent for people without disabilities. Over 25 percent of people with disabilities were living in poverty (Science Daily, 2007).
- Because civil rights, at least at the national level, have not been extended to nonheterosexual workers, the protection against discrimination afforded most workers by the Equal Employment Opportunity legislation is lacking for this group.
- The abandonment of workers by employers who relocate entire industries offshore and displace workers by outsourcing jobs continues at a high rate. Plunkett Research (2009) reports the following:

> Outsourcing will be an approximately $500 billion global industry in 2009, with the largest portions created in three broad areas: (1) logistics, sourcing

and distribution services; (2) information technology services, including the creation of software and the management of computer centers; and (3) business process outsourcing (BPO) areas such as call centers, financial transaction processing and human resources management.

IS A NEW MODEL FOR CAREER DEVELOPMENT PRACTICE NEEDED?

Publications (e.g., Blustein, McWhirter, & Perry, 2005; Peterson & Gonzalez, 2005) have indicated a need for the redefinition and overall reconceptualization of the theory and practice of career development. Peterson and Gonzalez believe that the underlying contemporary assumptions of career development are faulty; they suggest that linear logic, objective truth, and emphasis on empirical proof for career development practices be replaced with recursive thinking, relativism, and the subjective reality of postmodernism.

Blustein and colleagues concur that a new conceptual base is needed for career development, but, drawing on the work of Prilleltensky (1997), they come to a different conclusion regarding the new paradigm. Prilleltensky criticized the traditional approach as being a value-free model that embraces individualism and meritocracy. At the heart of this model is the belief that goal-oriented change is possible—that is, people can choose to better themselves and, as a result, do so. Advocates of the traditional model paid little attention to the factors that led to the oppression, discrimination, and marginalization of millions of people, and they did not address the inequitable distribution of power and money in U.S. society. The implementation of the traditional model focuses on the individual in an apolitical fashion and largely ignores issues such as racism, sexism, and political and economic disenfranchisement. Blustein and colleagues suggest that emphasis on meritocracy and free competition are misguided because the race for social attainment starts at different places for the poor, some racial and ethnic groups, and people with disabilities.

Empowerment is one alternative to the traditional approach. Prilleltensky (1997) identifies the empowerment model, as it is defined in feminist therapy, as the second candidate to underpin psychological practice, or, in our case, career development. This model is aimed at equalizing power and subscribes to a distributive philosophy that suggests that all people should have somewhat equal access to the benefits of society. Like Peterson and Gonzalez (2005), Prilleltensky identifies postmodernism as a third option to underpin psychological practice. However, he dismisses it, apparently because of its relativism on the issue of values. Blustein et. al. (2005) did not comment on options 2 and 3. Instead they endorsed option 4: emancipatory communitarianism. This approach, unlike the others discussed thus far, espouses the belief that the focus of practice should be on both individuals and the systems in which they function. Professionals who adopt emancipatory communitarianism endorse the value of social justice, value human diversity, subscribe to establishing mutual goals, engage in political action to correct inequities in the systems that impact students and workers, and orient themselves to nonclients who are discriminated against or marginalized by the educational and economic systems in the United States. Clearly, Prilleltensky is espousing a concept of social justice that goes beyond ensuring human rights to one that advocates a fairer division of the wealth, resources, and power in U.S. society.

The statistic quoted in the previous section regarding employment, wages, and poverty seem to support the assumption by Blustein and colleagues (2005) suggesting that the current models that underpin career development practice do not provide a basis for addressing the social ills of many of our client groups. Most career development models, including the ubiquitous Holland (1997) theory, focus on providing one-to-one assistance to client groups. Not one of the extant theories provides a basis for addressing the vocational and economic problems identified in the last section. They recommend that the constructs from emancipatory communitarianism (Prilleltensky, 1997) should be incorporated into existing theory, which would result in a focus on the interaction between the contexts in which the individual functions and the individual. Overcoming the barriers present in those contexts would help prepare individuals to make judicious career choices and transform the contexts into supportive elements.

Practice has almost always outstripped theory in the career development arena, and practitioners need not wait for theorists to provide models to move ahead. Career development practitioners can borrow from community psychology (Blustein et al., 2005), organizational development and change theory and practice, and the emerging literature dealing with collaboration in the change process (Brown, Pryzwansky, & Schulte, 2010). In fact, additional theory building may not be needed at all if career development specialists broaden their horizons and adopt theory and practices from other fields. The skills needed by career counselors dedicated to fostering social justice include the traditional skills of individual and small-group career counseling; career coaching; career and educational planning, assessment; job placement; design and delivery of psychoeducational learning experiences; and design and implementation of transitional experiences for a wide array of clients, such as students requiring special education, adults with disabilities, and adults who have been displaced. The skills needed by career development practitioners who wish to address some of the social injustices in U.S. society include consulting, collaboration, systemic assessment, program design, leadership, and advocacy. Additionally, career development practitioners must be fully knowledgeable about legislative initiatives, such as the American with Disabilities Act (ADA), the Ticket to Work and Work Incentives Improvement Act of 1990, and the Individuals with Disabilities Education Improvement Act (IDEA). Blustein et. al. (2005) indicate that knowledge about and use of qualitative research methodology is also an important tool for social activists as they strive to understand the systems in which our client groups function.

Adopting a social justice agenda is not without problems. Individualism is one of the core values of U.S. society (Brown, 2002), and it is difficult for many people in the United States to forgo the ideas that honesty and individual efforts are the prime ingredients for success in the workforce. However, sociologists have long realized the relationship between parental status and occupational attainment (Hotchkiss & Borow, 1996). The status attainment model, first articulated by Blau and Duncan (1967) and expanded by Sewell, Haller, and Portes (1969), suggests that family status and certain cognitive variables, such as intelligence and attitudes about education and occupations, transmitted through the family influence educational attainment, the level of occupation attained, and, ultimately, earnings. The research regarding this theory supports the assertion of Blustein and his colleagues that people begin the race for occupational attainment in vastly different places. Consider the following pairs of people:

- Two high school students, both of whom are white, are of equal intelligence. Student 1 comes from a family in which both parents completed college and have a combined income of $78,000; student 2's parents graduated from high school and went directly to work. No other family members attended college. Student 2's family income is at the median income level for white families, which is approximately $44,000.
- Two high school students are of equal intelligence. Student 1 is white and lives with his divorced mother. His father stopped paying child support several years ago and his mother makes $9.00 per hour in the local textile plant, which is expected to close within the next six months. Student 2 is also white but both her parents have stable jobs assembling computers for a leading computer manufacturer.

- An African American student and a white student both attend the same college. The African American student attended a substandard high school, whereas the white student attended a well-regarded public school in the suburbs. The African American student obtained a generous scholarship but will still have to work 15 hours per week to support himself, whereas the white student's parents are underwriting the entire expense for their son's college education. Both students want to attend law school after completing their bachelor of arts degrees.
- Two African American high school students with excellent grades both want to go to medical school. Because of their financial situations, both students will attend in-state, public universities. Both are admitted to Prestigious University (PU), but because her father was discriminated against when he attended PU, student 1 elects to attend a decidedly inferior university.

Although the emphasis of this book will be on the importance of getting a job, I do not wish to contribute to the myth that escaping from poverty is as easy as getting a job, although it is an essential first step. Jobs may be full-time or part-time, minimum wage or something higher. It is entirely possible to have a job or perhaps more than one full-time job and be among the working poor depending on the number of family members, the cost of housing, and a variety of other factors. In 2007 the Bureau of Labor Statistics published the results of a 2005 study by the U.S. Census Bureau regarding the working poor. In 2005 approximately 7.7 million people were classified as the "working poor." The Bureau of Labor Statistics (BLS, 2007) classified people as working poor if they spent at least 27 weeks working and were living below the poverty level. Not surprisingly, African American and Hispanic American workers were more likely to be classified as working poor than whites. In the survey reported by BLS, whites accounted for about seven in ten of the working poor although the ratio of working poor to nonworking poor was higher for African Americans and Hispanics than it was for whites. Factors that reduced the likelihood of falling into the working poor category were working full-time as opposed to working part-time, higher educational attainment, having no children, being older than 25, and being male.

Economic status, quality of basic and advanced education, and values passed on by the family and others influence career choice and occupational attainment. As Blustein and colleagues (2005) suggest, career development practitioners must assume a perspective that includes individuals within their contexts. The remainder of this book focuses on both traditional skills and some of the skills needed by the socially aware career development practitioner.

HISTORY OF VOCATIONAL GUIDANCE AND CAREER DEVELOPMENT

The current calls for the adoption of a new paradigm for the theory and practice of career counseling and the delivery of other career development services that focuses on both individuals and the social contexts are not new. They in fact reflect a century-old echo of the voices of the social reformers who founded the vocational guidance movement in education, business and industry, and elsewhere. Their concerns involved the immigrants from Europe, who came to the United States by the tens of thousands; high school dropouts, who were unprepared for the workplace; oppression in the workplace; substandard public schools; and the need to apply scientific principles to career planning and vocational education. These social reformers of the early twentieth century formed the National Society for the Promotion of Industrial Education (NSPIE) in 1906, which became the parent organization of the National Vocational Guidance Association (NVGA) in 1913. These early reformers were advocates for vocational education and they carried their fight to the legislative arena, to state legislators, to the National Education Association, and beyond. One of NSPIE's achievements was drafting and successfully lobbying for the passage of the Smith–Hughes act in 1917, legislation that laid the foundation for land grant universities and vocational education in public schools (Stephens, 1970).

These earlier reformers were advocates. One mechanism they used to initiate local reforms was the settlement house, which was a place in a working-class neighborhood that housed researchers who studied people's lives and problems in that neighborhood. In 1901, Frank Parsons founded the Civic Service House in Boston's North End, and in 1908, the Vocation Bureau, an adjunct of the Boston Civic Service House was opened in the North End. Leaders working out of the North End house established trade unions and generally conducted other activities aimed at empowering workers. These reformers also performed a variety of educational activities aimed at improving vocational skills. In the Boston Civic Service House, these activities were conducted under the auspices of the Breadwinners' Institute and the Vocation Bureau (Stephens, 1970).

A federal agency, the Employment Management Association (EMA) was formed in 1913. Its goal was to promote vocational guidance in business and in industry. EMA, NVGA, NSPIE, and other organizations lobbied aggressively for systemic changes in business, education, and governmental agencies during the early years of the twentieth century and were highly successful, perhaps because more than 50 groups united in collaborative efforts to lobby for needed reforms. By the late 1920s, the interest in reform had dissipated according to Stephens (1970) because of dissension within NVGA and disagreements among NVGA and other organizations, such as the National Education Association, with which they had partnered to pursue reform.

As can be seen in Table 1.1, formal interest in facilitating career development and occupational choice began in the nineteenth century in places such as San Francisco and Grand Rapids, Michigan. Pioneers such as George Merrill, Jesse B. Davis, Anna Y. Reed, and Frank Parson began a movement that still impacts the lives of millions in the twenty-first century. These social reformers gave the vocational guidance movement its direction. The development of psychometric instruments that could be used to promote self-exploration and as selection devices for business and industry during and after World War I introduced a scientific dimension to the movement and provided much needed tools for practitioners. However, it was not until the Great Depression of the 1930s that systematic occupational information became available in the form of the *Dictionary of Occupational Titles (DOT)*. This publication served as the basis for much of the occupational literature until the development of the Occupational Information Network (O*NET), which was published late in the twentieth century. The transition from the *DOT* to O*NET was completed in 2001.

The decade of the 1970s was an eventful time for career development in public schools because of federal support of a concept known as *career education,* in which funding was provided for 500 career education programs in school districts throughout the United States. However, more than 9,000 school districts experimented with career education in different forms according to Hoyt (2005) and remnants of these programs exist in various forms today. The 2003 American School Counselor Association (ASCA) model for comprehensive school counseling programs contains many of the same elements as the career development envisioned by Hoyt more than 35 years ago.

Serious efforts began in the mid-1960s to apply computer technology to career and educational planning and assessment and for the provision of educational and occupational information. Jo Ann Harris-Bowlsbey was instrumental in the planning that led to the development of the Computerized Vocational Information System (CVIS) in 1968. CVIS provided a method for storing information on about 400 occupations. It continued as a pilot program until 1972 when it was established as a demonstration project and widely adopted (Harris-Bowlsbey, 1990).

TABLE 1.1 Historical Highlights of Vocational Guidance, Career Development, and Career Counseling in the United States

Year	Event
1883	Salmon Richards publishes *Vacophy,* which calls for vacophers to be placed in every town. He envisioned the role of the vacophers as providing vocational assistance to all.
1895	George Merrill experiments with vocational guidance at the California School of Mechanical Arts in San Francisco.
1898–1907	Jesse B. Davis instructs students about the world of work at Central High School in Detroit. In 1907 Davis moves to a principalship in Grand Rapids, MI, where he encourages teachers to relate subject matter to vocations.
1905	Frank Parsons establishes Breadwinners' Institute, a continuing education center for immigrants and youth, in the Civic Service House in Boston.
About 1908	Anna Y. Reed, working in Seattle, WA, and Eli Weaver, in Brooklyn, NY, develop and organize vocational guidance programs in their respective schools.
1908	Philanthropist Mrs. Quincy Shaw organizes the Boston Guidance Bureau to provide assistance to young people based on the work of Frank Parsons, which stressed the importance of a systematic approach to selecting a vocation.
1909	Frank Parsons's book, *Choosing a Vocation,* is published posthumously. The book contains Parsons's tripartite theoretical model, which provided the basis for much of the vocational guidance in the first half of the twentieth century.
1913	The National Vocational Guidance Association (NVGA) is established in Grand Rapids, MI.
1917	The first group intelligence test, the Army Alpha, is used as the basis for placement in World War I. This test leads to an explosion of test and inventory development in the 1920s and a more measured approach to test construction since. During the 1920s and 1930s, assessment devices became important tools to psychologists and counselors interested in helping people make career decisions.
1921	The *National Vocational Guidance Bulletin,* first published in 1915, begins publication on a regular basis. The journal becomes *Occupations: The Vocational Guidance Journal.*
1933–1935	New Deal programs, such as the Civilian Conservation Corps and Work Progress Administration, create employment and educational opportunities for youths and adults.
1939	The first edition of the *Dictionary of Occupational Titles* is published by the U.S. Department of Labor.
1939	E. G. Williamson publishes *How to Counsel Students,* one of the early primers regarding career counseling.
1951	NVGA merges with the American College Personnel Association, the Student Personnel Association for Teacher Education, and the National Association of Guidance Supervisors to form the American Personnel and Guidance Association. The NVGA journal, *Occupations,* becomes the *Personnel and Guidance Association.* The American School Counselor Association joins the group in 1952.
1951	Ginzberg, Ginzburg, Axelrad, and Herma publish the first theory of career development in their book *Occupational Choice: An Approach to a General Theory.*
1952	NVGA begins publishing the *Vocational Guidance Quarterly,* currently published as the *Career Development Quarterly.*

(Continued)

TABLE 1.1 Historical Highlights of Vocational Guidance, Career Development, and Career Counseling in the United States (*Continued*)

Year	Event
1953	Donald Super publishes "A Theory of Vocational Development" in the *American Psychologist*. His is the second developmental theory of career development but becomes the most influential.
1956	Ann Roe publishes *The Psychology of Occupations,* which contains her personality-based theory of career development.
1957	The National Defense Education Act provides money to train school counselors and to support school counseling programs. The primary purpose of this legislation is to facilitate the recruitment of scientists, engineers, and mathematicians to aid in the U.S. response to the Soviet launch of the satellite *Sputnik*.
1959	John Holland publishes "A Theory of Vocational Guidance" in the *Journal of Counseling Psychology*, which lays the groundwork for his influential theory of vocational choice.
1963	The Vocational Education Act provides money for vocational guidance to vocational education students.
1982	The NVGA establishes competencies for career counselors.
1983	National Certified Career Counselor Certification is established by NVGA.
1984	NVGA changes its name to National Career Development Association (NCDA) and changes the name of its journal to *Career Development Quarterly.*
1984	The National Board for Certified Counselors assumes the management of the National Certified Career Counselor Certification program.
1987	NCDA holds its first national convention in Orlando, FL, since becoming part of the American Personnel Association in 1951. Currently NCDA holds annual conferences.
1989	NCDA, in concert with the National Occupational Information Coordinating Committee (NOICC) and the Vocational Education Research Center at Ohio State University, commissions the Gallup Organization to poll Americans to ascertain their use of career development services and information, their perceptions of the availability and quality of these services, and their perceptions of various aspects of the workplace, including discrimination. NCDA and NOICC commission similar polls in 1992, 1994, and 2000.
1990	Americans with Disabilities Act is passed by Congress. Act ensures, among other things, equal access to job opportunities and training for people who have disabilities.
1994	School to Work Opportunities Act is passed by Congress. It provides impetus for public schools to develop challenging educational programs for all, to relate academic subject matter to work, and to help students identify their interests and make educational and career plans.
1994	U.S. Department of Labor launches an effort to develop an occupational classification scheme to replace the *Dictionary of Occupational Titles (DOT)*. Technical reports detailing the development of the new system (O*NET) are published during the years 1995–1997, and the transition from the *DOT* to O*NET is completed by 2001.
2000	National Board for Certified Counselors opts to decommission the National Certified Career Counselor program. NCDA establishes a committee to explore the means of maintaining this program.
2001	NCDA establishes the Master Career Counselor membership category as a means of credentialing career counselors.

Sources: J. M. Brewer (1942); F. W. Miller (1968); A. P. Picchioni and E. C. Bonk (1983); M. Pope (2000); J. J. Schmidt (1999).

During this same period, Donald Super and Roger Myers of Columbia University were working with Frank Minor of IBM to develop the Educational and Career Exploration System (ECES). David Tiedeman, then of Harvard University, developed the Information System for Vocational Decisions (ISVD). These were ambitious projects that attempted to incorporate much of the career counseling process into their programs. From a technological point of view, these programs, which reached the operational stage between 1969 and 1970, were ahead of their time because of their heavy use of computer time (Harris-Bowlsbey, 1990). Today, desktop computers handle programs such as DISCOVER and SIGI PLUS, which are direct descendants of ISVD and ECES, with ease.

Career development has a rich history and, if people such as Hoyt (2005) are accurate, a bright future. However, the zeal with which the early leaders of the vocational guidance movement attacked the career-related problems of their time must be recaptured by twenty-first century practitioners because the problems confronting practitioners today have many parallels with the issues faced by the founders of the career development movement. There is a tide of legal and illegal immigrants entering the United States hoping to find work that will meet their economic needs. Providing career development services to illegal immigrants and their children is a unique challenge that has not been confronted previously because of the legal issues involved in the status of these people. Reaching the citizens in the United States who have been economically marginalized because of oppression and discrimination provides an entirely different, but equally important, challenge. Perhaps as Blustein and his colleagues (2005) suggest, we need a new model to underpin our work. Just as importantly, we need the courage to call into question the laws and practices that limit human development.

THE NEED FOR CAREER DEVELOPMENT SERVICES

It is probably not an exaggeration to say that the need for career development services is at its highest point since the Great Depression of the 1930s. In October 2009 the unemployment rate stood at 10.2 percent, which translated to 15.7 million unemployed. The number of long-term unemployed (27 weeks or more) stood at 5.6 million or approximately 35.6 percent of the unemployed. Of the employed, 9.3 million worked part-time because full-time employment was not available. Another category of workers, often referred to as discouraged workers because they have given up searching for a job, numbered 1.6 million. When the number of unemployed is added to the discouraged workers the number comes to 17.3 million people out of work. (BLS, 2009c) If the number of workers who are involuntarily employed part-time is added to the unemployed group, it is not a stretch to suggest that more than 25 million unemployed are suffering from some form of job loss angst. Moreover, this number does not include the workers who are employed in positions that do not allow them to use the job-related knowledge and skills they have developed. No reliable data exists regarding the number that fall into this underemployed category, but the numbers would likely be in the millions.

THE LANGUAGE OF CAREER DEVELOPMENT

Like all educational and psychological practitioners, career development practitioners, whether they are counselors, psychologists, or placement specialists, have a specialized vocabulary that must be mastered by the neophyte. Some words in this specialized vocabulary have already been introduced: *career, career development,* and *work.* Although jargon relating to career choice and development is interspersed throughout this book, some specialized vocabulary related to career development is defined and discussed in this section.

It should be noted that universal agreement regarding some of the words used to describe various aspects of career choice and development has not been reached. For example, some counselors and psychologists (e.g., Holland, 1997) have retained the word *vocation* and use it synonymously with the words *job* and *occupation*. However, many career counselors and psychologists reject the term *vocation* because it is associated with the idea that people are "called," sometimes by God, to their occupations instead of being active participants in choosing them. This latter group has adopted the term *career choice* to denote the process of selecting a career whereas some practitioners have retained the term *vocational choice*. Two of the leading publications of research dealing with career/vocational development are the *Journal of Vocational Behavior* and the *Career Development Quarterly*. Both journals publish material related to career choice and development, but their titles reflect the preferences of the groups that publish them. As will be seen, the semantic argument about which terms are most meaningful and descriptive is not restricted to the terms *career* and *vocation*. Disagreements abound about which terms are most useful to describe various aspects of career development.

Defining Position, Job, Occupation, Career, and Career Development

Just as *work* and *job* are often used interchangeably, so are the terms *position, job, occupation,* and *career*. More than five decades ago, occupational sociologists, such as Shartle (1959), advanced useful definitions of these terms that have since been endorsed by the NCDA. Shartle defined *position* as a group of tasks performed by one individual; thus, as many positions exist as the number of individuals working. A *job,* according to Shartle, is a group of similar positions in a single business, and an *occupation* is a group of similar jobs in several businesses.

The definitions of *position, job,* and *occupation* are relatively straightforward and are widely accepted, but there is some controversy over the meaning of *career,* as shown by the following five relatively recent definitions of *career*:

The totality of work one does in a lifetime (Sears, 1982).

Career = work + leisure (McDaniels, 1989).

A sequence of positions that one holds during a lifetime of which occupation is only one (Hansen, 1997).

The course of events which constitutes a life; the sequence of occupations and other life roles which combine to express one's commitment to work in his or her total pattern of self-development (Super, 1976, p. 4).

Careers are unique to each person and created by what one chooses or does not choose. They are dynamic and unfold throughout life. They include not only occupations but prevocational and postvocational concerns as well as integration of work with other roles: family, community, leisure (Herr & Cramer,1996).

By examining these five definitions, we can immediately get a sense of the problem involved in defining *career*. The definitions by Super (1976) and Herr and Cramer (1996) are based on a holistic lifestyle concept of career and reflect their beliefs that all life roles are interrelated. Although few people would dispute the idea that life roles are interrelated, it is obvious that the definition of *career* advanced by these authors is not universally accepted.The definition offered by McDaniels (1989) is more circumscribed in that it limits *career* to two roles that he sees as inseparable. The one offered by Sears (1982), which is the definition I have adopted for this book, is based on the concept that career is a series of paid or unpaid occupations or jobs that a person holds throughout his or her life.

I have also adopted Sears's (1982) definition of *career development*—a lifelong process involving psychological, sociological, educational, economic, and physical factors, as well as chance factors that interact to influence the career of an individual. However, I would add *culture* to Sears's list of factors that influence career development. Leong (1991), Luzzo (1992), and Fitzgerald and Betz (1994) correctly note that the influence of cultural background has not been adequately considered in theories of career development, in research on the process of career development, or in career development practice. Research suggests that important factors exist among cultural groups in areas such as career decision-making attitudes and work values (Leong, 1991; Luzzo, 1992). Given the increasingly multicultural nature of our society, our conceptualizations of career development, and our approaches to intervening in the process must take into consideration cultural background.

Career Interventions Defined

A *career intervention* is a deliberate act aimed at enhancing some aspect of a person's career development, including influencing the career decision-making process (Spokane, 1991). Many types of career interventions are available, including career guidance, career development programs, career education, career counseling, career information, and career coaching.

The concept of career intervention is general term that encompasses techniques ranging from career counseling to assessment. In the last decade a concerted effort has been made by the American Psychological Association (APA), the National Association of School Psychologists (NASP), the American School Counselor Association (ASCA), the Association of Counselor Education and Supervision (ACES), and others to identify *researched-based interventions*,—that is, those interventions that have been proved through rigorous research to make a difference in the lives of clients. In 2003 ACES and ASCA established a National Panel for Evidenced-Based School Counseling to establish a protocol for identifying researched-based practices (Carey et al, 2008). NASP and APA have established similar committees, but thus far no concerted effort has been made to identify research-based career interventions, except in schools. However, one of the long-term trends in the field of career development seems likely to be attempts to use stringent scientific standards to identify the best practices.

Career guidance is a broad construct that, like career intervention, encompasses most of the other strategies listed previously and has been used traditionally as the rubric under which all career development interventions were placed. Often, authors speak of career guidance programs (e.g., Herr & Cramer, 1996), which are organized, systematic efforts designed to influence various aspects of the career development of a client group, such as high school or college students (Herr & Cramer, 1996; Spokane, 1991). Career guidance programs may contain some or all of the following: systematic attempts to dispense career information, activities to enhance self-awareness, career planning classes or individual career counseling, job placement, and so forth. The term *career guidance programs* is increasingly being replaced by the term *career development programs,* but it is still widely used, particularly in referring to the career development efforts of counselors working in public schools.

Career education, a term coined in the 1970s (e.g., Hoyt, 1977), is a systematic attempt to influence the career development of students and adults through various types of educational strategies, including providing occupational information, infusing career-related concepts into the academic curriculum, taking field trips to businesses and industries, having guest speakers who represent various occupations talk about their jobs, offering classes devoted to the study of careers, establishing career internships and apprenticeships, and setting up laboratories that simulate career experiences. *Career education programs,* like career development programs, are sometimes used synonymously with career guidance programs, although the scope of career education programs has typically exceeded the scope of career guidance programs. The term *career education,* like *career guidance,* is being rapidly replaced by the term *career development programs* because of the efforts of the American School Counselor Association (2003).

Career counseling is a service provided to a single client or group of clients who come seeking assistance with career choice or career adjustment problems. The process of career counseling involves establishing rapport, assessing the nature of the problem, goal setting, intervention, and termination. The outcomes of career counseling are expected to be some or all of the following: the selection of a career, increased certainty about a career choice that was made prior to the beginning of counseling, enhanced self-understanding, increased understanding of one or more occupations, strategies for making adjustments within the work role, strategies for coordinating the work role with other life roles, and enhanced mental health (Brown & Brooks, 1991).

One aspect of the foregoing definition of career counseling that is receiving increasing attention is the relationship between career and mental health issues. Many researchers (e.g., Betz & Corning, 1993; Krumboltz, 1993) have argued that the two are inseparable though admitting that, at times, they may occur as independent processes. Others, such as Super (1993), have argued that, although career counseling and personal counseling are related, they fall on a continuum, with career counseling focusing on the specific, and personal counseling on the more general concerns of the individual. Still others (Brown, 1995; Brown & Brooks, 1991) argue that, although counselors may address both personal and career problems simultaneously, in some instances proceeding with career counseling is impossible because the psychological state (e.g., depression) of the individual precludes some clients from engaging in goal setting and rational approaches to career decision making.

Career information is sometimes referred to as labor market information (LMI), particularly when it involves providing comprehensive information about job trends, the industries in this country, or comprehensive information systems. Career information comes in a variety of formats including print, film, audiotape, and videotape. However, increasingly, career resource centers rely on information available on the Internet. For example, the U.S. Department of Labor now places all its major publications online, including the most used pieces of occupational information, the *Occupational Outlook Handbook,* all occupational projections, and the newly developed O*NET (the Occupational Information Network). O*NET is the most up-to-date source of information available today and is destined to become the basis for all types of occupational information. Thousands of other sources of information are also available on the Internet.

Career coaching is used in business and industry to signify managers' efforts to facilitate the career development of employees (Hall et al., 1986). Career coaching efforts help employees identify opportunities that exist within their work settings and prepare for and enter new positions. The motivation that underpins career coaching, according to Hall and his actually correct colleagues, is a result of company concern for the employee and the desire to help the business identify the talent it needs to be successful.

Recently career coaching has taken on a meaning that is in many ways akin to career counseling. Bench (2003) suggests that career coaches help clients clarify their values, become aware of the choices available to them, set goals, and move toward meeting those goals. Additionally, career coaches may help clients develop management skills, manage transitions, develop job search skills and conduct job searches, or simply become more effective in their current jobs. Bench (2003) envisions career coaching as a private practice enterprise, whereas Hall and his colleagues (1986) perceive career coaching more narrowly as a managerial function that occurs within the confines of the business.

ORGANIZATIONS AND PUBLICATIONS

As noted earlier in this chapter, the National Career Development Association, a division of the American Counseling Association, was founded in 1913 as the National Vocational Guidance Association. It publishes the *Career Development Quarterly*. Career counselors, school counselors, counseling psychologists, and other professionals who are interested in the career development process often affiliate with this division. Counseling psychologists, along with career counselors, have historically provided leadership for the career development movement. They typically belong to Division 17, Counseling Psychology, of the American Psychological Association. That division publishes the *Journal of Counseling Psychology,* which features a wide array of articles but typically has a section devoted to career development. The editorial board of the *Journal of Vocational Behavior*, a journal not affiliated with a professional organization, has traditionally been dominated by counseling psychologists. Another journal that focuses on career development and is not affiliated with a professional organization is the *Journal of Career Development*. Finally, the Association of Training and Development (ASTD) has a special interest group that focuses primarily on career development within business and industry.

WHY PEOPLE WORK

For most people work is primarily an economic enterprise, a way to earn money to pay for essential and nonessential goods and services. However, economics do not fully explain why people work. In fact many people continue to work long after their lifelong economic needs have been met. Moreover, work is seldom, if ever, only a means by which an individual sustains life. Work has many other functions of equal or sometimes greater importance to both society and the individual. It is one way in which the individual relates to society. Work provides the person, and often the family as well, with status, recognition, affiliation, and similar psychological and sociological products essential for participation in a complex society.

Historically work has had religious and theological meanings. In early Hebrew writings, work was viewed as punishment. Early Christians were offended by work for profit, but this view was reversed by the Middle Ages. During the Reformation, work was considered the only way to serve God. Luther and Calvin viewed work positively, and their attitude combined with Social Darwinism and laissez-faire liberalism to form the foundation of what is now called the Protestant work ethic.

Peterson and Gonzalez (2005) argue that not only is the Protestant work ethic outdated, but it is also the root of many of the ills in our society. They suggest that this ethic is the basis for blaming the poor and disenfranchised because they do not exert enough effort to improve themselves. They suggest that this blame-the-victim approach is deliberately and politically motivated as a means to justify oppressions and abuse in the workplace. They also suggest that the Judeo-Christian work ethic has limited multicultural applicability, is antiwomen, omits the debt that our culture has to our non-Protestant ancestors, and cannot be readily applied to the immigrant population.

There can be little doubt that there is some legitimacy to Peterson and Gonzalez's research, but they seem to be so dedicated to their position that they overlook some historical and current facts. For example, they begin their discussion of ant-Semitism with Martin Luther when in fact anti-Semitism was widespread long before he founded the Protestant movement. They rightly point out that many Asian students excel because of the roots of their culture in Confucian thought and, thus, the Protestant work ethic needs to be supplemented in our thinking with similar perspectives from other cultures. However, they contend that the idea that Asians are held up as the model minority is not to praise Asians but to uphold the belief that other minorities can achieve success by applying the Judeo-Protestant work ethic. Many individuals within all other minority groups have taken similar paths. Peterson and Gonzalez (2005) ignore the success of Hispanic immigrants when judged by unemployment rates and the amount of money returned to Mexico and elsewhere by Hispanics working in the United States.

Finally, their argument that the Judeo-Protestant work ethic is patriarchal, and thus antifeminist, is probably accurate. However, their view that it is an anti-women ethic depends entirely on your view of the role of women in our society. Some radical feminists have decried the role of woman as mother and caregiver because it a traditional role that can, in fact, be linked to the Judeo-Protestant position role. Many women have rejected feminism for this reason. It is probably more accurate to indicate that the current religious position on the role of women in our society is reflected by paraphrasing what is likely a feminist bumper sticker: The role of women is in the house—and Senate.

Another psychological product of work is the development of self-esteem. People feel a sense of mastery in dealing with objects of work, and their self-esteem is enhanced because they are engaging in activities that produce something other people value. Unemployed people often suffer low self-esteem because they believe they cannot produce something other people value.

If we assume that work is one of the central components of life activities for most adults, it is easy to assume that satisfaction derived from work is an important determinant in an individual's total satisfaction. This is obviously a nebulous concept. One research approach to determining job satisfaction has been to ask workers, "What type of work would you try to get into if you could start all over again?" One might logically infer that workers who choose the same occupation see greater likelihood of satisfaction in their present occupation than in any other field. Occupations named most frequently in response are those in which incumbents appear to have the greatest degree of control and the feeling that what they do is recognized as important by others. Such studies usually reveal that professions such as university professor, mathematician, biologist, and chemist show high percentages (80 or 90 percent) of practitioners stating that they would choose the same occupation again. Unskilled and blue-collar workers show the lowest percentages (in the teens or low twenties), and white-collar and skilled workers fall in the middle range. Hoyt and Lester (1995) found that nearly two-thirds of all workers would seek more information about jobs if they were starting over. Apparently many workers feel that they might find more satisfactory jobs than the ones they held at the time of the surveys.

The Future of Work

Futurists such as Toffler (1980), Johnston and Parker (1987), and Naisbett and Aburdene (1990) have correctly predicted many of the changes that have occurred in the labor force, although they have failed in many instances to gauge the magnitude of many of the recent shifts due to globalization. Most futurists anticipated the importance of the computer in the workplace. Predictions about the increasing decentralization of the workplace were also anticipated. Many work from their homes—called home sourcing in the parlance of the modern labor force—while many major airlines such as Delta have outsourced many of its reservation agent jobs to other countries. Similarly, it has long been predicted that computers would replace certain workers. Automatic teller machines (ATMs) have been replacing bank tellers, and clerical workers are being replaced by "smart" software that "learns" to interpret the voice of a user and type the message relayed.

In this same vein, most futurists who studied the workplace expected that, technology would decrease employment opportunities in some areas and would increase opportunities in others. Not surprisingly, given the use of computers in all phases of education, health care, business, and elsewhere, the demand for people who can create software that educates, monitors, and entertains is at an all-time high. Systems analysts who can design computer systems that increase efficiency and productivity are also in demand. Construction companies need specialists who can install fiber-optic cable to connect computers and telephones; technological equipment repairers are in demand; and knowledgeable salespeople who can explain the potential of various types of technological innovations are needed.

The rapid impact of the Internet on the dissemination of information and as a social networking and sales tool has surprised all but the most savvy prognosticators. Webmasters, the people who design and maintain Web sites on the Internet, are in demand. Salespeople with specialized skills needed to market products on the Internet are also in demand, along with people who can create software and hardware that take advantage of the Internet's potential. Finally, all experts agree that technology will continue to change the face of the workplace throughout the twenty-first century by eliminating and creating jobs, by changing the physical nature of the workplace, and by creating new tools for workers to use.

The shifts in the population makeup of this country will also have a significant impact on the workplace. Currently, approximately 3.5 in 10 workers in the United States are nonwhite. At some point during the first half of the twenty-first century nonwhites will make up a majority of workers. This may be why the U.S. Department of Labor noted in the Secretary's Commission on Achieving Necessary Skills (SCANS, 1991) that one of the skills needed by future workers was the ability to function in a multicultural workplace. Although the trend in the past has been toward earlier retirement, changes in Social Security that increase the age at which payments may be received and improved health care may reverse this trend, with the result that more older workers will work longer. Regardless of the impact of Social Security and longevity, it is likely that the average age of workers will increase in the short term because of the sheer number of workers in the cohort known as "baby boomers" who are now in their 50s and 60s.

Because one's occupation generally determines where and how one lives, the community activities and organizations in which one participates, and many other aspects of life, social status has long been associated with one's job. It is difficult to predict whether this relationship will become more or less intense. If, as some writers predict, technological change results in a small group of highly trained technical experts and a great mass of low-skilled workers who work infrequently at uninteresting and unrewarding positions, then it is likely that social status will become detached from occupation and shift to some other basis. However, if technological change produces a general upgrading of most workers and provides most people with an opportunity to participate in activities that not only appear to be worthwhile but also *are* challenging and satisfying, then social status may become even more closely related to one's job.

Although the discussion about the sources and extent of global warming continue to rage, the search for alternatives to fossil fuel is in full swing and will have a tremendous impact on the nature of the workplace. Hydrogen-powered automobiles, wind-driven turbines that generate electricity, and solar-powered energy cells are but a few of the ideas that have companies and governments engaging in a competitive frenzy for leadership. Change is in the offing, and some predictions will now be nade here:

• The demand for people who can create something out of nothing will increase dramatically. For centuries authors and musicians have produced something using minimal raw materials. More recently movie producers such as Walt Disney Studios use technology, imagination, and software engineers to produce entertainment. Others have found innovative ways to power ecommerce (e.g, Internet marketing) communication and to provide opportunities for social netwrorking through Web sites such as Facebook and Twitter. The demand for these creative people will grow.

• The demand for health care workers will increase dramatically as millions of citizens in the United States are given access to more affordable health care. The current use of nurse practitioners and physician assistants is likely to explode as the demand for primary care workers increase. Similarly, the demand for nurses, nurses' assistants, home care aides, and other primary care workers is set to explode.

• As the world population grows from its current level of 6.8 billion to nine to ten billion in 2050, food production will become increasingly important. Scientists who can reengineer and increase the food supply will be in great demand.

• Similarly, as the world's population grows current efforts focused on conserving water will not be sufficient and new sources of water will be required. The obvious places to look are the oceans and seas that cover more than half the earth, but new technology will be needed to turn undrinkable saltwater to freshwater that can be diverted for food production, leisure uses, and human consumption.

• The economies of the world will continue to produce many unskilled, primarily service jobs that can, as technology advances, be replaced thus displacing millions of workers. The result is that the need for workers skilled in helping displaced workers will grow,

• The academic skills required for new workers to be successful will escalate.

• In the future, not only will workers more often change jobs, they will more often change the types of jobs they do currently.

• Outsourcing in the United States and insourcing from other countries will continue to impact workers throughout the world. Unskilled workers in the United States, will be the hardest hit in the near term. Currently there is virtually an endless supply of workers in China, Africa, Asia, and South America who are willing to work for a fraction of the wages paid in the United States, Canada, and Europe. However, skilled and professional workers such as physicians, engineers, and software designers will be increasing displaced by workers in other countries.

• Paraprofessionals will be increasingly important sources of assistance to workers in government programs, such as One Stop Centers and Ticket to Work programs.

• Lifelong learning will lose its cliché status and take on new meanings as the rapidity of changes in the workplace accelerate.

• The centralized workplace will be increasingly decentralized as the global economy continues to grow. Although some workers will find themselves commuting to offices throughout the globe, the use of software that will facilitate communication between individuals and small groups will reduce the overall need for travel to the workplace.

THE GOALS OF THIS BOOK

Career development interventions are erroneously considered to be less interesting and certainly less potent than the work associated with personal counseling or psychotherapy. This line of reasoning also projects the idea that career interventions are in some ways simpler to understand and easier to apply. One of the goals of this book is to demonstrate that these beliefs do not reflect reality. Psychotherapy puts people back on the road of life. Career development interventions advances them down that road toward self-fulfillment, dignity, social equity, and self-esteem. Modern career development intervention are no longer based on simplistic "test 'em and tell'em" models, although assessment plays a key role in many career interventions. Career development interventions at one time could be classified as aligned solely with modern philosophy, but today many practitioners have embraced post modern philosophy and interventions.

The major purpose of this book is to provide a foundation for practitioners who are interested in facilitating the career development process of children, adolescents, and adults and all that this entails. In many instances fostering career development involves providing experiences that increase both self-awareness and knowledge of the occupational structure. However, to be successful in finding and succeeding in a career, much more than knowledge of self and careers is required. Successful workers are good decision makers and are sensitive to individual differences that other workers bring to the workplace. They have highly honed employability skills, including using the Internet to locate job openings, making employer contacts, and interviewing for jobs when invited to do so. Successful workers are also aware of the relationship between education and training and job success and they engage in lifelong learning. Not surprisingly, practitioners who hope to assist clients to take advantage of the opportunities presented to them by the occupational structure also need a wide variety of skills and knowledge, including understanding the theoretical foundations that underpin career development practice, the skills needed to select and use assessment devices with a wide variety of groups, culturally sensitive career counseling skills, and the ability to locate and use educational and career information. Each of these areas and others are addressed in this book.

Summary

Career development professionals face tremendous challenges as well as the opportunity to assist millions of students and workers in the twenty-first century. The biggest challenges lie in the areas of helping disenfranchised and marginalized workers gain meaningful employment in the modern workplace and getting a fair share of the economic benefits available in the economy. Just as it did at the turn of the twentieth century, the effort to help these workers today must begin with the educational process. However, all workers must begin to see themselves as members of a global workforce and understand how their occupations may be enriched or endangered by competition from workers throughout the world.

Chapter Quiz

T F **1.** Economists believe that the progress toward the establishment of a global economy is for the most part irreversible.

T F **2.** One of the major factors in the "flattening" of the earth according to Friedman was the failure of the economy of the former Soviet Union.

T F **3.** There is widespread agreement regarding the meaning of career.

T F **4.** Blustein suggests that we replace current models of career development in favor of one that emphasizes social justice.

T F **5.** African Americans account for just over 50 percent of the working poor in this country.

T F **6.** It seems likely that the number of discouraged workers who have stopped hunting for a job and the underemployed is larger than the number of unemployed.

T F **7.** The saying, "When the U.S. sneezes the rest of the world catches cold" refers to the fact that an economic downturn in the United States produces higher rates of unemployment with our trading partners than it does at home.

T F **8.** In 2009 it was entirely possible that the need for career development services was at its highest level since the Great Depression.

T F **9.** Job, occupation, and career are synonymous terms.

T F **10.** The concerns of the pioneers of the vocational development were focused primarily on immigrants and young people.

(1) T (2) T (3) F (4) T (5) F (6) T (7) F (8) T (9) F (10) T

References

Alliance for Excellence in Education (2009). Fact sheet. Retrieved from http://www.all4ed.org/files/Graduation Rates_FactSheet.pdf.

American School Counselor Association. (2003). *The ASCA National Model: A framework for school counseling programs.* Alexandria, VA: Author.

Bench, M. (2003). *Career coaching: An insider's guide.* Palo Alto, CA: Davis-Black.

Betz, N. E., & Corning, A. F. (1993). The inseparability of "career" and "personal" counseling. *Career Development Quarterly, 42,* 137–142.

Blau, P. M., & Duncan, O. D. (1967). *The American occupational structure.* New York: Wiley.

BLS (2007). A profile of the working poor. Retrieved from http://www.bls.gov/cps/cpswp2005.pdf.

BLS (2009a). Unemployment rates unadjusted by BLS, 10 European Union countries or areas, seasonally adjusted, 2007–2009. Retrieved from http://www.bls.gov/fls/ intl_unemployment_rates_monthly.htm#Rchart2.

BLS (2009b). International comparisons of hourly compensation costs in manufacturing, 2007. Retrieved from http://www.bls.gov/fls/

BLS (2009c). International comparisons of annual labor force statistics, adjusted to U.S. concepts, 10 countries, 1970–2008. Retrieved from www.bls.gov/fls/ flscomparelf/ unemployment.htm

BLS (2009d). Employment situation summary. Retrieved from http://www.bls.gov/news.release/empsit.nr0.htm.

Blustein, D. L., McWhirter, E. H., & Perry, J. C. (2005). An emancipatory communitarian approach to vocational development theory, research and practice. *Counseling Psychologist, 33,* 141–179.

Brewer, J. M. (1942). *History of vocational guidance: Origins of early development.* New York: Harper.

Brown, D. (1995). A values-based approach to facilitating career transitions. *Career Development Quarterly, 44,* 4–11.

Brown, D. (2002). The role of work values and cultural values in occupational choice, satisfaction, and success: A theoretical statement. In D. Brown et al., *Career choice and development* (4th ed., pp. 465–509). San Francisco: Jossey-Bass.

Brown, D., & Brooks, L. (1991). *Career counseling techniques.* Boston: Allyn & Bacon.

Brown, D., Pryzwansky, W. B., & Schulte, A. (2010). *Psychological consultation and collaboration: Introduction to theory and practice* (7th ed.). Boston: Allyn & Bacon.

Carey, J. C., Dimmit, C., Hatch, T. A., Lapan, R. T., & Whiston, S. (2008). Report of the National Panel for Evidenced-based school counseling outcome research coding protocol and evaluation of student success skills and second step. *Professional School Counseling, 11,* 197–206.

Fitzgerald, L. F., & Betz, N. E. (1994). Career development in a cultural context: Race, social class, and sexual orientation. In M. L. Savickas & R. W. Lent (Eds.), *Convergence in career development theories* (pp. 103–119). Palo Alto, CA: CPP Books.

Freidman, T. L. (2005). *The world is flat: A brief history of the twenty-first century.* New York: Farrar, Straus & Giroux.

Greenwell, M. (2009, April 24). IMF rally starts small with 75-person rally. *Washington Post.* Retrieved from http://www.washingtonpost.com/wp-dyn/content/article/2009/04/24/AR2009042402878.html.

Hall, D. T., et al. (1986). *Career development in organizations.* San Francisco: Jossey-Bass.

Hansen, L. S. (1997). *Integrative life planning: Critical tasks for career development and changing life patterns.* San Francisco: Jossey-Bass.

Harris-Bowlsbey, J. (1990). Computer-based guidance systems: Their past, present, and future. In J. P. Sampson, Jr., & R. C. Reardon (Eds.), *Enhancing the design and use of computer assisted career guidance systems* (pp. 128–149). Alexandria, VA: National Career Development Association.

Herr, E. L., & Cramer, S. H. (1996). *Career guidance and counseling through the lifespan: Systemic approaches.* New York: HarperCollins.

Holland, J. L. (1997). *Making vocational choices* (3rd ed.). Englewood Cliffs, NJ: Prentice-Hall.

Hotchkiss, L., & Borow, H. (1996). Sociological perspective on work and career development. In D. Brown, L. Brooks et al., *Career choice and development* (3rd ed.), (pp. 281–336). San Francisco: Jossey-Bass.

Hoyt, K. B. (1977). *A primer for career education.* Washington, DC: Department of Education.

Hoyt, K. B. (2005). *Career education: History and future.* Tulsa, OK: National Career Development Association.

Hoyt, K. B., & Lester, J. L. (1995). *Learning towork: The NCDA Gallup survey.* Alexandria, VA: National Career Development Association.

Johnston, W., & Parker, A. (1987). *Workforce 2000: Work and workers for the twenty-first century.* Indianapolis, IN: Hudson Institute.

Krumboltz, J. D. (1993). Integrating career and personal counseling. *Career Development Quarterly, 42,* 143–148.

Leong, F. T. L. (1991). Career development attributes and occupational values of Asian American and white American students. *Career Development Quarterly, 39,* 221–230.

Lim, L. (2009). Unemployment swells in China. Retrieved from http://www.npr.org/templates/story/story.php?storyId=103149269

Luzzo, D. A. (1992). Ethnic group and social class differences in college students' career development. *Career Development Quarterly, 41,* 161–173.

McDaniels, C. (1989). *The changing workplace.* San Francisco: Jossey-Bass.

Melamed, T. (1995). Career success: The moderating effects of gender. *Journal of Vocational Behavior, 47,* 295–314.

Melamed, T. (1996). Career success: An assessment of a gender specific model. *Journal of Occupational and Organizational Psychology, 69,* 217–226.

Miller, F. W. (1968). *Guidance principles and services.* Columbus, OH: Merrill.

Naisbitt, J., & Aburdene, P. (1990). *Megatrends 2000.* New York: Morrow.

National Career Development Association. (1999). *Career connecting in a changing context: A summary of the key findings of the 1999 national survey of working America.* Tulsa, OK: Author.

OpenMarket.org (2009). Unemployment skyrockets. Retrieved from http://www.openmarket.org/2009/11/10/unemployment-skyrockets-us-now-beating-european-unemployment-rates/

Peterson, N., & Gonzalez, R. C. (2005). *The role of work in people's lives: Applied career counseling and vocational psychology* (2nd ed.). Belmont, CA: Brooks/Cole.

Picchioni, A. P., & Bonk, E. C. (1983). *A comprehensive history of guidance in the United States.* Austin, TX: Texas Personnel and Guidance Association.

Plunkett Research (2009). Outsourcing and off shoring overview. Retrieved from http://www.plunkettresearch.com/Industries/OutsourcingOffshoring/Outsourcing-OffshoringTrends/tabid/183/Default.aspx

Pope, M. (2000). A brief history of career counseling in the United States. *Career Development Quarterly, 48,* 194–211.

Prilleltensky, I. (1997). Values, assumptions, and practices: Assessing the moral implications of psychological discourse and practice. *American Psychologist, 52,* 517–535.

SCANS (1991). Secretary's commission on achieving necessary skills. Retrieved from http://honolulu.hawaii.edu/intranet/committees/FacDevCom/guidebk/teachtip/scans.htm.

Schmidt, J. J. (1999). *Counseling in schools: Essential services and comprehensive Programs* (3rd ed.). Boston: Allyn & Bacon.

Science Daily (2007). Unemployment and poverty remain dramatically high among workers with disabilities. Retrieved from http://www.sciencedaily.com/releases/2007/11/071120111550.htm

Sears, S. (1982). A definition of career guidance terms. A National Vocational Guidance Association perspective. *Vocational Guidance Quarterly, 31,* 137–143.

Sewell, W. H., Haller, A. O., & Portes, A. (1969). The educational and early occupational attainment process. *American Sociological Review, 34,* 89–92.

Shartle, C. L. (1959). *Occupational information—Its development and application* (3rd ed.). Englewood Cliffs, NJ: Prentice-Hall.

Spokane, A. R. (1991). *Career interventions.* Englewood Cliffs, NJ: Prentice-Hall.

Stephens, W. R. (1970). *Social reform and the origins of vocational guidance.* Washington, DC: National Vocational Guidance Association.

Stiglitz, J.e. (2002, 2003). *Globalization and its discontents.* New York: Norton.

Super, D. E. (1951). Vocational adjustment: Implementing self-concept. *Occupations, 30,* 88–92.

Super, D. E. (1976). *Career education and the meaning of work.* Washington, DC: Office of Education.

Super, D. E. (1993). The two faces of counseling: Or is it three? *Career Development Quarterly, 42,* 132–136.

Toffler, A. (1980). *The third wave.* New York: Morrow.

TradingEconomics (2009). Japan unemployment rate. Retrieved from http://www.tradingeconomics.com/Economics/Unemployment-rate.aspx?Symbol=JPY

U.S. Census Bureau. (2005). People: Income and employment. Retrieved from http://factfinder.census.gov/jsp/saff/SAFFInfo.jsp?_pageId+tp6_income_employment

World Salaries (2005). China average salaries and expenditure. Retrieved from http://www.worldsalaries.org/china.shtml

Yingzi, T. (2009). China's unemployment rate climbs. Retrieved from. http://www.chinadaily.com.cn/bizchina/2009-01/21/content_7416242.htm

2

Trait-and-Factor and Developmental Theories of Career Choice and Development and Their Applications

Things to Remember

- Major historical events in the history of career development theorizing

- The major tenets of Holland's theory of vocational choice

- Cultural values and their role in human behavior from and Brown's values-based theory

- Similarities and differences between the theory of work adjustment and Holland's theory

- The major components of Super's life span, life space theory, particularly the developmental component

- Gottfredson's ideas about the sextyping of occupations and the order of factors that influence career choice

B uford Stefflre, a counselor educator at Michigan State University for many years, is reputed to have coined the phrase, "There is nothing as practical as a good theory." When this statement is conveyed to students, they are at best skeptical. Isn't using *theory* and *practical* in the same sentence oxymoronic? Theories are obviously not fact, and what most students want are proven practices that they can use to help their clients. The problem is that many of our practices have not been investigated to the degree that will allow us to say unequivocally that they work. A good theory provides a framework for designing practices. I believe Stefflre was right!

One aim of this chapter is to provide an overview of the history of theorizing about career choice and development. It is generally recognized that the forerunner of modern theories of career development appeared in 1909 in *Choosing Your Vocation* by Frank Parsons. Parsons's tripartite model—understanding one's self, understanding the requirements of the jobs available, and choosing one based on true logic—underpinned career counseling and career development practice into the middle of the twentieth century. However, in the 1950s and 1960s a period of intense theorizing about career development occurred. The result was eight new theories of career choice and development, many of which are still viable today. From 1970 to 1984 five new theories of career choice and development were advanced, three of which focused largely on women's career development. Another intense period of theorizing began in 1991, and since 1991 five new theories of career choice and development have been presented. A chronological account of these events can be found in Table 2.1.

I have tried to accomplish two additional tasks in this chapter. The first is to present five of the major theories of career development (others are presented in Chapter 3) that have been generated to explain career choice and development. Second, I have tried to illustrate how these theories can be put into practice and to indicate the groups into which the theories fit best. The implication of this last phrase is that not all theories apply to all groups; thus, caution is necessary when designing practices based on the theorist's assumptions. I believe it will be helpful before you read this chapter to consider your own personal theory about human behavior and career choice and development. Yes, you have your biases and perceptions about why people choose careers, although you may not have given them much thought previously. By identifying your own thoughts in this area, you take the first step toward the construction of a sophisticated theory of your own.

THE PURPOSES AND EVALUATION OF THEORY

In Chapter 1, career development was defined as a lifelong process involving psychological, sociological, educational, economic, physical, and cultural factors that influence individuals' selection of, adjustment to, and advancement in the occupations that collectively make up their careers. Career development is, to say the least, a complex process. Theories provide us with simplified pictures, or as Krumboltz (1994) prefers, road maps to the career development process.

There are "good" theories and "bad" theories. As Krumboltz (1994) states, "Our psychological theories are as good as we know how to make them so far, but in all probability they are far short of being accurate" (p. 11). However, good theories have distinct characteristics, such as well-defined terms and constructs, that can easily be interpreted by practitioners and researchers. Just as importantly, the relationships among the constructs in the theory are clearly articulated. If the terms are clearly defined and logically interrelated, practitioners can use them as guides to practice, and researchers can generate research to test the assumptions of the theory. Moreover, good theories are comprehensive in that they explain the career development process for all groups, including men and women, and individuals from various cultures and from all socioeconomic strata.

Well-constructed theories serve other purposes. For example, they help us understand why people choose careers but then become dissatisfied with them. They also allow us to interpret data about career development that have been generated in the past, are being generated in the present, and will be generated in the future. Researchers and practitioners have long been

TABLE 2.1   A History of Career Development Theorizing

Year	Event
1909	Parsons's book, *Choosing Your Vocation,* is published posthumously.
1951	Eli Ginzberg and associates publish *Occupational Choice: An Approach to a General Theory,* which outlines a developmental theory of career development.
1953	Donald Super publishes "A Theory of Vocational Development" in the *American Psychologist,* which outlines a second developmental theory of career development.
1956	Ann Roe publishes *The Psychology of Occupations,* which contains her personality-based theory of career development.
1959	John Holland publishes "A Theory of Vocational Choice" in the *Journal of Counseling Psychology,* which sets forth some of the propositions of his theory of vocational choice.
1963	David Tiedeman and Robert O'Hara publish *Career Development: Choice and Adjustment,* which contains a theory rooted in the idea that careers satisfy needs.
1963	Edward Bordin and associates publish "An Articulated Framework for Vocational Development" in the *Journal of Counseling Psychology,* which sets forth a psychodynamic framework for career development.
1967	Blau and Duncan publish *The American Occupational Structure,* which sets forth the premises of status attainment theory, a sociological theory of career development.
1969	Lloyd Lofquist and René Dawis publish *Adjustment to Work,* which outlines the premises of a trait-factor model of occupational selection and adjustment.
1976	John Krumboltz and associates publish "A Social Learning Theory of Career Selection" in *The Counseling Psychologist.*
1981	Linda Gottfredson publishes "Circumscription and Compromise: A Developmental Theory of Occupational Aspirations" in the *Journal of Counseling Psychology,* which focuses on how sex role identification limits occupational aspirations.
1981	Gail Hackett and Nancy Betz publish "A Self-Efficacy Approach to the Career-Development of Women" in the *Journal of Vocational Behavior,* which uses Bandura's self-efficacy construct to explain important aspects of the career decision-making process.
1984	Helen Astin publishes "The Meaning of Work in Women's Lives: A Sociopsychological Model of Career Choice and Work Behavior" in *The Counseling Psychologist,* which outlines a general theory of the career development of women.
1984	Tiedeman and Miller-Tiedeman publish "Career Decision Making: An Individualistic Perspective," which is one of the early attempts at framing a theory based on constructivist philosophy.
1991	Gary Peterson and associates publish *Career Development and Services: A Cognitive Approach,* which contains their cognitive information-processing model of career choice and development.
1994	Robert Lent and associates publish "Toward a Unifying Social Cognitive Theory of Career and Academic Interest, Choice and Performance" in the *Journal of Vocational Psychology,* which is based on Albert Bandura's (1986) sociocognitive theory. This theory was revised in 2002 to focus on the role of cultural and work values in occupational choice, success, and satisfaction.
1996	Duane Brown's "Values-Based Model of Career and Life-Role Choices and Satisfaction" is published in the *Career Development Quarterly* and *Career Choice and Development.* This theory was revised in 2002 to focus on the role of cultural and work values in occupational choice, success, and satisfaction.
1996	Richard Young and associates publish "A Contextual Explanation of Career," which is based on constructivist philosophy.
2005	Deborah Bloch and Jim E. H. Bright and Robert G. L. Pryor publish two independent versions of chaos theories of careers.

aware that children and adults sex-type careers and that these stereotypes influence career choices. Gottfredson's theory (1981, 2002a) helps us understand why this occurs. Well-developed theories also help us account for all internal and external factors that influence career development, including cognitions about careers and affective responses to various career-related events (Brown & Brooks, 1996; Krumboltz, 1994). Finally, well-constructed theories are parsimonious, which means they are set forth in the simplest, most succinct fashion necessary to describe the phenomena involved. To summarize, theories of career choice and development serve three functions:

1. Facilitate the understanding of the forces that influence career choice and development.
2. Stimulate research that will help to better clarify career choice and the development process.
3. Provide a guide to practice in the absence of empirical guidelines.

A History of Career Development Theorizing

The 19 publications listed in Table 2.1 are by no means the only attempts at developing theories of career choice and development, and as shown later, most of these theories have been revised numerous times. Today the theories of Holland (1997), Super (1990), Lofquist and Dawis (Dawis, 1996; Lofquist & Dawis, 1991), Lent, Brown, and Hackett (1995, 1996, 2002), and Gottfredson (1981, 1996) are making a major impact on research or practice. These theories are discussed in some detail later in this book in the developmental theories section and the socioeconomic theories section under the first subsection on status attainment theory (Blau & Duncan, 1967; Hotchkiss & Borow, 1996). These theories have become influential because they possess the characteristics of a "good" theory (described previously), although each of them has shortcomings.

It is difficult to say why some theories become influential whereas others do not. Bordin's psychodynamic theory (1984) was well constructed, but it may not have become popular because it was built on psychodynamic theory, which has never been widely accepted by counselors or counseling psychologists. Roe's theory (Roe, 1956, 1984; Roe & Lunneborg, 1990) gradually lost favor because researchers were unable to verify her basic propositions that early childhood environments give rise to personality types that in turn result in career selection. No perfect theory of career choice has yet to emerge and it is unlikely that this will occur. However, to return to Krumboltz's (1994) map metaphor, some theory builders do a better job than others of providing maps to the vast array of phenomena that influence career development.

Some relatively new theories of career choice and development may become influential in the future. For example, constructivist theories (e.g., Young, Valach, & Collin, 2002) are receiving a great deal of attention from scientists and practitioners alike. Some theories are so new that they have not had an opportunity to attract large numbers of adherents. The career information–processing model (Peterson, Sampson, & Reardon, 1991; Peterson, Sampson, Reardon, & Lenz, 1996) and the values-based theory of Brown (Brown, 1996, 2002a; Brown & Crace, 1995) are included in this group.

THEORIES FOR SPECIAL GROUPS   Some writers (e.g., Astin, 1984; Hackett & Betz, 1981) have proposed that, because many early theories (e.g., Super, 1953) were oriented primarily to white males, they are inappropriate explanations of the career development of women and of males and females from other-than-European backgrounds. Theorists such as Holland (1997) and Super (1990) contend that these criticisms are unwarranted, although Super made some changes in his theory over time to accommodate the changing career patterns of women. Efforts to develop alternative theories that focus on specific subgroups have not been met with much enthusiasm. For example, Astin's (1997) psychosociological model of career choice and work behavior has attracted few supporters. Moreover, Gail Hackett, who, in collaboration with Nancy Betz, addressed the role of self-efficacy in women's career choice making, is now a co-author of a more comprehensive theory that focuses on the social cognitive factors that influence the career development of both men and women (Lent, Brown, & Hackett, 1995, 1996, 2002). Interestingly, Betz, along with Fitzgerald (Fitzgerald & Betz, 1994) have argued forcefully that current theories have limited applicability to minority groups, persons with gay or lesbian sexual orientation, and women.

IS CAREER DEVELOPMENT THEORY UNINTENTIONALLY RACIST?   Sue and Sue (2000) and Pedersen (1991) have proposed that most of the theories included in training programs for professional counselors, psychologists, and others are culturally oppressive because they are rooted in Eurocentric beliefs. The Western European worldview is that people should act independently when they make career decisions, a belief that arises from the cultural belief that the individual is the most important social unit (Carter, 1991). However, many Native Americans, Asian Americans, and Hispanics believe that the welfare of the group should be placed ahead of the concerns of individuals. They hold a collateral, or collective, social value and thus may reject the ideas that independence and competition are acceptable. Leong (1991) found that the Asian American students in his sample had a dependent decision making style, not the independent style that would flow from Eurocentric values. One implication of this finding is that some Asian American students may find it perfectly appropriate to allow their parents to play a major role in the selection of their occupations. Unfortunately, most of the theories included in this chapter (e.g., Dawis, 1996; Gottfredson, 1996; Holland, 1997; Super, 1990) make this assumption, along with the assumption that job satisfaction is the result of the individual's interaction with his or her work environment. It seems entirely likely that job satisfaction and factors such as achievement in one's career are related to a much more complex set of variables, including family or group approval of the career choice and the individual's performance in it. Hartung (2002) joined the chorus of criticisms of career development theory based on cultural validity by reviewing some of the criticisms, which more or less echo those previously discussed. He, like the others mentioned here, suggests that there is a need to move from a monocultural approach to a multicultural perspective. However, Hartung (2002) admits that not all theory produced to date does not have a monocultural perspective. He cites Lent, Brown, and Hackett (1996) and Brown (1996) as examples of theories that have abandoned a monocultural perspective. Hartung (2002) also suggests that research literature is becoming available that supports the use of some of the traditional theories with cultural minorities. Monocultural theories are flawed because they often lack cultural validity. However, they provide a valid basis for practice for people who hold a Western European worldview. Further, it is a mistake to assume that they are inappropriate for use with cultural minorities based on phenotypic characteristics of individuals. Many cultural minorities have adopted a Western European worldview and function primarily in cultural contexts that reinforce these values. It is an ethical error to apply theories of any type without assessing the cultural perspective of the individual first.

A different set of criticisms of traditional theories have been advanced by Peterson and Gonzalez (2005), Bloch (2005), and Bright and Pryor (2005). These authors suggest that the modern philosophy that underpins most traditional theories is inappropriate based on advances in thinking and suggest that it be replaced with a postmodern perspective. The differences in these two philosophies are summarized below. As noted in Chapter 1, Blustein (2006) is also critical of current theories because they do not contain a social justice component. He and his colleagues

(Blustein, 2008; Blustein, Kenna, Gill, & DeVoy, 2008) suggest that career development specialists must become advocates for social change.

INTRODUCTION TO THE THEORIES

The theories that follow fall into several categories—trait-and-factor theories, developmental theories, learning theories, socioeconomic theories, and recent theoretical statements. Trait-and-factor theories stress that individuals need to develop their traits, which include their interests, values, personalities, and aptitudes, as well as select environments that are congruent with them. Developmental theories are based to some degree on the assumption that the factors that influence career choice and development are related to stages of personal and psychological development. The tenets of various learning theories have been used to describe both the process by which the individual develops and the choice-making process itself. Socioeconomic theories pay less attention to psychological traits, although they typically address the matter of intellect as a factor in career choice. However, these theories focus on the socioeconomic status of the decision maker and/or the influence of sociological and economic factors on occupational choice making. In the section on recent theoretical statements, two theories based on learning theory, one trait-and-factor theory and one constructivist theory, are presented.

All theories are based on certain philosophical assumptions that usually fall into two categories: positivist and postmodern. Trait-and-factor theories, developmental theories, and theories rooted in learning theory are based on modernist or positivist philosophical thinking. This position makes the following assumptions:

1. Human behavior can be measured objectively if reliable, valid instruments are utilized.
2. Human behavior can be studied outside the context in which it occurs.
3. Research processes should be value free. If the researcher's values enter into the process, the results are likely to be flawed.
4. Cause and effect relationships occur and can be measured.
5. If certain conditions are met, such as random sampling, the use of reliable, valid instruments, and lack of contamination of results by the researcher's values, results can be generalized to other people in similar settings.
6. As much as possible career counselors should maintain their objectivity, use instruments that are reliable and valid, and base their practice on well-designed empirical research.

Postmodern theories, often referred to as constructivist theories, are a relatively new addition to the theories of career choice and development. These theories depart radically from the assumptions of the theories based on positivist philosophy. The following assumptions underpin these theories:

1. Human behavior is nonlinear and thus cannot be studied objectively.
2. Cause and effect relationships cannot be determined.
3. Individuals cannot be studied outside the context in which they function.
4. Research data cannot be generalized.
5. Research is not a value-free process. The researcher's values should in fact guide the research process.
6. The stories (narratives) that students tell are legitimate sources of data.
7. Research is goal free: It is a search for actual effects based on demonstrated needs. Random samples are replaced with purposeful sampling—that is, studying individuals

who can respond to the research in a meaningful manner. For example, to understand sex-role stereotyping of occupational choice, a researcher might select subjects who knowingly chose careers because of stereotypes rather than selecting a random sample that included people who made decisions based on other variables.

8. Career counselors focus on the stories (narratives) of their clients, use qualitative assessment procedures, and help clients construct career goals based on their perceptions of the context in which they function.

These assumptions should be kept in mind as the theories are reviewed.

TRAIT-AND-FACTOR THEORIES

Holland's Theory of Vocational Choice

Holland developed a theoretical position gradually revealed in a series of published theoretical statements and research studies (Holland, 1959, 1962, 1963a, 1963b, 1963c, 1963d, 1966a, 1966b, 1968, 1972, 1973, 1985, 1987, 1997; Gottfredson and Johnstun, 2009; Holland & Gottfredson, 1976; Holland & Lutz, 1968; Holland & Nichols, 1964). Holland's theory of vocational choice is based on several assumptions:

1. An individual's personality is the primary factor in vocational choice.
2. Interest inventories are in fact personality inventories.
3. Individuals develop stereotypical views of occupations that have psychological relevance. These stereotypes play a major role in occupational choice.
4. Daydreams about occupations are often precursors to occupational choices.
5. Identity—the clarity of an individual's perceptions of his or her goals and personal characteristics—is related to having a small number of rather focused vocational goals.
6. To be successful and satisfied in one's career it is necessary to choose an occupation that is congruent with one's personality. A congruent occupation is one in which other people in the work environment have the same or similar characteristics as one's own.

Personality develops as a result of the interaction of inherited characteristics, the activities to which the individual is exposed, and the interests and competencies that grow out of the activities (Holland, 1997). Holland believes that to some degree "types beget types" but recognizes that children shape their own environments to an extent, and they are exposed to a number of people in addition to their parents who provide experiences and reinforce certain types of performance. The combination of these influences produces "a person who is predisposed to exhibit a characteristic self-concept and outlook and to acquire a characteristic disposition" (Holland, 1997, p. 19). Ultimately, the personality emerges. Holland posits the following "pure" personality types, which occur rarely if at all in their pure form: (1) realistic, (2) investigative, (3) artistic, (4) social, (5) enterprising, and (6) conventional. Let's look at these six types in more detail.

Realistic people deal with the environment in an objective, concrete, and physically manipulative manner. They avoid goals and tasks that demand subjectivity, intellectual or artistic expressions, or social abilities. They are described as masculine, unsociable, emotionally stable, and materialistic. They prefer agricultural, technical, skilled-trade, and engineering vocations. They like activities that involve motor skills, equipment, machines, tools, and structure, such as athletics, scouting, crafts, and shop work.

Investigative people deal with the environment by using intellect—manipulating ideas, words, and symbols. They prefer scientific vocations, theoretical tasks, reading, collecting, algebra, foreign languages, and such creative activities as art, music, and sculpture. They avoid social situations and see themselves as unsociable, masculine, persistent, scholarly, and introverted. They achieve primarily in academic and scientific areas and usually do poorly as leaders.

Artistic individuals deal with the environment by creating art forms and products. They rely on subjective impressions and fantasies in seeking solutions to problems. They prefer musical, artistic, literary, and dramatic vocations and activities that are creative in nature. They dislike masculine activities and roles, such as auto repair and athletics. They see themselves as unsociable, feminine, submissive, introspective, sensitive, impulsive, and flexible.

Social people deal with the environment by using skills to interact with and relate to others. They are typified by social skills and the need for social interaction. They prefer educational, therapeutic, and religious vocations and activities, such as church, government, community services, music, reading, and dramatics. They see themselves as sociable, nurturant, cheerful, conservative, responsible, achieving, and self-accepting.

Enterprising people cope with the environment by expressing adventurous, dominant, enthusiastic, and impulsive qualities. Characterized as persuasive, verbal, extroverted, self-accepting, self-confident, aggressive, and exhibitionistic, they prefer sales, supervisory, and leadership vocations and activities that satisfy needs for dominance, verbal expression, recognition, and power.

Conventional people deal with the environment by choosing goals and activities that carry social approval. Their approach to problems is stereotypical, correct, and unoriginal. They create a neat, sociable, conservative impression. They prefer clerical and computational tasks, identify with business, and put a high value on economic matters. They see themselves as masculine, shrewd, dominant, controlled, rigid, and stable and have more mathematical than verbal aptitude.

According to Holland, a person can be typed into one of these categories by expressed or demonstrated vocational or educational interests, by employment, or by scores obtained on such instruments as the Vocational Preference Inventory, the Strong Interest Inventory, or the Self-Directed Search. The last, an instrument developed by Holland, consists of occupational titles and activities that can be divided equally among the six type areas. Each method of determining personality type yields a score. Although Holland (1997) believes that all six types are descriptive of personality, he suggests that the top three scores are the most telling factors. Thus the result of the assessment of type is a three-letter code (e.g., SAE), known as a *Holland code.* If the three-letter code is consistent and differentiated, the primary (first type) is expected to be the most influential, the second type the second most influential, and the tertiary or third type the third most influential in describing vocational decisions and aspirations and academic achievement. The consistency of a personality profile can be determined by use of the hexagon shown in Figure 2.1. If the personality types are adjacent (e.g., realistic and investigative), they are said to be consistent. Inconsistent types are located opposite each other on the hexagon (e.g., investigative and enterprising). A personality profile is well differentiated if the scores on the primary type of the profile are significantly higher than the lowest score. Holland (1997) believes that consistency and differentiation are indirect estimates of identity, which he defines as the clarity of an individual's goals and self-perceptions. Identity can be measured directly by the My Vocational Situation instrument (Holland, Daiger, & Power, 1980).

Holland (1985, 1997) also proposes six work environments (realistic, investigative, artistic, social, enterprising, and conventional) analogous to the pure personality types just described. Work environments are assigned Holland codes based on the personality of the workers in those work environments. As already noted, individuals must select vocational environments congruent with their personalities to maximize their job satisfaction and achievements. These environments are described below.

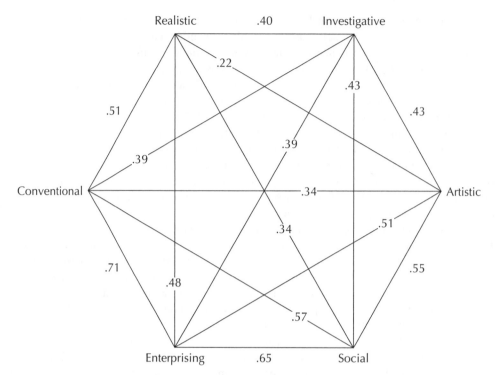

FIGURE 2.1   Holland's Model for Interpreting Interclass and Intraclass Relationships.
Source: Reproduced by special permission of the publisher, Psychological Assessment Resources, Inc., Odessa, FL 33556. From the *Self-Directed Search Technical Manual* by J. L. Holland, Copyright 1994, by PAR, Inc. Further reproduction is prohibited without permission from PAR, Inc.

The *realistic* environment involves concrete, physical tasks requiring mechanical skill, persistence, and physical movement. Only minimal interpersonal skills are needed. Typical realistic settings include a filling station, a machine shop, a farm, a construction site, and a barber shop.

The *investigative* environment requires the use of abstract and creative abilities rather than personal perceptiveness. Satisfactory performance demands imagination and intelligence; achievement usually requires a considerable time span. Problems encountered may vary in level of difficulty, but they are usually solved by applying intellectual skills and tools. The work revolves around ideas and things rather than people. Typical settings include a research laboratory; a diagnostic case conference; a library; and a work group of scientists, mathematicians, or research engineers.

The *artistic* environment demands the creative and interpretive use of artistic forms. One must be able to draw on knowledge, intuition, and emotional life in solving typical problems. Information is judged against personal, subjective criteria. The work usually requires intense involvement for prolonged periods. Typical settings include a play rehearsal, a concert hall, a dance studio, a study, a library, and an art or music studio.

The *social* environment demands the ability to interpret and modify human behavior and an interest in caring for and interacting with people. The work requires frequent and prolonged personal relationships. The work hazards are primarily emotional. Typical work situations include school and college classrooms, counseling offices, mental hospitals, churches, educational offices, and recreational centers.

The *enterprising* environment requires verbal skill in directing or persuading people. The work requires directing, controlling, or planning activities of others, and a more superficial interest in people than in the social environment, most of that interest centered on what can be had from people. Typical settings include a car lot, a real estate office, a political rally, and an advertising agency.

The *conventional* environment involves systematic, concrete, routine processing of verbal and mathematical information. The tasks frequently call for repetitive, short-cycle operations according to an established procedure. Minimal skill in interpersonal relations is required because the work mostly involves office equipment and materials. Typical settings include a bank, an accounting firm, a post office, a file room, and a business office.

Holland suggests that each work environment is sought by individuals whose personality type is similar to those controlling the environment. It is assumed that they will be comfortable and happy in a compatible environment and uneasy in an environment suited to a different personality type. A congruent person-environment match presumably results in a more stable vocational choice, greater vocational achievement, higher academic achievement, better maintenance of personal stability, and greater satisfaction.

Finally, Holland developed an occupational classification system based on the model environment construct. The first edition of his classification system was published in 1982. The latest edition of the *The Dictionary of Holland Occupational Codes* (Gottfredson & Holland, 1996) contains extensive listings of all major occupations, which are classified according to the extent to which they involve activities representing the different points on the hexagon. An occupation that is mainly realistic in nature but involves some investigative activities and a lesser amount of conventional characteristics would be labeled RIC. This code would be considered consistent because the types are adjacent on the hexagon. A code of RSC, however, would be inconsistent because it is work environment that involves activities that are on opposing sides of the hexagon.

STATUS AND USE OF HOLLAND'S THEORY   Holland's theory is the most influential of all of the extant theories. Instruments based on the theory, including his own Self-Directed Search (Holland, 1994a, 1994b) and Find Your Interests (Department of Defense [DOD], 2005), which is used by the Department of Defense along with the Armed Services Vocational Aptitude Battery in its military recruitment program of high school students throughout the country, are best sellers. His theory has stimulated hundreds of research studies as well (Gottfredson & Johnstun, 2009; Holland, 1997; Holland & Gottfredson, 1990). Moreover, Holland's conceptual scheme of interests is used exclusively in O*NET, the major occupational classification system in the United States. However, his theory has been criticized on the basis of its cultural validity and must be applied cautiously if at all with persons whose worldviews vary from that of the dominant culture. Much of the research defending the theory has taken the form of administering on the instruments that measure his constructs and then analyzing the data to see if it yields interest patterns that approximate his hexagon. For example, Sidiropoulou-Dimakakou, Mylonas, & Argyropoulou (2008) tested the Holland model with a sample of Greek students and concluded that Holland's model is useful for Greece and counseling in Greece. The presumption is that if the pattern of interests of a minority group (e.g., Greeks) approximates that found by Holland in his original research, construct validity has been established. While this argument has merit it does not follow that inventories administered to individual clients from different minority groups will produce valid results.

The goal of career exploration and counseling using Holland's (1997) theory is to help client groups identify occupations that include workers in them with the same personality characteristics as their own (congruence). This process, in all likelihood, begins with an assessment of a client's Holland type using one of the following instruments:

The Self-Directed Search (4th ed.)

The Strong Interest Inventory

The Harrington–O'Shea Career Decision-Making System, Revised

Find Your Interests (part of the Armed Services Vocational Aptitude Battery [ASVAB] Career Exploration Program)

The Career Key (online)

Interest Profiler (part of the O*NET system)

Wide Range Interest and Occupation Test (2nd ed.) (nonverbal inventory for special populations)

Although these instruments most often are used to measure Holland's constructs, they are by no means the only ones available for this purpose. All of the leading interest inventories produce Holland profiles.

Research generally supports the use of Holland's instruments with males and females as well as with people from diverse cultural backgrounds. Men generally score higher on realistic, investigative, and enterprising scales, whereas women tend to score higher on social, artistic, and conventional scales (Holland, 1997), and instruments tend to predict entry into occupations equally well for men and women. The newest version of Find Your Interests (DOD, 2005) includes norms for men and women. Much of the research regarding Holland's theory has focused on whether his conceptualization is appropriate for use with different minority groups. Typically, the answer is yes (e.g., Day, Rounds, & Swaney, 1998). However, research that suggests the interest patterns of cultural minorities approximate those of white persons begs the question of appropriateness of the theory to these groups because it does little to address the issue of the decision-making process. Arnold (2004) suggests that the congruence concept also needs a great deal more exploration as it pertains to minority and white persons.

Theory of Work Adjustment (TWA)

The theory of work adjustment (TWA) has been set forth in a series of publications (Dawis, 1996; Dawis, England, & Lofquist, 1964; Dawis & Lofquist, 1984; Dawis, Lofquist, & Weiss, 1968; Lofquist & Dawis, 1991). In each of these publications the theory has been changed somewhat, but with few exceptions the assumptions underpinning the theory have not changed. The basic assumption of TWA is that people have two types of needs: biological (or survival) needs, such as the need for food, and psychological needs, such as social acceptance. These needs give rise to drive states, which in turn lead to volitional behavior. Whenever the behavior results in the needs being satisfied, reinforcement occurs and the behavior is strengthened. A second assumption is that work environments have "requirements" that are analogous to the needs of individuals. Both individuals and environments develop mechanisms for satisfying their needs. When the needs of individuals in an environment (work) and those of the environment are satisfied, correspondence exists. Workers select jobs because of their perception that the job will satisfy their needs, and workers are selected because of the perceptions that their skills will meet the needs of the workplace. If the reinforcer pattern of the workplace matches the need pattern of the worker, satisfaction and satisfactoriness occur. Satisfaction results when the worker is reinforced. Workers are judged to be satisfactory when they reinforce the need pattern of the work environment. The tenure, or time spent in a job by workers, is the result of their satisfaction with the job and satisfactoriness in performance.

Three variables—skills, aptitudes, and personality structure—can be used to predict the success of the worker if the reinforcement pattern of the work environment is known. The skills referred to in this predictive equation are the job-related skills the individual can offer to a work environment. Aptitude is the potential an individual has to develop the skills needed by the work environment, and the personality structure of the individual is determined by a combination of aptitudes and values. Values are determined by the importance attached to classes of reinforcement (e.g., pay, independence of functioning). Gender and minority group status are assumed to be critical variables in the development of personality structure within TWA.

Figure 2.2 is a graphic description of the occupational choice-making process in TWA terms. As can be seen, decision making begins with an analysis of values and abilities, followed by an analysis of the ability patterns and value patterns of the several occupations. Ultimately individuals compare all occupations being considered in terms of the extent to which they can perform the job satisfactorily and the degree to which the occupation will satisfy their needs.

To understand work adjustment, the structure of the work environment and the characteristics of the worker must be known. Predictions of success depend on the celerity, pace, endurance, and rhythm of both the worker and the work environment. *Celerity* is the quickness with which workers engage their work environment to satisfy their needs. Successful workers quickly and

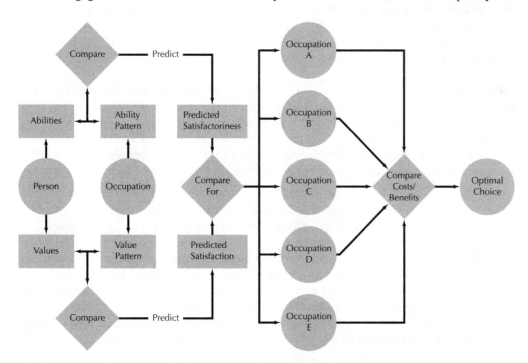

FIGURE 2.2 TWA's Graphic Explanation of Career Choice Correspondence. *Source:* From "The Theory of Work Adjustment and Person-Environment-Counseling," by R. V. Dawis, 1996, in D. Brown, L. Brooks, see earlier note et al., *Career Choice and Development* (3rd ed., pp. 75–120), San Francisco: Jossey-Bass. Reprinted by permission.

vigorously try to satisfy their needs prior to leaving a job. Moreover, work environments respond with varying degrees of speed when a worker is unsatisfactory. The vigor with which individuals and work environments try to satisfy their needs denotes *pace. Endurance* is used in TWA to indicate the tolerance of the individual or the work environment for dealing with unsatisfactory work conditions or workers in the case of the work environment. *Rhythm* denotes the pattern of attempts (e.g., steady, erratic) by individuals and work environments to satisfy their needs.

Another factor that must be considered in the adjustment to work process is whether individuals take an active or reactive approach. When workers take an active approach, they make a direct attempt to make the work environment more responsive to their needs. When workers respond reactively, they change themselves to respond to the perceived demands of the workplace. For example, reactive workers might reconsider the needs they deem important and substitute security for high pay. Some people have more tolerance (endurance) than others for unsatisfying situations and may make a series of reactive and active attempts to make the environment respond to their needs before ending their tenure in the job. Similarly, work environments may have greater or lesser tolerance for unsatisfactory efforts by workers. The development of work adjustment styles, including reactive and active approaches, celerity, endurance, pace, and rhythm is influenced by a variety of factors, including inherited characteristics, gender, and cultural background.

Counselors who want to apply TWA in their work will find that inventories and tests are available to measure the theoretical constructs of the theory (Dawis, 1996). Two scales, the Minnesota Satisfaction Questionnaire and the Minnesota Satisfactoriness Scales, can be used to measure satisfaction and satisfactoriness, respectively. The Minnesota Importance Questionnaire can be used to measure need preferences, and the Minnesota Ability Test Battery can be used to measure aptitudes. Occupational Reinforcer Patterns is an inventory that can be used to measure preferences for patterns of reinforcers.

STATUS AND USE OF TWA   TWA is not a widely practiced theory, probably because of its complexity. However, it has many similarities with Holland's theory in that the objective of the helping process is to help client groups match their aptitudes and values to occupations with jobs that provide appropriate occupational ability patterns and occupational reinforcer patterns. Holland (1997) uses the term *congruence* to indicate when an individual selects an occupation that matches his or her personality type. In TWA, the term is *correspondence.* The career counseling process would be as follows:

1. Assess ability patterns using the General Aptitude Test Battery (GATB). The U.S. Department of Labor has compiled a list of minimum requirements for jobs, as measured by the GATB, for success on the job.
2. Assess needs and values using the Minnesota Importance Questionnaire (MIQ). The results of the MIQ provide clients with a list of up to 180 occupations that match their needs.
3. Assist individuals in comparing their occupational ability patterns, needs, and values with those in the Minnesota Occupational Classification System.
4. Confirm that the outcome of this process benefits both the worker via increased job satisfaction and the employer by increased satisfactoriness in job performance.

It seems likely that the TWA could be used with both men and women, although there are no empirical data to support this observation. As Sharf (2002) notes, one drawback to using the TWA is that the testing process may involve many hours if the GATB is included. He suggests that estimates of aptitudes may suffice as a substitute for the actual administration of the GATB.

Estimates would have to be substituted for actual test results if this model were used for adults. Reading issues and the predictive validity of the tests and inventories for cultural and racial minorities are unresolved at this point. Additionally, the developers of the theory have not considered cultural values and how they may interact with work values and needs in their work on the theory. It may, therefore, be best for practitioners to consider TWA as a work in progress that may prove useful in the future.

A VALUES-BASED THEORY OF OCCUPATIONAL CHOICE

Brown (1996, 2002a; Brown & Crace, 1995) built on the work of Rokeach (1973), Super (1980, 1990), Beck (1976), and others to formulate a holistic model of career and life-role choice making. However, as he noted, the theory was aimed primarily at people with traditional Eurocentric values, including individualism, future time orientation, moderate need for self-control, emphasis on activity, and a core belief that humans should dominate nature.

Cultural values have been identified as important variables in career development and vocational behaviors (e.g., Fouad, 1995; Super & Sverko, 1995), but because these values vary across cultures, a comprehensive theory of career choice and development must take into account this variation. What is presented in this section is a major revision of Brown's (1996) theory that focuses for the most part on the values in a single life role: career.

However, cultural values are not the only variables that influence the career choice–making process or the resulting satisfaction and/or success. Contextual variables, such as socioeconomic status (SES) (e.g., Hotchkiss & Borow, 1996); family or group influence (e.g., Leong & Serifica, 1995); and discrimination (e.g., Melamed, 1996) are also considered in this revision, along with factors such as gender (e.g., Gottfredson, 1996; Melamed, 1995) and aptitudes (e.g., Jencks, Crouse, & Mueser, 1983; Phillips & Imhoff, 1997) because they have been linked empirically to career decision making and occupational attainment.

Variables That Influence Career Choice and Satisfaction

VALUES   Values are beliefs that are experienced by the individual as standards regarding how he or she should function. They are cognitive structures, but they have behavioral and affective dimensions. Values develop so that individuals can meet their needs in socially acceptable ways (Rokeach, 1973), and thus the behavioral aspect of values is shaped by the cultural context in which they develop. An individual's values are the basis for his or her self-evaluation and the evaluation of others, and they play a major role in the establishment of personal goals (Rokeach, 1973).

Work values are the values that individuals believe should be satisfied as a result of their participation in the work role. Values also play a central role in the decision-making process because they are the basis of goal setting. Goals, if properly constructed, move the individual toward desired end states (e.g., social acceptance). Financial prosperity, altruism, achievement, and responsibility are examples of work values. In addition to work values, individuals develop a number of other values that they expect to be satisfied in life roles other than work, such as family (Brown, 1996). The major underlying assumption of this theory that is advanced in this article is that cultural and work values are the primary variables that influence the occupational choice-making process, the occupation chosen, and the resulting satisfaction with and success in the chosen occupation.

Research (e.g., Carter, 1991; Kluckhorn & Strodtbeck, 1961) has indicated that some values seem to be more prevalent in certain cultural groups than others, although it is not uncommon for various cultural groups to hold some of the same values (Carter, 1991). Numerous efforts have been aimed at developing a taxonomy of cultural values that illustrates the similarities and differences among the values held by various cultural groups in this country (e.g., M. Ho, 1987; Ibrahim, 1985; Sue & Sue, 2000). These taxonomies draw on the pioneering research of Kluckhorn and Strodtbeck (1961), and typically they include categories for values regarding the following:

> *Human nature*   Human beings are good, bad, or neither.
>
> *Person-nature relationship*   Nature dominates people; people dominate nature; living in harmony with nature is important.
>
> *Time orientation*   Time is experienced as past, past-future, present, or circular—an orientation to changes that recur in nature as opposed to time being measured by watches and calendars.
>
> *Activity*   Being, that is, spontaneous self-expression, is important; being-in-becoming—that is, controlled self-expression,—is important; doing—that is, action-noriented self-expression—is important.
>
> *Self-control*   It is either highly or moderately important to control one's thoughts and emotions.
>
> *Social relationships*   Individualism is valued and the individual is the most important social unit.
>
> *Collateral*   Also referred to as filial piety, collateral lifestyle is highly or moderately valued (Lee, 1991).
>
> *Allocentrism*   It is important to put the group's concerns ahead of the concerns of the individual (Marin & Marin, 1991).

HOW VALUES DEVELOP   Enculturation is the process by which individuals incorporate the beliefs and values of their cultural group and form a values system (D. Ho, 1995; Rokeach, 1973). Although the process of enculturation is not fully understood, it seems likely that it occurs initially as a result of a complex process of modeling, reinforcement, and experience (Bandura, 1986; Rokeach, 1973). Cultural values and the work values that develop later may be vaguely perceived or crystallized. When values are crystallized, individuals can label them (I value competition) and apply them to their own behaviors (and that is why I try to work harder than other people). Values are relatively stable, but they may change throughout the life span as a result of conflict or contemplation (Rokeach, 1973).

The result of enculturation for most individuals is monoculturalism—that is, they incorporate the values and beliefs of one culture. Bienculturation or multienculturation occurs when the beliefs of two or more cultures are internalized. Biculturalism or multiculturalism may be the result of involvement in a bicultural or multicultural family (D. Ho, 1995) or acculturation resulting from sustained contact with other cultural groups.

Although the concept of biculturalism is often discussed in the context of multicultural literature (e.g., Leong & Gim-Chung, 1995), it is unlikely that an individual can adopt the values of two or more cultures because often these values conflict. However, this should not be interpreted to mean that individuals cannot understand and appreciate the cultural values of more than one cultural group and adapt some of their behaviors to match various cultural contexts. The enculturation process is influenced by the cultural group membership (M. Ho, 1987), gender (e.g., Brenner, Blazini, & Greenhaus, 1988; M. Brown, 1995), SES (Arbona, 1995; Blau & Duncan, 1967), and family membership (D. Ho, 1995; M. Ho, 1987).

Acculturation may or may not influence the cultural values that individuals incorporate into their values systems. Acculturation involves the enculturation of beliefs from a culture different from one's own (Berry, 1990). It may also involve adopting the language, customs, and traditions of the other culture. Individuals who are in contact with another culture often receive "messages" that conflict with their own beliefs. For example, an Asian American student who believes that it is important to make a career choice that is in keeping with his family's wishes may be "told" by members of his peer group and his counselor that the "appropriate" way to make a career choice is to act independently. The result of these conflicting messages is acculturative stress (Chan & Ostheimer, 1983; Smart & Smart, 1995). Acculturative stress can be resolved in several ways, including adopting the values of the dominant culture. However, as Rokeach (1973) noted, although values may change as a reaction to conflict, they may also change as a result of contemplation. Therefore, acculturation probably does not occur solely as a reaction to conflicts.

Members of minority groups are continuously exposed to the values of the dominant culture, values that are often at odds with those they have acquired from their own culture (e.g., McWhirter & Ryan, 1991; Smart & Smart, 1995). Acceptance and inclusion of Eurocentric values in the values system and the behavioral norms and traditions accompanying them result in acculturation. One of the outcomes of acculturation may be the rejection of one's cultural beliefs. If the conflicting images and messages that are transmitted from the different culture are rejected, no acculturation occurs (LaFromboise, Trimble, & Mohatt, 1990). Two additional points should be made at this time. First, acculturation is not necessarily a one-way process: it is reversible. Second, acculturation is a process that may affect individuals from all cultural groups, including members of the dominant culture who interact with cultural groups with different values (Berry, 1990). Because of the dynamic nature of the enculturation process in a multicultural society, it is a mistake to make assumptions based solely on cultural group membership.

CULTURAL GROUP MEMBERSHIP VERSUS INTERNALIZED CULTURE   Cultural group membership, which is a demographic designation, has typically been used in lieu of internalized culture (D. Ho, 1995). Ho recommends that the psychological characteristic—internalized culture—be substituted for demographic designations. Internalized culture consists of the beliefs and values of the individual. Research has consistently supported the idea that values systems differ among major cultural groups as well as *within* group variation (e.g., Carter, 1991), and, thus, assuming that an individual has a particular set of cultural values is likely to lead to erroneous conclusions.

FACTORS THAT RETARD MOTIVATION TO ACT ON VALUES   As noted previously, values are the major force in the goal-setting process (Feather, 1988; Rokeach, 1973). However, five factors may lead individuals to lower their expectations of success if they act on their values: mental health problems (Casserly, 1982; Pietromonaco & Rock, 1987), history of personal/cultural group discrimination (M. Brown, 1995; Leong & Serifica, 1995; Melamed, 1996), lack of information (Brown, 1996), poverty (Hotchkiss & Borow, 1996), and self-efficacy (e.g., Lent, Brown, & Hackett, 1996, 2002). These variables are all incorporated into the propositions that follow.

Propositions of Brown's Values-Based Theory

Several propositions are related to Brown's values-based theory (Brown, 1996):

1. Highly prioritized work values are the most important determinants of career choice for people who value individualism (i.e., the individual is the most important unit) if their work values are crystallized and prioritized. Such individuals are affected by several factors: They feel unconstrained to act on their work values; at least one occupational option is available that will satisfy the values held; values-based information about occupational options is available; the difficulty level of implementing the options is approximately the same; and the financial resources available are sufficient to support the implementation of the preferred option.

1. a. Factors that limit the number of occupational options considered for people who value individualism include low SES, minority status, mental health problems, physical disabilities, gender (Gottfredson, 1996), low scholastic aptitude, perception that they will be discriminated against in the occupation, and lack of values-based information. Women, minorities, people from lower-SES levels, and people with mental or physical limitations who value individualism choose occupations consistent with their work values, but they are likely to choose from a more restricted range of occupations than white European American males.

1. b. Self-efficacy becomes a constraining factor in the occupational decision-making process of individuals who value individualism when the options being considered require widely divergent skills and abilities.

2. Individuals who hold collective social values and come from families and/or groups who hold the same social values either defer to the wishes of the group or family members or are heavily influenced by them in the occupational decision-making process. The result is that the occupations chosen correlate less with the individual's work values than is the case with individuals who value individualism and make their own occupational choices.

2. a. Gender is a major factor in the occupations entered by individuals who value collectivism because of decision makers' sex-stereotyped perceptions of occupations. The result is that occupational choices are more likely to be stereotypically male or female. Women who value collectivism enter a more restricted range of occupations than men who value collectivism.

2. b. Perceptions that discrimination may occur if an occupation is chosen is a deterrent to choosing that occupation by decision makers who value collectivism.

2. c. Perceptions regarding resources available to implement an occupational choice are a major limiting factor in the occupational decision-making process of individuals who value collectivism.

2. d. The outcome of the occupational decision-making process for people who value collectivism is less influenced by the availability of the values-based occupational information than it is by the work values of their families or groups.

3. When taken individually, cultural values regarding activity (doing, being, being-in-becoming) do not constrain the occupational decision-making process. People who value individualism and have both a future/past-future time value and a doing/activity value are more likely to make decisions at important transition points, such as graduation from high school, and to act on those choices than people who value either collectivism or individualism and being or being-in-becoming.

4. Because of differing values systems, males and females and people from differing cultural groups enter occupations at varying rates.

5. The process of choosing an occupation value involves the following series of "estimates": (a) one's abilities and values, (b) the skills and abilities required to be successful in an occupation, and (c) the work values that the occupational alternatives being considered satisfy. For people who value individualism, the ability to make accurate estimates is a critical factor in their occupational success and satisfaction. For individuals who value collateral relationships, estimates made by the decision makers are the key factors in their occupational success and satisfaction.

> **5. a.** People who value individualism and who come from backgrounds where little emphasis is placed on feedback about individual strengths, weaknesses, and personal traits and who make their own occupational decisions make more errors in the process as defined by mismatches between their values and those values satisfied by the job. The result is lowered job satisfaction, lower levels of success, and shorter job tenure. In the case of people who value collateral, satisfaction, success, and tenure are based on the ability of the decision maker to make these estimates.

6. Occupational success is related to job-related skills acquired in formal and informal educational settings, job-related aptitudes and skills, SES, participation in the work role, and the extent to which discrimination is experienced regardless of which social relationship value is held.

> **6. a.** Because success in the occupational role requires an awareness of future events and the ability to accommodate the dynamic changes that occur in the workplace, success in the occupational role is related to time and activity values, with individuals having future or past/future values paired with doing/activity values being the most successful.

7. Occupational tenure is partially the result of the match between the cultural and work values of the worker, supervisors, and colleagues.

STATUS AND USE OF BROWN'S VALUES-BASED THEORY   Brown's first attempt at developing a values-based theory appeared in 1996. That theory attempted to account for the complexity of all life roles, admittedly a difficult task. His latest theory (first published in 2002) is a more modest attempt to account for occupational choice, satisfaction, and success and is thus more in line with the other theories in this section. Because of the newness of the theory, it is difficult to anticipate what its impact might be. Hopefully the theory will stimulate more thinking about the importance of cultural values and the need to consider cultural differences when examining the occupational choice-making process. A detailed example of an approach to career counseling using Brown's theory is presented in Chapter 4.

DEVELOPMENTAL THEORIES

Developmental theories focus on the biological, psychological, sociological, and cultural factors that influence career choice, adjustments to and changes in careers, and withdrawal from careers. These theories focus on stages of development (e.g., childhood and adolescence). The first developmental theory was presented in 1951 by Ginzberg, Ginzburg, Axelrad, and Herma, but their theory has been overshadowed by Super's life span, life space theory, which is discussed below. Another developmental theory has been presented by Gottfredson (1981, 1996), who focused on circumscription and compromise. Although her theory is not as comprehensive as Super's theory, it examines an extremely important aspect of the career development process—the impact that sex-typing occupations have on career choice.

Super's Life Span, Life Space Theory

Probably no one has written as extensively about career development or influenced the study of the topic as much as Donald Super. His writing on career development is so extensive that even a highly motivated student faces a major challenge in reviewing all of his work. The references cited here provide considerable depth but are not intended to be all-inclusive. (See the references at the end of this chapter for a listing of several works by Super.).

Super's earliest theoretical statements were influenced by researchers in differential psychology, developmental psychology, sociology, and personality theory. Super has often stated that his view is a "segmented" theory consisting of several related propositions, out of which he hopes an integrated theory ultimately emerges. He has, from time to time, restated these segments, broadening slightly earlier statements and on two occasions adding more segments. His 1953 article presented the initial 10 postulates. He added two more in the 1957 book written with Bachrach. The 1990 article expands the list to 14 propositions that are the basis for the following consideration of Super's life span theory. In this sequence, the original 10 propositions fall under items 1–6 and 9–12, and the additional propositions are identified by items 7, 8, 13, and 14. Super's 1990 statements are italicized, followed, where appropriate, with a brief discussion of the proposition.

1. *People differ in their abilities and personalities, needs, values, interests, traits, and self-concepts.*   The concept of individual differences is so widely recognized and accepted that no one seriously challenges it. The range of personal characteristics varies widely both within each individual and among individuals. Within each person are traits or abilities so pronounced that often they seem to caricature the individual. At the same time, in other areas each person is relatively weak or inept. Although most of us are more or less like other people in many traits, the uniqueness of each person is apparent in the individualized combination of strengths and weaknesses.

2. *People are qualified, by virtue of these characteristics, for a number of occupations.* The range of abilities, personality characteristics, and other traits is so wide that every person has within his or her makeup the requisites for success in many occupations. Research in the field of rehabilitation has demonstrated that even individuals with severe disabilities have the choice of many occupations in which they can perform satisfactorily. For people without serious physical or emotional impairment, the gamut of possibilities is wide indeed.

Few occupations require special abilities, skills, or traits in excessive quantity. Just as most athletic activities involve only certain muscles or muscle groups, so too most jobs require only a few specific characteristics. A person can thus perform successfully in any occupation for which he or she has the qualifying characteristics. The lack of a certain skill, or its presence in minute quantities, excludes the person from an occupation only if that skill is important in meeting the demands of a particular job.

3. *Each occupation requires a characteristic pattern of abilities and personality traits— with tolerances wide enough to allow both some variety of occupations for each individual and some variety of individuals in each occupation.*   For each ability or trait required in the performance of a particular occupation, we might expect to find a modal quantity that best fits the nature of the work. On either side of this amount, however, is a band or range of this characteristic that satisfactorily meets the demands of the work. For example, picture an extremely simple task that requires, hypothetically, only a single characteristic. In studying this task, we might ascertain the quantity of this trait that would best meet the requirements of the job. We would also expect that a person could perform satisfactorily even though he or she possessed less than the ideal amount of the trait, as long as the person surpassed the minimum demanded by the job. However, we could also expect satisfactory performance even if the worker possessed more of the trait than was required for optimum performance.

Because the patterns of abilities required in various occupations are rarely unique, we can expect to find considerable overlap. Thus, a number of occupations exist in which a particular distribution of assets can result in satisfactory performance, just as a number of patterns of ability exist that can result in satisfactory performance in a given occupation.

4. *Vocational preferences and competencies, the situations in which people live and work, and, hence, their self-concepts change with time and experience, although self-concepts, as products of social learning, are increasingly stable from late adolescence until late maturity, providing some continuity in choice and adjustment.* As individuals exercise certain skills or proficiencies, they may increase or expand them to a higher level. As these higher-level skills develop, workers may be drawn to occupational outlets that provide opportunities to use them. Similarly, as workers perform successfully in given work situations, they may realize that participating in more rewarding or more responsible positions may result in even more satisfaction. However, work situations may be so demanding on some workers that they may look for positions that do not tax the pattern of abilities so heavily.

Because the pattern of skills and preferences, as well as the work situation, undergoes constant change, it is likely that a job a worker once found entirely satisfactory is no longer viewed that way. The individual whose self-concept changes may also find that a once-satisfactory job is no longer so. Either of these changes may result in the worker seeking a new work situation or attempting to adjust the current position in some way so it again becomes comfortable and satisfying. Because neither the worker nor the job is static, either change or adjustment is necessary to keep the two in balance.

Super (1984, 1990) emphasizes that self-concept should be defined broadly to include not only an internalized personal view of self but also the individual's view of the situation or condition in which he or she exists. This is a significant factor because the situation surrounding the individual always bears on the person's behavior and self-understanding. Super suggests that *personal-construct* might be a more useful term than *self-concept* because it permits this broader definition.

5. *This process of change may be summed up in a series of life stages (a "maxicycle") characterized as a sequence of growth, exploration, establishment, maintenance, and decline, and these stages may in turn be subdivided into (a) the fantasy, tentative, and realistic phases of the exploratory stage and (b) the trial and stable phases of the establishment stage. A small (mini) cycle takes place in transitions from one stage to the next or each time an individual is destabilized by a reduction in force, changes in type of personnel needs, illness or injury, or other socioeconomic or personal events. Such unstable or multiple-trial careers involve new growth, reexploration, and reestablishment (recycling).*

The *growth* stage refers to physical and psychological growth. During this time the individual forms attitudes and behavior mechanisms that become important components of the self-concept for much of life. Simultaneously, experiences provide a background of knowledge of the world of work that is ultimately used in tentative choices and in final selections.

The *exploratory* stage begins with the individual's awareness that an occupation is an aspect of life. During the early or fantasy phase of this stage, the expressed choices are frequently unrealistic and often closely related to the play life of the individual. Examples can be seen in young children's choices of such careers as cowboy, movie star, pilot, and astronaut. These choices are nebulous and temporary and usually have little, if any, long-term significance for the individual. Some adolescents and even some adults, of course, have not advanced beyond the fantasy phase. Often, the understanding of themselves or of the world of work needed to make more effective choices is either missing or disregarded.

In the tentative phase of the exploratory stage, individuals narrow choices to a few possibilities. Because of uncertainty about ability, availability of training, or employment opportunity, the list may contain choices that later disappear. The final phase of the exploratory stage, still prior to actual entrance into the world of work, narrows the list to those occupations that individuals feel are within reach and provide the opportunities they feel are most important.

The *establishment* stage, as the name implies, relates to early encounters within actual work experiences. During this period the individual, at first perhaps by trial and error, attempts to ascertain whether choices and decisions made during the exploratory period have validity. Some of these attempts are simply tryouts. The individual may accept a job with the definite feeling that he or she will change jobs if this one does not fit. As he or she gains experience and proficiency, the individual becomes stabilized; that is, aspects of this occupation are brought into the self-concept, and the occupation is accepted as one that offers the best chance to obtain those satisfactions that are important.

During the *maintenance* stage, the individual attempts to continue or improve the occupational situation. Because both the occupation and the individual's self-concept have some fluidity, this involves a continual process of change or adjustment. Essentially, the person is concerned with continuing the satisfying parts of the work situation and revising or changing those unpleasant aspects that are annoying but not so disagreeable that they drive the individual from the field.

The *decline* stage includes the preretirement period, during which the individual's emphasis in work is focused on keeping the job and meeting the minimum standards of output. The worker is now more concerned with retaining the position than with enhancing it. This period terminates with the individual's withdrawal from the world of work.

Research by Levinson (1978) and by Gould (1972) on postadolescent male development appears to support Super's life stages approach. Both report patterns of adult male development consisting of relatively stable, structure-building periods separated by transitional, structure-changing periods. Levinson found that their subjects made occupational choices between ages 17 and 29 and often made different choices later. This age period is somewhat later than Super theorized. They also report that the preparatory phase of occupational development is completed in the 28–33 age period, also later than previously assumed. The discrepancy in ages may be because data for the Levinson subjects were obtained by interviewing adult men who were recalling earlier events in their lives.

Murphy and Burck (1976), using Super's life stages concept, suggest that the increasing frequency of midlife career changes may indicate that an additional stage, the renewal stage, be inserted between the establishment stage and the maintenance stage. During this period, approximately between ages 35 and 45, individuals reconsider earlier goals and plans, and then either rededicate themselves to pursuing those goals or decide to move in other directions with a midlife career change.

6. *The nature of the career pattern—that is, the occupational level attained and the sequence, frequency, and duration of trial and stable jobs—is determined by the individual's parental socioeconomic level, mental ability, education, skills, personality characteristics (needs, values, interests, traits, and self-concepts), and career maturity and by the opportunities to which he or she is exposed.*

All factors in the individual's experiential background contribute to attitudes and behavior. Some factors obviously contribute more significantly than others. The socioeconomic level of the individual's parents may be one of these because the individual's early contact with the world of work is largely brought about through parents, family, and friends. Hearing parents and their friends discuss experiences at work; observing the impact of occupational success, failure, or frustration within the family; and obtaining or losing chances at education, travel, or other experiences because of family circumstances all greatly influence the individual's later work history. The individual's mental ability is an important factor in academic success that can open or close doors to many occupations. Ability to deal with others is important in most work situations. "Being in the right place at the right time" or "getting the breaks" is also important because the individual must first have an opportunity to demonstrate competency before becoming established in a job.

We often think that, in the Horatio Alger tradition, anyone can attain any goal if he or she only tries hard enough. In reality, however, factors over which we often have no control set limits that can be surpassed or extended only by Herculean effort, if at all.

7. *Success in coping with the demands of the environment and of the organism in that context at any given life-career stage depends on the readiness of the individual to cope with these demands (that is, on his or her career maturity).* Super identifies career maturity as a group of physical, psychological, and social characteristics that represent the individual's readiness and ability to face and deal with developmental problems and challenges. These personal aspects have both emotional and intellectual components that produce the individual's response to the situation. The person whose maturity is equal to the problem probably resolves it with minimal difficulty or concern; when the maturity is not sufficient for the task, inadequate responses of procrastination, ineptness, or failure are likely to occur.

8. *Career maturity is a hypothetical construct. Its operational definition is perhaps as difficult to formulate as is that of intelligence, but its history is much briefer and its achievements even less definite.* Super's early research (e.g., the 25-year longitudinal study called the Career Pattern Study) addressed the concept of maturity as related to career or vocational development problems. He and coworkers searched for ways to define and assess this concept. Out of these efforts emerged Super's Career Development Inventory.

9. *Development through the life stages can be guided partly by facilitating the maturing of abilities and interests and partly by aiding in reality testing and in the development of self-concepts.* Individuals can be helped to move toward a satisfying vocational choice in two ways: (a) by helping them to develop abilities and interests and (b) by helping them to acquire an understanding of their strengths and weaknesses so they can make satisfying choices.

Both aspects of this postulate emphasize the role of the school and its guidance program in assisting the individual to maximize development as a person. The teacher, having frequent contacts with a young person, has the best opportunity to observe latent or underdeveloped abilities in the classroom. The teacher has numerous chances to challenge the individual to push toward higher, but nevertheless reachable, goals. The counselor, similarly, through data obtained from tests or other guidance techniques may encounter undeveloped potential. Out-of-school adults may need similar types of help.

Three questions have occasionally been found useful in the counseling relationship by providing some indication of the extent to which the counselee has already engaged in some reality testing of vocational aspirations:

What would you like to be if you could do anything you wanted?

What do you expect to be 10 years from now?

What is the least you would settle for 10 years from now?

The first question frequently evokes a fantasy response, which the individual usually soon labels as such. The second question often elicits a reply that still includes considerable fantasy but may also include a sizable display of self-evaluation and insight. The third question requires the client to discard fantasy entirely and to cope with strengths, weaknesses, and potential as the client sees them.

10. *The process of career development is essentially that of developing and implementing occupational self-concepts. It is a synthesizing and compromising process in which the self-concept is a product of the interaction of inherited aptitudes, physical makeup, opportunity to observe and play various roles, and evaluations of the extent to which the results of role playing meet the approval of superiors and fellows (interactive learning).*

As the individual develops and matures, he or she acquires a mental picture of self—a self-concept. Because one's position in the world of work is important in U.S. culture, this becomes a major influence on the individual's self-concept. During the educational period, before actual entrance into work, one's anticipated occupational role plays a part in the development of self-concept. Each person attempts to maintain or enhance a favorable self-concept and thus is led toward those activities that permit him or her to keep or improve the desired self-image. As the inner drive toward this ideal self-concept pushes the individual strongly, he or she encounters restricting factors, which may come from personal limitations or from the external environment. These factors interfere with attainment of the ideal self-concept and result in the individual compromising or accepting somewhat less than the ideal.

Another influence involves the extent to which individuals can gain insight into a variety of occupations and see to what extent each occupation permits them to be the kind of persons they want to be in their own eyes and in the eyes of family, teachers, peer group, and others whose opinions they value.

Super's (1980) description of a life-career rainbow, illustrated in Figure 2.3, emphasizes the different roles played by each individual during his or her lifetime and the influencethese

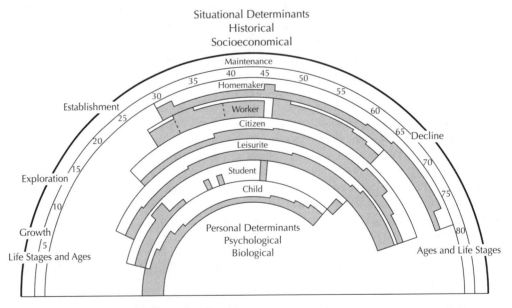

FIGURE 2.3 Super's Life-Career Rainbow: Six Life Roles in Schematic Life Space. *Source:* From "A Life Span, Life-Space Approach to Career Development," by D. E. Super, 1980, *Journal of Vocational Behavior, 16,* pp. 282–298. Copyright © 1980 by Academic Press. Reprinted with permission.

roles have on lifestyle and career. Typical roles for most people include child, student, citizen, worker, spouse, homemaker, parent, and pensioner. These roles emphasize the lifelong aspect of career development.

11. *The process of synthesis of or compromise between individual and social factors, between self-concepts and reality, is one of role playing and of learning from feedback, whether the role is played in fantasy, in the counseling interview, or in such real-life activities as classes, clubs, part-time work, and entry jobs.*

Modifications of the vocational aspects of the self-concept may occur in many ways. Because the world of work is so complex and entrance requirements in many areas so difficult, it is not feasible to experiment with actual participation in more than a few actual work situations. This leaves the necessity of matching the self-concept and its demands against what occupations have to offer in a situation that is essentially abstract. This may be a daydream or reverie, it may involve seeking professional assistance through counseling, or it may mean seeking related experiences that help the individual evaluate the suitability of the occupation in terms of self-concept.

12. *Work satisfactions and life satisfactions depend on the extent to which the individual finds adequate outlets for abilities, needs, values, interests, personality traits, and self-concepts. They depend on establishment in a type of work, a work situation, and a way of life in which one can play the kind of role that growth and exploratory experiences have led one to consider congenial and appropriate.*

The individual who finds pleasure and satisfaction in work does so because the position held permits characteristics and values to be used in a way that is seen as important. In other words, the experiences encountered in work are comparable with the individual's mental image of self—they give sufficient opportunity to be the kind of person one pictures oneself to be.

If the work performed does not provide individuals with the possibility of being the type of person they picture themselves to be, they becomes discontented. This dissatisfaction usually causes them to look for work situations where the possibility to play the desired role seems likelier.

13. *The degree of satisfaction people attain from work is proportional to the degree to which they have been able to implement self-concepts.* The relationship of the work situation to the individual's role must be thought of in the broad sense. The professions and higher managerial positions probably provide the greatest opportunities, as viewed by most people, for the intrinsic satisfactions that come from work itself. But many individuals gain great satisfaction from work that to some appears boring and monotonous. Other workers find satisfaction in jobs that they too may consider routine and unchallenging but that provide them the chance to be the kind of people they want to be, to do the things they want to do, and to think of themselves as they wish to think. Super proposes that the amount of satisfaction is directly related to the extent the job fits the self-concept. Super and Kidd (1979) explored career change and modification in adults, recognizing the increase in midlife career change. They suggest that *career adaptability* may be an appropriate term to identify the individual's ability to face, pursue, or accept changing career roles.

14. *Work and occupation provide a focus for personality organization for most men and women, although for some persons this focus is peripheral, incidental, or even nonexistent. Then other foci, such as leisure activities and homemaking, may be central. (Social traditions, such as gender-role stereotyping and modeling, racial and ethnic biases, and the opportunity structure, as well as individual differences, are important determinants of preferences for such roles as worker, student, leisurite, homemaker, and citizen.)*

Essentially, this proposition says that most adults are what they do—the individual is a reflection of that person's job or major role. To a large degree this proposition relates to the life-career rainbow (see again Figure 2.3), proposed by Super (1980) as representative of lifespan, life space career development, As indicated in this proposition, Super believes that the various segments of his theory apply to both men and women, if modified slightly to provide for women's childbearing role.

STATUS AND USE OF SUPER'S THEORY   At the time of his death in 1994, Super had authored or coauthored nearly 200 articles, books, book chapters, monographs, and other publications, many of them dealing with his theory. His students and others have also contributed dozens, if not hundreds, of publications to the professional literature, all stimulated by his theory. His theory is, by his own admission (Super, 1990), not well constructed because the various segments are not cemented together. This is probably the reason that many of the research studies stimulated by the theory focus on some of the constructs (e.g., career maturity) contained in the theory as opposed to testing its assumptions directly (Super, Savickas, & Super, 1996).

Super's (1990) theory has a number of applications. For example, it has been used as the framework for career development programs for children and adolescents. Growth is the developmental stage that covers pre–K to middle school and is subdivided into curiosity, fantasies, interests, and capacities (focusing on abilities). The exploration stage begins at about age 14 and continues until age 18, at which time a choice is crystallized. These stages are obviously approximations, but they can be useful when designing a career development program.

The theory can also be used as a basis for career counseling. The objective of the career counseling process would be the development of career maturity, which can be placed in six components, as measured by the Career Development Inventory (CDI) (Super, Thompson, Jordaan, & Myers, 1984):

- *Career planning (CP).* Career-mature individuals actively engage in the planning process and perceive themselves to be so engaged. The career planning scale is an effective tool that reveals how persons perceive themselves in relation to the planning process.
- *Career exploration (CE).* Career-mature individuals relate to the willingness of a client to engage in exploring careers—that is, their willingness to use materials. This scale is combined with the CP scale to produce a career development attitude (CDA) scale.
- *Decision making (DM).* Career-mature individuals know how to make decisions and have confidence in their abilities to do so.
- *World-of-work information (WWI).* The most obvious component of this scale involves having accurate information about work. Super believed that decision makers should have some knowledge of the time, developmentally speaking, in which people should acquire important information about work.
- *Knowledge of preferred occupations (PO).* Following, the CDI, people choose 20 occupations and answer questions about the jobs and qualifications needed to enter a particular occupation. WWI and PO are combined in the CDI to produce a career development knowledge and skill score (CDK).
- *Career orientation (COT).* The COT is the total score on the CDI, with the exception of the PO. In a sense this can be considered a global measure of career maturity.

Career counselors may or may not administer the CDI or another inventory, the Career Maturity Inventory (CMI) (Crites & Savickas, 1995), which also measures readiness to make a career decision and the amount of knowledge needed to make that decision. McDivitt (2002) suggests that the CMI can be used to teach clients the decision-making process, and the same can be said of the CDI. Counselors can raise some of the following issues to obtain the same information:

- *CP.* How would you rate your ability to make future plans on a scale of 1 to 10? How far along are you in the planning for your career?
- *CP.* Do you live in the past, focus on the present, or plan for the future? Why did you rate yourself as you did?
- *CE.* Estimate how many times you have sought information about careers by (1) talking to people, (2) reading occupational information, (3) using online sources of information about jobs, or (4) consulting other sources of information about jobs.
- *PO.* How much information do you have about your current occupational choice? What are the characteristics needed by successful workers in this occupation and how do these match your own characteristics?
- *DM.* Rate your ability to make a wise occupational choice on a scale of 1 to 10. Describe the process you followed when you last made a major decision.

Super's early theorizing (e.g., 1980, 1981) focused on what he perceived as the difference between the career development of men and women. It was and is a "white bread" theory because it was formulated based on research with white subjects. Sharf (2002) summarized the research on the career maturity of African Americans and concluded that they are likely to be lower in career maturity than white persons. However, stimulating career maturity, as defined by Super, and then helping clients develop and implement an occupational self-concept seems appropriate for most groups if they subscribe to an independence social value. Leong and Serifica (1995) questioned the application of Super's ideas to Asian American students because they are more likely to have a dependent decision-making style. It should be added that the dependent decision-making style is typical for individuals who subscribe to collateral social values. One of the goals implicit in the counseling process outlined here is the stimulation of an independent decision-making style.

Gottfredson's Theory of Circumscription and Compromise

The theory offered by Gottfredson (2002) is concerned with how career aspirations develop. It is predicated on four basic assumptions: (1) The career development process begins in childhood; (2) career aspirations are attempts to implement one's self-concept; (3) career satisfaction depends on the degree to which the career is congruent with self-perceptions; and (4) people develop occupational stereotypes that guide them in the selection process. Obviously, these assumptions about self-concept have much in common with Super (1990), and Gottfredson's views on occupational stereotypes are identical to Holland's (1997).

Gottfredson departs from other theorists in that she believes the self-concept consists of a social self and a psychological self, with the former being the more important determinant of occupational aspirations. The social self is made up of those aspects of self-perceptions regarding intelligence, social status, and gender, whereas the psychological self is made up of variables such as values and personality variables. Gottfredson believes that the major thrust of choosing a career is to establish a social identity based on the choice. According to Gottfredson (1996), people develop cognitive maps of occupations that are organized along three dimensions:

1. Masculinity/femininity of the occupation
2. Prestige of the occupation (see Table 2.2)
3. Fields of work

TABLE 2.2   Social Status of 25 Occupations: 1925, 1946, 1967, 1975, and 1992

Occupation	1925	1946	1967	1975	1992
Banker	1	2.5	4	3	5
Physician	2	1	1	1	1
Lawyer	3	2.5	2	5	2
Superintendent of Schools	4	4	3	4	4
Civil Engineer	5	5	5	2	3
Army Captain	6	6	8	8	6
Foreign Missionary	7	7	7	9	NR
Elementary School Teacher	8	8	6	6	7
Farmer	9	12	19	7	16
Machinist	10	9	12	11	14
Traveling Salesperson	11	16	13	16	13
Grocer	12	13	17	13	18
Electrician	13	11	9	10	8
Insurance Agent	14	10	10	14	9
Mail Carrier	15	14	18	17	15
Carpenter	16	15	11	12	10
Soldier	17	19	15	19	11
Plumber	18	17	16	15	12
Motorman (Bus Driver)	19	18	20	22	19
Barber	20	20	14	18	17
Truck Driver	21	21.5	21	21	20
Coal Miner	22	21.5	23	20	21
Janitor	23	23	22	24	23
Hod Carrier	24	24	24	23	22
Ditchdigger	25	25	25	25	24

Source: From "Fifty Years of Stability in the Social Status of Occupations," by G. A. Kanzaki, 1976, *Vocational Guidance Quarterly, 25,* pp. 101–105; and from "Social Status Ranking of Occupations in the People's Republic of China, Taiwan, and the United States," by R. H. Frederickson, J. G, Lin, & S. Xing, 1992, *Career Development Quarterly, 40,* pp. 351–360. Used by permission of NCDA.

For Gottfredson, prestige goes beyond the social status of the occupation and includes an intellectual complexity or ability dimension. Of these dimensions, the sex-type assigned to the occupation and the prestige associated with it are the most important in the career choice–making process, when individuals estimate the degree to which they are compatible with a given occupation. In making these estimates, preserving their self-perception regarding their masculinity or femininity is the most powerful concern, followed in descending order by protecting their social standing, and representing their interests and personality. Obviously, in the consideration of potential occupational choices, the accessibility of the occupation also must be considered. Career aspirations are the result of the interaction between estimates of accessibility and compatibility estimates.

As children grow, and develop perceptions of themselves and occupational fields, they begin to narrow or circumscribe their range of occupations based on their estimates of compatibility (sex-type, prestige, and interests) and accessibility. Gottfredson believes that once self-perceptions are developed and occupations discounted as incompatible with them, it is unlikely that the process will be reversed unless some type of intervention occurs, such as an influential person telling them that they have the intellectual capacity to perform the tasks associated with entering the occupation.

Often the final occupational choice is a compromise as adolescents and adults give up their most preferred choices in favor of those that are more accessible. Compromise, that is, the process of selecting an occupation that is viewed as a less-than-optimal fit with the self-view, occurs as a result of many factors, including the availability of work in some fields (e.g., artistic jobs), availability and quality of educational and employment opportunities, and discrimination. When people are forced to compromise, they give first consideration to sex-type, second consideration to prestige, and third consideration to interests. Using these three variables and their knowledge about the accessibility of careers, individuals develop a zone of acceptable occupations within their cognitive map of the occupational structure.

GOTTFREDSON'S DEVELOPMENTAL STAGES   Gottfredson (2002) has identified four developmental stages:

Ages 3–5: Orientation to size and power   During this stage children are laying the groundwork for later sex-role stereotypes as they observe play activities, orient themselves to same-sex adults, and learn about adult activities, such as occupations.

Ages 6–8: Orientation to sex roles   Children are not aware of social class at this stage, but they are beginning to develop perceptions of what is "acceptable" for men and women.

Ages 9–13: Orientation to social valuation   Children perceive that occupations have different social statuses and become critical of lower-status occupations. They also begin to recognize the symbols of social status. During this stage, they begin to develop ideas about their abilities, and using these perceptions, along with those associated with social class and sex typing (see Counselor's Report on Julio), they begin to develop tolerable boundaries of acceptable occupations. By the end of this period, or soon thereafter, numerous occupations will be eliminated as the circumscription process continues. Once eliminated, an occupation is unlikely to be considered without intervention.

Ages 14+: Choices explored   Occupational choices are explored but are limited to those jobs within the tolerable boundaries that have been constructed, beginning with the appropriateness of the sex-role associated with various occupations, the social status associated with occupations, and perceptions of their abilities. They reject occupational options perceived as being too difficult, either because of their perceptions of their abilities or accessibility. Compromises in preferred occupational choice are often made because of perceptions regarding accessibility.

Julio—Counselor's Report

Julio is a 19-year-old, single male of Cuban descent who has graduated from high school. At the time he began counseling, he was driving a bus that picked up and delivered guests to a large hotel. He was earning $7.50 per hour plus tips. His stated goal was to enter an occupation that would allow him to live well and support the family he expected to have in the future. Although he had been a good student in high school and indicated that attending the local community college either full or part time was something he had considered, he didn't know what course of study to follow.

Before we began to go through a complete process to identify alternatives, I suggested that the job with the most job openings that fit the description he had given was nursing. Big mistake! He sat up straight in his chair and declared, "You have to be kidding. My friends would crucify me."

STATUS AND USE OF GOTTFREDSON'S THEORY   Although Gottfredson (1996, 2002) suggests that her theory has two uses—as a career development program design and as a guide to career counseling—the fact is that it continues to stimulate needed research illuminating the role of gender and status on occupational choice. Tieg and Susskind (2008) explored the roles of sex-typed occupations and status in the occupational preferences of young children and found that girls preferred feminine occupations to masculine occupations. They also found that younger boys preferred masculine occupations with higher status, but that older boys' preferences were influenced by status alone.

According to Gottfredson, career development programs should be designed to break down sex-role stereotypes and limitations in occupational choice based on social status. She suggests that elementary school programs should focus on exploring a full range of occupations to prevent premature circumscription and to provide a basis for later occupational choice. Middle school programs should alert students that they already may be limiting their occupational choices and encourage their self-exploration. The process of identifying interests and abilities continues at the high school level and the issue of how to enter occupations should be introduced. In the author's view, the issue of breaking down occupation barriers should be a major part of this latter program.

Clearly, Gottfredson's theory has implications for career counseling. The second major application in her model involves diagnosing developmental problems. She lists five problems that should be assessed. I have taken the liberty altering questions to make the framework useful with racial and ethnic minorities and persons who have other than heterosexual orientations. The following questions will help identify the areas to be assessed:

1. Does the client have occupational alternatives? If not, is the problem a lack of self-knowledge, lack of occupational knowledge, or unwillingness to choose from among acceptable alternatives? Is the unwillingness the result of sex-role or racial/ethnic group stereotypes or because persons who are gay, lesbian, or bisexual are likely to be discriminated against?

2. Do the demands of entrants into an occupation match the characteristics of the client? Are the choices being considered appropriate?

3. Is the client satisfied with the alternatives being considered? If not, is the dissatisfaction a result of the necessity of compromising interests, or sex-type or racial/ethnic perceptions? Does sexual orientation cause concern about the appropriateness of one or more of the occupations being considered?

4. Has the client unduly restricted his or her occupational choices because of a lack of self-knowledge, knowledge about occupations, or unexamined sex-role or racial/ethnic stereotypes? Has the client's sexual orientation resulted in undue restrictions on occupational choice?

5. Is the client aware of the pathways to the occupations chosen, and is the client confident that she or he can negotiate those pathways? Have occupational alternatives been eliminated because of lack of skill or knowledge about these pathways?

Occupational information plays a major role in Gottfredson's approach to career counseling as it does in all the approaches outlined to this point. The strength of the theory itself is that it provides career counselors with a way to conceptualize how occupations may be limited by sex-role perceptions. Moreover, because it is likely that the process of circumscription and compromise may parallel the process that racial and ethnic minorities and persons with homosexual or bisexual orientations experience, it can be applied easily to these groups as well. However, because Gottfredson's theory is based on the supposition that the client will be the decision maker, the application to clients who do not have independent social values is thus problematic.

STUDENT LEARNING EXERCISE 2.1

Theories based on modern (logical positivism) versus postmodern theories have little in common. Circle the M or the P to indicate which of the following ideas are drawn from each positions.

M   P   1. Behavior is linear

M   P   2. It is not possible to establish cause and effect relationships

M   P   3. Meaningful research must be conducted using qualitative approaches

M   P   4. It is important to understand the laws of human behavior

M   P   5. It is impossible to understand an individual's behavior outside of the context in which it occurs

M   P   6. The theories in this chapter fall into the _____ tradition

Now check your answers

Summary

Five theories of career choice and development, three from the trait-and-factor perspective and two developmental theories, were discussed in this chapter. At the conclusion of each theory some of the applications of the theory were presented and the current status of the theory outlined. In each case, the application of the theory with multicultural populations was discussed. Although it was not pointed out specifically, one factor that limits the application of four of the five theories discussed in this chapter was the social value held by the client or group. All of the theories except Brown's (2002a) values-based theory are predicated on the belief that the individual holds an independence social value and will choose his or her own occupation. This supposition is not accurate for some members of the white majority culture and is patently false for many minority group members. The application of a theory indiscriminately is inappropriate and unethical.

Chapter Quiz

T   F   **1.** Of the theories presented in this chapter Super's developmental theory is probably the most parsimonious.

T   F   **2.** Super and Brown proposed that values are the major factors in occupational choice.

T   F   **3.** The importance of congruence between a person and the work environment was first identified by Frank Parsons.

T   F   **4.** Groups of people who hold collateral social values believe that the welfare of the group should be placed ahead of that of the individual.

T   F   **5.** Super has outlined a clear cut approach to career counseling based on his theory.

T   F   **6.** It is probably more appropriate to refer to an individual's self-concepts than a global self-concept if Super is correct.

T   F   **7.** Gottfried rank orders the factors that influence career choice beginning with interests as the most important.

T   F   **8.** Young girls are more likely than boys to take the sex-typing of occupations into account when stating their occupational preferences.

T F **9.** John Holland's theory of vocational personalities and work environments has been incorporated into material used by the military and the U.S. Department of Labor.

T F **10.** The theory of work adjustment is most like Holland's theory than any of the others presented in this chapter.

T (01) T (6) T (8) F (7) T (9) F (5) T (4) T (3) F (2) T (1)

References

Arbona, C. (1995). Theory and research on racial and ethnic minorities: Hispanic Americans. In F. T. L. Leong (Ed.), *Career development and vocational behavior of ethnic and racial minorities* (pp. 37–66). Mahwah, NJ: Erlbaum.

Arnold, J. (2004). The congruence problem in John Holland's theory of vocational decisions. *Journal of Occupational and Organizational Psychology, 77,* 95–113.

Astin, H. S. (1984). The meaning of work in women's lives: A sociopsychological perspective. *The Counseling Psychologist, 12,* 117–126.

Bandura, A. (1986). *Social foundations of thought and action: A social-cognitive theory.* Englewood Cliffs, NJ: Prentice-Hall.

Beck, A. (1976). *Cognitive therapy and the emotional disorders.* New York: International Universities Press.

Berry, J. W. (1990). Psychology of acculturation: Understanding people moving between cultures. In R. W. Brislin (Ed.), *Applied cross-cultural psychology* (pp. 232–253). Newbury Park, CA: Sage.

Blau, P. M., & Duncan, O. D. (1967). *The American occupational structure.* New York: Wiley.

Bloch, D. P. (2005). Complexity, chaos, and nonlinear dynamics: A new perspective on career development theory. *Career Development Quarterly, 53,* 194–207.

Blustein, D. L. (2006). *The psychology of working: A new perspective for career development and public policy.* Mahwah, NJ: Erlbaum.

Blustein, D. L. (2008). The role of work in psychological health and well being. A historical, conceptual, and public policy perspective. *American Psychologist 63,* 228–240.

Blustein, D. L., Kenna, A. C., Gill, N., & DeVoy, J. E. (2008). The psychology of working: A new framework for counseling practice and public policy. *Career Development Quarterly, 56,* 294–308.

Bordin, E. S. (1984). Psychodynamic model of career choice and satisfaction. In D. Brown, L. Brooks, et al., *Career choice and development* (pp. 94–136). San Francisco: Jossey-Bass.

Brenner, O. C., Blazini, A. P., & Greenhaus, J. H. (1988). An examination of race and sex differences in manager work values. *Journal of Vocational Behavior, 32,* 336–344.

Bright, J. E., & Pryor, R. G. L. (2005). The chaos theory of careers: A user's guide. *Career Development Quarterly, 53,* 291–305.

Brown, D. (1996). A holistic, values-based model of career and life role choice and satisfaction. In D. Brown, L. Brooks, et al., *Career choice and development* (3rd ed.). San Francisco: Jossey-Bass.

Brown, D. (2002a). The role of work values and cultural values in occupational choice, satisfaction, and success. In D. Brown et al., *Career choice and development* (4th ed., pp. 465–509). San Francisco: Jossey-Bass.

Brown, D. (2002b). The role of work and cultural values in occupational choice, success, and satisfaction. *Journal of Counseling and Development, 80,* 48–56.

Brown, D., & Brooks, L. (1996). Introduction to theories of career choice and development. In D. Brown, L. Brooks, et al., *Career choice and development* (3rd ed., pp. 1–32). San Francisco: Jossey-Bass.

Brown, D., & Crace, R. K. (1995). Values and life role decision making: A conceptual model. *Career Development Quarterly, 44,* 211–223.

Brown, M. T. (1995). The career development of African Americans: Theoretical and empirical issues. In F. T. L. Leong (Ed.), *Career development and vocational behavior of racial and ethnic minorities* (pp. 7–30). Mahwah, NJ: Erlbaum.

Carter, R. T. (1991). Cultural values: A review of empirical research and implications for counseling. *Journal of Counseling and Development, 70,* 164–173.

Casserly, M. (1982). *Effects of differentially structured career counseling on the decision quality of subjects with varying cognitive styles.* Unpublished doctoral dissertation, University of Maryland, College Park.

Chan, K. S., & Ostheimer, B. (1983). *Navajo youth and early school withdrawal.* Los Alamitis, CA: National Center for Bilingual Research.

Crites, J. D., & Savickas, M. L. (1995). *Career Maturity Inventory.* Ogdenburg, NY: Careerware.

Dawis, R. V. (1996). The theory of work adjustment and person–environment–correspondence counseling. In D. Brown, L. Brooks, et al., *Career choice and development* (3rd ed., pp. 75–120). San Francisco: Jossey-Bass.

Dawis, R. V., England, G. W., & Lofquist, L. H. (1964). A theory of work adjustment. *Minnesota Studies in Vocational Rehabilitation No. XV.* Minneapolis: University of Minnesota.

Dawis, R. V., & Lofquist, L. H. (1984). *A psychological theory of work adjustment.* Minneapolis: University of Minnesota Press.

Dawis, R. V., Lofquist, L. H., & Weiss, D. J. (1968). A theory of work adjustment (A revision). *Minnesota Studies in Vocational Rehabilitation No. XXIII.* Minneapolis: University of Minnesota.

Day, S. X., Rounds, J., & Swaney, K. (1998). The structure of vocational interests for diverse racial-ethnic groups. *Psychological Science, 9,* 40–44.

Department of Defense (DOD). (2005). *Finding your interests.* Washington, DC: Author.

Feather, N. T. (1988). Values systems across cultures: Australia and China. *International Journal of Psychology, 21,* 697–715.

Fitzgerald, L. F., & Betz, N. E. (1994). Career development in a cultural context. In M. L. Savickas & R. W. Lent (Eds.), *Convergence in career development theories* (pp. 103–118). Palo Alto, CA: CPP Books.

Fouad, N. A. (1995). Career behavior of Hispanics: Assessment and intervention. In F. T. L. Leong (Ed.), *Career development and vocational behavior of racial and ethnic minorities* (pp. 165–192). Mahwah, NJ: Erlbaum.

Ginsberg, E., Ginsburg, S., Axelrad, S., & herma, J. (1951). *Occupational choice: An approach to a general theory New York: Columbia University* (15-2 Gottfredson, G. D., & Holland, J. (1996). *The Dictionary of Holland's Occupational Codes* (3rd Ed.) Odessa, FL: PAR.

Gottfredson, G. D., & Johnstun, M. L. (2009). John Holland's contributions: A theory-ridden approach to career assistance. *Career Development Quarterly, 58,* 99–107.

Gottfredson, L. S. (1981). Circumscription and compromise: A developmental theory of occupational aspirations (Monograph). *Journal of Counseling Psychology, 28,* 545–579.

Gottfredson, L. S. (1996). A theory of circumscription and compromise. In D. Brown, L. Brooks, et al., *Career choice and development* (3rd ed.) pp. 179–281). San Francisco: Jossey-Bass.

Gottfredson, L. (2002). Gottfredson's theory of circumscription and compromise. In D. Brown et al., *Career choice and development* (4th ed., pp. 85–148). San Francisco: Jossey-Bass.

Gould, R. (1972). The phases of adult life: A study in developmental psychology. *American Journal of Psychiatry, 129,* 521–531.

Hackett, G., & Betz, N. E. (1981). A self-efficacy approach to the career development of women. *Journal of Vocational Behavior, 24,* 326–339.

Hartung, P. G. (2002). Cultural context in career theory: Role salience and values. *Career Development Quarterly, 51,* 12–25.

Ho, D. Y. F. (1995). Internal culture, culturocentrism, and transcendence. *The Counseling Psychologist, 23,* 4–24.

Ho, M. K. (1987). *Family therapy with ethnic minorities.* Newbury Park, CA: Sage.

Holland, J. L. (1959). A theory of vocational choice. *Journal of Counseling Psychology, 6,* 35–45.

Holland, J. L. (1962). Some explorations of a theory of vocational choice: I. One- and two-year longitudinal studies. *Psychological Monographs, 76* (26, Whole No. 545).

Holland, J. L. (1963a). Explorations of a theory of vocational choice and achievement: II. A four-year prediction study. *Psychological Reports, 12,* 547–594.

Holland, J. L. (1963b). A theory of vocational choice: Part I. Vocational images and choice. *Vocational Guidance Quarterly, 11,* 232–239.

Holland, J. L. (1963c). A theory of vocational choice: Part II. Self descriptions and vocational preferences. *Vocational Guidance Quarterly, 12,* 17–24.

Holland, J. L. (1963d). A theory of vocational choice: Part IV. Vocational daydreams. *Vocational Guidance Quarterly, 12,* 93–97.

Holland, J. L. (1966a). A psychological classification scheme for vocations and major fields. *Journal of Counseling Psychology, 13,* 278–288.

Holland, J. L. (1966b). *The psychology of vocational choice.* Waltham, MA: Blaisdell.

Holland, J. L. (1968). Explorations of a theory of vocational choice: Part VI. A longitudinal study using a sample of typical college students. *Journal of Applied Psychology, 52* (Monograph Suppl.).

Holland, J. L. (1972). The present status of a theory of vocational choice. In J. M. Whiteley & A. Resnikoff (Eds.), *Perspectives on vocational development* (pp. 8–32). Washington, DC: American Personnel and Guidance Association.

Holland, J. L. (1973). *Making vocational choices: A theory of careers.* Englewood Cliffs, NJ: Prentice-Hall.

Holland, J. L. (1985). *Making vocational choices: A theory of vocational personalities and work environments* (2nd ed.). Englewood Cliffs, NJ: Prentice-Hall.

Holland, J. L. (1987). Current status of Holland's theory of careers: Another perspective. *Career Development Quarterly, 36,* 31–44.

Holland, J. L. (1994a). *The self-directed search technical manual* (4th ed.). Odessa, FL: PAR.

Holland, J. L. (1994b). *The occupations locator* (4th ed.). Odessa, FL: PAR.

Holland, J. L. (1997). *Making vocational choices* (3rd ed.). Englewood Cliffs, NJ: Prentice-Hall.

Holland, J. L., Daiger, D.C., & Power, P. G. (1980). *My vocational situation.* Palo Alto, CA: Consulting Psychologist Press.

Holland, J. L., & Gottfredson, G. D. (1976). Using a typology of persons and environments to explain careers: Some extensions and clarifications. *Counseling Psychologist, 6,* 20–29.

Holland, J. L., & Gottfredson, G. D. (1990). *An annotated bibliography for Holland's theory of vocational personality and work environment.* Baltimore: Johns Hopkins University.

Holland, J. L., & Lutz, S. W. (1968). The predictive value of a student's choice of vocation. *Personnel and Guidance Journal, 46,* 428–436.

Holland, J. L., & Nichols, R. C. (1964). Explorations of a theory of vocational choice: III. A longitudinal study of change in major fields of study. *Personnel and Guidance Journal, 43,* 235–242.

Hotchkiss, L., & Borow, H. (1996). Sociological perspectives on work and career development. In D. Brown, L. Brooks, et al., *Career choice and development* (3rd ed., pp. 137–168). San Francisco: Jossey-Bass.

Ibrahim, F. A. (1985). Effective cross-cultural counseling and psychotherapy: A framework. *Counseling Psychologist, 13,* 625–638.

Jencks, C., Crouse, J. & Mueser, P. (1983). The Wisconsin model of status and attainment: A national replication with improved measures of ability and aspiration. *Sociology of Education, 56,* 3–19.

Kanzaki, G. A. (1976). Fifty years of stability in the social status of occupations. *Vocational Guidance Quarterly, 25,* 101–105.

Kluckhorn, F. R., & Strodtbeck, F. L. (1961). *Values in values orientations.* Evanston, IL: Row Peterson.

Krumboltz, J. D. (1994). Improving career development theory from a social learning theory perspective. In M. L. Savickas & R. W. Lent (Eds.), *Convergence in career development theory* (pp. 9–32). Palo Alto, CA: CPP Books.

LaFromboise, T. D., Trimble, J. E., & Mohatt, G. V. (1990). Counseling intervention and Native American tradition: An integrative approach. *Counseling Psychologist, 18,* 624–628.

Lee, K. C. (1991). The problem of the appropriateness of the Rokeach Values Survey in Korea, *International Journal of Psychology, 26,* 299–310.

Lent, R. W., Brown, S. D., & Hackett, G. (1995). Toward a unifying social cognitive theory of career and academic interest, choice, and performance. *Journal of Vocational Behavior, 45,* 79–122.

Lent, R. W., Brown, S. D., & Hackett, G. (1996). Career development from a social cognitive perspective. In D. Brown, L. Brooks, et al., *Career choice and development* (3rd ed., pp. 373–422). San Francisco: Jossey-Bass.

Lent, R. W., Brown, S. D., & Hackett, G. (2002). Career development from a social cognitive perspective. In D. Brown, L. Brooks, et al., *Career choice and development* (4th ed., pp. 255–311). San Francisco: Jossey-Bass.

Leong, F. T. L. (1991). Career development attributes and occupational values of Asian American and white high school students. *Career Development Quarterly, 39,* 221–230.

Leong, F. T. L., & Gim-Chung, R. H. (1995). Career assessment and intervention with Asian Americans. In F. T. L. Leong (Ed.), *Career development and vocational behavior of racial and ethnic minorities* (pp. 193–226). Mahwah, NJ: Erlbaum.

Leong, F. T. L., & Serifica, F. C. (1995). Career development of Asian Americans: A research area in need of a good theory. In F. T. L. Leong (Ed.), *Career development and vocational behavior of ethnic and racial minorities* (pp. 67–102). Mahwah, NJ: Erlbaum.

Levinson, D. J. (1978). *The seasons of a man's life.* New York: Knopf.

Lofquist, L. H., & Dawis, R. V. (1991). *Essentials of person–environment–correspondence counseling.* Minneapolis: University of Minnesota Press.

Marin, G., & Marin, V. M. (1991). *Research with Hispanic populations.* Newbury Park, CA: Sage.

McDivitt, P. J. (2002). Career Maturity Inventory. In J. T. Kapes & E. A. Whitfield (Eds.), *A counselor's guide to career development instruments* (4th ed., pp. 336–342). Tulsa, OK: National Career Development Association.

McWhirter, J. J., & Ryan, C. A. (1991). Counseling the Navajo: Cultural understanding. *Journal of Multicultural Counseling and Development, 19,* 74–82.

Melamed, T. (1995). Career success: The moderating effects of gender. *Journal of Vocational Behavior, 47,* 295–314.

Melamed, T. (1996). Career success: An assessment of a gender-specific model. *Journal of Occupational and Organizational Psychology, 69,* 217–226.

Murphy, P., & Burck, H. (1976). Career development of men in middle life. *Journal of Vocational Behavior, 9,* 337–343.

Parsons, F. (1909). *Choosing your vocation.* Boston: Houghton-Mifflin.

Pedersen, P. B. (1991). Multiculturalism as a generic approach to counseling. *Journal of Counseling and Development, 70,* 6–12.

Peterson, G. W., Sampson, J. P., Jr., & Reardon, R. C. (1991). *Career development and services: A cognitive approach.* Pacific Grove, CA: Brooks/Cole.

Peterson, G. W., Sampson, J. P., Jr., Reardon, R. C., & Lenz, J. G. (1996). A cognitive information processing approach. In D. Brown, L. Brooks, et al., *Career choice and development* (3rd ed., pp. 423–476). San Francisco: Jossey-Bass.

Peterson, N., & Gonzalez. R. C. (2005). *The role of work in people's lives: Applied career counseling and vocational psychology* (2nd ed.). Belmont, CA: Brooks/Cole.

Phillips, S. D., & Imhoff, A. R. (1997). Women and career development: A decade of research. *Annual Review of Psychology, 48,* 31–60.

Pietromonaco, J. G., & Rock, K. S. (1987). Decision style in depression: The contribution of perceived risks versus benefits. *Journal of Personality and Social Psychology, 52,* 399–408.

Roe, A. (1956). *The psychology of occupations.* New York: Wiley.

Roe, A. (1984). Personality development and career choice. In D. Brown, L. Brooks, et al., *Career choice and development* (pp. 31–53). San Francisco: Jossey-Bass.

Roe, A., & Lunneborg, P. W. (1990). Personality development and career choice. In D. Brown, L. Brooks, et al., *Career choice and development* (2nd ed., pp. 68–101). San Francisco: Jossey-Bass.

Rokeach, M. (1973). *The nature of human values.* New York: Free Press.

Sharf, R. S. (2002). *Applying career development theory to counseling* (3rd ed.). Pacific Grove, CA: Brooks/Cole.

Sidiropoulou-Dimakakou, D., Mylonas, K., & Argyropoulou, K. (2008). Holland's hexagonal personality model for a sample of Greek university students. *Journal of Educational and Vocational guidance, 8,* 11–125

Smart, J. F., & Smart, D. W. (1995). Acculturative stress: The experience of the Hispanic immigrant. *Counseling Psychologist, 23,* 25–42.

Sue, D. W., & Sue, D. (2000). *Counseling the culturally different* (3rd ed.). New York: Wiley.

Super, D. E. (1951). Vocational adjustment: Implementing a self-concept. *Occupations, 30,* 1–5.

Super, D. E. (1953). A theory of vocational development. *American Psychologist, 8,* 185–190.

Super, D. E. (1954). Career patterns as a basis for vocational counseling. *Journal of Counseling Psychology, 1,* 12–20.

Super, D. E. (1955). Personality integration through vocational counseling. *Journal of Counseling Psychology, 2,* 217–226.

Super, D. E. (1957). *The psychology of careers.* New York: Harper & Row.

Super, D. E. (1960). The critical ninth grade: Vocational choice or vocational exploration. *Personnel and Guidance Journal, 39,* 106–109.

Super, D. E. (1964a). A developmental approach to vocational guidance. *Vocational Guidance Quarterly, 13,* 1–10.

Super, D. E. (1964b). Goal specificity in the vocational counseling of future college students. *Personnel and Guidance Journal, 43,* 127–134.

Super, D. E. (1969). Vocational development theory. *The Counseling Psychologist, 1,* 2–30.

Super, D. E. (1972). Vocational development theory: Persons, positions, processes. In J. M. Whiteley & A. Resnikoff (Eds.), *Perspectives on vocational guidance.* Washington, DC: American Personnel and Guidance Association.

Super, D. E. (Ed.). (1974). *Measuring vocational maturity for counseling and evaluation.* Washington, DC: American Personnel and Guidance Association.

Super, D. E. (1977). Vocational maturity in midcareer. *Vocational Guidance Quarterly, 25,* 294–302.

Super, D. E. (1980). A life-span, life-space approach to career development. *Journal of Vocational Behavior, 16,* 282–298.

Super, D. E. (1981). A developmental theory: Implementing a self-concept. In D. H. Montros & C. J. Shinkman (Eds.), *Career development in the 1980s: Theory and practice* (pp. 185–215). Springfield, IL: Thomas.

Super, D. E. (1983). Assessment in career guidance: Toward truly developmental counseling. *Personnel and Guidance Journal, 61,* 555–562.

Super, D. E. (1984). Career and life development. In D. Brown, L. Brooks, et al. (Eds.), *Career choice and development.* San Francisco: Jossey-Bass.

Super, D. E. (1990). A life-span, life-space approach to career development. In D. Brown, L. Brooks, et al. (Eds.), *Career choice and development* (2nd ed.). San Francisco: Jossey-Bass.

Super, D. E., & Bachrach, P. B. (1957). *Scientific careers and vocational development theory.* New York: Teachers College, Columbia University.

Super, D. E., Crites, J. O., Hummel, R. C., Moser, H. P., Overstreet, P. L., & Warnath, C. F. (1957). *Vocational development: A framework for research.* New York: Teachers College, Columbia University.

Super, D. E., & Kidd, J. M. (1979). Vocational maturity in adulthood: Toward turning a model into a measure. *Journal of Vocational Behavior, 14,* 255–270.

Super, D. E., Savickas, M. L., & Super, C. (1996). A life-span, life-space approach to career development. In D. Brown, L. Brooks, et al., *Career choice and development* (3rd ed., pp. 121–178). San Francisco: Jossey-Bass.

Super, D. E., Starishevsky, R., Matlin, R., & Jordaan, J. P. (1963). *Career development: Selfconcept theory.* New York: College Entrance Examination Board.

Super, D. E., & Sverko, B. (Eds.). (1995). *Life roles, values, and careers: International findings of the work importance study.* San Francisco: Jossey-Bass.

Super, D. E., Thompson, A. S., Jordaan, J. P., & Myers, R. (1984). *Career Development Inventory.* Palo Alto, CA: Consulting Psychologist Press.

Tieg, S., & Susskind, J. (2008). Truck driver or nurse? The impact of gender roles and occupational status on children's occupational preferences. *Sex Roles, 58,* 848–863.

Young, R. A., Valach, L., & Collin, A. (2002). A contextual explanation of career. In D. Brown, L. Brooks, et al. (Eds.), *Career choice and development* (4th ed., pp. 206–254). San Francisco: Jossey-Bass.

3

Learning Theory-Based, Postmodern, Socioeconomic, and Decision-Making Theories and Their Applications

Things to Remember

- The major propositions of the theories rooted in learning theory

- The major propositions of the two postmodern approaches and why postmodern theories differ from those that are based in logical positivism

- The major propositions of socioeconomic theories of status attainment

- Two career counseling aids that were derived from decision-making theories

C hapter 3, like Chapter 2, is devoted to career development theory and its application. I hope you have accepted my hypothesis, which I borrowed from Bufford Steflre, that there is nothing as practical as a good theory. I also hope you have identified your own beliefs about human behavior and the process of career choice and development. Have you accepted the postmodern idea that suggests that it is at best difficult to determine cause-and-effect relationships and that it is impossible to generalize from one person to the other, or have you accepted the logical positivist position that both are possible? These issues are important. My own conclusion about this debate is revealed in this chapter and the next. Stay tuned. Two postmodern theories are presented in this chapter that may help you with your deliberations.

The learning theories presented in this chapter, particularly the social cognitive theory, have become increasingly popular. As you read this section try to guess why the cognitive perspective is receiving this increased attention. Keeping in mind that about 30 percent of your potential clients are likely to be from minority groups, which theory best provides an explanation of their choice-making processes?

In Chapter 2, five theories of career choice and development were presented and examples of how they could be applied were discussed. In this chapter, a diverse set of models and theories is presented following the same format used in Chapter 2. The presentation begins with learning-based theories, followed by a discussion of two postmodern theories. A socioeconomic theory of career attainment will precede the final section of this chapter, which deals with decision-making models that may be useful to career development practitioners.

THEORIES BASED IN LEARNING THEORY

In 1979 Krumboltz introduced a theory, based on the social learning theory of Albert Bandura (1977). Although Bandura's ideas about the acquisition of behavior have changed to some degree (e.g., Bandura, 1986), Krumboltz has not altered his theory in any significant way. What differentiates theories rooted in learning theory from trait-and-factor theories is that they are not as concerned about the role of traits, such as interests and values, in the career decision-making process. Rather, their focus is on the learning processes that lead to self-efficacy beliefs and interests and how these impact the career decision-making process. They differ from the developmentalists in some key aspects as well—namely, in that they are not concerned with developmental stages. Learning theorists believe that because many of the factors surrounding career choice and adjustment are learned, their theories need to account for the learning processes that lead to the acquisition of the beliefs and behaviors critical to the career development process.

Krumboltz's Social Learning Theory

Krumboltz (1979, 1996) and Mitchell and Krumboltz (1984, 1990, 1996) describe a social learning theory of career selection based on the behavioral theory of Bandura (1977) and others, emphasizing reinforcement theory. Krumboltz identifies four factors that influence career decision making:

1. *Genetic endowment and special abilities.*   Krumboltz recognizes that certain inherited characteristics can be restrictive influences on the individual. Other factors for which inheritance, at least in part, may set limits include various special abilities, such as intelligence, musical and artistic ability, and physical coordination.

2. *Environmental conditions and events.*   This factor includes those influences that may lie outside the control of individuals but that bear on them through the environment in which they exist. Some influences may be synthetic in the broadest sense; others may be a result of natural forces. These human or natural elements may cause events to occur that also bear on the individual in the educational and career decision process. Examples of influences of this type include the existence of job and training opportunities, social policies and procedures for selecting trainees or workers, rate of return for various occupations, labor and union laws and regulations, physical events such as earthquakes and floods, the existence of natural resources, technological developments, changes in social organization, family training experiences and resources, educational systems, and neighborhood and community influences.

3. *Learning experiences.*   All previous learning experiences influence the individual's educational and career decision making. Recognizing the extreme complexity of the learning process, Krumboltz identifies only two types of learning as examples: instrumental learning experiences and associative learning experiences. He describes *instrumental learning experiences* as those situations in which the individual acts on the environment to produce certain consequences. *Associative learning experiences* are described as situations in which the individual learns by reacting to external stimuli, by observing real or fictitious models, or by pairing two events in time or location.

4. *Task approach skills.* The skills that the individual applies to each new task or problem are called *task approach skills.* Examples of these include performance standards and values; work habits; and perceptual and cognitive processes, such as attending, selecting, symbolic rehearsing, coding, and so on. The application of these skills affects the outcome of each task or problem and in turn is modified by the results.

Krumboltz sees the individual as constantly encountering learning experiences, each of which is followed by rewards or punishments that in turn produce the uniqueness of each person. This continuous interaction with learning experiences produces three types of consequences, which Krumboltz labels as (1) self-observation generalizations, (2) task approach skills, and (3) actions. A *self-observation generalization* is an overt or covert self-statement that evaluates one's own actual or vicarious performance in relation to learned standards. The generalization may or may not be accurate, just as one's self-concept may or may not coincide with the concept others have of an individual. *Task approach skills* are thought to be efforts by the person to project into the future self-observation generalizations to make predictions about future events. They include work habits, mental sets, perceptual and thought processes, performance standards and values, and the like. *Actions* are implementations of behavior, such as applying for a job or changing a major field of study. The behavior produces certain consequences that affect future behavior.

In summary, an individual is born into the world with certain genetic characteristics: race, gender, physique, and special abilities or disabilities. As time passes, the individual encounters environmental, economic, social, and cultural events and conditions. The individual learns from these encounters, building self-observations and task approach skills that are applied to new events and encounters. The successes and failures that accrue in these encounters influence the individual in choosing courses of action in subsequent learning experiences, increasing the likelihood of making choices similar to previous ones that led to success and of avoiding choices similar to those that led to failure. The process is complicated by aspects of instability because the individual changes as a result of the continuous series of learning experiences, and the situation also changes because environmental, cultural, and social conditions are dynamic.

STATUS AND USE OF KRUMBOLTZ'S THEORY   Krumboltz's theory (Krumboltz, 1996; Mitchell & Krumboltz, 1996) has attracted only a modicum of attention from researchers and practitioners although it has much to recommend it. It is particularly attractive as the basis of career counseling. Krumboltz rejects the traditional notion that the goal of career counseling should be to choose an occupation based on the personal traits of the decision maker. Rather, he suggests that the goal should be to facilitate the acquisition of self-knowledge and the skills needed to negotiate an ever-changing world filled with uncertainty. He developed the Career Beliefs Inventory (Krumboltz, 1991) and an accompanying workbook (Levin, Krumboltz, & Krumboltz, 1995) to help people identify their beliefs and integrate them with their interests. According to Krumboltz, individuals who do not learn to take advantage of the learning opportunities that are presented to them on an ongoing basis are likely to make poor decisions.

Above all else, career counseling should prepare clients to recognize and benefit from the learning opportunities that are presented to them. Career counseling should proceed with four thoughts in mind:

1. Clients should prepare to expand their knowledge and skills instead of relying on their status when they enter the counseling process. Career counselors should help clients map their current status and outline a plan for change and growth. By planning to change, clients expand their opportunity structures.
2. Clients need to prepare for an occupational landscape that is ever changing.
3. Although diagnosing the client's current career development problem is a step in the career counseling process, it is not sufficient. Clients need to be empowered to cope with the stressors of a changing world.
4. Career counselors need to focus more broadly and help their clients tackle the array of job-related problems confronting them. Clients need to understand their values and, thus, the things that satisfy them. They need to seize control of their lives, to be able to deal with problems in the workplace, including how to advance in the workplace and plan for retirement.

Krumboltz's approach to career counseling has considerable merit, particularly for disenfranchised and marginalized groups in our society. Krumboltz would not be satisfied to let members of these groups accept the status quo. He would use positive reinforcement for effort and achievement, recognizing that some clients exist in negative environments. He would use behavior rehearsal and cognitive practice to prepare clients for career-related tasks and direct them to role models they can emulate. He would counter beliefs that limit growth and learning and assist clients to establish both proximal and terminal goals. In summary, Krumboltz outlines a dynamic approach to career counseling that can be applied to males and females, as well as to racial and ethnic minorities who have individualistic perspectives. I believe that Krumboltz's approach easily can be monitored to be useful with clients who hold collective perspectives as well. The client might be a family or group, rather than an individual, and some of the techniques would be tempered so that the decision maker in the family is shown the respect she or he deserves. The approach Krumboltz outlines is applicable to people who fear discrimination, including ethnic and racial minorities, and gay, lesbian, bisexual, and transgender clients.

A Social Cognitive Perspective

Social cognitive career theory (SCCT), which is based in the sociocognitive theory of Albert Bandura (1986), parallels Krumboltz's theory to some degree. It also departs from his theory in some significant ways. The most significant of the departures is that Lent, Brown, and Hackett (1995, 1996, 2002) place more emphasis on self-regulatory cognitions, particularly those associated with self-efficacy expectations, which is in keeping with Bandura's position. Self-efficacy beliefs are dynamic, ever-changing self-perceptions that individuals hold about their abilities to perform particular tasks. They state, "In formulating SCCT we tried to adapt, elaborate, and extend those aspects of Bandura's theory that seemed to be most relevant to the process of interest formation, career selection, and performance" (Lent et al., 2002, p. 258). The central propositions of social cognitive theory are as follows:

1. The interaction between people and their environments is highly dynamic; the result is that individuals are at once influenced by and have an influence on their environments.

2. Career-related behavior is influenced by four aspects of the person: behavior, self-efficacy beliefs, outcome expectations, and goals, in addition to genetically determined characteristics.

3. Self-efficacy beliefs and expectations of outcomes interact directly to influence interest development. People become interested in things they believe they can perform well to produce valued outcomes.

4. Gender, race, physical health, disabilities, and environmental variables influence self-efficacy development, as well as expectations of outcomes and, ultimately, goals and performance.

5. Actual career choice and implementation are influenced by a number of direct and indirect variables other than self-efficacy, expectations of outcomes, and goals. Direct influences on career choice and development include discrimination, economic variables that influence supply and demand, and the culture of the decision maker. Indirect influences include chance happenings.

6. Performance in educational activities and occupations is the result of the interactions among ability, self-efficacy beliefs, outcome expectations, and the goals that have been established. All things being equal, people with the highest levels of ability and the strongest self-efficacy beliefs perform at the highest level. However, self-efficacy beliefs and outcome expectations are altered continuously as individuals interact with their environments.

STUDENT LEARNING EXERCISE 3.1

You are a career counselor applying SCCT and a client of yours seems to be unmotivated to move forward toward the selection of an occupational goal. What would be your best guess about why that is the case assuming the absence of mental health problems?

Hint: The answer can be found in proposition 6 and there may be more than one.

Lent, Brown, and Hackett (1996) believe that their theory is in keeping with the increasing emphasis on cognitive functioning in psychology and that earlier theories, such as Krumboltz's social learning theory (Krumboltz, 1979; Mitchell & Krumboltz, 1996), rely too heavily on learning histories and not enough on cognitive processes to explain career-related behavior. For example, neither operant nor classical conditioning are mentioned in their theory, which is not the case in Krumboltz's work.

THE STATUS AND USE OF SOCIAL COGNITIVE CAREER THEORY   Social cognitive career theory was first published in 1994. Since that time SCCT has had a tremendous impact on research regarding career choice. It is also influencing the career assessment process (Betz & Borgen, 2000) in a number of significant ways. In addition there is increasing evidence that SCCT influences career counseling practice (Sharf, 2002). Patton and McIlveen (2009) conducted an extensive review of the career development literature published in 2008. They identified seven research studies and one "opinion piece" that were stimulated by SCCT. The modal number of articles stimulated by other theories appeared to be one.

One of the assumptions of SCCT is that self-efficacy and interests are linked and that interests can be developed or strengthened using modeling, encouragement, and, most powerfully, by performance enactments. Therefore, groups of clients, such as women who may have had little opportunity to engage in certain activities because of sex-typing, can benefit from the application of the theory. Lent, Brown, and Hackett (2002) also suggest that SCCT can be useful in working with other groups, such as members of ethnic and racial minorities, who, because of discrimination or poverty, may have had fewer opportunities to engage in occupationally relevant activities. These researchers report that the theory has been applied successfully to incarcerated women, lesbian women and gay men, and adults with mental illnesses.

Lent and colleagues (2002) recommend two career counseling applications of SCCT. The first begins with gathering traditional test data regarding needs, values, and aptitudes, similar to that which was proposed by Dawis (1996), discussed in Chapter 2. These data can be used to identify skills that have been developed and the situations in which those skills might be applied in a manner that would result in satisfaction.

The second application suggested by Lent and colleagues (2002) involves the use of a modified vocational card sort of occupations representative of the occupational structure. Initially, a client would be asked to sort the cards into two stacks: "In question" and "would choose." The two stacks are then divided into categories that reflect self-efficacy (*I might choose if I had the needed skills*) and outcome expectations (*I might choose if the occupation offered the things that I value*). This sorting process helps the counselor identify some of the cognitions that underpin the decisions to eliminate or retain certain occupations in the sorting process and to examine the accuracy of those cognitions with the client.

Finally, the recommendations for career counseling offered by Mitchell and Krumboltz (1996) in the preceding section should be examined for strategies for use with SCCT. Although Lent and his colleagues and Krumboltz reached various conclusions in their research, both theories are based in learning theory and rely heavily on the social learning theory of Albert Bandura (1977, 1986).

A Career Information–Processing Model of Career Choice

The career information–processing model (CIP) was first presented in 1991 (Peterson, Sampson, & Reardon, 1991) and was revised in 2002 by Peterson, Sampson, Reardon, and Lenz. Like the social cognitive model just described, it is based in learning theory. However, unlike Lent, Brown, and Hackett, who relied on Bandura's 1986 work as the basis for their theory, Peterson and and colleagues relied on the branch of learning theory that focuses on information processing. Additionally, they drew on the work of Meichenbaum (1977), a cognitive therapist, as the basis for some of their recommendations for interventions with career problems.

Figure 3.1 is a representation of CIP theory. It shows that, with regard to career decisions, people develop two types of knowledge: self-knowledge and knowledge about careers, which is identical to Parson's ideas first presented in 1909. However, what Parsons did not address is the decision-making process. When the time to make a career decision arrives, individuals draw on the information-processing skills they have developed, subsumed under self-knowledge about decision-making style. The decision-making process (deciding) can be

FIGURE 3.1 The CIP Model of Occupational Choice   *Source: From Career Development and Sevices: Cognitive Approach*, by G. W. Peterson, J. P. Sampson, Jr. and R. C. Reardon. © 1991. Reprinted with permission of Wadsworth, a division of Thomson Learning: www.thomsonrights.com.

subsumed under the acronym CASVE: communication, analysis, synthesis, valuing, and execution. The communication (C) phase begins with a signal from inside or outside the organism that a problem exists. In response to this signal individuals try to determine the aspects (A) of the problem. In the synthesis (S) stage, individuals generate potential solutions and then identify realistic options. In the valuing (V) stage, a costs-benefits analysis is conducted based on the values system of the individual. Finally, plans are developed and executed (E) to act on the alternatives that have been chosen.

The metacognitions used in the deciding process are the cognitive functions essential to monitoring and regulating the decision-making process. These include the acquisition, storage, retrieval, and processing of information relevant to the career problem at hand. The primary metacognitions involve self-talk, self-awareness, and monitoring and control. Self-talk is the internal dialogue carried on by decision makers with themselves. For the decision-making process to be optimal, the overall nature of this self-talk must be positive (e.g., "I am a good decision maker" and "There are many things I can do"). Self-awareness is the metacognition that keeps decision makers on task by producing the realizations that they are the ones most directly involved and by keeping out superfluous factors. The monitoring and control function has a temporal dimension ("Where am I in the decision-making process?" and, "Where do I need to be at this time?"). This metacognition also allows people to understand when they have collected enough information, when they need to backtrack, and when it is time to move from stage to stage in the process.

Of greatest concern to career counselors and counseling psychologists is the client who, for whatever reasons, is not a good decision maker. The Career Thoughts Inventory (CTI) was developed to diagnose various aspects of decision-making problems (Sampson, Peterson, Lenz, Reardon, & Saunders, 1996). The CTI has items relating to each compartment shown in the pyramid in Figure 3.1, including the executive processes, the CASVE cycle, self-knowledge, and occupational knowledge. This instrument should make the CIP theory more useful to practitioners and may stimulate research as well.

STATUS AND USE OF THE CAREER INFORMATION–PROCESSING MODEL   As noted above, the CIP model was first published in 1991. To date, the research and writing regarding the model have been the result of the effort of the authors of the theory. In 2008 two studies surfaced (Clemens & Milsom, 2008; Paivandy, Bullock, Reardon, & Kelly 2008), only one of which involved one of the authors of the theory (Reardon). This suggests that the theory may be attracting a wider audience.

The application of the CIP model begins with assessing the readiness of individuals to make well-reasoned career choices and their cognitive and affective capabilities to make those choices. When assessing readiness, career counselors examine four factors:

- A high level of self-knowledge and a willingness to use that knowledge in the decision-making process
- Willingness to explore the world of work
- Motivation to learn about and engage in the decision-making process
- Awareness of how negative thoughts influence problem solving and the willingness to seek assistance when needed

A second factor of concern to career counselors is what Peterson and his colleagues (1991) term the *complexity factor.* In a nutshell, complexity refers to contextual factors that will in all likelihood influence the process. These include family variables, employing organizations, society at large, economic variables, and so forth. These researchers concluded that people may either be coping with cognitive factors, such as expectations about discriminations, or complicated contextual factors. Readiness can be assessed using the Career Thoughts Inventory (Sampson et al., 1996), which consists of three scales: decision-making confusion, commitment anxiety, and external conflict.

Peterson and his colleagues (2002) outline the following seven-step model for career counseling:

1. *Conduct initial interview*   The career counselor meets with a client to establish their relationship, explain the career counseling process, and clarify the client's needs. At the conclusion of this session, clients are given information about the process that can be reviewed later.
2. *Conduct preliminary assessment*   The counselor and client determine the client's readiness to engage in career decision making.
3. *Mutually define problem and analyze causes*
4. *Formulate goals*
5. *Develop individual learning plan*   Consider resources who may be contacted and activities that will help the client reach his or her goals.
6. *Implement individual learning plan*
7. *Evaluate goal attainment*   Assist the client in using skills and knowledge gained for future decision making.

There is little information about the application of the CIP model to racial and ethnic minorities; people who are disabled; and gay, lesbian, bisexual, and transsexual clients. It is clear that the model applies primarily to persons who expect to make their own decisions. Moreover, the CTI (Sampson et al., 1996) is intrusive; clients must report their thoughts and this may not be appropriate for use with cultural minorities, such as some Asian Americans and Native Americans (Brown, 2002).

POSTMODERN THEORIES

A Contextualist Theory of Career

As mentioned in the introduction to this chapter, two of the theories presented are grounded in postmodern philosophy as opposed to logical positivism. One of the postmodern theories is the contextualist theory of Young, Valach, and Collin (2002), who suggest that the dichotomous approaches used by trait-and-factor theorists to describe the person and the work environment are inappropriate. They believe that the only way to understand individuals is in the context of their environments as they experience them and understand the meaning of these experiences.

Contexualists do not believe the actions of individuals are caused by past or present events. Career-related behaviors are goal-directed results of the individual's construction of the context in which she or he functions. To understand an event, one must start with the event, determine the individual's view of it, and proceed from that point.

Young and colleagues (2002) also maintain that actions taken with regard to a career involve a goal-oriented series of behaviors that is guided simultaneously by individuals and the social contexts in which they are participating. They break action into three parts: (1) unobservable behavior, (2) the internal processes that cannot be observed, and (3) the meaning or results as interpreted by the individuals and others who observe the action. Joint actions, such as those in career counseling, occur between people. In this process, joint goals are formed, and the players engage in joint actions that also have personal and social meaning. Projects are longer-term joint or individual actions, such as preparing for a career. When people construct meaning among actions and projects, they can engage in endeavors such as careers.

Actions take place in a series of sequential steps that occur in a social context from which the actor cannot be separated. The meaning associated by career-related actions and projects is interpreted not only in terms of its immediate context but also in terms of the goals of the individual (Young et al., 2002). Interpretations are also influenced by the gender and culture of the actor because of the variations in perceptions that develop as a result of those variables. Interpretation occurs at two levels: in the present context, which is built on a stream of actions, and in the anticipated context of the future. To describe these events, individuals construct narratives, which are temporal interpretations of life events that pertain to a career. If individuals are asked, "Why did you enter your present career?," they construct narratives based on their interpretations of the events that led to their careers as well as their interpretations of what the person who asked the question needs or wants to know. One role of career counselors is to assist clients to project their narratives into future contexts.

A number of publications are available that illustrate how contextual theory can be applied in career counseling (e.g., Savickas, 1995; Young et al., 2002). Savickas suggests a five-step approach beginning with evoking stories that allow the identification of themes. Themes are frequently mentioned ideas about the nature of the career problem. Once the theme or themes are described, the counselor "narrates" or describes the theme to the client. The client and counselor then interpret the problem in the context of the theme, edit or change the theme, and extend it into the future. The final step in the process involves helping the client develop the behavioral skills needed to implement the future narrative theme that has been developed.

STATUS AND USE OF THE CONTEXTUALISTS' THEORIES   Contextualist theories have attracted a great deal of attention and has generated a number of articles dealing with the career counseling process (see Young et al., 2002). The counseling applications of this theory are discussed later in this chapter.

Complexity, Chaos, and Nonlinear Dynamics: A Chaos Theory of Career Development and Spirituality

Bloch (2005) opens her theoretical statement with an attack on modernity and its philosophical underpinnings, which were presented in Chapter 2. She defines a career-adaptive entity and reiterates a theme that is central to postmodern thinking: Everything in the world is connected and nonpredictable. The movie *The Butterfly Effect* (2004) portrayed the idea that even the fragile movement of a butterfly's wings impacts everything else in our world and perhaps the universe. This same theme can be found in a theoretical statement by Bright and Pryor (2005), who adopt a constructivist point of view not unlike the one advanced by Young, Valach, and Collin (2002), with the difference being that Bright and Pryor relied on chaos theory, whereas Young and colleagues did not. I have chosen Bloch's ideas to illustrate chaos theory because they go beyond the theory to linking careers and spirituality.

Bloch (2005) begins the elaboration of her theory by listing the characteristics of adaptive entities, of which career is one. They can be briefly described as follows:

1. Adaptive entities of which clients are an example have the ability to maintain themselves even though their shapes and components may change.
2. They are open systems, taking energy from the environment and exporting energy in return.
3. They are parts of networks, engaging in the interchange of resources. These networks can be depicted as ever-widening, linked concentric circles (thus the butterfly effect).
4. They are parts of other entities such as career, families, and leisure groups. These parts are called fractals.
5. They are dynamic and thus ever changing. In this process of changing forms and components, they move between order and chaos.
6. They go through transitions and during these periods seek fitness peaks that maximize their chances of survival.
7. They behave in nonlinear ways because of multiple and unexplainable events that impinge on their functioning.
8. They react so that small changes may bring about large effects.
9. They move through transitions. As they do they may be constrained by what are termed attractors. They may return repeatedly to the same state (point attractors), swing from point to point in pendulum fashion (pendulum attractors), or move in circular, but nonconcentric, patterns (torus attractors).
10. Fractals may, as they move through transitions, create new fractals.
11. Fractals exist only as a part of the nested reality of the universe; they are interdependent. Spirituality is experiencing this unity with the universe.

Bloch (2005) applies these 11 principles in her theory of career development. She indicates that people are continuously regenerating their careers, moving freely among career pathways. Careers are fractals and are a part of people's lives, and they in turn are part of interlinked networks that shape and reshape themselves. As they work and participate in their careers, people experience an interchange of resources and energy similar to that envisioned in other fractals. People's careers, and thus their lives, range from orderly to chaotic. Small changes in a career often produce large, unanticipated changes. When people undergo transitions, which may or may not be a continuous process, their search for new careers becomes a search for fitness peaks, or the best for which the individual can hope. However, some people are "stuck" in a pattern when some changes revert to the status quo. Some swing from definable place to definable place (job to job), and some move in a circular fashion. Careers make sense only if nonlinear logic is used to examine them. The shifts in careers and the resulting shapes and states are not predictable; they can only be understood phenomenologically—that is, from the individual's perspective.

STATUS AND USE OF THE POSTMODERN THEORIES It is too early to tell whether Bloch's (2005) theory will be embraced by large numbers of practitioners. However, at this time Pryor and his colleagues (Bright & Pryor, 2006; Pryor, Admundson, & Bright, 2008; Pryor & Bright, 2008) are actively promoting their version of chaos theory, at least so far as practice is concerned. It also seems that an increasing number of professionals have accepted the philosophical underpinnings of chaos theory.

Postmodern Career Counseling

Pryor and Bright (2005) published a guide to the application of chaos theory in career counseling. Their recommendations include the following points:

1. It is important to adopt a perspective that perceives career development as a process that is influenced by a number of factors that are constantly undergoing changes that are occurring at different rates.
2. Many of the forces that influence career development are chance events that cannot be predicted, although it is possible to plan for responses to unknown and unknowable occurrences.
3. Inductive and deductive reasoning must be eschewed in favor of nonlinear abductive reasoning that deals with patterns and relationships and accepts the premise that all knowledge is open to questions. When patterns are identified (e.g., a client quickly became bored with last four jobs), clients should be encouraged to link these to past events.
4. When clients are considering past decisions, they should be encouraged to consider the context in which those decisions were made—that is, the environmental influencers that came to bear as the decision was made.
5. Clients should be encouraged to identify the attractors (constraints) in their systems. Bright and Pryor, like Bloch, identify three types of attractors that are based on the examination of repetitive patterns: point attractors, pendulum attractors, and Torus attractors. Bright and Pryor add a fourth type of attractor: strange attractors. The client who is oriented to a single goal is responding to a point attractor. The client who is torn between two influences or choices—for example, the college student who cannot choose between two majors—is responding to a pendulum attractor. Torus attractors are more complex, but characterized by repetitive patterns that ultimately yield unacceptable outcomes. Highly intelligent transoceanic pilots may perceive the complexity and importance of their jobs yet become dissatisfied and bored because of an unrecognized pattern associated with their job such as the repetitive tasks involved. Strange attractors are counterintuitive and unlike the others do not involve repetitive pattern. However, Bright and Pryor suggest that life pattern analysis, the use of myths and metaphors will ultimately reveal the similarities in the life patterns that lead to the current distress.

At least two perspectives on career counseling have arisen from postmodern philosophy. The goal of career counseling from one of these perspectives is assisting the client to construct a future career. This involves joint action between the counselor and the client, in contrast to a theory based on modernism, which depicts counselors and clients filling two different roles. Joint action taking suggests that joint goals may emerge in the process. Unlike the situations that have been described to this point, joint goals are not established in advance; they emerge spontaneously from the process. An example of a joint goal involves the development and telling of the client's life story, his or her narrative. Action taking is energized by the bond between the client and counselor that serves to encourage the creation of a life narrative, which is included in a career joint venture. Young, Valach, and Collin (2002) indicate that their theory emphasizes goals, so some postmodernists reject it because it makes the theory too rational. They hasten to add that, in their theory, goals are only one basis for the organization of action and often goals arise spontaneously from life events and are not predetermined.

It may be helpful to consider the work of Neimeyer (1988) to understand the development of vocational constructs. Most people begin the task of constructing a vocational narrative with a few useful constructs about themselves. However, they are unlikely to recognize useful concepts such as abilities and values. As they develop more constructs about themselves, clients begin to organize the constructs to examine themselves in terms of the occupational structure. As more constructs develop, they are differentiated into two or more classes of constructs—for example, those about the self and those about the world of work. Counselors must help their clients organize these constructs into themes using interpretation. A useful interpretation might be the emphasis on creativity, both as it relates to the workplace and to the remainder of the life space. Noting the need for collegiality in the workplace and how it relates to certain collateral family values may also be helpful. The final result of this process involves new constructs that are differentiated and organized (integrated) into themes.

Assessment devices are not necessarily employed in this approach to constructivist career counseling. As clients tell their stories, the career counselor should attend to the manner in which clients direct their energy—that is, their intentional behavior and its result in terms of producing pleasure, pain, joy, or sadness. Personal constructs can be identified in this manner. However, a few assessment techniques have evolved that can be used to help clients identify and organize new constructs. Card sorts, such as the Vocational Card Sort (Dolliver, 1967), can be used, as can the laddering technique developed by Neimeyer (1992). In the latter approach, clients are asked to identify three occupations and begin to spontaneously generate constructs related to them. In this strategy, the counselor records the constructs as they are generated. Clients are prompted to compare and contrast occupations, estimate the enjoyability of the occupations, or express emotions evoked in thinking about the occupation. These or similar prompts encourage the client to think of constructs. The objective is not to have the client select one of the occupations but to generate a list of positive constructs that can be used in the selection of an occupation. During the card sort, clients are asked to divide the cards into three piles based on whether they would consider, would not consider, or are uncertain about whether they would consider the occupation. Clients are then asked to identify the reasons why they accepted, are uncertain about, or rejected the occupations in each stack.

Young and his colleagues (2002) indicate that an essential aspect of career counseling is interpretation, which involves making sense of the client's experiences. As clients tell their life stories, the counselor and the client spontaneously interpret the story in a meaning-making effort. For the counselor, the purposes of the interpretive process are (1) to become aware of the client's worldview; (2) to help the client become aware of his or her conceptualizations and how these are workable within the life space; (3) to support the client in the application of the constructs; and (4) to maintain the client's construction and not abandon it in favor of more scientific ideas, such as traits and personality types. This process should enable the client to identify constructs that are related to his or her career choices. Often, these constructs will have meaning beyond the narrow confines of vocation. As the constructs are identified and valued or rejected, successful clients prioritize and integrate the constructs around certain themes, such as abilities and values. As the themes in the narratives change, the client's perspective changes (Savickas, 1997).

Constructivist approaches are, in theory at least, value free. Career counselors disregard their values during these sessions and join the client in the process of creating a life story that will encourage him or her in a career opportunity. This values–free perspective makes postmodern thinking and theories, such as the one constructed by Young and associates, ideal for use with all groups, including ethnic minorities. Being value free, the counselor can work with clients in the helping process unfettered by the counselor's own belief system.

A Second Approach to Postmodern Career Counseling: Solution-Focused Brief Career Counseling

As noted in the previous section, many postmodern theorists, such as Bloch (2005) and Neimeyer (1992), stress the importance of eliciting the clients' stories to help them identify their constructs and integrate their constructs into a plan for the future. Savickas (1995) has also taken this position. In the eighth edition of this book, a postmodern approach to career counseling based on the work of de Shazer (1985) was presented. Amundson (2003) presented a similar postmodern philosophy, but he added a step called *second-order questioning*, which is included in this presentation. The sequence of solution-focused brief career counseling (SFBCC) is as follows:

1. The client identifies the issue to be addressed.
2. The client identifies the changes (goals) to be made and scales the goals.
3. The client is encouraged to search for exceptions—that is, times when he or she was able to solve similar problems.
4. The client identifies personal strengths and strategies used in past successes that can be used to resolve the identified problem.
5. In follow up sessions the counselor and the client revisit the goal, scale it, and develop a plan to move toward problem resolutions.
6. The counselor may engage in second-order questioning if the client is "stuck."

Each of these steps is discussed in greater detail shortly, but prior to that presentation it should be noted the SFBCC was not developed to address mental health problems such as depression and decisional anxiety. Therefore, if depression or decisional anxiety or other mental health issues become a barrier to the career counseling process, the counselor should address it before proceeding.

1. *Relationship development.*   The career counselor avoids assuming the role of expert, instead encouraging clients to assume control of finding their own solution. Counselors may describe themselves as coaches or facilitators.

2. *Client presentation of issue.*   The counselor may encourage a client who has difficulty choosing from among several alternatives. to set a goal. The counselor's intent is to focus on the positive (goal attainment) and the future. In some instances it is important for the counselor to assist the client in taking ownership of the problem. For example, a worker who has lost his her job because of an economic downturn may blame the economy, the company, or the union. However, being unemployed is the client's problem and blaming others does not resolve this problem.

The goal or hoped-for outcome may be elicited with what de Shazar (1985) calls the magic question. This technique keeps the session focused on the future and on positive outcomes. The magic question typically takes the following form: "If you were to wake up one morning and this problem was resolved, what would have changed? How would you know that the problem was resolved? How would the people around you know that the problem was resolved?" It is important to note that the goals that are established must be positive and must involve behavior that is within the client's control. For example, a client who is having trouble with his or her supervisor might "wake up" to find that the supervisor is a nice, supportive person instead of the negative, critical person that he or she experiences every day. Because the client has no control over the supervisor, he or she would be asked to rethink the outcome in terms of factors that the client can control, such as the client's thoughts, emotions, and behaviors.

3. *Search for exceptions. The search for exceptions is actually a search for strengths. The counselor might prompt with some of the following leads,* "Think of a time when you made a difficult decision. What was different then (context, importance of the decision; people involved)? What was the decision-making process like? How did you feel as you made the decision? Who was helpful in the process? What resources did you use? The counselor reinforces past attempts and successes."

4. *After exceptions are found. Based on exceptions, what personal strengths can you identify that will help you achieve your goal?* What behaviors, emotions, or thoughts came to the fore when you made tough decisions in the past? If you never made difficult decisions in the past, what personal strengths do you possess (e.g., perseverance, mental toughness, intelligence, etc.) that will help you as you go forward? During this part of the process the career counselor might use devices such as self-estimates of abilities as aids to identifying strengths. Genograms, card sorts, and qualitative approaches to assessing self-efficacy might also be used at this time. These devices are discussed in Chapter 6.

5. *Develop a plan and scale the goal.* Near the end of the first session, ask the client to restate his or her goal and to scale it. Scaling involves rating the movement toward goal attainment and might be introduced as follows: "Your stated goal is to choose an occupation that will pay you at least $800 per week and one that matches your values and interests. On a 1-to-10 scale, with 1 being little progress toward the goal and 10 meaning that you have made your choice, rate where you are at this time in the process of attaining your goal." The counselor and the client then develop a plan that will move the client toward goal attainment and the session is ended.

6. *Follow up sessions.* These should probably begin with discussing the progress that has been made, road blocks that have developed, and the need to modify the plan. At each subsequent session, the goal that was established is scaled to determine progress.

7. *Ask second-order questions.* There are two approaches to second-order questioning, one growing rather directly from de Shazer's (1985) work and the other developed by Amundson (2003). Both have utility. From de Shazer's point of view, second-order questioning focuses the client on what would happen if the career problem that was identified at the outset is not addressed. Amundson uses second-order questioning to facilitate the client's understanding that the evidence suggests some of his or her beliefs may be off target. In de Shazer's approach, the client is asked, "Speculate about the future if the problem you identified is not addressed." Amundson would use a lead such as, "Tell me about how you arrived at the conclusion that you are not able to handle work-related stressors." From the latter perspective the client is asked to examine her or his private thoughts and encouraged to reflect on how they developed as well as their implications. De Shazer hopes to promote insight into the pros and cons of action and inaction as they relate to the presenting problem. Both of these approaches to second-order questioning have merit and should be incorporated into the model.

SOCIOECONOMIC THEORIES

The theories considered thus far are basically psychological in that they assume that individuals exert control over their lives. Although most theorists would agree that the degree of control varies from individual to individual and situation to situation, most would also agree with the proposition that individuals do have control and it is the job of the career counselor to increase the degree of self-direction.

Unlike psychologists, sociologists and economists are inclined to concern themselves with small- and large-group behavior. Sociologists often focus on small groups, such as the family, but they may be concerned with large groups, such as women or minority groups. Some economists may focus on the economic forces that influence the career development of the entire labor force, such as the global economy, the so-called dual labor market, or the impact of supply and demand of workers on wages and tenure. Hotchkiss and Borow (1990, 1996) report an increasing emphasis by sociologists and economists on structural variables, such as socioeconomic status, barriers to career development, such as discrimination and occupational segregation; and labor market considerations that influence careers. These broad-brush approaches place greater emphasis on factors outside the control of the individual than do the psychological approaches presented to this point.

Status Attainment Theory

According to Hotchkiss and Borow (1984, 1990, 1996), the publication of *The American Occupational Structure* (Blau & Duncan, 1967) marks the advent of status attainment theory (SAT). Initially, SAT posited that the socioeconomic status of one's family influences education, which in turn affects the occupation entered. Later variables, such as mental ability and what were termed *social-psychological processes,* were added to this model. Hotchkiss and Borow (1996) suggest that, as the model now stands, its basic assumption is that family status and cognitive variables combine through social-psychological processes to influence educational attainment, which in turn impacts occupational attainment and earnings. Some sociologists and economists have criticized SAT as being too simplistic and have sought alternatives to it. For example, some have tried to explain occupational attainment by focusing on the type of firm in which an individual is employed.

Dual Labor Market Theory

Dual labor market theory posits two types of businesses in our labor market: core and peripheral. Core firms have internal labor markets that have rather well-developed career paths and offer opportunities for upward mobility. These firms have dominant roles in the markets in which they compete. They make use of technology and other tools to enhance their positions in their markets. Peripheral firms make no long-term commitment to their employees. Instead, employees are paid by the job and furloughed when no longer needed. Workers in these firms have little chance of upward mobility according to the theory and research provides some support for this assertion (Hotchkiss & Borow, 1996).

Race, Gender, and Career

Sociologists have been at the forefront in the research of the impact of race and gender on occupational attainment and earnings. This research has consistently shown that African Americans earn less than whites (e.g., Saunders, 1995). Wage data regarding males and females show a similar pattern, with women earning consistently less than men (e.g., Johnson & Mortimer, 2002; Reskin, 1993). Reskin's research also suggests that males and females are largely segregated in the workplace, with women often relegated to occupations with lower earnings and status.

STATUS AND USE OF SOCIOECONOMIC THEORIES Socioeconomic theories have not been developed to advance practice. Their purpose is to help increase understanding of sociological and economic factors on career choice and development (Hotchkiss & Borow, 1996; Johnson & Mortimer, 2002). These theories, and the research growing out of them, indicate that the opportunity structure is not equal for all groups. The individual is an important variable in sociological thinking, which is particularly concerned with variables such as race, ethnicity, academic aptitude, and gender, all of which have been studied extensively. However, sociologists are more inclined to consider the social contexts in which people grow, develop, and aspire than are psychologists or counselors. Family social status as it relates to occupational choice has been a variable of great concern to sociologists for decades and has been found to be a powerful predictor of ultimate occupational attainment. Research, such as the occupational segregation of women and socioeconomic stratification of minority groups, should serve to remind career counselors and others that extraordinary efforts in practice and advocacy are required if these long-standing problems are to be addressed.

THEORIES OF DECISION MAKING

Each theory discussed in this chapter incorporates decision making as an important aspect of career choice and career development. However, with the exception of Krumboltz's (1979) social learning theory, most give little attention to how individuals make those decisions. The purpose of this section is to alert the reader to the importance of this process, to review briefly a few of the major approaches to understanding the decision-making process, and to direct the reader to more extended discussions of the topic.

Jepsen and Dilley (1974) and Wright (1984) provide discussions of several relevant models useful to the reader. Jepsen and Dilley separate the models they discuss into two groups: *prescriptive models* that describe how decisions ought to be made, and *descriptive models* that describe how decisions are actually made. They also state that the process involves a decision maker and a situation in which two or more alternatives exist that carry potential outcomes of variable significance for the decision maker. The essence of the process is for the decision maker to identify and assign relative values to the alternatives and their consequences so he or she can maximize the outcome. We examine briefly two models of each type.

Mitchell (1975) modifies a model proposed earlier by Restle (1961) so it can be applied to the career decision-making process. Restle states that the decision maker matches the confronting situation to his view of an ideal one and then chooses the alternative that most closely resembles that ideal situation. Mitchell identifies four elements of preferences held by the decision maker:

1. *Absolute constraints* are the factors that must be present or absent for the alternative to be viable.
2. *Negative characteristics* are undesirable aspects.
3. *Positive characteristics* are desirable aspects.
4. *Neutral characteristics* are aspects present but irrelevant to the choice to be made.

The decision maker can use these elements in a variety of ways, such as comparing only positive characteristics; considering alternatives singly, matching positive versus negative characteristics; rejecting an alternative because of negative characteristics; and other combinations.

Tversky (1972) proposes a model that he names *elimination by aspects*. This approach focuses on all choices simultaneously, with each choice having a variety of characteristics.

In this model, the characteristic (e.g., job security) for each alternative is matched, and those that fail to meet the decision maker's minimum standard are eliminated.

Examples of descriptive models include Vroom's expectancy model and Janis and Mann's conflict model. Vroom (1964) uses two key terms in developing his model: *valence,* which can be equated with preference, and *expectancies,* which are comparable to the belief that choices can be realized. Both aspects are crucial to each decision and interact in the process. The force or pressure to make a particular choice is directly related to the sum of the valences of all outcomes and the strength of the expectancies that the choice will result in the attainment of desired outcomes.

Janis and Mann (1977) assume that conflict is caused whenever a person is faced with making a decision, thus producing stress and uncertainty. The process starts when the decision maker becomes aware of a threat that he or she feels compelled to consider (e.g., the sounding of a fire alarm). The process continues through several steps that can be illustrated by a series of questions that, when answered positively, require action leading to the next question and when answered negatively interrupt the decision-making process. The questions are as follows:

1. Are risks involved if I do not change?
2. Are the risks serious if I do not change?
3. Can I hope to find a viable solution to the problem?
4. Is there sufficient time to search for viable alternatives?

The individual who answers the final question affirmatively is considered to be in a state of vigilance, in which attention can be given to acquiring information about alternatives and to weighing the advantages and disadvantages of each. This is considered to be the most favorable situation for reaching an appropriate decision.

The career counselor faces a serious dilemma in helping clients in the decision-making process. At present, none of the models described has been incorporated into the prevalent theories. It appears likely that one model may fit some clients and some situations better and another may be more satisfactory in different circumstances. The irony is that the counselor must apply a model in deciding which model is likely to be most useful to a client at a particular time.

Some of the major difficulties for counselors revolve around the inability to be certain of judgments of client characteristics (e.g., they cannot be certain of the client's motivation, clarity of self-understanding, and precision of values ascribed to various factors). It is often impossible to be sure that the client has incorporated her or his most important values and has weighted them properly. Nevertheless, the client must be helped and the counselor must choose a model or combination of models that appears most viable.

Status and Use of Decision-Making Theories

For the most part the theories of decision making outlined here do not have immediate application except to help career counselors better understand the career decision-making process with one exception. Janis and Mann (1977) developed the balance sheet as a means of helping high school students enhance their decision making as it related to college choice. The balance sheet can also be used as the basis for choosing a career. An outline of a modified balance sheet can be seen in Table 3.1. The process of using the balance sheet as an aid to decision making begins by eliminating all but four to five of the occupations being considered. This is typically done

TABLE 3.1   Modified Balance Sheet

Career Options	1	2	3	4
Criteria to Be Used	___	___	___	___
Salary	___	___	___	___
Benefits	___	___	___	___
Opportunity for Advancement	___	___	___	___
Opportunity to Use My Skills	___	___	___	___
Travel Requirements	___	___	___	___
Opportunities for Spouse	___	___	___	___
Quality of Schools	___	___	___	___
Recreational Opportunities	___	___	___	___
Other	___	___	___	___

based on factors such as an estimate of the minimum acceptable wage (e.g., *I want a job that pays at least $500 per week*), geographic region in which the work can be found (*I want to work in the Northeast because my family is there*), educational requirements (*I am willing to go to a community college for two years*), and interests (*A job must correspond to my interests*). Interest inventories, such as the Career Key (Jones, 2005), which is available in English, Korean, Spanish, and Chinese, can be used to identify occupations in this latter group and may be the place to start the winnowing process. The Career Key, which is an online interest inventory, produces Holland (1997) types. People who use the Career Key, or other similar devices, often discover more than a dozen occupations that correspond to their Holland profiles, thus leading to the need to reduce the number to acceptable alternatives. Individuals may use other factors, such as indoor versus outdoor work and preference for long vacation periods, in the process of eliminating choices. Once occupations are sorted into acceptable and unacceptable categories, individuals completing the balance sheet identify the criteria that will be used in making a final choice. Some of the criteria that are often used in the final selections of an occupation can be seen in Table 3.1.

Once the criteria to be used in the choice of an occupation have been listed, the next step is to rate the extent to which each of the occupations meets each criterion using a 1-to-10 scale, with 1 indicating that a career option satisfies the criterion to a small degree and 10 indicating that it satisfies the criterion to a considerable degree. Once the rating is complete, the columns are totaled and examined. If two or more occupations have similar ratings, other criteria may need to be considered or an in-depth examination of the options may be required in order to consider some of the subtle aspects of the job. If a client is considering specific jobs and employers (e.g., software engineer for Apple versus Microsoft), it is suggested that the nature of these employers be added to list of criteria in Table 3.1. These criteria may involve examining their stock value, earnings, offshore efforts, treatment of women and minorities, and outsourcing history, and a number of other variables. Finally, it should be stressed to clients that the numbers generated by the balance sheet are only a means of stimulating their thinking about the choice-making process. It is entirely likely that an individual will ultimately choose an occupation that is not the one with the highest quantitative score.

Summary

Career choice and development theories based on learning theory and a postmodern philosophy have been highlighted in this chapter. Socioeconomic theories and decision making have also been discussed. The learning theories have a number of similarities, particularly those of Krumboltz (Mitchell & Krumboltz, 1996) and Lent and colleagues (2002). Because they are based on the supposition that the individual (as opposed to the family or group) will be the decision maker, their application to people with collateral social values is limited. This is not a limitation of postmodern theory. Socioeconomic theory has produced research that should serve as reminders of the need to redouble our efforts with disenfranchised groups in our culture.

Chapter Quiz

T F   **1.** The importance of self-efficacy is stressed in Krumboltz's learning theory explanation of career decision making.

T F   **2.** The two themes that appear most often in the career development theories presented in this chapter are the importance of self-knowledge and knowledge about careers.

T F   **3.** The two models of postmodern career counseling presented in this chapter agree that the starting place for the process is having the client state a goal.

T F   **4.** In the postmodern approach to career counseling, career counselors are supposed to suspend their values.

T F   **5.** According to Bloch, the client can be perceived as a fractal.

T F   **6.** The client who vacillates between two occupational choices is constrained by a Torus attractor.

T F   **7.** The social cognitive theory and Krumboltz's learning theory were both based on Bandura's learning theory.

T F   **8.** Blau and Duncan, who are socioeconomic theorists, concluded initially that the social status of the family was the primary factor in occupational attainment.

T F   **9.** De Shazer used the magic question as a way of stimulating people to fantasize about their future.

T F **10.** In considering the role of the counselor in career counseling, the common theme among all the theories is the importance of the counselor in assessing a client's problem.

F (01) T (9) T (8) T (7) F (6) F (5) T (4) F (3) T (2) F (1)

References

Amundson, N. E. (2003). *Active engagement: Enhancing the career counseling process* (2nd ed.). Richmond, BC: Ergon Communications.

Bandura, A. (1977). *Social learning theory.* Englewood Cliffs, NJ: Prentice-Hall.

Bandura, A. (1986). *Social foundations of thought and action: A social-cognitive theory.* Englewood Cliffs, NJ: Prentice-Hall.

Betz, N. E., & Borgen, F. (2000). The future of career assessment: Integrating vocational interests with self-efficacy and personal style. *Journal of Career Assessment, 8,* 329–338.

Blau, P. M., & Duncan, O. D. (1967). *The American occupational structure.* New York: Wiley.

Bloch, D. P. (2003). *Salient beliefs review: Connecting spirit and work.* Indianapolis: JIST.

Bloch, D. P. (2005). Complexity, chaos, and nonlinear dynamics: A new perspective on career development theory. *Career Development Quarterly, 53,* 194–207.

Bloch, D. P., & Richmond, L. (1998). *Soul work: Finding the work you love, loving the work you have.* Palo Alto, CA: Davies-Black.

Bright, J. E., & Pryor, R. G. L. (2005). The chaos theory of careers: A user's guide. *Career Development Quarterly, 53,* 291–305.

Brown, D. (2002). The role of work and cultural values in occupational choice, success, and satisfaction. *Journal of Counseling and Development, 80,* 48–56.

Clemens, E. V., & Milsom, A. S. (2008). Enlisted service members' transition into the civilian world of work: A cognitive information processing approach. *Career Development Quarterly, 56I*, 246–256.

Dawis, R. V. (1996). The theory of work adjustment and person–environment–correspondence counseling. In D. Brown, L. Brooks, & Associates, *Career choice and development* (3rd ed., pp. 75–120). San Francisco: Jossey-Bass.

de Shazer, S. (1985). *Keys to solutions in brief therapy.* New York: Norton.

Dolliver, R. (1967). An adaptation of the Tyler vocational card sort. *Personnel and Guidance Journal, 45*, 916–920.

Holland, J. L. (1997). *Making vocational choices* (3rd ed.). Englewood Cliffs, NJ: Prentice-Hall.

Hotchkiss, L., & Borow, H. (1984). Sociological perspectives on career choice and attainment. In D. Brown, L. Brooks, & Associates, *Career choice and development* (pp. 137–168). San Francisco: Jossey-Bass.

Hotchkiss, L., & Borow, H. (1990). Sociological perspectives on work and career development. In D. Brown, L. Brooks, & Associates, *Career choice and development* (2nd ed., pp. 262–307). San Francisco: Jossey-Bass.

Hotchkiss, L., & Borow, H. (1996). Sociological perspectives on work and career development. In D. Brown, L. Brooks, et al., *Career choice and development* (3rd ed., pp. 281–336). San Francisco: Jossey-Bass.

Janis, I. L., & Mann, L. (1977). *Decision making: A psychological analysis of conflict, choice, and commitment.* New York: Free Press.

Jepsen, D. A., & Dilley, J. S. (1974). Vocational decision making models: A review and comparative analysis. *Review of Educational Research, 44*, 331–349.

Johnson, M. K., & Mortimer, J. J. (2002). Career choice and development from a sociological perspective. In D. Brown et al., *Career choice and development* (4th ed., pp. 37–84). San Francisco: Jossey-Bass.

Jones, L. (2005). *Career Key.* Retrieved from www.careerkey.org/index.asp.

Krumboltz, J. D. (1979). A social learning theory of career choice. In A. M. Mitchell, G. B. Jones, & J. D. Krumboltz (Eds.), *Social learning theory and career decision making.* Cranston, RI: Carroll Press.

Krumboltz, J. D. (1991). *Manual for the Career Beliefs Inventory.* Palo Alto, CA: CPP Books.

Krumboltz, J. D. (1996). A learning theory of career counseling. In M. Savickas & B. Walsh (Eds.), *Integrating career theory and practice* (pp. 313–360). Palo Alto, CA: CPP Books.

Krumboltz, J. D. (1998). Serendipity is not serendipitous. *Journal of Counseling Psychology, 45*, 390–392.

Krumboltz, J. D., Mitchell, A. M., & Jones, G. B. (1976). A social learning theory of career selection. *Counseling Psychologist, 6*, 71–81.

Lent, R. W., Brown, S. D., & Hackett, G. (1995). Toward a unifying social cognitive theory of career and academic interest, choice, and performance. *Journal of Vocational Behavior, 45*, 79–122.

Lent, R. W., Brown, S. D., & Hackett, G. (1996). Career development from a social cognitive perspective. In D. Brown, L. Brooks, and Associates, pp. 373–422) *Career choice and development* (3rd ed.). San Francisco: Jossey-Bass.

Lent, R. W., Brown, S. D., & Hackett, G. (2002). Career development from a social cognitive perspective. In D. Brown, L. Brooks, and Associates, *Career choice and development* (4th ed., pp. 255–311). San Francisco: Jossey-Bass.

Levin, A. S., Krumboltz, J. D., & Krumboltz, B. L. (1995). *Exploring your career beliefs: A workbook for the Career Beliefs Inventory with techniques for integrating your Strong and MBTI results.* Palo Alto, CA: CPP Books.

Meichenbaum, M. (1977). *Cognitive behavior modification.* New York: Plenum.

Mitchell, L. K., & Krumboltz, J. D. (1984). Social learning approach to career decisions: Krumboltz's theory. In D. Brown, L. Brooks, et al., *Career choice and development* (pp. 235–280). San Francisco: Jossey-Bass.

Mitchell, L. K., & Krumboltz, J. D. (1990). Social learning approach to career decisions: Krumboltz's theory. In D. Brown, L. Brooks, et al., *Career choice and development* (2nd ed., pp. 308–337). San Francisco: Jossey-Bass.

Mitchell, L. K., & Krumboltz, J. D. (1996). Krumboltz's theory of career choice and counseling. In D. Brown, L. Brooks, et al., *Career choice and development* (3rd ed., pp. 233–280). San Francisco: Jossey-Bass.

Mitchell, W. D. (1975). Restle's choice model: A reconceptualization. *Journal of Vocational Behavior, 9*, 315–330.

Neimeyer, G. J. (1988). Cognitive integration and differentiation in vocational behavior. *The Counseling Psychologist, 16*, 440–475.

Neimeyer, G. J. (1992). Personal constructs in career counseling and development. *Journal of Career Development, 18*, 163–174.

Paivandy, S., Bullock, E. F., Reardon, R. C., & Kelly, F. D. (2008). The effects of decision making style and cognitive thought patterns on negative career thoughts. *Journal of Career Assessment, 16*, 474–487.

Peterson, G. W., Sampson, J. P., Jr., & Reardon, R. C. (1991). *Career development and services: A cognitive approach.* Pacific Grove, CA: Brooks/Cole.

Peterson, G. W., Sampson, J. P., Jr., Reardon, R. C., & Lenz, J. G. (2002). A cognitive information processing approach. In D. Brown, L. Brooks, et al., *Career choice and development* (4th ed., pp. 312–373). San Francisco: Jossey-Bass.

Pryor, R. G., Amunson, N. E., & Bright, J. E. (2008). Probabilities and possibilities: The strategic counseling implications of the chaos theory application. *The Career Development Quarterly, 56,* 309–318.

Pryor, R. G., & Bright, J. (2008). Archetypal narratives in career counseling: A chaos theory application. *International Journal of Educational and vocational Guidance, 8,* 71–82.

Reskin, B. F. (1993). Sex segregation in the workplace. *Annual Review of Sociology, 19,* 241–271.

Restle, F. (1961). *Psychology of judgment and choice.* New York: Wiley.

Sampson, J. P., Jr., Peterson, G. W., Lenz, J. G., Reardon, R. C., & Saunders, D. (1996). *Career Thoughts Inventory.* Odessa, FL: Personality Assessment Resources.

Saunders, L. (1995). Relative earnings of black and white men by region. *Monthly Labor Review, 118,* 68–73.

Savickas, M. L. (1995). Constructivist counseling for career indecision. *Career Development Quarterly, 43,* 363–373.

Savickas, M. L. (1997). Constructivist career counseling: Models and methods. *Advances in Personal Construct Psychology, 4,* 149–182.

Sharf, R. S. (2002). *Applying career development theory to counseling* (3rd ed.). Pacific Grove, CA: Brooks/Cole.

Tversky, A. (1972). Elimination by aspects: A theory of choice. *Psychological Review, 79,* 281–291.

Vroom, V. H. (1964). *Work and motivation.* New York: Wiley.

Wright, G. (1984). *Behavioral decision theory.* Newbury Park, CA: Sage.

Young, R. A., Valach, L., & Collin, A. (2002). A contextual explanation of career. In D. Brown, L. Brooks, and associates *Career choice and development* (4th ed., pp. 206–254). San Francisco: Jossey-Bass.

4

Ethical and Legal Guidelines and Competencies Needed for Career Development Practice

Things to Remember

- The general principles of ethical career counseling and career development practice
- Guidelines for avoiding liability lawsuits
- Major competencies needed by career counselors

- Qualifications for three certificates: Master Career Counselor; Master Career Development Professional, and Global Career Development Facilitator

This chapter is in many ways the most important in Part I because ethical practice is the cornerstone of any profession and is essential if the public is to accept an individual practitioner or a professional group. Career development practice—the focus of Part II—will take up career counseling, assessment, and information, dissemination, all of which are topics where ethical pitfalls lurk. The major aim of this chapter is not to endorse one particular code of ethics, although I have relied heavily on the ethical standards of the American Counseling Association in the sections that follow. Although the principles on which codes of ethics are based are for the most part universal, there are to be sure nuances that pertain to the group drafting a position. The approach here will be to synthesize the principles of several codes of ethics. By looking at ethics using broad strokes I hope to avoid embroiling students in the mind-numbing details that characterize all codes of ethics. The details are important, but at this juncture a thorough knowledge of ethical principles should suffice to alert would-be practitioners to areas where the details become important and their particular code of ethics must be consulted.

Chief among the requirements of ethical practice is the importance of standards of competency. No one would knowingly hire a surgeon or an architect without first ascertaining their competence. Professional associations develop competency statements that are often embedded in program accrediting standards to make certain that people who enter their professional fields are competent. Additionally, graduates of professional programs are often required to take rigorous examinations prior to being licensed to practice and to engage in in-service education to maintain their credentials. This two-tiered approach to verifying that individuals are competent has served professions well, but history and current practice tell us that the two-tiered approach is not a foolproof way of ensuring competency.

Unfortunately the standards for career development practitioners in all states are subject to the same problems, and the public is not rigorously protected from incompetency, partially because standards for practice have only recently been developed and incorporated into training guidelines. The licensing of counselors in all 50 states was not complete until 2009 and the licensing of specialist career counselors is in its infancy. However, there is an exception of sorts. The licensure of psychologists, some of whom offer career counseling, has been in place for more than a quarter of century, although these licensing laws generally do not pertain to subspecialists such as vocational psychologists. Rather these laws depend on psychologists adhering to the code of ethics issued by the American Psychological Association (APA, 2002), which admonishes them to practice within the limits of their competence. Those who fail to heed the warning can have their licenses revoked as can counselors and others who are licensed by state licensing boards for professional counselors.

ETHICAL PRINCIPLES

Ethical codes for career counselors have been developed by the National Career Development Association, American School Counselor Association (1998), the American Counseling Association (2005), the National Board for Certified Counselors (1997b), the Commission on Rehabilitation Counselor Certification (1995), and a few other subspecialties. To a certain extent the sheer number of ethical codes within the counseling profession has resulted in a confusing mess in which some counselors are actually held accountable to a number of codes of ethics. Psychologists and social workers have done a much better job in this area and have arrived at a single set of ethical standards for their respective professions The purpose of this chapter is not to compare and contrast ethical codes. That would take a book, not a brief chapter. Instead, this chapter identifies principles of ethical standards that are embedded in all codes of ethics. If practitioners learn and follow,these principles, ethical practice will result.

Career development services such as career counseling, assessment, and career coaching are offered by a variety of practitioners—from school counselors, college counselors, and career counselors to mental health counselors, rehabilitation counselors, and counseling psychologists. Some of these practitioners are neither counselors nor psychologists and they may not necessarily be obligated to follow a code of ethics as a result of affiliation with a professional organization or state level licensure. Practitioners in private practice, as opposed to those who work in public institutions, typically are licensed in the states where they practice and must follow the code of ethics adopted by the licensing board of that state. However, no career development practitioners should be so foolish as to ignore the ethical principles of their professional group. To do otherwise is to place themselves at risk. Malpractice lawyers thrive when practitioners fail to follow the ethical canons of their professions and damage—real or imagined—occurs.

All practitioners should not only follow the extant codes of ethics of their professions but also maintain awareness of changes that are almost always in the works. The following are four examples of interim statements that deal with technology and assessment that have been issued since 1993:

Ethical Standards for Internet Online Counseling (American Counseling Association [ACA], 1997)

Standards for the Ethical Practice of Web-counseling (National Board for Certified Counselors [NBCC], 1998)

NCDA Guidelines for the Use of the Internet for the Provision of Information and Planning Services (National Career Development Association [NCDA], 1997b)

Multicultural Assessment Standards (Prediger, 1993)

In due time the standards set forth in these interim issues were incorporated into the codes of ethics of the organizations that promulgated them and perhaps codes of ethics of other organizations as well. For example, Prediger's (1993) statement has been largely incorporated into the ACA code of ethics (2005), as well as the NCDA (2003) ethical guidelines.

The remainder of this chapter focuses on the general principles of ethical practice as identified by VanHoose (1986), Koocher and Keith-Speigel (1998), Srebalus and Brown (2003), and others. The section numbers appearing with each principle refer to the ACA Code of Ethics (2005).

Principle 1: Above All, Do No Harm (Section A.4.a)

The do-no-harm principle puzzles most students until they consider that the misapplication of their knowledge and skills can, in fact, harm their clients. The career counselor who assumes that high school or college students will be their own decision makers may harm those clients' relationships with their parents if they follow up on the counselor's expectations. Furthermore, clients may perceive that they are being rejected because of their cultural values and, thus, their self-esteem may be lowered. The career counselor who fails to adhere to multicultural guidelines in the use of tests and inventories or misapplies them with people who are disabled is likely to generate faulty information that may harm clients prospects in the labor market. Clients may feel alienated by a counselor who maintains eye contact that is not in accordance with the norms in their own cultures. Doing no harm requires competence in the use of counseling techniques, coaching strategies, and assessment devices. It also requires counselors to provide up-to-date, accurate information about educational and occupational options. Furthermore, doing no harm requires that counselors develop knowledge of the cultural backgrounds and worldviews of their clients and an understanding of the cultural conflicts that may occur between the client's culture and the dominant culture.

Principle 2: Be Competent (Sections C.2.a, b, c, d, and f)

The last sentence in the foregoing section speaks to cultural competence, something that has been stressed from the beginning of this book. The competencies needed by counselors who engage in career counseling, coaching, assessment, and other aspects of career development practice are listed later in this chapter (NCDA, 1997a). It is worth noting that few, if any, practitioners master all of the competencies listed in the NCDA statement of career counseling competencies. Therefore, career development practitioners must know the limitations of their skills, knowledge, and abilities.

The acquisition of the knowledge and skills needed to be a competent practitioner is typically gained through formal coursework and under the supervision of professionals qualified to teach the needed skills. This is why licensing laws and certification standards typically require the completion of formal coursework from accredited preparation programs. However, the content of formal course offerings may, and often does, lag behind the developments in a field as dynamic as career development practice. For example, the technological innovations that have occurred with increasing rapidity in career development practice have forced counselors who wish to take advantage of these development to engage in self-study, attend accredited work-shops, and consult with other professionals. These educational approaches to competency development are acceptable as long as practitioners remember the importance of attending to the client's welfare by limiting their practice until skill development is completed.

Professionals are responsible for maintaining their competence through continuing education (ACA, 2005, sec. C.2.f) and monitoring their own competence. In the event a counselor becomes impaired and no longer able to practice effectively, the counselor is obligated to terminate the practice (ACA, 2005, sec. C.2.g). Finally, being competent involves sensitivity to multicultural issues (ACA, 2005, sec. A.2.c and sec. A Introduction) and the application of that knowledge to areas such as assessment and evaluation (ACA, 2005, sec. E.8).

Principle 3: Respect Clients' Rights to Choose Their Own Directions (Section A.4.b)

Respecting one's clients is the cornerstone of ethical practice. Respect in an ethical context means respecting clients' cultures, right to nondiscriminatory practice, approach to making decisions, and individualism. Clients have the right to choose their own paths.

I typically limit personal anecdotes to the introduction, but one experience that occurred during my training and a much more recent incident are worth illustrating here to show how the principle of a client's right to choose his or her own direction can be violated. The first incident involved a demonstration of the interpretation of the Strong Interest Inventory. The interpretation went well until the counselor asked the high school student to summarize what he had learned from the inventory and its interpretation. When the student hesitated, the counselor said, "I think this means mechanical engineering at Purdue University for you." Many career counselors forget that they are influential, and careless statements made without qualifications can have disastrous consequences. In another incident, a college counselor admitted that she had encouraged her Asian American student to leave his parents out of the decision-making process because of her lack of knowledge regarding her client's culture. She asked what she could do to make amends. I suggested that she apologize to the student and admit her ignorance. I also recommended that she become familiar with the cultural values and worldviews of all of the clients she advises.

In summary, clients have the right to choose to have others make their decisions. They also have the right to choose for themselves. How their right to choose a direction is implemented depends on a number of factors, but abridging it by declarative statements about what is "best" is unethical. Not understanding the worldview of clients is an egregious ethical error.

Principle 4: Honor Your Responsibilities (Section C)

Counselors and psychologists are responsible for maintaining their physical and psychological well-being so that they can adequately serve their clients. Professionals who deliver career development services also have responsibilities to their clients, professions, employers, and communities, including the laws of those communities. The problem is, how shall these responsibilities be prioritized? Most codes of ethics contain a statement such as the one found in Section A.1.a of the 1995 ACA code, which states that the counselor's primary responsibility is "to respect the dignity and to promote the welfare of clients." The 2005 ACA code has a similar statement, but it is much more specific, indicating that counselors have a responsibility to base their practice on research data.

What if there is a conflict between promoting the welfare of the client and the existing federal and community laws? The code of ethics of the American Psychological Association (2002) explicitly suggests that there may be times when the client's needs should be placed ahead of the laws of the community. The ACA Code of Ethics (2005) is less explicit about this matter. Consider the following ethical dilemma. Maria tells her counselor that her father has a fraudulent work permit and is in this country illegally. All codes of ethics require that disclosure between client and practitioner be held in confidence unless the client or the public is in jeopardy; therefore, keeping Maria's disclosure poses no immediate ethical dilemma. However, what if a client discloses the fact that she or he has a counterfeit green card and is using it to secure employment on a military base, which actually occurred at Camp Lejeune, North Carolina. This places the professional in an ethical bind because of national security issues for which there is no easy answer. However, given the potential consequences for the career counselor and the men and women in the military the counselor elected to call the personnel office of the military base and report the person with the bogus green card.

Codes of ethics are meant to serve as decision-making guides, but, in some instances, the path to take in the decision-making process is not altogether clear. Codes of ethics provide guidelines, not road maps. The career counselor's values and judgments fill in the gaps.

Principle 5: Make Accurate Public Statements (Section C.3)

Career counselors in private practice typically engage in various types of advertising to publicize their businesses. Ethical behavior requires that these advertising statements accurately reflect the practitioner's credentials and the limits of his or her practice. For example, counselors who earned doctorates in communication and master's degrees in counseling may not use the communications degrees in their advertisements because this may mislead clients into believing that they are consulting a person with a doctorate in counseling (ACA, 2005). Only degrees that relate to preparation for providing career development services may be used in advertisements.

Private practitioners are not the only career counselors who make public statements. Career counselors' opinions about a number of things, ranging from job hunting to jobs of the future, are often solicited by members of the media. Counselors may also be asked about the use of certain instruments in the career counseling process and aspects of career development practice as well. Statements made in interviews and press conferences should be based on factual information, and facts should be clearly delineated from opinion.

Principle 6: Respect Counselors and Practitioners from Other Professions (Section D)

As was stated at the outset of this chapter, career development professionals come from many subspecialties in counseling professions and other professions as well, including psychology and social work. Turf wars among these groups have occurred and continue to do so at this time. Two incidents may serve as useful examples. Psychologists in Indiana and elsewhere lobbied for legislation that would preclude counselors from using psychological tests and inventories in their practices on the grounds that only psychologists were sufficiently trained to use them. Until 2009, practitioners from other professions successfully lobbied against a licensing law for counselors in California. These battles have caused animosity among some groups, but such feelings should not preclude career development professionals from respecting the credentials and skills of other professionals. Offering career development services is not the domain of a single group.

One question in particular arises in discussions of respect for other professions: What should be the stance of career development specialists with regard to groups such as career coaches who may not be licensed or hold other recognized credentials and thus operate without oversight? One obligation of established professionals is to protect the public from unscrupulous practitioners within their own ranks. Does that obligation extend to protecting the public from unscrupulous practitioners from outside their professions? The answers is a qualified yes. The qualification has to do with how the public is protected. Educating nonprofessionals about the qualifications needed to provide career development services is a legitimate means of protecting the public. So is lobbying for the extension of credentialing legislation that regulates the practice of individuals who provide career development services. Attacking an individual is perilous from a legal point of view unless there is clear-cut evidence that she or he is harming the public. Even then a defamation suit may be lodged by the person who is being criticized.

Principle 7: Advocate for Clients in Need (Section A.6.a)

In 2005, the ACA included advocacy in its code of ethics. Until that time, only the code of ethics for rehabilitation counselors (Commission on Rehabilitation Counselor Certification, 1995) required practitioners to advocate for their clients. It expected that other professional organizations will follow suit. For example, the ASCA National Model for School Counseling Programs (ASCA, 2003) places considerable importance on advocacy as do the implications of the multicultural counseling standards (Arrendondo et al., 1996). It seems likely, therefore, that an advocacy standard will soon find its way into most of the codes of ethics for counselors, although the likelihood of this occurring for psychologists is less clear. The position here is that, with or without an ethical standard, it is a moral imperative that career development counselors take up some of the social and economic dilemmas of their clients through advocacy for them.

Advocacy is a process in which the career development professional assumes some or all of the responsibility for representing a client or group to another group, government agency, community agency, or business for the purpose of improving the client's access to resources, services, or jobs. To be effective, the effort must be data based, organized, and sustained. It often requires collaboration with other like-minded individuals or groups. The ultimate aim of advocacy is the empowerment of the group or individual being represented in a manner that will allow them to represent their own interests in the future. It is necessary, therefore, to include the disenfranchised group or individual in each step of the process (Brown & Trusty, 2005; Fiedler, 2000). The advocacy process outlined by Fiedler involves five steps: (1) define the problem, (2) collect information, (3) plan action, (4) take assertive action, and (5) evaluate and follow up. Of these steps, none is more important than planning action. At this point the desired outcomes of the action are identified, the positions of the targets of the advocacy are outlined, and the strategies needed to overcome their opposition are delineated in detail.

Advocacy requires some degree of risk taking, which may be many reason for professional groups to have avoided taking positive positions about its use on behalf of clients. However, it seems unlikely that groups such as legal and illegal immigrants as well as individuals who are disabled and those who live below the poverty level will overcome the obstacles that confront them in the labor market unless professionals in the field become their allies outside the office.

LEGAL ISSUES AND CAREER COUNSELING

We live in a litigious society where the threat of lawsuits has prompted most professionals to purchase liability insurance. Legal standards for career counselors and other professional are the result of laws such as the Family Educational Rights and Privacy Act (FERPA), which was passed in 1974 and ensured that parents have access to their children's records until they reach the age of 18, at which time the right to access the records passes to the student. This legal standard buttressed the ethical canon demanding that career counselors respect the right of their clients to confidentiality. However, FERPA focuses only on records, not on the verbal communication that occurs in the counseling context.

Privileged communication laws contained in some state licensing statutes and as free-standing legislation provide additional protection against disclosure of sensitive information. Privileged communication is a guarantee by a legal body, typically a state legislature, to clients that information given to practitioners will be held in confidence. Disclosure of the information by the practitioner is punishable by fines, short jail terms, or both. Additionally, career counselors can be sued for failure to protect sensitive records, test results, electronic communications, and verbal reports.

Liability suits, perhaps the most feared of all legal actions, may be lodged successfully against career counselors who practice outside their area of expertise (malpractice), fail to make appropriate and timely referrals, or abandon their client. Counselors become liable when there is a breach of the duty that they have toward clients, and harm or damage results. The 2005 ACA code of ethics is quite clear with regard to all of these issues, which suggest that following a personal code of ethics is perhaps the best protection against lawsuits.

Liability suits may also result when career counselors fail to select tests and inventories judiciously, misinterpret test results, or use counseling techniques that are not considered to be among the best practices by the profession. In addition, counselors who do not carefully craft recommendations for jobs and educational programs may find themselves face to face with a trial lawyer—a costly proposition where the defense in even an unsuccessful lawsuit can amount to fifty thousand dollars.

In summary, career counselors can avoid legal entanglements by being aware of legal statutes that impinge on the counseling relationship and following the guidelines set forth in them; following the ethical canons set forth in their codes of ethics, familiarizing themselves with the guidelines established by their profession for the selection, use, and interpretation of tests and materials, and carefully safeguarding the confidentiality of all information that results from the counseling process.

STUDENT LEARNING EXERCISE 4.1

1. Check to see if the state in which you are studying has a privilege communication law.

2. Call the chairperson of the state counseling, psychological association, or licensing board and ask about charges of unethical behavior that have been presented to the association or board. What is required to file a charge of unethical behavior?

3. Go to the yellow pages of your telephone directory or to the keyword search option on the Internet and find what appears to be the most highly qualified practitioners offering career development services. What are the credentials they list in their advertisements?

THE COMPETENCIES NEEDED BY CAREER COUNSELORS

The competency statement that follows is for those professionals interested in becoming proficient in career counseling, which is defined in the statement as the process of assisting individuals in the development of a life-career with focus on the definition of the worker role and how that role interacts with other life roles. NCDA's career counseling competencies (NCDA, 1997a) are intended to represent minimum competencies for those professionals at or above the master's degree level of education. These competencies are reviewed periodically by the NCDA Professional Standards Committee, the NCDA board, and other relevant associations.

Professional career counselors hold a masters degree or higher. Persons in career development positions must demonstrate the knowledge and skills for a specialty in career counseling that a school counselor or mental health counselor might not possess. The NCDA career counseling competency statement can serve as a guide for career counseling training programs or as a checklist for persons wanting to acquire or to enhance their skills in career counseling. The italicized competencies in the list that follows are those that must be met to obtain Master Career Counselor certification, which is discussed in the final section of this chapter.

NCDA Competencies and Performance Indicators

CAREER DEVELOPMENT THEORY   *Theory base and knowledge considered essential for professionals engaging in career counseling and development (Chapters 2, 3)*, who should demonstrate a knowledge of

1. Counseling theories and associated techniques.
2. Theories and models of career development.
3. Individual differences related to gender, sexual orientation, race, ethnicity, and physical and mental capacities.
4. Theoretical models for career development and associated counseling and information-delivery techniques and resources.
5. Human growth and development throughout the life span.
6. Role relationships that facilitate life-work planning.
7. Information, techniques, and models related to career planning and placement.

INDIVIDUAL AND GROUP COUNSELING SKILLS   *Individual and group counseling competencies considered essential for effective career counselors (Chapter 5; web counseling in Chapter 9)*, who should demonstrate the ability to

1. Establish and maintain productive personal relationships with individuals.
2. Establish and maintain a productive group climate.
3. Collaborate with clients in identifying personal goals.
4. Identify and select techniques appropriate to client or group goals and client needs, psychological states, and developmental tasks.
5. Identify and understand clients' personal characteristics as they relate to career.
6. Identify and understand social contextual conditions affecting clients' careers.
7. Identify and understand familial, subcultural, and cultural structures and functions as they relate to clients' careers.

8. Identify and understand clients' career decision-making processes.
9. Identify and understand clients' attitudes toward work and workers.
10. Identify and understand clients' biases toward work and workers based on gender, race, and cultural stereotypes.
11. Challenge and encourage clients to take action to prepare for and initiate role transitions by
    • Locating sources of relevant information and experience.
    • Obtaining and interpreting information and experiences, and acquiring skills needed to make role transitions.
12. Assist the client to acquire a set of employability and job-search skills.
13. Support and challenge clients to examine life-work roles, including the balance of work, leisure, family, and community in their careers.

INDIVIDUAL/GROUP ASSESSMENT   *Individual/group assessment skills considered essential for professionals engaging in career counseling (Chapter 7)*, who should demonstrate the ability to

1. Assess personal characteristics, such as aptitude, achievement, interests, values, and personality traits.
2. Assess leisure interests, learning style, life roles, self-concept, career maturity, vocational identity, career indecision, work environment preference (e.g., work satisfaction), and other related lifestyle/development issues.
3. Assess conditions of the work environment (such as tasks, expectations, norms, and qualities of the physical and social settings).
4. Evaluate and select valid and reliable instruments appropriate to the client's gender, sexual orientation, race, ethnicity, and physical and mental capacities.
5. Use computer-delivered assessment measures effectively and appropriately.
6. Select assessment techniques appropriate for group administration and those appropriate for individual administration.
7. Administer, score, and report findings from career assessment instruments appropriately.
8. Interpret data from assessment instruments and present the results to clients and to others.
9. Assist the client and others designated by the client to interpret data from assessment instruments.
10. Write an accurate report of assessment results.

INFORMATION/RESOURCES   *Information/resource base and knowledge essential for professionals engaging in career counseling (Chapter 8)*, who should demonstrate a knowledge of

1. Education, training, and employment trends; labor market information and resources that provide information about job tasks, functions, salaries, requirements, and future outlooks related to broad occupational fields and individual occupations.
2. Resources and skills that clients use in life-work planning and management.
3. Community/professional resources available to assist clients in career planning, including job search.
4. Changing roles of women and men and the implications that this has for education, family, and leisure.
5. Methods of good use of computer-based career information delivery systems (CIDS) and computer-assisted career guidance systems (CACGS) to assist with career planning.

PROGRAM MANAGEMENT AND IMPLEMENTATION   *Knowledge and skills necessary to develop, plan, implement, and manage comprehensive career development programs in a variety of settings (Chapters 11–14)*, including

1. Designs that can be used in the organization of career development programs.
2. Needs assessment and evaluation techniques and practices.
3. Organizational theories, including diagnosis, behavior, planning, organizational communication, and management useful in implementing and administering career development programs.
4. Methods of forecasting, budgeting, planning, costing, policy analysis, resource allocation, and quality control.
5. Leadership theories and approaches for evaluation and feedback, organizational change, decision making, and conflict resolution.
6. Professional standards and criteria for career development programs.
7. Societal trends and state and federal legislation that influence the development and implementation of career development programs. Career counselors should also demonstrate the ability to
   • Implement individual and group programs in career development for specified populations.
   • Train others about the appropriate use of computer-based systems for career information and planning.
   • Plan, organize, and manage a comprehensive career resource center.
   • Implement career development programs in collaboration with others.
   • Identify and evaluate staff competencies.
   • Mount a marketing and public relations campaign on behalf of career development activities and services.

COACHING, CONSULTATION, AND PERFORMANCE IMPROVEMENT   *Knowledge and skills considered essential in enabling individuals and organizations to effectively impact the career counseling and development process (Chapters 14, 15)*, including the ability to

1. Use consultation theories, strategies, and models.
2. Establish and maintain a productive consultative relationship with people who can influence a client's career.
3. Help the general public and legislators understand the importance of career counseling, career development, and life-work planning.
4. Impact public policy as it relates to career development and workforce planning.
5. Analyze future organizational needs and current level of employee skills and develop performance improvement training.
6. Mentor and coach employees.

DIVERSE POPULATIONS   *Knowledge and skills considered essential in providing career counseling and development processes to diverse populations* (Chapters 5, 6), including the ability to

1. Identify development models and multicultural counseling competencies.
2. Identify developmental needs unique to various diverse populations, including those of different gender, sexual orientation, ethnic group, race, and physical or mental capacity.
3. Define career development programs to accommodate needs unique to various diverse populations.

4. Find appropriate methods or resources to communicate with limited-English-proficient individuals.
5. Identify alternative approaches to meet career planning needs for individuals of diverse populations.
6. Identify community resources and establish linkages to assist clients with specific needs.
7. Assist other staff members, professionals, and community members in understanding the unique needs/characteristics of diverse populations with regard to career exploration, employment expectations, and economic/social issues.
8. Advocate for the career development and employment of diverse populations.
9. Design and deliver career development programs and materials to hard-to-reach populations.

SUPERVISION   *Knowledge and skills considered essential in critically evaluating counselor performance, maintaining and improving professional skills, and seeking assistance for others when needed in career counseling (typically covered in a separate course)*, including the ability to

1. Recognize own limitations as a career counselor and to seek supervision or refer clients when appropriate.
2. Utilize supervision on a regular basis to maintain and improve counselor skills.
3. Consult with supervisors and colleagues regarding client and counseling problems and issues related to one's own professional development as a career counselor.
4. Understand supervision models and theories.
5. Provide effective supervision to career counselors and career development facilitators at different levels of experience.
6. Provide effective supervision to career development facilitators at different levels of experience by
   • Understanding their roles, competencies, and ethical standards.
   • Determining their competence in each of the areas included in their certification.
   • Further training them in competencies, including interpretation of assessment instruments.
   • Monitoring and mentoring their activities in support of the professional career counselor, and scheduling regular consultations for the purpose of reviewing their activities.

ETHICAL/LEGAL ISSUES   *Information base and knowledge considered essential for the ethical and legal practice of career counseling (Chapter 4)*, including a knowledge of

1. Ethical codes and standards relevant to the profession of career counseling (e.g., NBCC, NCDA, and ACA).
2. Current ethical and legal issues that affect the practice of career counseling with all populations.
3. Current ethical/legal issues with regard to the use of computer-assisted career guidance systems.
4. Ethical standards relating to consultation issues.
5. State and federal statutes relating to client confidentiality.

RESEARCH/EVALUATION   *Knowledge and skills considered essential in understanding and conducting research and evaluation in career counseling and development (Chapter 17)*, including the ability to

1. Write a research proposal.
2. Use types of research and research designs appropriate to career counseling and development research.

3. Convey research findings related to the effectiveness of career counseling programs.
4. Design, conduct, and use the results of evaluation programs.
5. Design evaluation programs that take into account the needs of various diverse populations, including persons of both genders, differing sexual orientations, different ethnic and racial backgrounds, and differing physical and mental capacities.
6. Apply appropriate statistical procedures to career development research.

TECHNOLOGY *Knowledge and skills considered essential in using technology to assist individuals with career planning (Chapters 8, 9, 10)*, including a knowledge of

1. Various computer-based guidance and information systems as well as services available on the Internet.
2. Standards by which such systems and services are evaluated (e.g., NCDA and ACSCI).
3. Ways in which to use computer-based systems and Internet services to assist individuals with career planning that are consistent with ethical standards.
4. Characteristics of clients that make them profit more or less from the use of technology-driven systems.
5. Methods to evaluate and select a system to meet local needs.

CREDENTIALING CAREER DEVELOPMENT PRACTITIONERS

In 1981, the National Career Development Association (NCDA) established a certification program for career counselors as a means of recognizing individuals who meet minimum training, knowledge, and skill requirements to practice career counseling. Certification as a National Certified Career Counselor (NCCC) was administered by the National Board of Certified Counselors (NBCC) until 2000 when the credentialing program was terminated. In response to NBCC's decision, NCDA established two special membership categories in 2001 to credential career development specialists. These categories are Master Career Counselor (MCC) and Master Career Development Professional (MCDP). To qualify for MCC certification, counselors must meet the following standards:

- Be a member of the NCDA for one year
- Hold a master's degree in counseling or a closely related field from an accredited institution
- Complete three years of post–master's experience in career counseling
- Possess and maintain either the National Certified Counselor credential offered by the NBCC or a state-level license as a counselor or psychologist
- Complete at least three credits in each of six NCDA competencies that were italicized in the section dealing with counselor competencies
- Complete a supervised practicum in career counseling during training or two years of supervised postmaster's experience under a certified supervisor or a licensed counseling professional
- Document that at least 50 percent of the current job duties are directly related to career counseling

To qualify for membership as an MCDP, professionals must meet the following criteria:

- Be a member of NCDA for one year
- Hold a master's degree in counseling or a closely related field from an accredited institution

- Complete three years of post–master's experience in career development experience, training, teaching, program development, or materials development
- Document that at least 50 percent of current full-time job duties are directly related to career development

Clearly, the MCC and MCDP were developed to recognize two types of professionals, one who is actively engaged in career counseling and one who is engaged primarily in career development activities. However, the MCDP could ethically engage in career counseling. Another, and perhaps even more far-reaching, development is the credentialing of paraprofessionals in the United States and beyond. The Career Development Facilitators (CDF) program began at Oakland University in Michigan in the mid-1990s as a means of training specialists to facilitate career development groups, to serve as career coaches, to mentor people engaged in the job search, to coordinate career resource centers, to provide occupational information, and to provide a variety of other career development services (NCDA, 2005a). It is worth noting that career counseling is not included in the list of services that Career Development Facilitators can provide. To qualify for this credential, applicants must meet the following requirements:

- Complete 120 hours of training in a specified course of study.
- Possess one of the following: a graduate degree plus one year of career development work experience; a bachelor's degree plus two years of career development work experience; two years of college plus three years of career development work experience; or a high school diploma or GED plus approximately four years of career development work experience.

The CDF has now evolved into a credential called the Global Career Development Facilitator (GCDF) (Center for Credentialing and Education, 2010). Initially, this credential was developed in response to interest in Japan, but GCDF credentials are now available in eleven countries including Bulgaria, Canada, China, Turkey, Germany, South Korea, Greece, Japan, Romania, and New Zealand, as well as the United States (Center for Credentialing and Education, 2010).

Summary

Career development professionals follow a variety of ethical codes depending on their professional identities and credentialing. However, with the exception of advocacy, these codes of ethics have similar principles. In this chapter six principles that are embedded in most professional codes of ethics have been identified and discussed. A seventh principle, advocating for one's clients, has been added to this list because it seems that many of our clients' goals will be unrealized unless professionals assert themselves on their behalf.

Chapter Quiz

T F   **1.** Career counseling is one of the services that Global Career Development Facilitators may provide if an MCC is unavailable.

T F   **2.** The ethical canon, do no harm, means refers to the ethical guideline to maintain confidentiality because of the embarrassment that may result when information falls into the wrong hands.

T F   **3.** Privileged communication is a legal term that, when embedded in a law, protects clients from disclosure of information by their counselors.

T F   **4.** In order for a client to sue a career counselor, the client must first prove that he or she has suffered some type of loss.

T F **5.** People who qualify as Master Career Development Facilitators may ethically provide career counseling.

T F **6.** The National Board for Certified Counselors created the first certification program for career counselors.

T F **7.** After a number of years of wrangling, career counselors from a number of professional groups have agreed on a single code of ethics.

T F **8.** The NCDA has identified 11 competencies that must be acquired prior to certification as an MCC.

T F **9.** The APA code of ethics indicates that psychologists should base their practice on research; The ACA code does not contain the same suggestion.

T F **10.** Except for rehabilitation counselors, codes of ethics for career counseling practitioners have had no ethical guidelines pertaining to advocacy until quite recently.

T (10) T (9) F (8) F (7) F (6) T (5) F (4) T (3) F (2) F (1)

References

American Counseling Association. (1997). *Ethical standards for Internet online counseling.* Alexandria, VA: Author.

American Counseling Association. (2005). *American counseling association code of ethics.* Alexandria, VA: Author.

American Psychological Association. (2002). *Ethical principles of psychologists and code of conduct.* Washington, DC: Author.

American School Counselor Association. (1998). *Ethical standards for school counselors.* Alexandria, VA: Author.

American School Counselor Association. (2003). *ASCA national model for school counseling pro grams.* Alexandria, VA: Author.

Arrendondo, P., Toporek, R., Brown, S. P., Jones, J., Locke, D., Sanchez, J., & Sadler, H. (1996). Operationalization of the multicultural counseling competencies. *Journal of Multicultural Counseling and Development, 24,* 42–78.

Brown, D., & Trusty, J. (2005). *Designing and leading comprehensive school counseling programs.* Pacific Grove, CA: Brooks/Cole.

Center for Credentialing and Education. (2010). Credential for global career development facilitator. Retrieved from http://www.cce-global.org/credentials-offered/gcdf-home

Commission on Rehabilitation Counselor Certification. (1995). *American Rehabilitation Counselors Association/ National Association of Rehabilitation Counselors/ Commission on Rehabilitation Counselor Certification code of ethics for rehabilitation counselors.* Chicago: Author.

Fiedler, C. R. (2000). *Advocacy competencies for special education professionals.* Boston: Allyn & Bacon.

Koocher, G. P., & Keith-Speigel, P. (1998). *Ethics in psychology: Professional standards and cases* (2nd ed.). New York: Oxford University Press.

National Board for Certified Counselors. (1997a). *Code of ethics.* Greensboro, NC: Author.

National Board for Certified Counselors. (1997b). *Standards for the ethical practice of web counseling.* Greensboro, NC: Author.

National Career Development Association. (2005a). Career counselor training and credentialing. Retrieved from www.ncda.org,

National Career Development Association. (2005b). What is a career development facilitator? Retrieved from www.ncda.org

National Career Development Association. (1997a). *Career counseling competencies of the National Career Development Association.* Tulsa, OK: Author.

National Career Development Association. (1997b). *NCDA guidelines for the use of the Internet for the provision of information and planning services.* Tulsa, OK: Author.

National Career Development Association. (2003). *Ethical standards.* Tulsa, OK: Author.

Prediger, D. (1993). *Multicultural assessment standards.* Alexandria, VA: Association for Assessment in Counseling.

Srebalus, D. J., & Brown, D. (2003). *Introduction to the counseling profession* (3rd ed.). Boston: Allyn & Bacon.

VanHoose, W. H. (1986). Ethical principles in counseling. *Journal of Counseling and Development, 65,* 168–169.

P A R T

II

Career Counseling, Assessment, and Information Dissemination

5

A Values-Based, Multicultural Approach to Career Counseling and Advocacy

Things to Remember

- The process and techniques used in a culturally sensitive approach to career counseling

- The cultural values of the major racial and ethnic groups in the United States

- The advocacy process and the risks involved

In 1987, while serving as the president of the National Career Development Association, I had an opportunity to discuss various issues confronting career counselors from across the United States, particularly the issues of the changing demographics of this country and the impact it would have on counseling in general and career counseling in particular. I read and rejected several ideas about how best to tackle the issue of cross-cultural career counseling. I happened to on a report of English consultants who helped an African government design a health care intervention that failed miserably. The now-forgotten author concluded that the first step in the process should have been to assess the values of the people who were to be helped and then to design the intervention. The report of the failed consultation and the extensive work of the Association for Multicultural Counseling and Development on the need for cultural competence oriented my thinking to differences and similarities in cultural values.

In 1988, I embarked on a crash course in work and human values by reading literally dozens of research articles about values. Some of those articles discussed the differences in values in various cultures, including the impact those values had on the decision-making process, work satisfaction, and so forth. I also discovered that some people in the field of communications had focused on variations of communication styles based on differences in cultural values. This chapter is the culmination of a long process of discovery in an attempt to ascertain how effective, sensitive career counseling could be offered in a cross-cultural context.

In Chapter 1 Blustein and his colleagues (Blustein, McWhirter, & Perry, 2005) call for a change in the paradigms that guide the work of career development specialists was cited. In Chapters 2 and 3, seven career choice and development theories were presented along with suggestions for their applications in career counseling and career development programming. Each application was briefly critiqued with regard to its use for groups other than with representatives of the dominant culture, who are primarily white individuals with Eurocentric worldviews. Each of the approaches discussed in Chapters 2 and 3 have merit and some (e.g., the postmodern approaches) are applicable across cultures.

In this chapter a multicultural approach to career counseling is presented, based largely on Brown's (2002) values-based theory of occupational choice. The objective of this presentation is to provide a detailed, comprehensive approach to career counseling. I want to point out that the approach used does not rule out borrowing ideas from other theories. For example, I often use Bandura's ideas about elf-efficacy and appraisals to help my clients understand their motivation, or more likely their lack of motivation. This presentation is followed by a section focused on helping students and others build their own approaches to career counseling.

Implicit in many discussions on multiculturalism, and its extension to counseling, is the message that white counselors need to learn about the cultures of ethnic and racial minorities; persons who are disabled; and persons who are gay, lesbian, bisexual, and transgendered, and apply this knowledge to counseling. Consider the very real possibility of a lesbian counselor entering her office one day to find a white, Christian male who believes that homosexuality is a sin and freely expresses that view with everyone. One possibility is for the counselor to refer the client to another professional if she finds his views so repugnant that she cannot maintain her objectivity. The other is to try to understand his worldview, develop a working relationship with him, and proceed to help him with his career problem. The point here is a simple one: In a diverse culture such as ours, all counselors, regardless of race, ethnicity, or worldview, need a multicultural approach to career counseling.

CAREER COUNSELING DEFINED

There is a convergence in the definitions of career counseling, a process that probably began with the acceptance of Super's (1980) ideas regarding the interactive nature of life roles. In 1991, Linda Brooks and I (Brown & Brooks, 1991) defined career counseling as a process aimed at facilitating career development and one that may involve choosing, entering, adjusting to, or advancing in a career. We defined career problems as undecidedness growing out of too little information; indecisiveness growing out of choice anxiety; unsatisfactory work performance; incongruence between the person and the work role; and incongruence between the work roles and other life roles, such as family or leisure.

The National Career Development Association (NCDA, 1997) adopted a similar but simpler definition. This organization defined career counseling as a "process of assisting individuals in the development of a life-career with a focus on the definition of the worker role and how that role interacts with other life roles" (p. 2). For the most part, these definitions reflect the positions taken by Gysbers, Heppner, and Johnston (2003), Amundson (2003), and others.

As was illustrated in Chapters 2 and 3, the mechanics of career counseling, including approaches to the relationship and assessment, vary based on the theory being applied. Gysbers and colleagues (2003) developed a taxonomy of tasks that occur within career counseling simultaneously with the process of developing a working alliance. These tasks include identifying the presenting problem; structuring the counseling relationship; developing a counselor-client bond; gathering information about the client, including information about personal and contextual restraints; goal setting; intervention selection; action taking; and evaluation of outcomes. As will be shown later, the multicultural counseling model outlined in this chapter accepts most of these ideas regarding the structure of career counseling with minor changes.

FOUNDATION OF THE VALUES-BASED APPROACH

There are three aspects of culture. The *universal dimension* refers to the similarities among groups. The *general cultural dimension* refers to the characteristics of a particular group and typically refers to ethnicity, the group's common history, values, language, customs, religion, and politics. There are more than 200 national entities and 5,000 languages in the world. These broad groups can be broken down into countless subgroups. It is impossible for career counselors to study all of the cultures and subcultures of the world, although it is possible for counselors in the United States to learn about what are termed the *cultural generalizations* of the major cultural groups in this country. The third aspect of culture is the *personal dimension*, which is reflected in the individual's worldview and is based on the extent to which the general cultural values and worldview have been adopted by the individual. The process by which this occurs is called *enculturation* and the result is racial/ethnic identity development, a continuous process that results in a worldview (Peace Corps, 2005). An individual's worldview is the basis for his or her perception of reality (Ivey, D'Andrea, Ivey, & Simek-Morgan, 2009). Cultural generalization— that is, the assumption that the individual's characteristics resemble those of the broader group— is stereotyping and must be avoided (Ho, 1995). Skin color, dress, ethnicity, religious beliefs, customs, or traditions honored are not proxies for personal culture.

As was discussed in Chapter 2, there are two broad philosophical bases for our theories and approaches: logical positivism and postmodernism. Ivey and his colleagues (2002) adopted a postmodern underpinning for their general approach to multicultural counseling because it accommodates a "multiplicity of points of views" (p. 7). In fact, postmodernism accommodates an infinite number of points of view because each person is perceived as having a unique worldview. Not surprisingly, given the relative perspective of postmodernism, there are no guiding truths because truth is unknowable. Because there are no guiding truths, values are situational, not universal. It was this valueless perspective that led Prilleltensky (1997) to reject postmodernism as a philosophical basis for the practice of psychology. The assertion here is that career counseling should proceed based on the client's worldview, which is primarily based on the client's cultural values unless those value collide with the laws of the dominant culture. If advocacy is incorporated into the career counseling process it should also be based on the client's values. However, career counselors may also engage in advocacy aimed at legislative, community, and/or organizational change outside of the career counseling process based on their own values system.

Recently, I was confronted with a situation in which a young Chinese American high school student was being kept out of school to work in the family restaurant. Her parents believed their action was perfectly congruent with their worldview, but their behavior was in conflict with the laws of the state of North Carolina. Career counseling cannot be a value-free enterprise. For example, if I take the relativity perspective on values in postmodern approaches into a career counseling session with an unacculturated American Indian male and help him build a career plan based on his worldview, the plan must be implemented in a culture dominated by a totally different worldview. I may advocate for the client with prospective employers, but I may also find myself interpreting the employer's values and helping the client continue to prize his own views while adapting to those in the workplace so that he can find meaningful employment. In the next section, the informal assessment of cultural values is examined as the initial step in the values-based approach discussed there. Why use cultural values instead of variables such as identity development? Ivey and colleagues (2009) discuss individual identity development in terms of five levels and 10 factors, including many of those mentioned in the opening section of this chapter. Career counseling, unlike psychotherapy, is often necessarily a short-term process. Cultural values are assessed more easily than identity development; account for processes, such as enculturation and acculturation; and are understood easily by counselors and clients alike. They can also provide the basis for the selection of appropriate counseling techniques, assessment devices, and interventions (Brown, 2002). What should an approach to multicultural career counseling include? Bingham and Ward (2001) suggest seven components for an approach to career counseling for African Americans. These are presented here, with some modifications, including the addition of advocacy (Bingham & Ward, 2001, pp. 59–60). An approach to multicultural career counseling should provide the basis for the following components:

1. The assessment of cultural variables
2. A culturally appropriate relationship
3. The facilitation of the decision-making process
4. The identification of career issues (assessment)
5. The establishment of culturally appropriate goals
6. The selection of culturally appropriate interventions
7. The implementation and evaluation of the interventions used
8. Advocacy

VALUES-BASED MULTICULTURAL CAREER COUNSELING (VBMCC)

Step 1: Assessing Cultural Variables

Throughout this chapter and the two preceding it, several admonitions regarding making uninformed judgments about the culture of an individual have been issued. However, consider this situation. Sitting in your office, you note that you have an appointment with Lawrence Singh. You know that Singh is a very common name in India, comparable in many ways to Smith in the United States. However, the Eurocentric first name, Lawrence, suggests the possibility that the family has been acculturated and adopted Eurocentric values. If you are to be culturally sensitive, what do you do? The suggestion here is that you disclose your dilemma to Lawrence, perhaps beginning with, "I'm intrigued by your name. Singh is a common name in Asia and Lawrence is clearly an American name. Tell me how that came about?"

Another possible scenario is that you are sitting in your office and a grandmother appears with a student whose last name is Ho. Clearly, she wants to sit in on the conference to discuss Mr. Frederick Ho's career choice. You might wish to ask two questions. The first has to do with who the decision maker will be. In many cultures the family makes the career decision and the grandmother may be representing the family; thus, you begin, "I'm aware that for many Asian Americans families play a major role in the selection of their children's occupation. Before we begin, I would appreciate it if you would help me understand who will make the decision in Frederick's case." You might also compliment the grandmother for her willingness to participate in the career choice-making process and ask her if she is, in fact, a representative of the family. It is absolutely essential if the family is to be the decision maker that the counselor not suggest that it would be more appropriate if Frederick made his own career decision.

There are other means of determining cultural affiliation—for example, language spoken at home, customs and traditions observed, cultural affiliation of friends, cultural affiliation of parents, and section of the community in which the client resides—none of which are very precise (Garrett & Pichette, 2000; Thomason, 1995). The first career counseling interview should perhaps focus on these variables if uncertainty exists about the cultural affiliation of the client.

Step 2: Communication Style and Establishing the Relationship

One of the most powerful illustrations of how insensitivity in communication can occur was provided by Basso (1979) in a vignette involving a white male and a male Apache. The white male greets the Apache with a slap on the back, "Hello my friend. How are you feeling? You feeling good?" They continue on into the white man's house and the white man continues, "Look who is here; it's Little Man. Come in and sit right down. Are you hungry?" Then, facing Little Man, the white man continues. Altogether there are eight errors in cross-cultural communication in this vignette. Using the term *my friend* is considered to be a presumption and, thus, inappropriate. Asking about one's health may cause illness according to the beliefs of some Apaches. The white man may be considered as bossy because of the manner of the invitation to "sit right down." Repeating a question is seen as rude by many Apaches. The person may be viewed as foolish because of his verbosity. Making direct eye contact is considered aggressive in Apache culture and many others as well. Finally, touching in public is considered inappropriate by many Apaches, as is using the Native American's name without asking if it is appropriate. Clearly, the white man in this vignette did not considered the need to alter his communication style to one that is acceptable to Apaches.

In the preceding example, the white individual made two errors in nonverbal behavior (touching and eye contact) and six in his verbal communication style. Consider the acronym SOLER (Egan, 1994), illustrated in Table 5.1, which is commonly used to describe the approach that counselors in training should take in their work as counselors. To this acronym has been

TABLE 5.1   SOLER Approach in Counseling

		Nonverbal Communication Preferences
S	Squarely facing the client	Probably okay
O	Open posture	Probably okay
L	Forward lean (36–42 inches)	Asian Americans concerned by invasions of personal space; Hispanics may interpret as barrier
E	Eye contact—direct	Indirect preferred by many Native Americans, many Hispanics, most Asian Americans, and some African Americans
R	Relaxed	Probably okay, but not too informal with Asian American clients
FE	Facial expressions—smiles and nods signs	Smiles and nods may signal discomfort among Asian American clients; may be more important for Hispanic and African American clients

added facial expression (FE), which represents another major class of nonverbal behaviors (Ivey et al., 2009; Srebalus & Brown, 2001). As can be seen in Table 5.1, nonverbal behavior has different implications across cultures.

STUDENT LEARNING EXERCISE 5.1

Before proceeding, answer the following questions:

1. How would it feel to go for a day without access to a watch or clock?
2. How do you feel when others make decisions for you?
3. Are you punctual?
4. How comfortable are you when placed in a situation that requires you to disclose a great deal of personal information? Information about your family?
5. How do you feel when it is necessary to defer decisions to other people?
6. How competitive are you?
7. Are you tracking the "green jobs" trend in the United States and throughout the world and preparing yourself to take advantage of break throughs when they occur?

Before considering cultural differences in verbal styles, the typical values of major cultural subgroups are considered because of their implications for verbal communication. The taxonomy of cultural values in Table 5.2 is based on the pioneering work of Kluckhorn and Strodtbeck (1961), and a literature review by Carter (1991). It should be pointed out that these are generalized cultural values and should not be interpreted as personal value systems of members of these groups. The work of Kluckhorn and Strodtbeck, Carter, and others (e.g., Ho, 1987; Sue & Sue, 2009) reveals that these values can often be associated with the groups listed in Table 5.2, but the within-group variation in values is considerable.

As discussed in Chapter 2, values—whether they be cultural values, work values, or more general values—are highly prized beliefs (Rokeach, 1973). They are the basis on which we judge our own performance and our appraisal of others. They are also the primary basis for goal setting. Cultural values are the basis of ethnocentrism, or the belief that an individual's own culture

TABLE 5.2   Generalized Values of Major Racial/Ethnic Groups in the United States

Group	Importance of Self-Control	Time	Activity	Social Relationships	Relationships to Nature
White Eurocentric	Moderate	Future	Doing	Individual	Dominate
Native American	Very	Circular	Being-in-Becoming	Collateral	Harmony
Hispanic	Moderate	Present	Being	Collateral	Harmony/subjugation
African American	Moderate	Present	Doing	Collateral	Mixed
Asian American	Very	Past/future	Doing	Lineal/collateral	Harmony

is superior to others. As noted in Table 5.2 there are five basic cultural values: (1) importance of self-control, (2) time, (3)activity, (4) social relationships, and (5) relationships to nature. Groups that have a highly prized self-control value may be reluctant to disclose information about thoughts and feelings, whereas groups with a moderate self-control value may have considerably less concern about this type of self-disclosure.

The social relationships value is particularly important in career counseling because it may reflect the locus of the decision making (individual, family, or group) and it may also relate to preferred communication style (Basso, 1990; Kim, Shin, & Cai, 1998). Individuals with collateral/ collective social values may defer to the family or group in selecting a career or, at the very least, may be concerned about these others' expectations. Conversely, people who hold individual social values are quite likely to make their own decisions. There is one other implication of the social relationships value that has particular emphasis for career counselors: the structure of the relationship. Typically, it is recommended that these relations be collateral in nature, a relationship of equals. However, some subgroups, including many Chinese, Asian Indians, and Japanese, value what is termed a *lineal–collateral social relationship* (Sue & Sue, 2009). People who hold this value are likely to be more comfortable in hierarchical relationships, with the counselor in a position of authority.

Time and activity values are most likely to influence the nature of the interventions chosen and to contribute to the implementation of the interventions. Individuals with *doing* orientations are inclined to resolve problems once they present themselves, whereas people with *being* or *being-in-becoming* orientations may not immediately tackle issues, such as the need to choose an occupation or to secure employment once laid off. People who hold Eurocentric perspectives operate on the basis of calendars, clocks, deadlines, and due dates. The difference between people with future and past/future orientations is the attention paid to factors such as family history and cultural traditions in making choices. Persons with circular time orientations are not oriented to calendars and clocks. Rather they measure time in natural events, such as the seasons of the year or the cycles of the moon. Individuals with present time orientations may tend to enjoy the moment. In some instances, people who hold present time orientations believe they have little control over the future. The values of people's relationships to nature may have little impact on career development unless the client believes that nature dominates and, therefore, they lack control over their destinies (Brown, 2002).

VALUES AND COUNSELING TECHNIQUES   Table 5.3 presents the preferred verbal styles of the major cultural groups in the United States. As was the case with nonverbal behavior, the styles vary greatly. When taken together with the variations in the preferred nonverbal styles, counselors working in diverse setting face considerable challenges in crafting acceptable communication styles and selecting counseling techniques that will facilitate the career counseling process. For example, counseling techniques such as reflection of feeling, probing questions about thoughts and feelings, and questions that ask for personal disclosures about family members are likely to be inappropriate for the group that has a high level of concern about self-control (Ivey et al., 2009; Srebalus & Brown, 2001). Similarly, assessment strategies that involve personality inventories that ask for personal information and cognitive assessment strategies that require clients to disclose their thoughts should probably be avoided. The point made earlier that preferred communications style may be related to social value has merit, but it seems that other cultural values, such as self-control, also play a role in determining cultural communication style.

TABLE 5.3   Verbal Styles of the Major Cultural Groups in the United States

Group	Self-Disclosure	Loudness	Rapidity	Interruption	Pauses	Directness
White	Acceptable; content oriented	Moderate	Moderate	Acceptable	Okay; may be uncomfortable	Direct; task oriented
Native American	Unacceptable	Soft	Slow; controlled	Unacceptable	Okay; comfortable	Indirect
Hispanic	Acceptable	Moderate	Varies	Unacceptable	Okay; comfortable	Indirect
African American	Acceptable; expressive	Moderate	Moderate	Acceptable	Okay; may be uncomfortable	Indirect initially
Asian American	Unacceptable; sign of weakness	Soft	Slow	Unacceptable	Yes; comfortable	Indirect

Source: From David J. Srebalus and Duane Brown, *A Guide to the Helping Professions*. Published by Allyn and Bacon, Boston, MA. Copyright © 2001 by Pearson Education. Reprinted by permission of the publisher.

Step 3: Facilitating the Decision-Making Process

As previously discussed, the first step in facilitating career decision making is to determine who will make the decision. The next step is to determine the decision maker's expectations of the counselor and the counselor's expectations of the client and family. If the family or group is to make the decision, they may want more information about educational opportunities, financial resources, and occupational opportunities. They are not as likely to request help in assessing the characteristics of the student, but career counselors may wish to inquire whether they have considered abilities, interests, and values. I have interviewed a number of people who had their initial career decisions made for them, and rarely were their interests or aptitudes other than academic aptitudes considered in the process. Occupational prestige seemed to be a greater concern for the parents who made these decisions.

One almost inevitable problem for career counselors involves disputes between parents and their children about who will make the career choice. Individuals who have become acculturated may rebel when parents announce their choice of career, and students and parents may ask career counselors for assistance. Career counselors who would normally involve the parents in the occupational choice may find it difficult or impossible to get parents involved if the parents believe they have been disrespected.

Step 4: The Identification of Career Issues (Assessment)

One would expect that in the VBMCC model, early assessment would involve examining cultural, work, and lifestyle values. However, some clients who begin career counseling cannot meet their basic needs for food, clothing, and shelter. If this is the case, the career counselor may need to engage in short-term help to identify immediate sources of employment and the development of employment skills. Tactics such as identifying shelters, enlisting the support of social services agencies, and identifying health care resources may be required. Conventional career counseling using the VBMCC model can follow what can best be termed *crisis career counseling*.

The VBMCC is flexible enough that any number of assessment devices can be used to identify abilities; interests; personality variables; personal restraints such as disabilities, mental health problems, rigid sex-role stereotypes, or expectations of discrimination; and contextual constraints such as tribal and family expectations, geographic isolation, and so forth. In Chapter 6 quantitative and qualitative assessment devices are discussed in detail. However, three of the creative and exciting qualitative assessment devices compiled by Amundson (2003) are outlined at this point because of their particular relevance to nontraditional clients.

PATTERN IDENTIFICATION   According to the pattern identification assessment strategy, the individual thinks about an activity from one of the life roles in which she or he has participated. Once the activities are identified, clients are asked to think about times when the activities were enjoyable and times when they were not. They are also asked to describe in detail the positive and negative experiences, the people involved, the factors that made the experience positive or negative, and so forth. Amundson (2003) suggests that the salient points of the activity description be recorded on a flip chart after the story is complete. Once this phase is complete, the client is asked to conduct a pattern analysis by looking at the recorded information and describing how each piece of data reflects interests, values, and personal style. Themes should emerge from this discussion, which can be used as the basis for action taking. This process is summarized in Figure 5.1. Amundson (2003) suggests a similar approach to task analysis that involves identifying a routine activity, breaking it down into tasks, and then evaluating those tasks in terms of the satisfaction they produce, their importance, and the individual's competence in performing them.

ACHIEVEMENT PROFILING   The achievement profiling approach involves an in-depth analysis of an individual's achievement over a specified period of time lasting from a few weeks to a lifetime. This pattern is then analyzed by examining the goals the person was trying to accomplish; the skills and abilities used; the interaction with the context in which the achievement occurred, including restraining and facilitative forces; and the emotions (highs and lows) produced by the achievements. This activity can be used as a skills identification process (Amundson, 2003; Amundson & Poehnell, 1996; Westwood, Amundson, & Borgen, 1994) or for helping clients develop a more comprehensive understanding of themselves.

LIFELINE   Amundson (2003) uses a variation of the lifeline technique that traditionally asks clients to chart their future from their present age to retirement and to map the ups and downs of their occupational and educational lives. The result may be a depiction of their lives that looks very much like a roller coaster, or as he suggests, like a stock market index report. The roller coaster design grew out of research by Borgen and Amundson (1987) and can be useful in summarizing why clients come to counseling, particularly if they label the emotions and circumstances that led to the highs and lows on the lifeline.

Knowing a client's cultural values helps a counselor decide on the type of assessment devices to use. Understanding cultural values also presents a beginning point for appreciating the work and lifestyle values of the client. Kelly Crace and I developed the Life Values Inventory (Crace & Brown, 2004), which is designed to measure important life values and provide the basis for planning an overall lifestyle that will satisfy the individual's most prized values. The assumption underlying this assessment device and its subsequent application is that the work role is unlikely to satisfy all of the values held; thus, relationships with significant others (including family members), leisure, and the citizen role should be included in a life plan.

Other areas that require consideration in the assessment process include the role of disabilities, sexual orientation, concerns about discrimination, mental health problems, family and group issues, geographic location as it relates to preferred occupations, and socioeconomic

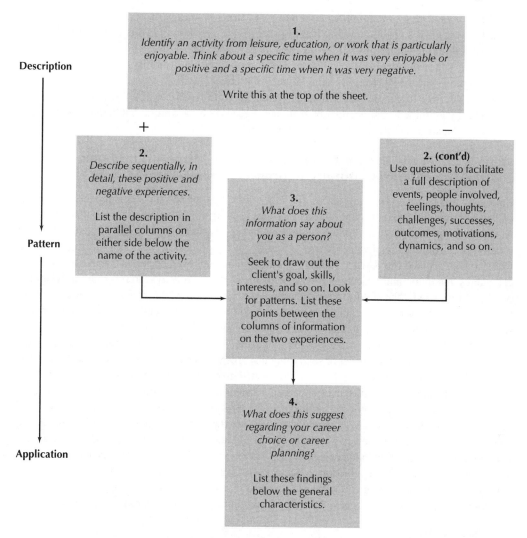

FIGURE 5.1 Problem Resolving Tasks: Systematic Self-Assessment. *Source*: Adapted from *Active Engagement: Enhancing the Career Counseling Process*, 2nd ed., by N. E. Admundson, 2003, p. 117, Fig. 8.

status. It is outside the scope of this discussion to outline the assessment of each of these areas in detail. However, the following questions should be answered during the process of assessing career-related problems.

1. Do you believe that you are limited by your cultural/ethnic background? If yes, what is the basis of this belief? Have you limited your occupational choices based on this belief? For example, have you only considered occupations that are traditionally entered by people of your ethnic/racial background?

2. Has your gender limited the occupational choices you have considered? If yes, how? Are these expectations related to planning for marriage? What nontraditional careers have you considered?

3. Has your sexual orientation entered into your career planning? If yes, how?

4. Do you have a chronic mental health problem? If yes, how has this problem influenced your thinking about jobs?

5. Have you ever been diagnosed with a mental or physical disability? If yes, how has this diagnosis influenced your thinking about your career?

6. Are you free to pursue occupations anyplace in North America? If no, why not?

7. Have you limited your occupational choices because of concerns about being able to afford the educational requirements needed for a job?

Steps 5 and 6: The Establishment of Culturally Appropriate Goals and the Selection of Culturally Appropriate Interventions

Culturally appropriate goals are set by the individual if he or she has an independence social value and by or with the family or reference groups (e.g., tribe) if the client has a collateral social value, all things being equal. As has already been suggested, when clients and their reference groups have different social values, expectations about the process and perhaps the goal itself are likely to conflict (see Ma & Yeh, 2005). The career counselor then becomes the translator of social values, mediator, and peacemaker who helps the parties involved search for mutually agreed on objectives. The father of a friend accepted his son's decision when the father offered to select the son's wife. However, the father disowned the son when he decided to pursue a career as a social scientist rather than in medicine and refused to pay for his college education.

Two cautions about the goal-setting process seem appropriate; one is related to Gottfredson's (2002) theory regarding the impact of sex-typing on career choice and the other is related to a meta-analysis by Fouad and Byars-Winston (2005). Gottfredson's theory was discussed extensively in Chapter 2 and will not be revisited except to say that career counselors should be alert to and prepared to challenge self-limiting stereotypes. Fouad and Byars-Winston found in their meta-analytic study that, whereas racial and ethnic group members aspired to the same occupations as white individuals, they were more inclined to perceive barriers that would keep them from realizing their aspirations. Perhaps a standard question in the career counselor's repertoire should be, "Once goals are set, have you lowered or limited your selection to occupations that you consider safe for someone of your ethnicity or race?" Depending on the answer, the goal may need to be adjusted. Gysbers and his colleagues (2003, pp. 354–355) suggest that career counseling goals have the following characteristics:

Are specific

Contain observable outcomes

Include a timeframe for attainment (as written in terms of the client's time perspective)

Are realistic, achievable

Are written

Are included in the intervention plan

Once goals, such as choosing an occupation, making an occupational transition, or restructuring the life space, are established, interventions must be selected. In some instances, the intervention may involve the use of a decision aid, such as the balance sheet (Janis & Mann, 1977) described in Chapter 3. Amundson and Poehnell (1996) use a technique similar to the balance sheet that they call the decision-making grid. Other systematic approaches involve using computer-assisted guidance systems (CAGS), such as DISCOVER, or Internet-based career exploration systems (IBCES), such as O*NET Online (Department of Labor, 2005), which allow individuals to find occupations using keywords or occupational codes. Users of O*NET Online may also conduct job searches by entering lists of their abilities. The Armed Services Vocational Aptitude Battery B Career Exploration Program (Department of Defense, 2005) can be used as a complete career exploration choice-making system or simply as a source of information. The components of this IBCES are shown in the table below.

Assessments	Information	Tools
Self-exploration	Explore careers	Plan for the future
Values	Links to interests	Educational options
Interests	Career information	Career planning tools (career and educational coursework) Skills, abilities

A number of qualitative interventions are also available, including vocational card sorts and the Achievement Pattern Profiler (APP) (Amundson, 2003). The APP can be used to identify skills and interests that could in turn be entered into O*NET Online (DOL, 2005). Behavioral rehearsal, homework assignments to consult with workers in occupations of interest, visits to job sites, internships and job shadowing, simulations, videos and compact disks that model skills or provide information, and many other strategies may be employed to help clients achieve their goals. Visual images, such as drawings or pie charts, may help clients understand their life space. Similarly, visual images in the form of drawings may help clients understand their sources of support and the expectations they must meet as they move forward.

Step 7: The Implementation and Evaluation of the Interventions Used

Implementation typically requires the client to carry out the strategies that have been identified to achieve the goals that have been set. I agree with Gysbers and his colleagues (2003), who suggest that preparing for each stage of the counseling process begins with the one that precedes it and perhaps an earlier one. At the outset Amundson (2003) recommends that career counselors frame the process in terms of the need for active involvement by both parties. Postmodernists, such as Ivey and colleagues (2009), also suggest that counseling of all types is a joint venture. They suggest, as has been a theme of this chapter, that the involvement of family and group members is essential to the success of many, if not all, clients. It seems that a key ingredient in implementation is the confidence with which clients approach the tasks that are set before them. Career counselors must teach the skills needed to take personal and contextual information that has been gained in the assessment process and apply it to the crafting of a new career or lifestyle. Follow-up and the evaluation of the success of the enterprise should focus both on the client's actions and on the quality of the counselor's work.

Step 8: Advocacy

The general goal of advocacy is to correct problems that influence job entry and in other ways limit and marginalize people in society (Fiedler, 2000). Advocacy may take many forms. One of these is preparing people for self-advocacy including taking individual action or organizing group action. Another approach to advocacy involves the career counselor advocating directly with an organization, agency, or business on behalf of the client. The third level of advocacy occurs outside of the career counseling process and involves action aimed at changing laws, policies, and practices that retard or preclude the involvement or advancement of minorities in the workplace.

Every effort should be made to identify barriers that might stymie clients' efforts to implement their career plans during career counseling and identify strategies for dealing with them. Many of the client groups served by career development specialists may benefit from advocacy on their behalf and in some instances advocacy is mandated by law or ethical standards. The 1997 amendments to the Individuals with Disabilities Education Act (IDEA) require that exceptional children have a transition to work plan incorporated into their individualized education plans (IEPs). Implementation of this part of IDEA requires that transitions coordinators work with businesses and industries to conduct on-the-job assessments and short- and long-term job placements. Rehabilitation counselors are required by their code of ethics to advocate for their clients with employers and others.

Groups other than the disabled that may benefit from advocacy efforts include newly arrived immigrants, particularly those with language deficiencies; persons with sexual orientations other than heterosexual; the poor; and many members of ethnic and cultural minorities.

Advocacy requires risk taking, and it also requires information, which is available in large measure on the Internet. For example, the Americans with Disabilities Act, which was passed to eliminate discrimination against individuals with disabilities, requires that employers make reasonable accommodations for people with disabilities. The Job Accommodation Network (found online at http://www.dol.gov/odep/pubs/fact/jan.htm) provides detailed information regarding accommodations that can be made for more than 40 categories of people with disabilities. The Ticket to Work and Work Incentives Improvement Act of 1999 (http://www.yourtickettowork.com/program_info) is another program aimed at helping people with disabilities increase their job opportunities. Other information, such as facts about the Age Discrimination in Employment Act of 1967 (http://www.eeoc.gov/facts/age.html), can also be found on the Internet. These Web sites and others provide legal information that can be passed along to clients and used in the advocacy process as well as keep career counselors informed of current developments.

SOME SPECIFICS FOR DIFFERENT MINORITY GROUPS

If there is any doubt about the rising importance of preparing to provide career counseling to minority clients, recent Bureau of Labor Statistics (BLS, 2009) projections should put them to rest. By 2018, African American and Hispanic workers are expected to make up 29.7 percent of the labor force, with Asian Americans, making up an additional 5.6 additional percent of the working population.

Much of this chapter has dealt with some general issues related to cross-cultural career counseling. At this point a few of the issues that may impact some of the sub-groups of minorities will be addressed. However, as has already been noted, becoming familiar with your own stereotypes and biases will help develop a foundation for your practice. Also, it is important to become familiar with the unique worldviews of the major groups but not to make the mistake of assuming that a client from any particular group holds the views and values of the larger group.

Career development specialists should also be knowledgeable about the history, religion, customs, and traditions of their clients' cultural groups. This information, along with knowledge about the typical values of various minority groups, can serve as a point of departure in designing and delivering career development services. However, even if the cultural group of the client is well understood, culturally sensitive career development specialists should realize that values can vary widely within each cultural group, and they should be careful to consider the "internal" culture of the client as opposed to external, demographic characteristics (Ho, 1995). For a fuller discussion of the issues that arise when providing career development services to minorities, Leong's *Career Development and Vocational Behavior of Ethnic Minorities* (1995) may be consulted. In the meantime, let's look now at some of the most salient special needs of the major ethnic groups.

African Americans

Until recently, African Americans were the largest minority group in the United States with most of them tracing their history to slavery in the South, although some have immigrated to this country from Africa in the past few years.

Historically, African Americans have been disadvantaged in the workplace because of discrimination and limited educational opportunities. The result of this has been lower earnings, higher unemployment rates, and growing family instability because of economic uncertainty. Some strides have been made in education in recent years, which are reflected in statistics indicating that the high school completion rate of African Americans is roughly equivalent (93.5% versus 87.8 %) to that of white European Americans (Cataldi, Laird, & KewalRamani, 2009). It should be noted that Cataldi and her colleagues focused on an age range of 18–24, which undoubtedly produced estimates of graduation rates higher than studies that looked at students aged 17–19, the typical ages of high school graduates. However, a review of the literature regarding dropouts shows that about one quarter of student who leave school prior to graduation return to earn a diploma or equivalency certificate (Brown, 1998). Therefore estimates that focus on the graduation rates of 17–18 year olds underestimate the graduation rate.

Hispanic Americans

Casas and Arbona (1992) and Arbona (1995) have described the career-related issues confronting Hispanics. Many of these issues have to do with recency of immigration, limited proficiency in English, substandard educational backgrounds, culture shock and alienation, and adapting to a new culture. It is worth noting that the dropout rate (17.3%) for Hispanic American exceeds that of all other minority groups. In 1995 Arbona suggested that Hispanics of African origin may be subject to greater discrimination because of their skin color.

Savickas (1991) noted that career development requires a future time orientation. Hispanics may be more oriented to the present than the future. They may also be less inclined to solve career development problems because of their being activity oriented, which may lead them to accept the current situation (Sue & Sue, 2009). Finally, many Hispanics hold collateral social values, which means they are more inclined to put the group's wishes ahead of their own, with the one implication that family members and godparents may need to be involved in the career planning process of youthful Hispanics.

Hispanics are racially diverse and may in fact be descended from European, African, or Asian ancestors, comprised of individuals of Caucasian, Negroid, and Mongoloid descent, respectively. They also come from diverse geographic backgrounds (Casas & Arbona, 1992). Large subgroups within this ethnic group include Mexicans, Puerto Ricans, Central and South Americans, and Cubans. Wide diversity also exists within and across Hispanic subgroups in factors that can be labeled demographic, sociohistorical, sociopolitical, socioeconomic, and socio-psychological. Some subgroups, even though dispersed across the country, have high concentrations in certain areas. For example, Mexican Americans are numerous in the Southwest; many Cuban Americans are found in south Florida and clusters of Puerto Rican Americans are found in New York City. Many people with roots in Central Americans can also be found in New York City as well as Los Angeles and San Francisco. Although there are large groups of Hispanic American in most cities, the fact is that clients with Hispanic heritages can be found in rural areas of most states as well. Because of the diversity within this group and the large number of recent immigrants who have limited facility with English, they pose a major challenge to career counselors.

Asian Americans

Asian Americans' high school graduation rate approximates that of white American (93.1% versus 93.5%) (Cataldi et al, 2009). Fukuyama (1992) discussed Asian Americans and career development and pointed out that this minority group includes individuals with a wide range of national origins, including Asian Indian, Pakistani, Thai, Chinese, Japanese, Filipino, Vietnamese, Laotian, Cambodian, Hmong, Hawaiian, Samoan, Guam, Korean, and others. Obviously, the cultural diversity within and across these national subgroups is wide.

Many Asian Americans have values that are markedly different from those of white European Americans. Their time orientation is more likely to be past future than is that of other ethnic groups, although other time orientations can be found among members of this highly diverse group. Some members (e.g., Chinese Americans) have collateral values, meaning they place the wishes of the group ahead of individual concerns. In other cases, Asian Americans hold what is termed *lineal social values* and allow elders or parents to make career decisions for them. A frequently occurring scenario in counselors' offices is conflicts between students who have begun to adopt individualism social values and parents who still hold lineal social values.

Mau (2004) reported the results of two studies that examined the career decision-making difficulties of high school and college students from various ethnic and racial backgrounds. Asian American college students reported more decision-making problems than either Hispanic or white students. Similarly, Asian American high school students reported more problems in making decisions than African American, white, or Hispanic students on many of the dependent variables dealing with the decision-making processes. Mau suggested that the differences found in the study may be attributable to differences in the social relationships (independent versus collateral) and values of the groups involved. Mau hypothesized that Hispanics in the studies may have been more acculturated than the Asian American studies and thus their similarities with white and African American students. Another study by Ma and Yeh (2005) found that Chinese American youth born in the United States were more likely to experience intergenerational conflict, and this in turn increased indecision in occupational decision-making processes. They suggest that this is likely the result of acculturation and, although it was not suggested by the author, the adoption of an independent decision-making style. Not unexpectedly, students in the study who were more closely connected to their parents when they had higher levels of occupational status. These findings of both studies are entirely supportive of the multicultural career counseling model described earlier.

American Indians

Currently, more than 450 American Indian tribes are recognized in the United States (Casas & Arbona, 1992). Not surprisingly, individuals are socialized to respect tribal values, traditions, and expectations. As suggested earlier, American Indians' time orientation may be more oriented to natural events than clocks and calendars, that they value self-control of their thoughts and emotions, a collateral social value, and they a somewhat unique communication style. However, research indicates that some tribes have values similar to those of European Americans (Carter, 1991), which suggests that they might have different expectations of individuals (i.e., might be accepting of individually oriented decision making versus deference to the group) than those tribes that subscribe to collateral values. Because of the potential of making an erroneous assumption about the value structure of American Indians, career development specialists should be careful to assess their values accurately.

Poverty, historic patterns of discrimination, geographic isolation, lack of occupational information, and geographic relocation resulting in loss of family and tribal support are major barriers to successful participation in the workforce for many American Indians. So is a cyclical time orientation that focuses on natural events as opposed to monitoring time mechanically. As noted previously, Savickas (1991) suggested that individuals who are successful in their careers look ahead and attempt to anticipate the future. Perhaps more importantly, participation in the workplace requires punctuality and attending to matters in a "timely" fashion. An orientation that does not acknowledge using clocks and calendars to monitor time may lead to serious problems for American Indian workers. So may tribal customs that dictate that healers or tribal elders spontaneously schedule unpredictable religious holidays and other ceremonies, thus interfering with the schedule of the worker.

Only about 54 percent of American Indian students complete high school (Greene and Forster, 2003) according to the most recent data available which was collected in 2000. This does not include the number of students who returned after leaving school prematurely or completed some form of equivalency certificate, which was the case for the data presented regarding white, African American, Hispanic, and Asian American students. However, the availability of high quality educational experiences and low graduation rates combined with other factors already listed limit the career opportunity structure for many if not most American Indians.

APPLICATION OF VBMCC TO GROUP CAREER COUNSELING

Career counseling is often provided in a group setting, which introduces a number of new concerns. The VBMCC can be used in a group setting as long as counselors accommodate the cultural values and preferred communication styles of clients and consider the impact of both of these variables on group dynamics. The Association for Specialists in Group Work (ASGW, 1999) published *Principles for Diversity Competent Group Workers*, which was developed as a guide for leaders who engage in group counseling with people who are racial/ethnic minorities, gay, lesbian, bisexual, disabled, and others. Group leaders should pursue the following general guidelines

1. Develop a high level of self-awareness, including self-awareness of the stereotypes they may hold of people different from themselves.
2. Acquire knowledge of the context characteristics of the groups with which they work.
3. Understand the interactions among group techniques, theory, and dynamics and the characteristics and worldviews of different client groups.
4. Respect differences in worldviews, religions, customs, and so forth.
5. Understand the sources and impacts of bias in assessment instruments.
6. Use culturally appropriate communication styles, respect language preferences, and make referrals when appropriate for the preferred language of group members.
7. Be sensitive to how oppression, discrimination, and prejudices may have impacted group members.

8. Educate group members about the counselor's approach to career counseling.
9. Work to eliminate stereotypes and other sources of bias and prejudice within the group.
10. Consult with tribal healers and religious and spiritual leaders of group members when appropriate.

Screening group members is the first step in the group leadership process (Jacobs, Masson, & Harvill, 2002). Assessing the cultural values of potential group members is one aspect of the screening process. Social and self-control values are particularly important. For example, social values influence the manner in which a member interacts with the leader and other group members. Members with collateral hierarchical social values are likely to be highly deferent to the leader, whereas those individuals with independence social values may perceive the leader as an equal. Decision-making preferences are dictated to a certain extent by the social values of group members, and these preferences should be ascertained during the screening process. Clearly, members who value self-control should not be placed in groups that require a high level of self-disclosure.

The screening process is also the best time to determine whether group members have biases that will preclude them from interacting in a positive manner with other group members. The following questions may be used to get at biases, prejudices, and stereotypes.

1. Would you feel comfortable being in a group with people who have a sexual orientation different from your own?
2. How would you feel about being in a group with people from different races? How about people from different ethnic backgrounds or with different religious views?
3. What are your experiences with people who are disabled? Would you be comfortable interacting with a person who is disabled in the group?
4. Is there any type of individual that should be excluded if you are to participate in the group?

The content of the group depends on the stage of career development of the individuals in the group and their immediate needs. However, as ASGW (1999) suggests, the group leader needs to accept the role of educator, or, preferably, cultural interpreter, to help group members understand each others' positions. Moreover, the group leader may have to resolve conflicts that arise in the group and should be prepared to intervene forcefully to reduce conflict. This involves dismissing people from the group who cannot respect the differences of others.

DEVELOPING YOUR OWN THEORY

Early in this book, several theories of occupational choice and career development were presented (see Chapters 2 and 3). Because of the rather brief treatment of these theories, it may not have been apparent that they would serve as a basis for career counseling. However, when many of the leading theorists were asked to apply their theories to a case description, most were able to do so without difficulty (Brown & Brooks, 1991). Nevertheless, as Srebalus, Maranelli, and Messing (1982) pointed out, the study of theory in most instances is meant to be a stimulus for the trainee to develop his or her own personal theory. They also suggest that theories of occupational choice and career development may need to be integrated with general counseling theory, personality theory, and behavior change theory, a recommendation that seems justified given the stage of evolution of theories of occupational choice and career development.

Most career counselors have developed their own approaches to career counseling. Srebalus and colleagues (1982) suggested that the following factors should be considered as the counselor trainee develops an approach to career counseling: foundation, description of clients, statements about client problems or goals, a conceptualization of how to counsel clients, conceptualizations of the counseling relationship, beliefs about how problems are diagnosed, development of counseling strategies that engender change, and approaches to evaluating counseling outcomes.

The foundation of most counselors' "theories" probably stems from two sources: formal theory and informal theory of human functioning (Strohmer & Newman, 1983). All trainees come to counselor preparation programs with a set of beliefs about how people develop and change, although these may not have been carefully articulated. At the outset of most training programs, trainees are exposed to numerous theories including those that attempt to explain human development, personality formation, learning, change via counseling and therapy, and occupational change and career development. In well-conceptualized training programs, students are then assisted to integrate these formal theories with their personal belief systems to develop their own models of counseling. More often, students are left to their own devices to develop personal approaches to counseling. It is suggested here that prospective career counselors begin to formulate their own models of career counseling by answering the following questions:

1. What are my personal beliefs about human nature? Are people essentially energetic and self-motivated or, by nature, lazy and in need of external motivation? What are the forces that cause people to grow and change? What retards that process?
2. With regard to formal theories of human development, how does normal development occur? What leads to abnormal functioning? How can abnormal behavior be changed? What circumstances may result in normal people becoming abnormal?
3. How do interests and work values develop? Why do they change? How can I measure them?
4. What are the indications of abnormal behavior? Why do they change? How can I measure them?
5. How does the work role interact with other life roles? How can they be interrelated? What happens when conflict between life roles occurs? How can the work role and other roles be brought into harmony?
6. How do I establish relationships with my clients?
7. How do I use information from tests and inventories in counseling?
8. How do I assess work satisfaction? How can I facilitate the process?
9. How do I motivate unmotivated clients?
10. What are the potential problems in providing career counseling to clients from other cultures? How can these be avoided or remedied if they arise?
11. How can I evaluate the outcomes of my work?

Summary

In Chapters 2–5 a number of approaches to career counseling have been discussed, primarily as they related to theories of career choice and development. Hopefully, these presentations served two purposes: (1) to illustrate the theories we use to explain career development with practical implications and (2) to provide practitioners with several models that can be used in their work or as the basis for building their own theories. The theme in all of these presentations has been to develop practices that are culturally sensitive. As has been shown, the ideas about multicultural career counseling are as diverse as the theories of career choice and development that have been advanced. The values-based approach presented in this chapter is based on the concept that cultural values are powerful determinants of the manner in which people approach problem solving, relationships, and communication. Career counselors who are able to sensitively discern the nature of the values of a client are less likely to make egregious errors of cultural insensitivity.

Chapter Quiz

T F **1.** Advocacy is a step in most career counseling models.

T F **2.** Most white people of European descent have a past-future time orientation.

T F **3.** Minority career counselors need not be concerned with learning the cultural values of white people who are a part of the dominant culture because they have learned their value structure through interaction.

T F **4.** Cross cultural career counseling begins with clarifying values.

T F **5.** Maintaining eye contact is seen as important in Eurocentric culture, but may be viewed as aggressive by some Asian Americans.

T F **6.** Acculturation is the process by which individuals acquire the values of their cultural group.

T F **7.** The major shortcoming of the Life Values Inventory as a tool in career counseling is that it does not measure all cultural values.

T F **8.** The code of ethics used by rehabilitation counselors specifies that advocacy, when needed, should be a part of the helping process.

T F **9.** Individuals with a collateral social value are more likely defer to the wishes of the group than individuals with other social values.

T F **10.** The concepts of worldview and values system are synonymous.

(1) F (2) F (3) F (4) F (5) T (6) F (7) T (8) T (9) T (10) F

References

Amundson, N. E. (2003). *Active engagement: Enhancing the career counseling process.* Richmond, BC: Ergon Communications.

Amundson, N. E., & Poehnell, G. (1996). *Career pathways* (2nd ed.). Richmond, BC: Ergon Communications.

Arbona, C. (1995). Theory and research on racial and ethnic minorities: Hispanic Americans. In F. T. L. Leong (Ed.), *Career development and vocational behavior of ethnic and racial minorities* (pp. 37–66). Mahwah, NJ: Erlbaum.

Association for Specialists in Group Work. (1999). *Principles for diversity-competent group workers.* Alexandria, VA: Author.

Basso, K. H. (1979). *Portrait of the white man: Linguistic play and cultural symbols among the western Apache.* New York: Cambridge University Press.

Basso, K. H. (1990). To give up words: Silence in western Apache culture. In D. Carbaugh (Ed.), *Cultural communication and intercultural contact* (pp. 303–327). Hillsdale, NJ: Erlbaum.

Bingham, R. P., & Ward, C. M. (2001). Career counseling with African American males and females. In W. B. Walsh, R. P. Bingham, M. T. Brown, & C. M. Ward (Eds.), *Career counseling for African Americans* (pp. 49–76). Mahwah, NJ: Erlbaum.

Blustein, D. L., McWhirter, E. H., & Perry, J. C. (2005). An emancipatory communitarian approach to vocational development theory, research and practice. *Counseling Psychologist, 33,* 141–179.

BLS (2009). Employment projections: 2008–2018. Retrieved from www.bls.gov/news.release/ecopro.nr0.htm

Borgen, W. A., & Amundson, N. E. (1987). The dynamics of unemployment. *Journal of Counseling and Development, 66,* 180–184.

Brown, D. (1998). *Manual: Dropping out or hanging in: Things you should know before you leave school.* New York: McGraw Hill

Brown, D. (2002). The role of work values and cultural values in occupational choice, satisfaction, and success. In D. Brown et al., *Career choice and development* (4th ed., pp. 465–509). San Francisco: Jossey-Bass.

Brown, D., & Brooks, L. (1991). *Career counseling techniques.* Boston: Allyn & Bacon.

Carter, R. T. (1991). Cultural values: A review of empirical research and implications for counseling. *Journal of Counseling and Development, 70,* 164–173.

Casas, J. M., & Arbona, C. (1992). Hispanic career related issues and research: A diverse perspective. In D. Brown & C. W. Minor (Eds.), *Report of second Gallup survey: Focus on minorities.* Alexandria, VA: National Career Development Association.

Cataldi, E. F., Laird, J, & KawalRamani, A.(2009). *High school dropout and completion rates in the United States: 2007.* Washington, DC: National Center for Education Statistics.

Crace, R. K., & Brown, D. (2004). *Life values inventory.* Williamsburg, VA: Applied Psychology Resources.

Department of Defense. (2005). ASVAB career exploration program. Retrieved from www.asvabprogram.com

Department of Labor). (2005). O*NET Online. Retrieved from http://online.onetcenter.org

Egan, G. (1994). *The skilled helper* (5th ed.). Pacific Grove, CA: Brooks/Cole.

Fiedler, C. R. (2000). *Making a difference: Advocacy competencies for special educational professionals.* Boston: Allyn & Bacon.

Fouad, N. A., & Byars-Winston, A. M. (2005). Cultural context of career choice. Metaanalysis of race/ethnicity differences. *Career Development Quarterly, 53,* 223–233.

Fukuyama, M. A. (1992). Asian–Pacific Islanders and career development. In D. Brown & C. W. Minor (Eds.), *Report of second Gallup survey: Focus on minorities.* (pp. 27–50) Alexandria, VA: National Career Development Association.

Garrett, M. T., & Pichette. E. F. (2000). Red as an apple: Native American acculturation and counseling without reservation. *Journal of Counseling and Development, 78,* 3–13.

Gottfredson, L. S. (2002). Gottfredson's theory of circumscription, compromise and self-creation. In D. Brown et al., *Career choice and development* (4th ed., pp. 85–148). San Francisco: Jossey-Bass.

Greene, J. P., & Forster, G. (2003). Public high school graduation and college readiness rates in the United States.

Retrieved from http://www.manhattan-institute.org/html/ewp_03.htm

Gysbers, N. C., Heppner, M. J., & Johnston, J. A. (2003). *Career counseling: Process, issues, and techniques* (2nd ed.). Boston: Allyn & Bacon.

Ho, D. F. (1995). Internal culture, culturocentrism, and transcendence. *Counseling Psychologist, 23,* 4–24.

Ho, M. K. (1987). *Family therapy with ethnic minorities.* Newbury Park, CA: Sage.

Ibrahim, F. A. (1985). Effective cross-cultural counseling and psychotherapy: A framework. *Counseling Psychologists, 13,* 625–638.

Ivey, A. E., D'Andrea, M., Ivey, M. B., & Simek-Morgan, L. (2009). *Theories of counseling and psychotherapy: A multicultural perspective* (7th ed.). Pacific Grove, CA: Brooks/Cole.

Jacobs, E. E., Masson, R. L., & Harvill, R. L. (2002). *Group counseling strategies and skills* (4th ed.). Pacific Grove, CA: Brooks/Cole.

Janis, I. L., & Mann, L. (1977). *Decision making: A psychological analysis of conflict, choice, and commitment.* New York: Free Press.

Kim, M., Shin, H., & Cai, D. (1998). Cultural influence in preferred forms of requesting and rerequesting. *Communications Monograph, 65,* 47–82.

Kluckhorn, F. R., & Strodtbeck, F. L. (1961). *Values in values orientations.* Evanston, IL: Row Paterson.

Leong, F. T. L. (Ed.). (1995). *Career development and vocational behavior of ethnic minorities.* Mahwah, NJ: Erlbaum.

Ma, P. W. W., & Yeh, C. J. (2005). Factors influencing the career decision status of Chinese American youth. *Career Development Quarterly, 53,* 337–347.

Mau, W. C. L. (2004). Cultural dimensions of decision-making difficulty. *Career Development Quarterly, 53,* 67–77.

National Career Development Association. (1997). *Career counseling competencies.* Tulsa, OK: Author.

Peace Corps. (2005). Cultural distinctions. Retrieved from www3.uop.edu/sisculture/pub/1.2.1-_Culture_Distinctions.htm

Prilleltensky, I. (1997). Values, assumptions, and practices: Assessing the moral implications of psychological discourse and practice. *American Psychologist, 52,* 517–535.

Rokeach, M. (1973). *The nature of human values.* New York: Free Press.

Savickas, M. L. (1991). Improving career time perspective. In D. Brown & L. Brooks, *Career counseling techniques* (pp. 236–249). Boston: Allyn & Bacon.

Srebalus, D. J., & Brown, D. (2001). *A guide to the helping professions.* Boston: Allyn & Bacon.

Srebalus, D. J., Maranelli, R. P., & Messing, J. K. (1982). *Career development: Concepts and practices.* Pacific Grove, CA: Brooks/Cole.

Strohmer, D. C., & Newman, J. L. (1983). Counselor hypothesis testing strategies. *Journal of Counseling Psychology 30,* 557–565.

Sue, D. W., & Sue, D. (2009). *Counseling the culturally different* (6th ed.). New York: Wiley.

Super, D. E. (1980). A life-span approach to career development. *Journal of Vocational Behavior, 16,* 282–298.

Thomason, T. C. (1995). *Introduction to counseling American Indians.* Flagstaff, AZ: American Indian Rehabilitation and Training Center.

Westwood, M., Amundson, N. E., & Borgen, W. A. (1994). *Starting points: Finding your route to employment.* Ottawa, Canada: Human Resources Development.

6

Clients with Special Needs

Things to Remember

- How the career counseling approaches discussed in earlier chapters apply to the groups highlighted in this chapter
- The groups that may require special consideration in the career counseling

    process and the issues they bring to the counselor
- One or two strategies that may be used in career counseling and career development programming for each group discussed

Chapter 5 was devoted entirely to providing career counseling to cultural and ethnic minorities. At this point readers may be wondering if they need to develop an unlimited number of approaches to helping in the career development process. Although that is not the case, this chapter may do little to allay that concern. One aspect of career counseling simply involves the application of sound counseling techniques. Another deals with cultural sensitivity and the ability to ascertain the values and worldviews of people who are different from you. Specific knowledge of the client and his or her unique needs is also required. Nowhere is this latter point more obvious than when dealing with clients who have disabilities. In this chapter we focus on these clients along with a number of other special groups—from displaced workers to gay, lesbian, and bisexual clients. However, after reading this chapter you will not be an expert in providing career counseling to the vast array of clients who request career counseling. If you expect to be successful, you will need additional study and supervised practice. Hopefully, this chapter will whet your appetite for more study and work with different types of clients.

Many classification systems could be used to categorize the clients requiring the specialized knowledge and skills of career counselors. Eight of these groups are addressed here:

1. Disabled individuals, including those with physical and mental disabilities
2. Women who wish to enter or who are now in the workforce
3. Workers who have been displaced because of economic conditions or other factors
4. Economically disadvantaged workers
5. Delayed entrants to the workforce, including retirees who return to work, military personnel transitioning from the civilian workforce, and ex-offenders

6. Midlife job changers, including those who change jobs voluntarily as a result of reevaluation of their current career

7. Older workers, including people who prefer work to retirement because of personal satisfaction and financial need

8. Workplace issues confronting gay, lesbian, bisexual and transgender clients

The primary objective of the discussion in each section is to develop increased sensitivity to the special needs that clients bring to the career counseling process. A second objective of each section is to raise readers' awareness of the distinct characteristics that influence the career development process. Some of these characteristics, such as physical limitations, may be quite obvious. Others, such as learning disabilities and values, may be less obvious. Although few well-trained career counselors and career development specialists would assume that all clients are alike, they might overlook some subtle details that determine success or failure in career counseling.

Because it is not possible to provide detailed descriptions of the groups considered in this chapters additional readings are suggested at the end of the chapter. These books and articles are readily available to professionals and should be accessed to expand the basic information provided here.

INDIVIDUALS WITH DISABILITIES

The words *disability* and *disabled* are often misunderstood and misused, suggesting that these labels imply deficits. As Mackelprang and Salsgiver (1999) indicate, people with disabilities have often been subjected to demeaning stereotypes, as being sick or deviant. The authors of the *Chartbook on Disability in the United States* (Kraus, Stoddard & Gilmartin, 1996) recommend that the definition of the World Health Organization be adopted: "A disability is any restriction or lack (resulting from an impairment) of ability to perform an activity in a manner or within the range considered normal for a human being," This definition has also been adopted in this discussion. The major classifications of disabled persons involve the following:

Mobility

Hearing

Vision

Developmental disorders (e.g., mental retardation, autism, epilepsy, Down syndrome)

Seizure disorders

Psychiatric disorders

Cognition (e.g., learning disabilities, attention deficit disorder)

Some estimates of the number of people with disabling conditions approach 20 percent of the population. However, according to the Current Population Survey (CPS, 2001, 2004) about 10.5 percent of the total U.S. population, or approximately 17 million people ages 16 to 64 were disabled. Of the people who classified themselves as disabled, 11.6 million were classified as severely disabled, which means they had a severe, long-term, physical or mental condition that kept them from working during the week they were surveyed; were unable to work the year before the survey; had an impairment, such as seeing, hearing, or walking; were impaired socially; or had a health condition that limited their ability to work. The CPS survey also reported the proportion of disabled people in the labor market. The percentages for people who were nondisabled, moderately disabled, and severely disabled were 85 percent, 81 percent, and 29.5 percent, respectively. Workers who were disabled, particularly those who were severely disabled, were concentrated in service occupations and earned considerably less than their nondisabled counterparts on the whole. People who have disabilities are often seen by rehabilitation counselors, but a wide array of career counselors may encounter people who have disabilities.

The term *rehabilitation*—the process by which people with disabilities are prepared for work and life in general—has gradually been broadened in concept to apply to overcoming many kinds of disabling problems, including physical disability, mental illness, mental retardation, alcoholism, drug addiction, delinquency, and chronic involvement in criminal activity. Rehabilitation may involve services such as education, improvement of physical functioning through physical therapy, enhancing psychological adjustment, increasing social adaptation, improving vocational capabilities, and/or identifying recreational activities.

Vocational rehabilitation traditionally has been referred to as the process of returning a disabled worker to a state of re-employability. However, when defined in this manner the conceptualization of vocational rehabilitation is unnecessarily narrow. The concept that employability is supposed to be a product of rehabilitations services would make some clients who are unlikely to join the workforce regardless of the services provided ineligible for other rehabilitation services that might deal with health or psychological issues. Fortunately, there has been movement toward eliminating the idea that rehabilitative services are aimed solely at the development of employability skills as the aforementioned definition suggests. For example, disabled people who have never worked may qualify for services and even those for whom assistance may result in greater self-esteem and self-satisfaction without clear certainty of employment may receive rehabilitation services.

Several pieces of federal legislation have reinforced and expanded existing laws. These include Public Law 93-112, the Rehabilitation Act of 1973; Public Law 94-142, the Education for All Handicapped Children Act of 1975; Public Law 95-602, the Rehabilitation, Comprehensive Services, and Developmental Disabilities Amendments of 1978; Public Law 101-476, the Individuals with Disabilities Act as amended in 1997 and 2004; and Public Law 101-336, the Americans with Disabilities Act of 1990. Such laws have raised awareness of the plight of the disabled and forced employers, educational institutions, and other public and private businesses and agencies to accommodate people with disabilities.

Rehabilitation services are provided by a number of professions—counseling, medical, nursing, psychological, social work, and others. Career counseling services are most frequently provided by rehabilitation counselors, whose counseling preparation has also usually included the medical and social aspects of various disabilities and their relationship to work. In 2008 there were 129,500 rehabilitation counselors in the United States according to the most recent version of the *Occupational Outlook Handbook* (*Bureau of Labor Statistics, 2010*). These counselors are employed by state level rehabilitation offices as well as a number of national, state, and local public and private social agencies. Among the well-known organizations involved in rehabilitation are Goodwill Industries, Jewish Vocational Service, and the Department of Veterans Affairs. Some rehabilitation counselors are assigned to work in public schools, community colleges, and postsecondary institutions to provide counseling and various educational services.

Like many other federal and state programs, rehabilitation programs exist in every state and are operated by state personnel under state policies within broad guidelines and provisions established by the federal agency. Funding for state services is provided on a shared or matching basis, with the formula used being a 4-to-1 ratio of federal to state funds. In other words, within the limits established by congressional authorization, for every $20 provided by state funds, the federal government matches it with $80. After the state makes its funds available, federal dollars are then allocated. Despite the generous matching formula, many states do not appropriate enough money to claim all the federal funds available to them. In these circumstances, unclaimed funds are reallocated to other states willing to provide additional matching monies. The obvious result is considerable variation in the quality and scope of public rehabilitation services from state to state. Costs vary greatly from one rehabilitation case to another, with some simple cases requiring small amounts of money to resolve the problem and other cases requiring much time and money. In general, data from annual federal reports show that the average age for rehabilitants is under 40, and that within three years the average client pays in federal income taxes as much as the rehabilitation services cost. Thus, an overwhelming case can be made in support of rehabilitation services on economic terms alone.

Disabled persons, like their nondisabled counterparts, seek to improve their employment prospects by enrolling in higher education institutions. In 2008, 11 percent of students enrolled in higher education had some type of disability, up from 9 percent in 2000 (Diamont, 2009). Diamont's statistics were taken from a study conducted in 2008 by the General Accounting Office (GAO, 2009). The GAO also reported that disabled students are more likely to be part-time and attend community colleges than students without disabilities. Their data suggest that the students with attention deficit disorder make up a larger proportion of disabled students than was the case in 2008 and that the coordination of services to disabled students and the types of assistive technology (e.g., voice recognition software to help with computer use) available to these students need to be improved.

Career Counseling for Individuals with Disabilities

Zunker (2006) described the career counseling process for clients with disabilities. He proposed a sequence that differs little from the approach used with all clients: assessment, occupational exploration and choice, vocational training, placement, and follow-up. The presence of a disability may require tailoring some of these steps to meet the specific needs of the client.

The purpose of assessment is to help both the client as well as the counselor understand the situation as completely as possible. Standardized tests as well as nonstandardized assessment devices may be used to obtain information about the client that is not readily available from other sources. More than 30 years ago Guidubaldi, Perry, and Walker (1989) stressed the importance of proper assessment procedures with students with disabilities, pointing out the failure of test developers to include disabled persons in their standardization samples. Zunker (2006) described a number of assessment devices appropriate for many clients with disabilities.

Zunker suggests that techniques other than traditional tests may be more useful for clients with disabilities. For example, clients with disabilities may have been isolated from experiences typical to their age group. Moreover, the impact of the disability on the client's physical and mental abilities may be such that psychometric measurement is inappropriate or produces imprecise results. The use of interview procedures with the client or with physicians and therapists who have evaluated the client may provide better evaluations of the disabling condition and its effect. Also, work samples and job tryouts may be much more significant indicators of the client's potential than many assessment devices. Evidence of what the client *can* do, such as strength factors and aptitudes, is even more important than identification of what he or she *cannot* do.

The occupational exploration process for clients with disabilities is similar to that followed by clients without disabilities, with the exception being that greater emphasis is placed on identifying occupations that correspond to the client's physical and mental abilities. O*NET, described in Chapter 8, promises to be a useful tool for helping clients relate their abilities and aptitudes to specific jobs. Some of the computer-based career guidance systems (for example, Guidance Information System, described later) include evaluations of physical demands and environmental conditions of occupations. Visits to work sites and actual job try-out experiences will be discussed in Chapter 8. These experiences are of special significance for disabled clients and their counselors in dealing with reality rather than conjecture. In the past, workers with disabilities were often restricted to narrow segments of the work world because of public attitudes and their own self-images. Nevertheless, the range of suitable occupations for most workers with disabilities should be nearly as wide as the universe of jobs.

Much of the literature dealing with the career development of students who are physically or mentally challenged focuses on adapting existing practices to meet their special needs. In a still relevant recommendation, Skinner and Schenck (1992) stress the importance of helping students with learning disabilities (LD) locate colleges that offer them specialized services and of helping them develop compensatory study skills. The Web site (http://www.college-scholarships.com/learning_disabilities.htm) harlene Colleges with Programs for Learning Disabled Students lists the programs offered by a number of colleges to aid learning disabled students. The 2009 GAO study cited earlier suggested that Skinner and Schenck's recommendation should be followed for all disabled students.

Over sixteen years ago Mather (1994) warned practitioners not to allow their clients with visual impairments to become too dependent on technology. The recommendation here is that disabled students learn to use assistive technology that will enhance their prospects in the workplace, advance their educational development, and increase the overall quality of their lives.

Job placement services for workers with disabilities is more complex than providing placement for workers without disabilities. Added complications arise because of the attitudes of employers and fellow workers who believe that disabled workers cannot perform at the same level as nondisabled workers. Involvement in job modifications to accommodate the disabled worker and helping clients with transpiration issues are but two of the issues that may need to be tackled as a part of the placement process.

Follow-up activities for recently placed workers with disabilities focuses on facilitating the adjustment between the worker and the work site. When problems are identified early and solved rapidly, they tend to be less severe and less disruptive. Sometimes minor adjustments at the work site are all that is needed to ensure that the worker can be as productive as workers without disabilities.

Kosciulek (2003) suggests that effective career counselors can empower clients with disabilities by fostering inclusion in the broader workforce and in society. He uses terms such as *dynamic*, *creative*, and *individualized* to describe the career counseling process, terms not unlike those used to describe career counseling in general. However, career counselors working with the disabled may find that these clients have limited experience from which to draw, poor decision-making abilities because of fewer opportunities to make decisions for themselves, and low self-esteem. To this list I would add that these clients have been exposed to fewer adequate role models, which limits their perspectives on their potential. Appropriate information and experiences, such as work-based assessment, internships, job shadowing, and sheltered workshops, can do much to offset some of the disabled's experiential deficits.

Experiential deficits also may limit the utility of traditional inventories such as those that are used to measure interests. Podmostko, Timmons, and Bremer (2009) suggest that the assessment portion of the career counseling process is more complex than it is for nondisabled clients. Counselors need to assess interests, knowledge, and career related abilities as they do for all clients. However, health issues, addictions, and life skills—that is, those skills needed to function at home, on the way to work, and after the workday is done—also need to be taken into account in the assessment process as needed to be assessed, often by professionals other than career counselors.

Counselors who provide services to disabled clients must also have a great deal of specific knowledge about their clients' rights and opportunities and the legal obligations of educational institutions and employers. For example, specialized knowledge in designing accommodations in the workplace, health care for people with specific disabilities, and use of prosthetic devices as a means of overcoming disabilities will help career counselors more effectively serve disabled clients. Knowledge of legislation, such as the Ticket to Work Program that establishes employment networks (ENs), will also be invaluable. Under this program, which can be accessed at www.tickettowork.com/program_info, the Social Security Administration (SSA) provides a ticket to disabled beneficiaries of Social Security that they may use to secure jobs from these networks. This program was designed to facilitate the movement of persons with disabilities into the labor without fear of losing their federally funded health insurance. Social Security beneficiaries who wish to work make an application to SSA, are given a ticket if qualified by SSA, and are provided with a telephone number that enables them to identify ENs in their area.

If it is discovered during placement and follow-up that the rights of disabled clients have been violated, counselors must be prepared to advocate for their clients. Discrimination, in any aspect of the lives of the disabled, is prohibited by the Americans with Disabilities Acts (ADA) of 1990, which is amended from time to time. The Rehabilitation Act Amendments of 1998 also specifically prohibit discrimination against the disabled and requires that employers make reasonable accommodations for workers with disabilities, as does ADA.

Career Counseling for Individuals with Mental Illness

In a sense the foregoing discussion regarding disabled clients applies in this section as well, particularly when a client's mental illness becomes a disabling condition. Many clients will suffer because of stigmas associated with their disabaility, race, ethnicity, or sexual orientation . In no case is this truer than for people who have chronic mental health problems. Caporoso and Kiselica (2004) point out that people with mental illness represent the second-largest group of clients with disabilities, and that the unemployment rate among this group may be as high as 85 percent. They suggest that career counselors *not* separate a client's mental health from his or her career problems. Rather, they suggest that the point of departure should be to consider how the client's personal lives and careers interact.

People with mental health problems are likely to experience multiple failures and lower occupational status than they would have achieved without the illness. Charlene is an example. She was a National Merit Finalist who went on to graduate from college with highest honors but then became bipolar. Stress precipitated the onset of mania or, more typically, depression followed by mania, resulting in long periods of time when she could not work and she needed to take a low-level, low-stress jobs. At times these jobs were more than she could handle.

The career counseling process outlined by Caporoso and Kiselica (2004) for people with mental illness is similar to a process discussed in Chapter 4 of this book. The first task is to determine the interest, abilities, and values of the client. If the client has limited work experience, a portion of this assessment may be done in work settings using short-term placements. Once the type and level of work that is appropriate for a client is determined, a job site should be secured and the counselor can then become an advocate for the client. Potential employers should be fully informed about the nature of the illness, the strengths and weaknesses of the client, and workplace modifications that may be needed. C needed a shortened work schedule that provided adequate time for therapy, exercise, and other stress-reducing activities.

WOMEN IN THE WORKFORCE

The relative earnings of men and women is an ongoing topic of debate. In the fourth quarter of 2009 the Bureau of Labor Statistics (BLS, 2010) reported that women who worked full-time had median earnings of $670 per week, or 81.2 percent of the $825 median for men. Why the discrepancy? Unquestionably, women have been discriminated against in the workplace. This is most obvious when women working in relatively the same jobs as men earn less. However, when the types of jobs held by men and women in the current labor force are examined, another reason becomes evident why women in general earn less than men. Service jobs, such as private household workers and protective services workers, have traditionally been low-paying occupations. Approximately 18 percent of female and 10.5 percent of male workers are in service occupations. Eighteen and one-half percent of men are in precision, production, craft, and repairs occupations compared to slightly less than 2 percent of women. These are among the higher-paid jobs in the workforce. Almost twice as many women as men (38.8 versus 19.6) are employed in sales areas, another category of largely low-paying jobs. Moreover, nearly four times as many men as women are in administrative support within the broader category of technical sales and administrative support, which is probably the lowest-paid sector of that group (Census Bureau, 2005).

An article posted by the Center for American Progress (Colquhoun, 2010) provided the following information acquired by analyzing 2007 U.S. Census Bureau reports:

• Almost half of the nearly 30 million employed women in 2007 were in 20 traditionally female job categories, with average annual earnings of $27,380.
• During child-rearing years, 23 percent of mothers are out of the workforce, compared to 1 percent of fathers, and 69 percent of unpaid caregivers of older adults in the home are women.

More education for women has often been touted as the solution to the problem, but the Current Population Survey (2004) statistics indicate that more education will not necessarily solve the problem. When male and female salary comparisons are made based on educational attainment, men earn more than women at almost every educational level. For example, male college graduates earn $1,089 per month, whereas female graduates earn $809. Some of this difference is undoubtedly attributable to men and women entering traditionally male and female jobs. It is true that women earn more college degrees than men, but only about a quarter of the jobs in the labor force require a college education.

Women spend less time in the labor force than men, probably to assume child-rearing and more recently to care for aging parents (Colquhoun, 2010; Melamed, 1995, 1996). Women must choose different occupations and must spend as much time in those jobs as men do if they are to close the gender gap in earnings. Additionally, women must become self-advocates and career counselors must become advocates for them.

Career Counseling for Women

Gysbers, Heppner, and Johnston (2003) suggest that the first step in helping women make career choices is to ascertain whether their preliminary choices were made as a result of socialization. Gottfredson's (2002) ideas about the circumscription process (see Chapter 3) could be one point of departure. Has the client been socialized to sex-type occupations in a manner that has led to the foreclosure of viable career options? Self-efficacy is another matter to explore, although it is likely that circumscribed choices and low self-efficacy will be related topics. The question to be answered is whether low self-confidence in areas such as math, equipment operation, the use of power tools, and other areas is limiting choices (Lent, Brown, & Hackett, 2002).

Ideas for the career counseling of women can also be drawn from feminist identity development. Downing and Rush (1985) suggest that women pass through several stages of development, beginning with the passive acceptance of sexism in society, followed by the realization that sexism is not valid. The third stage is characterized by dichotomous thinking and perhaps the rejection of men. Downing and Rush label this phase embeddedness-emancipation. In the fourth stage, synthesis, women begin to evaluate men as individuals, as opposed to an oppressive group, and in the last stage women make a commitment to taking control of their fates and assume roles in promoting social justice for all. Women in the first three stages of this developmental sequence may make career choices for the wrong reasons as follows:

Stage 1   I have little control so I'll follow tradition.
Stage 2   Sexism is not valid and I'm angry, but what can I do?
Stage 3   I'll reject male-dominated workplaces because sexism is bound to occur.

Career counselors should work to move clients to stages 4 and 5—that is, to the point where the women not only perceive themselves as powerful but they also believe that they can make a difference in their own lives and the lives of others.

Career counselors also need to prepare women for discrimination in the workplace and of their rights when subjected to sexual harassment in the workplace. Technically, sexual harassment occurs when a member or members of one sex create a hostile environment that either precludes or limits the functioning of a member of the opposite sex. Clients should be directed to the Web site for the Equal Employment Opportunity Commission (EEOC) in the event they have complaints about their employers. The EEOC receives complaints of discrimination and sexual harassment, investigates those complaints, and authorizes legal action if their investigation supports the allegations.

According to Duggan and Jergens (2007), women who have been the victims of violence and single mothers may require some special consideration in the career counseling process. They suggest that single parents may face six structural barriers: lack of affordable childcare, caring for aging parents, transportation, workplace discrimination, and sex-role stereotyping of occupations. Some of these variables have already been addressed in other discussions, but there listing here should serve as a reminder of the importance of these factors when helping single parents whether they be men or women. Duggan and Jergens also suggest that displaced homemakers may not have systemic support, may be coping with the aftermath of a divorce or death of a spouse, financial problems due to the failure of their ex-spouse to pay child support, and general inability to negotiate systemic organizations such as schools or departments of social services. Once again, specialized knowledge may be required for success as well as the willingness to step in the role of advocate.

DISPLACED WORKERS

The first wave of worker displacement began after the Civil War with the rapid mechanization of farming. Farm workers were forced to move to cities in search of employment, usually in manufacturing jobs. Technology also had a tremendous impact on mining and manufacturing as machines and computers displaced workers. Textile mills became more mechanized and, to exacerbate the problem further, mill owners moved their factories from New England to the South in searched of cheaper labor. Other industries also "headed south" for much the same reason and in doing so created what was widely known as the Rust Belt. Not surprisingly, millions of workers were displaced by technological innovations and the relocation of businesses inside the United States.

As was pointed out in Chapter 1, the movement of businesses out of the United States continues today. It is also the case that the U.S. economy has been undergoing its second structural change, the first being from agriculture and farming to manufacturing. The second structural change began in the middle of the twentieth century as an emphasis on manufacturing goods shifted to one based in offering services. We are now in what some call the information age, which indicates that creating and communicating information is at the core of our labor force. Another way of thinking about at least the direction the labor force is moving is to consider the idea that the worker of the future will be primarily involved in creating something out of nothing: software, analytical reports, art, sales and marketing campaigns, and financial strategies. Because our labor costs are higher than only those in most other countries. As both manufacturing and service jobs have been lost to technology and businesses have shipped jobs "offshore" to countries with lower labor costs and fewer environmental restrictions, workers have been displaced. Workers in those businesses and industries that are lost as a result of structural changes are forced to seek jobs in other businesses and industries, often in other geographic areas.

Currently, it is not uncommon to read of mass layoffs by companies such as Verizon, IBM, United Airlines, Boeing, and Ford Motor Company. Brown and Siegel (2005) studied two types of layoffs to better understand what occurs in these large-scale layoffs. One type of layoff occurs when work is moved from one company to another. This is known as outsourcing. Another results when jobs are transferred from the United States to another country, either to another company or within the same company, through the process earlier referred to as offshoring. During the 1995–2004 period, Brown and Siegel identified 17,000 layoffs involving 50 or more workers and impacting a total 1.8 million workers. About two-thirds of these layoffs occurred in the manufacturing sector. In 2004, about one in four of the layoffs involved moving the work out of the country, most often to China or Mexico.

The Brown and Siegel (2005) research illustrates the impact of the global economy and the problems it presents for U.S. workers. Other changes, such as the adoption of new business models, bankruptcies, and mergers, continue to displace workers for varying lengths of time. Some of these displaced workers will be offered outplacement services to aid them in their search for new jobs, but most will not. Public and private employment agencies will need to pick up the slack.

Career Counseling for Displaced Workers

The process of providing career counseling for displaced workers varies little from the models already presented with three exceptions. People who have lost their jobs may experience depression and loss of self-esteem because of the job loss, and economic factors may dictate the need for immediate employment or some type of economic assistance. In the latter case, simply getting a job that will help provide food and shelter may be the overriding consideration. When depression and loss of self-esteem are issues, they may need to be addressed prior to engaging the client in active decision making. Finally, as noted earlier, because there is often a mismatch between the skills required by available jobs and those required in jobs lost, locating suitable educational and training programs that prepare displaced workers for employment often becomes an important priority.

THE ECONOMICALLY DISADVANTAGED

Fitzgerald and Betz (1994) raised a provocative question: "Is career development a meaningful term in the lives of a majority of the population?" (p. 104). They make the point that, for many people, including the unemployed, discouraged workers who have given up looking for jobs, and marginally employed workers who teeter on the edge of poverty, work is not psychologically central to their lives. However, most of these people realize that meaningful employment is a way out of their current existence, and it becomes incumbent on career development specialists to find ways to facilitate this escape and to make career development a meaningful process.

The term *disadvantaged* can be interpreted very broadly. In its usual dictionary sense, it includes everyone who is in an unfavorable economic or social circumstance. Certainly, many members of minority groups, disabled workers, many women, particularly divorced or single women with children, the poor, educational dropouts, and several other large segments of the population are disadvantaged.

The same term can also be legitimately applied in a restricted or narrow sense. For example Miles (1984) used it to describe the economically disadvantaged, equating the term with *economically deprived* or *poor*. Typically, the circumstances of two subgroups in particular often land them in this category: those with limited education (either in quantity or quality) and those caught in geographic dislocation (often the rural poor or urban unemployed who have moved elsewhere searching for something better). Miles (1984) stated that three groups make up the economically disadvantaged:

> **The Chronically Poor**   These are individuals born into poverty and raised in families with inadequate resources to meet basic needs.
>
> **The Unemployed or Newly Disadvantaged**   Some unemployed can bridge brief periods of unemployment by using savings and other available resources. It is probably fair to assume that unemployment, sooner or later, puts each victim in the disadvantaged group. The structurally unemployed are in the greatest danger because they no longer have a job to which they can ultimately return. The cyclically unemployed can also be hurt if the economic recession outlasts their available resources. The recession that grips the United States and much of the world began in 2008 and is likely to extend in to 2011 and this without substantial support via unemployment insurance and other governmental aid, many workers will see their resources dwindle and expire.
>
> **The Underemployed**   Miles calls these the working poor because they are found mainly in low-wage, marginal jobs that involve little skill. Their wages are not sufficient to exceed poverty standards. One unfortunate result of plant closing and plant exportation is likely to be a rapid increase in this category as structurally unemployed skilled workers settle into low-paying unskilled jobs. Miles states that "approximately one sixth of the working population earn incomes that only barely exceed the poverty level; hence this group is constantly on the margin of falling into the poverty group." (pp. 386–389)

It should not be surprising that unemployed, economically deprived people develop low self-esteem and higher levels of depression (Waters & Moore, 2001). They often lack basic educational skills, have failed to adjust to the workplace, are unable to obtain vocational training, and periods of unemployment that have diminished their confidence that they can secure a "good" job.

Disadvantaged people need career development programs that address both short-term and long-term goals. As noted earlier, counselors often need to involve clients in short-term planning that will result in the client's ability to meet his or her basic needs. Once that is accomplished the counselor's role changes to help the client establish and pursue long-range goals. Many of the career-related problems of people with economic disadvantages can be confronted with the following four-part program:

1. Access to basic adult education and specific vocational training. Both are available in community colleges across the nation as well as vocational-technical schools.

2. Personal and/or career counseling.
3. Information about the world of work along with the skills to use the information in decision making.
4. Appropriate vocational training and placement.

Individuals with limited educational backgrounds are almost automatically relegated to the most marginal work opportunities. Literacy training, basic mathematics, and language proficiency are minimal essentials for almost every job in our society. Adult education programs exist in almost all metropolitan areas; however, individuals may be unable to capitalize on these services because of lack of transportation or unfamiliarity with local transportation systems, lack of child care, time schedule problems, and so forth. It is fairly safe to say that until basic educational skills are acquired, the individual has very little to sell to a prospective employer. The median income by educational attainment (BLS, 2009a) can be seen in Table 6.1. This table also shows that education provides at least a modicum of insurance against unemployment based on the data about unemployment rates across educational levels.

Career Counseling for the Economically Disadvantaged

Economically disadvantaged workers include workers who have lost their jobs due to structural changes, the working poor—that is people who have jobs that fail to meet their economic needs for food, shelter, clothing, and safety—homeless individuals, and welfare-to-work individuals. Displaced homemakers may also fall into this category.

As noted earlier, unemployment is typically accompanied by economic deprivation,—that is, a restriction of spending on necessities and meaningful leisure activities. Waters and Moore (2001) compared the psychological responses of employed and unemployed persons. They found that unemployed persons reported higher levels of depression, lower self-esteem, greater use of affective-based coping strategies aimed regulating the negative emotions associated with the deprivation and lower use of solution-focused coping behavior aimed at solving or moderating the problem that has given rise to the problem (unemployment and economic deprivations). Planned follow up analyses yielded two important findings for practitioners. As has been stated numerous times, career counselors should be prepared to deal with low self-esteem and depression when dealing with unemployed clients. Second, clients should be encouraged to use

TABLE 6.1   Median Weekly Income by Educational Attainment, 2008

	Median Weekly Income	Unemployment Rate
Less than high school diploma	$463	9.0
High school graduate, no college	$518	5.7
High school graduate, some college	$699	5.1
Associate's degree	$757	3.7
Bachelor's degree	$1,012	2.8
Master's degree	$1,233	2.4
Professional degree	$1,531	1.7
Doctoral degree	$1,561	2.0

Source: Bureau of Labor Statistics (BLS, 2009a).

solution-focused coping mechanisms such as job hunting and skills development as a means not only to increase the likelihood of securing employment but as a way to raise self-esteem and lower depression. Jacobs and Blustein (2008) suggested another strategy that may be useful to career counselors engaged in providing assistance to clients with what they term employment uncertainty, which they defined as those workers experiencing uncertainty about their future in their jobs. They suggested that clients may benefit from mindfulness—a technique that is learned through meditation, where the goal is to pay attention to the present and dismiss fearful, stress-inducing thoughts that occur.

Not all economically disadvantaged clients will require personal counseling prior to career counseling or integrated into the process. However, the devastating impact that job loss and economic deprivation has on the psychological well being has been well documented (Waters & Moore, 2001) and career counselors should be alert to the possibility that the counseling process needs to be broadened.

Realistic and practical information about the world of work can also be used to help the disadvantaged to see potential opportunities to break out of what is frequently viewed as a hopeless morass. Interviews with workers, work samples, plant visits, and synthetic work situations may help the person understand the job, relate that job to self and to attainable goals, and perhaps acquire usable role models.

Access to realistic skill training is necessary for all jobs but those at the lowest skill level. One problem is that many disadvantaged students withdraw from school before they reach the grade level at which vocational skills are taught. This situation limits their access to skill training, to Job Training Program Administration (JTPA) services, or to similar efforts provided at the local level. Compared with the numbers of people who truly need such preparation, the few training positions available are far too limited.

GAY, LESBIAN, BISEXUAL, AND TRANSGENDER INDIVIDUALS

As discussed in Chapter 4, sexual orientation is one of the many factors that may influence the career development process. Because of developmental processes and the omnipresent threat of discrimination, people with other than heterosexual orientations have a variety of special needs. One of these needs may be how to overcome the barriers that mainstream society places in their career paths. Coping with discrimination may also result in lower self-esteem and insecurity (Elliot, 1993). Gay, lesbian, bisexual, and transgender individuals may also experience rejection by their families, isolation in the workplace, isolation from heterosexual communities, rejection by their religious communities, and so forth (Fassinger, 1995; Pope et al., 1995).

Although many of the groups discussed in this chapter experience various forms of discrimination, they are protected to some degree by federal legislation that protects their civil rights. This legal leverage typically is not available to gay, lesbian, and bisexual individuals. Fassinger observes that lesbians may experience discrimination both because they are homosexual and because they are women, which can have serious emotional consequences. Further, lesbian women of color may experience the "triple whammy" of discrimination—gender, race, and sexual orientation. Finally, career decision making may be more difficult for gay, lesbian, and bisexual people because of nontraditional interest patterns (Chung & Harmon, 1994) and because of the stereotypes that mainstream society has of the occupations they choose. Some people may actually avoid occupations chosen by gay, lesbian, and bisexual people because of these stereotypes.

Counseling Gay, Lesbian, Bisexual, and Transgendered Clients

Chung (2003) reviewed the literature relating to counseling gay, lesbian, bisexual, and transgendered (GLBT) clients and concluded that bisexual and transgendered persons are virtually ignored in the research literature and that lesbians are underrepresented. Pope and his colleagues (2004) reached a similar conclusion. However, they went on to recommend that career counselors who work with GLBT clients begin with a bit of soul searching about their own beliefs, stereotypes, and prejudices about people who have sexual orientations that differ from heterosexuality. Counselors who cannot work in an affirming fashion with this group have an ethical duty to refer clients to other counselors. Pope and colleagues also suggest that counselors must understand the identity development of people in this group. They point out that "coming out" is a two-pronged process, the first of which is accepting one's own sexuality and the second, coming out to others. They view the process as perhaps the most important step in the development of sexual identity development for GLBT clients. Other issues that GLBT clients must confront include discrimination and becoming familiar with the unique assessment issues for GLBT clients. However, the Gay Rights Movement has taken strides toward gaining protection from discrimination and the struggle continues. Twenty-one states plus the District of Columbia currently have laws that prohibit sexual orientation discrimination in both public and private jobs. These states include California, Colorado, Connecticut, Hawaii, Illinois, Iowa, Maine, Maryland, Massachusetts, Minnesota, Nevada, New Hampshire, New Jersey, New Mexico, New York, Oregon, Rhode Island, Vermont, Washington, and Wisconsin. Finally, Pope and colleagues (2004) suggest that career counselors need to become advocates for their GLBT clients.

ATYPICAL TIME OF ENTRANCE TO THE LABOR FORCE

Although it is increasingly difficult to define what is common or typical for workers to enter the workforce, I have assumed that this occurs most often at the point at which they terminate their educational programs, usually between 16 and 26. Veterans, men and women who stay at home to engage in child or elder care delay their entrance to the civilian work force and will be discussed in this section. Voluntary and involuntary job changers will also be discussed as will older workers who decide to return to work after exiting from the labor force.

Former Military Personnel

In 2008, there were nearly 12 million veterans in the labor force and 573,000 unemployed veterans, an unemployment rate of 4.6 percent. Fast-forward to 2009 and the unemployment rate for veterans returning from Afghanistan and Iraq who are 18 years of age or older stood at 11.2 percent compared to 8.8 percent of nonveterans in the same age groups (Zoroyo, 2009). The unemployment rate for nonveterans in 2008 stood at 5.6 in the same period (BLS, 2009c) which suggests the current unemployment situation for veterans may be an anomaly that will change as our recession ends.

Individuals who return to civilian life after a period of military service can be divided into three groups:

1. Those who serve 20 to 30 years and retire from military duty and draw a pension and other benefits. Retiree pay begins at 50 percent of a veteran's base salary when terminating his or her military career after 20 years of service. Retirement compensation grows to three-quarters of base pay at the time of termination if the service member has served 30 years.

2. Those members of the military who incur a service-related disability that prevents them from continuing in military service will be paid disability benefits, which are based on the extent of the disability.

3. Those leave after a relatively brief period (often a single enlistment of 3 to 6 years).

Military retirees are considered in the next section because they are in fact voluntary midlife career changers for the most part. The second group, if individuals attempt to enter civilian employment, qualifies for rehabilitation benefits as described earlier in addition to those provided by the Veterans Administration. Therefore the primary focus in this section is on individuals who delay entrance into the civilian workforce because of a period of military service that may qualify them for certain benefits but not long enough to justify a pension.

Many young people volunteer for military service for quite different reasons. The majority of voluntary enlistees are probably recent high school graduates. A few are colleges graduates, many of whom enter officer candidate training programs. Some enlistees, recognizing that they have no clear-cut educational or occupational plan, decide to join one of the four branches of the military to give themselves time to decide what they want to do. Others, unable to obtain acceptable civilian employment either because of economic factors or the lack of salable skills, enlist as an alternative course of action. Still others may volunteer to escape an array of problems—difficult family situations, unsatisfactory living conditions, or a desire for affiliation and belonging. A few have clearly formed long-range civilian goals (e.g., law enforcement; air transport pilot) in mind and may enlist to acquire the specialized training that they expect to use in a civilian position, or to accrue educational benefits that permit completion of civilian college programs after the enlistment period is completed.

Many military occupations have equivalent civilian counterparts, and individuals who acquire the skills in military service necessary to perform these jobs can transfer with little difficulty from one to the other, just as other workers move from one employer to another. Some military personnel complete specialized training in medicine, law, and other fields. "Payment" for the specialized training requires extended periods of service.

Personnel who elect not to reenlist or are not eligible to do so, and who have had military assignments that provided no opportunity to develop transferable skills are most likely to need career counseling. Some in this group may view themselves as disadvantaged because they are competing against younger individuals for entry-level jobs. Similarly, they may have only vague ideas about their work values and occupational goals. This latter group may fail to see that, although they lack specific job skills, they have skills and attitudes (self-discipline, reliability) that employers value highly. However, there can be a downside to military service for some enlistees who, as a result of having lived in a tightly structured and directed environment, need help learning to make their own decisions.

CAREER COUNSELING FOR FORMER MILITARY PERSONNEL Men and women who are terminating their military service are typically offered transitional services including career counseling and a review of benefits available to them. Military counselors use many of the same tools and procedures employed by other career counselors. However, over time I have collected a fair amount of anecdotal evidence that some military counselors may press people who leave the service prior to retirement age to reenlist. In many instances, depending upon the person's specialty in the military, attractive bonuses are offered for "re-upping," military slang for reenlisting.

Career counselors who deal with returning veterans must be prepared to deal with the same range of problems encountered by other career counselors, including low self-esteem, lack of self understanding, problems with interpersonal relations, and negative attitudes toward work and society. Veterans who have been in combat positions may also be suffering from post-traumatic stress disorder or depression. Suicide rates among active duty military personnel and veterans is on the rise (US Army, 2010) and should be a concern for career counselors helping this group. Psychological problems may be exacerbated by the veteran's inability to secure employment. Added complications may be encountered because of stressors in the family and simply returning to the routine of civilian life.

Veterans who require vocational training or higher education degrees in order to implement their career plans may be eligible to receive funds from sources such as the Montgomery GI Bill. The U.S. Department of Veterans Affair Web site provides an array of information about this and other programs designed to facilitate the entry of veterans into the civilian labor force.

Ex-Offenders

In 2008 1.6 million criminals were incarcerated in the United States (BJS, 2009b). Of a more immediate concern to career counselors 5.1 million prior offenders were on probation or parole in our communities (BJS, 2008a) and overall nearly one-third of adults in the United States have criminal records (National Employment Law Project, 2008). Studies of recidivism show that overwhelming numbers soon find themselves incarcerated again, particularly if they cannot find employment.

State and federal penal institutions vary widely in fundamental philosophy with respect to the goal of rehabilitation versus custodial care. The range of variation is probably even greater when one examines the services actually provided in these two areas. Many prison officials confirm that even in those institutions that emphasize rehabilitation programs, the primary attention is still given to security and custody. We must conclude that very few inmates acquire significant occupational training during their imprisonment. Deming and Gulliver (1981) described an exemplary program in five New York correctional facilities aimed at helping inmates begin or complete college-level training that prepares them for professional careers. More recently the California Department of Corrections and Rehabilitation (2007) introduced an innovative rehabilitation program that will be discussed in the next section.

CAREER COUNSELING FOR EX-OFFENDERS   Most prior offenders need extensive personal counseling before effective career counseling can be initiated. In many cases, the factors that originally led the person into difficulty with the law may still exist. These factors are often compounded by the experiences of confinement, producing an explosive mixture of hostility, anger, and frustration. California has embarked on an ambitious effort to reform the rehabilitation program for criminal offenders in that state. The program, the California Logic Model: Evidenced-based Rehabilitation for Offender Success, is carried out in eight steps:

1. Assess risk and target offenders who pose the highest risk of reoffending.
2. Assess needs by examining the seven factors (e.g., educational-vocational-financial deficits) that are the best predictors of re-offending.
3. Develop a behavior management program.
4. Deliver cognitive-behavioral programs that target offenders' needs.
5. Conduct periodic measures of an offender's progress toward the objectives.
6. Prepare offender for reentry.
7. Reintegrate offender in collaboration with community agency.
8. Follow-up and collect outcome data.

Although the California rehabilitation model is a promising approach because it seems to contain most of the elements needed to prepare the offender for reintegration in the community, it may not be useful in states that mount only feeble efforts to help the offender become law-abiding, productive citizens.

Clearly the California Logic Model requires counselors to be advocates for their clients in the business community and to possess the ability to establish collaborative relationships with community agencies. It also requires counselors to be skilled in helping their clients deal with anger management and impulse control, family and marital relationships, abuse of drugs and alcohol, academic, vocational, and financial deficits, and for some, issues of sex offending. Unfortunately, probation and parole officers are usually overloaded and often provide only cursory assistance. The resources available to assist in this difficult transition are generally very few, frequently of limited quality, and rarely able to overcome the opposing pressures.

Midlife Job Changers

In Chapter 2 Super (1990) posited that people move through a maxicycle consisting of five stages: growth, exploration, establishment, maintenance, and decline. He also suggests that many people pass through several minicycles made up of these same stages as they change jobs throughout their lives. Bejian and Salamone (1995), drawing on the work of Murphy and Burck (1976), suggested that a sixth developmental stage occurs during the 35–45 age period, a stage they call midlife career renewal. Described as a transitional stage, career renewal is a time for reevaluation and self-analysis, which may lead the individual to change careers or to reaffirm his or her original career direction. The developmental tasks to be performed during the renewal stage are (1) reconsideration of the original career choice, (2) dealing with the polarities that may have developed in the personality, and (3) modifying the structure of one's life to fit the conclusions reached. Bejian and Salamone (1995) proceed to provide support for the validity of adding a sixth career development stage for both men and women. It should be noted that although the idea of a sixth developmental stage is relatively new, the tasks described by Bejian and Salamone parallel the substages of the minicycle posed by Super (1990). However, whereas Murphy and Burck suggest that renewal occurs within a certain period (midlife), Super suggests that a recycling of the career choice process (the minicycle) can occur several times throughout the life cycle.

The idea of a sixth developmental stage advanced by Bejian and Salamone, along with the ideas of Super (1990), certainly seems to provide viable explanations for what we call voluntary midlife career change in this review. However, as already noted, an unprecedented number of people at midlife have been forced to change jobs because of structural changes in the labor market, competition from foreign businesses, and many other factors. These workers, along with other groups who are discussed in this section, are involuntary midlife career changers who are often involved with outplacement specialists and career counselors. As noted earlier, these clients may need different types of assistance from voluntary changers because of the trauma associated with the job loss and the lack of planning for change. Researchers working in 1980s produced a number of studies and opinion type articles relating to midlife career changer. (Armstrong, 1981; Brown, 1984; Kanchier & Unruh, Perosa & Perosa, 1987; Schlossberg, 1984; Stark & Zytowski, 1988) . The thrust of many of the articles was focused on abandoning unsatisfying career and finding values that produced higher levels of satisfaction.

Finnegan, Westerfeld, and Elmore (1981) described a workshop approach to helping midlife changers. Helping midlife individuals deal with job loss was discussed by Davenport

(1984), Mallinckrodt and Fretz (1988), and Schlossberg and Leibowitz (1980) during this period. Much of the emphasis on midlife changers has migrated to older workers, women, displaced workers and minorities since the 1980s. However, some of the information generated is useful for a small subset of clients and will be examined here.

Voluntary Changers

The deliberate decision to redirect one's career goals can be caused by many factors. Some of these reflect increased maturity and self-understanding, clearer identification of values and goals, changing needs, or perhaps the appearance of new opportunities. Levinson and colleagues (1978) found that most of their sample reviewed their past during the early forties and began to make new plans or confirm already developed plans. In the case of retiring members of the military who have reached the point in their service (20 to 30 years) that qualify them for substantial pensions and perhaps benefits that will allow them to retrain. Also, it is not unusual for men and women who retire from the military to assume civilian jobs similar to those filled during their military service.

Midlife career changers typical pass through a period of intense reevaluation by matching earlier dreams and aspirations against present and potential realities to judge the possibility of reaching those early goals. When the discrepancy seems insurmountable, change is likely to occur. More than 30 years ago Thomas (1979) found that many in his sample gave up high-status positions to search for "more meaningful" work, thus demonstrating that there are still people willing to trade income and status for rewarding careers. The operative phrase in the foregoing sentence is "meaningful work." Needs interests and values often change as an individual ages and the youthful desire for travel that resulted in a career choice at age 22 may have been replaced by the desire to become more involved with one's family at age 40.

Changing circumstances in one's work may also lead workers to consider change. For example, revision of one's assignment, changes in company management, failure to win a desired promotion, relocation of the work site, anticipated changes in process or quality, and similar factors can produce a desire for change. Feelings of dissatisfaction may lead the worker to look for other options. Sometimes those new opportunities appear even when the worker feels content with the present position—for example, when a new industry moves to town or new educational opportunities make options available that previously appeared closed. More than 30 years ago Snyder, Howard, and Hammer (1978) provided career counselors with a still useful concept of many job changers. They posited that an occupational change occurs when the attractiveness of the new opportunity plus the expectation of successful entry exceeds the pressure to remain in the current position.

An additional factor in midlife career change might be called an *enabling option*. The increase in the number of two-income families, with approximately half of U.S. wives now employed for pay, decreases the financial pressure that previously deterred many men from contemplating any type of occupational change. The presence of the second income allows some room for risk taking. Also, a spouse who finds self-satisfaction and fulfillment in work may encourage the partner to look for similar compensations.

Most counselors would concur that individuals who are moving to careers that are more personally satisfying or more lucrative are mostly acting from positions of strength and are likely to need limited help, if any. Clarification of personal values, needs, and goals may help some, especially the worker who feels dissatisfied and has not focused on the causes of discontent. Some may desire information about job requirements and opportunities or educational preparation needed to qualify in a particular occupation. Others may want information about job search procedures or how to start a business. The Small Business Administration can be a useful source for this type of help.

Vaitenas and Wiener (1977) reported some causes of midcareer change that may be less healthy than the aforementioned situations. They compared career changers and nonchangers in two age groups—a younger group (median age 29.4) and an older group (median age 43.0). They found significant differences between changers and nonchangers but not between age groups. The changers had less stable interest patterns, more emotional problems, and greater fear of failure. These results suggest that some changers are running away because of lack of self-understanding, inconsistent interest patterns, or concern that they will be unable to succeed in their jobs. Where these behavioral patterns are evident, personal counseling aimed at expanding self-understanding is need before any attention can be given to career counseling (Bejian & Salamone, 1995).

OLDER WORKERS

The maxicycle described in Super's (1990) developmental model suggests that deceleration typically begins at age 60 with disengagement from work following thereafter. His model also suggests that age 60 may be the line of demarcation between older and younger workers. However, the average 60-year-old male has a life expectancy of 17 more years, and females the same age can expect to live an additional 25 years. Perhaps more importantly, many 60-year-olds are at the peak of their careers and do not consider themselves to be older workers.

The Age Discrimination in Employment Act adopted in 1967 and amended in 1986 prohibits discrimination against workers older than 40, which means that anyone who is 40 or older is according to legal statutes an older worker. Age, like beauty, is thus very much in the eye of the beholder. For purposes of this discussion, Super's (1990) idea that one becomes an older worker at about age 60 has been adopted.

The stereotype of older workers spending their golden years playing golf, fishing, traveling, and grandparenting is as faulty as most stereotypes. What seems certain based on a number of surveys and discussions (e.g., BLS, 2009d) is that the number of persons older than 60 will continue to increase, particularly since the first cohort of baby boomers turned 64 in 2010. Also, the current recession that has pushed unemployment to double digits coupled with a falling stock market that has eroded retirement savings has increased uncertainty about the future and is likely to keep older workers in their jobs. One older worker lamented that his 401-K had become a 201-K as he announced that he was postponing his retirement plans.

It is also worth noting that a number of older retired workers have reentered or are attempting to reenter the labor force. Many of them have discovered that retirement is an unsatisfactory experience; other have lost income because of the same conditions that are keeping some workers from retiring. Even when the economy was not as shaky as it is today, one in three workers who retired returned to work within a year (Brown, 1995).

Until recently the median age of retirement has decreased steadily to 62 since 1950 when it was 67, but it may well be that a greater proportion of older workers will remain in the labor force beyond this age in the future. Changes in Social Security and Medicare benefits are making it mandatory that more workers stay in the work force to protect their economic well-being. Other older workers will take advantage of changes in the tax code and Social Security laws that allow them to have unlimited earnings after age 65. Another change that may keep older workers in the workplace is that in the future full Social Security benefits will be available only to people who are 67 and older. The elimination of compulsory retirement in all but a few occupations will also contribute to people staying in the labor force beyond the traditional retirement age.

However, the decision to stay in the labor force is not purely an economic one. Most older workers continue in their careers for the same reasons that younger workers do: desire to improve the quality of their lives and the lives of others around them, fellowship with other workers, social status, desire to make a contribution to society, maintaining a sense of self-worth, and simply having something to do.

Career Counseling for Older Workers

The process of helping older workers change careers has been addressed by counseling professionals as well as book publishers. Quintessential Careers is an example of a publisher offering a variety of books for mature and older workers.

One problem older workers experience is age discrimination (Cahill & Salamone, 1987). The American Association of Retired Persons (AARP) has sponsored two studies that explore the extent of age discrimination in the workplace. In the first of these studies the Gallup Organization polled 1,300 workers over the age of 40. Six percent of the respondents reported experiencing age discrimination directly (AARP, 1989). In the second study, Bendick, Jackson, and Romero (1993) sent nearly identical résumés of two fictional workers, one 32 years old and one 57 years old, to a randomly selected national sample of 775 large firms and employment agencies. They concluded that the older worker with identical job qualifications received less favorable responses approximately one-quarter of the time than did the "younger" counterpart. The researchers also concluded that job application strategies that deemphasize age and that emphasize youthful qualities of the applicant are superior to strategies that emphasize the importance of experience and maturity in the job hunt for older workers.

Although two studies do not offer conclusive evidence that age discrimination exists, they do support the long-held belief that employers respond less positively to older workers. The number of age discrimination suits filed in federal and state courts indicates than an increasing number of older workers are less inclined to accept discrimination. In 1982, 11,397 suits were brought against employers for age discrimination. In 2008 this number had increased to 24,582 (EEOC, 2009) probably because of increased awareness that age discrimination in the workplace is illegal.

The book, along with others that can be found in most major bookstores identify some of the problems associated with changing careers and working later in one's life.

Career development specialists must prepare workers to deal with the following myths (AARP, 1993; Brown, 1995):

1. Older workers have more health problems; they have higher absentee rates.
2. Older workers are inflexible.
3. Older workers are less productive than younger workers.
4. Older workers are likely to be unhappy in jobs for which they are "overqualified."
5. Older workers will be unhappy working for a younger supervisor.
6. Older workers have diminished strength and learning capacity.

Of these six beliefs, only one has any basis in fact. It is true that the older a worker is, the greater the likelihood that major health problems will occur. For this reason Brown (1995) suggested that older workers who wish to change jobs (1) focus on improving their appearance by losing weight, (2) go on an exercise program that includes both lower-body and upper-body exercise, (3) have a physical examination and take the results with them to job interviews as one means of preempting this concern, and (4) use health insurance benefits from previous employment when possible to offset the cost of insurance for a new job. Older workers also need to know that, as a group, they have the lowest incidence of all mental health problems except depression, and thus the costs associated with mental health problems are lower for them than for younger workers. Finally, older workers have better attendance records than younger workers who often have to miss work because of dependents.

With regard to the misconceptions previously listed, the unfortunate thing is that many older workers have internalized them. Therefore, the first task for the career counselor to undertake may be to help the older clients identify and eliminate some of their own beliefs about themselves. To counter their own stereotypical thoughts, older workers need to know the following (AARP, 1993; Brown, 1995):

1. As we age, our personality traits do become more fixed; however, if we were flexible as a young person, we become more flexible as an older person. The point is that the traits that make us good young workers as well as poor young workers become more salient as we age.
2. Older workers are as productive as younger workers, and in some instances they are more productive.
3. Being overqualified for a job may be a source of unhappiness for an older worker. However, because older workers sometimes take jobs to supplement existing incomes such as Social Security or pensions, they may be more interested in factors such as flexibility of schedule than in their qualifications to do the job.
4. The characteristics of the supervisor are the most important determinant of the supervisory relationship, not the age of the supervisor.
5. There is evidence that brain cells are destroyed as we age. However, unless older workers have Alzheimer's disease or dementia, they learn just as well as younger workers, primarily because they develop successful learning strategies as they age.
6. Strength decline is more a function of lack of exercise than it is of age, at least up to a point. However, few jobs in our labor force require unusual strength, and thus the absence or presence of strength is typically not a limiting factor.
7. Although senses such as sight and hearing decline with age, compensatory devices make these losses of negligible importance in the performance of all but a few jobs.

The process of changing careers or reentering the workforce is little different for older workers than it is for younger workers, with the possible exception that consideration of other life roles in the job selection, particularly leisure, may be more important (Brown, 1995). Once choices are made, many older workers require substantial assistance with the development of employability skills because they may not have been involved in a job hunt for many years. For example, older workers may have developed the skills and personal flexibility needed to hold several jobs and they may need several resumes as a result. Fortunately, in this day of personal computers this is easy to accomplish. They also need to develop interviewing skills that can help them counteract the misconceptions about older workers. AARP has been quite active in providing assistance to the older job hunter (Stern, 1993), both in the development of materials and in the sponsorship of workshops for employability skills development. Most major bookstores carry books regarding all facets of the job search process that can be useful to older workers.

STUDENT LEARNING EXERCISE 6.1

Identify the issues in the following client groups which might bring to career counseling.

1. Disabled individuals, including those with physical and mental disabilities
2. Women who wish to enter or who are now in the workforce
3. Workers displaced because of economic conditions or other factors
4. Economically disadvantaged workers (e.g., the working poor)
5. Delayed entrants to the workforce, including retirees who return to work, military personnel transitioning from the civilian workforce
6. Ex-offenders
7. Midlife job changers, including those who change jobs voluntarily as a result of reevaluation of their current career
8. Older workers, including people who prefer work to retirement because of personal satisfaction and financial need
9. Gay, lesbian, bisexual, and transgendered (GLBT) clients

Summary

The focus in this chapter has been on several groups for whom the usual career development pattern does not apply. Consideration has been given to why the individuals differ, as well as to how the career development professional can assist them.

Clients with physical or other restrictions find some occupations inaccessible because the work requires a physical act which they are unable to perform. Vocational rehabilitation services can assist them in preparing for activities that do not require that particular physical act. Economically disadvantaged clients can obtain training or other services to compensate for the restriction they are experiencing.

Some individuals enter the workplace at a later time in life than typical members of their age group. Examples include the woman who devotes her early posteducation years to homemaking and child rearing, the individual who spends some years in the military before moving to civilian life, and the individual who is released from a penal institution. All must be helped to understand the world of work as it exists at the time of their entrance into it. They also usually need help in dealing with the age differential between themselves and other entering workers.

Other workers face major occupational change at midcareer periods. Those who initiate such changes voluntarily need help primarily in the transitional process. Those who find themselves unexpectedly switching jobs may need help in dealing with factors related to the change process: grief over loss of the old job; readjustment to a new, undesired situation; and learning how to seek and find a new position.

The final group considered in this chapter is those who are approaching or have reached the usual retirement age, but who either wish to or are forced to continue to work. They may need help in developing realistic plans that fit their physical, emotional, and economic conditions.

Every person seeking career development help can be served best when attention is focused on the interaction between personal characteristics and the total environment in which that person exists.

Additional Resources

Farley, J. I. *Military-to-civilian career transition guide: The essential job search handbook for service members.* Indianapolis: JIS.

Gregory, R. F. *Age Discrimination in the workplace: Young at an old age.* New Brunswick, NJ: Rutgers University Press.

Jans, L., & Stoddard, S. (1999). *Chartbook on women and disability in the United States.* An InfoUse Report. Washington, DC: U.S. National Institute on Disability and Rehabilitation Research. Retrieved from http://www.infouse.com/disabilitydata/womendisability/7.php.

Masters, R. E. *Counseling criminal justice offenders.* Englewood Cliffs, NJ: Prentice Hall.

Riggar, T. F., & Maki, D. R. *Handbook of rehabilitation counseling* (Springer Series on Rehabilitation), Available at Amazon.com.

Stoddard, S., Jans, L., Ripple, J., & Kraus, L. (1998). *Chartbook on work and disability in the United States.* An InfoUse Report. Washington, DC: U.S. National Institute on Disability and Rehabilitation Research. Retrieved from http://www.infouse.com/disabilitydata/disability/.

Chapter Quiz

T F   **1.** According to the Age Discrimination in Employment Act a worker is classified as older at age 55.

T F   **2.** Three of the factors that contribute to women earning less than men is initial career choice, discrimination in the workplace, and lower aspirations for higher-level jobs because of concern for their families.

T F   **3.** Veterans have lower unemployment rates than nonveterans, but the veterans of the Iraq and Afghanistan wars are an exception.

T F   **4.** The label that best describes the current evolution of the U.S. labor force is post manufacturing.

T F   **5.** It appears that jobs have been placed off shore to avoid strikes and other entanglements with union contracts.

T F   **6.** The stress of financial deprivation results in solution focused and stress management mechanisms, both of which serve as a source of motivation for job seeking.

T F   **7.** It can be expected that high school dropouts will earn about $20,000 dollars per year on average and are less likely to lose their jobs in economic downturns because of their lower pay.

T F   **8.** The Logic Model being developed in California for use with offenders relies on cognitive behavioral psychology for its approaches to changing attitudes and behavior.

T F   **9.** The California Logic Model targets those at the lowest risk of recidivism because the likelihood of success is greater.

T F   **10.** People who leave the military after 20 years of service can expect a pension of approximately 50 percent of their base pay.

(1) T (2) F (3) F (4) F (5) F (6) T (7) T (8) T (9) F (10) T

References

American Association of Retired Persons. (1989). *Work and retirement: Employees over 40 and their views.* Washington, DC: Author.

American Association of Retired Persons. (1993). *America's changing work force: Statistics in brief.* Washington, DC: Author.

Armstrong, J. C. (1981). Decision behavior and outcome of midlife career changers. *Vocational Guidance Quarterly, 29,* 205–212.

Bejian, D. V., & Salamone, P. R. (1995). Understanding midlife renewal: Implications for counseling. *Career Development Quarterly, 44,* 52–63.

Bendick, M., Jr., Jackson, C. W., & Romero, J. H. (1993). *Employment discrimination against older workers: An experimental study.* Washington, DC: Fair Employment Council of Greater Washington.

BJS (2009a). Bureau of Justice statistics: Probation and parole in the United States. Retrieved from http://jfactivist.typepad.com/jfactivist/2009/10/more-postsecondary-students-than-ever-have-disabilities.html.

BJS (2009b). Bureau of Justice statistics: Prisoners in 2008. Retrieved from http://bjs.ojp.usdoj.gov/index.cfm?ty=pbdetail&iid=1763.

BLS (2010). *Occupational Outlook Handbool. U. S. Department of Labor: Washing to, DC.*

BLS (2009a). Education pays. Retrieved from http://www.bls.gov/emp/ep_chart_001/htm.

BLS (2009c). Employment status of persons 18 years and over by veteran status, period of service, sex, race, and Hispanic or Latino ethnicity, annual averages. Table 1. Retrieved from http://www.bls.gov/news.release/vet.toc.htm.

BLS (2009d). Older workers. Retrieved from http://www.bls.gov/spotlight/2008/older_workers/

Brown, D. (1984). Mid-life career change. In D. Brown, L. Brooks, et al. (Eds.), *Career choice and development.* San Francisco: Jossey-Bass.

Brown, D. (1995). *How to choose a career upon retirement.* Lincolnwood, IL: VGM Books.

Brown, S. P., & Siegel, L. B. (2005, August). Mass layoff data indicate outsourcing and offshoring work. *Monthly Labor Review. Retrieved at http://business.highbeam.com/4857/article-1G1-139172113/mass-layoff-data-indicate-outsourcing-and-offshoring.*

Cahill, M., & Salomone, P. R. (1987). Career counseling for worklife extension: Integrating the older worker into the labor force. *Career Development Quarterly, 35,* 188–196.

California Department of Corrections and Rehabilitation (2007). The logic model.Retrieved from http://www.cdcr.ca.gov/Divisions_Boards/Adult_Programs/docs/FS_CA%20_Logic_ Model_Final_1-8-09.pdf.

Caporoso, R. A., & Kiselica, M. S. (2004). Career counseling with clients who have a severe mental illness. *Career Development Quarterly, 52,* 235–245.

Census Bureau. (2005). Income and employment—American factfinder. Retrieved from http://census.gov/jsp/saff/SAFFInfo.jsp_pageId=tp6_income_employment.

Chung, Y. B. (2003). Career counseling with gay, lesbian, bisexual, and transgendered persons: The next decade. *Career Development Quarterly, 52,* 78–86.

Chung, Y. B., & Harmon, L. W. (1994). The career interests and career aspirations of gay men: How sex-role orientation is related. *Journal of Vocational Behavior, 45,* 223–239.

Colquhoun, H. (2010). Women as breadwinners with half a loaf. Retrieved from http://technorati.com/lifestyle/family/article/women-as-breadwinners-with-half-a/.

Center for Population Statistics (2001). Disability: Selected characteristics of persons 16 to 74: 2001. Retrieved from www.census.gov/hhes/www/disability/cps/cps2001.html.

Center for Population Statistics (2004). Income in 2003 by educational attainment of the population of 18 years and over, by age, sex, race alone or in combination, and Hispanic origin. Table 8a. Retrieved from http://www.census.gov/population/www/socdemo/education/cps2004.html

Davenport, D. W. (1984). Outplacement counseling: Whither the counselor. *Vocational Guidance Quarterly, 32,* 185–191.

Deming, A. L., & Gulliver, K. (1981). Career planning in prison: Ex-inmates help inmates. *Vocational Guidance Quarterly, 30,* 78–83.

Diamont, M. (2009). Disability accommodations vary widely at nations colleges. Retrieved from http://www.disabilityscoop.com/2009/10/30/disabilities:college/5988/

Downing, N. E., & Rush, K. L. (1985). From passive acceptance to active commitment: A model of feminist identity development for women. *The Counseling Psychologist, 13,* 695–709.

Duggan, M. H., & Jurgens, J. C. (2007). *Career Interventions and Techniques: A complete Guide for Human Service Professionals.* Boston: Pearson.

EEOC. (2005). Sexual harassment charges: EEOC and FEDA combined: FV 1992–2005. Retrieved from at www.eeoc.gov/stats/harass.html.

EEOC. (2009). Catholic charities settles eeoc age discrimination suit. Retrieved from www.eeoc.gov/eeoc/newsroom/release/6-18-09b.cfm-23k-2010-01-12.

EEOC. (2010). EEOC complaints remain flat, but more suits filed. Retrieved from http://www.arkansasbusiness.com/article.aspx?aID=119503.54928.131647.

Elliot, J. E. (1993). Career development of lesbians and gays. *Career Development Quarterly, 41,* 210–226.

Farmer, H. S. (1985). Model of career and achievement motivation for women and men. *Journal of Counseling Psychology, 32,* 363–389.

Fassinger, R. E. (1995). From invisibility to integration: Lesbian identity in the workplace. *Career Development Quarterly, 44,* 148–167.

Finnegan, R., Westerfeld, J., & Elmore, R. (1981). A model for midlife career—Decision-making workshop. *Vocational Guidance Quarterly, 30,* 69–72.

Fitzgerald, L. F., & Betz, N. (1994). Career development in a cultural context. In M. L. Savickas & R. W. Lent (Eds.), *Convergence in career development theories* (pp. 103–118). Palo Alto, CA: CPP Books.

GAO (2009). Education Needs a Coordinated Approach to Improve Its Assistance to Schools in Supporting Students. Retrieved from http://www.gao.gov/new.items/d1033.pdf.

Gottfredson, L. S. (2002). Gottfredson's theory of circumscription, compromise, and self-creation. In D. Brown et al. (Eds.), *Career choice and development* (4th ed., pp. 85–148). San Francisco: Jossey-Bass.

Guidubaldi, J., Perry, J. D., & Walker, M. (1989). Assessment strategies for students with disabilities. *Journal of Counseling and Development, 68,* 160–165.

Gysbers, N. C., Heppner, M. J., & Johnston, J. A. (2003). *Career counseling: Process, techniques and issues* (2nd ed.). Boston: Allyn & Bacon.

Haverkamp, B. E., & Moore, D. (1993). The career-personal dichotomy: Perceptual reality, practical illusion, and workplace integration. *Career Development Quarterly, 42,* 154–160.

Jacobs, S. J., & Blustein, D. L. (2008). Mindfulness as a coping mechanism for employment uncertainty. *Career Development Quarterly, 57,* 174–180.

Kanchier, C., & Unruh, W. R. (1988). The career cycle meets the life cycle. *Career Development Quarterly, 37,* 127–137.

Kosciulek, J. F. (2003). An empowerment approach to career counseling for people with disabilities. In N. C. Gysbers, M. J. Heppner, & J. A. Johnston (Eds.), *Career counseling: Process, techniques and issues* (2nd ed., pp. 139–153). Boston: Allyn & Bacon.

Kraus, L., Stoddard, S., & Gilmartin, D. (1996). *Chartbook on Disability in the United States.* An InfoUse Report. Washington, DC: U.S. National Institute on Disability and Rehabilitation Research. Retrieved from http://www.infouse.com/disabilitydata/disability/)

Lent, R. W., Brown, S. D., & Hackett, G. (2002). Social cognitive career theory. In D. Brown & Associates (Eds.), *Career choice and development* (4th ed., pp. 255–312). San Francisco: Jossey-Bass.

Levinson, D. J., Darrow, C. N., Klein, E. B., Levinson, M. H., & McKee, B. (1978). *The seasons of a man's life.* New York: Knopf.

Mackelprang, R. W., & Salsgiver, R. O. (1999). *Disability: A diversity model approach in human service practice.* Pacific Grove, CA: Brooks/Cole.

Mallinckrodt, B., & Fretz, B. R. (1988). Social support and the impact of job loss on older professionals. *Journal of Counseling Psychology, 35,* 281–286.

Mather, J. (1994). Computers, automation and the employment of the blind and visually impaired. *Journal of Visual Impairment and Blindness, 88,* 544–549.

Melamed, T. (1995). Career success: The moderating effects of gender. *Journal of Vocational Behavior, 47,* 295–314.

Melamed, T. (1996). Career success: An assessment of a gender-specific model. *Journal of Occupational and Organizational Psychology, 69,* 217–226.

Miles, J. H. (1984). Serving the career guidance needs of the economically disadvantaged. In N. C. Gysbers et al. (Eds.), *Designing careers.* San Francisco: Jossey-Bass.

Murphy, P., & Burck, H. (1976). Career development of men at midlife. *Journal of Vocational Behavior, 9,* 337–343.

National Employment Law Project (2008). Employment rights of people with criminal records. Retrieved at http://www.nelp.org/. 9/16/2010.

Perosa, S. L., & Perosa, L. M. (1987). Strategies for counseling midcareer changers: A conceptual framework. *Journal of Counseling and Development, 65,* 558–561.

Podmostko, M., Timmons, J., & Bremer, C. D. (2009). Assessing youth and adults with education and career challenges. In E. A. Whitfield, R. W. Feller, & C. Wood (Eds.), *A Counselor's Guide to Career Assessment Instruments* (pp. 69–80) Broken Arrow, OK: National Career Development Association.

Pope, M. (1995). Career interventions for gay and lesbian clients: A synopsis of practice, knowledge, and research needs. *Career Development Quarterly, 44,* 191–203.

Pope, M., Barret, B., Szymanski, D., Chung, Y. B., Singaravelu, H., McLean, M., & Sambria. S. (2004). Culturally appropriate career counseling with gay and lesbian clients. *Career Development Quarterly, 53,* 158–177.

Prince, J. P. (1995). Influences on the career development of gay men. *Career Development Quarterly, 44,* 168–177.

Schlossberg, N. K. (1984). *Counseling adults in transition: Linking practice with theory.* New York: Springer.

Schlossberg, N. K., & Leibowitz, Z. (1980). Organizational support systems as buffers to job loss. *Journal of Vocational Behavior, 17,* 204–217.

Skinner, M. E., & Schenck, S. J. (1992). Counseling the college bound student with a learning disability. *School Counselor, 39,* 369–376.

Snyder, R., Howard, A., & Hammer, T. (1978). Midcareer change in academia: The decision to become an administrator. *Journal of Vocational Behavior, 13,* 229–241.

Stark, S., & Zytowski, D. G. (1988). Searching for the glass slipper: A case study in midlife career counseling. *Journal of Counseling and Development, 66,* 474–476.

Stern, L. (1993). Modern maturity report: How to find a job. *Modern Maturity, 36,* 24–43.

Super, D. E. (1990). A life-span, life-space approach to career development. In D. Brown, L. Brooks, et al. (Eds.),

Career choice and development (3rd ed.). San Francisco: Jossey-Bass.

Thomas, K. R., & Berven, N. L. (1984). Providing career counseling for individuals with handicapping conditions. In N. C. Gysbers et al. (Eds.), *Designing careers.* San Francisco: Jossey-Bass.

Thomas, L. E. (1979). Causes of mid-life change from high status careers. *Vocational Guidance Quarterly, 27,* 202–208.

U.S. General Accounting Office (GAO). (1995). *Vocational education: Two-year colleges improve programs, maintain access for special populations.* Washington, DC: Author.

U.S. Army (2010). Army suicides increasing. Washington, DC: McGlacty News Bureau. Found in *Wilmington Star-News,* p. 9A.

U. S. Department of Employment and Training Administration (2001).

Vaitenas, R., & Wiener, Y. (1977). Development, emotional, and interest factors in voluntary midcareer change. *Journal of Vocational Behavior, 11,* 291–304.

Waters, L., E., & Moore, K. A., (2001). Coping with economic deprivation during unemployment. *Journal of Economic Psychology, 22, 461–483.*

Zoroyo, G. (2009). Jobless rate at 11.2 % for veterans of Iraq, Afghanistan. *USA Today.* Retrieved from http://www.usatoday.com/news/nation/2009-03-19-jobless-veterans_N.htm.

Zunker, V. G. (2006). *Using assessment results in career counseling* (7th ed.). Monterey, CA: Brooks/Cole.

7

Assessment in Career Counseling and Development

Things to Remember

- The major approaches used in the career assessment process including some of the most important quantitative and qualitative assessment techniques

- The criteria that should be used when selecting assessment approaches

- The strategies to be used when interpreting assessment results

- The differences between modern (logical positivism) and postmodern approaches to assessment

Some type of assessment must be an integral part of the career development and career counseling process. Career assessment may range from self-estimates of skills, interests, and values by the client to the administration of a standardized battery of inventories and tests. Assessment techniques and devices may be paper-and-pencil inventories and exercises, computerized administered tests and/or online inventories that are essentially self-administered. After the assessment is complete, results may be self-interpreted, counselor interpreted, or interpreted by computer programs . In fact there is an almost unlimited number of assessment instruments. *A Counselor's Guide to Career Assessment Instruments* (Whitfield, Feller, & Wood, 2009) includes professional reviews of more than 60 career assessment instruments and lists nearly 200 additional instruments that are not reviewed. Some assessment approaches may not include tests or inventories, particularly those chosen by postmodern counselors. They may opt for qualitative devices such as occupational genograms or card sorts.

Contrast the assessment processes you might use when counseling a senior citizen looking for a part-time job to supplement her income with an 18-year-old woman who is looking for her first job. Traditional instruments that were developed to help young workers would be of little use with a mature woman who may have held a number of jobs, raised children, and served as a volunteer in her church and in civic clubs. It is likely that you would examine her life experiences to determine her interests, values, and past work experience to ascertain her abilities. The number of hours she wants to work and the amount of money she needs to supplement her income will be important things to assess. Formal assessment using traditional interest and values inventories is more likely to be included in the career assessment process of the 18-year-old. Likes and dislikes of various subjects and performance in various subject matter areas may provide clues to values, interests, and abilities as well. The principle is simple: One assessment strategy will not fit all clients.

The first model of vocational development (Parsons, 1909) emphasized the importance of personal analysis in promoting self-understanding and as a basis for career selection. Career counselors still adhere to the idea that self-understanding as well as knowledge of occupations are at the foundation of making informed career choices. However, today's career counselors are much more likely to explore personal factors, lifestyle concerns, and spiritual issues (Andersen & Vanderhey, 2006) in the process as a means of determining contextual variables that should be included in the decision-making process. In the section that follows some of the factors that may be assessed in the career counseling process are defined.

PERSONAL-PSYCHOLOGICAL CHARACTERISTICS

Aptitude

Aptitudes are defined as specific capacities and abilities required of an individual to learn or adequately perform a task or job duty. Recent research suggests that *aptitudes* refers to specific psychological factors that contribute in varying degrees to success in occupations. It is a capacity or potential that has stability, unity, and independence. However, the developers of O*NET identified 52 *abilities* (U.S. Department of Labor, 1998). Ultimately the O*NET development team identified nine "abilities" which are in fact aptitudes as defined here:

Verbal Ability	Clerical Perception
Arithmetic Reasoning	Motor Coordination
Computation	Finger Dexterity
Spatial Ability	Manual Dexterity
Form Perception	

Not all of these aptitudes are required for skill acquisition and performance in all jobs.

Interests

Perhaps the most-used type of information to determine the appropriateness of occupations for individuals is interests—the likes or preferences, or, stated somewhat differently, the things that they enjoy. More than half a century ago, Super (1957) described four types of interests varying primarily with the method of assessment:

Expressed interests: Verbal statements or claims of interest

Manifest interests: Interests exhibited through actions and participation

Inventoried interests: Estimates of interest based on responses to a set of questions concerning likes and dislikes

Tested interests: Interests revealed under controlled situations

As can be seen in Super's taxonomy, interest may be assessed in a number of ways. Although interests are most frequently assessed using psychometric devices, stated or expressed interests are as valid a predictor of factors such as occupational choice, satisfaction, and achievement as are inventoried interests (Whitney, 1969). However, when individuals involved in career decision making have limited experiences, the likelihood that either stated or inventoried interests will be good predictors of occupational behavior is reduced. Moreover, interest measures are aimed at quantifying what individuals like or prefer, not why they like or prefer them. Personality and values measures are more likely to provide this type of information.

Personality

The theoretical positions of Holland (1997) and Super (1990) identify personality as a key factor in vocational choice and career development. However, although Holland claims that interest inventories are personality inventories, his assertion is probably not accepted outside the realm of career development, and his instruments are typically classified as interest inventories because they measure likes and preferences (cf. Whitfield, Feller, & Wood, 2009). *Personality* is typically defined as the sum total of an individual's beliefs, perceptions, emotions, and attitudes and may be extended to include the behavior of the individual as well. Historically, the role of personality in career choice has been secondary to interests, a situation that still exists. However, since the development of the Myers-Briggs Type Indicator (MBTI), there has been a resurgence in interest in the role of personality in occupational selection, and it is likely that many of the millions of people who have taken the MBTI did so as a means to facilitate their career choice and development. This interest in the MBTI as a career assessment instrument was fueled partially by the career data collected with this instrument, which are presented in the appendix to the technical manual of the MBTI (Myers & McCaulley, 1998). The MBTI yields includes four bi-polar scales:

Extroversion _____ Introversion

Sensing _____ Intuition

Thinking _____ Feeling

Judging _____ Perceiving

The personality profile resulting from the Myers-Briggs consists of the highest scores on Introversion versus Extroversion, Sensing versus Intuition, Thinking versus Feeling, and Judging versus Perceiving. Thus each individual is categorized as one of 16 personality types, such as ENFP or ISTJ. Each personality type has certain preferences, including preferences for work environments. For example, approximately half the individuals in the helping professions surveyed by Myers and McCaulley (1998) have NF in their personality profile. This means that their preferred way of taking in data is through intuition (versus the five senses, or Ss), and their preferred manner of using information is on the basis of their feelings (as opposed to their thoughts, as would be the case for Ts).

Values

The most widely accepted definition of values stems from the seminal work of Rokeach (1973, 1979), who defined *values* as cognized needs that guide our behaviors and serve as standards against which we judge our behaviors and the behaviors of others. Needs, particularly basic biological needs, are transitory because once they are satisfied they no longer motivate behavior; Values function across situations and are not transitory. Values differ from interests in that they serve as standards whereas interests do not. While interest do not serve as standards they are relatively stable across time and situations. Super (1990), Srebalus and Brown (2001), and others, such as Leong (1991), have identified values as important determinants of various aspects of career development, career choice, and career satisfaction, propositions that have received wide support.

THE MARRIAGE BETWEEN TESTS AND CAREER COUNSELING

In 1972 Goldman observed that the marriage between testing and counseling had failed and that it was time to look for other approaches to facilitating growth and development. Specifically, Goldman (1972, 1982) raised concerns about the use of tests and inventories to predict vocational success and/or satisfaction. Goldman's 1972 criticism had been voiced earlier by Crites (1969) and has been rehashed since by Ivey (1982) and Weinrach (1979). However, Prediger (1974, 2001), taking a different path, discussed how the "failed marriage" between tests and inventories could be revived by using comprehensive assessment programs, providing test results to help those being tested bridge the gap between the tests results and career choice implementation, and relying more on self-administered and self-interpreted instruments.

Healy (1990) also contended that the traditional trait-and-factor approaches to testing and assessment have had certain shortcomings that are inconsistent with the goal of promoting client growth and development. One of these inconsistencies is that because assessment devices are typically selected by counselors, people being assessed are placed in dependent roles. Healy also contended that trait-and-factor approaches to assessment do not strengthen clients' abilities to assess their own strengths and weaknesses, which he believes is inconsistent with the ideal of promoting independence. Moreover, relying on tests and inventories as the principal personal assessment tools denies the influence of environmental and contextual (i.e., work setting) variables, such as qualities of supervision, that may interact with clients' characteristics. Finally, Healy criticized traditional approaches to assessment because they emphasize helping clients find careers that "fit" them rather than actively involve them in identifying and implementing career choices. Healy's comments, like the scathing criticisms of traditional assessment by Peterson and Gonzalez (2005) caricaturize traditional career counselors who use traditional approaches as noncaring statisticians who are interested only in the three interviews and a cloud of dust ("test em, tell em, and say good-bye") described by Crites, (1969) nearly half a century ago. For the most part, nothing could be further from the truth, but like most stereotypes, they contain a grain of accuracy.

Peterson and Gonzalez (2005) suggest that the cure for the malpractice they see is a turn to postmodern approaches that consider factors such as interests in values in the context of the client's lifestyle. Healy also enumerated certain remedies for the problems he sees with traditional approaches to assessment. For example, he suggests that clients be prepared to act as collaborators in the appraisal process by giving them more information about appraisal and its potential use in career choice and implementation, a recommendation that Peterson and Gonzalez endorse. Peterson and Gonzales also concur that career counselors should also accentuate the development of self-assessment skills, such as the ability to estimate aptitudes. Not surprisingly, Healy advocates that clients be made more aware of how their characteristics interact with workplace variables and how these interactions influence their performance and ultimately their success or failure. Healy (1990) believes that in addition to the foregoing reforms in the appraisal process, new approaches to appraisal devices need to be designed to improve not only decision making but the implementation of decisions as well.

The degree to which clients are engaged as collaborators in developing self-evaluation skills, including using assessment data to make as well as implement choices, depends on a number of variables. For example, one application of career development assessment is to facilitate exploration and planning over a period of time, as opposed to providing information for decision making at a specific point in time (Prediger, 1974). In the former, assessment is used to promote readiness by developing self-awareness, whereas in the latter the use of assessment data is to inform decision making and implementation of decisions once made. Prediger (1974, 2001) also pointed out that counselors may use assessment devices to diagnose various aspects of students' (and presumably nonstudents') career development for the purpose of designing programs to meet career needs. For example, counselors might give an interest inventory to ninth graders to stimulate self-awareness. This inventory might be selected, administered, and interpreted by counselors because only the most preliminary career decisions are being made at the time the inventory is administered, and assessment of large numbers of students precludes the use of highly individualized strategies. However, a career counselor working with a college senior who is deciding among various career options could implement all of Healy's (1990) suggestions.

In the future the criticisms by Goldman, Healy and Peterson and Gonzalez, and others will only be valid if career counselors fail to follow the best practices of their professions. We know how to avoid all of the pitfalls that have been identified. However, for those who insist that traditional assessments are biased, mechanized, and reductionistic, the rise of postmodern approaches to career counseling have stimulated interests in what is termed *qualitative* assessment (Peterson & Gonzalez, 2005). In the next section, objective, or quantitative, approaches to assessment are contrasted to qualitative assessment. A third type, clinical assessment, is also touched on in the discussion.

CLINICAL, QUANTITATIVE, AND QUALITATIVE APPROACHES TO ASSESSMENT

Clinical assessment occurs whenever a career counselor applies information gained through training and experience to classify, diagnose, or predict a client's behavior or problem (Gregory, 2006). Career counselors may engage in clinical assessment as they conduct the counseling process, including administering and interpreting various type of quantitative and qualitative assessment. Clinical judgment (e.g., the suspicion that the client is depressed) often leads to additional formal assessment to confirm the assessment. Astute career counselors share their judgments with their clients as one means of confirming of disconfirming the judgment they have made. Once the judgment has been confirmed it can be used to determine a course of action with the client. (Gregory, 2006). Clinical assessment is at best an adjunct for use with other types of assessment.

Quantitative Assessment

Quantitative assessment devices are those most familiar to clients because they have taken achievement test batteries in response to mandates such as the No Child Left Behind legislation, the Scholastic Aptitude Test, or other similar tests as they progressed through public or private schools. Many clients will also have completed inventories that measure interests, values, or personality. These are also quantitative assessment devices. Tests such as scholastic aptitude tests, sometimes referred to as intelligence tests, are presumed to be measures of maximum or optimal performance, whereas inventories are presumed to measure typical performance. However, both tests and inventories have standardized administration and scoring procedures.

Typically, tests are time-limited while assessments such as interest inventories are usually not time limited.

Most tests and inventories including paper-and-pencil instruments are typically scored and profiled using computerized algorithms. Sampson (1990, 2001) and Sampson, Carr, Lunsden, Smission, & Dozier (2009) identified a number of distinct assessment trends related to computer applications in testing. Among the most salient of these are the use of computer-based interpretational systems to support the interpretations made by practitioners, the use of computers to generate cutoff scores when aptitude tests are used as the basis for job or educational placement decisions, and the use of computer-controlled videodisk technology to reduce dialectic and language barriers in the interpretation process. Sampson also notes that adaptive devices, such as Braille keyboards, are being used to enable some people with disabilities to take tests with relatively little assistance.

Qualitative assessment approaches, in contrast to objective approaches, are bound by less rigid parameters. For example, there may be no standardized set of directions and the "scoring" is more subjective; in fact, often there is no scoring at all. The results of these devices are not profiled, and they are interpreted ideographically as opposed to normatively. Goldman (1990) pointed out that qualitative assessments tend to involve clients more actively than standardized or objective tests and inventories because the objective approach gives the client very little voice in where or how the instrument is administered and scored. Goldman goes on to identify several qualitative assessment devices, including card sorts, values clarifications exercises, simulations such as the use of work samples, and observations. Peterson and Gonzalez (2005) add early recollections of occupational daydreams, and life themes to this list.

Some of the "qualitative" devices identified by Goldman (1990) can be developed into objective approaches to assessment. Behavioral psychologists have developed highly sophisticated observational systems, as well as procedures for establishing interobserver reliability, that are as standardized as any test or inventory.

Throughout the history of the career counseling and development movement, objective or standardized tests have been emphasized (Brown, 1990). However, some of the earliest writings (e.g., Williamson, 1939) about career counseling also discussed qualitative methods of assessment such as job shadowing, which is used to help individuals "assess" their potential interests in, and aptitude for, particular occupations. Perhaps what is different is that currently more qualitative assessment approaches are available than ever before. Role play, self-efficacy assessment, and cognitive assessment are all useful strategies with some clients. All of these are qualitative assessment devices, although, as will be shown later in this chapter, the assessment of self-efficacy can be quantified.

Assessment is a major field of academic study with many facets. As noted at the outset of this chapter, literally hundreds of quantitative and qualitative assessment approaches could be included in this chapter. The question is what to include? A few of the most useful qualitative assessment devices are discussed in this chapter, most of them selected on the basis of the author's perceptions of their utility in career development programming and counseling. They were also selected to a large degree on the basis of the latest reviews by Kapes and Whitfield (2002) and Whitfield, Feller, and Wood (2009). These editors used professionals to review the technical and practical merits of various instruments used to assess interest, aptitudes, career development, and values. A few inventories that did not surface on any of these lists are also discussed, as are some instruments that may be useful in assessing certain decisional problems, such as career indecisiveness.

Qualitative Assessment and Constructivist Theory

Chapter 2 focused on theories of career choice and development stem from two major philosophical positions, postmodernism and logical positivism. Theories based on these philosophical positions differ in a number of important ways, as do the career counseling approaches based on them. One of the major practical differences between these two perspectives lies in the assessment area. Logical positivists, such as Holland (1997), rely heavily on traditional measurement devices, such as interest and personality inventories, whereas postmodern approaches, such as the constructivist approach advanced by Young, Valach, and Collins (1996), do not. Career counselors who base their work on postmodern philosophy believe that each individual constructs his or her own unique reality; they use assessments designed to elicit the individual's perspective. Thorgren and Feit (2001) indicate that the logical positivists search for fit whereas the postmodernists search for meaning. Additionally, Brott (2001) noted that, when postmodernists use instruments such as interest inventories, they use them to help clients understand (make meaning of) their career stories, which explain how they got to their current state, and extend their stories into the future.

Some of the postmodern approaches to assessment, such as the repertory grid technique, or reptest, are quite complex and require extensive training before they can be used in career counseling. However, many postmodern assessment strategies are relatively easy to use. Some of these strategies, including the Career-O-Gram, role play, card sorts, and genograms, are discussed in this section. Self-efficacy measurements, which can be assessed both quantitatively and qualitatively, are discussed in the section that follows.

CAREER-O-GRAMS The Career-O-Gram assessment, as described by Thorgren and Feit (2001), begins when the career counselor asks the client to identify his or her earliest career ambition and the factors that encouraged the client either to pursue or discard it. The following questions might be posed during the assessment process:

- What was your first career goal?
- How old were you when this goal surfaced?
- What aspects of this career most appealed to you? Least appealed to you?
- What did you think you would have to do to enter this career?
- Was this choice similar to the choices of other people in your culture?
- What messages did you receive about the appropriateness of career choices for males and females?
- How powerful did you feel in regard to making a career choice?
- If the initial choice changed, what factors influenced the changes and your current position?
- What were and are the influential interpersonal relationships in your life?
- How did (do) these relationships influence your choices?
- What was going on historically at the time you made each of your choices?
- What rules did your family have for discussing career choice?

As each goal (i.e., initial and subsequent) is identified, it should be represented by a symbol, for example, a rectangle (□) for the initial goal, a triangle (▼) for the next goal, and so forth. Each choice should be surrounded by symbols representing contextual factors that influenced that particular choice, for example, a dollar sign ($) for economic factors, an up arrow (↑) for positive interpersonal relationships, a down arrow (↓) for negative interpersonal influences, and a heart (♥) for parental involvement in the process. The result should be a developmental, symbolic representation of the factors that influenced the career choice-making process throughout the client's life. Major life events are also depicted in the Career-O-Gram, for example, drug usage, an unexpected pregnancy, illness, divorce, or child bearing and rearing. A Career-O-Gram is a symbolic illustration of a client's career decision-making process resulting from the verbal interaction between the counselor and the client. The expected outcome of the Career-O-Gram is increased understanding of the contextual factors that influenced the career decision-making process up to the point of the assessment. Brott (2001) indicated that clients benefit from techniques such as the Career-O-Gram because they discover heretofore unsuspected relationships among the constructs that guide their lives.

ROLE PLAY Role play can be used both as an intervention and as an assessment strategy. Although this discussion focuses largely on assessment, a brief description presents the uses of role play as an intervention. Role play is the process of acting out a social situation to demonstrate how one would, or has, performed. For example, a career counseling client may report that she "blew her last job interview." The counselor needs to determine why the interview was blown and ask the client to report verbally what occurred. Verbal reports may be enlightening, but situations involving social skills may not be described accurately.

Role play represents an alternative to verbal descriptions. The career counselor may begin by asking the client to describe the interviewer or, better still, to imitate the interviewer's behavior. Once the counselor has a relatively full understanding of how the interview went, the client is asked to reenact the job interview with the counselor acting as the interviewer. If the client agrees to reenact the interview, she is asked to illustrate through her behavior how she actually performed in the job interview. Then the role play begins.

During the role play, the counselor observes the client, making mental notes about strengths and weaknesses. After the role play is completed, the counselor's observations may be shared with the client, or if the counselor wants to "clench" the assessment, the counselor may engage in role reversal. In role reversal, the counselor assumes the role of the client and the client assumes the role of the job interviewer, and a new role play of the interview is performed. Once completed, the counselor asks the client whether the client's behavior was accurately depicted. If the client answers yes, she is asked to evaluate her own performance during role reversal. The counselor may then provide additional evaluations, and the client and the counselor can construct a list of interviewing strengths and weaknesses. Intervention follows and usually entails presenting models of desired behaviors, practice through behavioral rehearsal, and feedback. Role play can be used to assess clients' social skills in a wide variety of areas, such as job interviews, telephone contacts, and employee-employer interactions (e.g., asking for a raise).

CARD SORTS Card sorts are typically used to assess a variety of variables, including values, interests, job skills, and lifestyle preferences. Potential options are placed on 3″ by 5″ cards, and clients are asked to sort the cards, usually into three to five stacks. The following lifestyle variables are examples of potential options:

1. Ballet available
2. Symphony available
3. Theater available
4. Skiing within commuting distance
5. Short commute to work

6. High-quality schools for children
7. Golf course nearby
8. Educational opportunities for client
9. Warm climate
10. Cold climate
11. Moderate climate (has all four seasons)
12. Close to parents
13. Intramural sports program for children
14. Near a large city
15. Near recreational water

The client sorts these 15 cards into stacks of no importance, some importance, or great importance while discussing the reasons for the selections with the counselor. Tyler (1961), Dolliver (1967), and Dewey (1974) pioneered the use of card sorts to measure interests. More recently Knowdell (1998) developed the Career Values Card Sort Kit.

GENOGRAMS The genogram was developed for use in family therapy. McGoldrick and Gerson (1985) wrote an excellent book on its use with families. The third edition of the same book, differently titled and authored (McGoldrick, Shelleneberger, & Perry, 2008) also focuses on the family, but generalizing their work on genogram for families is relatively simple. In career counseling the genogram is used to create a graphic representation of a family tree of careers engaged in by the client's immediate or extended family—namely, parents, grandparents, aunts, uncles, and any other relatives who might have influenced the client's career-related attitudes. If used correctly, the genogram can assess sources of self-limiting stereotypes, expectations about the outcomes of various career choices, and development of career values and interests (Brown & Brooks, 1991; Okiishi, 1987).

The construction of a total genogram, as outlined by McGoldrick and colleagues (2008) is quite time consuming, but because the use of this device in career counseling has somewhat more limited objectives, an abbreviated version can be developed. Typically, generations of family members are listed in order of descent, with grandparents listed on line 1, parents and their brothers and sisters on line 2, influential cousins on line 3, and siblings on line 4. This organization is shown in Figure 7.1. Other individuals outside the family who had a significant impact on the "career thinking" of the client, such as teachers, early employers, and so forth, can also be added to the family tree (see Gibson, 2005; Malott & Magnuson, 2004).

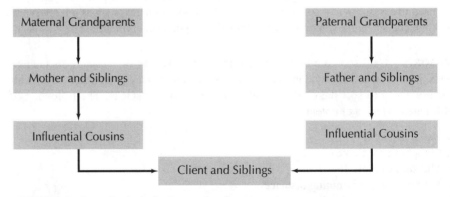

FIGURE 7.1 Organization of a Career Genogram

Once a chart of the family tree is organized, the occupations of each person (including homemaking) are listed. Clients are then asked to report how their relatives felt about their occupations, what values they tried to engender in the client, and why they believe each person in the chart influenced them either positively or negatively.

SUPPORT FOR QUALITATIVE ASSESSMENT   Empirical support for the use of qualitative devices is not extensive. There is widespread support for the use of card sorts (e.g., Gysbers & Moore, 1987) and role play (e.g., Brown & Brooks, 1991). However, qualitative assessment strategies are widely used and can provide much needed data when dealing with clients with diverse perspectives and should be included in the repertoire of all career counselors.

Quantitative and Objective Assessment Devices

Some assessment devices can serve as either qualitative or objective assessment devices although most are used as one or the other. The first assessment strategy introduced in this section, self-efficacy assessment measurements can serve in either capacity.

SELF-EFFICACY MEASUREMENTS   Self-efficacy is the individual's judgment regarding her or his ability to perform a task at a certain level (Bandura, 1977, 1986). These self-efficacy cognitions mediate action with the result that individuals avoid tasks or activities they believe are beyond their capabilities and instead engage in those they judge themselves capable of performing (Bandura, 1986). Betz and Hacket (1981, 1986) were the first to emphasize the importance of self-efficacy expectations on career decision making and, drawing on Bandura's work (1977, 1986), set forth a model of career decision making based primarily on this construct. Self-efficacy has traditionally been measured by first identifying a task to be performed (e.g., complete algebra successfully); second, asking clients to estimate the degree of difficulty of the task and the extent of the confidence with which they can perform the task; and third, estimating their performance in related situations (range) (Bandura, 1986). The following conversation is an example of how self-efficacy expectations might be assessed during career counseling:

COUNSELOR: We've been discussing engineering as a possible career option for you. On a 1-to-10 scale, with 1 being extremely difficult, how would you rate the difficulty of engineering?

CLIENT: A 10—definitely a 10.

COUNSELOR: Then how confident are you that you can complete an engineering curriculum with at least a 2.5 GPA, again using the 1-to-10 scale, with 1 being not very confident and 10 being extremely confident?

CLIENT: That's tough. Probably a 7. I'm pretty good in math and science.

COUNSELOR: OK, just one more rating. We've discussed several options that are related to engineering, such as engineering technology, architecture, and industrial relations. Using the 1-to-10 scale, how would you rate your confidence that you can enter and complete courses of study in these areas?

CLIENT: Engineering technology a 10, definitely; architecture, a 5 or a 6. I'm just not sure I can do some of the things that are needed. Industrial relations probably a 9 or a 10.

Self-efficacy ratings can be used on an ongoing basis to assess clients' perceptions of their abilities to find information about jobs, complete interviews with employers, or even complete career counseling successfully.

One of the most interesting trends in assessment in the past decade is away from assessing self-efficacy qualitatively to quantitative measures of perceived self-efficacy. Additionally, perceived self-efficacy measures are now being integrated into interest assessment. Betz (2000) outlined the general principles of the self-efficacy assessment. First, self-efficacy assessment should focus on a specific behavioral domain. As noted earlier the rationale for this principle is based on Bandura's (1986) definition that self-efficacy is a person's judgment that he or she can perform a specific task. Career self-efficacy, therefore, is a misnomer according to Betz because careers entail the performance of a complex set of behaviors, not a single specific task. The assessment process should focus each specific domain of behavior, not the entire career (Betz, 2000).

After a domain of behaviors is identified (using a software package, for example), the second step of the self-efficacy assessment is to establish an assessment measure. Betz (2000) points out that most self-efficacy measures use what she terms a 1-point or 10-point confidence range. These scales, much like the one shown in Figure 7.2, ask students to indicate from 1 to 5 or from 5 to 10 the confidence with which they can perform certain tasks.

Betz and Hackett (1981) first studied perceived self-efficacy using the Occupational Self-Efficacy Scale, which was designed to measure the confidence with which college students could perform the educational requirements and job duties of 20 occupations. Mathematics self-efficacy or the confidence with which students could perform the tasks associated with Holland's types (RIASEC) has been studied extensively. The Skills Confidence Inventory (Betz, Borgen, & Harmon, 2005) has been used to assess individuals' self-efficacy expectations regarding occupations in the various Holland types. However, according to Betz, the most widely used instrument, and most studied, is the Career Decision-Making Self-Efficacy Scale (Betz & Taylor, 2001).

SUPPORT FOR SELF-EFFICACY MEASURES   Support for the inclusion of self-efficacy measures in the career assessment process is overwhelming. In the 1981 study mentioned previously, Betz and Hackett found significant gender differences in self-efficacy expectations for traditional male and female occupations. Similarly, Rotberg, Brown, and Ware (1987) found that occupational self-efficacy is related to the range of occupations being considered. Research also supports the importance of counseling interventions to improve self-efficacy as a means of reducing career indecision (e.g., Luzzo & Taylor, 1994). Finally, researchers have turned to studying the relationship between interests and self-efficacy. Betz and Borgen (2000) contend that assessment data on interests and self-efficacy provide extensive empirical support for their position (e.g., Donnay & Borgen, 1999). Generally speaking, pairing self-efficacy data with information about interests provides a better predictor of occupational choice than using either assessment alone. Two measures of self-efficacy are now available for use: the Skills Confidence Inventory (Betz, Borgen, & Harmon, 1996) for use with the Strong Interest Inventory and the Kuder Task Self-Efficacy Scale (Lucas, Wanberg, & Zytowski, 1997) for the use with the Kuder Occupational Interest Survey.

VALUES: FOUR WORK VALUES INVENTORIES   Needs and values are sometimes confused in discussions, or the differences simply are not addressed. Similarly, values and interests are sometimes equated, even though they are actually two separate constructs (Rokeach, 1979). Some needs are assumed to stem from the physiological functioning of the individual (e.g., the need for air and water), and unless they are met, the individual perishes. Psychological needs also stem

Please complete the following by indicating how certain you are that you could, if you elected to do so, perform the duties involved in the following occupations by circling a number on the scale provided. One (1) indicates that you are very uncertain that you could perform the task and five (5) indicates that you are very certain you could perform the task

---

1. *Secondary School Teacher:* Instructs junior or senior high school students, usually in a specific subject.

1	2	3	4	5
Very Uncertain		Somewhat Certain		Very Certain

2. *Psychologist:* Concerned with the collection, interpretation, and application of scientific data to human behavior.

1	2	3	4	5
Very Uncertain		Somewhat Certain		Very Certain

3. *Pharmacist:* Mixes and dispenses medicines, gives medication advice to health practitioners and the public.

1	2	3	4	5
Very Uncertain		Somewhat Certain		Very Certain

4. *Dental Hygienist:* Provides dental treatment, gives instruction on teeth care, takes x-rays, and assists dentists.

1	2	3	4	5
Very Uncertain		Somewhat Certain		Very Certain

5. *Buyer, wholesale or retail:* Purchases merchandise from manufacturers or wholesales merchandise that is then sold to the public.

1	2	3	4	5
Very Uncertain		Somewhat Certain		Very Certain

6. *Sales Manager:* Directs staffing and training of sales staff, and develops and controls a sales program.

1	2	3	4	5
Very Uncertain		Somewhat Certain		Very Certain

7. *Primary School Teacher:* Teaches elementary school students, teaching several subjects and supervising various activities.

1	2	3	4	5
Very Uncertain		Somewhat Certain		Very Certain

FIGURE 7.2 A Career Self-Efficacy Rating Scale: Certainty of Performing Job Duties. *Source:* From *Career Self-Efficiency Expectations and Perceived Range of Career Options in Community College Students* (pp. 96–98), by H. L. Rotberg, 1984. Unpublished doctoral dissertation, University of North Carolina at Chapel Hill. Reprinted with permission.

8. *Stocks and Bonds Salesperson:* Gives information and advice in the buying and selling of stocks and bonds.

1	2	3	4	5
Very Uncertain		Somewhat Certain		Very Certain

9. *Editor:* Assigns, stimulates, prepares, accepts or rejects, and sometimes writes articles for publication.

1	2	3	4	5
Very Uncertain		Somewhat Certain		Very Certain

10. *Registered Nurse:* Administers nursing care to the ill and injured, using skills, experience, and education.

1	2	3	4	5
Very Uncertain		Somewhat Certain		Very Certain

11. *Engineer:* Uses practical applications of mathematics, physics and chemistry to solve applied problems dealing with construction, use of chemicals, machine design, etc.

1	2	3	4	5
Very Uncertain		Somewhat Certain		Very Certain

12. *Personnel Relations:* Hires and assigns people to jobs that they can do, to benefit themselves and their employer.

1	2	3	4	5
Very Uncertain		Somewhat Certain		Very Certain

13. *Laboratory Technician:* Works with other health professionals in the laboratory analysis of biological materials.

1	2	3	4	5
Very Uncertain		Somewhat Certain		Very Certain

14. *Designer:* Creates original designs for new types and styles of clothing, leather goods, and textiles.

1	2	3	4	5
Very Uncertain		Somewhat Certain		Very Certain

15. *Librarian:* Maintains library collections of books and other materials, and aids people in using library material.

1	2	3	4	5
Very Uncertain		Somewhat Certain		Very Certain

FIGURE 7.2 (*Continued*)

from the functioning of the individual, and unless they are met, the individual's development is arrested with various consequences (Rokeach, 1973, 1979). Values, however, are learned or may grow out of needs and are assumed to be a basic source of human motivation. Values may have either a positive or negative valence; that is, individuals are assumed to seek or move toward values with a positive valence and move away from values that hold negative valences (Rokeach, 1973, 1979). Interests typically are viewed as less basic than values and as growing out of values

(Holland, 1985; Rokeach, 1979). The following descriptions of four work values inventories may be helpful in identifying areas for client exploration:

Super's Work Values Inventory—Revised SWI-R

Donald E. Super and Donald G. Zytowski

> **Purpose:** Measures client preferences for an array of careers. Yields scores on 12 work values: (1) Achievement, (2) Co-workers, (3) Creativity, (4) Income, (5) Independence, (6) Lifestyle, (7) Mental Challenge, (8) Prestige, (9) Security, (10) Supervision, (11) Variety, and (12) Workplace
>
> **Target Audience:** Middle school through adult.
>
> **Date of Publication:** SWI-R Technical Manual 2006.
>
> **Publisher:** Kuder, Inc. (www.Kuder.com/downloads/SWV-Tech-Manual.pdf).

Work Importance Locator and Work Importance Profiler

DOLETA

> **Purpose:** The Work Importance Locator (WIL)* is a paper-and-pencil measure; the Work Importance Profiler is a computerized version of the same inventory. Both instruments measure six work values: (1) Achievement, (2) Independence, (3) Recognition, (4) Relationships, (5)Support, and (6) Working Conditions. The WIL, which is self-administered and self-scored, uses a color-coded card-sort approach to measuring these values. Work values can be combined with interest information from the O*NET Interest Profiler and used to access the *O*NET Occupations Combined List: Interests and Work Values.* This document classifies occupations according to the Holland type associated with them, the extent of preparation required (little, some, medium, and considerable), and work values. For example, under Realistic one can find a classification labeled Job Zone 1 (little preparation), Realistic, and Achievement. This classification contains forest and conservation officers and semiconductor processors.
>
> **Target Population:** High school students and adults.
>
> **Date of Publication:** Work Importance Locator, 2001; Work Importance Profiler, 2002.
>
> **Publisher:** U.S. Department of Labor (www.onetcenter.org/WIP/html).
>
> **Note:** A Web-based Work Importance Locator is currently being revised by the O*NET Development staff. No date for the completion of this inventory has been established.

Life Values Inventory (LVI)

R. Kelly Crace and Duane Brown

> **Purpose:** The LVI was developed both as a measure of values that guide normal behavior and as an intervention to assist clients to crystallize and prioritize their values within life roles. It measures 13 values: (1) Belonging, (2) Concern for Others, (3) Creativity, (4) Prosperity, (5) Dependability, (6) Health and Activity, (7) Scientific Understanding,

(8) Privacy, (9) Spirituality, (10) Loyalty to Family or Group, (11) Achievement, (12) Concern for the Environment, and (13) Humility.

Target Population: Grade 9 and up.

Date of Publication: Technical Manual 1996; revised 2002.

Publisher: Applied Psychology Resources, 1581 River Ridge, Williamsburg, VA 23188.

Career Orientations Placement and Evaluation Survey (COPES)

Kna, R. R. and Knap-Lee, L. J.

> *Purpose:* To measure vocational values. Reported in eight work dichotomous values clusters: (1) Investigative vs. Accepting; (2) Practical vs. Carefree; (3) Independence vs. Conformity; (4) Leadership vs. Supportive; (5) Orderliness vs. Flexibility; (6) Recognition vs. Privacy; (7) Aesthetic vs. Realistic; (8) Social vs. Reserved.
>
> *Target Population:* Junior high through adults.
>
> *Date of Publication:* Technical Manual 1996.
>
> *Publisher:* EDITS PO Box 7235, San Diego, CA 92167

SUPPORT FOR WORK VALUES INVENTORIES   Cochran (1983) asked high school students (1) to generate and rank-order a list of 10 occupational alternatives and (2) to study and rank-order a list of values-laden career constructs (e.g., higher salary). He concluded that their explicit ranking of career values did not correlate well with their implicit values, which seemed to guide their selection of career alternatives. Pryor and Taylor (1980) also studied high school students in an effort to determine whether it was beneficial to use both values and interests measures. Their conclusion was that counselors are justified in using both. Their findings also support the conclusion of Knapp and Knapp (1979) that values and interests are two separate constructs. However, as we see in the next section, interest measures are the most widely used career counseling tools. This is probably because instruments measuring values have not received as much attention as have interest inventories.

Practitioners who assist their clients to consider their values as a part of the career counseling process may use checklists (Cochran, 1983) to "measure" values or they may use values clarification exercises or imagery (Brown & Brooks, 1991). Some practitioners may also infer values clinically from verbal reports. These approaches, as well as the use of psychometric instruments, appear useful as long as the limitations of the approaches used are kept clearly in mind.

INTEREST INVENTORIES   Literally hundreds of thousands of interests inventories are administered each year. Regardless of the theoretical or empirical origin of these scales, they are presumed to measure liking or preferences for engaging in certain specific occupations.

Once scores on interest inventories are obtained, they may be compared to those of others in a reference or norm group, compared to some absolute criterion such as the interest levels of other pilots, or interpreted as raw scores (Blocher, 1987). Typically, inventories used in career development programs to promote awareness use either the normative or the raw score approach. For example, the individual's scores or the Strong Interest Inventory Assessment Tool are compared to a series of norm groups comprising successful workers in managerial, technical, and professional occupations. However, the raw scale scores on the Self-Directed Search (Holland, 1994) are used to construct a scale profile to locate jobs of interest. Whether the normative approach to scoring and interpretation is superior to the raw score approach has been a hotly debated area. Career counselors who accept the logical positivism perspective are likely to favor comparison to norm or reference groups, which is admittedly a risky approach if the norm group is not representative of the client. Postmodernists are more likely to argue for the raw score approach because the emphasis is placed on self-understanding. What follows are a few examples of frequently used inventories.

Career Occupational Preference System (COPS)

R. R. Knapp, L. Knapp, and L. Knapp-Lee

Purpose: The COPS was designed to reveal preferences for job activities in the following areas: (1) Science Professional, (2) Science Skilled, (3) Technology Professional, (4) Technology Skilled, (5) Consumer Economics, (6) Outdoor, (7) Business Professional, (8) Business Skilled, (9) Clerical, (10) Communication, (11) Arts Skilled, (12) Service Professional, and (13) Service Skilled.

Target Population: Junior high through college: norm groups include junior high, high school, and college students.

Date of Publication: COPS System Technical Manual, 2001.

Publisher: EDITS, PO Box 7234, San Diego, CA 92107.

Self-Directed Search (SDS-R) (4th ed.)

John Holland

Purpose: The SDS was developed to be a self-administered, self-scored, and self-interpreted instrument to measure Holland's types: Realistic, Investigative, Artistic, Social, Enterprising, and Conventional. Depending on the form, the inventory yields two- or three-letter personal profiles that can be used with an Occupations Finder to locate a career that should be of interest to the individual.

Target Population: Junior high through adult. Raw scores are reported. Inventory was developed using high school and college students as well as adults.

Dates of Publication: Form R, 1994; Form E, 1996; Form CP, 1991; Manual, 1991; Occupations Finder, 1994.

Publisher: Psychological Assessment Resources, 16204 North Florida Avenue, Lutz, FL 33549.

Career Decision–Making (CDM) System

Thomas F. Harrington and Arthur O'Shea

Purpose: The CDM is based on Holland's theory of occupational choice and yields six scores that are analogous to his types: (1) Crafts (Realistic), (2) Scientific (Investigative),

(3) the Arts (Artistic), (4) Business (Enterprising), (5) Clerical (Conventional), and (6) Social (Social). The raw scores in the highest two or three interest scales are assessed to identify career clusters for exploration. Self-estimates of abilities, work values, future plans, and preferences for school subjects are incorporated into the overall career decision–making system.

Target Population: Junior high through adult. Norms drawn from junior high schools and senior high schools from across the country.

Dates of Publication: Self-scored and machine-scored versions, 2000; user's guide, 2000; technical manual, 2000; college finder, 2000.

Publisher: AGS, Publishers Building, 4201 Woodland Road, Circle Pines, MN 55014.

Strong Interest Inventory Assessment Tool (SII)

E. K. Strong Jr.

Purpose: The SII was originally developed to help people interested in managerial, technical, and professional careers identify career options. It is now widely used in business and industry and adult counseling centers to assist people interested in making career changes as well as initial career choices. The SII yields a wealth of data, including basic interest scales, general interest scales, and general occupational themes, as well as administrative indices and special scales (e.g., Extroversion–Introversion). The 23 basic interest scales and six general occupational themes (GOT) are organized around Holland's six types (RIASEC), and the 207 occupational interest scales (OIS) are also reported in this context.

Target Population: Late adolescents and adults. Norm groups for OIS were drawn from successful and satisfied people; those for GOT were composed of women and men from each of the six Holland types and from various educational levels.

Dates of Publication: Latest revision form, 2004; manual, user's guide, 2005.

Publisher: Consulting Psychologists Press and Davies-Black Publishing, 1056 Joaquin Road., Mountain View, CA 94043.

Kuder Occupational Interest Survey (KOIS) Form DD

G. Frederick Kuder and D. G. Zytowski

Purpose: The purpose of Form DD is to provide data on 104 occupational scales, 39 college major scales, 10 vocational interest estimates, and Holland type scale information to be used in educational and career planning, using norms based on successful workers or graduating students.

Target Population: Grade 10 through adult. Norms provide occupational and educational scales for males and females.

Dates of Publication: Latest revision inventory, 2005; manual 2005.

Publisher: Kuder, 302 Visions Parkway, Adel, IA 50003.

Reading-Free Vocational Interest Inventory (2nd ed.)

Ralph L. Becker

Purpose: The purpose of the revised RFVII is to determine the interests of special need students and adults with cognitive and learning disabilities. It yields scale scores in 11 areas: (1) Automotive, (2) Building Trades, (3) Clerical, (4) Animal Care, (5) Food Service, (6) Patient Care, (7) Horticulture, (8) Housekeeping, (9) Personal Service, (10) Laundry, and (11) Materials Handling.

Target Population: 13- to 60-year-old people with cognitive and learning disabilities. Norms drawn from people with cognitive and learning disabilities; adults in sheltered workshops; adults who have environmental disadvantages.

Dates of Publication: Inventory, 2000; manual, 2000; Hand scoring only.

Publisher: Elbern Publications, PO Box 9497, Columbus, OH 43209.

Campbell Interest and Skill Survey (CISS)

David P. Campbell

Purpose: The CISS was developed to measure career interests and self-estimates of skills. The instrument yields interests and skill scores on seven Orientation Scales, 29 Basic Interest and Skill Scales, and three special scales. The Orientation Scales include (1) Influencing, (2) Organizing, (3) Helping, (4) Creating, (5) Analyzing, (6) Producing, and (7) Adventuring. The Basic Interest and Skill Scales are subscales of the Orientation Scales. The special scales include Academic Focus, Extraversion, and Variety.

Target Population: Fifteen-year-old students and up.

Date of Publication: 1992.

Publisher: Pearson Assessment, 5601 Green Valley Drive, Bloomington, MN 55437.

Ashland Interest Assessment (AIA)

Douglas N. Jackson and Connie W. Marshall

Purpose: The AIA consists of 144 pairs of work-related items and yields scores in 12 interest areas: (1) Arts and Crafts, (2) Personal Services, (3) Food Service, (4) Clerical, (5) Sales, (6) General Service, (7) Protective Service, (8) Health Care, (9) Mechanical, (10) Construction, (11) Plant or Animal Care, and (12) Transportation. It is written at a third-grade reading level and is printed in larger type than most inventories. At this time it uses Canadian norms and thus must be evaluated carefully by U.S. users.

Target Population: Adults or older adolescents who have learning disabilities, developmental disabilities, limited use of English, limited education, brain injury, or a chronic emotional or psychiatric conditions. Also useful for students who do not want to finish high school. The instrument can be hand-scored or mailed to the publisher for scoring; or users can purchase software that administers, scores, and provides an interpretive report.

Date of Publication: All materials, 1997.

Publisher: Sigma Assessment Systems, Inc., 4110 Military Street, PO Box 610984, Port Huron, MI 48061.

O*NET Interest Profiler

U.S. Department of Labor

> **Purpose:** One of the newest interest inventories is the Interest Profiler (IP) developed by the U.S. Department of Labor to help individuals access the O*NET database. The questions on the IP are answered using Like (L), Dislike (D), Uncertain (?) format and yield Holland type scores (RIASEC). The instrument is self-administering and self-scoring and is linked to O*NET via an *Interest Profiler O*NET Occupations Master List.* The jobs in this publication are organized by Holland type and by the amount of preparation required. That is, Holland types are categorized by four levels of preparation: (1) little or no, (2) some, (3) medium, and(4) considerable. One caveat is important: Some of the occupations in the master list are organized by the second letter in the Holland type profile to extend the number of occupations listed under each level of preparation. The IP is available on paper and a computerized version was published in 2002.
>
> **Target Population:** High school students and adults.
>
> **Date of Publication:** 2001.
>
> **Publisher:** U.S. Department of Labor (www.onetcenter.org).
>
> **Note:** The Interest Profiler is currently undergoing revision by the O*NET development staff. No date has been posted for its completion.

SUPPORT FOR INTEREST INVENTORIES   Studies and opinion articles on the use of interest inventories abound. as is demonstrated in the annual reviews of the career development literature published annually in *The Career Development* Quarterly (e.g., Chope, 2008; Patton & McIlven, 2009). Typically articles about career assessment leads the list of published studies with interest assessment being the most researched topic. Generally, the use of interest inventories is supported in studies of longitudinal predictive validity, which is generally the holy grail for psychometric research. Rottinghaus, Coon, Gaffey, & Zytowskis (2007) reported that the results of Kuder Occupational Interest Survey administered to 107 high school juniors in 1975 and again in 2005 were moderately stable and that the 1975 scores matched occupations in 20005.

It comes as no surprise that the Strong Interest Inventory (SII) and the Self-Directed Search (SDS) are the most researched instruments year after year. The SII is the oldest (and perhaps best) of the currently published inventories and the SDS is one of the most popular.

Hansen and Swanson (1983) studied the validity of the SII as a predictor of college majors and concluded that it was valid for this purpose, although slightly less so for males than females. Johnson and Hoese (1988) also studied the SII and concluded that it cannot be used as the sole career planning device because many of the college students in this sample had a wide variety of personal and career development problems. The SII was *not* developed as a stand-alone career planning instrument. Galassi, Jones, and Britt (1985) also studied the SII to determine to what degree it suggests nontraditional options for women. The instruments studied, in addition to the SII, were the Kuder Occupational Interest Survey (KOIS), Career Assessment Inventory (CAI), Harrington–O'Shea Career Decision–Making (CDM) Systems, the Self-Directed Search (SDS), Non-Sexist Vocational Card Sort (NSVCS), and the Occ-U-Sort. The SII suggested 46 nontraditional occupations, whereas the Occ-USort guide suggested 382 jobs; the SDS Job Finder, 327 jobs; the CDM, 164 jobs; the KOIS, 65 jobs; the CAI, 50 jobs; and NSVCS, 41 jobs. In another comparative study, the SII was compared to the Vocational Card Sort (VCS) for expressed and inventoried interests of college women. Slaney and Slaney (1986) found that 42 percent of the expressed and inventoried interests were incongruent. They found that interests measured by the VCS were more highly related to expressed interests than were those measured by the SII, suggesting that the VCS may be a superior means of measuring interests, at least for some groups.

The Self-Directed Search, as an interest inventory, has also been explored extensively. For example, Gottfredson and Holland (1975) studied the predictive validity of the SDS and found it to be a moderately efficient predictor of choices for both men and women. However, the section of the SDS that asks for expressed career choice proved to be the best predictor of career choice. Numerous studies (e.g., Holland, Gottfredson, & Baker 1990; Noeth, 1983) have supported this finding.

Maddux and Cummings (1980) compared the test–retest reliability of the SDS and the SDS Form E (Easy) with high school students with learning disabilities and found that Form E may be more appropriate for this group because test–retest reliabilities are higher with Form E. In another comparative study, Jones, Gorman, and Schroeder (1989) compared the utility of the SDS with the Career Key (CK) in helping undecided college students choose academic majors. Students rated the CK more positively than the SDS and spent more time exploring career resources after testing than did those who took the SDS. Finally, Gault and Meyers (1987) compared the SDS with the Vocational Interest, Experience, and Skills Assessment (VIESA) to determine which would best serve college and adult populations. In this study the SDS was rated more positively and as being more effective.

An argument arose about 30 years ago over the validity of using raw scores, particularly with women (e.g., Holland, Gottfredson, & Gottfredson, 1975; Prediger, 1981). In 1981 Prediger questioned the validity of the SDS for females. His meta-analytic research suggested that using raw scores instead of normative scores restricts the range of occupations suggested for women and has less construct validity than when normed scores are reported. The crux of Prediger's arguments rests on the relative value of construct versus predictive validity. Holland (1982) asserted the importance of predictive validity in his reply, suggesting that "the depreciation of predictive validity by Prediger is a step backward" (p. 197).

In the twenty-first century the debate about the SDS shifted to focus on its utility with cultural minorities. Much of this research has focused on the validity of the RIASEC model, perhaps better stated as the construct validity of the inventories and Holland's model in general. The conclusions reached by Gupta, Tracey, and Gore (2008) that there was no difference in the fit of Holland's model among the five groups studied (Caucasians, African Americans, Latinos, Asian Americans, and American Indians) is typical. Many recent studies have also focused on the cultural validity of the instruments that measure Holland's (1997) theory and have come to somewhat different conclusions. The approach used in much of this research (e.g., Rounds & Tracey, 1996) has been to administer an instrument, such as the SDS or SII, to a non-Eurocentric sample and analyze the data to determine whether the scores yield the classic hexagonal figure that characterizes data from U.S. samples. Leong and Hartung (2000) summarized much of this research and suggested that in most instances cross-cultural differences were found. Hansen, Scullard, and Haviland (2000) tested the construct validity of the SII with Native American college students. They found that the distribution of female students in their sample more closely resembled the hexagon than did the scores from the male sample. Leung and Hou (2001) examined the concurrent validity of the SDS for students in Hong Kong by examining the correspondence between the scores on this instrument and choices of academic tracks, university majors, and careers. The researchers found that the correspondence between SDS scores and the

STUDENT LEARNING EXERCISE 7.1

Complete the Self-Directed Search or other paper-and-pencil measures of Holland types, and the Web-based O*NET Interest Profiler which also reports Holland types and then compare your results.

1. Do the inventories yield the same profiles?
2. Which one was easiest to use? To score? To interpret?
3. Which inventory produced the most useful list of occupations?

criteria was generally lower for Hong Kong students than the results reported for students in the United States, but their data yielded some support for the concurrent validity of the SDS. Tang (2001) studied Chinese college students using the SII with similar results.

Probably the safest conclusion than can be drawn from the research on the cross-cultural use of interest inventories is that caution is required, based on both the research data and an intriguing question raised by Soh and Leong (2001): Do people from cultures other than mainstream U.S. culture who have identical scores perceive themselves and occupations in the same manner? They offered some limited evidence that they do not, which, if supported in future research, invalidates the use of these instruments.

The SII and the SDS are not the only instruments that have received attention from researchers. For example, the Harrington–O'Shea has been shown to have moderate predictive validity for high school students' choice of a college major in a longitudinal study (Brown, Ware, & Brown, 1985). Generally speaking, research supports the continued use of these inventories.

PERSONALITY INVENTORIES   Few personality inventories have captured the interest of career counselors, perhaps because many of those available were developed to measure abnormal behavior. As a result, only two personality inventories are discussed here.

Myers–Briggs Type Indicator (MBTI)

Isabel Briggs Myers and Katharine C. Briggs

> *Purpose:* The MBTI was developed to provide a measure of Jung's types and yields scores of four dipolar scales: (1) Extroversion–Introversion; (2) Sensing–INtuition; (3) Thinking–Feeling; and (4) Judgment–Perception. A profile is constructed based on the person's highest score on each of the scales (e.g., ENTJ). An interpretive profile is available if the MBTI is taken in conjunction with the Strong Interest Assessment Tool.
>
> *Target Population:* High school students and adults. Norms are available on junior high, high school, and college students, and various adult groups.
>
> *Dates of Publication:* Standard Form (6), 1977; Revised Form (F), 1985;
>
> Abbreviated Form (AV), 1985; Manual, 1998.
>
> *Publisher:* Consulting Psychologists Press and Davies-Black Publishing 1056 Joaquin Rd. 2nd Floor, Mountain View, CA 94043.

Sixteen P. F. Personal Career Development Profile (16PFQ)

Raymond Cattell and colleagues

Purpose: The interpretive profile (Personal Career Development Profile [PCDP]) provides an interpretation of personality and its potential influence on career choice and development. The profile is in actuality a computer-generated, occupationally oriented interpretation of the 16 personality factors measured by the Sixteen Personality Factors Questionnaire.

Target Population: High school students and adults. Norms available for high school and college students, and general adult population.

Dates of Publication: 16 PFQ, 1993; 16 PF manual, 1994.

Publisher: IPAT, 1801 Woodfield Drive, Savoy, IL 61874.

SUPPORT FOR PERSONALITY INVENTORIES Willis and Ham (1988) reviewed the MBTI and suggested that it has three uses: (1) helping clients build cognitive frameworks for organizing career information, (2) work adjustment counseling, and (3) as a self-assessment device. They also provided some cautionary notes. For example, they suggested that the MBTI is not a comprehensive personality test and that it would be a mistake to overestimate the utility of the information gained from the scales. However, it is worth noting that the MBTI manual lists data on more than 180 occupations. Perhaps the most striking feature of these tables is that most types are found in most occupations.

Wholeben (1988) stated that the PCDP, which was derived from the 16PF, "is an excellent tool for career awareness in the high school curriculum and occupational exploration of adults" (p. 241). However, little construct or predictive validity information has been developed and, thus, much caution is in order.

It seems likely that the MBTI will receive increasing use in career counseling, although other personality inventories may not fare so well.

MULTIPLE APTITUDE TEST BATTERIES Theoretically, aptitude tests measure a person's potential to acquire a skill or learn some specialized knowledge. In reality, they measure what has already been learned, which is an indicator of future performance. Unfortunately, not everyone has the opportunity to acquire knowledge and/or skill to the same degree. However, when taken as *one* indicator of potential aptitude, tests can be of assistance to clients attempting to make career plans or can simply be one way of promoting self-awareness.

Differential Aptitude Test (DAT)

G. K. Bennett, H. G. Seashore, and A. G. Wesman

Purpose: The DAT yields data that are potentially useful in the career/educational planning process. The subtests on the DAT are (1) Verbal Reasoning, (2) Numerical Ability, (3) Abstract Reasoning, (4) Clerical Speed and Accuracy, (5) Mechanical Reasoning, (6) Space Relations, (7) Spelling, and (8) Language Use.

Target Population: Grade 8 through adult. Norms for grades 8 through 12.

Dates of Publication: Latest edition of all documents, 1991.

Publisher: The Psychological Corporation, 555 Academic Court, San Antonio, TX 78204.

Armed Services Vocational Aptitude Battery (ASVAB)

Department of Defense

Purpose: This test provides data that may be useful to counselors and students in planning a military career. It is also used by military recruiters to determine applicants' suitability for military careers. The ASVAB yields seven composite scores: (1) Academic Ability; (2) Math; (3) Verbal; (4) Mechanical and Crafts; (5) Business and Clerical; (6) Electronics and Electrical; and (7) Health, Social, and Technology. There are also 10 subtest scores in (1) General Science, (2) Word Knowledge, (3) Paragraph Comprehension, (4) Numerical Operations, (5) Arithmetic Reasoning, (6) Math Knowledge, (7) Auto and Shop Information, (8) Mechanical Comprehension, (9) Electronics Information, and (10) Coding Speed.

Target Population: High school (grades 10 through 12) and adults. Norms available for target groups.

Dates of Publication: Counselor's manual, 1995; ASVAB test manual, 2000; student workbook, 2005.

Publisher: U.S. Military Entrance Processing Command, 2500 Green Bay Road, North Chicago, IL 60064.

O*NET Ability Profiler

U.S. Department of Labor

Purpose: The Ability Profiler (AP) is designed to help individuals identify occupations that fit their strengths as well as areas where they might want to engage in more training. It measures (1) Verbal Ability, (2) Arithmetic Reasoning, (3) Computation, (4) Spatial Ability, (5) Form Perception, (6) Clerical Perception, (7) Motor Coordination, (8) Finger Dexterity, and (9) Manual Dexterity. Administration takes two to three hours if both paper-and-pencil and apparatus sections are administered. The paper-and-pencil sections take one and a half to two hours to administer. The results of the AP are reported on computer-generated, customized score reports that include O*NET links and data. The U.S. Department of Labor indicates that AP information can be used in conjunction with other O*NET tools. The AP can be downloaded and printed along with support material (www.onetcenter.org/AP.html).

Target Population: High school students and adults.

Date of Publication: 2002.

Publisher: U.S. Department of Labor. Available online through the O*NET Center Website (www.onetcenter.org).

SUPPORT FOR MULTIPLE APTITUDE TEST BATTERIES   Support for the use of all aptitude tests was probably summed up best by Anastasi and Urbina's (1997) and Gregory's (2006) discussions of the Differential Aptitude Test (DAT). They observed that the support for the predictive validity of the DAT is relatively high when the criterion is success in high school, academic, and/or vocational education programs and quite modest when used to predict success in specific occupations. Ghiselli (1973) reviewed research prior to 1965 and concluded that the average correlation between test scores and educational performance was in the order of .30 and for occupational proficiency about .20. However, as Hogan, DeSoto, and Solano (1977) noted, average correlations are of little value, and in some instances validity coefficients for occupational performance reach .60. Career counselors should carefully inspect validity studies to determine whether the test being used has adequate predictive validity generally and whether the norm groups are sufficiently representative to include the client with whom they are working. It is also important to keep in mind that even if a validity coefficient approaches .60, only 36 percent of the variance associated with performance is being accounted for by the test, and thus a combination of other variables, such as work or study habits, motivation, family support, and person–environment, are likely to be more important than aptitude to the success of the individual.

DIAGNOSTIC INVENTORIES   A number of inventories have been developed to measure certain career development "problems." These inventories are often used in research but also have reliability in determining problems that may limit or retard the career development or career decision-making process.

Career Decision Scale (CDS)

Samuel H. Osipow

> *Purpose:* The CDS provides explanatory information regarding a failure to make career decisions. It yields two scale scores: (1) Certainty and (2) Indecision. The scales provide an estimate of indecision as well as data regarding the antecedents of indecision.
>
> *Target Population:* High school through adult. Norms available on high school students, college students, continuing education students, and returning adults.
>
> *Date of Publication:* Most recent edition, 1987.
>
> *Publisher:* Psychological Assessment Resources, 1604 N. Florida Avenue, Lutz, FL 33549.

My Vocational Situation

John L. Holland, Denise C. Daiger, and Paul G. Power

> *Purpose:* My Vocational Situation was developed primarily to identify lack of vocational identity, but it also provides information about lack of information and environmental or personal barriers to occupational choice. Three scale scores (Vocational Identity, Occupational Information, and Barriers) provide evidence regarding these areas.
>
> *Target Population:* High school through adult. Norm groups made up of high school students through adult.
>
> *Date of Publication:* All information, 1980.
>
> *Publisher:* Psychological Assessment Resources, 16204 North Florida Avenue, Lutz, FL 33549.

Career Beliefs Inventory

John D. Krumboltz

Purpose: This inventory assists individuals in identifying problematic self-perceptions and worldviews.

Target Population: High school students through adults.

Date of Publication: All documents, 1988.

Publisher: Consulting Psychologists Press, 3803 East Bayshore Road, Palo Alto, CA 94303.

Career Thoughts Inventory

James P. Sampson, Jr., Gary W. Peterson, Janet G. Lenz, Robert Reardon, and Denise E. Saunders

Purpose: This inventory provides career counselors with a means of identifying dysfunctional thinking in career problem solving and decision making. The instrument yields a single global score of dysfunctional thinking and problem solving in the career decision–making and problem–solving areas. It also yields three construct scales: (1) Decision-Making Confusion, (2) Commitment Anxiety, and (3) External Conflict. The instrument can be completed by most students in 7 to 15 minutes. The manual identifies methods for dealing with the concerns identified by the instrument.

Target Population: High school and college students and adults.

Dates of Publication: 1994; latest revision, 1996.

Publisher: Psychological Assessment Resources, 16204 North Florida Avenue, Lutz, FL 33549.

SUPPORT FOR DIAGNOSTIC INVENTORIES   The aforementioned diagnostic inventories fall into two categories: (1) those that can be used to measure normal development, such as the Career Development Inventory, and (2) those that can be used to diagnose some aspect of abnormal development, such as the Career Decision Scale. Psychologists and counselors have generally been concerned with both of these areas, although recent research has focused on diagnosing decisional difficulties.

With two exceptions, the diagnostic inventories described should probably not be used for any purpose other than research because their authors and others have failed to produce the necessary criterion-related empirical support to justify their usage. The exceptions to this recommendation are the Career Decision Scale (CDS) and the Career Thoughts Inventory. Numerous studies (Fuqua, Blum, & Hartman, 1988; Hartman, Fuqua, & Blum, 1984; Hartman, Fuqua, & Hartman, 1983) have demonstrated that the CDS may be a useful tool when used as a preliminary screening device to differentiate undecided clients, who can benefit from traditional career counseling strategies such as testing and the provision of occupational information, and indecisive clients, who have decisional difficulties that must be addressed prior to using traditional strategies. Studies (Fuqua, Blum, Newman, & Seaworth, 1988; Larsen, Heppner, Harm, & Dugan, 1988; Vondracek, Hostetler, Schulenberg, & Shimiza, 1990), as well as some of the previous studies, suggest that the constructs *undecidedness* and *indecisive* have correlates in other personality variables, such as *anxiety* and *locus of control*. With regard to the CTI, Feller and Daly (2009) report that the CTI provides career counselors with a model that allows counselors to facilitate the process by which clients talk back to their dysfunctional thoughts. However, they caution that the CTI may have limited utility with high school students because of reliability issues.

MULTIPURPOSE TESTS AND INVENTORIES Most tests and inventories are designed to measure a single construct (e.g., career interests) or dimensions of a construct (e.g., aptitudes). However, a few tests and inventories have been developed to measure more than one construct (e.g., interests and aptitudes). A few of the potentially useful ones are presented here.

Occupational Aptitude Survey and Interest Schedule (OASIS)

Randall M. Parker

> *Purpose:* The OASIS was developed to help junior and senior high school students engage in career planning. The instrument yields scores in 12 interest scales: (1) Artistic, (2) Scientific, (3) Nature, (4) Protective, (5) Mechanical, (6) Industrial, (7) Business Detail, (8) Selling, (9) Accommodating, (10) Humanitarian, (11) Leading–Influencing, and (12) Physical Performing. It also provides measures of five aptitudes: (1) General Ability, (2) Perceptual Aptitudes, (3) Spatial Aptitudes, (4) Numerical Aptitudes, and (5) Verbal Aptitudes.

> *Target Population:* Students in grades 8 through 12; norm groups made up of twelfth graders.

> *Date of Publication:* All documents, 2001.

> *Publisher:* PRO-ED, 8700 Creek Boulevard, Austin, TX 78757.

McCarron–Dial System (MDS)

Lawrence T. McCarron and Jack G. Dial

> *Purpose:* The MDS was developed for use with special education and rehabilitation groups. It yields five scores: (1) Verbal–Spatial–Cognitive, (2) Sensory, (3) Motor, (4) Emotional, and (5) Integration–Coping. The basic purpose of the MDS is to predict how clients will function after training, and it is an instrument that can be used in counseling or placement activities. The actual subtests included in the battery are the Peabody Picture Vocabulary Test, Bender Visual Motor Gestalt Test, Behavior Rating Scale, Observational Emotional Inventory, Haptic Visual Discrimination Test, and McCarron Assessment of Neuromuscular Development.

> *Target Population:* Adolescents and adults who have learning disabilities, emotional disturbances, cognitive disabilities, cerebral palsy, head injuries, or social disadvantages.

> Norms are available for target groups.

> *Date of Publication:* User's manual, 1986.

> *Publisher:* McCarron–Dial Systems, PO Box 45628, Dallas, TX 75245.

PESCO 2001/ Online

Chuck Loch, Charles Kass, and Joseph Kass

> *Purpose:* PESCO is used as a screening instrument that produces scores in (1) Reading, (2) Math, (3) Language–GED Levels, (4) General Verbal, (5) Numerical Spatial, (6) Form, (7) Clerical Finger, (8) Eye–Hand–Foot, (9) Color Discrimination, (10) Motor Coordination, (11) Vocational Interest, (12) Learning Styles, (13) Job Temperament, (14) Work Ethics, and (15) Work Attitude. There are 13 timed and four untimed units for measuring math, reasoning, and language skills, and 11 untimed subtests that measure the other variables included in the battery.
>
> *Target Population:* Students in grades 8 through 12, employed workers, welfare recipients, clients with disabilities, and vocational–technical students.
>
> *Date of Publication:* 2001
>
> *Publisher:* PESCO International, 21 Paulding Avenue, Pleasantville, NY 10570 (http://www.kazette.com/pesco2001.htm.)

SUPPORT FOR MULTIPURPOSE TESTS AND INVENTORIES   Multipurpose inventories have been developed for specific purposes, typically for use with special populations. Test manuals should be consulted to determine whether the inventory is appropriate for the client and if the psychometric characteristics of the inventory justify its use.

SELECTING ASSESSMENT DEVICES

Career counselors may select from among hundreds of tests, inventories, and qualitative assessment strategies. Schwiebert (2009) outlined a step-by-step procedure for selecting appropriate assessment devices beginning first with the user's and technical manual and comparing the needs of the client with the purpose of the instrument being considered. Once the client's needs and the purpose of the instrument are aligned, the technical characteristics of the instrument should be examined. Reliability and validity issues and the representativeness of the norm groups deserve special consideration. The ethical principles developed by the American Counseling Association (ACA, 2005) and the American Psychological Association (APA, 2002) as well as documents such as *The Responsibilities of Users of Standardized Tests* (AAC, 2003) The responsibilities of users of standardized tests should guide the final steps in the selection process of both objective and qualitative assessment devices. Specifically, counselors must be competent in the use of any assessment device selected; the welfare of the client must be maintained as the uppermost consideration when selecting an assessment strategy; and cultural and gender issues must be carefully weighed prior to using an assessment approach with a client. However, some additional guidelines are outlined in more specific terms in the next sections.

Technical Qualities

The reliability, validity, and representativeness of the norm group (standardization) are of utmost importance in the selection of tests and inventories. The exact type of reliability (test–retest versus internal consistency) is, to some degree, determined by the type of test or inventory, but test–retest reliability is generally preferred when measuring those traits of importance in career planning.

Both predictive and construct validity are of concern to career counselors, although the degree of importance of each is determined by the purpose of the test. If the test is to be used for screening purposes or placement, predictive validity is of utmost importance. Construct validity becomes particularly important when one purpose of the assessment is to promote self-awareness. For example, the Self-Directed Search was developed by Holland (1994) to measure his theoretical personality types. These types and their descriptions became important aspects of the way students and adults see themselves, and thus any inventory purporting to measure Holland types should have construct validity. These inventories should also have predictive validity, but construct validity is the first consideration.

Gender and Cultural Bias

Gender and culture bias have received widespread attention in the counseling literature. Thirty years ago, Tittle and Zytowski (1980) provided a full discussion of gender issues in assessing interest. More recently, Lonner (1988), Mehrens (2002), and Peterson and Gonzalez (2005) discussed the cross-cultural issues in testing and assessment. At the center of these discussions is the question, "Do the tests used by career counselors produce information that may mislead either the person taking the test or persons (e.g., personnel managers) who may use tests to make decisions?" (Sundberg & Gonzales, 1981, p. 482).

It is probably fair to say that tests and inventories are biased to some degree but that most counselors attempt to use these products in a nondiscriminatory fashion. There are, of course, a number of legal prohibitions against the use of tests in a discriminatory manner, particularly in the employment process. The Equal Employment Opportunity Act (Title VII of the Civil Rights Act of 1964) and its subsequent amendments (Anastasi & Urbina, 1997) prohibits the use of inventories that do not include rigorous studies of predictive validity. Professional and ethical standards regarding the use of tests have also been developed and published and prohibit the use of biased assessment practices.

Obviously, career development workers need to avoid using inventories and tests that have not been developed properly. However, even given the safeguards built into the development of tests and the legal prohibitions against using them inappropriately, subtle forms of bias do exist in the use of tests and inventories, particularly as they relate to minorities. The sections that follow focus on the concerns that must be addressed in the assessment process if bias is to minimized.

THE TEST OR INVENTORY ITSELF   The relevance of the content of the assessment device is a major concern when assessing minorities, women, and clients who are culturally isolated, such as those from certain parts of Appalachia or other rural areas (Peterson & Gonzalez, 2005). If the following question is posed—Are you more interested in going to an art gallery or reading quietly at home?—a number of clients who never had any experience with art galleries or a quiet place to read may begin to see the entire process as irrelevant to them. Similarly, the question— Would you rather repair a small engine or complete a crossword puzzle?—is biased against many females who have not been accorded the opportunity to repair a small engine and against those people who do not receive newspapers and may have had little opportunity to do crossword puzzles. Careful examination of the content of tests and inventories as well as a thorough knowledge of the people to whom the devices are to be given is perhaps the only way to avoid this subtle form of bias.

THE TESTING PROCESS Anastasi and Urbina (1997) pointed out a number of factors that contribute to bias in the assessment process, including lack of previous experience with assessment; lack of motivation to do well or to present a representative picture of self; and the inability of the test administrator to establish rapport, particularly with culturally different people. However, Anastasi and Urbina indicate that the most important consideration in assessment pertains to the interpretation of the results. The interpretation process is discussed in detail later in this chapter.

DIFFERENTIAL PREDICTION One of the legitimate complaints about tests such as the Scholastic Aptitude Test and other tests of scholastic aptitude by members of minority groups is that they are biased in favor of white, middle-class students. One way to look at this issue is by answering the question, Does the test and/or inventory predict a criterion, such as grades, differentially? If it does, it is biased and should not be used with minority clients.

NORMING (STANDARDIZATION) BIAS The Interest Finder (IF), which is a part of the U.S. Department of Defense–sponsored ASVAB career exploration program, contains norms for males and females. For these norms to be useful, they must contain a representative sample of men and women. Unless this is the case (which is the case with the IF), the test or inventory should not be used.

LANGUAGE Many of the bias issues in assessment can be summed up in a single word: *language.* Obviously clients, whose primary language is not English, may not score as well on tests of maximum performance and may not respond to words and phrases in a manner that produces accurate responses on inventories that are designed to produce profiles of typical interests or personality variables. However, socioeconomically disadvantaged individuals and individuals raised out of the mainstream of U.S. culture may also have language deficiencies that produce biased results. Many groups of minorities live in culturally encapsulated areas. Hispanics who spend most of their time speaking Spanish may become victims rather than the beneficiaries of the assessment process, as may Native Americans who live in remote regions of Arizona, New Mexico, and South Dakota. As mentioned in Chapter 4, career counselors need to be particularly careful when using any techniques that require high levels of self-disclosure with Native Americans and Asian Americans because of their concern about self-control. Assessment may become an alienating process for these groups if questions are too personal.

Language bias can also spill over into the interpretation process and preclude the client from gaining an understanding of the results of the test. It is important to recall that a client who speaks English as a second language or is disadvantaged in any way has at least two "opportunities" to be discriminated against in the assessment process. The first of these is during the assessment process itself; the second is in the interpretative process. These concerns have prompted many career counselors to turn to qualitative assessment procedures. However, even qualitative assessment is subject to bias. For example, using a card sort that contains occupational titles or values on the cards or a genogram that asks clients who have high concerns about self-disclosure about their families may produce biased information. The bottom line is a simple one. Great caution needs to be exercised in the assessment process, particularly with minority clients and clients who have language deficits or are concerned about self-disclosure.

At least one other issue related to cultural bias should be raised: the use of Internet-based assessment and computer-assisted career guidance system (CACGS) to deliver assessment devices. Several authors (e.g., Oliver & Zack, 1999; Robinson, Meyer, Prince, McLean, & Low,

2000) have been critical of Internet-based assessment because of a concern for cultural and other issues. In addition to the usual concerns about reliability and validity of computer-delivered assessment services, a related concern, involves experience (or lack thereof) with computers and the Internet and it may play a role in the assessment process. Soh and Leong (2001) also raise the issue that people from different cultures may attach different meanings to identical results based on their cultural experiences. Furthermore, they present some preliminary research suggesting that college students from Singapore and the United States who have a type I in their Holland profiles do, in fact, interpret that type differently. Clearly, concerns about cultural biases that may exist in computer-assisted assessment warrant extensive exploration.

When an inventory includes questions oriented to middle-class whites, it is clearly culturally biased (Fouad, 1993; Lonner, 1988). There are numerous other sources of cultural bias, including language used and making assumptions about the motivation to take the test. The possibility that the norm group used is inappropriate because of underrepresentation of minorities can also be a problem (Lonner, 1988; Peterson & Gonzalez, 2005). Moreover, when items are selected that are outside the experiences of females or, because of gender-role socialization, interact negatively with past experiences, the test or inventory is gender biased.

Other Issues

The time needed to take the test or inventory, the cost, the reading level, the availability of computerized or hand scoring, and the counselor's preference are all factors to take into consideration when selecting tests or inventories.

INTERPRETING TEST AND INVENTORY RESULTS

The interpretation of test results may be the most important step in the assessment process (Goodyear, 1990). Five approaches to interpretation of quantitative assessment devices may be used. Computerized interpretations (e.g., SII), self-interpretation using materials provided by the publisher (e.g., SDS), interactive approaches in which the client leads, interactive approaches in which the counselor leads, and combinations of these approaches. Goodyear compared counselor-led and client-led interpretational approaches and found no difference in the amount of information gained. However, clients appeared to prefer counselor-led approaches. Hanson, Claiborn, and Kerr (2001) studied the same issue and their findings echoed those of Goodyear.

The first step in the interpretation process is for the counselor to become thoroughly familiar with the instrument (Andersen & Vanderhey, 2006; Tinsley & Bradley, 1986, 1988). This may involve reviewing the technical and counselor's manual, but perhaps the best initial approach is actually to take the test or inventory to be interpreted. This familiarization process should involve reviewing norms if they are available, identifying any cultural or gender issues or limitations that may arise, and reviewing the statistical concepts used.

The second step is to review the results of the tests and inventories prior to meeting with the client. If more than one assessment device has been administered, the results of each device should be inspected, compared, and contrasted. Counselors should anticipate issues that may arise in the interpretational process, such as discrepancies that are evident in the results.

The third step in interpreting the results of tests and inventories is to consider the clients involved. If there are language barriers, should a person fluent in the language of the client be involved? What are the client's values? What are their preferred verbal and nonverbal communication styles? Who should receive the results? If the family or group is involved, are there likely to be conflicts about the implications of the results for the career plan? Should the counselor present and interpret the results or should the client be the one who does the interpretation of the results? These questions can only be answered if the career counselor is familiar with the individual and his or her cultural context.

Once tentative answers to the foregoing questions are determined, a plan for interpreting the assessment results can be formulated. Prince and Heiser (2000), in their excellent book on interpretation, provide specific guidelines for interpreting three popular interest inventories: the Campbell Interest and Skills Survey, the Strong Interest Inventory, and the Self-Directed Search. The general steps in the interpretation process that follow are based to some degree on an amalgamation of their ideas.

1. Check to see if any unusual factors influenced the client during the administration of the instrument, such as personal or family issues, illness, and so forth.
2. Check to see if the client was motivated during the test. Did language or assessment conditions influence performance?
3. Provide an overview of the instrument to be interpreted. What are its purposes?
4. Give a brief description of the scales and what they mean.
5. Check for understanding.
6. Explain how scores are presented (e.g., percentiles) and present scores.
7. Check for agreement with the results.
8. Interpret the scores or allow the client to make his or her own interpretation.
9. Compare assessment results with information gained qualitatively in the interview, such as sources of frustration and satisfaction, best and least liked subjects, and information about abilities. Are the results consistent with real-life events?
10. Troubleshoot as necessary.
    a. *Flat, low-interest inventory profile.* Is this the result of experience? Lack of planning? Information about training or careers? Safeguarding because of fear of discrimination? Gender or racial stereotyping of careers? Personal issues, such as low self-esteem? Mental health issues? Are there conflicts with family or group expectations? Remedies include using occupational information, interviews with workers, job shadowing, debunking gender and racial stereotypes, developing planning skills, and personal counseling.
    b. *Too many options.* Some SDS profiles may result in more than 50 occupational options. Is the client multipotentialed? Is the client reluctant to check *dislike* as an option on the SII (Prince & Heiser, 2000)? Remedies include using values as an additional means of eliminating options and discussion of crafting a lifestyle that enables individuals to satisfy interests in roles other than work.
    c. *Conflicts in the family or group.* Is acculturation an issue? Are there misperceptions about the skills and abilities needed to enter a training program or occupation? Remedies include explaining values, mediation, and using information such as O*NET regarding the skills and abilities needed for success in an occupation.
    d. *Bad news.* Aptitude tests may yield scores that are lower than the expectations of the client, and interest inventories profiles may not match those of preferred occupations. Remedies include explanations about other measures of interests (e.g., stated, manifest) and their validity, and explanations of testing error. Also, Super's idea that each occupation is broad enough to accommodate a wide range of people may be considered. Interviews with workers and job shadowing may also be helpful. Finally, Tinsley and

Bradley (1988) suggest that tests and inventory results not be viewed as "the last word." Motivation can overcome aptitude in many instances and interest inventories rarely predict a great deal of the variance associated with occupational success.

11. Complete the interpretation with a summary of the results and by providing self-interpreting material that can be used for future reference by the client.

Summary

Assessment is an essential ingredient in career counseling and other career development activities aimed at promoting self-understanding. However, unlike some activities associated with career development, the appropriate use of tests requires a high level of expertise that must be gained through careful training and supervision. It is inappropriate for untrained people to use tests and inventories for any purpose.

The two approaches to assessment discussed in this chapter, qualitative and quantitative, are both important and have long been used by career counselors.

It may be that the effective use of qualitative assessment procedures requires a higher level of clinical skill because fewer guidelines are provided to guide this work. However, both qualitative and quantitative approaches require counselors to be sensitive to issues related to race, ethnicity, gender, and socioeconomic status if they are to be used appropriately. Moreover, if these approaches are to be used effectively with the counseling process for any group, a high level of counseling skills is a prerequisite to administering and interpreting tests and inventories.

Chapter Quiz

T F **1.** The interest in testing and assessment has waned since 2000 because of the influence of postmodern career counselors.

T F **2.** Computers are extremely useful tools in the assessment process, but their utility is confined to routine tasks such as scoring.

T F **3.** Self-efficacy measures can be adapted for use in either quantitative or qualitative assessment.

T F **4.** The original use of the genogram was in genealogical studies.

T F **5.** Postmodern career counselors prefer clinical assessment to qualitative assessment because of its phenomenological basis.

T F **6.** Generally speaking psychometricians would prefer that an inventory have construct validity as opposed to predictive validity.

T F **7.** The Self-Directed Search, the Harrington-O'Shea Career Decision Making Inventory, and the Interest Profiler all produce scores based on Holland's theory.

T F **8.** The O*NET Ability Profiler is actually an aptitude test.

T F **9.** Cultural bias in an assessment device occurs primarily because of the norming process.

T F **10.** Unfortunately, there are no interest inventories available for clients who either have language deficits of cannot read.

(1) F (2) F (3) T (4) F (5) F (6) F (7) T (8) T (9) F (10) F

References

Association for Assessment in Counseling (2003) Responsibilities of Users of Standardized Tests (3rd Ed.) Alexandria, VA: author

American Counseling Association (2005). *ACA code of ethics and standards of practice*. Alexandria, VA: Author.

American Psychological Association. (2002). Ethical principles of psychologists and code of conduct. Washington, DC: Author.

Anastasi, A., & Urbina, G. (1997). *Psychological testing* (7th ed.). New York: Macmillan.

Andersen, P., & Vanderhey, M. (2006) *Career Counseling and Development in a Global Economy*. Boston: Houghton Mifflin.

Association for Assessment in Counseling (2003). *The Responsibilities of users of Standardized Tests* (3rd ed.). Alexandria, VA: Author.

Bandura, A. (1977). Toward a unifying theory of behavior change. *Psychological Review, 89,* 191–125.

Bandura, A. (1986). *Social foundations of thought and action: A social–cognitive theory.* Englewood Cliffs, NJ: Prentice Hall.

Betz, N. E. (2000). Self-efficacy theory as a basis of career assessment. *Journal of Career Assessment, 8,* 205–222.

Betz, N. E., & Borgen, F. H. (2000). The future of career assessment: Integrating interests with self-efficacy and personal styles. *Journal of Career Assessment, 8,* 329–338.

Betz, N. E., Borgen, F. H., & Harmon, L. (2005). *Skills Confidence Inventory Applications and Technical Guide* (2nd ed.) Palo Alto, CA: Consulting Psychologists Press.

Betz, N. E., & Hackett, G. (1981). The relationship of career-related self-efficacy expectations to perceived career options in college women and men. *Journal of Counseling Psychology, 28,* 399–410.

Betz, N. E., & Hackett, G. (1986). Applications of self-efficacy theory to understanding career choice behavior. *Journal of Social and Clinical Psychology, 4,* 279–289.

Betz, N. E., & Taylor, K. M. (2001). *Career Decision Self-Efficacy Scale: Technical Manual.* Worthington, OH: Author.

Blocher, D. H. (1987). *The professional counselor.* New York: Macmillan.

Brott, P. E. (2001). A storied approach: A postmodern perspective for career counseling. *Career Development Quarterly, 49,* 304–313.

Brown D. (1990). Trait and factor theory. In D. Brown, L. Brooks, et al. (Eds.), *Career choice and development* (2nd ed., pp. 13–36). San Francisco: Jossey-Bass.

Brown, D., & Brooks, L. (1991). *Career counseling techniques.* Boston: Allyn & Bacon.

Brown, D., Ware, W. B., & Brown, S. T. (1985). A predictive validation of the career decision–making inventory. *Measurement and Evaluation in Counseling and Development, 18,* 81–85.

Chope, R. C. (2008). Practice and research in career counseling and development. *The Career Development Quarterly, 57,* 198–173.

Cochran, L. (1983). Implicit versus explicit importance of career values in making a career decision. *Journal of Counseling Psychology, 30,* 188–193.

Crites, J. O. (1969). *Vocational psychology.* New York: McGraw-Hill.

Dewey, C. R. (1974). Exploring interests: The nonsexist card sort. *Personnel and Guidance Journal, 52,* 348–351.

Dolliver, R. H. (1967). An adaptation of the Tyler Vocational Card Sort. *Personnel and Guidance Journal, 45,* 916–920.

Donnay, D. A., & Borgen, F. H. (1999). The incremental validity of vocational self-efficacy: An examination of interest, efficacy, and occupation. *Journal of Counseling Psychology, 46,* 432–447.

Feller, R. W., & Daly, J. (2009). Career Thoughts Inventory :Review. In *A Counselor's Guide to Career Assessment Instrument* (5th ed., pp. 352–355). Broken Arrow, OK: National Career Development Association.

Fouad, N. A. (1993). Cross-cultural vocational assessment. *Vocational Guidance Quarterly, 42,* 4–13.

Fuqua, D. R., Blum, C. R., & Hartman, B. W. (1988). Empirical support for the diagnosis of career indecision. *Vocational Guidance Quarterly, 36,* 363–373.

Fuqua, D. R., Blum, C. R., Newman, J. L., & Seaworth, T. B. (1988). *Journal of Counseling, 35,* 154–158.

Galassi, M. D., Jones, L. K., & Britt, M. N. (1985). Nontraditional career options for women: An evaluation of career guidance instruments. *Vocational Guidance Quarterly, 34,* 124–130.

Gault, F. M., & Myers, H. H. (1987). A comparison of two career-planning inventories. *Career Development Quarterly, 35,* 332–336.

Ghiselli, E. E. (1973). The validity of aptitude tests in personnel selection. *Personnel Psychology, 26,* 461–477.

Gibson, D. M. (2005). The use of genograms in career counseling with elementary, middle, and high school students. *Career Development Quarterly, 53,* 178–186.

Goldman, L. (1972). Tests and counseling: The marriage that failed. *Measurement and Evaluation in Guidance, 4,* 213–220.

Goldman, L. (1982). Assessment in counseling: A better way. *Measurement and Evaluation in Guidance, 4,* 213–220.

Goldman, L. (1990). Qualitative assessment. *The Counseling Psychologist, 18,* 205–213.

Goodyear, R. K. (1990). Research on the effects of test interpretation: A review. *The Counseling Psychologist, 18,* 240–257.

Gottfredson, G. D., & Holland, J. L. (1975). Vocational choices of men and women: A comparison of predictors from the Self-Directed Search. *Journal of Applied Psychology, 22,* 28–34.

Gregory, R. J. (2006). *Psychological testing: History, principles and applications* (5th ed.). Boston: Allyn & Bacon.

Gupta, S.,Tracey, T. J. G., & Gore, P. A. (2008). Structural examination of RIASEC scales in high school students: Variations across ethnicity and methods. *Journal of Vocational Behavior, 72,* 1–13.

Gysbers, N. C., & Moore, E. J. (1987). *Career counseling: Skills and techniques for practitioners.* Englewood Cliffs, NJ: Prentice Hall.

Hansen, J. C., Scullard, M. G., & Haviland, M. G. (2000). The interest structure of Native American college students. *Journal of Career Assessment, 8,* 159–172.

Hansen, J. C., & Swanson, J. L. (1983). Stability of interests and predictive and concurrent validity of the 1981 Strong–Cambell Interest Inventory for college majors. *Journal of Counseling Psychology, 30,* 194–201.

Hanson, W. E., Claiborn, C. D., & Kerr, B. (2001). Differential effects of two approaches to test interpretation: A field study. In C. E. Hill (Ed.), *Helping skills: The empirical foundation.* Washington, DC: American Psychological Association.

Hartman, B. W., Fuqua, D. R., & Blum, C. R. (1984). A path-analytic model of indecision. *Vocational Guidance Quarterly, 33,* 231–240.

Hartman, B. W., Fuqua, D. R., & Hartman, P. T. (1983). The predictive potential of the Career Decision Scale in identifying chronic career indecision. *Vocational Guidance Quarterly, 32,* 103–108.

Healy, C. C. (1990). Reforming career appraisals to meet the needs of clients in the 1990s. *The Counseling Psychologist, 18,* 214–226.

Hogan, R., DeSoto, C. B., & Solano, C. (1977). Traits, tests, and personality research. *American Psychologist, 32,* 255–264.

Holland, J. L. (1982). The SDS helps both females and males: A comment. *Vocational Guidance Quarterly, 30,* 195–197.

Holland, J. L. (1985). *Making vocational choices: A theory of vocational personalities and work environments* (2nd ed.). Englewood Cliffs, NJ: Prentice Hall.

Holland, J. L. (1994). *Manual—Self-Directed Search.* Odessa, FL: Psychological Assessment Resources.

Holland, J. L. (1997). *Making vocational choices: A theory of vocational personalities and work environments* (3rd ed.). Odessa, FL: Psychological Association Resources.

Holland, J. L., Gottfredson, G. D., & Baker, H. G. (1990). Validity of vocational aspirations and interest inventories, extended, replicated, and reinterpreted. *Journal of Counseling Psychology, 37,* 337–342.

Holland, J. L., Gottfredson, G. D., & Gottfredson, L. S. (1975). Read our reports and examine the data: A response to Prediger and Cole. *Journal of Vocational Behavior, 7,* 253–259.

Ivey, A. E. (1982). Toward less of the same. Rethinking the assessment process. *Measurement and Evaluation in Guidance, 15,* 82–86.

Johnson, R. W., & Hoese, J. C. (1988). Career planning concerns of SCII clients. *Journal of Career Development, 36,* 251–258.

Jones, L. K., Gorman, S., & Schroeder, C. G. (1989). A comparison of the SDS and career key among undecided college students. *Career Development Quarterly, 37,* 334–344.

Kapes, J. T., & Whitfield, E. A. (Eds.). (2002). *A counselor's guide to career assessment instruments* (4th ed.). Tulsa, OK: National Career Development Association.

Knapp, R. R., & Knapp, L. (1979). Relationship of work values to occupational activity interests. *Measurement and Evaluation in Guidance, 12,* 71–76.

Knowdell, R. L. (1998). Career values card sort kit. San Jose, CA: Career Research and Testing.

Larsen, L. M., Heppner, P. P., Harm, T., & Dugan, K. (1988). Investigating multiple subtypes of career indecision through cluster analysis. *Journal of Counseling Psychology, 35,* 439–446.

Leong, F. T. L. (1991). Career development attributes and occupational values of Asian American and white college students.*Career Development Quarterly, 39,* 221–230.

Leong, F. T. L., & Hartung, P. J. (2000). Crosscultural career assessment: Review and prospects for the new millennium. *Journal of Career Assessment, 8,* 391–402.

Leung, S. A., & Hou, Z. (2001). Concurrent validity of the 1994 Self-Directed Search for Chinese high school students in Hong Kong. *Journal of Career Assessment, 8,* 282–296.

Lonner, W. J. (1988). Issues in testing and assessment in cross-cultural counseling. *The Counseling Psychologist, 18,* 599–614.

Lucas, J. L., Wanberg, C. R., & Zytowski, D. G. (1997). Development of a career self-efficacy scale. *Journal of Vocational Behavior, 50,* 437–459.

Luzzo, D. A., & Taylor, M. (1994). Effects of verbal persuasion on the career self-efficacy of college freshmen. *California Journal of Counseling and Development, 14,* 31–34.

Malott, K. M., & Magnuson, S. (2004). Using genograms to facilitate undergraduate students' career development: A group model. *Career Development Quarterly, 53,* 353–362.

McGoldrick, M., & Gerson, R. (1985). *Genograms in family assessment.* New York: Norton.

McGoldrick, M., Shellenberger, S. & Perry, S. (2008). *Genograms Assessment and Intervention.* New York: Norton.

Mehrens, W. A. (2002). Selecting a career assessment instrument. In J. T. Kapes & E. A. Whitfield (Eds.), *A counselor's guide to career assessment instruments* (4th ed., pp. 27–34). Tulsa, OK: National Career Development Association.

Myers, I.B., & McCawley, D. (1998). *BTI manual* (3rd ed.). Palo Alto, CA: Consulting Psychologist Press.

Noeth, R. J. (1983). The effects of enhancing expressed vocational choice with career development measures to predict occupational field. *Journal of Vocational Behavior, 22,* 365–375.

Okiishi, R. W. (1987). The genogram as a tool in career counseling. *Journal of Counseling and Development, 66,* 139–143.

Oliver, L. W., & Zack, J. S. (1999). Career assessment on the Internet. *Journal of Career Assessment, 7,* 323–336.

Parsons, F. (1909). *Choosing a vocation.* Boston: Houghton Mifflin.

Patton, W., & McIlven, P. (2009). Practice and research in career counseling and development—2008. *Career Development Quarterly, 58.* 116–161.

Peterson, N., & Gonzalez, R. C. (2005). *The role of work in people's lives: Applied career counseling and vocational psychology.* Pacific Grove, CA: Brooks/Cole.

Prediger, D. J. (1974). The role of assessment in career guidance. In E. L. Herr (Ed.), *Vocational guidance and human development* (pp. 325– 349). Boston: Houghton Mifflin.

Prediger, D. J. (1981). A note on Self-Directed Search validity for females. *Vocational Guidance Quarterly, 30,* 117–129.

Prediger, D. J. (2001). Assessment in career counseling. In G. R. Walz & J. C. Bleuer (Eds.), *Assessment: Issues and challenges for the millennium* (pp. 329–334). Greensboro, NC: ERIC-CASS.

Prince, J. P., & Heiser, L. J. (2000). *Essentials of career interest assessment.* New York: Wiley.

Pryor, R. G. L., & Taylor, N. B. (1980). On combining scores from interest and value measures for counseling. *Vocational Guidance Quarterly, 34,* 178–187.

Robinson, N. K., Meyer, D., Prince, J. P., McClean, C., & Low, R. (2000). Mining the Internet for career information: A model approach for college students. *Journal of Career Assessment, 8,* 37–54.

Rokeach, M. (1973). *The nature of human values.* New York: Free Press.

Rokeach, M. (1979). *Understanding human values: Individual and societal.* New York: Free Press.

Rotberg, H. L. (1984). *Career self-efficacy expectations and perceived range of career options in community college*

students. Unpublished doctoral dissertation, University of North Carolina, Chapel Hill.

Rotberg, H. L., Brown, D., & Ware, W. B. (1987). Career self-efficacy expectation and perceived range of career options in community college students. *Journal of Counseling Psychology, 34,* 164–170.

Rottinghaus, R. J., Coon, K. L., Gaffey, A. B., & Zytowski, D. G. (2007). Thirty-year stability and predictive validity of vocational interests. *Journal of Career Assessment, 15,* 5–22.

Rounds, J., & Tracey, T. J. (1996). Cross-cultural structural equivalence of the RIASEC models and measures. *Journal of Counseling Psychology, 43,* 310–329.

Sampson, J. P., Jr. (1990). Computer-assisted testing and the goals of counseling psychology. *The Counseling Psychologist, 18,* 227–234.

Sampson, J. P., Jr. (2001). Using the Internet to enhance test interpretation. In G. R. Walz & J. C. Bleuer (Eds.), *Assessment: Issues and challenges for the millennium* (pp. 189–202). Greensboro, NC: ERIC-CASS.

Sampson, J. P., Jr., Carr, D. L., Lunsden, J. A., Smission, C. & Dozier, C. (2009). Computer-assisted career assessment: State of the art. In *A counselor's guide to Career assessment instruments* (5th ed., pp. 43–60). Broken Arrow, OK: National Career development Association.

Savickas, M. L. (1984). Career maturity: The construct and its measurements. *Vocational Guidance Quarterly, 32,* 222–231.

Schwiebert, V. L. (2009). Selecting a career assessment instrument. In E. A. Whitfield, R. W. Feller, & C. Wood, *A counselor's guide to career assessment instruments* (5th ed., pp. 27–34.) Broken Arrow, OK: National Career Development Association.

Slaney, R. B., & Slaney, F. M. (1986). Relationship of expressed and inventoried vocational interests of female career counseling clients. *Career Development Quarterly, 35,* 24–33.

Soh, S., & Leong, F. T. L. (2001). Cross-cultural validity of Holland's theory in Singapore: Beyond structural validity of RIASEC. *Journal of Career Assessment, 9,* 115–134.

Srebalus, D. J., & Brown, D. (2001). *A guide to the helping professions.* Boston: Allyn & Bacon.

Sundberg, N. D., & Gonzales, L. R. (1981). Crosscultural and cross-ethnic assessment: Overview and issues. In P. McReynolds (Ed.), *Advances in psychological assessment* (Vol. 5, pp. 475–491). San Francisco: Jossey-Bass.

Super, D. E. (1957). *The psychology of careers.* New York: HarperCollins.

Super, D. E. (1990). A life-span approach to career development. In D. Brown & L. Brooks (Eds.), *Career choice and development* (2nd ed., pp. 107–261). San Francisco: Jossey-Bass.

Super, D. E., & Thompson, A. S. (1979). A six-scale, two-factor measure of adolescent career or vocational maturity. *Vocational Guidance Quarterly, 28,* 6–15.

Tang, M. (2001). Investigation of the structure of vocational interests of Chinese college students. *Journal of Career Assessment, 9,* 365–379.

Taylor, K. M., & Betz, N. E. (1983). Application of self-efficacy theory to the treatment of career indecision. *Journal of Vocational Behavior, 22,* 63–81.

Thorgren, J. M., & Feit, S. S. (2001). The Career- O-Gram: A postmodern career intervention. *Career Development Quarterly, 49,* 291–303.

Tinsley, H. E. A., & Bradley, R. W. (1986). Test interpretation. *Journal of Counseling and Development, 64,* 462–466.

Tinsley, H. E. A., & Bradley, R. W. (1988). Interpretation of psychometric instruments in career counseling. In J. T. Kapes & M. M. Mastie (Eds.), *A counselor's guide to career assessment instruments* (2nd ed., pp. 37–46). Alexandria, VA: National Career Development Association.

Tittle, C. K., & Zytowski, D. G. (Eds.). (1980). *Sex-fair interest measurement: Research and complications.* Washington, DC: Institute of Education, U.S. Government Printing Office.

Tyler, L. E. (1961). Research explorations in the realm of choice. *Journal of Counseling Psychology, 8,* 195–202.

Tyler, L. E. (1978). *Individuality.* San Francisco: Jossey-Bass.

U.S. Department of Labor. (1998). *The occupational information network.* Retrieved from www.doleta/gov/programs/onet.

Vondracek, F. W., Hostetler, M., Schulenberg, J. E., & Shimiza, K. (1990). Dimensions of career indecision. *Journal of Counseling Psychology, 37,* 98–106.

Weinrach, S. G. (1979). Trait and factor counseling: Yesterday and today. In S. G. Weinrach (Ed.), *Career counseling: Theoretical and practical perspectives.* New York: McGraw-Hill.

Weinrach, S. G. (1984). Determinants of vocational choice: Holland's theory. In D. Brown, L. Brooks, et al. (Eds.), *Career choice and development* (pp. 61–93). San Francisco: Jossey-Bass.

Whitfield, E. A., Feller, R. W., & Wood, C. (Eds.) (2009). *A counselor's guide to career assessment instruments* (5th ed.). Broken Arrow, OK: National Career Development Association.

Whitney, D. R. (1969). Predicting from expressed choice. *Personnel and Guidance Journal, 48,* 279–286.

Wholeben, B. E. (1988). Sixteen PF personal career development profiles: Review. In J. T. Kapes & M. M. Mastie (Eds.), *A counselor's guide to career assessment instruments* (2nd ed., pp. 238–242). Alexandria, VA: National Career Development Association.

Williamson, E. G. (1939). *How to counsel students.* New York: McGraw-Hill.

Willis, C. G., & Ham, T. L. (1988). Myers–Briggs Type Indicator: Review. In J. T. Kapes & M. M. Mastie (Eds.), *A counselor's guide to career assessment instruments* (2nd ed., pp. 228–233). Alexandria, VA: National Career Development Association.

Womer, F. B. (1988). Selecting an instrument: Choice or challenge. In J. T. Kapes & M. M. Mastie (Eds.), *A counselor's guide to career assessment instruments* (2nd ed., pp. 25–36). Alexandria, VA: National Career Development Association.

Young, R. A., Valach, L., & Collins, A. (1996). A contextual explanation of career. In D. Brown, L. Brooks, et al. (Eds.), *Career choice and development* (pp. 477–513). San Francisco: Jossey-Bass.

8

Using Information to Facilitate Career Development

Things to Remember

■ The major types of occupational information and the places where they can be found

■ The potential uses of O*NET

■ How to select and use educational occupational information with individuals and groups

When I introduce the topic of occupational information to my classes, I hear sighs and the posture of the students signals a mood of silent resignation. They know at this juncture that there is nothing as practical as a good theory and they think that there is nothing as boring as occupational information. They may be right, but when I ask them, "How many occupations can you describe in detail?" most indicate that their knowledge of occupations is limited. In fact, most students can describe the preparation for and duties of fewer than half-a-dozen of the more than 1,000 occupations in the U.S. occupational structure, and these are mostly jobs that require college degrees. Approximately 22 percent of the occupations in this country require a bachelor's degree. In order to be effective, career counselors must help their clients to choose from among 1,000 occupations and to prepare for them, and to find ways to implement their choices. However, occupational information has a more extensive use than facilitating individual choice: It is an invaluable tool in also facilitating career development of children, adolescents, and adults. Let's begin with the latter assumption, that career information has important uses, some of which are as follows:

Children

- To develop an awareness of the diversity of the occupational structure
- To develop an awareness of their parents' occupations and the nature of workers in their community and beyond
- To break down racial and sex-role stereotypes and the stereotypes about people with disabilities

- To develop an appreciation for the link between education and work
- To develop economic awareness of the relationship of occupation to lifestyle

Adolescents

- To sharpen their focus on personal identity as it relates to work
- To help provide motivation to complete high school and enroll in postsecondary education and training programs
- Begin reality testing by contacting and observing workers
- To provide a basis for lifestyle planning
- To eliminate stereotypes
- To compare career opportunities in the private and public sectors as well as in the military

Adults

- To provide information about training opportunities that will enhance their current occupational performance
- To provide information that allows them to evaluate their earnings as it relates to others with similar jobs
- To enhance those skills that will allow them to conduct job searches across the nation and the world
- To develop employability skills that will allow them to apply and interview for other jobs
- To provide information about the rights of workers who are disabled, older, female, or minorities and how to lodge grievances when those rights are abridged

Retirees

- To identify part-time or full-time job opportunities if retirees decide to return to work
- To help them use the skills they have developed as workers or as volunteers
- To assist them to continue lifestyle planning

To repeat, occupational and educational information is an essential ingredient in a comprehensive career development program and as a tool in career counseling. The complexity of the occupational structure is staggering. Information can be used to help clients not only understand the occupational structure but to negotiate it in a manner that is beneficial to them and to society. A few editions ago this chapter focused largely on commercially produced print materials, but that is no longer the case. Much of the focus of the chapter will be on government-produced on-line and computer-based materials. This chapter deals with computer-assisted career guidance systems (CACGS), most of which also provide occupational and educational information. Therefore most of the discussion of these systems and the materials in them will be postponed until the next chapter.

OCCUPATIONAL AND LABOR MARKET INFORMATION

Occupational information includes educational, occupational, and psychosocial facts related to work. This type of information comes almost entirely from governmental sources and for the most part focuses on individual jobs. Labor market information is also generated by government agencies for the purpose of informing both individuals and policymakers. For example, the unemployment rate in a particular geographic area of our country is usually of interest to individual clients because it may be one indicator of the difficulty or ease of their job search. On the other hand, Congress, the U.S. Employment Security Commission, the Federal Reserve System, and a host of other agencies are interested in the overall unemployment rate because it may (1) indicate a need for legislation authorizing increases or decreases in funds for training and retraining programs, (2) suggest that the demand for employment placement services will increase or decrease, or (3) signal a positive or negative trend in the nation's economy.

Labor market information includes data about the occupational structure and the trends that shape it. For example, the U.S. Census Bureau collects and disseminates information about the numbers of people employed in various occupations. The Bureau of Labor Statistics, located in the Department of Labor, collects information about hiring, plant closings, and layoffs, and it uses the data to make predictions about the future of individual jobs (demand for workers) as well as the overall occupational structure. Their predictions also include projections regarding demographic characteristics of the people employed in the labor market (e.g., women in the workforce). The Departments of Defense, Commerce, Interior, Agriculture, and Treasury also collect and disseminate labor market information.

Not unexpectedly, given the differences in occupational and labor market statistics, information is generated in decidedly different ways. Historically, information about specific occupations was generated using job analysis techniques. Job analysis requires the observation of workers on the job to ascertain the functions they perform, the machines and tools required to perform their functions, the materials used on the job, the products produced, the nature of the work environment, and the worker traits (aptitudes, abilities, and temperaments) required to perform the job. The first comprehensive database about jobs in the United States, the *Dictionary of Occupational Titles (DOT)*, was published in 1939. The information in the DOT was developed using observational strategies known as job analysis, but the architects of O*NET, the replacement for the DOT, asked workers in the jobs described in the O*NET system to rate the nature of work they performed, the abilities needed to perform the job, and the nature of the work environment.

TWO IMPORTANT SOURCES OF INFORMATION

Occupational and labor force information is typically produced and distributed in combination with each other. The most important occupational/labor force information databases are available both online and in print. Two of these, O*NET and *The Occupational Outlook Handbook (OOH)*, will be discussed at this time.

The Occupational Information Network (O*NET)

The Dictionary of Occupational Titles, was last published by the United States Department of Labor in 1991 because it failed to provide an adequate basis for helping workers who were laid off locate other jobs in which they could use their skills. The Occupational Information Network (O*NET), which corrects this deficiency, can be accessed both by governmental agencies, private and public institutions, and the general public.

The content model adopted for O*NET can be seen in Figure 8.1. It contains some of the same types of data formerly found in the *Dictionary of Occupational Titles* (e.g., general knowledge and education required for job performance). Some of the data in O*NET that can also be found in the *Occupational Outlook Handbook* (e.g., occupational forecasts and wage information), and the *Guide for Occupational Information* (e.g., data not currently included in current labor market and occupational information, such as cross-functional skills, which are skills that can be

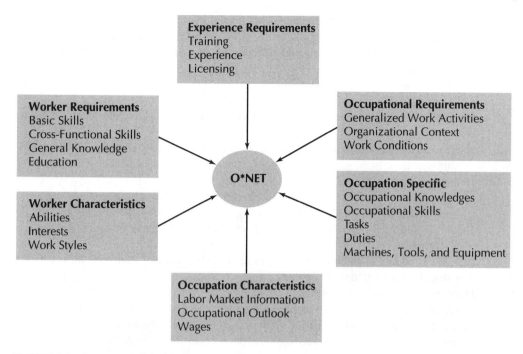

FIGURE 8.1   Content Model of the O*NET.   *Source*: From *Prototype Development of the O*Net: The Occupational Information Network*, by J. Nottingham and J. Gulec, undated. Raleigh: North Carolina Occupational Analysis Field Center.

used in more than one job). Data regarding approximately 906 occupations can be found in O*NET.

DEFINITIONS   The content model of O*NET contains six domains of information:

1. Worker characteristics—individuals' enduring characteristics that influence their motivation and capacity to function in an occupation. Three types of worker characteristics are included in O*NET:
   a. Abilities—characteristics, such as aptitudes, needed to perform an occupation.
   b. Occupational values and interests—values are preferences for certain types of occupational reinforcers, such as autonomy; interests are likes and preferences.
   c. Work styles—characteristics that influence typical performance as well as the individuals' ongoing adaptation to and performance of work.
2. Worker requirements—individuals' attributes that influence occupational performance across a range of work activities:
   a. Basic skills—skills, such as reading, that facilitate the acquisition of new knowledge.
   b. Cross-functional skills—skills, such as problem solving and social skills, that enable worker to function across a broad range of work activities.
   c. Knowledge—information about related principles and procedures, such as customer and personal service, that influence job performance across a number of work activities.
   d. Education—the amount and type (course of study and specific subjects) of formal education required to enter a job.

3. Experience requirements—prerequisite experiences in various types of jobs, specific job preparation, on-the-job training, and certification and licensure requirements:
   a. Training—highest level of specialized training needed to perform the job (related to 2(d), education, above).
   b. Experience—total time spent on a job.
   c. Licensing—specific licenses needed to perform the job.
4. Occupational requirements—job requirements established for individuals across domains of work:
   a. Generalized work activities—a cluster of similar occupational activities, such as communicating with people outside the organization, that underlie the performance of major job activities.
   b. Organizational context—includes the types of industry, the structure of the organization, the human resources practices, the organizational culture, the goals of the organization, and the roles expected of workers in the organization in which the work is performed.
   c. Work conditions—the physical, structural, and interpersonal environment in which a particular occupation is conducted.
5. Occupation-specific requirements:
   a. Occupational knowledge—specific knowledge needed to perform the work.
   b. Occupational skills—specific job skills needed to perform the work.
   c. Tasks—specific tasks to be carried out by workers in the occupation.
   d. Duties
   e. Machines, tools, and equipment—specific machines, tools, and equipment used by workers on the job.
6. Occupation characteristics:
   a. Labor market information—information about the labor market context in which the job is performed.
   b. Occupational outlook—projections, such as number of job vacancies as a result of growth and replacement of existing workers.
   c. Wages—amount of earnings and types of remuneration systems.

USING O*NET The O*NET database was not developed for use in print form, but print copies of the online assessment inventories used in conjunction with O*NET are available for sale from the U.S. Government Printing Office. The entire system can also be downloaded from the O*NET Web site (http://onet.center.org/using.html), which indicates that school, career, and rehabilitation counselors may use the O*NET database as a career exploration tool and that it can also be used by human resource managers in business and industry to design training programs and to develop job descriptions.

Students and adults may view summary reports that include the most important characteristics of the workers in various jobs and the requirements of a particular job. Once the user locates jobs that match their interests and skills, related occupations can be found and explored. Moreover, there are links to other classification systems and other sources of occupational information.

The way that O*NET databases are accessed depends on the needs of the user. As noted above, an employer who wishes to write job descriptions based on O*NET might simply access the portion of the database dealing with specific occupational skills required to perform a particular job. On the other hand, high school students can either type in an occupation of interest in the search box or complete either the O*NET Interest Profiler or other inventories that measure Holland types, such as the Self-Directed Search. Once users have entered their three letters, they can go to Interests Search (http://online.onetcenter.org/explore/interests/) and click on any of the six Holland codes. A second page occurs where users enter their three-letter code. Clicking on the "Go" button produces a list of occupations associated with Holland codes, some of which are highlighted as "In demand." After Holland code information is inserted to the system additional information about the occupations associated with the Holland code including abilities needed to perform the work and level of training required.

It is interesting to note that (Department of Labor Employment and Training Administration) DOLETA has not integrated an online Interest Profiler into the O*NET database. If you wish to examine an online version of the Interest Profiler the staff who designed the Arizona State University Virtual Counseling Center has placed what they term an "in-house" version of the Interest Profiler online at http://vcc.asu.edu/oip/index.shtml. It is expected that the Interest Profiler will become integrated into the system in the near future.

Another of the almost endless possibilities for the use of O*NET is that after rehabilitation counselors have done a careful evaluation of a client's physical attributes, they can search for occupational options based on physical characteristics. Educational policymakers may look at the skills and "knowledges" included in O*NET to set standards for the jobs in their institutions, and business leaders can look at the data dealing with work and organizational context to ascertain information about high-performance workplaces.

The Occupational Outlook Handbook

The Occupational Outlook Handbook (OOH) is available in print and online and provides predictions about the future of both occupational clusters and individual occupations, brief descriptions of the duties performed on the job, working conditions, average salary data, and information regarding preparing for each job listed. The wage information, which is the average wages for the workers from entry level to those near retirement, will be of little use to entry-level workers, but this data may be extremely interesting and useful to midlife career changers.

STUDENT LEARNING EXERCISE 8.1 USING O*NET

What follows is a suggested approach for accessing and using O*NET, one based largely on recommendations by Janet Wall, a member of the O*NET development staff. Using either a keyword search or the URL provided, go to O*NET and follow each of the recommended steps.

1. Access the Web site at http://online.onetcenter.org.
2. In the keyword or O*NET SOC code box, type in "electrical engineer."
3. Receive a list of occupations; click on one of the "in demand" occupations.
4. Review the information provided about the occupation you selected.
5. Rate helpfulness of information in terms of understanding the occupation on a 1–10 scale.

INFORMATION ABOUT THE MILITARY   Neither O*NET nor the OOH provides highly useful information for clients considering the military as a career. The OOH contains a general section on military service as well as salary information, but specific information about careers in the information and their civilian workforce counterparts is lacking. O*NET can be useful in helping people transitioning from the military to the civilian labor force, but it is generally not of much help to people at the beginning of their exploration of the military. However, each of the armed services publishes handbooks and brochures and posts Web sites describing career opportunities within their specific branch of service. These sources provide information regarding the relationship of each military specialty to civilian jobs.

The Department of Defense is also responsible for many other Web sites. Their online information is also available in print form by contacting the local recruiting command station. Some of the available Web sites include the following:

1. Military Education Online (www.Education4Military.com) provides information about educational benefits available to people in the military.
2. Today's Military (http://www.todaysmilitary.com/?WT.term=military+information& WT.campaign=281&WT.source=google&WT.medium=cpc&WT.content=801846&cshi ft_ck=1317764942cs801846&WT.srch=1) provides an overview of life in the military as an enlisted person and as an officer. This site contains links to each of the four services, descriptions of some of the skills learned during military service, and information about transitioning to civilian careers It also contains an explanation of the ASVAB (Armed Services Vocational Aptitude Battery) Career Exploration Program, the use of the ASVAB in the recruitment process, how the site visitor can take the ASVAB, and links to recruiters.
3. Military Career Guide contains a vast array of links to sites related to military careers at their Web site (http://www.khake.com/page33.html).

COMPUTER-ASSISTED CAREER GUIDANCE SYSTEMS (CACGS)   use both passive and interactive CD-ROM technology software programs as well as streaming audiovisual materials to provide an invaluable source of information. CACGS are typically quite expensive to acquire, and maintain—especially those that are proprietary in nature—and they usually require that learners be given special instructions before use. CACGS do have several advantages when compared to most types of materials, however. These systems can incorporate several components, including assessment, career exploration, and occupational information, and they are interactive in nature. O*NET, which is free but may not be as easy to use because the assessment instruments are not yet integrated into the system, contains the same components.

STATE SYSTEMS   Online state systems are produced by the remnants of the State Occupational Information Coordinating Committee (SOICC). This network provides databases that contain vast amounts of material to individuals who have Internet access. They typically include access to listings of jobs available in the state. The material in these online systems is often also available in software packages. Some of these online systems include links to information outside the state-level database.

OTHER TYPES OF OCCUPATIONAL INFORMATION

Occupational information can be found in a wide variety of other sources.

SIMULATIONS   Simulations may range from simple role-playing exercises, wherein a client assumes the role of the worker, to the use of highly sophisticated programs, such as those used in the training of airline pilots and astronauts. A middle ground between the simplistic role play and the sophisticated computer-assisted trainer is the simulation of rather complex work settings—such as cities and hospitals—that are used in many public school career development programs. As early as 1989 computer games such as SIMCITY have been produced using CD-ROM technology and placed online. Simulations place clients in interactive modes, and they can be developed to suit large groups. It is also worth noting that such simulations may be more useful to teach decision making than as a means of teaching about occupations.

Elementary teachers have used simulations frequently to enhance classroom learning activities. For example, the class establishes a "store" where class members acquire commonly used supplies, such as paper, crayons, pencils, and markers, or perhaps a "bank," in which each student maintains a small savings account while the class makes decisions about interest to be paid to depositors, loans, and other financial transactions.

High school vocational education classes also have used simulations extensively to teach specific vocational skills. Many trade and industry departments assign construction craft students to a class project involving the complete building of a home that then is sold to provide the materials for next year's project. In the construction process, the students, under proper faculty supervision, actually do the work of carpenters, electricians, plasterers, plumbers, painters, masons, and so on.

GAMES   Games can be used at any age level, are inexpensive, and can be stored and maintained easily. Miller and Knippers (1992), capitalizing on an idea first developed by Sandler (1990), used the format of the popular *Jeopardy!* television quiz show to teach high school students occupational concepts ranging from Holland types (Holland, 1997) to occupational information. They developed a *Jeopardy!* board using five categories: Holland Types, Holland II, Self-Awareness, Occupational Information, and Potpourri. They then wrote questions of varying difficulty and divided their class into teams to compete by determining which team had acquired the most information.

INTERVIEWS WITH EXPERTS   The logical step to providing credible occupational information is to enlist the assistance of an expert working in the field. Interviews with experts are appropriate experiences in all phases of the career development process; from the awareness level onward. Obviously, the interview itself should be adjusted to the level of development of the individuals involved, and other steps should be taken to make the experience valuable. In the awareness and early exploratory phases of career development, interviews can be used best with groups of students; adults will probably benefit most from individual interviews.

In some instances, workers can leave their work sites and come to schools or training centers to discuss their jobs. However, these experiences take away the learners' opportunities to observe the work environment.

DIRECT OBSERVATION   Observation of workers on their jobs is probably preferred to off-site interviews, but these experiences can add additional cost, particularly when the expenses associated with arranging these experiences is considered. Costs mount if transportation and supervision must be provided, which is usually the case when elementary, middle, and high school students are involved. Another problem that often presents itself when providing information through direct observation is whether a wide range of jobs is available to observe.

JOB SHADOWING A visit by students to shadow an individual may offer students one of the best opportunities to gain insight into a job of interest. Sometimes these visits involve an entire day. If time permits students may observe more than one worker. Shadowing allows the students to see a variety of aspects of the job and to ask questions about the job as well.

Many high schools and some middle schools have adopted Groundhog Day as their job shadowing day. Typically, counselors and teachers bus large groups of students to work sites where students can observe workers in action. Students are prepared for their observation experiences by discussing the nature of the job site they will visit in their classrooms. They are also given tips of things to observe. Hospitals, government agencies, and large businesses are favorite visitation sites because they employ a variety of workers. Rural schools that have difficulty accessing businesses and industries can take students to hospitals, the courthouse, and to the school district central office to observe jobs. Job shadowing experiences should be followed up with debriefings in which students tell what they have learned and are given an opportunity to ask questions. Ideally they are also given sources of additional information about the jobs they observed that are of interest to them.

Heppner's (1981) description of using alumni contacts to establish an externship of a day or more experience for college students is an application of the shadowing technique. A similar approach was reported by Sampson (1980) using local alumni. Tomlinson and DiLeo (1980) described a field trip to local work sites as part of a seminar designed to assist college women considering careers in science. Finally, job shadowing is used outside of the United States. Herr and Watts (1988) described shadowing as it is being used in Britain to help students learn about work.

CAREER DAYS On career day in most schools, groups of students are given an opportunity for direct contact with representatives of selected occupations. The career day program is designed to provide students with pertinent and accurate information about specific fields of work. If properly organized, it can help them broaden their understanding of fields in which they have expressed interest. It also gives them contact with at least one individual in the occupation from whom they may be able to obtain additional information.

Once the date has been set, the next question concerns the best part of the day for the program. Whether morning or afternoon is chosen depends largely on the local situation, the normal school schedule, and which portion of the day best lends itself to the objectives of the program. A schedule that permits the maximum number of parents to be included has many obvious advantages, and an evening program should be considered if the school wishes to include parents in the activity.

Career day programs have been criticized in some instances because the occupations included have not been representative of student interest. One way to prevent this is to begin planning with a survey of the students who will be involved in the program. Students may be asked to list the occupations they would most like included in a career day program. Sometimes a checklist is used, on which the student indicates from three to five preferences. The list can be compiled from a survey of occupations entered by students from the school or from a listing of the occupations most prevalent in the geographic area. It is rarely possible to include all occupations listed by students in a single school day. A tally of the checklists, however, indicates areas in which student interest is sufficient to plan for one or more groups. Frequently, one can meet specialized interests by grouping on a broader base than student response. For example, if only a few indicate interest in carpentry, stonemasonry, and construction trades workers may appear in a single session labeled building trades. When student interest is too small to include the requested occupations, the students making the requests should be helped individually to obtain the desired information in other ways.

Once student interests have been inventoried and tallied, the occupations to be included can be identified. Every effort should be made to cover the entire range of student interests. Securing speakers for each occupation may be difficult and time consuming. Members of the faculty, members of local service clubs, employers, and union members may be able to suggest individuals who can represent particular occupations. Speakers should be sought who can present their occupations fairly to interested students. Years of experience in the field may not necessarily be a major concern, particularly in a field in which changes have occurred recently. Giving speakers appropriate materials regarding expectations (e.g., tools used, education required, working conditions, and typical earnings) well in advance can assist them in preparing for their participation.

Because career days are basically learning activities, students should be prepared properly for their part. They should be provided with ample opportunity to read material about occupations of interest before the career day program, which should put them in a better position to ask appropriate questions. Groups of students can be encouraged to prepare questions in advance and to complete other preparatory steps that will increase the effectiveness of the program.

Soon after the program has been held, it should be evaluated by all participants to determine whether such a program should be used in subsequent years and, if so, how it should be modified to improve its effectiveness. Ideally, evaluation should include reactions from students, faculty members, and occupational representatives. Most schools use a brief evaluation form for gathering reactions from students and speakers.

Follow-up is as crucial as preparation of students. Many opportunities for follow-up exist in every school situation; these should be identified and capitalized on. Several of the classes in which students are enrolled naturally lend themselves to further discussion of the topics in the program. Others, such as English classes, can be used for stimulating student thought and reaction through assigned papers, preparation of letters, role-playing interviews, and similar activities. Counselors should follow up with student interviews to help them obtain further information; discuss tentative career choices; arrange visits to businesses, industries, or advanced schools, or schedule further activities that help them develop career plans.

CAREER CONFERENCES   If a school prefers not to interrupt its schedule, a series of career conferences can be arranged within the framework of the regular school calendar. Basically, the career conference is a briefer more circumscribed career day program in which an occupational representative is brought together with a group of interested students to discuss a specific field. Often a series of these, extending over a considerable period of time, can be strung together to provide the same coverage as a career day program.

Organizing and developing a series of career conferences involves the same steps as those described for the career day program. The major difference between the two activities is simply that the career day implements the whole program in a single day or portion of a day, whereas the career conferences may number one or two per day over a period of a month or more, depending on the number of occupations to be included.

WORK EXPERIENCE PROGRAMS   Exploratory work experience programs aim at helping students understand various types of work, work settings, tools and equipment used by workers, demands placed on workers, and similar factors. General work experience programs are designed to assist students in the development of attitudes and skills that are not narrowly vocational in nature, including punctuality, dependability, acceptance of supervision, interpersonal relations, and similar characteristics that apply to all work situations.

Another example of work experience programs is the college-level cooperative programs. Typically these involve alternating periods of full-time study and work assignments. An experience of this kind usually comes late in the preparatory program and is designed to develop and sharpen work-related skills rather than to provide exploratory insight into the occupation. Nevertheless, it does offer meaningful contact with work that the individual can use to confirm the appropriateness of an earlier choice or to begin the process of realigning plans.

CAREER FAIRS   Career fairs are often a part of the career development programs of colleges, community colleges, and vocational technical programs. Four-year colleges may have career fairs for each of their colleges (e.g., Business, Education Liberal Arts) and community colleges and vocational technical colleges nay concentrate their efforts on their vocational programs. Career fairs begin by issuing invitations to employers who may be interested in hiring the graduates of the various programs offered by the institution. Once a listing of employers who will attend the career fair is obtained, students are apprised of the date, time, and location of the fair, the names and affiliations of the employers, and if provided, the types of jobs the employers wish to fill (e.g., accountants, electrical engineers), The announcement regarding the career fair usually includes an invitation to students to attend resume and interviewing skills workshops that are offered prior to the fair.

Career fairs provide employers with an opportunity to identify a list of potential employees. Although some hiring may occur at the fair, the typical scenario is for potential hires to be interviewed at the institution or business with job offers following in some instances. Job fairs provide students to practice their resume development and interview skills with real employers.

Children's Materials

Almost all the material described thus far has been useful for adolescents and/or adults. However, in Chapter 1 career development is defined as a lifelong process, and as we shall see later, many school districts have career development programs in their elementary and middle schools. Fortunately many excellent print and nonprint materials are available to support these programs. A list of some of these can be found in Table 8.1. Children can also benefit from interviews with workers, direct observation, and many of the approaches described in subsequent sections of this chapter.

TABLE 8.1   Children's Occupational Information

Material	Available From
Children's Dictionary of Occupations (CD-Rom)	Impact Publishers
Videos (http://www.kids.gov/6_8/6_8_careers.shtml)	Dept of Labor
Print materials (http://www.careerkids.com/)	Career Kids
Online materials (http://www.bls.gov/k12/computers.htm)	BLS
Online (http://www.careerkids.com/1152x864/WOOHS.html)	Career Kids

Educational Information

Much of the occupational information produced today includes explanations of the kinds of education or training needed to qualify for a particular occupation. However, most occupational materials include some discussions of the preparation needed for entrance and advancement in the job, but they do not identify specific schools or organizations where that preparation is available. Some of the Web sites produced by state agencies do provide specific information about training opportunities, but sources such as O*NET and OOH do not contain the names of institutions that offer training, Unfortunately, some clients, particularly high school students access educational information first and may not consult occupational education until late in their second year in college, if then. For both of these groups, career counselors must be prepared to provide information about two-year and four-year colleges, universities, technical and trade schools, and apprenticeship programs.

EDUCATIONAL INSTITUTIONS   Prior to the rise of the Internet as a search tool, many career centers kept copies of college catalogs and directories that contained nationwide listings of colleges ands universities coupled with some basic information about the colleges most often attended by their graduates. For the most part, this is no longer necessary. The Yahoo! Directory (found at http://dir.yahoo.com/Education/Higher_Education/Colleges_and_Universities/By_Region/U_S__States/) has replaced the old fashioned directories of colleges and the majors they offered. This Web site contains listings of all of the colleges, universities, community colleges, and technical schools in a particular state, whether the schools are public or private, a map showing the location of the institution, and a link to each school's Web site. The directory also provides links to schools in Canada, the United Kingdom, India, and Australia, as well as listings of the top universities in the United States and other countries, college search tips, and many other types of helpful information.

Although the Yahoo Directory may be the most comprehensive Web site available, there are others that are also useful. Many two-year and four-year colleges and universities can be accessed through one of the following clearinghouses: University Worldwide (http://univ.cc/) contains 8,450 links to colleges in 201 countries. College Board's College Search (http://collegesearch. collegeboard.com/search/index.jsps) provides links to 3,500 colleges, and the American Association of Community Colleges College Finder database (http://www.aacc.nche.edu/pages/ ccfinder.aspx) provides links to community colleges in all 50 states.

APPRENTICESHIPS   Printed material about specific apprenticeship opportunities is almost non-existent. The best source of information about apprenticeships can be found in the Education + Training section of the One-Stop Career Centers Web site for each state. General information about apprenticeship programs can be obtained from the Bureau of Apprenticeships in U.S. Department of Labor. Information about local and regional offices also can be obtained there. If the state government offices include a Department of Labor that agency will post information related to apprenticeships.

POST–HIGH SCHOOL OPPORTUNITY PROGRAMS   As is the case with occupational information, students should be encouraged to make direct contacts with training institutions. Many high schools have organized programs or special days labeled as Postsecondary Opportunity Nights or some similar title. These programs resemble the career day described earlier except that speakers are drawn from educational institutions. Historically, these programs developed because school and college officials recognize that high school students need an opportunity to discuss post–high school educational plans with representatives of institutions. Because every school has students whose future plans do not include continuing their education, only a portion of the student group is served by such a program, which accounts for the fact that many of these programs are scheduled after school hours. This also permits many parents to attend the sessions with their children. The format of these programs is similar to that used in career day programs, and the organization and development of such programs should be similar.

Another difficulty that may be encountered in the typical postsecondary opportunity session is college and technical school representatives who are not fully cognizant of the programs offered at their institutions or the nature of other factors such as student life. Student questions to the representative will often cover the entire range of services and experiences available to students at the institution. Representatives who may be alumni who graduated several years earlier may be unable to provide adequate answers to students' questions. Coordinators should thus be prepared to help students follow up the session by having them access Web sites and talk to others familiar with a particular institution.

Many schools have developed a modified version of the postsecondary opportunity program that is particularly advantageous. It involves asking recent graduates of the high school or community college to conduct discussions with students when they return to the community during vacations or summer breaks. The major advantages of this approach are obvious: (1) The former students arouse personal interest among the listeners because they are probably known to them; (2) their experiences are accepted because they are recent; (3) the concerns and problems experienced by recent graduates have meaning for the students.

Summary

The sheer volume of occupational and educational information can be intimidating. Fortunately the development of computer software and online systems has made retrieval and storage of information much easier. However, technology has created additional concerns for those students whose level of knowledge of computers and skills needed to use them is lacking. Serious students will familiarize themselves with the OOH and the O*NET system because they are free, continuously updated, and user friendly.

Although technology has made a tremendous impact on the dissemination of information, it is also important to note that some of the traditional sources of materials such as printed documents and direct contact with workers and educational institutions have not lost their importance. Career counselors are forced to answer the age-old question: "What information is required at this point in my client's development and what is the best medium to use in delivering it?"

Chapter Quiz

T F **1.** The first comprehensive occupational classification system in the United States was published in *The Dictionary of Occupational Titles.*

T F **2.** O*NET, the current comprehensive occupational classification system, came about because of concerns about the assessment component of the DOT.

T F **3.** The assessment component in O*NET allows user to assess their values, interests, and aptitudes online.

T F **4.** Both O*NET and the OOH contain projections about occupational growth.

T F **5.** Both the OOH and O*NET were originally designed to be used as print systems.

T F   **6.** The knowledge and abilities needed to perform an occupation can be found in the OOH.

T F   **7.** O*NET contains information regarding well over 2,000 occupations

T F   **8.** The search engine Google has produced a comprehensive Web site dealing with postsecondary educational institutions.

T F   **9.** Of the various types of postsecondary training programs, it is probably most difficult to find information about apprenticeships.

T F   **10.** An 18-year-old seeking information about a career in the military would be well advised to begin the exploration process by using OOH.

(1) T (2) F (3) F (4) T (5) F (6) F (7) F (8) F (9) T (10) F

References

Heppner, M. J. (1981). Alumni sharing knowledge (ASK): High quality, cost-effective career resources. *Journal of College Student Personnel, 22,* 173–174.

Herr, E. L., & Watts, A. G. (1988). Work shadowing and work-related learning. *Career Development Quarterly, 37,* 78–86.

Holland, J. L. (1997). *Making vocational choices: A theory of vocational personalities and work environments* (3rd ed.). Odessa, FL: Psychological Association Resources.

Miller, M. J., & Knippers, J. A. (1992). *Jeopardy:* A career information game for school counselors. *Career Development Quarterly, 41,* 55–61.

Sampson, J. P., Jr. (1980). Using college alumni as resource persons for providing occupational information. *Journal of College Student Personnel, 21,* 172.

Sandler, S. B. (1990). *Jeopardy!* The counselor as a classroom teacher. *School Counselor, 38,* 65–66.

Tomlinson, E., & DiLeo, J. C. (1980). Broadening horizons: Careers for women in science. *Journal of College Student Personnel, 21,* 570–571.

9

Virtual and Brick and Mortar Career Exploration Centers: Design and Implementation

Things to Remember

- The services provided by One-Stop Career Centers
- The process to be followed when establishing a career exploration center
- Criteria to be used in locating and designing a CEC

- The technological competencies needed by CEC coordinators
- Ethical guidelines to be followed when providing Web-based career counseling
- Uses of CEC Web sites as adjuncts to career counseling

Traditionally, career exploration centers (CECs) have been labeled as career resource centers (CRCs) (Schutt, 2008). Why the change? The connotation associated with CRCs is that it is a depository for print, audiovisual, and other informational resources. The current thinking about these centers is that they are places where people needing a variety of services can go to engage in action that will yield information about needs, values, interests, abilities, training, and education. Occupational information can also be found here—including information about opportunities in the military, job openings, job-hunting strategies, and ultimately employment.

In 1994 the Department of Labor Employment and Training Agency (DOLETA) responded to the criticism that their services overlapped and in some instances were difficult to access by developing what is now termed One-Stop Career Centers. These centers are now located throughout the country in U.S. Employment Services (USES) offices and in other agencies that serve job hunters (Ettinger, 2008b). They are also available online. One-Stop Career Centers, as the name suggests are designed to provide a full range of assistance to job seekers under one roof. These centers offer referrals to training facilities, career counseling and job listings, and similar employment-related services. Subtopics on the One-Stop Career Center home page include the following:

1. Explore careers with links to the O*NET self-assessment devices
2. Education + Training with links to goal setting and planning and training opportunities
3. Resumes + Interviews with links to employability skill development resources
4. Salary + Benefits with links to salary information, unemployment benefits and relocations information
5. Job Search with links to developing a job hunting plans and lists of available jobs by state
6. People + Places to help with links to employment and training, unemployment benefits, and agencies that can help

As suggested in the definition of CECs and illustrated by One-Stop Career Center home page, virtual career exploration centers place assessment instruments, occupational information such as OOH, access to O*NET'S more than 900 occupational profiles, readings and exercises about employability skills, job posting opportunities for employers, and links to an array of agencies where the job hunter can receive assistance such as career counseling and counselor-directed assessment.

The only resources needed to access virtual career exploration centers is a computer and an Internet connection. One-Stop CECs were set up for use by individuals, professionals, and businesses for individuals. They have been incorporated into brick and mortar centers in community colleges and vocational technical schools, four-year institutions, U.S. employment security offices, and other agencies.

Not all virtual CECs are as comprehensive as One-Stop Career Centers. Canada's WORK*ink* (http://www.workink.com/province_template.php?id=11152&pid&pr=11152), which focuses on employment for disabled people, is an example of a more focused virtual exploration center. Government agencies are not alone in their interest in virtual CECs. The University of Illinois and many other colleges and universities have used technology to create their own virtual CECs for both students and alumni.

STUDENT LEARNING EXERCISE 9.1

Before moving on to "visit" a virtual career resource center such as the U.S. One-Stop Career Center or Canada's WORK*ink*, which focuses on disabled persons, take stock of the resources offered. If your career focus is on two-year or four-year institutions, check out the CEC sites for one of those institutions (e.g., the University of Illinois or Arizona State University) and their efforts to use virtual resources such as O*NET or the resources they have developed for their own students. A "trip" to a virtual center should help you better judge the resources that need to be made available in brick and mortar centers.

ESTABLISHING A CEC

The development of the One-Stop Career Centers involved an extensive developmental program that incorporated the occupational projections from the Bureau of Labor Statistics, O*NET occupational profiles and assessment tools, apprenticeship data from the Department of Labor Bureau of Apprenticeships, Department of Defense information about the four branches of military services and crosswalks between jobs the military and civilian jobs, and literally scores of other sources including some from commercial publishers. Career counselors aiming to establish CECs would do well to utilize the mass of materials and resources available in these resources. However, because high schools, two-year institutions, colleges, and other agencies have limited resources, their developmental approaches must be much more circumscribed. What then are the factors that should be considered in the development of what in all likelihood will be a combination of online (virtual) resources and the delivery of information in a traditional manner?

Basic Criteria for Locating and Designing a CEC

At least five factors must be considered as plans which are made to develop a career exploration center:

1. *Accessibility*   Although there are many general questions about the accessibility of the CECs, the issue of accessibility for persons with disabilities raise both ethical and legal concerns. The Americans with Disabilities Act mandates that all facilities must be accessible to people with disabilities, including those with mobility, hearing, and visual disabilities. Schutt (2008) and Ettinger (2008a) compiled list of concerns for these groups that included:

> ***For People with Visual Disabilities***
>> Well-lighted areas for those with limited visual acuity
>> Tactile directions, signs, and elevators
>> Closed caption videos
>> Alternatives to keyboard and mouse use (e.g., voice activated)
>> Audio version of graphics
> ***For People with Hearing Disabilities***
>> Rooms equipped with alternative emergency notices, such as flashing lights in place of bells and sirens
>> Available telecommunication devices for the deaf (TDD)
> ***For People with Mobility Disabilities***
>> Wheel chair accessible entrances, registration desks, telephones, and restrooms
>> Easy access to buildings

Other general accessibility issues include nearness to parking lots and entrances close to career counselors' offices and in the mainstream of client traffic flow. In public schools this typically means that the center should be accessible from one of the main corridors. CECs on college campuses and in businesses career centers should be located in buildings near the center of the campuses. Community centers should be easily accessible by automobile and should provide adequate parking.

2. *Attractiveness*   The center should be well lit and the overall appearance should be inviting. Posters, audiovisual invitations at the entrance of the center, and comfortable furniture enhance the CEC's appeal.

3. *Ease of Operation*   Ease of operation covers a variety of areas, including the filing system used, storage and display of material, policies regarding checking out material, and the nature of the assistance provided to users of the CEC. With regard to the latter, a staff member should always be available to explain and demonstrate the use of complex machines, online materials, and computer software packages. Perhaps it goes without saying that the more information and assessment devices stored in computers and online, the easier the task of storing, organizing, and perhaps delivering material becomes.

4. *Responsiveness*   A CEC is typically designed and stocked with the materials and machines that will serve the needs of client populations, regardless of whether it is in a One-Stop Career Center, a school, college, or a business. By identifying and programming to client needs, the center becomes immediately responsive. However, needs change. The group or individual may come with a request for information that has not been acquired. Responsive centers have budgets that allow them to act on requests from individuals and groups as long as they are within reason.

5. *Reflection of Diversity Issues*   Throughout this book addressing the unique needs of individuals who are other than white and middle class has been stressed. CECs should have materials that allow individuals to "see themselves in a particular job or educational opportunity." Seeing themselves in the material means that the material addresses the unique needs of clients and that it has appropriate pictures and examples. All centers should contain material that deals with the concerns of women; members of racial and ethnic minorities; persons who are disabled; and persons who are gay, lesbian, or bisexual.

RENOVATING A CEC   Most career counselors will enter workplaces that have some type of CEC. Schutt (2008) and Schnell and Schaefer (1999) have issued some useful guidelines for revising an existing CEC. The first step in either developing or renovating a CEC is to select a coordinator who understands technology and its application in information provision, testing and assessment, and Web-based career counseling.

BASIC TECHNOLOGICAL COMPETENCIES

In response to the growing need for counselors and others to be technologically competent, the Association of Counselor Education and Supervision (ACES) established a list of minimum technological competencies needed by counselor education students at the time they complete their programs of study (ACES, 1999). Some of the competencies on this list are relatively low level (e.g., using email and participating in listservs) and some are now out of date and will not be discussed. However, coordinators of CECs need a relatively high-level technology and its application in career development. What follows is my revision of the ACES list.

1. Use available software to develop Web pages.
2. Use videoconferencing equipment that provides outreach and educational programs.
3. Identify and evaluate Web-based career decision–making programs and assessment packages that can be used in the CEC.
4. Help clients search for career-related information via the Internet, including information about careers, employment opportunities, educational and training opportunities, financial assistance/scholarships, salary data, and social and personal information.
5. Help clients prepare online résumés and conduct virtual job interviews.
6. Apply the legal standards and ethical codes that relate to career services on the Internet.
7. Design and deliver ethically and legally sound Web-based career counseling programs.
8. Evaluate the quality of Computer Assisted Career Guidance Systems.
9. Evaluate the efficacy of Internet-based job placement programs.

Once a technologically competent coordinator is in place, the development of the CEC can move forward. Many of the steps listed separately here will in fact be pursued simultaneously. At the outset the coordinator must enlist the support of the CEO, vice-chancellor, president, or principal of the organizations in which the CEC is located. Although there are many reasons why the support of the leader is needed, the most fundamental of these is budget. The administrative officers are typically the key persons in the preparation and defense of the organization's budgetary requests and, while they will ask for input from the coordinator of the program, unless the CEC is an important priority it is likely to languish without administrative support.

Other steps in the developmental process include establishing a steering committee that can assist in establishing objectives and designing the programs that will be offered to client groups. Members of the steering committee can also help in developing policies that guide the CEC's operation. The steering committee, if comprised of people who are representative of the institution and community, can also assist in identifying clients' needs, and publicizing the CEC. Finally, the steering committee may be useful in the design of a plan to evaluate the CEC. The objectives of the CEC should serve as the starting point for the evaluation plan (i.e., are we meeting our objectives). For example, it is quite reasonable that one of the objectives pertain to the number of people who will be involved in the activities offered by the center. However, the answer to the question suggested by this objective does little to answer the more important question, "How effective is the CEC in meeting student needs?" Effectiveness may be measured by satisfaction with the activities, ratings of new knowledge or skill required, or estimates of progress toward reaching a career decision, or gaining self-understanding.

CRITERIA FOR COLLECTING MATERIAL Ultimately the materials to be made available to clients must be collected and organized. Several factors should be considered while assembling the resources for the center, one of which is obvious: include online material that is useful and free. However, other perhaps more important criteria should be applied in the selection process:

1. *The Group That Will Make Major Use of the Materials* Different materials will be used in a middle school, where students are only beginning to explore concepts about themselves and occupations, than in a vocational rehabilitation center for adults. Even where the differences are less extreme, materials should be appropriate to the group or groups being served.

2. *The Nature of the Community* A knowledge of the community where the school or agency is situated provides additional information about the group that will use the career resource center. Although the high mobility of Americans decreases the likelihood that they will remain within the community throughout their lives, the range and scope of occupations within the community may provide the framework for the evaluation and consideration of career fields by students and their parents. That is, it will be more difficult to stimulate students to consider a wide range of occupational choices if they have grown up in a stable community dominated by a single industry than if the town has many businesses and factories and the population is constantly changing.

The socioeconomic range within the community and the extent to which community attitudes encourage educational achievement and individual development are other factors to be considered.

3. *The Staff Who Will Use the Materials* Logically, materials used only by the counselor differ from those used by aides or teachers. The use of "packages" such as O*NET presupposes some understanding of the system. Tests and other assessment devices must be used judiciously and ethically. It is the coordinator's responsibility to ensure that ethical standards are maintained.

4. *How the materials will be used* Closely related to *who* use the career resource center is the question of *how* the materials are to be used. If career materials are used only in individual counseling concerning vocational plans, it may be possible to locate and print single copies found in online databases or CACGS. However, if materials are used for instructional purposes in small groups or classroom setting, the range of materials is probably narrowed to make available the number of copies needed for the entire group.

5. *Auxiliary Local Resources*   Almost every community has agencies that work with youth or adults and hence might have materials, including career materials, that relate to their problems. The local public library is an obvious location for materials of this type. Other local resources that may have materials would be 4-H clubs, youth centers, the YMCA, YWCA, and churches or other groups that operate active youth or adult programs.

6. *Critical CEC Resources*   Schutt and Finkle (2008) developed a list of critical resources for CECs. These include assessment tools, such as those in paper-and-pencil format and computer-assisted assessment programs. Also, many states such as California, Texas, and California have placed the O*NET Interest Profiler online. In such settings, it is suggested that the uses of paper-and-pencil measures be minimized. CACGS, career and labor market information and strategy-based references that can be used to improve decision making and employability services should also be included. The latter category includes materials that help clients take action, such as preparing a résumé, conducting a job interview, and preparing for a test. Material should also be included that provides clients with information about their legal rights in the workplace as well as bias and discrimination and how to handle it.

INITIATING A COLLECTION   Historically CECs in public schools, two-year institutions, and colleges have occupied large rooms or sections of libraries while CECs in businesses and other organizations have been located in smaller spaces. The size of the space and the equipment included in the center should be based on the activities to be conducted by the CEC staff. Schutt and Finkle (2008) suggested that assessment tools, video collections, occupational and educational print materials, employability skill development materials, and computer-assisted career guidance resources may be housed in the center. The online O*NET assessment tools may be considered as substitutes for other paper tests and inventories, and the information contained in One-Stop Career Centers can replace print guides to job hunting, resume development, and interviewing skills.

Evaluating materials is an integral part of building a good CEC. The. National Career Development Association (NCDA) has established, and regularly revises, *Guidelines for the Preparation and Evaluation of Career Information Literature*, the *Career and Occupational Information Rating Form*, and *Software Evaluation Criteria*, all of which are available by going to the NCDA Web site at http://associationdatabase.com/aws/NCDA/pt/sp/Home_Page and then clicking on the guidelines button.

Should CACGS Be Included in the CEC?

CACGS are typically self-contained systems that offer many of the same components included in O*NET and, if they are connected to the Internet, may allow users to access the services offered by One-Stop Career Centers. The question about including them in the CEC is often based on economics; unless the system is available through a state agency at a reduced cost, the expense of commercially produced costs may be prohibitive. The State Occupational Information Coordinating Committee (SOICC) network was defunded by Congress in 2000, but many of the services providing including CACGS offered for individual states have been continued as result of state funding or by charging licensing fees. The typical fees levied for access to state level CACGS are quite modest when contrasted to the licensing fee charged by commercial publishers.

CAGS should be affordable, but prior to purchasing a system there are other factors to be considered.

WHO BENEFITS FROM CACGS?   Although it is somewhat of an oversimplification, the career development process can be summarized as (1) developing self-awareness, (2) developing an awareness of the occupations that may be suitable, (3) choosing an occupation, and (4) implementing the choice that is made. Implementation of one's career choice involves selecting an educational or training site, unless on-the-job training is provided by the employer. Implementation also includes developing the skills to find and secure jobs, and then using those skills in the job search. CACGS can be useful for *most* client groups in each of these steps. The question then becomes, "Who benefits from using CACGS?" Sampson (1997a, 1997b, 1997c) has attempted to answer this question and provides the following guidelines for potential users of CACGS:

1. Users should have the verbal ability necessary to use the systems. Users who have low reading ability should probably be precluded from use of these systems or use them in conjunction with counselors or paraprofessionals.
2. Students with goal instability or low self-efficacy may not benefit from the systems and may need to engage in traditional career counseling or engage in what Sampson terms "supported use." Supported use of CACGS simply means that clients use them with the support of a professional or paraprofessional.
3. Poorly motivated clients—that is, clients who are not greatly concerned about getting more information about themselves or occupations or engaging in career planning—are unlikely to benefit from CACGS and thus should probably be involved in either traditional career counseling or supported use of CACGS.
4. Students with low self-esteem or negative thinking about careers or themselves are unlikely to benefit from CACGS. These individuals may distort the information they receive from CACGS and therefore must have this problem resolved prior to using one of these systems.
5. Clients with anxiety and depression may encounter barriers to effective decision making. Such issues need to be dealt with prior to accessing CACGS.
6. Lack of information or misconceptions about CACGS are deterrents to effective use. Although these problems can be dealt with in brief interventions, it is inappropriate to allow people to use CACGS who are either unskilled in their use of the computer and may overestimate or underestimate their potential based on the results.
7. People who have significant barriers including economic limitations or role conflicts (married persons) to making career choices or implementing those choices should not rely solely on CACGS. Counselor support is necessary for these clients. Sampson (1997b) also raises the questions of the utility of CACGS for people who have intuitive (versus reflexive) decision-making styles and people who have Holland interest codes that are either social or enterprising. However, no compelling data suggest that these people will not benefit from CACGS.

Sampson suggests that CECs need to establish procedures for screening potential users of CACGS to ascertain who can take advantage of self-directed experiences and who cannot. Once this screening has been completed, various scenarios for helping clients can be established based on the conclusions reached in the screening process. Sampson's recommendations for these scenarios are summarized next, with some modifications based on the recommendations of Brown and Brooks (1991).

Group A contains three categories of people who are ready for independent use of CACGS. In addition to being computer literate, these individuals share certain characteristics: (1) they have relatively simple questions, such as the salaries or occupational duties of two or three occupations; (2) they are motivated to use CACGS and are free from negative thinking, anxiety, depression, decisional anxiety, and role conflicts; and (3) they have the reading skills needed to use the system. Group B contains those individuals who are ready for independent use of CACGS, except for orientation to the system—that is, all members of group A who are not computer literate. Group C contains two categories of people who are not ready for independent use but for whom CACGS with support can be used without prior counseling interventions: (1) individuals who have low reading abilities or economic limitations and (2) multipotentialed individuals. Finally, group D contains three categories of people who are not ready for independent use and for whom counseling intervention should precede use of CACGS: (1) individuals with low self-esteem and negative thoughts, (2) individuals who have decisional anxiety, and (3) individuals who are highly anxious or depressed.

HOW EFFECTIVE ARE CACGS AND WHAT ARE THEIR BENEFITS? The literature regarding the effectiveness of CACGS is basically supportive of their use. Kapes, Borman, and Frazier (1989), Niles and Garis (1990), and Marin and Splete (1991) found that counselor intervention or counselors plus computers are more effective than CACGS alone, but in each case the researchers concluded that CACGS alone have a positive effect on clients. Earlier studies (e.g., Campbell, 1983; Garis & Harris-Bowlsbey, 1984) found no significant differences between the effectiveness of career counselors and CACGS.

Sampson (1997c) contended that the use of CACGS can produce numerous benefits for users and summarized 30 years of research to identify positive outcomes. The benefits include the generation of an increased number of occupational alternatives that are more related to personal characteristics, increased knowledge of occupations and labor market information, increased certainty regarding occupational choice, and increased career maturity. As noted earlier, it is also expected that individuals will receive better career development services and that the career development specialist will be freed from repetitive tasks. Sampson (1997c) goes on to suggest that when CACGS are presented using multimedia technology, other benefits, such as increased motivation and opportunities for reality testing, may result. As yet, the impact of multimedia presentations have not been evaluated, however.

What Are Some Frequently Used CACGS?

CACGS developed for use in individual states such as WISCareers, Virginia Career View, Georgia Career Information System, and Eureka—The California Career Information System are but a few of the career information systems produced by states. As was noted in the introduction to this section, state-level sites are linked to jobs and job openings in the state training institutions, financial aid information and other state agencies. Some systems, like Virginia Career View, offer packages for various public school levels, adults, and parents. Other systems, like the Georgia system (GCIS), offer only two packages: one for middle-elementary school students and the other for high schools. The search for a CACGS system should probably begin with these state-level programs.

There are a number of commercially developed programs, two of which will be discussed here: DISCOVER and SIGI Plus. The development of DISCOVER has been largely the work of Jo Ann Harris-Bowlsbey and, in part, is an extension of her previous effort on CVIS, one of the earliest systems that gained widespread usage. DISCOVER was developed as a systematic career guidance program to assist in career development activities at the secondary school level. From its earliest days, its emphasis has been on the career planning process. Harris-Bowlsbey (1990) stressed that competitive pressures among the various systems require updating and redevelopment on a regular basis. American College Testing (ACT) has followed such a pattern and has been very successful in anticipating market needs. ACT offers five CACGS: DISCOVER for high schools; DISCOVER for colleges and adults; VISIONS for middle schools and VISIONS PLUS, both of which were developed for the Maryland SOICC; and DISCOVER for the military.

The middle school/junior high school version, designed for students in grades 6 to 9, is focused on helping these students plan for high school. The conceptual approach, is intended to give students a start in career exploration with an overview of the world of work and identification of personal characteristics. The middle school/junior high version has an entry/exit section and three major modules. The individual may choose to use any one or all three of the modules. The entry/exit section explains how to use the system, how to collect identifying information to store student records, and the career planning process used in the modules. When ready to sign off, students can save the results for later use or reference. The modules are as follows:

1. *You and the World of Work*   This module uses the ACT World-of-Work Map (see Figure 9.1). Users can participate in a World-of-Work Map game that requires identifying basic work tasks involved in nine job-related activities. These activities are required to become familiar with the basic work tasks (working with people, data, things, or combinations of these) and include examples of typical activities for each. Users are asked to identify whether they would enjoy the activity, thus initiating awareness of their reactions to work activities.

2. *Exploring Occupations*   In this module students systematically explore occupations using the World-of-Work Map and Holland's typology. Students can enter their scores on any of several achievement tests, grades earned in selected courses, or self-ratings in several ability areas, to relate specific achievement or ability to various occupational clusters. Occupational information can be accessed by adding the anticipated educational level students hope to attain before going to work.

3. *Planning Your High School Program*   This module uses the student's tentative career and educational aspirations to plan a high school program of studies. If desired, schools can incorporate local graduation requirements and course offerings into this section.

The high school version places primary emphasis on career direction and thereby proposes to offer help to both students whose plans are beginning to crystallize and students who are still undecided or uncertain. This version provides modules at each step of the career planning process. There are seven in all, and each is divided into subparts that can be used independently if desired. Several activities (e.g., interest assessment) are available either online or in paper-and-pencil format not requiring computer time. The seven modules are as follows:

1. *Beginning the Career Journey*   In this module the user checks his or her level of career decision–making maturity to determine which later modules will be most useful. A 36-item inventory, taken either online or offline, is keyed to the remaining modules and provides a list of modules most likely to be helpful.

2. *Learning About the World of Work*   This section presents the ACT World-of-Work Map and explains the concepts of work tasks, map regions, clusters, and job families.

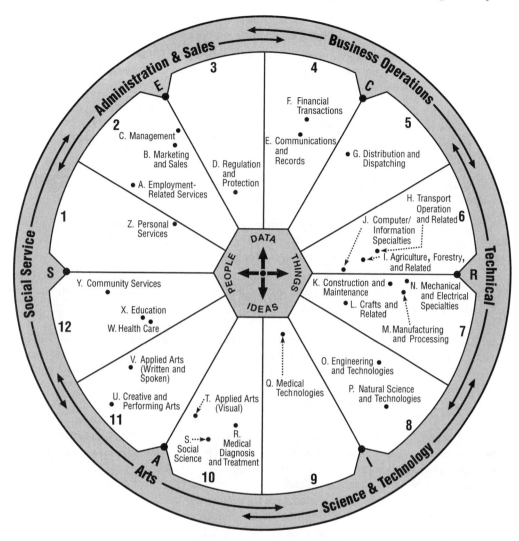

FIGURE 9.1 The New World-of-Work Map (Counselor Version). *Source:* American College Testing, Iowa City, IA. Copyright 2001, by ACT, Inc. All rights reserved.

3. *Learning About Yourself* This module helps users acquire information about themselves through a series of exercises, including interest assessment and other devices that also can be completed online or offline. Factors besides interest include abilities, work-related values, and experiences. The module can also accept data from a range of previously completed interest and aptitude measures.

4. *Finding Occupations* This module generates lists of occupations for consideration and exploration. Users can select suboptions from an array of categories, such as employment outlook, job setting, work hours, amount of supervision, job pressure, and education needed.

5. *Learning About Occupations* This module provides detailed information about any of the 458 occupations included in the file. Information is updated annually. As new occupations become significant in the labor market, they are added to the file. ACT claims that the occupations within DISCOVER represent 95 percent of the employment opportunities in the United States.

6. *Making Educational Choices*   This module presents information on educational preparation leading to the occupations identified in module 5. Appropriate majors or programs of study are also listed for chosen occupations.

7. *Planning Next Steps*   This module provides information about postsecondary educational opportunities. The file includes 2,921 vocational-technical schools, 1,458 two-year colleges, 1,731 four-year colleges, 1,241 graduate schools, 144 external degree programs, and 212 military programs.

The college and adult version of DISCOVER consists of modules 1 through 7 of the high school version, with two additional modules:

8. *Planning a Career*   This module is designed for adults in transition or others beyond the college age group. It uses Super's life/career rainbow (1990) as the basis for exploring the various roles in each person's life. Users can apply the module to plan for changes in their futures.

9. *Making Transitions*   This module helps users understand career transitions that are increasingly common, the pressures and tensions that one encounters in such transitions, and how to deal with and control these factors.

RESEARCH REGARDING DISCOVER   Roselle and Hummel (1988) report a study of 12 college students that examines the relationship between intellectual development and effective use of DISCOVER. Students with higher scores on the Measure of Intellectual Development showed higher ability to use DISCOVER as one more tool in career planning, to adapt easily to the system, and greater self-knowledge. This suggests that most users need assistance in using the system for maximum advantage in reverse proportion to intellectual development. Fukuyama, Robert, Neimeyer, Nevill, and Metzler (1988) reported that completion of the college system resulted in higher self-efficacy scores for undergraduates. The students who had completed the system were much more certain of their occupational plans than students who had not used DISCOVER. Garis and Niles (1990) reported a study using DISCOVER and SIGI PLUS with career planning courses matched against students taking the courses without access to CACGS. Their results did not show significant increases in career planning when computer systems are added.

Maples and Luzzo (2005) evaluated the impact of DISCOVER, career counseling only, and DISCOVER Plus counseling on career decision-making self-efficacy. They found that students in the study increased their career decision-making self-efficacy, whereas those who participated in the counseling-only treatment did not. The impact of the DISCOVER plus career counseling was not reported. It should be noted that the counseling treatment consisted of a 45- to 50-minute session and thus was not an adequate test of this intervention.

SIGI PLUS is the product of developmental adds to effort by a research group led by Martin Katz at Educational Testing Service. Katz (1990) describes the early activities that resulted in SIGI. It was originally intended for use by students in or about to enter two-year colleges. It is now applied more broadly, including usage in four-year schools and with out-of-school adults in a variety of settings.

The philosophical basis for SIGI proposes that values identification and clarification are basic to an effective career decision process involving evaluation of the rewards and risks that accompany each option. The system covers the major aspects of career decision making, using nine separate modules or sections. Each module provides an array of user activities that can be used selectively or entirely. The introductory section can recommend specific pathways based on user-provided personal information about present career status. Like DISCOVER, the system provides a means of storing client records that permits the client to recall information from previous system usage. Included in the following brief descriptions of the nine modules is a question that indicates the purpose of the section, a description of what the client can do, and some of the special features built into the module.

1. ***Introduction***   What is in SIGI PLUS?

    Included: An overview of SIGI PLUS and a recommended pathway based on client-provided information.

    Features: Clear explanations; directs clients to sections that apply to them; permits requests for additional information about subsequent parts.

2. ***Self-Assessment***   What do I want? What am I good at?

    Included: Work-related values and personal choices of most importance; choice of main interest fields; consideration of work activities and evaluation of likes and what one does well; a game to help clarify values.

    Features: Chance to clarify personal values, interests, and skills; helps identify what is most important personally; maintains emphasis on personal values; uses an activities inventory that links interests and skills; relates these to everyday life.

3. ***Search***   What occupations might I like?

    Included: Identification of preferred work features; identification of work features client wishes to avoid; creates a list of occupations having the preferred features.

    Features: Helps client develop a personal list of occupational alternatives; allows any combination of values, interests, skills, level of education, and features to be avoided; permits exclusion of occupations client does not want to consider; explains which factor eliminated a specific occupation not on the list.

4. ***Information***   What occupations might I like?

    Included: Selection of one or two occupations at a time to match against information such as skills required, advancement possibilities, potential income, national employment outlook, and educational requirements.

    Features: Answers 27 questions about each selected occupation; gives alternate job titles; provides sources for additional information; local information may be added.

5. ***Skills***   Can I do what's required?

    Included: Lists specific skills required for any listed occupation; self-rating on skills required.

    Features: Selection of any included occupation; shows how work skills are applied in the specific occupation; provides examples of how these skills are applied in everyday life; includes information on managerial and supervisory skills.

6. ***Preparing***   Can I do what's required?

    Included: Shows typical preparatory paths, estimates client's likelihood of completing preparation.

    Features: Links career planning to preparatory programs; shows typical preparation for each specific field, including courses and course descriptions if desired; considers factors related to acquiring preparation, such as finding time, finding money, handling the difficulty, staying motivated.

7. ***Coping***   Can I do what's required?

    Included: Suggestions on dealing with issues related to preparation, such as finding time and money; arranging care for others; obtaining school credit for present knowledge; learning to handle preparation-related worries.

>   *Features:* Provides specific suggestions for time management and financing alterna-
>   tives; responds to common preparation worries; provides information on establish-
>   ing academic credit; permits addition of local information.

8. *Deciding*   What's right for me?

>   *Included:* Client can match three occupations at a time for rewards, anticipated employ-
>   ment, chances for entrance and success, overall evaluation.
>   *Features:* Summarizes information from previous sections; provides a decision-making
>   strategy; permits comparison of occupation with possible new careers; introduces
>   basis for graphic comparison of alternatives.

9. *Next Steps*   How do I put my plan into action?

>   *Included:* Clients can start toward career goal by planning short-term goals such as
>   more education or training; developing new skills; proving they can do the work;
>   building a network of contacts; writing a résumé; overcoming obstacles.
>   *Features:* Helps identify specific steps; provides concrete suggestions, tips, and models
>   for résumé writing; prompts planning immediate first steps.

RESEARCH REGARDING SIGI PLUS   Mazel and Cummings (1982) reported that the average user spends 3.5 hours completing the process, which may pose a problem for CECs that have limited time available for students who wish to use SIGI PLUS. Like other systems, the strengths and weaknesses of SIGI PLUS depend on how those characteristics are valued by site users. SIGI PLUS is based on a clearly conceived theoretical position that emphasizes the importance of values, and some will see it as underplaying other important attributes. Because it focuses on an education-ally affiliated clientele, some will see it as serving other groups less adequately. It requires the user to progress methodically through its conception of the career decision process, so some will see it as more rigid and less flexible than systems that do not adhere to a clear philosophical position.

Other CACGS

Two other CACGS are used widely in the United States. The first is CHOICES (Computerized Heuristic Occupational Information and Career Exploration System), which was originally developed for Canadian users but has now been adopted by a number of states plus the District of Columbia. Although largely aimed toward information access and retrieval, CHOICES does include aspects of career exploration.

The second system is C-LECT (Computer-Linked Exploration of Careers and Training), which is marketed by Chronicle Guidance Publicationsand also includes identification of per-sonal temperament and interest patterns in addition to occupational and educational information.

Both CHOICES and C-LECT are designed for general use in the career development process and therefore are used mainly in educational settings. C-LECT is quite brief compared to the more extensive programs described earlier and usually requires less than an hour to complete.

PRESENT STATUS OF CACGS

The most important recent technological breakthroughs in the use of CACGS is technology that permits the inclusion of extensive video and audio clips in the programs and the development of Web-based versions. In the future it seems likely that almost all CACGS will be delivered via the Internet. Users can be guided through a system such as DISCOVER via auditory instructions and can view clips of individuals in the workplace. This has the distinct advantage of providing various models (e.g., females in male-dominated occupations) to users. The memory requirement and the need for more powerful computers increases the overall cost of using DISCOVER and similar systems. Fortunately, the overall cost of computers has been in a downward trend that seems likely to continue. The insertion of video clips introduces a problem heretofore associated with print materials. Images, like data, become dated. Dated images can deter potential users, even if the information contained in the system is up-to-date.

CACGS have become an important feature in many career development programs in the United States and Canada, as well as in several other countries, such as Australia, France, Hungary, Luxembourg, Belgium, and the Netherlands. Not surprisingly, given this international interest, CACGS are available in several different languages. CHOICES, and Career Futures are available in Canada in both French and English, and CHOICES is available in Dutch, Flemish, and Hungarian to accommodate users in these countries (Sampson et al., 1998).

The ASVAB Career Exploration Program

TheArmed Services Vocational Aptitude Battery (ASVAB) Career Exploration Program Has been designed by the Department of Defense to aid military recruiters.It does not comfortably into an online or CACGS category because of the assessment process. It was begun in 1968 and serves between 800,000 and 900,000 people annually according to Baker (2002). A new version became available in late 2005, and the DOD is committed to maintenance and upgrading the system.

The process of the ASVAB Career Exploration Program begins when the student takes the ASVAB, which yields an Armed Forces Qualification Test (AFQT) score that is used by military recruiters to determine a student's qualifications to enter various branches and job specialties within those branches. It also yields math, verbal, and science Career Explorations Scores and eight subtest scores. The Finding Your Interests (FYI) inventory (formerly called the Interest-Finder) yields Holland types in much the same way that other inventories (e.g., the Self Directed Search) that measure Holland's personality types do.

Counselors can arrange to have the ASVAB and FYI administered and interpreted by the local military recruiting command. Students may also take the ASVAB and FYI by contacting the local recruitment office. The report of the results of the ASVAB includes an access code (e.g., **123456789X**) that can be used to access Occu-Find. Currently, the Career Exploration Scores generated using ASVAB scores can be used in Occu-Find to explore 400 military careers and educational options. Students are able to explore both military and civilian careers using FYI and ASVAB. Baker (2002) conducted an independent evaluation of the ASVAB Career Exploration Program and found that students who completed the program increased their career exploration knowledge and had lower levels of career indecision.

USING THE INTERNET TO PROVIDE CAREER COUNSELING AND ASSESSMENT

The CEC may include, and often does, career counseling services. One question that must be answered is, "Will counseling services be offered via the Internet?" Internet-based career counseling has some obvious advantages, particularly for students who have difficult commutes as is often the case in rural areas and for students who have disabilities. However, few career counselors have received training and supervision in the art of Web-based career counseling. In the final analysis two major factors will probably dominate the decision of whether to offer Web-counseling: meeting student needs and counselor comfort with the process.

Career counselors who plan to use the Internet as a counseling tool have several options available to them. They may use e-mail to correspond with their clients and to provide support and encouragement to clients dealing with issues such as being laid off or changing jobs. E-mail also enables career counselors to request feedback from clients about aspects of the process, such as their success in completing homework assignments (e.g., an interview with a worker). Career counselors may also interact with clients using chat rooms. Communicating in chat rooms is an immediate and interactive process that simulates to some degree the type of conversation that one might have in a person-to-person or group session, as long as the session is synchronous, meaning the counselor and the client are online at the same time. Career counselors may also use asynchronous chat rooms, which simply means that not all the people involved in the cyber conversation are online at the same time. Nevertheless, career counselors can pose questions, make homework assignments, and conduct other types of processes using asynchronous chat. Asynchronous chat has few if any advantages over email.

The process of synchronous chat begins when one person, typically the counselor, types a question or statement. Others who are "in" the chat room may then type responses to what was "said." Chat rooms have the distinct advantage of allowing several people to join the session. For example, it is often useful to have clients interact with other people who have their same concerns to learn how they dealt with a problem. Career counselors can form support groups for job hunters, and participants can participate synchronously or asynchronously. If synchronous chat is used, regular meetings are scheduled and clients simply log on and participate. Arranging chat rooms and schedules can be difficult. However, schedules and distances are often much easier to accommodate when the interaction occurs online. Obvious drawbacks of using chat rooms to provide counseling services are that neither counselors nor clients have visual or auditory contact during the counseling session.

The development of computers equipped with cameras opens the possibility of "face to face" career counseling so long as both counselors and clients have computers equipped with cameras. This process approximates many of the aspects associated with traditional person-to-person counseling and is likely to become the preferred mode of providing career counseling on the Internet. The National Board for Certified Counselors developed a set of ethical standards in 1997 and updated them in 2001 and 2007 (Haberstroh, Parr, Bradley, Morgan-Fleming, & Gee, 2008) to guide practitioners who provide Web counseling. The American Counseling Association (2005) included a set of best practices in its latest ethical statement for the same purpose. Some of the guidelines include the following suggestions:

1. Obtain parental permission when providing services to minors.
2. Make sure that any information obtained from clients is stored in a secure place. Encrypted systems should be used if possible as an additional protection of the client's confidentiality.
3. Ensure that the quality of services provided via the Internet is of the same quality that would be provided in person from a counselor.
4. Get permission from clients when releasing information.
5. Make clients aware that technical difficulties may interrupt the service from time to time.
6. Inform clients that miscommunication can occur when nonverbal cues are not available, as may occur during chat room conversations.
7. Find out whether clients can contact the service provider at times other than when services are being provided.

8. Provide clients with hyperlinks to licensing boards and professional associations so that ethical complaints can be lodged if necessary.
9. Maintain a list of referral sources in the client's locale in the event that online counseling becomes inappropriate or nonproductive.
10. Discuss cultural or language differences that might impact the counseling process.

Career Assessment Devices Online

As was noted earlier, assessment is an integral part of career counseling and thus the practitioner who elects to use Web-counseling must be prepared to identify resources that can be accessed using the Internet. Several publishers provide opportunities for individuals to go online, enter a credit card number, and complete an interest or personality inventory. Once the inventory is completed, the individual receives a computer-generated printout with a detailed interpretation of the results. Some of the inventories and the Web sites where they can be accessed are as follows:

Strong Interest Inventory	https://www.cpp.com/products/strong/index.aspx
Myers-Briggs Type Inventory	http://www.myersbriggsreports.com
Self-Directed Search (SDS)	http://www.self-directed-search.com/
Career Key	http://www.careerkey.org/
Kuder Career Planning System	http://www.kuder.com/

ESTABLISHING WEB SITES AS ADJUNCTS TO WEB-COUNSELING   A brief surfing expedition on the Internet using keyword searches reveals that many CECs have developed Web sites to publicize the activities of the center, to provide online assessment services, to help students and others develop job-hunting skills including crafting resumes and interviewing skill, to link jobs posted in the career placement service to students and alumni, and to provide services to satellite campuses. Web sites can also include hyperlinks to useful sites containing occupational and educational information, assessment instruments, and job openings. Before linking the CEC Web site to another Web site, a careful evaluation of the site should occur by answering the following questions:

- When was the site last updated? This information usually appears on the home page. Useful sites are updated regularly.
- Who developed and maintains the site? Can this person or agency be contacted via e-mail to answer questions?
- Are the sources of the information on the Web site reputable? For example, are there excerpts from professional journals or government publications?
- Is the reading level of the material appropriate for your clients?
- Can the material on the Web site be accessed easily? For example, do icons allow easy return to the home page?

Summary

Three types of CECs have been discussed in this center: virtual, brick and mortar, and a blend of the two. If properly designed, CECs become the hub of the career development Web site by offering career counseling, assessment services, career and educational information, employability skills development opportunities, and a host of other services. Perhaps the most important aspect of this presentation is that it is increasingly possible to offer many CEC services virtually using a computer and an ISP. Perhaps the most controversial and so far unresearched aspect of CECs is Web counseling. Uncertainty about the effectiveness of this approach has deterred many agencies from offering the service, but given the sheer number of people who have Internet access it seems likely that the practice will grow.

Chapter Quiz

T F **1.** Because of the rapid increase in the amount and quality of information on the Internet, the CRC of the future may be a series of computer sites.

T F **2.** One-Stop Career Centers are the Department of Labor's attempt to simplify and eliminate duplication among the many types of data they produce.

T F **3.** Offering career counseling using the Internet poses few ethical issues,

T F **4.** Web-based career assessment tools are little different from computer-based assessments

T F **5.** Web counseling using e-mail is synonymous with using synchronous chat rooms.

T F **6.** The major weakness of One-Stop Career Centers is their failure to deal with cross-functional skills and thus the ability of unemployed workers to find jobs.

T F **7.** The Association for Counselor Education and Supervision has developed guidelines for evaluating the credentials of CEC coordinators.

T F **8.** The strongest rationale for installing CACGS is that research shows that all groups benefit from using them.

T F **9.** CACGS are available for all educational levels and adults.

T F **10.** ASVAB is an interest inventory that is used by military recruiters to assist potential enlistees to select military jobs that have links to civilian jobs.

(1) T (2) T (3) F (4) T (5) T (6) F (7) F (8) F (9) T (10) F

References

American Counseling Association. (1995). *Code of ethics and ethical standards.* Alexandria, VA: Author.

Association of Counselor Education and Supervision. (1999). *Technical competencies for counselor education students: Recommended guidelines for program development.* Alexandria, VA: Author.

Baker, H. E. (2002). Reducing adolescent career indecision: The ASVAB career exploration pro gram. *Career Development Quarterly, 50,* 359–370.

Brown, D., & Brooks, L. (1991). *Career counseling techniques.* Boston: Allyn & Bacon.

Campbell, R. B. (1983). *Assessing the effectiveness of DIS-COVER in a small campus career development program.* York, PA: Career Development and Placement Center. (ERIC Document Reproduction Service NO. ED 253 782).

Ettinger, J. (2008a). Serving diverse populations. In D. A. Schutt Jr. (Ed.) *How to plan and develop a career center* (2nd ed., pp. 105–118) New York: Ferguson.

Ettinger, J. (2008b) One-stop career centers for adults. In D. A. Schutt Jr. (Ed.) *How to plan and develop a career center* (2nd ed., pp. 135–144) New York: Ferguson. Jossey-Bass.

Fukuyama, M. A., Robert, B. S., Neimeyer, G. J., Nevill, D. D., & Metzler, M. A. (1988). Effects of DISCOVER on career self-efficacy and decision-making of undergraduates. *Career Development Quarterly, 37,* 56–62.

Garis, J. W., & Harris-Bowlsbey, J. (1984). *DISCOVER and the counselor: Their effects upon college student career planning progress* (Research Report #85). Hunt Valley, MD: American College Testing.

Garis, J. W., & Niles, S. G. (1990). The separate and combined effects of SIGI or DISCOVER and a career planning course on undecided university students. *Career Development Quarterly, 38,* 261–274.

Haberstroh, S. Parr, G., Bradley, L., Morgan-Fleming, B., & Gee, R. (2008). Facilitating online counseling: perspectives from counselors in training. *Journal of Counseling and Development, 87,* 381–390.

Harris-Bowlsbey, J. (1990). Computer-based guidance systems: Their past, present, and future. In J. P. Sampson,

Jr., & R. C. Reardon (Eds.), *Enhancing the design and use of computer-assisted career guidance systems.* Alexandria, VA:

Kapes, J. T., Borman, C. A., & Frazier, N. (1989). An evaluation of SIGI and DISCOVER microcomputer-based career guidance systems. *Measurement and Evaluation in Counseling and Development, 22,* 126–136.

Katz, M. R. (1990). Yesterday, today, and tomorrow. In J. P. Sampson, Jr., & R. C. Reardon (Eds.), *Enhancing the design and use of computer-assisted career guidance systems.* Alexandria, VA:

Maples, M. R., & Luzzo, D. A. (2005). Evaluating DISCOVER's effectiveness in enhancing college students' social cognitive career development. *Career Development Quarterly, 53,* 274–285.

Marin, P. A., & Splete, H. (1991). A comparison of the effect of two computer-based counseling interventions on the decidedness of adults. *Career Development Quarterly, 39,* 360–371.

Mazel, M., & Cummings, R. (1982). *How to select a computer assisted guidance system.* Madison: Wisconsin Vocational Studies Center.

Niles, S., & Garis, J. W. (1990). The effects of a career planning course and a computer-assisted career guidance program (SIGI PLUS) on undecided college students. *Journal of Career Development, 16,* 237–248.

Roselle, B. E., & Hummel, T. J. (1988). Intellectual development and interaction effectiveness with DISCOVER. *Career Development Quarterly, 36,* 241–250.

Sampson, J. P., Jr. (1997a, January). Ethical delivery of computer-assisted career guidance services: Supported vs. stand-alone system use. Paper presented at the National Career Development Association Convention, Daytona Beach, FL.

Sampson, J. P., Jr. (1997b, April). Helping clients get the most from computer-assisted career guidance systems. Paper presented at the Australian Association of Career Counselors Seventh National/ International Conference, Brisbane, Australia.

Sampson, J. P., Jr. (1997c, October). Enhancing the use of career information with computer-assisted career guidance systems. Paper presented at symposium "The Present and Future of Computer-Assisted Career Guidance Systems in Japan," Tokyo, Japan.

Sampson, J. P., Jr., Reardon, R. C., Reed, C., Rudd, E., Lumsden, J., Epstein, J. (1998). A differential feature–cost analysis of 17 computer-assisted career guidance systems: Technical Report Number 10 (8th ed.). Tallahassee: Florida State University, Center for the Study of Technology in Counseling and Career Development.

Schnell, A., & Schaefer, K. (1999). Adult career centers: An overview. In D. Schutt et al., *How to plan and develop a career center* (pp. 109–130). New York: Ferguson.

Schutt, D. A. Jr. (2008). Developing your facilities, In D. A. Schutt Jr (Ed.) *How to plan and develop a career center* (2nd ed., pp. 18–37). New York: Ferguson.

Schutt, D. A., Jr., & Finkle, J. (2008). Critical center resources. In D. A. Schutt Jr (Ed.) *How to plan and develop a career center* (2nd ed., pp. 53–71). New York: Ferguson.

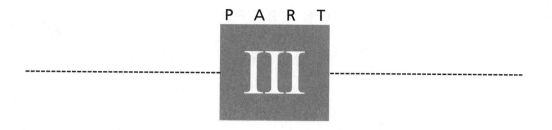

Facilitating Action Taking

10

Preparing for Work

Things to Remember

- The many options open to American workers to attain the education and training they need prior to employment
- The magnitude of the high school dropout problem and sources of assistance and training for dropouts
- The major sources of financial aid for postsecondary education and how it can be located

I t is common knowledge that there is a positive relationship between the educational level attained and lifetime earnings. To be sure, a tackle in the National Football League makes more than the orthopedic surgeon that reconstructed his broken arm and rock stars make more money than almost everyone. It is also the case that educational attainment is not accompanied by a written guarantee that the completion of a bachelor's degree comes with a written guarantee of employment or, if graduates are able to land a job, a salary that guarantees a comfortable lifestyle. College graduates are very often underemployed, which in plain English means they make less money than their educational attainment would suggest is likely. The fact is I that many people who graduated from college made poor occupational choices that offered little opportunity after graduation.

Preparing for work begins with choosing a job that suits the individual's talents, getting the best possible education or training for that job, and developing employability skills that allows the aspiring worker to locate and secure the best possible employment. Chapters 5 through 9 addressed the processes and resources need to help the people make appropriate occupational choices. Chapter 11, which follows, deals with the job hunt and the skills needed for success in that endeavor, and it outlines some of the training and educational options open to clients who have chosen an occupation.

Education is often touted as the road out of poverty, but there is increasing doubt that our schools are up to setting poor people on the right path. Some believe that our educational institutions, particularly our public K–12 schools, are rapidly becoming second class institutions that serve our society badly. They point to National Educational Assessment Program data that compares U.S. students with those in other developed countries and other test results to support their case. The bottom line is that typical American students do less well than students in other countries, but that is not the entire story. Jerry Trusty and I (Brown & Trusty, 2005) reviewed the data and came to a different conclusion. That conclusion is that our schools are failing poor white and minority students. If that conclusion is correct, our goal of helping marginalized groups attain economic equity is, at best, difficult.

As a career counselor, you have two tasks to perform. First, familiarize yourself with the educational opportunities that are available to your clients and teach them how to negotiate the system to prepare themselves for a high-quality occupation. Second, advocate for better schools, colleges, and training programs for the adolescents and adults in this country. The information in this chapter will set you on the path to the knowledge you need to perform these tasks.

TRAINING TIME

Training time can be divided into two broad types: general education and specific vocational preparation. The first includes all the general academic preparation that develops reasoning and adaptability, decision-making skills, the ability to understand and follow directions, and the ability to work cooperatively with others. It also includes the development of basic educational skills, such as mathematics, language usage, reading, and writing. Acquisition of these skills starts no later than an individual's first day of kindergarten and, in most cases, many months earlier. To the general education requirements I would add foreign language skills. The global job market requires workers to have the ability to read, write, and speak the language of the country in which they are employed. It is already the case that many jobs in this country require the ability to speak Spanish because many of the workers and the clients of the businesses are of Hispanic origin and have limited ability to speak English. Although much general education is acquired outside the classroom and supplements the school curriculum, most is learned in school.

Specific vocational preparation is training directed toward learning techniques, knowledge, and skills needed for a specific job and situation. In general, an individual becomes concerned with obtaining specific vocational preparation after a tentative career decision has been made and the person recognizes (usually in the planning period) that she or he must acquire certain skills and knowledge to implement the decision.

Every occupation requires some combination of these two types of preparation. Continued attendance in public or private school typically enhances the development of a student's general education development. However, specific vocational preparation is typically gained outside of K–12 schools, although there are exceptions for students who choose to pursue a vocational curriculum. For these students, preparation for work is included in the high school program. Other students may leave school prior to graduation and enter a training program in a community college, vocational technical school, or as an OJT trainee. On-the-job training is typically the route followed by high school dropouts and graduates who do choose not to pursue some form of postsecondary education. Many high school graduates do elect a postsecondary educational route that may or may not include a college degree, a graduate program, or some form of professional education.

It is important to note that students who do decide not to complete high school increase the likelihood of sustained periods of unemployment and lower wages when they are employed. Each year 1.2 million or nearly 29 percent of enrolled students leave high school prematurely (Alliance for Excellent Education, 2009). Put differently, about 7,000 students leave high school each day (Monrad, 2009). Dropouts are more likely to be Hispanic or African American and to attend schools in western and northern cities, and throughout the South. The Alliance for Excellent Education points out that some high schools are what they term dropout factories and that about 12 percent of U.S. high schools produce 50 percent of the dropouts. Although the factors that lead students to leave school before they graduate are many, a well developed career development program that begins as early as sixth grade can reduce the dropout rate. Well-designed programs can answer the question, "Why do I have to learn this stuff?"—a question that has to be answered for many students if they are to be kept in school.

HIGH SCHOOL AND PREPARATION FOR WORK

Preparing high school students to enter the labor market has been a longstanding concern in this country. In contrast to some European countries, students in the United States are not tracked into college and noncollege options based on test scores and grades. The U.S. approach has the advantage of not foreclosing educational and career options prematurely. The disadvantage of the system is that when students complete their secondary schooling, many have difficulty making the transition to work. One legislative effort, the School-to-Work Opportunity Act (STWOA) of 1994, was developed to address this concern. This legislation provides money to schools to develop instructional programs based on both academic and occupational standards; to provide opportunities to all students to engage in work-based learning, including work experience, mentoring, and apprenticeships; and to provide what are termed *connecting activities*, which develop links between the workplace and schools. The STWOA has been reinforced by several other pieces of legislation, including the amendments to the Individuals with Disabilities Education Improvement Act of 2004, Goals 2000: Educate America Act, No Child Left Behind Act of 2001, and the National Skills Standards Act of 1994. There are several implications related to these acts:

1. School-to-work (STW) activities may begin as early as kindergarten.
2. Students with disabilities must have STW transition plans as a part of their individualized education programs (IEPs).
3. Coordination of school activities with the other agencies is required.
4. Work-based learning should be a part of the program.
5. Employers should be involved in the design and implementation of the program.
6. Career exploration and counseling are an integral part of the program, and students involved in the program must choose a career major no later than grade 11.

In North Carolina middle school students complete a plan for their four-year course of study that is intended to lead to one of four options: college or university, postsecondary education to include technical careers or college (tech-prep), occupational education, or nondiploma. Although vocational education programs may not be included in every high school, such programs may be offered at specialized school in the district. In addition to vocational education, some schools offer a variety of work experience programs that directly address the need to prepare high school graduates for the workforce. The school-to-work initiative was not intended to supplant these approaches, which are discussed in next section in some detail. However, STWOA was intended to address a concern that schools often ignore, the transition from school to work.

Vocational Education

Vocational education programs were formally established in the United States during World War I and have received continuing support since then. Such programs offer specific vocational preparation in a variety of occupations ranging from cosmetology and the building trades to printing and auto repair. Many vocational education programs require the completion of rigorous educational programs and thus are open primarily to students with relatively high academic ability. However, some schools offer vocational education programs such as shoe repair that accommodate students with relatively low academic ability. Often the admission to vocational education programs that require high levels of academic aptitude is highly competitive The result is that many students who wish to enter them are precluded from doing so.

Work Experience Programs

Many secondary schools include in their curricula some opportunities for students to combine study in the classroom with experience in an employment situation. These opportunities vary slightly from school to school and are known by a range of titles: cooperative work experience, distributive education, office practice, job experience, and diversified training. These programs are usually incorporated into the school's vocational curriculum. The general purpose of these programs is to prepare selected students for employment while they complete their high school education. Successful participation in a work experience program results in high school graduation, a sound basic general education, and preparation for full-time employment in a chosen occupation.

Operationally, work study programs depart from traditional high school instructional procedures. Often the students in the group are involved in widely varied occupations; in fact, one of the titles used for this type of program—diversified cooperative education—stresses the variety. The programs require cooperation between high school coordinators and local employers who divide instructional and supervisory responsibilities to assist the student in gaining occupational competence. In general, then, this is a school-community program of vocational instruction that uses the training and educational resources, facilities, and personnel of both the local school and the community. The program is expected to accomplish the following objectives:

1. The student establishes an occupational objective consistent with abilities and interests.
2. The student develops skills necessary for full-time employment as a worker or as an apprentice in a chosen occupation.
3. The student acquires related and technical information necessary for occupational performance.
4. The student develops appropriate attitudes and personal characteristics enhancing adjustment, success, and progress in the occupational field.
5. The student becomes increasingly mature in his or her relationship to school and to economic, social, and home life.

The specific objectives can be thought of in terms of (1) the job skills that the student needs to master, (2) the knowledge that must be gained to perform the work with intelligence and judgment, and (3) the personal and social traits that must be developed to get along well on the job and in the community. The instruction in job skills is provided by the employer under actual employment conditions. Students usually work a minimum of 15 hours a week, most of which is scheduled during the regular school day.

The typical program permits a student, usually in the junior or senior year, to attend classes half-time and to work in an assigned employment position the other half. In a few large city systems, the student spends one week in school and the following week at work, alternating with a fellow student on a reverse schedule. The most common situation, however, has the student in school in the morning and on the job in the afternoon. The student is supervised by the employer in the work assignment, but a school staff member serves as a liaison between the school and the employer and maintains close contact with both the student and the employer. The student earns academic credit for the work assignment as part of the school's vocational education curriculum.

All participants are enrolled in a related study class or classes that meet for at least one regular class period each school day. The classes taught by the school staff members are responsible for the program. Most of the instruction is technical and has a direct relationship to the student's work assignment. The courses provide trainees with information that helps them in their work. Because the students are usually involved in a wide range of occupational assignments, they have a similar variety of individual training plans; so the class work is provided necessarily on an individual basis, using special instructional materials.

General information for beginning workers is included in the program of classes. Topics covered usually include units on employer–employee relations, Social Security provisions, money management, income tax problems, personality and work, and labor organizations. Some schools arrange the program so that each day includes one period of general related instruction and another period of specialized or individualized instruction based on the placement.

Work experience in these programs is totally realistic because it has every characteristic of a regular job, including pay. The student has an opportunity to face the same situation that every worker encounters, with the added advantage of having a coordinator to assist in making adjustments or solving the problems encountered in the position.

The placement of students may not be completely aligned with their career goals, but even in these situations the students are advantaged in several ways. They are provided an opportunity to gain insight into the work situation and their responsibility in it. They learn to adjust to the employer, fellow workers, the public served and to the overall demands of the work situation. They also learn the importance of punctuality, cooperation, responsibility, paths for advancement, and similar factors that are beyond simple vocational skill. It is not unusual for participants, on completing their schooling, to accept full-time employment with the companies in which they were placed for work experience, although employment after school is not necessarily an expectation. Participants gain an additional advantage later because they can list actual experience on their resumes when seeking full-time employment.

Inevitably, work experience programs also have some disadvantages. It is not always possible to acquire placement sites that serve the best interests of the students. Some employers are primarily concerned with obtaining inexpensive workers when they should be interested in training each student. Similarly, students may enter the programs principally for the financial benefits rather than for vocational preparation. Some programs have such strict admission requirements that the student who most needs assistance are ineligible to participate. Because of the time consumed in field supervision, in consultation with employers, and in observation of student workers on the job, program coordinators can effectively handle only a limited number of students; consequently, the program is rarely as extensive as it should be to meet the needs of most non–college-bound students in a particular high school.

Though rarely used to the fullest extent, the work experience program offers an opportunity for most secondary schools to render a service to both students and community by helping students prepare themselves realistically for post–high school employment. Close cooperation between the coordinator and the school counselor brings more effective selection and placement in the program and more satisfying results to the student, school, and community.

Advocates for career development programs point to the work experience program as illustrative of the close school-community cooperation considered essential for effective career education. They suggest that all students should have work experience placements beginning in grade 9 with exploratory programs and culminating in grade 12 with work skills development.

Early placements would not involve pay. Placements extending over several school years and incorporating a variety of work assignments would provide students with a better understanding of the workplace as well as a set of marketable skills. It also seems likely that schools and the business community would be drawn together into cooperative relationships that would be mutually beneficial. The Crowley Independent School District of Crowley, Texas (www.crowley.k12. tx.us) offers a number of career and cooperative education programs including horticulture, science and technology; business education; computer/technology education; family and consumer sciences, and cosmetology.

Academies

One of the newest approaches to preparing students for the labor market is the academy, which was developed in response to initiatives from business and industry. An academy, much like many vocational education programs, is a program designed to prepare students to work in a specific occupation. One of the best-known academies was developed by Cisco Systems, the major manufacturer of devices called routers that link together computer and telephone systems. This highly successful corporation found that there was a substantial shortage of technicians who could repair their equipment. In response to this shortage, executives from Cisco Systems designed a high school curriculum for training technicians and a certification examination that would ensure that graduates of the program were sufficiently trained to perform the tasks required.

Health science academies have been developed that provide specific vocational preparation and introduce students to the broad array of health science occupations typically under the auspices of vocational education. At the conclusion of one such academy, students are eligible to sit for the Emergency Medical Technician examination, which many successfully pass. However, many others decide to pursue postsecondary training that leads to other careers in health science. Both Cisco academies and the health science academies bridge academic and vocational programs and provide students the options of electing to continue their educations at the postsecondary level or going directly to work.

OUTSIDE THE CLASSROOM—NO DIPLOMA REQUIRED

As noted in the introduction, U.S. schools have difficulty retaining all of their students until they graduate. The group, usually referred to as high school dropouts, includes many who might more appropriately be labeled "pushouts" or "lost-outs." Some individuals decide that the school program has nothing to offer them and voluntarily leave when they reach the legal age or shortly thereafter. Others, confronting difficult problems—poverty, parental discouragement, lack of family, pregnancy, personal adjustment or behavioral problems, addiction, and so forth—do not receive sufficient help from the school to overcome the difficulties they face. With some obvious exceptions, most of those who leave before graduation are likely to face the greatest problems in finding, obtaining, and keeping jobs. Dropouts rarely leave school with a carefully developed career plan. The result is that they have no specific vocational preparation and only a marginal general education. Unfamiliarity with the world of work makes them ignorant of how to seek work, what kinds of jobs might fit their qualifications, and where those jobs are. Those who find their way to state employment security agencies are helped by referral to other local agencies that may be able to provide some of the needed services or by referral to employers who are seeking unskilled, entry-level workers. In general, two possibilities are available for this group unless they complete their high school work—on-the-job training (OJT) or skill acquisition through programs such as the Job Training Partnership Act.

On-the-Job Training

Some employment situations require neither specialized educational preparation nor specific vocational experience as a prerequisite. The absence of such requirements usually means that the work either can be learned readily during a brief demonstration period or is such that only a minimal general education is necessary to prepare the worker. The employer may prefer, for a variety of reasons, to hire inexperienced workers who can be trained as desired, paid little or nothing in fringe benefits, and let go without fear of legal retribution.

For the most part employers offer on-the-job training when the essentials of job performance can be learned in a relatively brief period of time. However, there are exceptions. When the job is performed by a team or crew of skilled workers, new employees may be assigned to a team as helpers, where they learn the complexities of the job by observing and assisting skilled practitioners for a specified period. Some employers may rotate beginners' assignments so that they serve a period with several teams involved in different aspects of the work, thus becoming familiar with several phases before assignment to a specific job.

Job Training Partnership Act as Amended by STWOA of 1994

Since World War II, the United States has attempted to develop a system for training or retraining workers needed in certain parts of the economy. The Manpower Defense Training Act served this purpose during the war years, training workers to fill positions in rapidly expanding defense and war-related industries. This was followed by the Manpower Development and Training Act (MDTA), which provided workers with skills needed in new and expanding industries. Training was aimed especially at unemployed or underemployed individuals. Next, the Comprehensive Employment and Training Act (CETA) was developed to provide a decentralized program in which state and local units of government could develop training programs to meet local conditions and the needs of prospective employers as well as those of unemployed or underemployed workers. CETA was replaced by the Job Training Partnership Act (JTPA) in 1982. More than 1 million people receive training under the auspices of JTPA each year.

JTPA authorizes state-level officials to designate "service delivery areas"—that is, geographic regions consisting of contiguous counties or other political units that constitute a "labor market." Within each service delivery area, a Private Industry Council is created, consisting primarily of representatives of businesses or industries in the area, with responsibility for policy guidance and administrative oversight of job training in the area. The Private Industry Council and local government officials must concur on the local plan and its administration; this local plan then must be approved by the state governor's office. The law requires that 70 percent of the funds available to a service delivery area be spent on training. Each state, through the governor's office, is required to monitor programs in service delivery areas.

The legislation that established JTPA authorizes a wide range of training activities aimed at economically disadvantaged youth and adults to prepare them for unsubsidized employment. Programs may include on-the-job training, classroom training, remedial education, basic skills training, and job-search assistance. At least 40 percent of the funds must be spent for disadvantaged youth between the ages of 16 and 21. Ninety percent of the participants must be economically disadvantaged. The other 10 percent must have identifiable labor market disadvantages, and might include individuals with disabilities, prior offenders, displaced homemakers, older workers, teenage parents, and others.

JTPA legislation also authorized state-administered programs to assist dislocated workers and homemakers, including workers from permanently closed plants, offenders, veterans of the Vietnam War, disabled veterans, and the long-term unemployed who have little prospect of obtaining local employment. Services provided may include job-search assistance, retraining, pre-layoff assistance, and relocation. Currently many of these services are offered through One-Stop Career Centers.

The 1994 School-to-Work Opportunities Act (STWOA) was initiated to facilitate partnerships between public schools and business organizations. It is typically operated by a board or council comprised primarily of representatives from businesses and schools and strives to integrate academic and vocational education. Hollenbeck (1997) reports that the intent of STWOA was to stimulate educational reform and to enhance the career preparation of high school students. He also suggests that the program has fallen far short of its primary goals. Apparently much of the activity in these programs involves activities such as job shadowing and career fairs which are essentially devoted to career exploration.

The Job Corps

The Job Corps (http://jobcorps.doleta.gov), which is a no cost, residential program with more than 120 centers throughout the United States, was first established in 1964 as a result of the passage of the Equal Opportunity Act. Originally intended to serve high school dropouts, The Job Corps currently serves individuals ranging from ages 16 to 24, unless they have disabilities, whereupon no age restriction applies. Job Corps Centers provide the following services:

- Intensive counseling designed to increase students' self-esteem
- Medical services
- Remedial education
- Specific realistic vocational education
- Social skills development aimed at helping enrollees obtain and keep jobs
- Educational experiences intended to lead to high school diplomas or GED certificates
- Citizenship training

Eligibility to enroll in Job Corps, in addition to the age parameters noted previously, is based on the following criteria:

- Being a U.S. citizen or a legally admitted alien
- Having a low income
- Being a school dropout or an individual who requires additional academic or vocational education, intensive career counseling, or is homeless or a runaway
- Having parental consent if a minor
- Being drug free and agreeing to a no-tolerance drug use policy
- Having a child care plan if applicant is a parent
- Not having face-to-face court supervision or court-imposed fines

Job Corps Centers vary in the types of services they offer. Some offer English as a second language programs to help legal immigrant and others develop the language skills they need to succeed in school and at work. Others offer family living support skills, and still others offer specific vocational preparations such as the Cisco Academy, mentioned previously.

OUTSIDE THE CLASSROOM—HIGH SCHOOL DIPLOMA PREFERRED OR REQUIRED

As noted earlier, high school graduates may have had access to work experience programs in some situations. They may also be eligible for certain government training programs already discussed depending on the socioeconomic background and the presence of disabling conditions. In addition, there are at least two other types of training situations available that are more likely to be available to high school graduates than early school leavers. Apprenticeship programs and military services offer training in a vast array of occupations.

Apprenticeship Programs

The use of apprenticeships for transmitting knowledge and skills to new workers dates back at least to the Middle Ages. The various guilds of skilled artisans developed the regular practice of indenturing young workers to master crafters. During the period of indenture, often seven years, the young worker served or worked for the master; in return, the master provided food and lodging for the boy, usually in the master's own home, and taught him the skills and secrets of the craft. On successful completion of the indenture, the worker was accepted by the guild as a journeyman or independent craftsman. As the practice of his craft grew and expanded, he in turn became a master and took in apprentices who were taught job skills (see www.doleta.gov/atels_bat).

The National Apprenticeship Program was established by Congress in 1937 with the support of both labor and management organizations. The Fitzgerald Act authorized the Secretary of Labor to set up standards to guide industry in employing and training apprentices; to bring management and labor together to work out plans for training apprentices; to appoint such national committees as needed; and to promote general acceptance of the standards and procedures agreed on. The agency, now known as the Bureau of Apprenticeship and Training (BAT), was created to put the program into effect. A committee, known as the Federal Committee on Apprenticeship, representing management, labor, and government was appointed to develop standards and policies.

A basic tenet of the BAT has been that employers and employees should jointly develop programs for employment and training of apprentices to their mutual satisfaction. Because apprenticeship programs exist in a wide range of trades, the standards recommended by the Federal Committee on Apprenticeship are quite general, thus permitting the employer and employee groups in various trades to work out in concert the details for the training programs. Under the provisions of the BAT, an apprentice is a person at least 16 years of age (most programs require 18 years of age) who works under a written agreement registered with the state apprenticeship council (or with the BAT if there is no state council). The regulation provides for a specified period of reasonably continuous employment for the person, and for participation in an approved schedule of work experiences supplemented by at least 144 hours per year of related classroom instruction. The bureau has established certain basic standards by which an apprenticeship program functions:

1. An apprenticeable occupation usually requires from one to six years of employment to learn. Most last about four years.
2. The employment must be organized into a schedule of work processes to be learned so that the apprentice gains experience in all phases of the work. This prevents assignment to only one or a few specific tasks during the period of training and is intended to ensure the development of skill and knowledge in all aspects of the work.

3. A progressively increasing wage scale should be set for the apprentice, starting at about half the regular worker's rate.
4. Related classroom instruction should amount to at least 144 hours per year.
5. A written agreement, including the terms and conditions of employment and training of each apprentice, is registered with the State Apprenticeship Council.
6. The State Apprenticeship Council provides reviews of local apprenticeships.
7. Programs are established jointly by employer and employees.
8. Adequate supervision and records are required for all programs.
9. Full and fair opportunity to apply for apprenticeship is provided, with selection made on the basis of qualifications alone without discrimination.
10. Periodic evaluation of the apprentice's progress is made, both in job performance and in related instruction.
11. Recognition of successful completion is provided.

Apprenticeship programs have a number of easily identified advantages:

1. They provide the most efficient way to train all-around craftspeople to meet present and future needs.
2. They ensure an adequate supply of skilled craftspeople for employment opportunities.
3. They ensure a supply of competent craftspeople in the community, skilled in all aspects of their trades.
4. They offer the consuming public a supply of high-quality products and services that only trained hands and minds can produce.
5. They increase the individual worker's productivity.
6. They give the individual worker a greater sense of security.
7. They improve employer-employee relations.
8. They eliminate close supervision because the craftsperson is trained to use initiative, imagination, and ability in planning and performing work.
9. They provide a source of future supervision.
10. They provide the versatility necessary to meet changing conditions.
11. They attract capable young people to the industry.
12. They generally raise skill levels in the industry.

State departments of labor have been asked to establish apprenticeship councils at the state level. These councils are intended to serve as liaison agencies between federal local levels and to encourage cooperation between state agencies and employers and employee groups. Where formed, these groups include an equal number of representatives of employers and employees, as well as representatives from appropriate state agencies. The state organization, using standards recommended by the federal committee as guides, sets up state standards and procedures to be followed by industries in employing and training apprentices. Once established and recognized by the bureau, the state council becomes part of the national apprenticeship program.

In some industries, national employer groups and national trade unions appoint apprenticeship committees. These committees meet as joint management-labor groups to develop national apprenticeship standards and to encourage the establishment of training programs in accordance with the adopted standards. These organizations grow out of specific industries and are concerned with programs within the specific industry; they are therefore independent of the BAT. The usual practice has been for a close relationship to develop between the national committees and the federal bureau, with each assisting the other through sharing information and consultation.

Both the federal and the state organizations are primarily concerned with the establishment and development of standards. The actual employment and training of apprentices occur at the local level. Employers who are members of the local groups and other employers who subscribe to the program establish local joint apprenticeship committees to organize the development of standards for employment and training for all apprentices in the specific trade.

Qualifications for employment, such as age, education, aptitude, wages, hours of work, the term of the apprenticeship, the schedule of job processes, and the amount of class time required, are usually spelled out in detail in the local standards. Also included are procedures for executing and registering the agreement and methods of supervising apprentices at work and at school. The classroom instruction is provided by local and state vocational schools. The local committee often serves as an advisory group in developing an appropriate program of instruction.

Admission requirements are set by the local apprenticeship council in compliance with general standards set at the state and national level. Considerable variation can be found from trade to trade and even within a particular trade among geographic regions. The number of applicants usually far exceeds the number of vacancies. For example, in the construction trades, applicants usually exceed openings about eight to one.

Nearly 35,000 programs are registered for apprenticeships in more than 1,000 occupations (U.S. Department of Labor, 2010). Table 10.1 provides a partial list of apprenticeable occupations. Though not comprehensive, the list does show the range of programs that can be included. Currently nearly one million people are involved in registered and nonregistered apprenticeship programs according to an estimate by Lerman (2009). He recommends the expansion of the number of apprenticeship programs through a collaborative effort by labor unions, businesses, and community colleges focusing on those occupations that are predicted to have high growth rates during the next decade (e.g., licensed practical nurses). Lerman admits that implementing will take a higher level of collaboration than is generally the case but points to bright spots such as South Carolina.

Information about apprenticeships can be obtained from several sources. Perhaps the easiest way to find information is to go to the One-Stop Career Center Web site, click on the Education + Training button, which will yield a variety of educational options. Under FIND click on apprenticeships, where you can view listings of registered apprenticeship programs, view an apprenticeship video, or find apprenticeships in your state. Students and workers interested in apprenticeships may also consult local unions and employment security offices, and/or the Web site of the department of labor within their states.

Military Training

Although a number of specialized occupations actually exist only within the military—infantryman is a prime example—many more military occupations have civilian counterparts to which military training and experience are directly transferable. Of the approximately 4,100 occupational specialties in the military services, 2,600 have civilian equivalents. Those that do not have civilian counterparts are primarily combat specialties.

One of two military programs may be especially important to interested individuals. One is college-level training, either in one of the service academies, where a four-year program leads to both a commission and a degree, or in a civilian college or university, where a four-year Reserve Officer Training Corps (ROTC) program can produce the same results. A second option is a matched savings program in which enlisted personnel can designate pay set-asides that are supplemented by additional two-for-one grants from the military to pay for college education after completing the military enlistment.

TABLE 10.1   Examples of Apprenticeable Occupations

1. Airframe and Power Plant Mechanic	38. Instrument Mechanic
2. Automobile Body Repairer	39. Insulation Worker
3. Automobile Mechanic	40. Legal Secretary
4. Baker	41. Line Erector
5. Biomedical Equipment Technician	42. Line Maintainer
6. Boatbuilder, Wood	43. Machine Repairer, Maintenance
7. Boilermaker I	44. Machinist
8. Boiler Operator	45. Maintenance Machinist
9. Butcher, Meat	46. Maintenance Mechanic
10. Bricklayer	47. Medical Laboratory Technician
11. Cabinetmaker	48. Millwright
12. Car Repairer (Railroad)	49. Mine-Car Repairer
13. Carpenter	50. Miner I
14. Cement Mason	51. Model Maker
15. Compositor	52. Mold Maker Die Casting and Plastic Molding
16. Computer Peripheral Equipment Operator (Clerical)	53. Office Machine Servicer
17. Construction-Equipment Mechanic	54. Offset Press Operator I
18. Cook	55. Ornamental Ironworker
19. Coremaker	56. Painter
20. Cosmetologist	57. Patternmaker, All-Around
21. Dairy Equipment Mechanic	58. Patternmaker, Wood
22. Dental Laboratory Technician	59. Pipefitter
23. Drafter, Architectural	60. Plumber
24. Drafter, Mechanical	61. Powerhouse Mechanic
25. Drilling Machine Operator	62. Precision Lens Grinder
26. Electrician	63. Programmer, Business
27. Electrical Repairer	64. Programmer, Engineering and Scientific
28. Electronics Mechanic	65. Refrigeration Mechanic
29. Electronics Technician	66. Sheet Metal Worker
30. Emergency Medical Technician	67. Shipfitter
31. Environmental-Control System Installer–Servicer	68. Shoemaker, Custom
32. Farm Equipment Mechanic I	69. Stationary Engineer
33. Firefighter	70. Structural Steel Worker
34. Fire Medic	71. Television and Radio Repairer
35. Furniture Finisher	72. Tool Maker
36. Glazier	73. Tool and Die Maker
37. Heavy Forger	74. Water Treatment Plant Operator
	75. Welder, Combination
	76. Welding Machine Operator, Arc

Source: From U.S. Department of Labor, "Appendix D: Apprenticeship Programs in the Military and Facts on Apprenticeships." Retrieved from www.dol.gov/csp/medialreports/credentialing/appendix.htm

Enlistment periods can be as brief as two years in the Army, three years in the Navy, and four years in all other branches. Six years is the maximum commitment in all branches except the Coast Guard, where the ceiling is four years. Pay and allowances are uniform through the branches. High school graduation is highly preferred for all recruits and is required for all Coast Guard recruits and for some training programs in other branches of the service. Some high school seniors who want to acquire specialized occupational training in a specific occupation can assure themselves of this by participating in the delayed-entry program, whereby they enlist for a specific training program in which reporting to active duty is delayed until high school graduation is completed.

Typically, new enlistees complete a basic training program that ranges from 6 to 10 weeks and consists of rigorous physical training along with classroom study and fieldwork on weapons, military law, drill, and so on. After completing basic training, the recruit enters the specific training program for the selected occupation. This is usually a classroom-based program, but it may combine classwork with field experience or may even be primarily practical training. Table 10.2 lists the occupations for which apprenticeships are available in the military services.

In addition to job-oriented training, the military services provide several other educational advantages. These include tuition assistance (up to 90 percent) for off-duty study at accredited schools; payment of fees for tests that establish college credit, such as CLEP or SAT; independent study courses; and similar programs. Information regarding the branches of the military and the military academies is easily obtained from recruiting offices that exist throughout the country, from toll-free telephone numbers, and on the Internet (see Chapter 8).

POSTSECONDARY SCHOOLS: ASSOCIATE'S DEGREES OR CERTIFICATES

As we look at the current labor force, it is apparent that the complexity of jobs has increased and the preparation jobs time is longer. Only about one-quarter of the jobs in the labor force require a college education to perform, but the need for advanced, postsecondary education is clear. Community colleges and private and public vocational-technical schools are proving the training needed to perform many twenty-first century jobs. Some of these programs are as short as eight weeks while other stretch beyond two academic years. At the end of these programs graduates typically receive either a certificate attesting to the completion of a program of studies or an associate's degree typically signifying the completion of a two-year program of studies.

Trade, Vocational, and Technical Schools

One by-product of the increasing need for postsecondary education is greater attention on specific vocational preparation. Frequently, during periods of economic downturn such as the one in progress in 2010, high unemployment rates, and general uncertainty, vocational school enrollments experience upsurges. Some of this is a search for assistance that might ensure employment or even an opportunity for employment. In many states, the expansion of the community college program or the establishment of publicly supported technical schools has met the major need for specialized education. Such expansion has not been uniform across the United States, however. Some states have established public area vocational schools; other states have established programs of postsecondary specialized public education through contractual arrangements with local secondary schools, universities, or other agencies equipped to offer vocational training to groups of students. Part of the impetus producing these rapid changes has come from the Vocational Education Amendments enacted by Congress, which have broadened and redefined vocational education.

Obtaining accurate, usable information about a vocational school, particularly private schools, is often much more difficult than finding similar information about a degree-public institutions. Some of the state information systems mentioned in Chapter 8 include links to private school Web sites that have eased this problem to some degree. Not every state career

TABLE 10.2 Some Apprenticeable Occupations in the Military

Apprenticeships in the following occupations are offered in the military. All are available in the Army unless otherwise indicated

Air-traffic communication technician (Marine Corps only)
Air-traffic control radar technician (Marine Corps only)
Air-traffic navigational aids technician (Marine Corps only)
Aircraft electrical mechanic
Aircraft engine mechanic (turbine)
Aircraft mechanic, armament
Airplane mechanic
Artillery repairer
Automatic equipment technician
Automobile body repairer and painter
Automobile mechanic (Marine Corps only)
Automotive electrical systems repairer
Baker (Marine Corps only)
Cable splicer
Camera repairer (Navy only)
Carpenter (Marine Corps only)
Central office telephone installer and repairer (Marine Corps only)
Construction equipment mechanic (Marine Corps only)
Cook (Marine Corps and Navy)
Drafter (architectural)
Electrical instrument repairer

Electrical mechanic (aircraft)
Electrical repairer (Marine Corps also)
Electrician (Marine Corps and Navy)
Electrician, radio
Electromechanical technician
Electronic mechanic (Marine Corps also)
Electronic mechanic (radar)
Electronic technician
Electronic technician (communications)
Electronic technician (radar)
Electronic technician (radio/TV)
Electronic warfare intercept systems repairer
Field engineer (microwave)
Fire control instrument repairer
Fire control system repairer
Firefighter
Fuel systems repairer
Grading and paving equipment operator
Heavy-duty equipment mechanic
Heavy-duty repairer (construction equipment)
Helicopter mechanic
Hydraulic equipment mechanic
Illustrator

Industrial electrician/repairer
Industrial welder
Instrument repairer (electronic)
Laboratory technician (petroleum)
Land surveyor (Marine Corps only)
Line installer/repairer
Lithographer (offset press operator)
Lithographer platemaker (Navy only)
Machinist (Navy also)
Maintenance mechanic (Navy only)
Maintenance mechanic, hydraulic equipment (aircraft)
Marine heavy-duty mechanic (heavy-duty mechanic—diesel)
Marine hull repairer, ironworker (boatbuilder—steel)
Meteorologist (Navy only)
Molder (Navy only)
Office machine servicer (Navy also)
Offset press operator (Marine Corps only)
Ordnance artificer
Photograph interpreter
Photographer, motion picture
Photographer, still (Navy also)
Photographic equipment maintenance technician
Plant equipment operator

Plumber (Marine Corps only)
Plumber, pipefitter
Powerhouse electrician/repairer
Production coordinator (radio/TV broadcasting)
Pumper–gauger (petrochemical)
Radio communications technician
Radio mechanic (Marine Corps also)
Radio operator
Radio/television repairer
Refrigeration/airconditioning repairer/servicer
Refrigeration mechanic (Marine Corps only)
Rigger
Sewing machine repairer
Sheet-metal worker (aircraft)
Small weapons repairer
Station installer/repairer (wire systems)
Stationary engineer (Navy only)
Surveyor (artillery)
Surveyor, engineering
Telegraphic-teletypewriter operator
Television cable installer
Truck mechanic
Universal equipment operator (construction equipment)
Welder, combination (Marine Corps only)

Source: From U.S. Department of Labor, "Appendix D: Apprentice Programs in the Military and Facts on Apprenticeships." Retrieved from www.dol.gov/csp/medialreports/credentialing/appendix.htm

information delivery system incorporates current data about private trade and technical institutions, which is unfortunate. However, information about both private and public vocational training programs can also be found at (http://features.yahoo.com/college/search.html) and at http://www.allschools.com.

Community Colleges and Junior Colleges

Community colleges and junior colleges have existed in this country for many years. Some states—California and Florida, for example—have included community colleges as an integral part of the statewide education program by synchronizing the two-year programs offered by community colleges with those of their four-year institutions so that students who transfer can do so seamlessly and complete their program of studies in two additional years of full-time study.

Originally, two-year institutions were developed as a downward thrust of the college or university and as a means of serving students in geographically remote locations. More recently community colleges have been developed and their curricula expanded as a means of allowing students with limited finances to complete a part of their education while living at home and usually paying less in tuition than they would to attend a four-year institution. Community colleges also save state governments money because they require neither elaborate facilities nor senior faculty members.

Whether called community college or junior college, these schools offer full- and part-time programs that include the following options:

1. The traditional college-related program for students who plan to transfer to four-year institutions to complete baccalaureate degrees.
2. A technical–terminal program to prepare students to enter employment on completion of the two-year, or shorter, curriculum.
3. Short courses of various sorts needed locally for retraining or further education.
4. An adult basic education program that offers adults the opportunity to increase their literacy and math skills.

Among the four types of programs, the greatest expansion has occurred in the technical–terminal area as the occupations in our labor force have become more complex. This growth in the occupationally oriented part of the curriculum will increase the significance of these institutions in the educational plans of students who are not interested in programs offered in baccalaureate level institutions.

One of their greatest advantages of community colleges may well be the flexibility that permits them to respond to local needs and interests. The two-year transfer programs and those technical–terminal programs that extend over two academic years often culminate in an associate of arts degree on satisfactory completion. Programs that ordinarily are completed in less than this amount of time recognize successful completion with certificates.

Admission to all community college programs, whether they are college transfer or occupationally oriented, vary with the demand and the resources available to meet the demand. Admission requirements are usually less stringent in two-year schools than they are in four-year schools. However, schools offering college transfer programs may establish entrance requirements that parallel those used by the schools to which their graduates transfer. Technical–terminal programs are more likely to have skill-based or experience-based requirements and are unlikely to specify particular academic records as prerequisites for admission. However, they may require certain scores on entrance examinations that measure math and literacy skills. Terminal programs and adult education programs often operate on totally open admission plans within the community served by the school.

The most reliable source of information about any school is the school itself, including visits, Web sites, and catalogs. Because data in most state career information delivery systems are revised at least annually, these materials may be more current than institutional print publications.

COLLEGES AND UNIVERSITIES

Harvard College was the first private college to open its doors in what is now the United States, and the University of North Carolina at Chapel Hill was the first public university to admit students. The University of Georgia, which was chattered before the University of North Carolina, opened its doors a few months later. Currently, tens of thousands of colleges and universities that offer a vast array of academic possibilities are open to students who meet entrance requirements. This wealth of options can be bewildering to students who are just graduating from high school and to adults who decide to return to school to earn degrees. Some of these schools are highly competitive and are open only to the most academically talented. Others operate under a policy of open admissions, as is the case in Indiana, where state-supported universities are required by law to admit any student who graduates from an accredited Indiana high school.

The programs range from those that prepare students for specific careers (e.g., engineering) and some that offer more general courses of study (e.g., English, usually under the auspices of a college of liberal arts). Because of the variation in institutions as well as the courses of study they offer, choosing a college is one of the major life decisions faced by students and adults. To be sure, many decisions regarding choice of college are made by default; that is, they are made on the basis of geography or financial concerns. Few students can afford the $45,000-per-year price tag now attached to some of the most prestigious U.S. colleges; others cannot pursue options outside their immediate geographic location because of a variety of personal considerations. However, even students who are faced with financial or geographic constraints need to consider their options carefully as they choose a college or university. In the remainder of this section, some concerns of this decision-making process are addressed.

Admissions Requirements

The restriction of admission by a school, either because of its desire to limit student body size or because its facilities, such as number of classrooms or dormitory rooms, often creates competition among applicants. If a school has a generally favorable reputation, the competitiveness is accentuated and the school's prestige is enhanced. Unfortunately, many prospective applicants and their parents assume that limitation of enrollment automatically reflects the quality of the educational program. This may be true to some extent, but it is often the case that students can find academic opportunities of equal standing at nearby public or private institution that have less stringent admission policies.

Generalizations based on admission standards are risky. Various institutions are moving in opposite directions on admission policies for different reasons. As mentioned earlier, enrollment ceilings may mean only that the school's philosophy is that small is better or that it has limited space. Other institutions have moved in exactly the opposite direction and adopted a policy of open admissions under which anyone with a high school diploma or other basic qualification may be permitted to enroll. In a few instances students who left high school before graduation can qualify for admission on the basis of significant employment experience, examination results, or completion of the GED.

For many years, most institutions have asked applicants to support the usual application data, a transcript of high school or preparatory school courses completed, grades, and class rank, with admissions test data. Colleges and universities require test scores for many reasons. Most large schools serve students from wide geographic regions, often nationwide or worldwide. In such a broad area, considerable difference in academic standards of high schools can be anticipated; as a result, high school grades are difficult to compare, and test scores are a valuable source of information about the students' potential. Some schools may seek to serve a particular type of student. For example, they may choose to focus on the development of writing skills and thus would be anxious to identify those students with high verbal skill. These schools are likely to request a sample of the student's writing as well. Often schools with restricted enrollments give priority to only the most able students. These schools often believe that college admission tests provide some of the information they need to select the students they wish to admit. Finally, many schools base their financial aid programs partly on consideration of ability and, therefore, require scholarship applicants to submit test scores for this purpose.

Most degree-granting schools now require applicants to submit, with their application materials, scores obtained on either the College Entrance Examination Board (CEEB) Scholastic Aptitude Test (SAT), or the American College Testing Program (ACT). Most schools specify the test they require, but many institutions now accept either one. These tests are now so widely used and so generally available in U.S. high schools that they require no special discussion here. Some colleges and universities using SAT scores also may ask applicants to submit scores on achievement tests in subject areas relevant to the field they plan to study.

The College Level Examination Program (CLEP) is one method many colleges and universities use to determine whether an applicant qualifies for advance standing and college credit. The program consists of a group of achievement tests more difficult than those just described. The basic assumption of this program is that an applicant might acquire the knowledge or competencies taught in beginning-level college courses in many ways. Many high schools now provide advanced study for highly motivated students; some students undertake self-teaching projects because of interest or other reasons; tutorial assistance may push other students beyond the levels usually accomplished in high school; and some students may acquire these skills through travel, employment, or other out-of-school activity. Assuming that many colleges would willingly recognize such claims for advance standing as legitimate if properly documented, the CEEB established the CLEP plan. This program enables the student to move ahead to an appropriate level in those areas in which advanced skill has been developed and to obtain credit for the bypassed courses. CEEB reports at least two separate studies demonstrating that students given CLEP advanced standing do as well or better in advanced courses as students who have completed the usual prerequisite courses.

QUOTAS IN THE ADMISSIONS PROCESS   One of the most controversial aspects of the admission process has to do with attaining a diverse student body and racial quotas. Some schools have provided preferential treatment to minorities, men, and women in order to meet this goal, but they place themselves in legal peril when they do. On June 23, 2003, the U.S. Supreme Court ruled that subtle policies aimed at increasing the diversity of the student body of the Law School were acceptable (*Grutter v. the Universiy of Michigan Law School*). It also struck down the University of Michigan affirmative action program, which assigned extra points to minorities in the undergraduate admission process and was therefore too mechanistic (*Gratz v. Bollinger*, 2003). The University of Michigan had established an admission system in which a perfect SAT score was awarded 12 points and minority status 20 points. One hundred and fifty points was the maximum any student could attain. Although it is not clear why the court ruled as it did in *Grutter v. University of*

Michigan Law School, it appears that the court viewed the undergraduate admission policy as at least similar to a quota system, which the court has banned in a number of settings (e.g., *Bakke v. University California Board of Regents*, 1976). In 1996 Californians passed Proposition 209, which banned the use of race, gender, or ethnicity in the college admissions process.

Financial Aid

As the costs of higher education increase steadily, many students and their families need accurate information about the sources and extent of financial assistance available. Frequent changes in federally funded and state-funded programs not only affect specific programs included in federal and state support but impinge on all other aid programs as well. Consequently, the basic data needed for financial planning are seldom available far enough in advance to permit broad publication of the information. Even the institution's financial aid office often encounters difficulty answering questions about next year's aid.

Information about financial aid for individual states and the entire country are on the Web sites of most schools and on the Internet. For example, FastWEB (http://www.fastweb.com) is a comprehensive database that provides information about scholarships, fellowships, and grants. Information about grants and loans subsidized by the federal government can be obtained at http://www.ed.gov/finaid/landing.jthml?sec=rt. Both sites provide links to other online sources of information.

The Financial Aid Form is a program operated by the CEEB. This service is designed to simplify the process of applicants providing family financial information for financial aid to colleges and universities. It provides a Parents' Confidential Statement form that the applicant's parent completes, describing the family's financial situation. The report is analyzed, and a copy of the form and the analysis are forwarded to the schools specified by the applicant. A comparable form, the Family Financial Statement (FFS), is provided by the American College Testing Program. These forms are used by scholarship program sponsors as well as by financial aid officers in colleges and universities, and they are available online. Students applying for federal loans must complete the Free Application for Federal Student Aid (FAFSA). An online application can be found at http://www.fafsa.ed.gov.

STUDENT LEARNING EXERCISE 10.1

Visit the following financial aid Web sites and rate them on the points below.

1. FinAid! http://www.finaid.org/
2. Student Aid on the Web http://studentaid.ed.gov/PORTALSWebApp/students/english/index.jsp

	Poor	Average	Good
1. Appearance of Web site	1	2	3
2. Ease of navigation	1	2	3
3. Helpfulness of information on the site	1	2	3

Factors to Consider When Choosing a College

School administrators, teachers, and counselors can anticipate a greater demand for accurate, usable information about college preparation. Inevitably, concerned students and parents expect secondary schools to exert effort to assist its graduates in preparing for college and in gaining admission. Such assistance usually requires planning over an extended period as well as developing extensive information about available institutions and involving staff in the transitional process.

Because institutions of higher education come in an almost limitless variety of size, kind, and purpose, one can find almost as many individual differences among them as among people. One can properly conclude, then, that specific schools will better fit the particular needs of certain students than will others. If an appropriate matching process is to occur, accurate information is imperative. Many high school students assume that one perfect college, like one perfect mate, exactly fits their needs and personality. This romantic notion is prevalent among individuals in this age group. In reality, several colleges or universities will suit most individuals equally well.

HELPING STUDENTS DECIDE   Although a particular student's selection of a few schools for final consideration depends on a great many factors, several general characteristics can be used to reduce the number of schools to be studied in detail:

1. *Type and Compatibility of Program*   Does the college offer the major that the student intends to study in a package that matches the student's plans and expectations?
2. *School Environment*   The geographic location and the size of the community should meet the student's needs.
3. *Admission Requirements*   Can the student meet the institution's demands, and do they reflect the level of rigor desired?
4. *Size*   Many students have preferences of a general nature, such as small, medium, or large.
5. *Type of School*   A school may be tax supported, church supported, or independent; each type may offer particular advantages desired by the student.
6. *Type of Student Body*   Factors such as gender, geographic range, cultural homogeneity, and degree of competitiveness need to be considered.
7. *Expenses and Financial Aid*   Costs vary extensively, with public schools usually being less expensive than private institutions; however, financial aid may help balance some of these differences.
8. *Student Activities, Social and Cultural Life*   If desired by the student, are these other aspects of college life available?
9. *Campus Facilities*   Are the facilities adequate to provide the program and educational experience desired?

Gaining Admission to College: An Application Strategy

School counselors and others have devised a number of plans for gaining admission to a preferred institution by developing zones of likelihood of admissions. Zone 1 includes preferred colleges that are typically competitive, but there may be a low probability of the student being admitted even if the student has great credentials. The prospective applicant, with the help of a counselor, carefully compares his or her class rank, SAT or ACT scores, and other characteristics with the admission profile of the school. These may be posted by the college or located in a college directory. Once this comparison has been completed, one or more zone 1 colleges are chosen and applications submitted. Zone 2 schools are colleges that seem likely to admit the candidate, and zone 3 schools are colleges that will admit the student under almost all conditions. The colleges in zone 3 are called "safety schools."

Accreditation

Much of our time is spent in a world in which regulation and control are obvious— speed limits, building permits, Social Security numbers, consumer protection agencies. We sometimes forget the ancient warning *caveat emptor.* The commitment to a college education, in terms of time, effort, and money, is so great that both student and parent need to be assured that their investment is sound and will yield real value. Accreditation is one means by which the potential purchaser of a college education can have some assurance about the quality of the purchase.

Accreditation of colleges and universities is usually performed by two different types of organizations. In some academic areas, programs are evaluated by established agencies formed by the appropriate professional organization based on the types of graduates. The American Psychological Association accredits programs that train psychologists and the Council for the Accreditation of Counseling and Related Programs (CACREP) accredits counselor education programs. The second type of accrediting agency is an association of educational institutions that focus on accrediting institutions as a whole. The North Central Association of Colleges and Secondary Schools is an example of this type of associations.

Many prospective students or their parents raise questions about the ranking of a college or university or of a specific department or section within the school. It is often difficult to convince them that such rankings are not made by the accrediting agencies. Generally, the accrediting groups simply list schools that meet certain minimum standards. Occasionally, this list is arranged into appropriate groups related to the scope of the program, the areas included, or similar factors, but a numerical list in order of quality is seldom made. The variety of programs among schools, even in highly specialized subject areas, precludes the possibility of such ranking in terms of quality.

Public conviction that rankings exist stems primarily from two sources. Many loyal alumni remember their alma mater as "the best in the country," "tops in such and such," or "highly recognized." Such evaluation is, of course, subjective and not based on comparative criteria. Second, many popular magazines, such as *U.S. News and World Report*, newspapers, and Sunday supplements run feature stories based on the judgment of a single person or a panel of so-called experts who often purport to evaluate institutions in various subject fields or by type of school. Again, the published judgments may be made by highly knowledgeable individuals who have a wide acquaintance with many schools, but these reports are nevertheless, subjective in nature and are not based on detailed studies of the type and scope that justify a precise ranking.

Continuing Education Needed

Because of the rapidity with which jobs change in today's dynamic workplace, preparation for work continues throughout most workers' lives. In an older but still illustrative survey a national sample of employed adults was asked, "Do you think you will need more formal training or education to maintain or increase your earning power during the next few years?" Fifty-six percent answered yes. Not unexpectedly, the percentage of workers who expected to need more training to maintain or improve their earnings was highest in the 18 to 25 age group (83 percent said yes) and lowest in the 66 and over age group (17 percent said yes). Also, more African Americans than whites (66 percent versus 51 percent) indicated they would need additional training in the years ahead if they were to maintain or improve their incomes. When these workers were asked where they expected to go to get the training they needed, more than 30 percent said four-year colleges, 23 percent said courses offered by their employers, 13 percent said community colleges, and the same percentage expected to enroll in business or technical schools. Smaller percentages of employed adults expected to engage in training activities in adult education courses, special courses offered by their professional associations or trade unions, or some form of public job training program (Hoyt & Lester, 1995; NCDA, 1999).

Perhaps the only thing surprising about the survey results just cited is that the percentages were low. Except for those jobs requiring only minimal skills, continuing education is a fact of life for almost all workers, even if they stay with their current job. Job changes, whether within the current business or changing employers completely, inevitably involve additional training. More than 25 percent of the workers surveyed in the NCDA Gallup polls expect either to change voluntarily or to be forced to change jobs (Hoyt & Lester, 1995; NCDA 1999). This figure does not account for the number of people who make either lateral changes or are promoted to jobs with greater responsibility within their current workplace. Neither do these figures account for the continuing education required of workers when changes in computer hardware or software packages, new accounting systems, new production strategies, and so on occur. I suspect the percentages would have been much higher if the question posed had been, "Do you expect to be involved in additional training either to maintain your ability to perform your job at a satisfactory level or because of a change in your current job status?"

Many people belong to professional associations that provide continuing education opportunities online, in workshops, and in extended training sessions. Forward looking businesses also provide continuing education on a regular basis and some labor unions are also involved in offering educational experiences to their members. On the other hand, workers who do not have regular opportunities to upgrade current skills and learn new skills that will be needed as their job evolves, are in jeopardy of becoming obsolete. The only option for this group is to consult regularly with leaders and educators in their field and to consult publications such as the *Occupational Outlook Handbook* for adv ice and directions.

Summary

Students and adults have a variety of educational options open to them once they make a career choice. Choosing from among these options may in fact be as bewildering as choosing a career itself. The ultimate option chosen depends on a variety of factors, including the career chosen, the wishes of the student, the ability of the student to finance the education, the academic record of the individual, and so forth. A carelessly chosen preparation program can lead to personal dissatisfaction and even to a change in career plans. Thus, it becomes incumbent on career counselors to be fully abreast of educational information and to develop the skills necessary to facilitate educational exploration because career and educational choices are inextricably linked.

Chapter Quiz

T F **1.** If the dropout statistics presented in this chapter are accurate, approximately 300 students drop out of high school each day in the United States.

T F **2.** High schools in large cities seem to be the ones that contribute most to the dropout problem.

T F **3.** The program that is most oriented to getting high school dropouts into the labor force is School to Work.

T F **4.** Admissions standards for colleges and universities are relatively the same except for a few of the elite institutions.

T F **5.** Community colleges have open door admissions policies, which means that all students who apply can be admitted and typically get into the program of studies they choose.

T F **6.** High school math and science courses are part of the specific vocational preparation of most scientific careers.

T F **7.** Vocational education in high schools is a relatively new innovation and was prompted by the Great Depression.

T F **8.** Although it is difficult to account for people in apprenticeship programs that are not registered with the government, it seems likely that the number of people in some type of apprenticeship is approximately 1 million.

T F **9.** The U.S. Department of Labor has identified approximately 1,000 apprenticeable jobs.

T F **10.** Regional accrediting agencies such as the Southern Association of Colleges and Schools rank the overall quality of colleges and universities in their geographic region.

(1) T (2) T (3) F (4) 4 (5) F (6) F (7) F (8) T (9) T (10) F

References

Alliance for Excellent Education (2009). Drop out factories. Retrieved from http://www.all4ed.org/about_the_crisis/schools/dropout

Brown, D., & Trusty, J. (1995). *Designing and leading comprehensive school counseling programs.* Belmont, CA: Brooks/Cole.

Hollenebeck, K. M. (1997). School to work: Promise and effectiveness. Retrieved from http://www.upjohninst.org/publications/newsletter/kh-f97.pdf

Hoyt, K. B., & Lester, J. N. (1995). *Learning to work: The NCDA Gallup survey.* Alexandria, VA: National Career Development Association.

Lerman, R. L. (2009). Training tomorrow's workers: Community colleges and apprenticeships as collaborative routes to rewarding careers. Retrieved from http://www.gatesfoundation.org/united-states/Documents/community-colleges-apprenticeships.pdf

National Career Development Association (NCDA). (1999). National survey of working America. Retrieved from http://www.ncda.org

Monrad, M. (2009). High school dropout: A quick stats fact sheet. Retrieved from http://www.betterhighschools.org/docs/NHSC_DropoutFactSheet.pdf.

OATELS (2004). *The national registered apprenticeship system.* Washington, DC: Author.

U.S. Department of Labor. (2005). Appendix D: Apprenticeship programs in the military and fast facts on apprenticeship in the U.S. Retrieved from http://www.dol/asp/media/reports/credentialing/appendix.htm.

U.S. Department of Labor (2010). Registered apprenticeships. Retrieved from http://www.doleta.gov/OA.

Facilitating the Global Job Search: Employability Skills and Placement Services

Things to Remember

- The numerous uses of the Internet in the job search process

- The employability skills needed by the job hunter

- Types of job placement services available to the job hunter

- The approaches to job placement used by educational institutions

I have tried to make it clear that the economies of the world are interlinked and that many of the careers once found in the United States have been relocated to other countries. It also seems clear that job growth in some of the economies of other countries, particularly China and India, may outpace job growth in the United States. It seems certain that serious job hunters will consider international jobs with increasing frequency now and in the future. However, this does not indicate that dropouts, high school and college graduates, displaced adults, and others should ignore the American workplace. It does mean that individuals who decide to seek employment abroad need to broaden their perspective and develop some additional skills such as posting resumes on the Internet and virtual job interviews if they are to negotiate the job search to locate suitable employment. It also means that cultural competency and understanding must take center stage for workers who hope to be successful in securing employment in other countries. This chapter begins by addressing the job search and then focuses on using placement services and other agencies in the job search.

THE JOB SEARCH

The job-search process is fraught with anxiety for job seekers, whether they are seeking their first jobs or looking for new ones. Gaining employment not only ensures economic stability but also validates the worth of an individual to some degree. Those who have lost their jobs as a result of economic downturns, technological advances or other reasons may have already suffered blows to their self-esteem, thus, success in the job-search process may become even more important for them. Social support may offset some of the anxiety experienced by job seekers and in doing so increase their potential for success. The point is that career development specialists engaged in facilitating the job search must attend to psychological issues and the emotional state of the job seeker (Brewington, Nassar-McMillan, Flowers, & Furr, 2004; Subich, 1994).

EMPLOYABILITY SKILLS

Job seekers need a wide range of employability skills ranging from locating jobs to interviewing. Historically, job seekers have relied on self-help books and attended group meetings in high schools, colleges, and as a part of the career development programs in their workplaces to develop these skills. Fortunately, the One-Stop Career Center's Web site, state level department of labor sites such as Virginia Career View, and a number of proprietary sites offer instruction and advice that can aid job seekers gain the skills they need. The Riley Guide (http://www. RileyGuide.com) lists more than a dozen sections devoted to improving job search skills, ranging from using the Internet to avoiding the scams that promise job seekers more than they intend to deliver for a "small fee." The sites also contains job postings for North and South America, Western Europe, Eastern Europe, the British Isles, Scandinavia, and Asia and the Pacific Rim countries, including Australia. Monster (http://www.monster.com/geo/siteselection.aspx) also offers many of the same types of tips and publications found on Riley and instead of offering job listing by region provides job opening listings for over 50 countries.

The questions for each job seeker are these: What is the best means of developing the skills I need to be successful in the job hunt? Self-help guides? Internet publications and tips? Classes or small groups? Based on a study by Eden and Avarim (1993), which provides a partial answer, some job seekers need more than self-directed activities. They designed an eight-week workshop that employed cognitive strategies to increase job hunters' self-efficacy and job-search activities. They found that their intervention was more helpful for people who had low self-efficacy at the outset and that reemployment increased dramatically for this group. Platt, Husband, Hermalin, Cater, and Metzger (1993) also used cognitive behavioral approaches in an attempt to increase the reemployment of drug abusers on methadone maintenance. They found that African American clients in the treatment groups were far more likely to be employed than their counterparts in the control groups, but they found no significant difference in the employment of white clients in the experimental and control groups.

Whereas these two studies illustrate that group interventions can be useful in the development of employability skills, two other observations can also be made on the basis of the results of these studies. First, the treatments did not work equally well for all groups involved, suggesting the need to tailor the types of interventions used to the needs of the clients. Second, in the study conducted by Platt and colleagues (1993), only 15 percent of the people in the experimental groups had jobs after one year. This suggests that employability skills training cannot overcome other obstacles to employment, such as substance abuse or inadequate preparation for the job. Not surprisingly, Eck (1993) found a direct link between the ability of job hunters to secure jobs and the extent to which their education prepared them to perform the job.

Finally, employability skills training and initial employment and reemployment may be tempered by another variable: social support. Rife and Belcher (1993) found that workers who had the greatest degree of social support for their job-hunting activities spent more hours searching for jobs and made more employer contacts than those who did not have this support. Unemployed friends were judged to be better sources of support than employed friends and relatives in this study. This finding provides direct support for many of the group-oriented activities, such as job clubs, described later in this section.

Legislation, including the School to Work Opportunity Act, the Individuals with Disabilities Education Act, and the Job Training Partnership Act, includes provisions for supplying *transitional activities*—a term that includes teaching and helping individuals locate and obtain jobs. JTPA programs are in a position to provide this type of group help to disadvantaged individuals, including school dropouts, displaced homemakers, dislocated workers, and some others. Obviously, secondary and postsecondary institutions are in a position to provide help to enrollees who are about to complete their educational programs. Community agencies often sponsor support groups or directly operate programs that provide this assistance to other members of the community who need and want help.

At the high school level, units on job-search techniques can be incorporated into several courses established as electives or offered as special activities during or outside regular school hours. The content is usually based either on a brief textbook or, more often, on a workbook or manual. Examples of materials available for this purpose include those by Bloch (2000); Wegman, Chapman, and Johnson (1989); and Farr (2005). It is worth noting that the state informational sites such as Texas Workforce: Youth Information and Services (http://www.twc.state.tx.us/svcs/youthinit/youth_links. html) or the North Carolina Career Resource Network (http://www.soicc.state.nc.us/soicc/planning/ job_search.htm) include material that can be used with high school students. A wide range of materials that can be used in classes and small groups college-level students and adults is available. Most of these materials were designed for self-help, but can easily be adapted for group activities.

One development that is being used in JTPA and community groups to help those actually engaged in the job-search process is job clubs (Azrin & Besadel, 1979; Hansen, 2010; Murray, 1993). These authors propose the formation of a group that not only provides support and encouragement but also helps members improve their interview skills through role playing; clarifies and sharpens their goals through group efforts; shares tips with other members as possible leads appear; and seeks group solutions to problems such as child care, transportation, and others facing individual members.

When job clubs include a support group whose members face common problems, the advantages of this approach are even more obvious as members work together to resolve problems that frequently cause failure in the job search, to improve access to information about possible openings through networking, and to build skills in job-seeking techniques. The approach is clearly appropriate not only for the so-called disadvantaged groups but also for dislocated workers, the structurally unemployed, and late entrants.

Local labor market information is particularly useful to job clubs because members are seeking jobs within the local area. Some communities have formed advisory committees consisting of representatives of local employers who are able to add further realism to job club activities through role-playing application interviews, alerting members to potential vacancies, and educating members about what employers look for in applicants. Although I can find no research on the topic, it appears to me that FaceBook, Twitter, and personal blogs are potentially useful for job clubs and others that are recruiting members, spreading the word about successes and failures, providing social support, and as a means of posting personalized job hunting tips. I went to the Twitter Web site on March 10, 2010, and entered "job hunting" into the search box. There were 15 postings in the hour before I conducted the search. A newly published book, *The Twitter Job Search Guide* (Whitcomb, Bryam, & Dib, 2010) provides tips for using Twitter in the job search.

Job Seekers with Disabilities and Those with Criminal Records

When considered in general terms, the process of placing people with mental and physical disabilities is essentially the same as that for those without disabilities. However, the specifics of the process vary considerably (Hall & Parker, 2010). When clients with severe mental retardation or developmental disabilities have limited potential for competitive employment, two options exist. One is to develop sheltered workshops that subcontract with other businesses to produce various products, although states such as Vermont have eliminated these workshops. Criticisms have been levied by Taylor (2002), who concluded that very few disabled workers move from sheltered workshops to regular employment (3.5%) and people in sheltered workshops are paid relatively little.

The second alternative for helping disabled clients is to develop job skills through supported work programs that include job-site training, job coaching, placement, and long-term follow-up to determine work adjustment. In both types of programs extensive assessment of medical and psychomotor conditions, intellectual and academic abilities, interests, interpersonal skills, and work skills must be conducted (Kanchier, 1990). This is followed by training, coaching, counseling, observation, and evaluation. People in supported work programs typically work in restaurants, motels, hospitals, or similar situations (Lam, 1986). Lam also found that the supported work program is a more cost-effective means of servicing clients with mental retardation, whereas sheltered workshops may be more cost effective with clients having moderate to severe mental retardation.

When clients with disabilities have the potential for competitive employment, as is the case with many individuals with physical disabilities, additional support in the form of counseling, training, and work with employers to overcome stereotypes is necessary, much as it is for clients with mental disabilities (Caporoso & Kiselica, 2004; Hall & Parker, 2010; Jones, Ulicny, Czyzewski, & Plante, 1987). In a disturbing finding, Hall and Parker found that clients with disabilities felt that One-Stop Career Center counselors did not understand their problems, were not very helpful, and too often used the "library model" of helping in which, after a brief orientation, clients were expected to work independently.

In Chapter 6, I tried to make it clear that persons who have broken the law and are in the job market face a number of barriers in the job search. I will not rehash those issues at this point except to add that the stigma of having a criminal record may be worse for people from minority groups and that offenders who were convicted of substance abuse crimes and sex offenders may have a more difficult time find a job than other offenders (Thompson & Cummings, 2010).

EXECUTING THE JOB SEARCH

The typical job search generally follows the three steps presented below: establish career goals by taking an inventory of self and skills; identify and investigate the job market; and finally develop employability skills, such as résumé preparation, letter writing, and interviewing to wage a job-search campaign or as the Monster Web site seems to suggest, multiple job searches. Here are some details to consider.

Step 1: Taking an Inventory of Self and Skills

The first step is essentially one of taking an inventory—that is, establishing what one has for sale. If a counselor has been working with a client in a career counseling process, this step has already been identified and clarified. If the counselor or para professional is starting at the job-search stage, some backtracking is necessary to be sure that the client has thorough and accurate self-knowledge and can identify personal strengths and weaknesses. Identifying skills and strengths may be difficult for the individual who has only limited work experience. For example, the displaced homemaker may discount or overlook skills that were used in homemaking responsibilities because they did not produce a paycheck.

The period devoted to clarifying self-knowledge should be expanded to include consideration of short-term and long-term goals that can be used as a partial guide for evaluating the wisdom of accepting a job offer. Though often postponed until later, at this stage a basic résumé can be prepared as a working tool to inventory personal characteristics and accumulated experiences related to what a job seeker has to offer an employer. Zunker (2006) suggests that clients can use self-estimates to classify and evaluate job skills and then to use these ratings to estimate the types of positions for which they are best qualified. To return to an earlier chapter for a moment, the various assessment and self-rating scales that were identified in Chapter 7 could also be used for this purpose.

Step 2: Investigating the Job Market

The second step is to identify the individual's job market by first circumscribing a geographic area and second identifying information resources within that specified territory. Ordinarily, an individual's labor market area must be described in terms of personal factors, such as one's access to transportation; how long and far one is willing to travel to and from the work site; whether geographic, personal, or family barriers exist; and similar items relating to the individual.

Individuals must next identify resources for obtaining information about possible job openings, some of which are often overlooked. One such source is the "hidden job market," which exists almost everywhere and is not hidden. Many openings in large corporations are never advertised through the usual sources unless they cannot be filled from within and thus are "hidden" in a sense. Vacancies that are about to develop, perhaps through promotion, retirement, reorganization, or expansion in a business become known to job seekers through networking strategies—for example, through conversations with people who work in the business. Perhaps the basic question for the job hunter is, "How well do you know what is happening inside the companies in which you hope to work?"

The second source of information is closely related to the hidden market and consists of the network of acquaintances in the local area where a job is sought. Those who are employed in businesses that are potential sites for a client may know the state of the hidden job market in their companies. They may also know what trends are beginning to influence their industries and how competing companies plan to respond. Job clubs which were mentioned earlier in this chapter, first described by Azrin and Besadel in 1979, still operate in many parts of the country. These clubs have traditionally emphasized the importance of networking in the job search. Silliker (1993) found that unemployed workers over age 50 who were in Conventional, Enterprising, or Realistic occupations found new jobs primarily through networking with relatives and friends. People in Social, Artistic, and Investigative occupations were more likely to find jobs through agencies or by consulting newspaper advertisements. In a related study, Ports (1993) studied trends in job seeking beginning in 1970 and found that more and more workers used newspaper articles as a means of locating jobs. It is doubtful that this trend toward greater use has continued, but newspapers are still a valuable source of job listings.

Pencom, an employee recruiting firm, surveyed personnel officers to determine what they considered the most effective means of recruiting new workers. The results were as follows: 36.4 percent of the personnel officers favored the use of professional recruiters, 32.3 percent found that getting referrals from other workers or acquaintances (networking) worked best for them, and 10.1 percent preferred to retrain existing workers for new positions. Among other preferred methods of recruiting workers, personnel officers included newspaper advertisements

(9.1%), Internet postings (6.1%), and job fairs (6.0%). These findings have many implications for the job hunter, perhaps the most important being that they are going to have to consult many sources of job openings if they are to be successful (Eisenstadt, 1995).

As has already been noted, the Internet can be an invaluable tool if job seekers elect to take advantage of online job placement centers. Moreover, the Internet can also be used as a means of identifying job openings by accessing traditional sources of job listings. For example, newspapers that have Web sites, and most major newspapers do, post the jobs listed in their classified advertisements. In addition, the following five Web sites may be useful to several types of job seekers: (1) RecruitAbility (http://www.disabledperson.com) for information about jobs for people with disabilities; (2) Riley's Guide (http://www.rileyguide.com) for information about jobs for students in college; (3) CareerPath (www.careerpath.com) for information about jobs listed in newspapers; (4) IHispano (http://www.ihispano.com/careers/searchjob/) for information about jobs for Hispanics; and (5) Veteran Employment (http://www.veteranemployment.com/) for information about jobs for veterans.

Step 3: Developing Employability Skills

The third step in the job-search process is developing a strategy for selling oneself to prospective employers and polishing the employability skills needed to complete this phase. The appropriate strategy depends on many factors and must be developed essentially according to rules set by the employer. After a potential position has been identified, a properly written, well-stated letter containing a résumé should be sent to the employer. If the advertisement asks applicants to telephone for an appointment, telephone manners may become quite important. The immediate goal is to secure an interview; the long-range goal is to complete the interview in a way that produces a job offer.

THE JOB HUNT   Clients may need assistance in translating what want ads are saying about jobs, and they almost certainly will need help in preparing letters of application, résumés, and skills for interviews. Both research and the experiences of job hunters provide some additional clues about how to make this process more successful. For example, Helwig (1987) surveyed career and placement specialists to rate what they perceived to be the most important information needed by job hunters. Out of 99 items, 15 were rated most important and 15 rated least important on a scale from 1 to 7 (see Table 11.1). Perhaps the most obvious finding, as Helwig noted, is that all items in his questionnaire were viewed as at least somewhat important by the respondents.

Yates (1987) took a somewhat different approach in her research than Helwig did. She asked job seekers to rate the information and skills they needed during the job search. She found that, generally, among job hunters, self-assessment skills, decision-making skills, and job-hunting knowledge and skills were considered most important, whereas occupational and educational information were considered less important. The top 10 needs of job seekers, according to their own ratings, are (1) selling yourself, (2) preparing for a typical interview, (3) writing a résumé, (4) self-assessment skills, (5) salary information, (6) budgeting until a job is found, (7) legal and illegal questions that may be posed by interviewers, (8) understanding the career decision-making process, (9) how to use skills acquired in past jobs in a new occupation, and (10) information about entry-level requirements of various jobs.

INTERVIEWS   Many job applicants, especially first-timers, may be unaware of how interviews are influenced by personal grooming and appropriateness of attire; eye contact; proper grammar and self-expression; poise, posture, and composure; and the ability to explain what one can give to a job and what one expects in return. Role playing and practice interviews are the most

TABLE 11.1   Counselors' Perceptions of Most and Least Important Information Needed by Job Seekers (N = 1,121)

Most Important
 1. Ability to identify one's aptitudes (6.35)
 2. Ability to identify one's skills (6.34)
 3. Ability to identify one's interests (6.31)
 4. Knowledge of the importance of personal appearance and hygiene in getting a job (6.29)
 5. Ability to sell one's skills to get a job (6.28)
 6. Awareness of the importance of a properly completed application (6.28)
 7. Ability to relate one's skills, interests, aptitudes, and values to a job (6.26)
 8. Knowledge of how to participate in a job interview (6.23)
 9. Ability to prepare for an interview (6.18)
10. Knowledge of the personal characteristics that are considered important by employers (6.17)
11. Knowledge of the importance of proper language and dress in the workplace (6.13)
12. Knowledge of the importance of personal responsibility in finding a job (6.11)
13. Ability to understand the employer's expectations for a specific position (5.99)
14. Knowledge of the steps in job hunting (5.97)
15. Knowledge of where to find job openings (5.97)

Least Important
 1. Knowledge of military information (4.01)
 2. Knowledge of labor organizations (4.27)
 3. Knowledge of the regional history of employment changes and attitudes (4.28)
 4. Knowledge of how the natural environment influences the jobs that are available (4.40)
 5. Knowledge of seasonal jobs (4.52)
 6. Information about starting one's own business (4.58)
 7. Knowledge of the relationship between work and leisure time (4.58)
 8. Knowledge of the General Educational Development (GED) certificate (4.63)
 9. Knowledge of how cycles in the economy affect the number of job openings (4.63)
10. Knowledge of the different parts of a cover letter (4.67)
11. Knowledge of how public transportation may affect job choice (4.74)
12. Knowledge of how family and friends may influence occupational choice (4.74)
13. Ability to use the *Dictionary of Occupational Titles* and the *Occupational Outlook Handbook* (4.75)
14. Ability to ascertain employer differences regarding worker benefits (4.76)
15. Knowledge of illegal questions that may occur during the interview (4.78)

Source: From "Information Required for Job Hunting: 1121 Counselors Respond," by A. A. Helwig, 1987, *Journal of Employment Counseling, 24,* pp. 184–190. Reprinted by permission.

common techniques for sharpening these skills. Many of the resources listed previously include sample questions likely to be asked in the interview.

The job interview has been the focus of some important and enlightening research. Atkins and Kent (1988) asked 95 business recruiters at West Virginia University to rate the most important variable involved in the job interview. The recruiters' rankings can be seen in Table 11.2.

Riggio and Throckmorton (1987) examined the nature of errors in oral communication committed during mock job interviews and found that the most common problem was responses that failed to provide enough information. Other errors identified were extreme difficulty in answering a question, complaining about either employers or the quality of their education, providing negative

TABLE 11.2   College Recruiters' Rankings of the Most Important Considerations in the Employment Interview

1. Overall oral communication skills	11. Overall appearance
2. Enthusiasm	12. Assertiveness
3. Motivation	13. Manners
4. Credentials	14. References
5. Degree	15. Preparation or knowledge of employer
6. Career maturity	16. Sense of humor
7. Initiative	17. Report-writing skills
8. Grade-point average	18. Summer or part-time job experience
9. Listening skills	19. Ability to resolve conflict
10. Punctuality	20. Extracurricular activities

Source: From "What Do Recruiters Consider Important during the Employment Interview?" by C. P. Atkins and R. L. Kent, 1988, *Journal of Employment Counseling, 25,* p. 102. Reprinted by permission.

personal information, lack of emphasis on their careers, too much emphasis on salary, inability to communicate skills, and poor grammar. Often oral communication problems included answers that were too long, too vague, or bizarre, such as thoughts about committing suicide. Riggio and Throckmorton (1987) also found that students who received a 40-minute lecture on interviewing skills did no better in their oral communication than did those who had not been exposed to the lecture.

RÉSUMÉS   Some empirical guidelines for résumé and cover letter preparation have also come forth. Helwig (1985) surveyed 71 recruiters from 50 corporations and found that they had a clear preference for a résumé that is one page in length, is clearly labeled, has headings on the left side, uses action verbs to describe work experience, and looks uncluttered. Neatness, use of proper English, and correct spelling have also been found to be important to corporate recruiters, as has the order of the presentation of data (Stephens, Watt, & Hobbs, 1979).

In a particularly significant study, Ryland and Rosen (1987) found that 230 personnel professionals preferred the functional résumé format as compared to the standard chronological format (see Figure 11.1). Ryland and Rosen also found that functional résumés are particularly helpful when applying for highly skilled careers. Apparently, personnel managers want to see education listed first and work experience second, whereas they have mixed opinions about the presentation of personal data, according to Stephens and colleagues (1979). How should the résumé be structured? Rated as the most important items to include on the résumé were current address, past work experience, major in college, job objectives, permanent address, tenure on previous jobs, colleges attended, and specific physical limitations. The least important items were listed as religious preference, race, personal data on parents, high school transcripts, photograph, sex, spouse's education, spouse's occupation, typing skills, and number of children.

Résumés that are posted online on Web sites such as Monster should be prepared somewhat differently than the traditional résumé. The most obvious difference between traditional résumés and the electronic résumé is the format. Traditional résumés typically include bullets, italics, underlined words or topics (see Figure 11.1a and b). None of these formatting features is acceptable. As is shown in Figure 11.2 (p. 244), capitals may be used to denote sections and asterisks (or dashes) to bring attention to special elements. The other main difference between electronic and traditional résumés is the addition of a section for keywords. The job hunter is

Jane E. Taylor
105 Oakdale Road
Columbus, Ohio 45710
614-554-3934

JOB OBJECTIVE: Sales representative for large pharmaceutical company

SALES
Sold merchandise in busy neighborhood store, handled purchase orders for stock, and trained three other successful sales clerks.

MANAGEMENT
Assisted store manager of large discount department store with maintaining stock, supervising sales clerks, ordering inventory, developing displays for new merchandise, and handling customer returns and complaints.

Founded amateur photographers' club, increasing membership to 103 in one year. Coordinated convention for national photographers' organization, and organized and implemented photo show, featuring 30 artists.

ADMINISTRATION
Evaluated jobs for manufacturer of office furniture and supplies, determined job grading system, gathered wage survey data, determined and justified merit increases and adjustments, approved job descriptions, established salary ranges, and counseled employees.

Studied jobs, categorized positions, interviewed prospective applicants, conducted exit interviews, assisted with annual employee attitude surveys and with administration of pension programs.

EDUCATION AND EXPERIENCE
1980 to present	APEX OFFICE FURNITURE AND SUPPLY COMPANY Wage and Salary Specialist
1976–1980	Apex Office Furniture and Supply— Personnel Assistant
1974–1976	$-Mart Department Stores—Assistant Store Manager
1971–1973	ABC Drugstores—Sales Clerk (summers)
1970–1974	B.A. in Business Administration, Florida State University
INTERESTS:	Tennis, Photography

References available upon request   Willing to relocate

FIGURE 11.1a   The Functional Résumé Format.

Jane E. Taylor
105 Oakdale Road
Columbus, Ohio 45710
614-554-3934

OBJECTIVE: Sales representative for large pharmaceutical company

WORK EXPERIENCE:
1980 to present: APEX OFFICE FURNITURE AND SUPPLY COMPANY
                     Wage and Salary Specialist: Evaluate jobs for manufacturer of
                     office furniture and supplies, determine job grading system,
                     gather wage survey data, determine and justify merit increases
                     and adjustments, approve job descriptions, establish salary
                     ranges, and counsel employees.

1976–1980   APEX OFFICE FURNITURE AND SUPPLY COMPANY
                     Personnel Assistant: Studied jobs, categorized positions,
                     interviewed prospective applicants, conducted exit interviews,
                     assisted with annual employee attitude survey and with
                     administration of pension programs.

1974–1976 $-MARK DEPARTMENT STORES
                     Assistant Store Manager: Assisted store manager with
                     maintaining stock, supervising sales clerks, ordering inventory,
                     developing displays for new merchandise, and handling
                     customer returns and complaints.

1971–1973   ABC DRUGSTORES
                     Sales Clerk (summers): Sold merchandise in busy neighborhood
                     store, handled purchase orders for stock, and trained three
                     other successful sales clerks.

EDUCATION: B.A. in Business Administration, Florida State University
  1974

INTERESTS: Tennis, Photography

References available upon request   Willing to relocate

FIGURE 11.1b The Chronological Résumé Format. *Source:* From "Personnel Professionals'
Reactions to Chronological and Functional Résumé Formats," by E. K. Ryland and B. Rosen,
1987, *Career Development Quarterly, 35,* p. 231. Reprinted with permission.

E-mailed or database résumés are written in plain text without columns, bullets, bold, or italics.

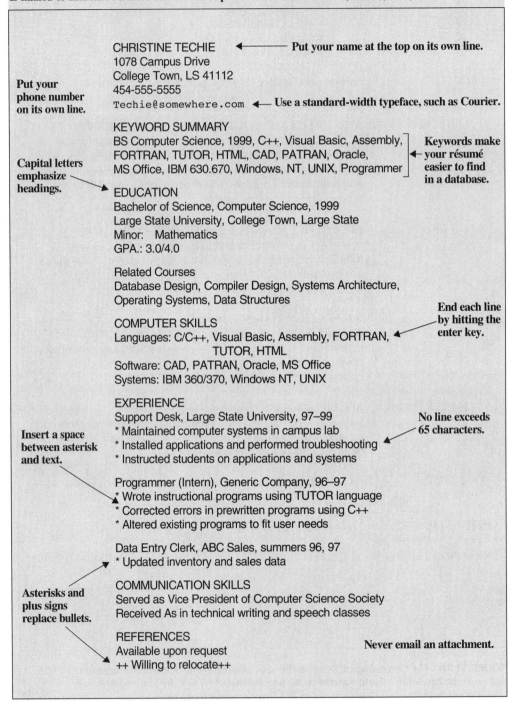

CHRISTINE TECHIE ← Put your name at the top on its own line.
1078 Campus Drive
College Town, LS 41112
454-555-5555
Techie@somewhere.com ← Use a standard-width typeface, such as Courier.

Put your phone number on its own line.

KEYWORD SUMMARY
BS Computer Science, 1999, C++, Visual Basic, Assembly, FORTRAN, TUTOR, HTML, CAD, PATRAN, Oracle, MS Office, IBM 630.670, Windows, NT, UNIX, Programmer

Keywords make your résumé easier to find in a database.

Capital letters emphasize headings.

EDUCATION
Bachelor of Science, Computer Science, 1999
Large State University, College Town, Large State
Minor: Mathematics
GPA.: 3.0/4.0

Related Courses
Database Design, Compiler Design, Systems Architecture, Operating Systems, Data Structures

COMPUTER SKILLS
Languages: C/C++, Visual Basic, Assembly, FORTRAN, TUTOR, HTML
Software: CAD, PATRAN, Oracle, MS Office
Systems: IBM 360/370, Windows NT, UNIX

End each line by hitting the enter key.

EXPERIENCE
Support Desk, Large State University, 97–99
* Maintained computer systems in campus lab
* Installed applications and performed troubleshooting
* Instructed students on applications and systems

No line exceeds 65 characters.

Insert a space between asterisk and text.

Programmer (Intern), Generic Company, 96–97
* Wrote instructional programs using TUTOR language
* Corrected errors in prewritten programs using C++
* Altered existing programs to fit user needs

Data Entry Clerk, ABC Sales, summers 96, 97
* Updated inventory and sales data

COMMUNICATION SKILLS
Served as Vice President of Computer Science Society
Received As in technical writing and speech classes

Asterisks and plus signs replace bullets.

REFERENCES
Available upon request
++ Willing to relocate++

Never email an attachment.

FIGURE 11.2 Sample Plain Text Resumé. *Source:* From "Résumés, Applications, and Cover Letters," by O. Crosby, 1999, *Occupational Outlook Quarterly* (Summer), p. 11.

asked to provide keywords that highlight his or her skills, job qualifications, or past experience. These keywords are crucial because the search engines used are text-based. Employers search the database containing the résumés using a keyword methodology, not unlike the one used by people who are searching the Internet for other types of information. Typically no fee is charged for posting a résumé on one of these online sites, but there are exceptions.

Finally, assistance with résumés, preparation for interviews, and writing cover letters is as close as the Internet. The One-Stop Career Center's Web site provides a host of tips and guidelines for preparing and improving resumes. The clearinghouse Riley's Guide (http://www.rileyguide.com) provides information particularly helpful to college students and others who wish to get tips in these areas. People who wish to know more about the salaries as well as how to negotiate a salary if they are offered a job should visit Monster & Salary (http://monster.salary.com/salarywizard/layoutscripts/swzl_newsearch.asp http://monster.salary.com/salarywizard/layoutscripts/swzl_newsearch.asp) or the One-Stop Career Center Web site, which offers salary information for 800 jobs.

JOB PLACEMENT SERVICES

Astute job hunters take advantage of the resources available to them. Job placement centers can be an invaluable tool if used as a part of the search for employment. Placement services, like many other career development resources, come in many forms ranging from virtual placement services such as Monster to public brick and mortar private services and public agencies such as U.S. Employment Service offices. Colleges and universities, community colleges, public schools, and other public institution also offer job placement services to their graduating seniors as well as to alumni.

Perhaps the most unusual of the placement services offered to job seekers is outplacement. As the name suggests, job placement services are offered to workers outside of the firm. Outplacement firms were started by entrepreneurs who saw an opportunity to help displaced workers and make money in the process. Imagine this scene: You are finishing up the workweek and there is an announcement that you and a number of other people are to report to a large conference room. On entering the conference room, you are told that your job is being phased out and this is your last day on the job. The company spokesperson introduces an outplacement counselor who tells you that her firm's job is to help you in your transition to your next job. This not the way all outplacement work begins, but it is not an unusual event either. Outplacement and job placement are vital components of the career development process. A 2009 movie, *Up in the Air* starring George Clooney as an outplacement counselor, offers a glimpse into the world of the outplacement specialist, albeit a caricatured glimpse.

Each year institutions and federal and state governments spend tens of millions of dollars to staff high school, college, and public job placement offices that offer free services to help place individuals seeking employment. Employers pay large sums of money to private employment agencies, headhunters, and others to facilitate the process of locating workers. Businesses also pay large sums of money to outplacement firms to assist individuals whose jobs have been eliminated to find new careers. Individuals also spend large sums of money to private job placement firms to assist them with their search. The amounts of money spent on the job placement processes attest to the importance placed on it by the government, business, individuals, and institutions.

The reason large sums of money are spent on job placement are fairly clear, with the most obvious being why individuals spend money for assistance with job placement. Most people must work to maintain their current standard of living, or to move toward a desired lifestyle. People also work for psychological reasons some of which are discussed in the next paragraph. Institutions—particularly colleges, community colleges, and vocational–technical colleges—invest in job placement services for both altruistic and self-serving reasons. The altruistic reasons relate to the perception that it is incumbent on institutions, particularly educational institutions, to facilitate the transition from education to the next life stage, which is typically work. The self-serving motive is that inevitably these institutions are evaluated on the basis of their services to students, particularly services related to success in life. Businesses also have altruistic and selfish reasons for hiring private outplacement agencies to assist their employees who have been dismissed from their jobs. Private outplacement agencies can often reduce severance pay and extended benefits, forestall lawsuits, and eliminate payments for unemployment insurance if workers that have been "laid off" secure new jobs. Outplacement firms also help corporations maintain their public images as caring institutions, and assuage corporate guilt.

Public Employment Services

Every state has a state employment security agency (SESA). In some states it is called the Job Service; in others it is referred to as the Employment Service. These state-operated services work within the general structure, regulations, and operating procedures established by the U.S. Employment Service (USES).

Public employment services in the United States have a history that spans more than a century and a half. New York City organized a municipal service as early as 1834, and San Francisco established programs before the turn of the twentieth century. Ohio did so in 1890, Montana in 1895, New York in 1896, Nebraska in 1897, and Illinois and Missouri in 1899. The federal government entered the scene in 1907 with the formation of the U.S. Employment Service to help arriving immigrants find jobs across the country. During World War I, its task was changed to assist all unemployed people seeking work and to help employers find needed workers. After the war, many local offices were closed, and the agency was relatively inactive until the impact of the Great Depression in the 1930s resulted in the reestablishment of a federal system of state offices. These state offices were nationalized during World War II and returned to state control in 1946. They are still the most-used source of assistance by people who lose their jobs (Ports, 1993).

Because each SESA is state operated, there is some variation in structure and operating procedures from state to state. Overall, however, SESAs have far more similarities than differences, and most offer parallel services. Most states have established local offices in all metropolitan areas and conveniently located regional offices that serve less populated areas. These offices usually provide the following services:

1. *Placement*   Applicants are registered, classified, selected, and referred to prospective employers. Orders for workers are received, and applicants' qualifications are matched with the employers' specifications so that referrals can be made.
2. *Counseling*   Applicants without previous work records or with inadequate experience are provided assistance through aptitude testing and counseling, so that appropriate classification and referral can be made.
3. *Service to Veterans*   Each office is charged with providing special assistance to veterans seeking employment.
4. *Service to Applicants with Disabilities*   Each office is also responsible for providing placement assistance to job seekers with disabilities.

5. *Collection of Labor Market Information*   Changes and trends in the local employment situation are assessed regularly; pooling this information at the state and federal levels increases the services available to those seeking work and provides a current picture of employment across the nation.

6. *Cooperation with Community Agencies*   The local office helps keep the public informed, attracts applicants and possible employers, and maintains close contact with local employment conditions. They also are linked to One-Stop Career Centers, which are government agencies that help the unemployed.

In addition to the foregoing, SESAs handle the registration and processing of unemployed workers who qualify for unemployment compensation payments. They also cooperate in the operation of the state level jobs bank, a computerized list of unfilled jobs. Because of the specific responsibilities assigned to such local public employment agencies, they offer many services and advantages to job seekers. Liaison with other local offices through the state provides useful information to workers on employment opportunities at both a statewide and nationwide level. The services of the local office are available without charge to applicants seeking work, who are served by a professional staff concerned with matching applicants' abilities with employers' needs.

Besides providing direct service to the individual job seeker and the unemployed worker, SESAs are a prime source of information that can be used by counselors and those in charge of career resource centers. Because they are the basic collecting unit for local labor market information, SESA staff members are usually more knowledgeable about local job conditions and trends than any other agency. Local data are pooled at the state level and, in turn, at the national level. SESAs have access to the latest available data on the employment situation at these broader levels as well. Most state offices issue regular labor market information reports as part of the occupational employment survey, and current local data are available online.

STUDENT LEARNING EXERCISE 11.1

Before reading the remainder of this section, find a local telephone book, turn to the employment section in the yellow pages, and answer the following questions.

1. How many private agencies are listed? _____
2. Do any of them indicate specializations such as education? _____
3. Are their indications of the fees charged by the agencies listed? _____
   If yes, who pays the fee? _____
4. Are any of the employment agencies linked to providing part-time or temporary workers? _____
5. Is the local public employment office listed in the yellow pages? _____

Private Employment Agencies

Probably every large metropolitan area has several private employment agencies. A quick survey of the telephone directory's yellow pages usually reveals more listings than most people would expect. Because they have many different purposes, it is difficult to provide a simple classification system. Some are regular profit-seeking businesses. Some serve the general public; others limit their clientele to a particular occupational group. Some work primarily for the job seeker; others serve the employer. Some list only regular, full-time positions; others handle only short-term, temporary jobs.

For-profit job placement organizations serve a role similar to the agent who represents a popular entertainer. The agency contracts with the job seekers to assist them in finding satisfactory positions with the understanding that a fee is charged for the service if the person accepts a job. Some businesses contract with for-profit agencies to screen prospective employees and thereby reduce the load on the company's personnel office. When this arrangement exists, the employer often pays the fee charged by the private agency. As with any other group of businesses, the quality of service covers a wide range.

More than 30 years ago Lilley (1978) described some of the problems that arise from involvement with unethical private placement agencies, and during the 1980s and 1990s, thousands of complaints were lodged against some of these agencies. It is clear that complaints rise during recessions when people desperate for a job are willing to take chances. However, it would be unfair to label all or most agencies as fraudulent.

Fees may be on a sliding scale, with higher-paying positions carrying a decidedly heavier fee. As a rough rule of thumb, most fees approximate at least one month's pay, due in full the moment the individual accepts a position. The exact fee should be determined in advance. Special-purpose placement agencies may restrict their clientele to a specific occupational or professional group. For example, some agencies serve only technical occupations at the professional or subprofessional level; others may handle only educational positions such as teacher, school administrator, and related jobs. Closely related to this type of placement agency is the union hiring hall, which serves only members of the organization, or the professional registry—for example, nurses in some metropolitan areas who accept private cases.

A few placement agencies limit their activities to what they label executive searches, or more popularly, headhunting. These companies are employed by organizations to find a person for a specific position rather than the more customary reverse situation. The position to be filled is usually top-level management or some particularly sensitive position where those most qualified would be reluctant to be identified as candidates because of the impact that information would have on their present positions. Fees are typically paid by the employing organization for these services.

Secondary and Postsecondary School Placement Services

The most obvious time for individuals to need placement assistance is at the point when they complete their preparatory programs. Logically, one would thus expect placement services to be an automatic part of a public educational system although this is not always the case. Public schools are rarely evaluated based on the number of graduates who obtain jobs and are therefore less likely to engage in job placement, but many do offer the service.

Public schools have several options available in organizing a placement service, ranging from transferring full responsibility to the local public employment security office to retaining total responsibility within the school itself. The major arguments for full use of the local public employment agency to meet the placement needs of the local school usually are as follows:

1. The state employment service, including the local office, is set up uniquely for placement services, with a trained staff, close contact with employers, and current and accurate local information on the labor market.

2. It is uneconomical to operate two parallel systems.
3. Developing a competing placement service within the school would arouse ill will among the public, who would oppose duplication.
4. The state employment service is where workers go to get a new job, so this facility might just as well be available to those looking for a first job.

Despite the foregoing points, a strong argument can be made in support of job placement services within the school. Advocates of this position usually argue as follows:

1. Our educational institutions are responsible for the adjustment of the individual. Changing from the classroom to the job is part of the adjustment process.
2. The best placements are made when each individual's previous experience and abilities are considered. The educational institution is in the best position to know this information.
3. If the school provides vocational education, it should logically include placement as part of the total process.

Of special importance in school-based placement activities is the opportunity to help students obtain part-time and vacation employment. Valuable experience, as well as a more realistic understanding of the relationship of worker to job, can be acquired by teenagers and young adults who engage in work after school hours, on weekends, or during vacations. These experiences can be helpful to students in their career planning. Often, part-time placements can be arranged to give students exploratory experiences that have direct relationships to career fields. Even when this is not possible, the student can expect to profit in various ways from participation in work experience, such as becoming familiar with supervisory styles.

Some of the reasons that high school students and recent graduates fail to obtain jobs include some rather easily corrected problems, such as unsatisfactory appearance, unrealistic attitude about the nature of work, and unrealistic wage demands; insufficient training; expectations of employment though unqualified; impatience and unwillingness to adapt to entry requirements; insistence on own concept of job duties; and general ignorance of labor market facts. These problems can be reduced or even eliminated by an effective combination of training and practice.

Another argument for providing placement services within the school is the basic philosophical assumption that publicly funded schools have an obligation to students and society to help students find suitable jobs. As has been noted from time to time, American public schools are under fire because of perceptions that students underachieve in the academic arena. Students who are unprepared to make the leap from education to work are underachievers in a different sense. Rudderless students who leave school without making some type of transition to the adult world flounder economically and psychologically, spend longer periods of time being dependent on their parents, and provide poor models for students who are considering whether to stay in or leave school.

School districts that elect to provide placement services to their students have three main options available: (1) create a decentralized system, (2) a centralized program, or (3) create a cooperative program with the local SESA office. The decentralized plan places responsibility for job placement at the lowest functional level: the high school The advantages of this approach are that students are in familiar surroundings, with staff members who probably already know them well, so little or no delay is involved in identifying students who require job placement services. The disadvantages of a decentralized system are also apparent: (1) the program serves a smaller group of students and may not be able to supply the best applicants when employers ask for recommendations; (2) little time may be available for developing employer contacts and conducting follow-up; (3) there is duplication of effort and competition among the schools in the system;

and (4) employers may be uncertain about which school to contact or must make several calls to place job orders.

In a centralized job placement program, a single office is established for the school district that develops pertinent information about students desiring placement and employers who may send notifications of job openings. The advantages of this approach are convenience and efficiency and the likelihood of better staffing, uniform policies, and better community relations. One disadvantage of this system used to be that student records were not as readily available to the placement staff, but this problem has been eliminated by the computerization of records and the electronic transmission of data. However, locating the placement service away from the school may discourage students from accessing it. This geographic gap can be bridged electronically using e-mail and maintaining a job-posting Web site as well as another Web site that contains the resumes of job hunters in the school district.

A cooperative program involving both a school placement service and the local public employment service may provide the best approach to solving job placement problems. The school and employment agency will need to appoint liaison staff who will work together to meet the needs of graduates and dropouts.

Postsecondary schools are involved in placement, and many of them operate placement offices for their students and alumni. Typically, these offices operate as part of the services provided by the educational institution and charge either no fee or a very modest registration fee.

Many university placement offices operate placement activities in a way that might be compared to a dating bureau, where the major objective is to facilitate the meeting of two people—the student and an employer's representative. In these situations the agency focuses its attention on inviting employer representatives to campus and establishing interviewing schedules so that as many students as time permits can have an opportunity to meet with the representatives. Student records are maintained by the registrar and can be accessed by students and provided to prospective employers. In addition, placement officers may keep a file with a résumé but it is more likely that student files will contain only a registration card. When students register, they will usually be asked to identify type of company or industry, geographic preference, and/or occupational goal on their registration card. A notification system, typically an e-mail, alerts students when representatives of companies that relate to their preferences will be on campus, and students can sign up electronically for an interview. Interviewers are provided with a list of students prior to or upon arriving on campus and a room assignment where interviews are to be held. Placement staff members may hold receptions or other public relations activities for business representatives. They are also available to handle problems that arise and to pass out and collect evaluation instruments to interviewers if the data are not being collected as apart of an electronic survey.

Online Job Placement Centers

The most recent innovation in job placement is online or virtual job placement centers. As is the case with other centers, some of these are privately operated and require a fee for their services. Others, primarily those operated by governmental agencies, are free to both employers and job seekers. Both the private and public placement centers allow résumé and job postings by job seekers and employers, respectively. They also allow employers to conduct a résumé search to identify prospective workers; create a hyperlink between their Web sites and the Web sites of businesses that have posted jobs; and provide e-mail addresses so that employees can contact employers directly, résumé screening to ensure that the information on résumés is correct, and user support services to provide assistance when problems are encountered. The fees charged by these private job placement centers vary, and in some instances no fees are charged to job seekers who wish to post their résumés online. Some examples of private and public online job placement services were listed earlier, but one of the oldest and largest is Monster.

Job hunting on the Internet has one major advantage: efficiency. While sitting at a personal computer, connected online to a job placement Web site, job seekers can investigate thousands of job postings from around the world and post résumés that reach vast geographic areas without ever leaving their chairs. This approach to job seeking has the advantage of lowering costs associated with the job search, not only because transportation costs are eliminated but also because résumés posted online bypass development and printing costs. These costs must be weighed against the fees charged by the placement agency, however. Given the rapid expansion of online job placement centers, it seems reasonable to expect that future job seekers need to be aware of these services and include them in their overall plans to gain employment.

Job seekers who use online services may search the same database for jobs in many instances. Except for government-sponsored services, such as those in the state-level Web sites, job listings in each state can be found by going to the One-Stop Career Center Web site, finding the state box on the home page, and scrolling down to the state of interest.

Outplacement Services

Outplacement is a $4 billion industry according to the *Wall Street Journal* (Dvorak & Lublin, 2009). Outplacement services perform many functions, providing assistance to workers whose jobs have been terminated because of technological advances, business mergers, relocation of businesses outside this country, the need to increase competitiveness by reducing costs, employee dismissal for poor performance, or a number of other reasons. Outplacement services are most often provided to exempt employees (salaried; not reimbursed for overtime), but they are also provided in some instances to nonexempt (salaried; reimbursed for overtime) and hourly workers. Dvorak and Lublin reported that more than two-thirds of the U.S. employers offered some form of outplacement service in the two years prior to their 2009 article at an average cost of $3,589 per employee. When these costs were broken down the average cost per executive was $7,518, manager $3,793, salaried employee $2,615, and hourly employee $1,472.

The source of assistance for outplacement typically is offered by an external consulting firm, such as Drake Beam Morin (DBM Career Services) or Right Management. In a few instances outplacement services are offered as an extension of the internal career development program. The services offered, which begin on the day the employee is terminated, usually include resume development, interviewing skills, job location strategies, and supportive counseling. Workshop session may be made available online or on site depending on the contract. One outplacement company, RiseSmart Inc., offers no on-site services. Their entire outplacement program is offered online or via telephone and is understandably cheaper at $2,500 per worker. Assistance may be made available for as long as one year, although the term of outplacement contract is often much shorter, sometimes lasting for only one month.

Morin and York (1982) suggested that a comprehensive outplacement counseling service should be aimed at diffusing the employees' feelings of frustration, depression, and anger; establishing a contract with them to proceed with a job search and to help them develop a job-search plan and the skills to implement it; and following up employees' efforts as they search for a job. Brammer and Humberger (1984) offered a similar outline, although they placed more emphasis than did Morin and York (1982) on assisting workers to engage in self-assessment strategies as prerequisites to establishing career goals.

A 2005 qualitative study of the critical incidents in the outplacement counseling process by Butterfield and Borgen yielded information regarding clients' perspectives of the helpfulness of the outplacement process they experienced. Eighty seven percent of skills development activities were viewed as helpful. Assessment activities were more likely to be judged as helpful than not helpful. Participants' reports of incidents dealing with provision of reference materials and the overall design of the program were evenly rated between helpful and not helpful. The intensity of the outplacement process is reflected in Brammer and Humberger's (1984) observation that a counselor may spend 30 to 65 hours for each candidate for outplacement. The counselor may spend five hours orienting the candidate to the process of outplacement: 20 hours helping the candidate conduct a self-assessment of interests, values, and attitudes; and 40 more hours helping with job selection and mounting the job-search campaign. Brammer and Humberger (1984) note that candidates themselves may spend 310 hours on these same activities. Information uncovered by Dvorak (2009) and Lublin suggest that the information reported by Brammer and Humbarger may be an overestimate of the amount of time spent by counselors in these programs.

Finally, offering an outplacement service is not a guarantee of a job, only a guarantee of assistance in finding a new position. The quality of the personnel and the availability of a full support system, including stationery, clerical help, occupational information, message services, and other similar services, seem to be the most important features involved when outplacement agencies are being selected. Having a full support service and offering a quality experience are key factors in the success of these programs.

Summary

Placement has traditionally been viewed as the culmination of either the career counseling or vocational training process. Although this is still true to a degree, many individuals need job placement services because they have lost their current job. In some instances, these individuals may engage in some type of career planning; in other situations, they are more concerned with getting the first available job. It is apparent that regardless of the reasons for undergoing a job search, today's job hunters must be properly equipped with a set of specific skills if they are to be successful. Personnel officers have definite preferences regarding résumés and biases against certain types of interview behavior. Unless job hunters have the skills to search out available jobs, write appropriate letters, develop attractive résumés, and interview properly, they are severely limited in the job search. Fortunately, career development specialists have the tools they need to develop job-hunting skills and have proved to be effective in this area.

It is also clear that several different types of placement operations are needed in a workforce where literally millions of people seek to enter first jobs or find replacements for old ones. Part-time placement offices in high schools and postsecondary institutions can not only provide students with jobs but also facilitate their career development. Private placement agencies can provide specialized job placement services, and outplacement operations can help relocate the displaced worker. Placement offices in high schools, vocational-technical schools, colleges, and elsewhere can help students find that critical first job. These job placement agencies working independently, but with the same purpose, can alleviate much of the anxiety of being without a job.

Chapter Quiz

T F **1.** Job clubs are primarily aimed at helping people who are out of work deal with the stress of unemployment.

T F **2.** The preferred resume among personnel officers appears to be one that uses the chronological style.

T F **3.** The author suggests that FaceBook and Twitter may be useful job hunting tools.

T F **4.** Private businesses that help people acquire jobs are carefully monitored by law enforcement officials and thus job hunter need not worry about unscrupulous behavior.

T F **5.** State employment agencies also handle applications for unemployment insurance.

T F **6.** Perhaps the best source of job openings can be found on the Web site of a One-Stop Career Center.

T F **7.** State employment agencies provide job hunters with almost all services except career counseling.

T F **8.** Businesses hire outplacement firms to assist their employees find jobs for a variety of reasons, some of which are altruistic and others financial.

T F **9.** "The hidden job market" is a phrase coined to define jobs growing out of government created jobs because they are not advertised in usual channels.

T F **10.** Private job placement agencies are often paid by the employer.

(1) T (2) F (3) T (4) F (5) T (6) T (7) F (8) T (9) F (10) T

References

Atkins, C. P., & Kent, R. L. (1988). What do recruiters consider important during the employment interview? *Journal of Employment Counseling, 25,* 98–103.

Azrin, N. H., & Besadel, V. B. (1979). *Job club counselor's manual: A behavioral approach to vocational counseling.* Baltimore: University Park Press.

Bloch, D. (2000). *The job winning resume* (3rd ed.). Lincolnwood, IL: VGM Books.

Brammer, L. M., & Humberger, F. E. (1984). *Outplacement and inplacement counseling.* Englewood Cliffs, NJ: Prentice-Hall.

Brewington, J. O., Nassar-McMillan, S. C., Flowers, C. P., & Furr, S. R. (2004). A preliminary investigation of factors associated with job loss grief. *Career Development Quarterly, 53,* 78–83.

Butterfield, L. D., & Borgen, W. A. (2005). Outplacement counseling from the client's perspective. *Career Development Quarterly, 53,* 306–316.

Caporoso, R. A., & Kiselica, M. S. (2004). Career counseling with clients with severe mental illness. *Career Development Quarterly, 52,* 235–245.

Dvorak, P., & Lublin, J. S. (2009, August 20). Outplacement firms struggle to do job. *Wall Street Journal* . Retrieved from http://online.wsj.com/article/SB125069793645343423.html#articleTabs%3Darticle

Eck, A. (1993, October). Job-related education and training: Their impact on earnings. *Monthly Labor Review,* 21–38.

Eden, D., & Avarim, A. (1993). Self-efficacy training to speed reemployment: Helping people to help themselves. *Journal of Applied Psychology, 78,* 352–360.

Eisenstadt, S. (1995, October 24). Information highway offers new route to jobs. *The News and Observer,* Raleigh, NC.

Farr, J. M. (1989). *Getting the job you really want.* Indianapolis, IN: JIST.

Hall, J. P., & Parker, K. (2010). Stuck in a loop: Individual and System Barriers for Job seekers with disabilities, *Career Development Quarterly, 58,* 246–256.

Hansen, K (2010). For networking and support, join or start a job club. Retrieved from http://www.quintcareers.com/job_club.html

Helwig, A. A. (1987). Information required for job hunting: 1121 counselors respond. *Journal of Employment Counseling, 24,* 184–190.

Helwig, A. A. (1985). Corporate recruits preferences for three résumé styles. *Vocational Guidance Quarterly, 34,* 99–105.

Jones, M. L., Ulicny, G. R., Czyzewski, M. J., & Plante, T. G. (1987). Employment in care-giving jobs for mentally disabled young adults: A feasibility study. *Journal of Employment Counseling, 24,* 122–129.

Kanchier, C. (1990). Career education for adults with mental disabilities. *Journal of Employment Counseling, 27,* 23–36.

Lam, C. S. (1986). Comparison of sheltered and supported work programs: A pilot study. *Rehabilitation Counseling Bulletin, 30,* 66–82.

Lilley, W. (1978). Job hunters, beware. *Canadian Business, 51,* 36–37, 99–100.

Morin, W. J., & York, L. (1982). *Outplacement techniques: A positive approach to terminating employees.* New York: AMACON.

Murray, N. (1993, Spring). Bridge for the X's: A new career services model. *Journal of Career Planning and Employment, 3,* 28–35.

Platt, J. J., Husband, S. D., Hermalin, J., Cater, J., & Metzger, D. (1993). A cognitive problem solving employment readiness intervention for methadone clients. *Journal of Cognitive Psychotherapy: An International Quarterly, 7,* 21–33.

Ports, M. H. (1993, October). Trends in job search methods. *Monthly Labor Review,* 63–67.

Rife, J. C., & Belcher, J. R. (1993). Social support and job search intensity among older unemployed workers. Implications for employment counselors. *Journal of Employment Counseling, 30,* 98–107.

Riggio, R. E., & Throckmorton, B. (1987). Effects of prior training and verbal errors on students' performance in job interviews. *Journal of Employment Counseling, 29,* 10–16.

Ryland, E. K., & Rosen, B. (1987). Personnel professionals' reactions to chronological and functional résumé formats. *Career Development Quarterly, 35,* 228–238.

Silliker, S. A. (1993). The role of social contacts in the successful job search. *Journal of Employment Counseling, 30,* 25–34.

Stephens, D. B., Watt, J. T., & Hobbs, W. S. (1979). Getting through the resume preparation image: Some empirically based guidelines for resume format. *Vocational Guidance Quarterly, 28,* 25–34.

Subich, L. (1994). Annual review: Practice and research in career counseling and development. *Career Development Quarterly, 43,* 114–151.

Taylor, S. (2002). Disabled workers deserve real choices, real jobs. Retrieved from http://www.accessiblesociety.org/topics/economics-employment/shelteredwksps.html.

Thompson, M. N., & Cummings, D. L. (2010). Enhancing the career development of individuals with criminal records. *Career Development Quarterly, 58,* 209–218.

Wegman, L., Chapman, I., & Johnson, T. (1989). *Work in the new economy.* Indianapolis, IN: JIST.

Whitcomb, S. B., Bryan, C., & Dib, D. (2010) *The Twitter Job Search Guide.* Indianapolis, IN: JIST Publishing.

Yates, C. J. (1987). Job hunters' perspective on their needs during the job search process. *Journal of Employment Counseling, 24,* 155–165.

Zunker, V. G. (2006). *Career counseling: Applied concepts of life planning* (5th ed.). Monterey, CA: Brooks/Cole.

Managing Career Development Programs in Private and Public Domains

Designing and Implementing Comprehensive K–12 Career Development Programs Within the Framework of the ASCA National Model

Things to Remember

- The components of the ASCA Model
- The steps in the program planning and implementation process
- At least one scheme for organizing the delivery of career development

interventions from kindergarten through grade 12

- The major techniques used for delivering career development content

There are many critical periods in the career development process. However, if we are to develop the foundation for a lifelong developmental process, we must take advantage of the years when students are in school. Fortunately, the American School Counselor Association (ASCA, 2003, 2005) has taken the lead in this area by publishing the *ASCA National Model: A Framework for School Counseling Programs* (ANM). The ANM is a developmental framework that emphasizes the importance of career, academic, and personal social development. It also provides an outline for developing a comprehensive career development program, the competencies that should result from such a program, and other valuable information. In this chapter the basics of designing and implementing a K–12 career development program based on the ANM are presented. The intent is to show that career development is a part of the larger framework for the school counseling program, not a stand-alone entity.

HISTORICAL BACKGROUND

Career development is a lifelong process (Ginzberg, Ginzburg, Axelrad, & Herma, 1951; Super, 1957), and crucial aspects of this development occur during the school years. Over the past four decades numerous educational thrusts have been aimed at promoting career development in elementary, middle, and high schools. The most ambitious of these programs was the career education movement that developed during the Nixon administration under the leadership of then-Secretary of Education Sidney Marland. Many prominent counselor educators, including K. B. Hoyt (2005), were prominently involved in this movement, which saw the establishment of extensive programs to help children and adolescents broaden their career horizons, learn decision-making skills, acquire vocational skills, and generally develop an appreciation for themselves. Hoyt (1977) defined career education as follows:

> Career education is an effort aimed at refocusing American education and the actions of the broader community in ways that will help individuals acquire and utilize the knowledge, skills, and attitudes necessary for each person to make work a meaningful, productive and satisfying part of his or her way of living. (p. 5)

Marland (1974) describes eight elements of career education identified by the Center for Research in Vocational Education at Ohio State University:

1. Career Awareness—knowledge of the total spectrum of careers.
2. Self-Awareness—knowledge of the components that make up self.
3. Appreciations, Attitudes—life roles; feelings toward self and others in respect to society and economics.
4. Decision-Making Skills—applying information to rational processes in order to reach decisions.
5. Economic Awareness—perception of processes in production, distribution, and consumption.
6. Skill Awareness and Beginning Competence—skills in ways in which humans extend their behaviors.
7. Employability Skills—social and communication skills appropriate to career placement.
8. Educational Awareness—perception of the relationship between education and life roles. (pp. 100–102)

By the mid-1980s, most of the remnants of the career education movement in the 1970s had been swept from U.S. schools by the back-to-basics educational movement. Advocates of back to basics were particularly critical of career education programs in elementary schools that focused children's attention on workers, developing skills with tools through hands-on approaches, and field trips to work sites because these activities took time away from core subjects. However, the failure of career education in the elementary school cannot be laid solely at the doorstep of the back-to-basics movement. Many mistakes were made in the design and implementation of those programs, including the following: (1) they were funded with monies external to the school district with no plans to provide internal financial support once external funding was withdrawn; (2) they added to the workload of an already overloaded group: teachers; (3) the term *career education* was negatively associated with vocational education by many middle-class parents, who were concerned that their children might be diverted from the college preparatory curriculum; and (4) local political support among educators, parents, and the business community was not carefully developed in many instances.

However, career education, and particularly the idea that education and career should be linked, was more resilient than many people believed. In 1989 the National Occupational Information Coordinating Committee (NOICC, 1989a, 1989b, 1989c, 1989d) published four extensive publications that outlined how career development programs in schools and elsewhere could be implemented. These were consolidated into a single publication in 1996 (Kobylarz, 1996). In 1994 the School-to-Work Opportunities Act (STWOA) was passed by Congress. This legislation provided the impetus for public schools to develop challenging educational programs for all, to relate academic subject matter to work, to help students identify their interests, and to stimulate students to make educational and career plans. One outgrowth of STW and the school reform movement was the adoption of four courses of study for students who wished to graduate from high school in North Carolina: (1) occupational, (2) career, (3) tech-prep, and (4) college bound. Although students were able to switch courses of study during their high school years, they had to finish all the curricular requirements of one of the courses of study in order to graduate.

More recently another professional organization, the American School Counselor Association, published *The National Standards for School Counseling Programs* (Campbell & Dahir, 1997), which emphasized the importance of developing career development competencies in school-age youth in the context of a school counseling program. *The National Standards* set forth nine standards that are subsumed under three broad areas: academic, career, and personal/social development. The standards for career development include three key points: (1) students should develop the skills needed to explore the world of work in relationship to knowledge about self and use this information to make career decisions; (2) students will employ strategies to achieve future career choice and satisfaction; and (3) students will develop an understanding of the relationship of personal qualities, education, and the world of work. The standards then proceed to identify specific competencies that, if developed, allow school counseling programs to meet the standards.

The publication of *The National Standards for School Counseling Programs* (Campbell & Dahir, 1997) was a prelude to a much more important publication, one that seems destined to have a profound impact on K–12 career development programs. Published in 2003 and revised in 2005, *ASCA National Model: A Framework for School Counseling Programs* (ANM) includes the national standards, and describes the process for establishing a comprehensive school counseling program among many other components.

THE ASCA MODEL AND CAREER DEVELOPMENT

The ANM contains what "ASCA believes to be the essential elements of a quality and effective school counseling program" (ASCA, 2003, p. 3) and a brief description of the delivery mechanisms used in a comprehensive school counseling program. It also contains a listing of the competencies that students should develop as a result of the school counseling program.

As can be seen in Figure 12.1, the ANM contains four components: foundation, delivery systems, accountability, and management system. The foundation of the program serves as the basis of the delivery and management systems. As the arrows in the model illustrate, the foundation for a comprehensive school counseling program should be based on a statement of beliefs; a mission statement; and the national standards for academic, career, and educational development. The career development standards are not entirely original. Campbell and Dahir (1997) report that the career development standards have their roots in standards developed by the NOICC (1989a, 1989b, 1989c, 1989d) as well as other sources.

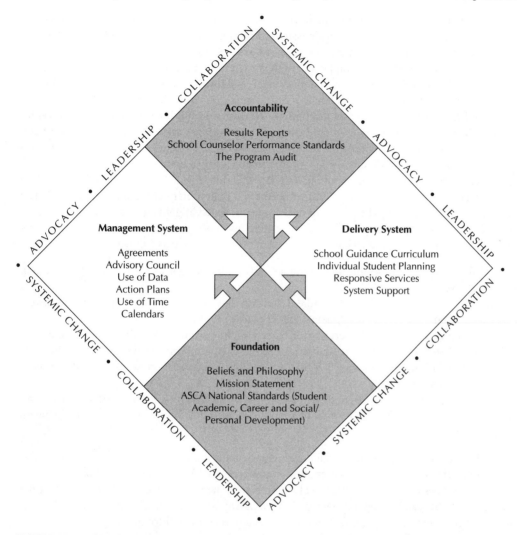

FIGURE 12.1 The ASCA National Model Schematic.   *Source:* From the *ASCA National Model: A Framework for School Counseling Programs.* Reprinted with permission of the American School Counselor Association, http://www.schoolcounselor.org.

The delivery systems in the ASCA model involve those strategies used by school counselors to deliver services to students and others. The elements within the delivery systems were taken directly from the comprehensive guidance program model (Gysbers & Henderson, 2000). The guidance curriculum contains classroom guidance, structured group activities, parent education, and classroom units taught by teachers. These are the primary strategies used in the delivery of the career development program, with the exception of individual planning. Individual student planning is essentially an advising process that incorporates the assessment needed to serve as the basis for advising and developing students' long- and short-term educational and career plans.

Responsive services include teacher and parent consultation, referral, counseling, responses to crises, and peer-facilitated activities. Career counseling falls under this rubric as does the provision of information. System support involves collaboration with other stakeholders in and outside the school, management of the school counseling program, and professional development. Collaboration with businesses and with agencies such as Employment Security facilitates the development of internship sites and job placement.

Accountability, the third component of the program, consists of the evaluation of the effectiveness of the delivery systems and the personnel, and the dissemination of data in the form of results reports to support the effectiveness of the program. A combination of factors including No Child Left Behind (2002) and the Individuals with Disabilities Education Act (2004) has prompted professionals working in public schools to engage in what are termed evidence-based interventions in order to demonstrate the effectiveness of the strategies employed to produce desired outcomes. The ANM embraced this position and set up a committee to establish standards for determining evidence-based approaches (Carey, Dimmitt, Hatch, Lapan, & Whiston, 2008).

Earlier Whiston & Sexton (1998) combed the research literature in an attempt to identify evidence-based practices. They focused on 12 studies related to guidance curriculum, 10 studies related to individual planning services, 25 related to responsive services, and three related to system support. Their conclusions based on a total of 50 studies were as follows:

1. We cannot conclude that the guidance curriculum activities positively affect student achievement.
2. The results of these reports (studies) indicate that individual planning interventions can have a positive impact on students' career plans.
3. With regard to responsive services: Group counseling seems to be effective with elementary school students and students in general experiencing difficulties with their families . . . Social skills training may be helpful to students and that peer counseling may also be helpful in a number of areas.
4. With regard to system support: Sample limitations restrict our ability to draw general conclusions about the effectiveness of school counseling activities with the typical student. (pp. 423–424)

The fourth component, the management system, includes when, why, and on whose authority various aspects of the program are implemented. The *when* of the school counseling program includes calendars of events and action plans. The *why* is based on data suggesting that the actions to be taken are appropriate, and the *authority* issue is addressed through the development of agreements among school leaders and the advisory council for the program.

As noted earlier, the content for the school counseling program was first articulated in 1997 in *The National Standards for School Counseling Programs* (Campbell & Dahir, 1997). Nine standards for school counseling programs were identified that are related to the three content areas. These standards are included in the ANM; they list the student competencies that are to be developed by the school counseling program and the indicators that the competencies have, in fact, been developed. The standards for the career development domain and the competency indicators are shown in Table 12.1. This table is a modified version of ASCA's developmental and curriculum crosswalks, which can be used to plan one facet of the program: the guidance curriculum.

Program planners have two decisions to make regarding the development of competencies. The first is from a developmental point of view: At what age should the competency be developed? The second issue involves the activities and materials that are required to develop the competency. As noted previously, the guidance curriculum consists of classroom guidance, structured group activities, parent education, and classroom units taught by teachers. School

TABLE 12.1   ASCA National Standards: Modified Guidance Curriculum Crosswalk

	Grade Level(s)	Dates	Activity	Materials	Person Responsible
CAREER DEVELOPMENT DOMAIN					
STANDARD A: Students will acquire the skills to investigate the world of work in relation to knowledge of self and to make informed career decisions.					
Competency A:1: Develop Career Awareness					
C:A1.1 Develop skills to locate, evaluate, and interpret career information					
C:A1.2 Learn about the variety of traditional and nontraditional occupations					
C:A1.3 Develop an awareness of personal abilities, skills, interests, and motivations					
C:A1.4 Learn how to interact and work cooperatively in teams					
C:A1.5 Learn to make decisions					
C:A1.6 Learn how to set goals					
C:A1.7 Understand the importance of planning					
C:A1.8 Pursue and develop competency in areas of interest					
C:A1.9 Develop hobbies and vocational interests					
C:A1.10 Balance between work and leisure time					
Competency A:2: Develop Employment Readiness					
C:A2.1 Acquire employability skills, such as working on a team, problem-solving, and organizational skills					
C:A2.2 Apply job readiness skills to seek employment opportunities					
C:A2.3 Demonstrate knowledge about the changing workplace					
C:A2.4 Learn about the rights and responsibilities of employers and employees					
C:A2.5 Learn to respect individual uniqueness in the workplace					
C:A2.6 Learn how to write a résumé					
C:A2.7 Develop a positive attitude toward work and learning					

(Continued)

TABLE 12.1   ASCA National Standards: Modified Guidance Curriculum Crosswalk   (*Continued*)

	Grade Level(s)	Dates	Activity	Materials	Person Responsible
C:A2.8 Understand the importance of responsibility, dependability, punctuality, integrity, and effort in the workplace					
C:A2.9 Utilize time- and task-management skills					

STANDARD B: Students will employ strategies to achieve future career goals with success and satisfaction.

Competency B:1: Acquire Career Information

C:B1.1 Apply decision-making skills to career planning, course selection, and career transition					
C:B1.2 Identify personal skills, interests, and abilities, and relate them to current career choice					
C:B1.3 Demonstrate knowledge of the career planning process					
C:B1.4 Know the various ways in which occupations can be classified					
C:B1.5 Use research and information resources to obtain career information					
C:B1.6 Learn to use the Internet to access career planning information					
C:B1.7 Describe traditional and nontraditional career choices and how they relate to career choice					
C:B1.8 Understand how changing economic and societal needs influence employment trends and future training					

Competency B:2: Identify Career Goals

C:B2.1 Demonstrate awareness of the education and training needed to achieve career goals					
C:B2.2 Assess and modify the educational plan to support career goals					
C:B2.3 Use employability and job readiness skills in internship, mentoring, shadowing, and/or other work experience					
C:B2.4 Select coursework that is related to career interests					
C:B2.5 Maintain a career planning portfolio					

(*Continued*)

TABLE 12.1   ASCA National Standards: Modified Guidance Curriculum Crosswalk (*Continued*)

	Grade Level(s)	Dates	Activity	Materials	Person Responsible
STANDARD C: Students will understand the relationship between personal qualities, education, training, and the world of work.					
Competency C:1: Acquire Knowledge to Achieve Career Goals					
C:C1.1 Understand the relationship between educational achievement and career success					
C:C1.2 Explain how work can help to achieve personal success and satisfaction					
C:C1.3 Identify personal preferences and interests influencing career choice and success					
C:C1.4 Understand that the changing workplace requires lifelong learning and acquiring new skills					
C:C1.5 Describe the effect of work on lifestyle					
C:C1.6 Understand the importance of equity and access in career choice					
C:C1.7 Understand that work is an important and satisfying means of personal expression					
Competency C:2: Apply Skills to Achieve Career Goals					
C:C2.1 Demonstrate how interests, abilities, and achievement relate to achieving personal, social, educational, and career goals					
C:C2.2 Learn how to use conflict-management skills with peers and adults					
C:C2.3 Learn to work cooperatively with others as a team member					
C:C2.4 Apply academic and employment readiness skills in work-based learning situations, such as internships, shadowing, and/or mentoring experiences					

Source: From the *ASCA National Model: A Framework for School Counseling Programs*. Reprinted with permission of the American School Counselor Association. http://www.schoolcounselor.org.

counselors engaged in planning the guidance curriculum should consider the nature of the activities to be offered and the grade level at which the competency will be developed.

It is worth noting that the competencies listed in the ANM are not broken down by grade level; thus, the competencies to be developed at each grade level must be determined by the planning committee. It seems likely that many of the competencies will be addressed at several points in the curriculum. For example competency C:A1.1, "develop skills to locate, evaluate, and interpret career information," might be addressed as follows:

> *Grade 4*—As part of a unit on nontraditional careers, students interview workers who have entered nontraditional careers.
>
> *Grade 7*—As part of unit on self-exploration, students identify three occupations related to their Holland code and, using the *Occupational Outlook Handbook* (online or print versions), develop brief job descriptions and salary information.
>
> *Grade 11*—Using online data sources, students identify jobs, their descriptions, likely geographic locations, and entry-level salaries regarding either their postsecondary education plans (majors) or their expected occupations after graduation.

In summary, the ANM contains four components, four themes, four delivery strategies, and several accountability measures and approaches. These components, themes, delivery strategies, and accountability approaches serve as an integrated model that can be used to design and implement a comprehensive school counseling program. ASCA also provides a process by which program development should occur.

THE PROCESS OF PROGRAM DEVELOPMENT

The planning of a comprehensive program includes several steps: (1) gaining administrative support, (2) establishing preconditions, (3) forming a planning committee, (4) conducting a needs assessment to determine which competencies need to be developed, (5) planning the program to develop competencies, (6) implementing the program, and (7) establishing an accountability system (ASCA, 2003).

Gaining Administrative Support

Although the ANM was developed to serve as a guide for the development or renovation of district-wide programs, the model applies equally well to individual schools. In either case, the top-level administrator or the building-level principal must agree to endorse the career development program if it is to succeed. If the program development effort is aimed at an entire district, endorsement from the school board should be sought. This becomes particularly important if new money is to be allocated to support the program.

Although gaining administrative support for changes in the career development program is essential, it is also necessary to develop support among other stakeholders, including teachers, parents, community agencies, and businesses (Brown, Pryzwansky, & Schulte, 2010). Successful career development programs involve all these groups, and their support at the outset is crucial.

Establishing Preconditions

To be successful, programs must have the staff, budget, facilities, materials and supplies, and technology appropriate to operate the program. Before a great deal of effort is put into the design of the program, school counselors should estimate the cost of each component needed in the program. This estimate should be presented to top-level administrators during the process of gaining administrative support. The school counselors involved should also expect to present rationales for the expenditures. Endorsement for the concept of providing career development services is most likely to be forthcoming if it is reasonable and is couched in terms of the overall goals of the individual school or district (Brown & Trusty, 2005a). Some of these overall goals might include the following:

- Reducing the dropout rate
- Increasing student achievement
- Decreasing the achievement gap between white and minority students
- Increasing postsecondary enrollment

It is important to not promise more than is possible as a consequence of the implementation of a career development program, but there is some evidence that the variables listed here can be affected by well-designed programs (Brown & Trusty, 2005b).

Forming a Planning Committee

Once support for the development of the program is gained and the preconditions are established, the ASCA recommends that, the next step be the formation of a planning committee. This committee has a number of responsibilities, including writing a mission statement, drafting a philosophy for the program, conducting a needs assessment, selecting the competencies that will be developed based on the needs assessment, and planning the program.

The planning committee should include representatives from the administrative staff, the teaching faculty, school counselors, parents, members of the business community, and at least one student representative. Some of the tasks to be performed by the committee are described in more detail in the paragraphs below.

The mission and philosophy statements are essential. The mission statement reflects what the career development program entails, and the philosophy statement is a brief letter to the public about the program (National Consortium of State Guidance Leaders, 2000). For example, the mission statement might indicate that the program is an integral part of the school counseling program that has as its basic aim facilitating career choice and career implementation for all students. A variation of part of this statement, "facilitating career choices and their implementation for all students," would be appropriate on the letterhead of the program chair. The statement of philosophy sets forth the values on which the program is built. It might include the following points:

- Serves all students and is dedicated to advancing their educational and career development
- Staffed by knowledgeable professionals, counselors, and teachers
- Facilitates transition
- Serves as a key part of a K–12, coordinated program
- Becomes an integral part of the school counseling program, the school, and the community
- Dedicated to advancing the educational mission of the school (district)

The statement of philosophy may be presented in either a narrative or bulleted list format. Its purpose is to inform the stakeholders of the program and to serve as a guide in the planning process.

Conducting a Needs Assessment

School districts located in rural West Virginia, suburban Indianapolis, inner-city Chicago, and Chapel Hill, North Carolina, have different types of students and thus need different types of career development programs. Many of the students in rural West Virginia go directly into the military or the civilian workplace, as do the students in inner-city Chicago. However, students in rural West Virginia probably relocate to other geographic areas within the state or even outside the state to find suitable employment. If students from an inner city are minority students, they are likely to be confronted with varying degrees of discrimination. It is likely that large numbers of students from Chapel Hill and suburban Indianapolis school districts will attend some form of postsecondary educational institution; therefore, their initial career decision process will be somewhat more protracted. However, all these students need to be able to incorporate career planning into their educational planning processes. To determine what type of program best serves the students in these school districts, it is imperative that a full understanding of the characteristics of students and their families be developed. The process of developing this profile is usually termed *needs assessment*.

Data about the needs of students are available from a variety of sources, including demographic data about the community; the results of achievement testing; information about the dropout rate; follow-up of studies of graduates and dropouts; and direct surveys of students, teachers, business leaders, and parents. The questions to be answered through needs assessment are (1) What are the students' needs as they relate to the career development program? and (2) What is the best approach to meeting the needs that are identified? (Brown & Trusty, 2005a). When data from needs assessment devices, such as the one shown in Figure 12.2, are combined with information collected from graduates and business leaders as well as other sources, planners can begin to get a sense of the type of program that needs to be delivered.

The needs assessment may be directed by a steering committee as suggested in the *NCDG Handbook* (Kobylarz, 1996). However, it is more likely that the needs assessment is directed by a school counselor, the district-wide director of school counseling services, or a representative from the vocational education division. Steering committees are typically put into place once needs are established and top-level administrative support is gained. Once the need for the career development program has been documented, two courses of action are possible. One is to appoint an advisory committee to lobby for the program. The other is to have the person or persons who conducted the needs assessment use the data gathered about the needs of the students to gain approval from school administrators and the school board. Regardless of how it is sought, an administrative endorsement of the program should be secured before launching a full-scale planning process.

Writing Goals and Objectives and Establishing Criteria for Success

Although the steering committee for a district-wide program should establish goals, specific program objectives should be established for each school. Goals are usually stated in rather broad terms—for example, "Students will increase their knowledge of the types of careers available to them." Broad goal statements are then broken down into their behavioral objectives, which are sequenced chronologically.

Behavioral objectives contain four components: who will accomplish them, what they will accomplish and to what degree they will be accomplished, by when they will be accomplished, and by what means they will be accomplished (Burns, 1972; Morris, Fitz-Gibbon, & Lindheim, 1987). The following is an example of a series of behavioral objectives that might be written for the aforementioned goal:

Goal: Students will increase their knowledge of the types of careers available to them.

Kindergarten—By the end of kindergarten, students will be able to identify their parents' jobs and be able to list at least three of the duties they perform on those jobs, as a result of homework assignments to interview their parents about their jobs.

First grade—By the end of grade 1, all students will be able to identify three community helpers and three of their duties as a result of a speakers' program featuring community workers.

	Level of Importance		
	Little	**Moderate**	**Great**
Self Knowledge: Students will develop			
Knowledge of the importance of a positive self-concept	1	2	3
Skills to interact positively with others	1	2	3
Awareness of need for continued emotional growth	1	2	3
Educational and Occupational Exploration: Students will develop			
Awareness of the importance of educational achievement	1	2	3
Awareness of the relationship between work and learning	1	2	3
Skills to understand and use career information	1	2	3
Awareness of the importance of personal responsibility and good work habits	1	2	3
Awareness of how work relates to the needs and functions of society	1	2	3
Career Planning: Students will develop	1	2	3
Understanding of how to make decisions	1	2	3
Awareness of the interrelationships among life roles	1	2	3
Awareness of the changing roles of men and women in the workforce	1	2	3
Awareness of the career planning process	1	2	3

FIGURE 12.2 Needs Assessment Survey Form—Elementary School. *Source:* Adapted from *National Career Development Guidelines: K–Adult Handbook* by L. Kobylarz, 1996 (p. A.3). Stillwater, OK: Career Development Training Institute.

Second grade—By the end of grade 2, all students will be able to identify three workers who work in their county along with two tasks they perform and how they use reading on their jobs, as a result of a classroom unit titled "Workers in Our County."

Third grade—By the end of grade 3, all students will be able to identify five workers employed by the state, identify their major responsibilities, and tell two ways they use mathematics on their jobs, as a result of a field trip to the state capitol and follow-up activities.

Fourth grade—By the end of grade 4, all students will be able to identify five workers who are unique to the Southeast, describe their major job responsibilities, and tell how they use information learned in at least two school subjects on their jobs, as a result of completing an out-of-class assignment "Workers in Our Region."

Fifth grade—By the end of grade 5, all students will be able to identify 10 U.S. workers who hold jobs outside of the Southeast, the major duties they perform, and how they use information from school on their jobs, as a result of writing an essay on jobs in the United States, viewing D at a workstation established for this purpose, and class assignments.

Sixth grade—Students learn about careers in our hemisphere and the world as a result of infusion in all classes. Students complete an English essay "If I Could Be Anything." Counselor-led monthly seminars will feature speakers who represent international careers.

Seventh grade—Students complete an interest inventory and then participate in counselor-led groups to discuss the sources of interests and how interests influence career choice making.

Eighth grade—Students complete a nine-week class on choosing a career that focuses on decision making and using occupational information along with data about self to make career choices. The culminating experience is for students to select three careers of interest and to do a self-analysis regarding their potential to enter those careers and to lay out an educational path to the most desired career. By the end of grade 8, students will have identified three jobs that may be of interest to them in the future, determined what academic skills that are needed to enter those jobs, and analyzed how their aptitudes and academic performance may prepare them for or provide a barrier to entering those jobs,

Grades nine through twelve (*High school*)—Each student will make a preliminary career choice along with an alternative choice and construct educational plans to enter those careers, as a result of counselor-directed activities, such as career seminars, individual planning sessions, bibliotherapy, job shadowing, participation in career day, interest and aptitude assessment, and so forth.

Another approach to writing objectives is to tie them to the competencies listed in the ASCA (2003, 2005) model. Table 12.2 presents a subset of the ASCA career development standards and competencies.

As can be seen in Table 12.2, the competencies are not written in observable, behavioral terms, which complicates the evaluation process. It is, therefore, necessary to rewrite them so they

---

TABLE 12.2   ASCA Standards: Career Development Domain, Standard A, Competency A.1 and Indicators

Competency A:1: Develop Career Awareness

C:A1.1 Develop skills to locate, evaluate, and interpret career information

C:A1.2 Learn about the variety of traditional and nontraditional occupations

C:A1.3 Develop an awareness of personal abilities, skills, interests, and motivations

C:A1.4 Learn how to interact and work cooperatively in teams

C:A1.5 Learn to make decisions

C:A1.6 Learn how to set goals

C:A1.7 Understand the importance of planning

C:A1.8 Pursue and develop competency in areas of interest

C:A1.9 Develop hobbies and vocational interests

C:A1.10 Balance between work and leisure time

Source: From the *ASCA National Model: A Framework for School Counseling Programs*. Reprinted with permission of the American School Counselor Association, http://www.schoolcounselor.org.

TABLE 12.3   ASCA Standards Career Development Domain, Standard A, Competency A.1 and Rewritten Indicators

---

Competency A:1: Develop Career Awareness in Middle School Career Development Unit

C:A1.1 Each student will identify three sources of information about occupations related to their Holland code and use that information to describe the occupation

C:A1.2 Each student will identify three occupations that contain less than 25 percent males or females and tell whether these are nontraditional for men or women in a single page report

C:A1.3 As the result of the Self-Directed Search and a self-analysis of skills and abilities, each student will identify his or her Holland code and his or her most important abilities and skills as they relate to their current occupational choice

C:A1.4 After a one-hour-long, unstructured, cooperative project on using the Internet to find career information, students in groups of three will provide anonymous ratings of the quality of the cooperative behavior of other group members using a scale constructed for the exercise

C:A1.5 After an introduction on the balance sheet, student will construct a matrix that identifies two occupations that they consider as possible occupational choices, generate criteria that can be used to test the validity of the choices, and apply the balance sheet to make a preliminary occupational choice

C:A1.6 Students will set one-week goals for some aspect of their behavior and rate the extent to which that goal was achieved at the end of the week; this procedure will also be used for two- and three-week goals

C:A1.7 Small groups of students will set up a small school-based business; some groups will be given planning guidelines and others will not; progress is judged after one hour of deliberations

C:A1.8 After identifying one occupation based on their Holland code, students will use O*NET to identify one ability needed in the performance of the job and develop a plan to develop that ability

C:A1.9 As a result of a field trip to the hospital, students will identify one new job of interest and two leisure options that a person in that occupation might enjoy

C:A1.10 As a result of shadowing one of his or her parents or guardians or another person who works, students will identify (1) how that person spends his or her time and (2) how the requirements of the occupation might interfere with family and leisure activities

---

Source: From the *ASCA National Model: A Framework for School Counseling Programs.* Reprinted with permission of the American School Counselor Association, http://www.schoolcounselor.org.

fit nicely into the evaluation process. A rewrite of the competencies is presented in Table 12.3, which suggests not only how the competency can be written in behavioral terms but also how the competency might be developed. This rewrite also contains one of the essential aspects of the plan: *when* the competency is to be developed. Although these objectives were written for a middle school career development unit, similar objectives and plans could be developed for elementary and high school activities. The information in Table 12.3 is one step in the planning of the guidance curriculum.

Designing the Career Development Program

Gaining administrative support, establishing preconditions, forming a planning committee, assessing student needs, and establishing objectives set the stage for the most important phase in the planning process, the actual design of the program. Several questions need to be answered at this juncture. Perhaps the most important of these is which of the delivery systems in the ASCA model will be used in the effort to help students develop the competencies that are important. The guidance curriculum must be a major aspect in the development of the competencies if the program is to serve all students, a value that underpins the ANM (ASCA, 2003, 2005). This leads to a series of subquestions, the first of them related to the guidance curriculum:

1. What opportunities are available or can be made available for career development units in classrooms?
2. What opportunities are there to infuse career development material into existing units?
3. What types of small-group activities can be offered?
4. How can the parent aspect of the guidance curriculum be designed and delivered effectively?
5. How can the parents of minority and poor students be incorporated into the program?
6. What materials will be needed to support the guidance curriculum?
7. How can technology, such as the Internet, be used to deliver the guidance curriculum?
8. How can the Career Resource Center staff be involved in the guidance curriculum?
9. How can each aspect of the guidance curriculum be evaluated?

Several questions are related to individual student planning:

1. At what point in the schooling process do students have to choose a curriculum? What activities should precede this process?
2. How can parents be involved in this process?
3. What assessments are needed to support the individual and group educational and career planning efforts?
4. What is the best approach to providing the educational and career planning needed by all students (e.g., teacher advisors, counselor led, peer led)?
5. Are there students with special needs that require different types of assessment and planning activities?
6. What types of accommodations will be required for minority and/or English as a second language (ESL) students?

During the planning of responsive services the following questions must be considered:

1. How can consultation services be offered to teachers and others involved in the program?
2. How can students who require career counseling be identified?
3. What types of career counseling are needed for students who are disabled, minorities, and ESL students?

Several questions are likely to arise when planning for system support:

1. What is the budget?
2. What types of professional development are required in order to prepare for program implementation?
3. How can the school counseling staff support the operation of the school using consultation and collaboration?
4. What type of community outreach is required to familiarize counselors with community resources?
5. How will the program be managed?
6. How will staff be assigned?

Finally, the overall plan for the career development program as a part of the school counseling program must deal with the issues of program coordination, developing a calendar of events for the program, accountability, staff performance evaluation, the overall approach of the program, and evaluation of the program.

ADDRESSING THE ISSUE: PROGRAM IMPLEMENTATION

Budgeting

It is uncertain how long the current economic downturn will continue to cause shortfall in the budgets of school districts, but what is certain is that the money available to underwrite the career development program rarely provides all of the resources needed to furnish the materials, test and assessment instruments, staff and extra school activities that would optimize the program if available. School counselors need to learn to take advantage of materials available to them on the Intranet. What follows are some money-saving suggestions:

- Have the local military recruiter administer, score, and interpret the Finding Your Interests and Armed Services Vocational Aptitude Battery to all juniors.
- Take eighth-graders to the computer lab (assuming computers are linked to the Internet) and have them take the Interest Profiler (IP) (which should be available at http://www.onetcenter.gov by the time this book is published). Students can use IP scores to explore occupations of interest in subsequent sessions once the scores are properly interpreted.
- Assemble and post the Web site addresses of the four-year colleges, community colleges, and technical schools that most graduates attend.
- Hold One-Stop Career Center orientation sessions aimed at potential dropouts beginning no later than eighth grade. These sessions should be repeated beginning late in the sophomore year for graduates who are likely to go directly to work.
- Explore links to materials and exercises such as budgeting for college posted on the Internet by your state department of labor or state occupational information coordinating committee for elementary, middle, and high school students.
- Hold orientation sessions to the *Occupational Outlook Handbook* for teachers interested in incorporating more information about careers into their curriculum.
- Staff the career resources center with paraprofessionals instead of school counselors. This will result in a cost saving of 33 to 50 percent of a counselor's salary and fringe benefits. If possible hire staff that has attained the Global Career Development Center certificate described in Chapter 4.

Selecting a Management System

Because the career development program is an integral part of the school counseling program, the coordinator of the school counseling program at the district and building levels would ordinarily coordinate the career development aspect of the program. Others, such as the Career Resource Center coordinator, the school-to-work transition director for exceptional children, and vocational education representatives, would ordinarily be involved in the coordination of the overall school counseling program and the career development portion of it. Regardless of who is involved on the management team, the overall approach to managing the program should be a collaborative one.

Johnson, Johnson, and Downs (2005) indicate that the role of the program coordinator is to review the plans that the program staff produces; monitor the activities associated with those plans; audit results reports; and, with the staff, validate accomplishments, facilitate staff development, and participate in the establishment of agreements among the staff and with administrators. Brown and Trusty (2005a) suggested that the program coordinator should also be prepared to engage in conflict resolution, facilitate problem solving, establish collaborative relationships within and outside the program, coordinate the public relations effort, disseminate results reports, and advocate for the program when necessary.

Planning and Implementing the Guidance Curriculum

The goals of the guidance curriculum are to provide basic information to students using what can best be described as an educational or psychoeducational model. Although the discussion to this point has focused on helping students develop the career development competencies identified in the ANM (2003), a comprehensive career development program is aimed at developing academic and personal social competencies because of the obvious linkages among these competencies and educational, career, and personal functioning. Consider Standard A, the academic competency, and indicators that competency A1 has been developed, as listed in Table 12.4. Which of the indicators are not required for success in choosing, preparing for, entering, and becoming successful in an occupation? Of course, successful workers should have developed a sound academic self-concept as indicated by the variables A:A1.1 through A.A1.5.

Now consider Table 12.5. Once again the competency and the indicators that the competency has been developed are essential to personal, social functioning, and to occupational success as well. How often has the importance of self-knowledge been expressed in the first 11 chapters of this book? Hopefully often enough to impress on the reader that, without self-knowledge, it is impossible to make an informed career choice. The classroom units and small groups included in the guidance curriculum should be planned in a manner that focuses on multiple competencies, regardless of the domain in which they have been placed.

The needs assessment discussed earlier suggests the competencies that should be the focus of the school counseling program and the career development aspect of the program. The guidance curriculum classroom units and small-group activities are chosen to target at least some of those competencies. A grid such as the one shown in Table 12.6 may be helpful in planning the K–12 guidance curriculum.

TABLE 12.4   ASCA Standards: Academic Domain, Standard A, Competency A.1 and Indicators

---

Standard A: Students will acquire the attitudes, knowledge, and skills that contribute to effective learning in school and across the life span.

Competency A:1: Improve Academic Self-Concept

A:A1.1 Articulate feelings of competence and confidence as learners

A:A1.2 Display a positive interest in learning

A:A1.3 Take pride in work and achievement

A:A1.4 Accept mistakes as essential to the learning process

A:A1.5 Identify attitudes and behaviors that lead to successful learning

---

Source: From the *ASCA National Model: A Framework for School Counseling Programs*. Reprinted with permission of the American School Counselor Association, http://www.schoolcounselor.org.

TABLE 12.5 ASCA Personal Social Domain, Standard A, Competency A.1 and Indicators

Standard A: Students will acquire the knowledge, attitudes, and interpersonal skills to help them understand and respect self and others.

Competency A:1: Acquire Self-Knowledge

PS:A1.1 Develop positive attitudes toward self as a unique and worthy person

PS:A1.2 Identify values, attitudes, and beliefs

PS:A1.3 Learn the goal-setting process

PS:A1.4 Understand that change is a part of growth

PS:A1.5 Identify and express feelings

PS:A1.6 Distinguish between appropriate and inappropriate behavior

PS:A1.7 Recognize personal boundaries, rights, and privacy needs

PS:A1.8 Understand the need for self-control and how to practice it

PS:A1.9 Demonstrate cooperative behavior in groups

PS:A1.10 Identify personal strengths and assets

PS:A1.11 Identify and discuss changing personal and social roles

PS:A1.12 Identify and recognize changing family roles

Source: From the *ASCA National Model: A Framework for School Counseling Programs*. Reprinted with permission of the American School Counselor Association, http://www.schoolcounselor.org.

TABLE 12.6 K–12 Guidance Curriculum Planning Grid

Grade Level and Month	ANM Competencies	Objective	Activity	Material Needed	Evaluation Strategy
2; October	PS:A1; C:A1—Self-Knowledge	Each student will identify three skills that he/she does well and one to develop	Four-session classroom guidance	Red and green crayons; paper	Student lists will be collected and evaluated for competency
8; April	A:B2; C:A1—Goal Setting	Students will demonstrate the ability to set short- and long-range goals	Six 40-minute classroom guidance sessions on goal setting	None	Small groups of students will be asked to evaluate the short- and long-term goals that have been written
11; September	C:C2; PS:B1—Conflict Management	Students will demonstrate the use of one conflict management model—win-win	Three classroom guidance sessions	None	Small groups will evaluate and provide feedback based on role-play application of the model

Two things should be obvious from the data shown in Table 12.6. First, the development of a K–12 guidance curriculum is a laborious task, albeit a necessary one. Second, once it is complete, the grid provides much of the information needed to develop a calendar for the school counseling program, which is a real advantage. By adding the names of the people who are to deliver the units and small groups to the grid, responsibility is fixed and, thus, another important task has been completed.

PLANNING AND IMPLEMENTING INDIVIDUAL STUDENT PLANNING

In a sense, individual student planning (ISP) is a misnomer because this service includes individual and group educational and career planning activities. One concern about ISP raised by Brown and Trusty (2005a) is that it may be viewed as mundane and thus overlooked, resulting in students suffering. These researchers point to work by Adelman (1999) and Trusty and Niles (2004) that deals with the factors that influence completing bachelor's degrees. Men are less likely than women to complete degrees, and white and Asian American students are more likely than African Americans and Native Americans to complete degrees. This points to the need for careful planning with males and minorities. The research cited by Brown and Trusty (2005a) also concluded that completing advanced-level math and science classes was a key factor in completing undergraduate degrees. Therefore, encouraging students who might not take advanced courses in these areas should be a high priority in ISP. The question remains, How should the ISP be structured and delivered?

In 2002, a joint publication by the U.S. Army Recruiting Command and the ASCA titled *Planning for Life* provided some answers regarding the design of the ISP. This publication featured exemplary career planning programs from across the United States. The authors suggested that each student should have an individualized career plan (ICP), which includes career and educational goals, assessment data, leisure and extracurricular activities, part-time jobs, community service activities, and other information that could be useful in career and educational planning. The document shown in Figure 12.3 could be used as the basis of the ICP.

STUDENT LEARNING EXERCISE 12.1

Go to the Planning for Life Web site at (http://www.planningforlife.com/video/video.html) and watch the videos available. How would you rate the program (poor–average–good) based on what you have observed? Discuss your reaction with at least one of your classmates.

In addition to some general guidelines for developing the ISP service, *Planning for Life* contains descriptions of outstanding districtwide and single-school programs. The outstanding district-wide program described in the report is located in Hillsboro, Oregon, and has the following characteristics:

K–12   As early as kindergarten the ideas of educational and career planning are stressed. This activity culminates in activities focusing on school-to-work transitions in the senior year.

Assessment   The Self-Directed Search is given to all ninth graders.

Technology   The district developed a searchable database on its Web site that allowed teachers to identify units that could be used in their classes. They also used the Oregon-based career information system (CIS) to provide career and educational information to students.

This activity suggests a technique to help staff monitor and strengthen student achievement of the career guidance and counseling competencies and to assist in developing an educational and career plan.

Instructions
1. It is recommended that an individual career plan be maintained for each student throughout the high school experience.
2. The counselor or counselors to whom a student is assigned will be responsible for meeting with that student to develop, review, revise, and implement the plan.
3. As product evaluation is completed, an individual profile of student attainment of the standards will be added to the plan.

Name _____
       Last   First   Middle

School _____

1. My interests are:
   9th Grade   10th Grade   11th Grade   12th Grade
   _____   _____   _____   _____
   _____   _____   _____   _____
   _____   _____   _____   _____

2. My abilities and skills are:
   9th Grade   10th Grade   11th Grade   12th Grade
   _____   _____   _____   _____
   _____   _____   _____   _____
   _____   _____   _____   _____

3. My hobbies and recreational/leisure activities are:
   9th Grade   10th Grade   11th Grade   12th Grade
   _____   _____   _____   _____
   _____   _____   _____   _____
   _____   _____   _____   _____

4. The school subjects in which I do best are:
   9th Grade   10th Grade   11th Grade   12th Grade
   _____   _____   _____   _____
   _____   _____   _____   _____
   _____   _____   _____   _____

5. I have explored careers in the following occupation clusters:
   9th Grade   10th Grade   11th Grade   12th Grade
   _____   _____   _____   _____
   _____   _____   _____   _____
   _____   _____   _____   _____

FIGURE 12.3 Individual Career Plan Form: High School Level. *Source*: From *National Career Development Guidelines: Local Handbook for High Schools* (pp. 81–87), by National Occupational Information Coordinating Committee, 1989, Washington, DC: Author.

6. I have worked part time or had some experience with the following jobs or work tasks:

9th Grade	10th Grade	11th Grade	12th Grade
_____	_____	_____	_____
_____	_____	_____	_____
_____	_____	_____	_____

7. My tentative career goal(s) is (are):

9th Grade	10th Grade	11th Grade	12th Grade
_____	_____	_____	_____
_____	_____	_____	_____
_____	_____	_____	_____

8. I have chosen the following curriculum to study in high school. Courses are outlined on my high school studies plan, which is part of my cumulative record.
   (20) Credit Diploma _____
   (22) Credit Diploma _____
   Other _____

9. I plan to pursue further training beyond high school in the following programs, schools, or colleges:

   _____
   _____
   _____
   _____

OR

   I plan to obtain work in one of the following jobs (businesses, industries):

   _____
   _____
   _____
   _____

10. I have attained the indicators specified in the local student career development standards. If not, I have met with my counselor to determine activities I can do to strengthen each indicator that I have not attained. Also attach individual profile summarizing student attainment of indicators each year.

		Grade		
Competency	9th	10th	11th	12th
Understanding the influence of a positive self-concept.	____	____	____	____
Skills to interact positively with others.	____	____	____	____
Understanding the relationship between educational achievement and career planning.	____	____	____	____
Understanding the need for positive attitudes toward work and learning.	____	____	____	____
Skills to locate, evaluate, and interpret career information.	____	____	____	____
Skills to prepare to seek, obtain, maintain, and change jobs.	____	____	____	____
Understanding how societal needs and functions influence the nature and structure of work.	____	____	____	____
Skills to make decisions.	____	____	____	____
Understanding the interrelationship of life roles.	____	____	____	____
Understanding the continuous changes in male/female roles.	____	____	____	____
Skills in career planning.	____	____	____	____

Signatures:
Student_____
Parent_____
Counselor _____

FIGURE 12.3 (Continued)

Staffing   Parent volunteers were recruited to train students and serve as advisors. Each parent-advisor was assigned a caseload. The ICP, which is housed in the Career Research Center, is revised and updated each year. Students meet with their counselors one time per year as well.

Facilities   Advising activities took place in the Career Resource Center as did other activities.

Other   Worksite visits, job shadowing, and guest speakers were promoted.

Bearcreek Middle School in Fairburn, Georgia, was one of the individual schools singled out for recognition. This school's program is organized around three questions:

Grade 6: Who am I?

Grade 7: Where am I going?

Grade 8: How am I going to get there?

There are several interesting aspects related to the Bearcreek Middle School program:

Coordination   The program is organized by the career center coordinator.

Staffing   Career center coordinator, works with teachers to integrate concepts into the curricula, with support from school counselors.

Assessment   The Career Decision Making Inventory is administered in eighth grade; other informal devices are used to assess aptitudes and abilities.

Technology   The Georgia Career Information System is a source of educational and career information.

Facilities   The Career Resource Center is used for most activities.

Recordkeeping   A portfolio system is used, similar to the one in Figure 12.3.

Other   Students may participate in job shadowing.

Not unexpectedly, no elementary school ISP was included in *Planning for Life.* However, beginning as quickly as the students have the academic foundation needed, which is probably near the end of third grade, students should be engaged in goal setting and planning activities that will prepare them for the transition to middle school. This should involve visits to the middle school, seminars conducted by middle school students about the life of a "middle-schooler," pretransition parent conferences, and so forth. They should also be exposed to activities that link education and career, develop systematic decision-making skills, promote self-awareness, and minimize racial and gender-based stereotypes. E. K. Powe Elementary in Durham, North Carolina, sponsors an annual Career Day for grades 4 and 5 that links many of these concepts together.

The ISP programs described in this section are totally integrated into the broader career development program, and that is likely why they have been singled out by the joint U.S. Army/ASCA project, which is aimed at identifying exemplary programs and at promoting career and educational program planning generally. As is the case with all of the so-called parts of career development programs, it is often difficult to tell where one component begins and another leaves off.

Assessment

Assessment is a key portion of the ISP program. The developers of the Hillsboro, Oregon, district-wide ISP used interest inventories in the middle school as their only formal assessment. The career development specialists in the Bearcreek Middle School's ISP indicated that they used other forms of assessment but were not specific. Brown and Trusty (2005a) suggest that achievement data is needed to inform the individual planning process. Counselor-constructed self-estimates of skills and abilities can be used to replace more expensive commercially produced estimates. Self-estimates of skills and abilities from the O*NET system can also be used as inexpensive measures of skills and abilities. Locally constructed self-estimate scales that measure Holland types also can be useful if the budget for these and other instruments precludes their purchase. Teachers familiar with students can be surveyed to get estimates of interpersonal skills and decision-making styles and abilities. Finally, estimates regarding the obstacles that individuals face in achieving their goals can give planners insight into the perceptiveness of the students about real-world issues, and target them for assertive action to diminish or eliminate barriers that may stand in the way of goals.

The End Product

ISP should begin no later than the eighth grade and should culminate when the student graduates from high school or leaves school prior to graduation. All planning sessions should end with an up-to-date portfolio (see again Figure 12.3) and or other record of the events that occurred and the decisions made. Students who expect to leave school prior to graduation should have a transition plan to another educational institution or to work. The transition plan may include returning to school once the issues that are precipitating the withdrawal are resolved. As has been noted elsewhere, students in special education must have transition plans in their IEP and a detailed listing of the strategies needed to bring the plan to fruition. Students who plan to graduate also need transition plans, whether they involve attending some form of postsecondary education or going directly into the workforce. It has been an unfortunate fact that many high school counselors consider a student's transition plan complete once the student has been accepted to one of her or his choices. This plan is inadequate for the simple reason that some students who plan to go to college never reach the campus, some must postpone attending for a few years to earn money or to attend to family issues, and a far greater number enter college only to drop out prior to graduation. Without contingency plans (What-if? plans), these students must begin the search for an occupation that should have been determined on a preliminary basis. The competencies listed in the ANM (ASCA, 2003, 2005) are not only for those students who expect to go directly to work after high school. They are useful skills for every student who attends high school.

PLANNING AND IMPLEMENTING RESPONSIVE SERVICES

Responsive services include consultation, individual and small-group counseling, crisis counseling and response to crises, referral, and peer facilitation. Of these responsive services, the two that require the greatest attention in the planning of the career development program are consultation and individual and group counseling. It is suggested here that, for the most part, the idea of consultation be forgone in favor of collaboration. Consultation involves a co-equal relationship in which the consultee and consultant identify the consultee's problem, establish goals, and design interventions. The implementation of the intervention is left to the consultee, who is typically a teacher. Collaboration follows the same process with a single exception. In collaboration the collaborators share joint responsibility for the implementation of the intervention (Brown et al., 2010). In a collaborative approach, career development professionals share the responsibility of designing and implementing career development interventions. This might mean that counselors and teachers would work together to design and deliver a classroom unit on transition from school to work. Similarly, they might share the responsibilities involved in designing a middle school career day or a job shadowing day. For example, counselors, vocational education teachers, and representatives from businesses collaborate to design and deliver a job shadowing on Groundhog Day each year at Athens Drive High School in Raleigh, North Carolina.

Not all students will need career counseling if the ISP portion of the career development program is implemented properly. However, some students will have decisional anxiety and will require career counseling to overcome this problem. Students who are gifted may have so many options open to them that career counseling is necessary to narrow the choices to a manageable few. Students who are disabled may require specialized services from a rehabilitation counselor in order to identify career options and the accommodations required by employers under the auspices of the Americans with Disabilities Act. Some high schools have full- or part-time rehabilitation counselors on staff who are employed by the State Division of Rehabilitation Counseling.

Identifying students who require career counseling should begin by training advisers to recognize students who could benefit from the service, particularly those with decisional anxiety and indecision. Students who experience decisional anxiety may exhibit one of three symptoms: avoidance, impetuous decision making, or dependent decision making. Dependent decision makers are not to be confused with members of minority groups who have collective social values and defer to their parents in the occupational choice–making process. Students who believe they should make their own decisions because they have an independent social value and are unable to do so should be classified as having decisional anxiety. These students may want the counselor to make the decisions for them and may ask over and over, What do you think I should do? They may also choose an occupation because one or more of their friends have chosen it. Students who avoid making decisions may be uncomfortable when the topic of choosing an occupation arises or may not show up for planning sessions. Impetuous decision makers appear to be careless because they give little thought to the process. When presented with a list of occupations related to their interests, they may choose one very quickly and be unable to present an adequate rationale for the choice.

Career counselors should recall that decisional anxiety is created by irrational thoughts about the student's ability to make choices (I'll mess this up) or the need to make the perfect decision (I need to make the perfect choice). The cognitive behavioral approach to career counseling described in Chapter 3 is probably the preferred approach to dealing with decisional anxiety. Using this approach, the career counselor identifies the irrational thoughts that precipitate the anxiety and, using techniques such as thought stopping, altering self-talk, and relaxation strategies (e.g., breathing and deep muscle relaxation) reduces the anxiety.

An issue that may need to be resolved in career counseling may appear to be decisional anxiety, but it is more accurately classified as indecision. Career indecision arises because of too little information and can be dealt with by providing more personal or occupational information. The following counseling leads may be helpful in differentiating decisional anxiety from career indecision:

1. When you think about actually choosing a career, rate your anxiety on a 1- to-10 scale with 10 being very high and 1 being very low.
2. Using a rating scale of 1 to 10, with 10 being very high and 1 being very low, rate your ability to make a career choice if you have information about the options available and how they correspond to your interests and abilities.

Students with decisional anxiety are likely to have relatively high ratings for item 1 and low ratings for item 2. Students who manifest career indecision may have high ratings on item 1 and they are likely to have high ratings on item 2 as well. The difference is that indecisive students, that is, those with decisional anxiety, doubt their ability to make decisions, whereas students with indecision do not.

Other students may require career counseling, such as those with lifestyle issues, minority students, students who are gay or lesbian, and so forth. For example, an African American student who had spent most of his school years in mostly white schools wanted to explore the pros and cons of attending a traditionally African American college that was less prestigious than the other schools to which he had been accepted. At issue was his recognition that his experiences to that point had not allowed him to consider what it meant to be African American in U.S. culture. Students who are gay and lesbian who have not "come out" may seek help finding "safe" careers. Female students may want to explore the impact of choosing certain careers on their plans to be wives and mothers. When these and other issues, such as the ones identified earlier in this section, arise, career counseling is indicated.

PLANNING AND IMPLEMENTING EVALUATION AND ACCOUNTABILITY: SOME GENERAL CONSIDERATIONS

Evaluation is the process by which the impact of the career development program on student development and behavior is assessed and is, therefore, the core element of the accountability effort. The process of accountability continues with the distribution of results reports to the stakeholders of the program and is complete when the data developed in the evaluation effort are used in the improvement of the career development program (ASCA, 2003, 2005). The overall accountability effort is dynamic and ongoing. Some instruments that might be helpful in the evaluation and accountability process are displayed in Figures 12.4, 12.5, and 12.6.

There are two general strategies that may be pursued when evaluating the career development program. One of these is to look at the overall impact of the program. For example, a meta-analysis of 18 career development programs by Baker and Popowicz (1983) suggested that, generally speaking, career development programs can be effective. The developers of the

---

My overall purpose in the unit we just completed was to help you learn about how your education is important in the future when you choose an occupation. Please rate the extent to which you acquired the following knowledge by marking yes, no, or uncertain.

Yes   No   Uncertain

_____ _____ _____   1. I understand why math is important if I want to go to community college or college. (C:C1.1)

_____ _____ _____   2. I learned why adults who work have to continue to learn. (C:C1.4)

_____ _____ _____   3. I learned that everyone makes mistakes when they are learning new skills. (A:A1.4)

_____ _____ _____   4. Perseverance (sticking with it) is an important attitude for students learning difficult material. (A:A1.5)

_____ _____ _____   5. I learned how to plan my time so that I can do schoolwork and have fun. (A:C1.1)

FIGURE 12.4 Classroom Guidance Evaluation Form (Elementary).

The purpose of this group was to help you develop three competencies. These are

C:A1.5   Learn how to make decisions
C:A1.6   Learn how to set goals
C:A1.7   Understand the importance of planning

Please rate the extent to which you have confidence that you have acquired these competencies as a result of participating in this group and your overall satisfaction with the group. Using a scale of 1 to 10, with 1 indicating that you have little confidence that you have the skill or knowledge and 10 meaning that you have a very high level of confidence that you have the skill or knowledge, rate your confidence in each area.

Rating
_____ 1. I can use a systematic decision-making model to make my career choice.

_____ 2. I can set short-term goals that are attainable.

_____ 3. I can set long-term goals that are attainable.

_____ 4. I understand the importance of planning as it relates to career choice.

My overall satisfaction with the group is (check one)

_____ 1. Satisfied

_____ 2. Somewhat satisfied

_____ 3. Dissatisfied

FIGURE 12.5   Group Evaluation Form (Middle School).

Satisfied	Uncertain	Dissatisfied	
_____	_____	_____	1. The person who conducted the session helped me understand the importance of planning. (C:A1.7)
_____	_____	_____	2. I was actively involved in the decision-making process in the planning session. (C:A1.5)
_____	_____	_____	3. I acquired knowledge of the educational planning process and how to make important decisions. (C:B1.1; C:B1.3)
_____	_____	_____	4. I was encouraged to think about how my personal characteristics, such as interests and abilities, should be considered in course selection. (C:B1.1)
_____	_____	_____	5. The session help me clarify the relationships among my personal characteristics, course selection, and my future career. (C:B1.20)

My overall satisfaction with the group is (check one)

_____ 1. Satisfied

_____ 2. Somewhat satisfied

_____ 3. Dissatisfied

FIGURE 12.6   Individual Student Planning Session Evaluation Form (High School).

National Career Counseling and Guidance Guidelines for high schools (Kobylarz, 1996) concluded that these programs would have several positive outcomes—they would benefit students, their parents, and their schools—based on the literature reviews of Campbell, Connell, Boyle, and Bhaerman (1983); Crites (1987); Herr (1982); and Spokane and Oliver (1983).

However, the evaluation of the impact of an entire program is a laborious task and may not provide the data needed for program improvement. Brown and Trusty (2005a) have also noted that, when entire programs are the target of research or evaluation, it is difficult to establish which aspects of the program actually produce the observed results. They recommended that school counselors embark on an evaluation effort to establish the effectiveness of the delivery strategies used, such as individual planning, career counseling, and assessment. Three sample evaluation forms that could be used to evaluate certain aspects of the program can be seen in Figures 12.4, 12.5, and 12.6. However, sophisticated research methodology based upon the objectives, the nature of the intervention, the context of the intervention and other variables will be needed if evidence-based practices are to be produced. These strategies will be taken up in detail in Chapter 16.

Program Planning Tips: Elementary School

Elementary school career development programs should probably be organized around a theme that parallels that used in social studies or other curricular areas. For example, some states organize their programs around a geographic theme starting with the home and neighborhood and progressing to the community, state, nation, and world. A program of this type might appear as follows

Kindergarten	Workers at school and home
First grade	Community helpers
Second grade	Workers in my county
Third grade	Workers in my state
Fourth grade	Workers in the nation
Fifth grade	Workers in the world

Classroom guidance units could be built around these themes and could be enhanced by speakers; walking or riding field trips that allow students to view workers; role-playing exercises using workers' hats in which students wear the hats and tell what the workers do; exercises that involve the tools that workers from various areas use; visits from firefighters, public safety officers, and sanitation workers; and so forth.

The program outlined here begins with workers at school and home. Presentations by teachers, administrators, custodians, groundskeepers, administrative assistants, aides, school nurses, social workers, school psychologists, cafeteria workers, and perhaps specialists from the district administrative offices provide students with interesting insights about work, occupational stereotyping, the relationship of education to work, and the use of tools that are properly selected and oriented.

Field trips provide students with insight into the working conditions of various occupations, but they are expensive and somewhat time consuming. When possible, field trips should be taken to work sites that include a wide variety of occupations. Hospitals, banks, post offices, school district administrative offices, government offices, and businesses that employ large numbers of workers are ideal sites. Students need to be oriented to the types of jobs that they will see in their visits, know what questions to ask, and understand safety issues. Follow-up to determine what the students learned about the occupations and their interests should be conducted.

The school can also serve as a fertile teaching tool for older students. Counselors can identify a list of aides for each of the occupations in the school and have fourth- or fifth-grade students fill out job applications, develop résumés, and interview for assistant positions. Those that are hired can assume some of the duties for those positions. After students serve a week or two as assistants, they can be rotated into other assistantships. Periodically, students should be engaged in the things that they learn about the work that they are doing, the education required in the job, and what they are learning about themselves. The only caution about placing students in the position of assistants is to keep them out of harm's way. For example, aides to the cafeteria staff should not be allowed to participate in activities in which they might be burned or injured by sharp instruments.

Some counselors have engaged children in starting and operating businesses as a means of teaching them about occupations. Businesses that sell candy or school supplies at breaks introduce students to planning, raising capital, budgeting, personnel selection and evaluation, marketing, and inventory control to name a few of the activities required to start and operate a business. Each of these activities has a number of occupations associated with it and students can be introduced to these occupations using the experiential format of operating a business.

Career days, if properly planned, can provide exciting career-related experiences for students. The process of developing a career day begins with helping students identify occupations that they want to explore and compiling a list of occupations for the grade level being targeted. Workers in these occupations are then invited to come to school and meet with groups of students. Prior to career day, students should be oriented to information-gathering strategies, such as questions to ask about the desirable and undesirable aspects of the worker's job, the education that is required, working conditions, hours, and wages. During career days, students meet in small groups with three or four workers for about 30 minutes. Follow-up to career day involves having students discuss what they learned from the workers and whether their interest in various jobs was increased or decreased. Students should also write thank you notes to the workers who participated in the program.

Perhaps the most important tip for implementing the elementary school career development program is that it should be fun. Games, interesting speakers, and field trips to places such as art museums and zoos in which the objective is to explore the occupations in those settings can set the tone for the program. Additionally, occupational stereotypes should be addressed in the program and every effort should be made to help students learn about the relationship between education and work, and gain knowledge about themselves and occupations.

Program Planning Tips: Middle School

Most students in middle school have begun the process of making occupational choices. Jessell and Boyer (1989) surveyed 5,464 seventh- and eighth-grade students and found that only 6 percent had not given at least some consideration to their future careers. Interestingly, 94 percent of the students expected to finish high school. Although estimates of the high school dropout rate vary, it is expected that at least 25 percent of students entering high school will leave before they graduate (Brown, 1998).

In elementary school, the primary objectives are to increase students' awareness of their choices by providing occupational information in an interesting format and by challenging their occupational stereotypes. Although these goals are still important at the middle-school level, increasing their self-awareness and enhancing their goal setting, planning, and decision-making ability become important. Assessment devices can be used to accomplish and promote self-awareness, but students should be engaged in self-assessment exercises as well. Self-assessment skills can be enhanced by asking students to estimate their interests and aptitudes prior to completing measures of their traits, and comparing their self-estimates with test and inventory results.

As was the case in the elementary school, an organizing theme for the exploration of occupations must be chosen. Because much of the information that is available to students is organized around Holland's (1997) theory, his RIASEC model might be used as that theme. Students who have taken one of the many interest scales that measure Realistic, Investigative Artistic, Social, Enterprising, and Conventional occupations will be able to relate their interests to those occupations. However, it is also important for students to think in terms of the skills and abilities needed to perform the occupations that interest them and relate these to their educational choices.

Lifestyle planning begins in middle school, and thus units that deal with economic awareness should be included in the program. One useful exercise is to assign students a salary and have them try to make certain lifestyle choices. For example students might be placed into groups that make $20,000, $30,000, and $40,000, respectively. Then, using the local newspaper, they try to determine where they will live (e.g., apartment, house, or at home), the car they will drive, and the leisure activities in which they will participate. Parts of this exercise require them to explore after-tax income as opposed to gross income, the cost of utilities, auto and homeowners insurance, transportation to work, and so forth. This type of information can be obtained from parents, relatives, or friends. After each group has completed its work, they report the decisions they made to the other groups. At the conclusion of this exercise, students research the occupations they are considering using Internet-based information to determine salaries earned by people in those occupations.

Computer-assisted career guidance systems (CACGS) can be used to enhance the career development process at the middle school level. Luzzo and Pierce (1996) found that students' career maturity increased when they used DISCOVER in their career explorations.

Small-group procedures are popular means of promoting career development in both middle and high school, but because of the structure of the middle school, groups are easier to organize at this level.

Group career development activities may be quite varied. For example, it is possible to hold career seminars in which a representative of an occupation, such as an insurance salesperson or over-the-road truck driver, can discuss the nature of their jobs, the training requirements, hiring requirements, lifestyle advantages and disadvantages, and so forth with a small group of interested students. Groups can also be organized for exploratory purposes; to focus on the career decision-making process; or for field trips to explore hospitals, industrial sites, and so forth.

Dropout prevention groups that center on career development activities are increasingly popular. In *Dropping Out or Hanging In* (Brown, 1998), which is a manual for students to use in dropout prevention groups, students are first taken through a series of self-awareness activities. These are followed by activities designed to teach decision-making skills, and then students are encouraged to practice using their skills in setting career, educational, and other life goals. The culmination of these small groups is preparing students to "drop into" school if they do drop out but decide that they have made an error.

As has been noted throughout this book, support is increasing for broader career experiences that involve integrating career planning with other life roles. Brown (1980) outlined what he terms a life planning group, which consists of seven components: (1) understanding human behavior, (2) conceptualizing one's self as a winner, (3) the importance of fantasy in planning, (4) matching fantasy and reality, (5) setting goals, (6) short-term planning, and (7) long-term planning.

Amatea, Clark, and Cross (1984) evaluated a two-week high school course called Lifestyles that was aimed at (1) increasing students' awareness of their values and their preferences for various life roles, (2) increasing students' awareness of the costs and benefits associated with various lifestyles, and (3) helping students establish life-role priorities. They found that their course did seem to increase students' decisiveness about their career choices. They also found that, at the end of the group sessions, males and females did not vary in their attitudes toward the family role.

Prior to involving students in a group activity, a screening interview should be held to determine the students' objectives, degree of motivation, and the extent to which they will work collaboratively with other group members. Unmotivated students and potential discipline problems may be precluded from groups unless the counselor feels that the problems can be corrected in the group setting.

Careers Classes

Some middle schools offer "careers classes" ranging in length from 9 to 18 weeks. At one time these courses were taught at the ninth-grade level, but with the reorganization of high schools and middle schools, they are more likely to be offered at the seventh- or eighth-grade levels.

Organized classes in careers permit more extensive consideration of the topic than is possible in a short unit studied in another class. Nevertheless, any course is not of limited value to the student if it is approached in textbook fashion with the aim of thorough familiarization with the world of work. The goal of such a course should be to maximize self-actualization through the development of concepts appropriate to the student's level of maturity and proximity to the world of work.

One advantage of an organized course in occupations or careers is that it can be closely tied to the total school counseling program and properly staffed. In some schools the course is taught by a member of the counseling staff, whose academic preparation may be more appropriate for teaching such a course than is that of a subject-area teacher. Even though this arrangement gives the counselor contact with students, it also reduces the time available for individual counseling and other activities.

A regularly scheduled course taught by a counselor may offer the best opportunity to meet the individual needs of the students enrolled. It should be possible to relate class activities to individual counseling and to develop an approach based on both group procedures and individual counseling, with the student being involved in both phases to whatever extent is appropriate. When this dual approach can be arranged, the student has the maximum opportunity to benefit.

The adoption of an organized course may cause a school faculty to assume that it has met its responsibility for helping students in the career development process. When this happens, the course becomes a one-shot effort, and the basic axiom that career choice and development should start in the early years and continue throughout one's life is disregarded. Two- and four-year colleges often adopt this view and offer an elective course called Life and Career Planning or Career Exploration. Although the course is useful to those who enroll, it is not enough to meet the needs of all students.

Involving Parents

Beginning in Chapter 2, the issue of identifying the decision maker was discussed. Although parents who hold an independence social values may not be involved in the decision-making process, they should be involved in the process (Young, 1994). Parents who have collective social values expect to be involved in the career choice-making process as do their children. In the middle school, parents should be involved in educational planning and made aware of the relationship between education and careers. Web sites are available to help parents become involved in their children's career planning, such as http://www.jobweb.com/Resources/Library/Parents/A_Parents_Guide_to136_01.htm, where *A Parents' Guide to Career Development* is posted. Career Connect (http://www.afb.org/section/asp?DocumentID=2843), which is produced by the American Foundation for the Blind, can be particularly useful to parents of students who are visually impaired. Career Connect can be downloaded to parents' computers. Parents of elementary and middle school students may wish to access the U.S. government Web site for kids and students (http://benshuide.gpo. gov/subject.html), which contains a wealth of information ranging from careers in the sciences to those in the military.

The most difficult part of parental involvement is getting parents to participate who are poor, do not speak English, or do not have well-developed skills themselves. Some of these parents come from cultures that do not encourage parental involvement. Others have had negative experiences in school and thus avoid contact with educators. Still others have child care and transportation problems. It is suggested here that career development be taken into the community by holding sessions for parents in community centers and churches and providing baby sitting services along with refreshments. The information should be provided in English as well as the language of the participants.

PROGRAM PLANNING TIPS: HIGH SCHOOL

Many of the suggestions offered in the two previous sections can be adapted to the high school setting. However, students at this level should be preparing for the transition to the next educational level or to the work world. In order to make wise occupational choices, they need in-depth career exploration experiences that will allow them to make informed decisions about their knowledge, skills, interests, and values as these relate to entry-level jobs. This can be accomplished best through job shadowing, internships, part-time job placements, and interviews with workers. Students going directly to work need employability skills, such as locating and applying for jobs on the Internet, filling out job applications, developing résumés, interviewing, writing letters to employers, and so forth. These skills can be developed in small groups or in classroom settings.

Targeting High School Students with Special Needs

STUDENTS WITH DISABILITIES   High school career development programs should pay particular attention to students with disabilities. The National Center on Secondary Education and Transition (2005) produced *Essential Tools: Handbook for Implementing a Comprehensive Work-Based Learning Program According to the Fair Labor Standards Act*, which identifies four components of successful transition programs for students with disabilities. These include career exploration, career assessment, work-related training, and cooperative work experience. Grayson (1999) described two such transitional programs. The first is supported school to work (SSW), which provides a flexible program of academic studies and paid work experiences in entry-level jobs, all of which is supervised by a director of transition services or employment coordinator. The second approach, coordinated employment, involves an employment coordinator who develops jobs, places students, and serves as a job coach. The SSW approach works hand in hand with vocational educators, whereas the coordinated employment approach involves on-the-job training. Both approaches also work to develop self-advocacy skills, employability skills, and social skills.

Conway (2003/2004) suggests that greater emphasis is also needed to help students with disabilities make the transition to higher education. He indicates that this effort begins by preparing at the high school level students with disabilities by carefully advising them about entry requirements, encouraging self-advocacy, and helping them access technology that supports academic achievement. Colleges and universities must continue the efforts begun in high school if students with disabilities are to achieve success.

Biller and Horn (1991) have suggested that career development specialists may need to tailor their efforts if they are to be helpful to students with learning disabilities. Biller and Horn admonish counselors to consider the possibility that students with learning disabilities may not be as ready as their peers to engage in career planning and that, because of lower reading levels, they may have more difficulty absorbing information from printed material, reading instructions on computer screens, and completing assessment devices. In another study, Humes (1992) found that students with learning disabilities have somewhat different career interests than other students and suggests that counselors need to be prepared to assist them to explore careers related to those interests.

Roessler, Johnson, and Schrimmer (1988) identify several barriers to the implementation of a comprehensive program for career development for students with disabilities: "assessment, planning, curriculum materials, generalization and maintenance (from the school to the community), and system commitment" (p. 24). The processes outlined in the *National Career Development Guidelines* (Kobylarz, 1996; NOICC, 1989b) can be used if applied appropriately as a guide to overcoming the planning and school system commitment barrier. Measures for assessing the occupational potential of students with disabilities are improving steadily, and Roessler and his colleagues (1988) validate materials that can be used in the assessment of students with disabilities. Roessler also concludes that the Life-Centered Career Education curriculum materials may solve the previous deficit in this area.

MINORITY STUDENTS   Career development programs for minority students are the cornerstone of any effort to promote economic equity. The disparity between rates and earnings for white and minority students begins at their entry into the labor force and widens with time and experience, regardless of whether the students are disabled (Cameto, Marder, Wagner, & Cardosa, 2003). Some of the programs for minority students are much like those for white students, but the intensity of the efforts for minorities should be greater. Others, such as the one described by Grover (1999) at Whitehorse High School in Utah, are quite different. Located on a Navajo reservation, this school has a unique student population: 55 percent of the students are classified as homeless, 93 percent qualify for free or reduced-rate lunches, 14 percent are in special education, and many students are absent as much as 30 percent of the time. Every student in the program, which is geared to the development of technology skills, must make a career choice and participate in one week of job shadowing experience as a part of the fourth-year language arts class. Parents are involved in twice yearly conferences. There are 300 students in the program and 265 computers are available for their use. Some of the graduates of the program have been hired into jobs typically requiring college degrees. Research by Karunanayake and Nauta (2004) suggests that a portion of any program for minority students should include same-race role models. Minority students in their study identified as many influential models as did white students and most of the models listed were of their same race.

MULTIPOTENTIALED STUDENTS   It is probably a truism that counselors consistently underestimate the needs of students who are gifted, or as Pask-McCartney and Salamone (1988) termed them, *multipotentialed students*, because they have so many avenues to pursue. It is also the case that having so many career avenues open is a curse of sorts. Post-Kammer and Perrone (1983) report that more than 30 percent of students who are gifted in their studies felt unprepared to make career decisions when they left high school. It is probably the case that the types of programs needed by these students do not vary dramatically from those required by their less talented counterparts, although a report by Borman, Nash, and Colson (1978) suggests that the students who are gifted in their program did not like the testing component. It is certainly possible that these students have been tested so extensively that they are alienated from the formal assessment process.

In a study that has implications for career development programming for gifted boys and girls, Gassin, Kelly, and Feldhusen (1993) found no difference in the certainty of career choice between gifted girls and boys in middle school. However, as they matured, girls became progressively less certain about their career choices, perhaps because they were beginning to consider their roles as spouses and mothers in their plans. Interestingly, girls were more involved in career planning than were boys during the high school years. This study suggests that efforts directed toward girls may need to focus on identifying the factors that lead to uncertainty and help them deal with them, whereas efforts may need to be mounted to stimulate career planning among high school boys.

INVOLVING COMMUNITY RESOURCES IN THE PROGRAM

The use of community resources is important at all educational levels, but employing them at the high school level is critical. Businesses can provide advanced level job-shadowing experiences, internships, and ultimately part- and full-time employment. Public and private job placement agencies may provide career counseling and job placement services. Community resources, if employed properly, can add an important dimension to the high school career development program.

In most cases, local businesses and industries already have close ties with the school. They have a continuing interest in the students of the local school, which is often their main source of employees, particularly for positions that do not require post–high school training. Because of this natural relationship, they are usually interested in cooperating in any way possible to improve the quality of those students. This provides the school with an entree to representatives of local businesses and industries, who may be able to inform students about their fields of activity. Local professional groups may also be eager to render the same kind of service to interested students.

Local service clubs, whose members are drawn from local businesses, industries, and professions, are also frequently eager to provide assistance to the school or to specific students in problems related to career information. They can be helpful in organizing career day conferences or community occupational surveys. Members often are encouraged to make themselves available to students to discuss career opportunities in their fields.

Local labor union representatives or officials can provide information on training requirements, apprenticeship programs, employment opportunities, membership requirements, and benefits. Government offices located in the community, at the local, state, or national level, often can provide information to assist students. Government service opportunities and requirements are areas that can be covered by such representatives. Agencies such as county extension offices and employment services already are involved, by the nature of their work, in career information activities.

Every community includes some social agencies that are involved in career information activities. Particularly likely to be involved are agencies whose services are directed primarily at youth, such as Boy Scouts, Girl Scouts, YMCA, YWCA, and 4-H clubs. Many of these serve the same young people as the school. Special career information projects that they may develop can be of genuine assistance to the school. They may also have access to information in specialized fields that can help the school in its career information program.

Many churches organize special activity programs for school-age youth. Often these programs focus on the concerns and problems of the age group involved; for teenagers, this inevitably includes career-related problems. Many churches support or maintain church-related colleges or other educational institutions that may be of particular significance to members of the church's youth group. A number of churches operate summer camp programs for school-age youth, thus providing an additional means of reaching young people.

Cooperation with the local library may lead to a more comprehensive collection of career information materials as well as to the development of special services that are of assistance to school-age youth.

Many resources cut across more than one of the categories we have considered. In many ways, these may be the most valuable of all. Counselors and teachers may find it advantageous to establish networks involving contact with as many school and community resources as possible so that each of those contacts can provide information on new resources.

Summary

The *ASCA National Model* (ANM) incorporates career development into a comprehensive model. In keeping with the ANM, the approach outlined in this chapter is competency based—that is, it is oriented to developing certain key academic, career, and personal social competencies. A program might not target all of the competencies listed in the ANM. Rather, program planners should choose to target the development of competencies based on an assessment of the needs of their students.

The process of planning a career development program that meets the needs of all students is an arduous one that only begins at the point at which the program is implemented. Evaluation data should be collected and disseminated on an ongoing basis and the results used to improve the program. Hopefully, a key element of the program will be to improve the career development of minority students and students who are disabled. Career development professionals have a unique opportunity to improve the economic and social standing of these and other students.

Chapter Quiz

T F **1.** Career counseling is found in the foundation component of the ANM.

T F **2.** The school counselor who engages in teacher consultation to facilitate the inclusion of career development content into the classroom services is engaging in responsive services.

T F **3.** Although the competencies students are expected to acquire are supposedly drawn from a developmental perspective, they are not listed by grade or age level.

T F **4.** One of the problems with the ASCA model is that the context in which students function is not considered.

T F **5.** The accountability portion of the ASCA model is in tune with legislation such as No Child Left Behind.

T F **6.** Qualitative research designs are not in keeping with the national approach to evidence-based practice in education.

T F   **7.** Because the student competencies to be developed are spelled out in the model, needs assessment can be ignored prior to establishing objectives.

T F   **8.** Goals and objectives are essentially two words for the same concept: performance outcomes.

T F   **9.** Behavioral objectives are established for students who come in for career counseling and small group activities, but not for students who are involved in classroom guidance activities.

T F   **10.** Ultimately the plan for the SNM should reflect who will be involved, what activities to be used, when the activities are to be conducted, and what the outcomes of the activities will be.

T (10)   F (9)   F (8)   F (7)   F (6)   T (5)   F (4)   T (3)   T (2)   F (1)

References

Adelman, C. (1999). Answers in the tool box: Academic intensity, attendance patterns, and bachelor's degree attainment. Retrieved from Department of Education, www.ed.gov/pubs/Toolbox/title/htm

Amatea, E. S., Clark, J. E., & Cross, E. G. (1984). Lifestyles: Evaluating a life role planning program for high school students. *Vocational Guidance Quarterly, 32,* 249–259.

American School Counselor Association. (2003). *ASCA national model: A framework for school counseling programs (Rev).* Alexandria, VA: Author.

American School Counselor Association. (2003). *ASCA national model: A framework for school counseling programs.* Alexandria, VA: Author.

Baker, S. B., & Popowicz, C. L. (1983). Metaanalysis as a strategy for evaluating effects of career education interventions. *Vocational Guidance Quarterly, 31,* 178–186.

Biller, E. F., & Horn, E. E. (1991). A career guidance model for adolescents with learning disabilities. *School Counselor, 38,* 279–286.

Borman, G., Nash, W., & Colson, S. (1978). Career guidance for gifted and talented students. *Vocational Guidance Quarterly, 27,* 72–76.

Brown, D. (1980). A life-planning workshop for high school students. *Vocational Guidance Quarterly, 29,* 77–83.

Brown, D. (1998). *Dropping out or hanging in* (2nd ed.). Lincolnwood, IL: National Textbook Center.

Brown, D., Pryzwansky, W. B., & Schulte, A. (2010). *Psychological consultation: Introduction to theory and practice* (7th ed.). Boston: Allyn & Bacon.

Brown, D., & Trusty, J. (2005a). *Organizing and leading comprehensive school counseling programs.* Pacific Grove, CA: Brooks/Cole.

Brown, D., & Trusty, J. (2005b). School counselors and comprehensive school counseling programs: Are school counselors practicing more than they can deliver? *Professional School Counseling, 19,* 1–8.

Burck, H. D. (1978). Evaluating programs: Models and strategies. In L. Goldman (Ed.), *Research methods for counselors: Practical approaches in field settings* (pp. 177–197). New York: Wiley.

Burns, R. W. (1972). *New approaches to behavioral objectives.* Dubuque, IA: Wm. C. Brown.

Cameto, R., Marder, C., Wagner, M., & Cardosa, D. (2003). *Youth employment.* Minneapolis, MN: National Center on Secondary Education and Transition.

Campbell, C. A., & Dahir, C. A. (1997). *The national standards for school counseling programs.* Alexandria, VA: American School Counselors Association.

Campbell, R. E., Connell, J. G., Boyle, K. K., & Bhaerman, R. D. (1983). *Enhancing career development: Recommendations for action.* Columbus: NCRVE, Ohio State University.

Carey, J. C., Dimmit, C., Hatch, T. A., Lapan, R. T., & Whiston, S. (2008). Report of the National panel for evidenced-based school counseling outcome research coding protocol and evaluation of student success skills and second step. *Professional School Counseling, 11,* 197–206.

Conway, M. A. (2003/2004). Improving post secondary education success and results for youth with disabilities. *Impact, 16,* 8–9.

Crites, J. O. (1987). *Evaluation of career guidance programs: Models, methods, and microcomputers.* Columbus: NCRVE, Ohio State University.

Gassin, E. A., Kelly, R. R., and Feldhusen, J. F. (1993). Sex differences in the career development of gifted students. *School Counselor, 41,* 90–95.

Ginzberg, E., Ginzburg, S. W., Axelrad, S., & Herma, J. L. (1951). *Occupational choice: An approach to a general theory.* New York: Columbia University Press.

Grayson, T. E. (1999) Including all learners: Models for success. *Impact, 12,* 4–5.

Grover, L. (1999). School-to-careers on a Navajo reservation. *Impact, 12,* 13.

Gysbers, N. C., & Henderson, P. (2000). *Developing and managing your school guidance program* (3rd ed.). Alexandria, VA: American Counseling Association.

Herr, E. L. (1982). The effects of guidance and counseling: Three domains. In E. L. Herr & N. M. Pirson (Eds.), *Foundations of policy in guidance and counseling* (pp. 22–64). Alexandria, VA: American Association of Counseling and Development (formerly APGA).

Holland, J. L. (1997). *Vocational choices: A theory of vocational personalities and work environment* (3rd ed.). Odessa, FL: PAR.

Hoyt, K. B. (1977). *A primer for career education.* Washington, DC: U.S. Government Printing Office. (ERIC Document Reproduction Service No. 145 252)

Hoyt, K. B. (2005). *Career education: History and future.* Tulsa, OK: National Career Development Association.

Humes, C. W. (1992). Career planning implications for learning disabled students using the MBTl and SDS. *School Counselor, 39,* 362–368.

IDEA (2004). Individuals with Disabilities Education Act. Retrieved from http://www.copyright.gov/legislation/pl108-446.pdf

Jessell, J., & Boyer, M. (1989). *Career expectations among Indiana junior high and middle school students: A second survey.* Terre Haute: Indiana State University.

Johnson, S., Johnson, C., & Downs, L. (2005). *Building results-based student support programs.* Boston: Houghton-Mifflin.

Karunanayake, D., & Nauta, M. N. (2004). The relationship between race and students' identified career models and perceived role model influence. *Career Development Quarterly, 52,* 225–234.

Kobylarz, L. (1996). *National career development guidelines: K–adult handbook.* Stillwater, OK: Career Development Training Institute.

Luzzo, D. A., & Pierce, G. (1996). The effects of DISCOVER on the career maturity of middle school students. *Career Development Quarterly, 45,* 170–172.

Marland, S. P., Jr. (1974). *Career education.* New York: McGraw-Hill.

Morris, L. L., Fitz-Gibbon, C. T., & Lindheim, E. (1987). *How to measure performance and use tests.* Beverly Hills, CA: Sage.

National Center on Secondary Education and Transition. (2005). *Essential Tools: Handbook for implementing a comprehensive work-based learning program according to the Fair Labor Standards Act.* Minneapolis, MN: Author.

National Consortium of State Guidance Leaders. (2000). *A state guidance leadership implementation and resource guide.* Columbus, OH: Center on Education and Training for Employment.

National Occupational Information Coordinating Committee. (1989a). *The national career development guidelines: Local handbook for elementary schools.* Washington, DC: Author.

National Occupational Information Coordinating Committee. (1989b). *The national career development guidelines: Local handbook for high schools.* Washington, DC: Author.

National Occupational Information Coordinating Committee. (1989c). *The national career development guidelines: Local handbook for middle/junior schools.* Washington, DC: Author.

National Occupational Information Coordinating Committee. (1989d). *The national career development guidelines: Local handbook for postsecondary institutions.* Washington, DC: Author.

No Child Left Behind PL 107-110. (2002). Retrieved from http://www.wrightslaw.com/nclb/law/nclb.107-110.pdf.

Pask-McCartney, C., & Salamone, P. (1988). Difficult cases in career counseling III: The multi-potentialed client. *Career Development Quarterly, 36,* 231–240.

Post-Kammer, P., & Perrone, P. (1983). Career perceptions of talented individuals. *Vocational Guidance Quarterly, 37,* 22–30.

Roessler, R. T., Johnson, J., & Schrimmer, L. (1988). Implementing career education: Barriers and potential solutions. *Career Development Quarterly, 37,* 22–30.

Spokane, A. R., & Oliver, L. W. (1983). The outcomes of vocational interventions. In W. B. Walsh & S. H. Osipow (Eds.), *Handbook of vocational psychology.* Hillsdale, NJ: Erlbaum.

Super, D. E. (1957). *The psychology of career.* New York: Harper & Row.

Trusty, J., & Niles, S. G. (2004). Realized potential or lost talent: High school variables and bachelor's degree completion. *Career Development Quarterly, 53,* 2–15.

U.S. Army/ASCA. (2002). *Planning for life: Developing and recognizing exemplary career planning programs.* Alexandria, VA: ASCA.

Whiston, S. C., & Sexton, T. L. (1998). A review of school counseling outcome research: Implications for best practice. *Journal of Counseling & Developemt 74,* 412–426

Young, R. A. (1994). Helping adolescents with career development: The active role of parents. *Career Development Quarterly, 42,* 198–203.

13

Career Development in Postsecondary Educational Institutions

Things to Remember

- What graduates can do about underemployment after completing a baccalaureate degree
- The steps in the design/redesign of career development programs in postsecondary institutions

- At least two self-directed, brief, and case-managed activities that can be used in the implementation of career programs in postsecondary institutions
- The major purposes of program evaluation

In March 2010, the Bureau of Labor Statistics reported that the unemployment rate among workers with at least a college degree stood at 4.9 percent as compared to the overall unemployment rate of 9.7 percent (BLS, 2010). In February 2010 the Gallup Daily Tracking Poll (Gallup, 2010a) reported that nearly one-fifth of employed workers were underemployed, which was defined as working part-time and wanting to work full-time. In another report the Gallup Organization (Gallup, 2010b) reported that substantially fewer, perhaps 50 percent less, of college graduate reported that they were underemployed. The problem with the Gallup Organization's survey was that their definition of underemployment—working part-time and wanting to work full-time—does not include many college graduates, and thus there is every reason to believe that their estimate is woefully inadequate. As has been noted previously, underemployed workers also includes workers who are in jobs, either full or part-time, that do not allow them to use the skills and knowledge gained in their education. When the Gallup estimate of the percentage of underemployed graduates (e.g., College grad.com, 2004 = 18%) is combined with the percentage of graduates who are not in position to use the skills they acquired in college it is certain that the percentage of underemployed college graduates is quite high. Fifty-four percent of the respondents to a Gallup survey (Hoyt & Lester, 1995) who attended college indicated that their current job did not allow them to fully utilize their skills. Students need access to high quality career services if they are to minimize the risk of both unemployment and underemployment.

Career services at the postsecondary level are particularly important for students who are entering community college vocational programs, vocational–technical schools, and technically oriented four-year colleges and universities. Students who enter some of these institutions must have chosen a major prior to matriculation or have a very short period of time after their education begins before a major must be chosen. These majors lead directly to certain occupations and, thus, the choice of a major is by default a career choice. Students who have been in high schools with weak career development programs are at a decided disadvantage.

Jeremy represents a typical example. After flunking out of a major technically oriented university, he held a variety of construction jobs to support himself, completed a one-year program to become an optician, rejected the occupation because it was too boring, and finally landed a job as an electrician's apprentice that he enjoyed. What was the elapsed time from entry into college to occupational satisfaction? Seven years! Lost time and lost wages are only a part of the loss. Years of frustration and self-doubt were also a part of the price Jeremy paid during this period of his life. Had Jeremy not had family support, his occupational story might have been such that he took the only job available to him, or worse. Getting an education is important. Getting an education that prepares you for a satisfactory occupation is much more important.

More than half the students who graduate from high school attend some form of postsecondary educational institution, including four-year colleges, community colleges, or vocational–technical schools. Whereas one of the primary reasons for pursuing a college education is to train for a career, only approximately 54 percent of college graduates report being in their present career as a result of following a conscious plan. Of those adults who either did not finish college or who attended two-year institutions, about 35 percent followed a conscious plan to their current careers. Approximately one-quarter of those who attended some form of postsecondary education never used occupational information (Hoyt & Lester, 1995). This study plus an earlier one by Hatcher and Crook (1988) suggests that certain aspects of the career development of students are not being addressed. They surveyed graduates of a small liberal arts institution to determine what surprises they had encountered on their jobs. They found that students were better workers than they expected they would be, they perceived themselves to be criticized for poor work more than expected, and the organization's demand for good work was greater than they had anticipated. They also found that when expectations regarding work did not coincide with reality, particularly if that was a negative reality, students expressed intentions to leave their current jobs.

Although not every student pursuing postsecondary education does so for the sole purpose of preparing for a career, many expect this to be a product of their educational experience. It is important that the career development needs of these students be met. Healy and Reilly (1989) tried to determine whether the career development needs of vocational–technical students enrolled in 10 California community colleges were being met. Older students indicated that they had less need to set career goals, become certain of career plans, explore career-related goals, select courses relevant to career goals, develop employability skills, and/or obtain jobs than did younger students. However, about 25 to 50 percent of all age groups studied rated these needs of major concern. They also rated knowing more about their interests and abilities as important needs. The authors reported that the finding that older students have less need for career development activities was not unexpected. However, one suspects that younger respondents did not rate their needs for career development activities higher because of lack of awareness of the problems encountered by college graduates. in the workplace.

Sixty-four percent of college graduates would try to get more career information if they were starting over. This may be because only 54 percent of adults who attended or graduated from college believe that their skills are being fully utilized on their current job. Moreover, approximately 6 percent of this group expected to be forced out of their jobs within three years after the 1993 NCDA survey (Hoyt & Lester, 1995).

THE STUDENTS

The stereotype of community college and college students is that they are 18 to 22 years old and pursuing their first postsecondary educational experience. However, it is now projected that as many as two-thirds of the students entering postsecondary education will be nontraditional students (deBlois, 1992; Healy & Reilly, 1989). Nontraditional students fall into several categories, including those older than age 22, those who are reentering school because of previous academic failure, those who have been displaced from their marriages or jobs, or who have decided to change careers.

The influx of older-than-average students into postsecondary institutions is not the only change that has occurred in the demographic makeup of student populations. The diversity of college students increasingly reflects the diversity of our society. Minorities representing almost all ethnic groups make up sizable portions of the enrollments of most community and four-year colleges. The Americans with Disabilities Act has made it mandatory that all educational institutions provide access to people regardless of the nature of their disabilities. This has made it possible for students with physical disabilities, such as visual impairment, and students with learning disabilities, such as dyslexia, to avail themselves of a college education. Two other groups present on campuses of postsecondary institutions, gays and lesbians, also present challenges to career development specialists who hope to meet the needs of all students.

Several authors have indicated that many students enrolled in postsecondary institutions need specialized career development services. For example, Leong (1993) suggested that both the content and the process of career counseling must be altered to accommodate the interpersonal styles, cultural values, attitudes, and beliefs of Asian students. Padula (1994) and Luzzo (1995) have both addressed the special needs of college women, with Padula focusing more on reentry women and Luzzo on gender differences in career maturity. Like Padula's literature review, Luzzo's research identified a recurring theme in the literature dealing with women's career choice–making: conflicts between career and other life roles. Belz (1993) indicates that counselors working with gay and lesbian students may have to address their homosexual identity concurrently with career development concerns. Student athletes are another group that may require special attention because of their failure to set academic and career goals (Blan, 1985; Lanning, 1982; Petrie & Russell, 1995). Wilkes, Davis, and Dever (1989) outlined a joint planning effort between the career planning and placement office that attempted to address these problems. This litany of special needs could be extended to each group of students present on today's campuses.

It would be easy to conclude that career development programs must be tailored to each student, and this conclusion contains more than a grain of truth. However, Griff (1987) indicates that groups of students share common needs, and the career development services available to students should include some or all of the following:

1. Career and self-awareness activities
2. Exploration of interests, values, goals, and decisions
3. Realities of the job market and future trends

4. Practical, accurate information about careers

5. Workshops that deal with special needs, such as risk taking, résumé development, interviewing, and so forth

6. An academic advising system that makes it possible for students to get the assistance they need in academic planning

THE INSTITUTIONS

Three general types of institutions vocational technical schools, community colleges, and four-year colleges are of concern here. The first of these, vocational–technical schools, are extensions of high school vocational education programs and provide skills training in a variety of careers ranging from semiskilled to professional (such as heating and air conditioning equipment installation and maintenance, licensed practical nurses, registered nurses, and drafters). Because of the vocational nature of these programs, students often select an area of study at the time of entry and pursue it to completion. In many instances the necessity to make an early decision leads to mistakes.

Community colleges often have a vocational–technical component along with a college transfer program. In many states the college transfer program is coordinated with the programs in colleges and universities so that students transferring to four-year institutions do so as "junior transfers." Students select community colleges because of financial reasons (they can live at home and thus save money), because of the need for remedial study to make up for academic deficits, because they want to explore whether post–high school study is actually something they want to pursue, and for a variety of other reasons. Students who have had academic difficulty may also regain their eligibility to reenroll in four-year institutions by demonstrating their competency in community college courses. A remarkable aspect of community colleges is their open-door admissions policy, which enables students to begin at their academic competency level and advance their education. This open-door policy does not extend to all programs offered in these institutions, however. Vocational–technical programs as well as programs such as nursing, accounting, and others have established standards that must be met prior to entry.

Four-year colleges and universities are nearly as diverse as vocational–technical schools and community colleges. Highly prestigious colleges, such as Harvard, Stanford, Yale, Williams, and Brown, turn away hundreds and in some instances thousands of highly qualified applicants, whereas some other colleges are barely able to attract sufficient numbers of minimally qualified applicants to maintain their enrollments. Some colleges are predominantly female whereas others are comprised largely of males. Predominantly African American colleges, such as Howard University, have led the way in providing quality education to African American students, whereas Gallaudet has focused on students with hearing impairments. Enrollments range from a few hundred to more than 50,000, and the cost can vary from $8,000 a year to more than $50,000 a year. Not surprisingly, the curriculums can vary widely. Some colleges emphasize liberal arts preparation, which focuses on the arts, sciences, and humanities, whereas others concentrate on technical areas, such as engineering, or on preparing people for educational careers.

Resources, philosophy, mission, size and characteristics of the student body, curriculum offerings, location, and a variety of other factors influence the career development program. Career development specialists in liberal arts institutions must be prepared to help students choose careers that appear to have little relevance to their majors. Law schools have historically given preferential treatment to English and to a lesser extent history and political science majors all other things such as grades and Law School Admission Test (LSAT) scores, being equal. It is also the case that some laws schools now make concerted efforts to enroll students with technical backgrounds such as computer science or engineering. Psychology majors may be able to use their skills in a variety of related areas, but they need to know that personnel officers, human services workers, and researchers draw on psychological principles in their work.

CAREER DEVELOPMENT PROGRAMS

Johnson and Figler (1984) suggested that many issues confront career development specialists as they plan programs for postsecondary institutions. Among these are philosophical issues of whether to (1) emphasize counseling or placement; (2) send clients out on their own to collect information; (3) focus students on the "vocational" aspects of their training; (4) involve significant others, such as parents, in the career planning process; and (5) emphasize risk taking or security in the career planning process. Dealing with the issues identified by Johnson and Figler and planning to meet new demands require decisions about programming that must be considered carefully.

The National Career Development Guidelines for postsecondary institutions (Kobylarz, 1996; NOICC, 1989) lay out a process for developing a comprehensive program that is quite similar to the processes outlined in Chapter 12 for building or improving programs in elementary, middle, and high schools. *The National Career Development Guidelines: Local Handbook for Postsecondary Institutions* lays out two sets of competencies: those for young adults and those for adults. The 1996 version of the *Guidelines* (Kobylarz, 1996) consolidated the adult and young adult competencies into a single set of competencies. A combination of the 1989 and 1996 competencies for adults is shown in Table 13.1. As can be seen in that table, the *Guidelines* emphasize that adults need to (1) identify positive self-images, (2) be able to identify career information and use that information to make informed career decisions, (3) engage in lifelong learning, (4) prepare for transitions in their careers, (5) understand the interaction of career and other life roles, (6) understand the changing roles of men and women in our society, and (7) understand the interrelationships that exist between the needs of society and the world of work. To the list I would add an eighth competency: understanding the nature of the global economy and its impact on jobs.

Career Resource Centers

The Career Resource Center will be the hub around which the career services program revolves. Reardon, Zunker, and Dyal (1979) surveyed four-year institutions of higher learning to investigate whether institutions had a separately budgeted career resource center. At that time, 51 percent responded affirmatively. This number has grown dramatically in the time since the survey, although exact numbers are not available. However, an institution that does not have a career resource center and a well developed career services program should be shunned by prospective students. College graduates list the college career center as the second most often used source of information about careers, followed by newspapers. Nearly 48 percent of the college-educated adults in a Gallup poll (Gallup Organization, 1989) indicated that they had used *college career centers*, as they were termed in the survey. A later Gallup poll (NCDA, 1999) produced similar results. Clearly, the career resource center is one of the keys to the career development program on college campuses.

TABLE 13.1 Adult Competencies and Indicators

Competency	Sample Indicator: The Adult Will
1. Maintenance of a positive view of self in terms of potential and preferences and self-assessment of transferability to the world of work.	1. Identify achievements related to work, learning, and leisure and state their influence on his/her perception of self.
2. Ability to assess self-defeating behaviors and reduce their impact on career decisions.	2. Understand physical changes that occur with age and adapt work performance to accommodate these.
3. Skills for entering, adjusting to, and maintaining performance in educational and training situations.	3. Document prior learning experiences and know how to use their information to obtain credit from educational institutions.
4. Skills for locating, evaluating, and interpreting information about career opportunities.	4. Assess how skills used in one occupation may be used in other occupations.
5. Skills required for seeking, obtaining, keeping, and advancing in a job.	5. Develop a résumé appropriate for an identified career objective.
6. Skills in making decisions about educational and career goals.	6. Develop skills to assess career opportunities in terms of advancement, management styles, work environment, benefits, and other conditions of employment.
7. Understanding of the impact of careers on individual and family life.	7. Describe how family and leisure roles affect and may be affected by career roles and decisions.
8. Skills in making career transitions.	8. Accept that career transitions (e.g., reassessment of current position, job changes, or occupational changes) are normal aspects of career development.
9. Skills in retirement planning.	9. Recognize the importance of retirement planning and commit to early involvement in the retirement planning process.
10. Understand how the needs and functions of society influence the nature and structure of work.	10. Recognize economic trends that influence workers.
11. Understanding the continuing changes in male and female roles.	11. Identify changes in the job and family roles held by men and women.

Source: From *National Career Development Guidelines: K–Adult Handbook,* by L. Kobylarz, 1996, Stillwater, OK: Career Development Training Institute; and *The National Career Development Guidelines: Local Handbook for Postsecondary Institutions* by National Occupational Information Coordinating Committee, 1989, Washington, DC: Author.

Developing the Program

The staff of the Florida State University career resource center has been at the forefront in the thinking about the design and implementation for career programs on college campuses and elsewhere, Recently Sampson (2008) drawing on his work with Robert Reardon, Janet Lenz and others published *Designing and Implementing Career Programs: A Handbook for Effective Practice*, which I believe is the best resource available to practitioners hoping to filed well designed programs at the postsecondary level. The career program design process that Sampson suggests involves eight steps: (1) evaluate current career resources, service tools, and services; (2) select, adapt, revise, and develop improved career resources, service tools, and services; (3) integrate improved career resources, service tools, and services into existing program; (4) train staff to use new services tools and approaches; (5) conduct a pilot test of the new program; (6) if applicable, train staff in all career centers and schools; (7) implement program; and (8) conduct ongoing evaluation and continue accountability.

At the end of each step in the process Sampson (2008) inserts, "communicate with stakeholders" (pp. 52–53) to emphasize a point that has been made repeatedly—that it is important to keep everyone from administrators to clerical staff not only informed but fully involved in the program design or redesign process.

It is expected that the final career development plan will include a statement of the purpose of the program as well as the competencies that are to be developed as a result of the program (see again Table 13.1). Like the elementary, middle/junior high school, and high school plans, the processes (e.g., counseling, placement) to be employed in the program along with specific activities, staff expected to deliver the activities, and a time line for delivery should be included in the plan (Kobylarz, 1996; NOICC, 1989).

Conducting a needs assessment is the first step as the staff prepares the design of a new program or the redesign of an existing program. Evans (1985) compared two general approaches to needs assessment in postsecondary educational institutions: interviews and questionnaires. Within these general categories, Evans also tried to discern whether questionnaires and interviews based on developmental theory were superior to needs assessment procedures that had been empirically derived. She concluded that questionnaires provided a more efficient means of collecting and tabulating data about needs whereas interviews produced a richer database that provided more insight into the individual's concern. However, data for all the approaches suggested the same areas of need, including academic performance, career and lifestyle concerns, and issues relating to personal identity. Once needs are identified, indicators should be selected and then standards of performance established. This process is shown in Table 13.1.

The actual competencies to be developed in the career development program, the processes to be used, and the specific activities depend on the overall philosophy and nature of the school itself. Because students in vocational–technical schools begin specific vocational preparation immediately, it is important that their abilities to relate educational and occupational preparation to career opportunities (Competency 3 in Table 13.2) and use skills in making decisions about educational career goals (Competency 6 in Table 13.2) be developed early, perhaps prior to beginning the training program. Orientation, initial advising, and perhaps screening devices might be relied on to develop these competencies. Table 13.3 includes some suggested activities that may be used in conjunction with each of the processes identified in the postsecondary career development guidelines (Kobylarz, 1996; NOICC, 1989). Sampson (2008) breaks career services into three broad categories: self-help, brief staff-assisted, and individual case-managed. An example of a self-help services would be self-administered assessments, some of which have been discussed in earlier chapters. Brief staff-assisted services include workshops, short-term group counseling, and large sections of career courses. Individual counseling and long-term group counseling are examples of individual case-managed approaches. These and other activities will be discussed later in this chapter under the rubrics of brief and case-managed interventions.

Sampson, Peterson, Reardon, and Lenz (2000) and Sampson (2008) suggested an approach to service delivery based on the cognitive information processing (CIP) (Peterson, Sampson, Lenz, & Reardon, 2002) model discussed in Chapter 3. They suggest that the delivery of career services should begin with an assessment of the client's readiness to make a career decision so that an estimate can be made about the need for a practitioner to support or facilitate the decision-making process. They also indicate that there are two levels of readiness assessment, which they refer to as *intervention planning assessment* and *aggregate assessment for program*

TABLE 13.2   Selecting Indicators and Establishing Standards of Performance

Needs Assessment: Sixty percent of sophomores uncertain about the relationship between their educational and career plans

Develop Competency 3	**Ability to relate educational and occupational preparation to career opportunities**		
Indicators	*Processes Involved*	*Activities*	*Standard*
1. Assess education and training alternatives and selected field of study or training post	Information	Advising begins at matriculation	100% by end of sophomore year
2. Identify education or training requirements of specific occupations that are related to field of study	Classroom instruction	Required class on careers	100% will select appropriate occupation
3. Develop an action plan to achieve educational goal	Classroom instruction	Required class on careers; counseling	100% will develop action plan
4. Not chosen			
5. Develop long- and short-range plans to achieve identified career goals	Classroom instruction; counseling information	Required class; counseling, advising	100% will develop short- and long-range plan

Develop Competency 6	**Skills in making decisions about educational and career goals**		
Indicators	*Processes Involved*	*Activities*	*Standard*
1. Establish personal criteria for making decision about educational and career goals	Classroom instruction	Required class on careers	100% will meet criteria
6. Make and implement effective career and educational decisions	Classroom instruction, information counseling	Career Resource Center (CRC) advising, career counseling, required class	100% will complete

planning. Aggregate assessment precedes program development because it yields information about the group to be served. Intervention assessment comes prior to the selection of the intervention with an individual.

The readiness assessment model outlined by Sampson and colleagues (2000) focuses on individual assessment using the Career Thoughts Inventory (CTI) (Sampson, Peterson, Lenz, Reardon, & Saunders, 1996), which measures two factors: capability and complexity. Capability to make a decision involves both the commitment to make a decision and the skills needed to make that decision. Complexity refers to factors such as family issues, economic concerns, and other environmental factors that may impinge on the decision-making process. Using CTI data,

TABLE 13.3 Processes/Approaches to Career Development

Outreach

1. Career seminars in housing units
2. Informal rap sessions in housing units to establish contacts
3. Activities designed for special groups delivered at their meetings (e.g., international students)
4. Mentoring programs using alumni or upper classpeople.
5. Parent involvement, such as career development seminars

Classroom Instruction

1. Required classes for credit
2. Optional classes for credit
3. Noncredit, short-term classes
4. Employability skills training classes
5. Units in regular classes dealing with careers

Counseling

1. Individual career counseling
2. Group career counseling
3. Employability skills groups
4. Special programs for alumni, such as group counseling activities
5. Support groups for job hunters

Assessment

1. Screening examinations given at entry to focus on career/decision making
2. Ongoing assessment offered to students in counseling/career planning and placement center
3. As part of career counseling
4. Computer-assisted services
5. Self-directed assessment (e.g., self-directed search)
6. Needs assessments

Information

1. Orientation sessions/information
2. Catalogs
3. Advising information/careers
4. Career information center
5. Articles in student newspapers
6. Computer-assisted systems
7. Handouts that relate educational programs to career opportunities
8. Alumni newsletters

Placement

1. Regular job placement activities for students
2. Job fairs to link employers and workers

Work Experience

1. Internship programs
2. Placement for part-time work
3. Cooperative educational/work programs
4. Work–study programs

Consultation

1. With faculty advisors to make them aware of education–career connection; needs of certain students
2. With residence hall assistants and directors to provide assistance
3. With instructors who wish to infuse more career information
4. With club/social activities advisors to suggest career-related activities

Referral

1. To workers in the community for career information
2. To mental health professionals to get assistance with personal problems blocking career-related decisions

the client and the counselor decide on one of three courses of action: (1) self-help, brief, assisted services, such as assistance by a librarian or aide; (2) a career course or short-term group counseling; or (3) extensive services that may include an array of interventions, such as assessment, career counseling, and decision-making training.

The career information processing (CIP) planning model can serve as a basis for planning an entire program. It would require administering the CTI to the entire population to be served, providing feedback to them based on the assessment, and then developing the appropriate interventions for those who wish to participate in the career development program. When conceptualized in this manner, it seems that the CTI replaces the traditional needs assessment, but Sampson's model includes a needs assessment.

There is one concern, which was raised in Chapter 5. The CTI tends to be intrusive and may be offensive to groups that value a high level of self-control. Moreover, the complexity factor measured by the CTI seems to depict the family as a potential barrier to decision making, which is inconsistent with the beliefs of people who hold collective social values.

AN IN-DEPTH LOOK AT CAREER PROGRAM ACTIVITIES

Career interventions can be effective if properly implemented, but some professionals question the use of brief interventions (Sampson, 2008; Sampson et al., 2000). What is a brief intervention. In this context it is defined as one that takes relatively less staff time per student, not the number of hours expended by students. Goodson (1982) found that relatively short interventions, such as workshops and seminars, were available on 87 percent of the campuses surveyed. Pickering and Vacc (1984) reported, after a review of the literature on career-related interventions, that the most commonly researched areas were those with six sessions or less, including a variety of activities. They also reported that longer-term interventions (more than five sessions) were usually more effective than short-term interventions. However, Buescher, Johnston, Lucas, and Hughey (1989) reported that a brief intervention consisting of a 1.5-hour meeting with a career counselor, the completion of an occupational card sort, a discussion of career options, and a tour of the career center resulted in positive changes for undecided students.

STUDENT LEARNING EXERCISE 13.1

From a list of postsecondary institutions in your state, choose one community college, one small school (less than 5,000 students), and one large school (over 12,00 students). Visit the career services Web site of the three schools you have chosen, make a list of the career services offered via the Web site, and then make a list of other uses of this site.

	Web site Uses
Community college	
Small college	
Large college/university	

Brief Activity: Web Sites

As was noted in earlier chapters, the Internet provides a number of unique opportunities for career resource centers on college campuses to extend and expand the services they offer. Sampson (1999, 2008) and Srebalus and Brown (2001) also discussed the use of the Internet as a means of increasing both the effectiveness and the efficiency of counseling centers. Sampson suggested that centers can develop Web sites and post career and educational information on them, thus allowing students to download needed information without coming to the center. He also suggested that career resource center Web sites could be used to market the center's services, to deliver services such as the development of employability skills, and to provide links to prescreened Web sites. To this list should probably be added the development of an intranet that links the career resource center, the college counseling center, the advising service, and other services within the college or university. Web-based career counseling and assessment services can also be offered to off-campus students and alumni. Appointments for services can be scheduled using the career resource center's Web site, and intake data can be collected prior to the first appointment.

Brief Activity: Advising

Advising is the backbone of the educational planning process in postsecondary institutions and it appears that the quality of this process varies greatly. If competencies dealing with the integration of educational and career planning are to be developed, it seems logical that one goal must be the development of an outstanding advising system. Dailey (1986) suggests that advisers use decision trees to aid in the academic/career planning process at the time the student must select a major. A decision tree is little more than a graphic representation of life decision points, with the branches of the tree representing options. The process of decision making using a decision tree approach is illustrated in Figure 13.1. Dailey believes that the decision tree approach may be particularly applicable for use with business majors because they probably have been oriented to this approach in their courses. However, use of the tree concept should not be limited to business.

Advisers, who are not typically career specialists, need to be oriented to the implications of educational programs for careers. This can be done through consultation (if advisers are open to this process). However, advisers need data from follow-up studies that examine the career success of graduates. They also need information from business recruiters who come on campus. Recruiters should be invited to provide seminars for advisers that focus on the criteria used by

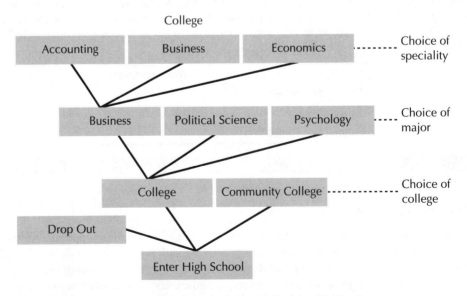

FIGURE 13.1 Decision Tree of College Sophomore's Decision-Making Process.

their businesses to make hiring decisions. Finally, advisers should receive information regularly about the jobs entered by graduates of various programs.

Brief Activity: Major Fairs

Elliot (1988) described a Pennsylvania State University program aimed at fostering educational planning. Undecided students, along with faculty representatives of various academic programs, were invited to attend an evening program in which students and faculty could interact about major areas of study. Although no formal evaluation was conducted, those involved believed that the program was an effective way to stimulate educational exploration.

Brief Activity: Career Courses

As noted in Table 13.2 and by Sampson (2008), there are numerous approaches to delivering career exploration courses to students, including modules, credit courses, and noncredit courses. Quinn and Lewis (1989) found that certainty of career choices was increased by inserting career-related material into a traditional academic course.

Savickas (1990) designed and field-tested a career exploration course that tried to develop the following attitudes and concepts: (1) Become involved now, (2) explore your future, (3) choose based on how things look to you, (4) control your future, (5) work: problem or opportunity? (6) view work positively, (7) conceptualize career choice, (8) clear up career choice misconceptions, (9) base your choice on yourself, and (10) use four aspects of self as choice bases. He found support for the idea that the course generally had a positive impact on ability to engage in career decision making and on long-term time perspectives, with students enrolled in the course being somewhat more oriented to a future time perspective. Savickas's findings generally support the earlier research of Lent, Larkin, and Haşequa (1980), who found that a 10-week career planning course focusing primarily on technical and scientific careers was helpful in facilitating career planning.

The availability of career planning classes is widespread. Typically, these courses focus on career exploration and development; career decision making; employability skills; and, to a lesser extent, on careers for special groups, field experiences, and self-assessment. Allyn (1989) described a departure from this traditional curricular approach. She tried to "focus on the learning styles associated with the left and right hemispheres [of the brain]" (p. 281) and to apply the 4MAT System, which attempts to capitalize on learning styles using an experiential approach. The objectives of her course were to have students learn more about themselves, their support systems, and careers that might be of interest. The first step in the course has students deal with the *why* question (e.g., "Why is this course important?"). Then students focus on the *what* question ("What is the content of the course?"). After answering the *what* question, students engage in hands-on activities to answer the *how* question ("How will I fit into the world of work?"). Finally, students answer the *if* question ("If the information I have learned applies to me [or doesn't], what are the consequences?"). The content of Allyn's (1989) course does not vary greatly from that covered in other courses previously described, but the techniques employed, which include guided imageries, are worth serious consideration.

Finally, the results of a study by Johnson and Smouse (1993) found no significant increase in career decidedness, knowledge of occupations, and certainty of occupational choices among students who completed a career planning course versus a control group. They suggest that for these courses to be effective they must be developed to meet the specific needs of the students who are enrolled in them.

Brief Activity: Workshops and Seminars

Kahnweiler and Kahnweiler (1980) reported on a dual-career family workshop that has particular relevance given the likelihood that married couples will face this situation. The workshop was divided into didactic input, models of dual-career families, and discussion. In the didactic phase, the benefits (e.g., extra income) and liabilities (e.g., gender-role conflicts) were presented. In the modeling section, the workshop leaders, who were involved in a dual-career marriage, discussed the pros and cons of their relationships. Finally, students were engaged in a discussion focusing on their backgrounds and the problems they might have with dual-career marriages.

Unfortunately, many career seminars and other more didactic career interventions are not evaluated systematically. However, if the needs of the target audience are clearly identified and seminars and other experiences are carefully designed to meet these needs, these approaches can be highly effective for students who do not have decisional anxiety or other personal problems that preclude them from benefiting from the experience.

An example of a carefully designed and evaluated seminar that addressed specific student needs is presented by Robbins and Tucker (1986). Their concern, like that of many career counselors, was career goal instability, and they tried to discern whether small groups that are primarily self-directed are more effective than those involving leader-directed interaction. They found that students with high and moderate goal instability engage in greater numbers of career information–seeking behaviors as a result of the interactional groups than those who participate in the self-directed groups. However, the type of group appears to make little difference on the information-seeking behaviors of students with low-goal instability. Students enrolled in the groups that are interactionally oriented are more satisfied with their groups than those where the leaders emphasize self-direction.

Brief Activity: Self-Directed Activities

Many colleges provide opportunities for students to engage in self-directed activities including assessment, computer-assisted career exploration, and career exploration books. Pickering (1984) compared the results of a career planning seminar run by career counselors, a similar seminar run by peer tutors, and a self-directed group where students were oriented to using a career exploration workbook. The analysis of the outcome yielded no significant differences among the treatment groups. Unfortunately, Pickering did not include a no-treatment control group in the design. However, Pickering concluded that the self-study method was the most cost-effective method, an inference that must be interpreted very cautiously because Pickering and Vacc (1984) had earlier concluded that self-help approaches were the least-effective approaches based on their review of the research literature.

For those individuals who wish to establish a self-help section in their career information centers, Nachreiner's (1987) description of the material housed in the University of Wisconsin–Madison Center is instructive. Their materials are placed in four color-coordinated stations:

Station I: Who Am I—Includes materials about life transitions, values, interests, and skills

Station II: Job Search—Includes information about employability skills, such as résumé development

Station III: Education and Career Research—Includes study skills information as well as educational and career information

Station IV: Bibliographies—Includes lists of readings on various topics

Brief Activity: Information Dispensation

Earlier chapters were devoted to discussions of various informational approaches, including types of information and the establishment and operation of a career information center. That discussion will not be duplicated here. However, the CareerLine approach once used at Michigan State University is worth consideration (Forrest & Backes, 1988). CareerLine is a 300- to 400-word career information column that appears weekly in the student newspaper at Michigan State. It addresses such topics as planning for summer jobs, various types of careers, and related topics. One by-product of the program has been the development of a *CareerLine* booklet that includes some of the better columns.

Individualized Case-Managed Activities Internships

Students in postsecondary education need opportunities that will help them finalize their career choices. Students in vocationally oriented courses of study are immediately involved in laboratory experiences and field assignments that allow them to see, smell, feel, hear, and taste the occupations they expect to enter. Students in liberal arts programs, such as English and history, have no such opportunities. Internships involving editing of and research on historical events help these students get this type of experience. One criminal justice major enrolled in an internship that involved observation of police operations, visits to trials, discussions with law enforcement officers and probation and parole counselors, and nighttime patrols with peace officers. One student changed majors when he witnessed a brief exchange of shots between police and a would-be armed robber. His explanation was that it had not occurred to him that criminals shoot back.

Consultation

Spokane (1991) discusses career development consultation and prevention together, and though he does not link them directly, he suggests that both are linked to promoting career competence. Brown, Pryzwansky, and Schulte (2010) go one step beyond Spokane's position and link consultation to the prevention process, asserting that consultants can be instrumental in preventing problems from arising if they can effectively intervene in programs and activities that promote developmental processes. As was suggested in Table 13.2, consultation from internal consultants can be offered to advisers, residence hall advisers, instructors who wish to make their courses more career relevant, and the advisers of students who may wish to promote career development. Campus activities from the ski club to the student newspaper can have relevance to career and lifestyle decisions and should be included in the career development program.

Career development specialists have numerous opportunities to engage in consultation with faculty members, club sponsors, resident assistants, and others to assist them in planning programs that facilitate career development. However, one variation is to use alumni to consult with students about their career options. Willamette College developed such a program by creating a file of alumni who would be willing to consult with students and then providing their names to any interested students (Bjorkquist, 1988). The staff at Willamette College also uses this alumni file as a basis for securing speakers for on-campus seminars. Ohio State University has also developed a program of this type.

Career Counseling

Chapter 5 is devoted entirely to the career counseling process, so the discussion here is brief. However, many colleges and universities now offer career counseling services to alumni and some, such as the University of South Carolina, devote a great deal of attention to this area. It is also noteworthy that some colleges and universities have developed cooperative arrangements with other institutions to provide counseling and informational services when geographic location makes it impossible for alumni to return to their alma maters.

Career counseling is probably the most widely offered of the career-related services. Typically, career counseling services are offered through specialized agencies called career planning and placement, the university counseling center, or both. Magoon (1989) reports that more than one-fifth of the counseling centers offered no career counseling, whereas 40 percent of the counseling centers in large universities and 53 percent of the centers in small universities reported sharing the responsibility of offering career counseling with another agency on campus. Career counseling is offered exclusively at the remaining counseling centers (30 percent of the large and 24 percent of the small centers). If Stone and Archer (1990) are correct, interest is decreasing among the counselors and counseling psychologists who have traditionally offered career counseling in university counseling centers. This may result in career counseling services being offered more frequently through career planning and placement centers.

Career counseling is offered in three modes: individual, group, and computerized services. Some career counselors would take exception to including computerized services in this list, and perhaps they have a legitimate case because career counseling is an interpersonal process between two or more people aimed at solving a career-related problem. However the CACGS discussed in Chapter 9 do approximate traditional career counseling, and Hoyt and Lester (1995) report that 10.6 percent of adults in their nationwide survey who attended college used one of these systems. However, 48 percent of adults who had attended community colleges and 52 percent of college grads reported that they had consulted a professional counselor about their career choices at some point in their lives. In all likelihood this consultation occurred on a one-to-one basis.

Some agencies that provide career counseling services have developed intake procedures in an effort to identify the best approach to dealing with students' problems. Intake interviews are conducted by counselors to determine students' needs and expectations. After this interview, students are referred variously to a psychometrician for testing; individual counseling; group counseling; or group guidance activities, such as those for developing employability skills. The goal of the intake process is to deliver career development services effectively and efficiently.

Group career counseling has not received the same degree of investigation or discussion that individual career counseling has, although Oliver and Spokane (1988) concluded after a review of the literature that group interventions are as effective or more effective than other types. Suggestions from Butcher (1982) and Sampson and colleagues (2000) that students be carefully screened prior to group counseling seem appropriate. They recommend that students need to be ready to engage in counseling, by which they mean they are prepared to accept the responsibility of the process. They also suggest that some determination be made as to whether students have pervasive decisional problems (are indecisive) because students who have decisional problems must have that concern addressed prior to engaging in the decision-making process.

Based on suggestions by Niles and Harris-Bowlsbey (2005), Pyle (2000), and Posthuma (2002), and the career counseling model set forth in Chapter 5, several other suggestions about career counseling are in order.

1. Students who are at very different stages in their career development should not be placed in the same group. For example, college students in liberal arts universities are asked to choose a major during the latter half of their sophomore years. This often prompts them to consider their career options and, thus, they are in the early stages of career exploration. Other students may be in the throes of deciding among several choices and need assistance with the decision-making process. Still others may be at the point of choosing from among the specialties in law, dentistry, medicine, or business. Students in each of these categories need to be placed in groups with students who are at the same developmental stage.

2. Groups move through discernible stages and each stage presents different challenges to the leader. These stages are assigned different names by different authors (Niles & Harris-Bowlsbey, 2005; Pyle, 2000), but essentially they can be distilled into four stages.

a. *Socialization*—accepting similarities and differences, trust building
b. *Problem identification*—identifying the concerns of the individual
c. *Problem solving*—exploration of approaches to dealing with the problem
d. *Termination*—summing up and planning for postgroup experiences

Careful prescreening can help to ensure success in the socialization stage. Students should be in the same developmental stage and have other common characteristics. Race, gender, and sexual orientation only become concerns if people with prejudicial attitudes are placed in groups. A simple screening question can eliminate many of these problems: How would you feel about being in a group with women (or men, if the candidate is a woman), people of color (white people, if a person of color), or people who have a sexual orientation different from yours? Prescreening should also focus on preferred verbal and nonverbal communications styles and cultural values, particularly those that may influence decision making or communication style (see Chapter 5 discussion). Prescreening may not identify all of the problems that may arise in the group. Niles, Anderson, and Cover (2000) found little correlation between the problems presented at intake and during the career counseling sessions themselves.

3. We assume that the leadership skills required in other types of groupwork generalize to career counseling. However, Kivlighan (1999) reviewed the literature in this area and found that this assumption has not been tested.

4. Once socialization occurs and group members accept and trust each other, group counseling becomes individual counseling in a group setting, and the application of his or her theory dictates how the career counselor deals with individuals.

5. Structured groups have set agendas, whereas unstructured groups do not. It is suggested here that career development groups that are aimed at the typical problems of self-exploration, exploring occupations, or decision making have agendas and structures, such as a set of exercises or lessons to support those structures, with one cautionary note. Career counselors should be flexible enough to depart from the structure to solve interpersonal problems that arise in the group, or to deal with emergencies that arise in the lives of the group members (for example, a group member may lose his or her job while in the process of seeking an alternative career).

6. Less structured groups that offer emotional support and assistance with career development issues for job hunters; displaced workers; women; minorities; and gay, lesbian, bisexual, and transgender students should be available.

Peer Counseling Programs

Postsecondary institutions facing personnel shortages have, at times, turned to peer programs of various types, including tutorial and counseling programs. As Holly (1987) notes, careful screening and training of counselors is an essential aspect of a successful program. Screening criteria should include motivation, psychological openness, freedom from psychological concerns, communications skills, and interpersonal style. The nature of the training program depends on the goals of the program, but with proper supervision, peer counselors might orient students to computer-assisted career planning systems, assist students in locating and interpreting occupational information, train students in job shadowing and information interviewing, and answer questions about self-directed self-assessment devices. It is imperative that supervisors be available to answer immediate questions and that regular, ongoing supervision is established to protect both the client and the peer counselor. It is also important to note that serving as a peer counselor can provide a valuable career development experience for students who aspire to careers in the mental health field. The University of Maryland, Cornell University, and Dickinson College have at various times offered peer counseling programs (Johnson & Figler, 1984).

PROGRAM EVALUATION

A more detailed look at the issues involved in program evaluation will be taken up in Chapter 16 and thus the discussion here will be brief. Step 7 in Sampson's (2008) program development process was program evaluation, and a careful inspection suggests that the process informs the continued redesign of the program and program accountability. From this point of view, the process of program development of redevelopment is most appropriately portrayed as a circular process, not a linear one. Evaluation data should be used to activate the entire process of program improvement.

In a practical sense program evaluation is meant to answer two questions: (1) Did we accomplish the objectives that we set forth? and (2) Which activities contributed to their development? However, career development programs may have other objectives that deal with broader institutional concerns. Some of these objectives might be to increase the graduation rate, increase satisfaction with the advising program, increase the effectiveness of the job placement services, increase the satisfaction with the internship programs, and so forth. These objectives might be evaluated using a variety of techniques, such as follow-up studies, and qualitative strategies such as focus groups.

Reed, Reardon, Lenz, and Leierer (2001) illustrated how evaluation also may be based on the CIP theory (Peterson et al., 2002). They evaluated the extent to which a semester-long career course impacted career thoughts as measured by the Career Thought Inventory (Sampson et al., 1996). They found that there was a significant decrease in negative thoughts about career decision–making at the end of the course. This outcome is consistent with competency 2 in Table 13.1. However, it is likely that a semester-long course would also target entering, adjusting to, and maintaining performance in educational and training institutions; locating and evaluating occupational information; employability skills; decision making; and lifestyle considerations, which are competencies 3 through 7 in Table 13.1. The development of these skills and others could have been assessed using a rating scale, such as the one shown in Figure 13.2, in addition to the CTI.

At this point our discussion has been focused on answering the question regarding the evaluation of outcomes. Although outcome evaluation helps answer some of the *what things were accomplished* questions, some answers to the *how* questions must come from process evaluation.

Process evaluation looks at decision making, staffing, resources, management variables, and other program process variables that may contribute to, or detract from, attainment of program

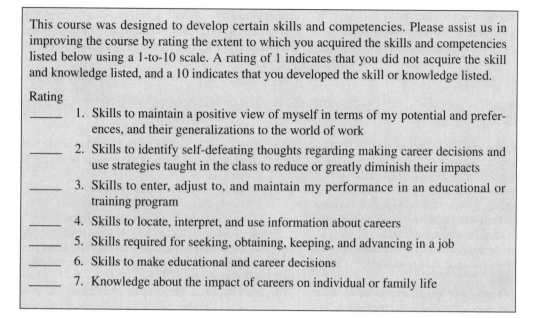

This course was designed to develop certain skills and competencies. Please assist us in improving the course by rating the extent to which you acquired the skills and competencies listed below using a 1-to-10 scale. A rating of 1 indicates that you did not acquire the skill and knowledge listed, and a 10 indicates that you developed the skill or knowledge listed.

Rating

_____ 1. Skills to maintain a positive view of myself in terms of my potential and preferences, and their generalizations to the world of work

_____ 2. Skills to identify self-defeating thoughts regarding making career decisions and use strategies taught in the class to reduce or greatly diminish their impacts

_____ 3. Skills to enter, adjust to, and maintain my performance in an educational or training program

_____ 4. Skills to locate, interpret, and use information about careers

_____ 5. Skills required for seeking, obtaining, keeping, and advancing in a job

_____ 6. Skills to make educational and career decisions

_____ 7. Knowledge about the impact of careers on individual or family life

FIGURE 13.2   Course Evaluation.

goals. If these processes are perfect (which they will not be) and if the programs themselves are perfectly designed (which they will not be), some failure will occur because of the interaction of development and the environment. An example of the results of a process evaluation was presented by Reardon and Regan (1981). The objective of their evaluation was to determine student reactions to a career development course at Florida State University. The course, which consisted of three units (Self and Environmental Analysis, Decision Making, and Job Acquisition), was evaluated by two types of student rankings and by looking at academic records. Reardon and Regan found that students learned about the course from friends, faculty advisors, and the schedule of classes. They also discovered that students enrolled in the class to develop a fuller understanding of the career planning and decision-making process, to increase their motivation to engage in career planning, to find out more information about careers, and to determine how careers and majors are linked. Finally, they found that students valued the organization of the course and the level of instructor–student interaction. Reardon and Regan concluded that the information resulting from their evaluation was helpful in determining how the course could be marketed and as an aid in course redesign.

Summary

Career development activities in postsecondary educational institutions can assist students to crystallize their career plans and begin the process of implementing them by linking education and career. However, not all students perceive that they need these activities. In some instances, students do not need career development activities, but in others it is just as obvious that students' perceptions of the relevance of career development activities is based on naivete, not information. It is also clear that students enrolled in postsecondary institutions are diverse, both by virtue of their development and because of their age, ethnicity, and reasons for being in college. Good programming requires that these needs be carefully considered and that attempts be made to meet them. It is likely that only those programs that use multiple approaches—including information, career counseling, classes, small groups, and units in classes—and that link advising and career planning will be successful.

Chapter Quiz

T F **1.** During the peak of the recession,of 2007–2010 the unemployment rate for college graduates was approximately 25 percent lower than that of the general population.

T F **2.** According to the author, underemployment should be defined as people working part-time who wish to be working full time.

T F **3.** The percentages of college graduates who are in the workforce and underemployed is about 10 percent.

T F **4.** Program evaluation should be considered as the final step in program design and implementation.

T F **5.** Sampson, Reardon, and others have concluded that career development theory is of little use in the design of career programs for colleges.

T F **6.** It would be defensible to assert that nearly half of college students use the services of the career program.

T F **7.** Early in the program development or redevelopment process, the stakeholders that should be involved are the career program staff and students.

T F **8.** At least one college has developed a self-directed career development program for its students.

T F **9.** Career counseling is probably the most often offered career service.

T F **10.** Sampson's classification of career services seems to be based on the amount of time required per student rather than the overall amount of time required to deliver the service.

(1) T (2) F (3) F (4) F (5) F (6) T (7) F (8) T (9) T (10) T

References

Allyn, D. P. (1989). Application of the 4MAT model of career guidance. *Career Development Quarterly, 37,* 280–288.

Belz, J. R. (1993). Sexual orientation as a factor in career development. *Career Development Quarterly, 41,* 197–200.

Bjorkquist, P. M. (1988). Creating an alumni career consultant program in a liberal arts college. *Journal of College Student Development, 29,* 77–78.

Blan, F. W. (1985). Inter-collegiate athletic competition and students' educational and career plans. *Journal of College Student Development, 26,* 115–118.

BLS (2010). Employment status of the civilian population 25 years and over by educational attainment. Retrieved from http://www.bls.gov/news.release/empsit.t04.htm.

Brown, D., Pryzwansky, W. P., & Schulte, A. (2010). *Psychological consultation and collaboration: Introduction to theory and practice* (7th ed.). Boston: Allyn & Bacon.

Buescher, K. L., Johnston, J. A., Lucas, C. B., & Hughey, K. F. (1989). Early interventions with undecided college students. *Journal of College Student Development, 30,* 375–377.

Butcher, E. (1982). Changing by choice: A process model of group counseling. *Vocational Guidance Quarterly, 30,* 200–209.

College Grad. Com (2010). Underemployment affects 18 percent of entry level job seekers Retrieved from http://www.collegegrad.com/press/underemployed.shtml.

Dailey, M. J. (1986). Using decision trees to assist students through academic and career advising. *Journal of College Student Development, 27,* 457–458.

deBlois, C. S. (1992, July). *The emerging role of the female nontraditional education student–family and professional development.* Paper presented at the annual meeting of the Association of Teacher Educators, Orlando, FL.

Elliot, E. S. (1988). Major fairs and undergraduate student exploration. *Journal of College Student Development, 29,* 278–280.

Evans, N. J. (1985). Needs assessment methodology: A comparison of results. *Journal of College Student Development, 26,* 107–114.

Forrest, L., & Backes, P. (1988). CareerLine: Career resources delivered to students. *Journal of College Student Development, 29,* 165–166.

Gallup (2010a). Underemployment 19.8% in February, on par with January. Retrieved from http://www.gallup.com/poll/126272/Underemployment-February-Par-January.aspx.

Gallup (2010b). Focus on education may reduce underemployment. Retrieved from http://www.gallup.com/poll/126995/focus-education-may-reduce-underemployment.aspx/

Gallup Organization. (1989). *A Gallup survey regarding career development.* Princeton, NJ: Author.

Goodson, W. D. (1982). Status of career guidance programs on college campuses. *Vocational Guidance Quarterly, 30,* 230–235.

Griff, N. (1987). Meeting the career development needs of returning students. *Journal of College Student Development, 28,* 469–470.

Hatcher, L., & Crook, J. C. (1988). First-job surprises for college graduates: An exploratory investigation. *Journal of College Student Development, 29,* 441–448.

Healy, C. C., & Reilly, K. C. (1989). Career needs of community college students: Implications for theory and practice. *Journal of College Student Development, 30,* 541–545.

Holly, K. A. (1987). Development of a college peer counselor program. *Journal of College Student Development, 28,* 285–286.

Hoyt, K. B., & Lester, J. N. (1995). *Learning to work: The National Career Development Association Gallup survey.* Alexandria, VA: National Career Development Association.

Johnson, C. A., & Figler, H. E. (1984). Career development and placement services in postsecondary institutions. In N. C. Gysberg (Ed.), *Designing careers* (pp. 458–481). San Francisco: Jossey-Bass.

Johnson, D.C., & Smouse, A.D. (1993). Assessing a career planning course: A multidimensional approach. *Journal of College Student Development, 34,* 145–147.

Kahnweiler, J. B., & Kahnweiler, W. M. (1980). A dual-career workshop for college undergraduates. *Vocational Guidance Quarterly, 28,* 225–230.

Kivlighan, K. M. (1999). Career group therapy. *Counseling Psychologist, 18,* 64–79.

Kobylarz, L. (Ed.). (1996). *National career development guidelines: K–adult handbook.* Stillwater, OK: Career Development Training Institute.

Lanning, W. (1982). The privileged few: Special counseling needs of athletes. *Journal of Sports Psychology, 4,* 19–23.

Lent, R. W., Larkin, K. C., & Hasequa, C. S. (1980). Effects of a "focused" interest career counseling approach for college students. *Vocational Guidance Quarterly, 34,* 151–159.

Leong, F. T. L. (1993). The career counseling process with racial-ethnic minorities: The case of Asian Americans. *Career Development Quarterly, 42,* 26–40.

Luzzo, D. A. (1995). Gender differences in college students' career maturity and perceived barriers in career development. *Journal of Counseling and Development, 73,* 319–322.

Magoon, T. M. (1989). *The 1988/1989 college and university counseling center data bank.* College Park: University of Maryland Counseling Center.

Nachreiner, J. A. (1987). A self-help education and career planning resource for adult students. *Journal of College Student Development, 28,* 277–278.

National Career Development Association. (1999). Survey of working America. Retrieved from http://www.Ncda.org

National Occupational Information Coordinating Committee. (1989). *The national career development guidelines: Local handbook for postsecondary institutions.* Washington, DC: Author.

Niles, S. G., Anderson, W. P., Jr., & Cover, S. (2000). Comparing intake concerns and goals with career counseling concerns. *Career Development Quarterly, 49,* 135–145.

Niles, S. G., & Harris-Bowlsbey, J. (2005). *Career development interventions in the twenty-first century.* Columbus, OH: Merrill/Prentice-Hall.

Oliver, L., & Spokane, A. R. (1988). Career intervention outcome: What contributes to client gain? *Journal of Counseling Psychology, 35,* 447–462.

Padula, M. A. (1994). Reentry women: A literature review with recommendations for counseling and research. *Journal of Counseling and Development, 73,* 10–16.

Peterson, G. W., Sampson, J. P., Jr., Lenz, J. G., & Reardon, R. C. (2002). A cognitive information processing approach to career problem solving and decision making. In D. Brown et al. (Eds.), *Career choice and development* (4th ed.). San Francisco: Jossey-Bass.

Petrie, T. A., & Russell, R. K. (1995). Academic and psychosocial antecedents of academic performance for minority and nonminority college football players. *Journal of Counseling and Development, 73,* 615–620.

Pickering, J. W. (1984). A comparison of three methods of career planning for liberal arts majors. *Career Development Quarterly, 35,* 102–111.

Pickering, J. W., & Vacc, N. A. (1984). Effectiveness of career development interventions for college students: A recovery of published research. *Vocational Guidance Quarterly, 32,* 149–159.

Posthuma, B. W. (2002). *Small groups in counseling and therapy: Process and leadership* (4th ed.). Boston: Allyn & Bacon.

Pyle, K. R. (2000). A group approach to career decision making. In N. Peterson & R. C. Gonzalez (Eds.), *Career counseling models for diverse populations: Hands-on applications for practitioners.* Belmont, CA: Wadsworth/ Thompson Learning.

Quinn, M. T., & Lewis, R. J. (1989). An attempt to measure a career-planning intervention in a traditional course. *Journal of College Student Development, 30,* 371–372.

Reardon, R., & Regan, K. (1981). Process evaluation of a career planning course. *Vocational Guidance Quarterly, 29,* 265–269.

Reardon, R., Zunker, V., & Dyal, M. A. (1979). The status of career planning programs in career centers in colleges and universities. *Vocational Guidance Quarterly, 28,* 154–159.

Reed, C. A., Reardon, R. C., Lenz, J. G., Leierer, S. J. (2001). A cognitive career course: From theory to practice. *Career Development Quarterly, 50,* 158–167.

Robbins, S. B., & Tucker, K. R., Jr. (1986). Relation of good instability to self-directed and interactional career counseling workshops. *Journal of Counseling Psychology, 33,* 418–424.

Sampson, J. P., Jr. (1999). Integrating Internet-based distance guidance with services provided in career centers. *Career Development Quarterly, 47,* 243–254.

Sampson, J. P., Jr. (2008). *Designing and Implementing Career Programs: A Handbook for Effective Practice.* Broken Arrow, OK: National Career Development Association.

Sampson, J. P., Jr., Peterson, G. W., Lenz, J. G., Reardon, R. C., & Saunders, D. E. (1996). *Career Thoughts Inventory.* Lutz, FL: Psychological Assessment Resources.

Sampson, J. P., Jr., Peterson, G. W., Reardon, R. C., & Lenz, J. G. (2000). Using readiness assessment to improve career services: A cognitive information-processing approach. *Career Development Quarterly, 49,* 146–174.

Savickas, M. L. (1990). The career decision making course: Description and field test. *Journal of College Student Development, 38,* 275–284.

Spokane, A. (1991). *Career interventions.* Englewood Cliffs, NJ: Prentice-Hall.

Srebalus, D. J., & Brown, D. (2001). *Introduction to the counseling profession.* Boston: Allyn & Bacon.

Stone, G. L., & Archer, J. A., Jr. (1990). College and university counseling centers in the 1990s: Challenges and limits. *Counseling Psychologist, 18,* 539–607.

Wilkes, S. B., Davis, L., & Dever, L. (1989). Fostering career development in student athletes. *Journal of College Student Development, 30,* 567–568.

14

Career Counselors in Private Practice: Counseling, Coaching, and Consulting

Things to Remember

- The factors that contribute to the success of private practices

- The types of private practice licensing laws and the implications of each

- The steps in starting a successful private practice

The current numbers of unemployed and underemployed workers has created an unprecedented need for career development services. Unfortunately, these same conditions have reduced the ability of many workers who need career counseling and other services to pay for them. Unlike mental health counseling, which is often at least partially paid for by health insurance, the client must underwrite the entire cost of career counseling unless there is a coexisting mental health problem.

Private practice is about offering career development services to earn money. Most career development practitioners work in educational or governmental agencies for a salary. Career counselors who choose private practice do so for a variety of reasons, including the opportunity to manage their own careers and increase their earnings. Some career counselors want to establish relatively limited part-time practices in their homes, whereas others aspire to the development of a multifaceted consulting firm that offers an array of services to the public. Regardless of the goal, establishing a private practice depends on the practitioner's ability to market the services she or he is offering. In this chapter some of the services that can be marketed are discussed and some of the rudimentary aspects of establishing a private practice outlined. One service that has not been discussed elsewhere, career coaching, is discussed in this chapter. It is relatively new and, for reasons that will be obvious, controversial.

Literally thousands of counselors, psychologists, social workers, and other mental health professionals in private practice are delivering a variety of mental health services. It is likely that a few thousand of these professionals, primarily counselors and counseling psychologists, provide career counseling services to the public. It is also likely that this number will grow because adults in our society seem to be relying increasingly on career counselors for assistance. The results of two surveys (Hoyt & Lester, 1995; NCDA, 1999) found that almost 9 percent of the respondents responded affirmatively to a question about using a private practitioner to get help with their careers. This means that approximately 11 million adults paid to receive some type of assistance with their careers in the two periods covered by the survey. Because of the number of people changing jobs voluntarily and involuntarily today, it seems likely that increasing numbers of people will seek assistance from private practitioners in the future if they can find the funds to do so.

QUALIFICATIONS FOR PRIVATE PRACTICE

At the outset it is worth mentioning that qualifications come under two categories: ethical and legal. Both issues were discussed to some extent in Chapter 4 and will only be revisited briefly at this time. It is important to note that all states have licensure, certification, and registry laws that regulate the practice of psychologists and counselors. For the most part, the licensure laws for psychologists require that people who purport to be psychologists must be licensed whether they practice in public institutions or are engaged in private practice. However, the statutes for counselors are primarily aimed at regulating practice in the private domain. Licensing laws fall into two broad categories: title acts and practice regulation acts.

Those states that have licensing laws regulating practitioners titles afford consumers little protection. In these states people may provide career development services as long as they do not call themselves counselors or psychologists. This opens the door to some poorly qualified persons calling themselves career coaches and career specialists to offer a wide variety of services to the public. Fortunately, many states, such as Idaho, North Carolina, Florida, Texas, Ohio, and Virginia, have adopted regulatory statutes that limit both title and practice. These states have included career counseling as a service that should be offered only by licensed counselors or other licensed professionals. Ideally, all states will adopt these types of laws in the future.

GUIDELINES FOR CONSUMERS

Caveat emptor, or "let the consumer beware," is probably the best advice for consumers who are seeking assistance with career-related problems. The reason for this, as already noted, is that in some states the practice of career counseling is not sufficiently regulated. To assist consumers to make wise choices, the National Career Development Association first issued consumer guidelines for selecting a career counselor in 1988 and has updated them periodically. The latest guidelines, posted in 2010 (NCDA, 2010), are paraphrased in the following section

Credentials

Career counselors should have earned graduate degrees in an appropriate mental health specialty, such as career counseling, counseling psychology, or social work. As part of their training, career counselors should have completed supervised field experience that involved career counseling. They should have appropriate work experience. They should have developed knowledge bases that support their activities as career counselors, including knowledge about career development, assessment, occupational information, employability skills, the integration of life roles, and the stresses of working, job loss, and/or career transitions.

Fees

Career counselors should have established fees and allow clients to choose the services they need, terminate whenever they deem appropriate, and pay for only those services that have been provided. (Many state licensing boards require private practitioners to place a fee schedule on file in their offices in case a dispute between the client and practitioner arises over a billing issue and a complaint is filed with the board.)

Promises

Professional career counselors should refrain from promising careers that have higher salaries or claiming that they can provide immediate resolution to career problems.

Ethics

As noted in the introduction, Chapter 4 was dedicated to ethical issues in career counseling. Generally speaking, licensed career counselors follow the ethical codes published by the American Psychological Association or the American Counseling Association. Clients should be informed that these codes can be found online and that complaints of ethical misconduct can be lodged through the ethics committees of these organizations. Many private practitioners develop brochures that list their services, the fees for the services, their professional affiliations and information regarding filing complaints.

Even if consumers are aware of the guidelines developed by the National Career Development Association, it is likely that they may still be confused by the number of people who call themselves career counselors and offer a wide range of services—from job placement specialists who offer résumé preparation services to outplacement specialists who assist people whose jobs have been terminated to find suitable employment. Unfortunately, some of these people have little training in career counseling, whereas others may have completed a one- or two-week training course and received impressive certificates from what appear to be creditable organizations.

Career Coaching

What is career coaching, who does it, and how is the career coaching industry regulated? Career coaching has not been discussed in detail elsewhere in the book because it is primarily something done by private practitioners. Knowdell (1996) explained that the focus of career coaching is narrower than that of career counseling. He went on to indicate that the job of the career coach is to help a client negotiate a short-term or long-term career transition.

Bench (2003) reported that the career coaching movement in this country was less than 20 years old, but had grown into a multimillion dollar business. Seven years later there are no reliable estimates of the dollars earned by career counselors. Currently, there are thousands of career coaches at work in this country and abroad, Bench's observation that it is impossible to determine exact numbers is still true. The reason for this lack of information is simple: There are no licenses or certificates needed before becoming a career coach. This lack of regulation has caused some professional career counselors to speak of career coaching in pejorative terms. Also, because much career coaching occurs via the telephone, some career counselors have questioned its validity. Career coaching as well as preparation to be a career coach can also be conducted online. Some career counselors have elected to add career coaching to their repertoire of skills and to their practices. Because most career counselors are already skilled in the development of career plans and job-hunting skills, which is one major role filled by career coaches, they

---

TABLE 14.1   Skills Needed in QuantumShift! Coaching

Core Competencies	Preparing for the call Establishing rapport and the agenda Elaborating on the client's agenda Eliciting action
Level 1 Competencies	Use Cartesian coordinates, which involves examining all aspect of the presenting problem (systematic questioning) Draw on past successes[*] Find an expert who has solved a similar problem Change the perspective by asking what others might see if they looked at the problem[*]
Level 2 Competencies	Determine client's motivation by asking or inference Involve client in the interpretation of the events surrounding their issue Challenge assumptions Ask why the goal or issue has become important Use visualizations, help select role models who have accomplished the client's goal, teach self-affirmations, prescribing mediation, and journal entries
Level 3 Competencies	Question beliefs clients have about themselves (confrontation) Question identity Help client identify beliefs, establish identity based on core beliefs, and take action based on the new identity

---

*The level 1 techniques have a great deal of similarity to the Brief Solution-Focused Counseling Model.

need to learn performance enhancement (the level 1 skills shown in Table 14.1) and other job coaching skills. Because the practice of career coaching is unregulated, there is nothing other than ethical guidelines that preclude career counselors from adding "coach" to their titles.

What are the skills of the career coach other than facilitating career decision making and developing employability skills? Bench (2003) has developed a model of coaching that she terms QuantumShift! Coaching (QSC). QSC has as its goal helping clients "leap" to an authentic career, which is a career that corresponds to their core belief systems. According to Bench, career coaching can be viewed as occurring at three levels; level 1 is aimed at changing behavior and improving performance. This is very similar to managerial coaching, which will be discussed briefly in Chapter 15. Level 2 coaching involves the belief system and the unconscious motivators of the client, and level 3 addresses the identity of the individual and is aimed at a change in self-perception, an identity transformation. Bench identified the skills needed in general and at each of these stages, as shown in Table 14.1.

Bench (2003) indicates that there are more than 120 coaching training programs in existence and in all likelihood the number is growing. CareerTrainer, a publishing and consulting firm headed by Richard Knowdell, operates a program to train job and career transition coaches. Knowdell, who is a National Certified Career Counselor, leads the three-day certification workshop. The agenda for the workshop is as follows:

• Changes in the World of Work, the Composition and Configuration of Jobs, Careers Paths in the Twenty-First Century, the Important Impact of Emotions, and Job and Career Transitions

- Career Assessment Tools
- How to Focus on an Immediate Job Objective or a Long-Term Career Goal
- Building and Managing a Career Strategy Plan
- The Coach as ASSESSOR
- The Coach as INFORMATION PROVIDER
- The Coach as REFERRAL AGENT
- The Coach as GUIDE
- The Coach as TUTOR
- Introduction to Job Search Techniques

For more information go to www.careertrainer.com. Other career coaching certification programs require self-directed study and from 12 to 250 hours of documented coaching (see www.careercoachinstitute.com). Marcia Bench also offers an online program for dealing with building a private practice involving coaching at www.6figurecoach.com and numerous publications through CTS, her publishing company.

ESTABLISHING A PRIVATE PRACTICE

Almost everyone who has been involved in setting up a private practice will attest to the difficulty involved in the process, particularly if the practitioner chooses not to join a group practice where referrals are immediately available from other professionals. Many psychologists and counselors who enter private practice enter a group practice, and then choose to offer both personal and career counseling. Often they find that their group practice colleagues refer their "career cases" to them because they lack the skill to provide the service themselves. Other career counselors choose to set up independent practices and offer only career development services. In this section some general concerns regarding establishing a private practice are discussed.

Practice Pointer (u.d.) (http://www.counseling.org/Counselors/PrivatePracticePointers. aspx, a Web site dedicate to providing private practitioners with tips regarding the initiation and improvement of private practices, suggests that the would-be private practitioner should develop a marketing plan early on. However, before that is done the question, "Market what?" must be answered.

STUDENT LEARNING EXERCISE 14.1

Before reading the next session, make a list of services that you as a private practitioner might offer the public.

1.
2.
3.
4.
5.

Types of Services

Career counselors often offer a wide variety of services, including career counseling with individuals and groups, consultations, job placement, testing, outplacement, résumé development and the development of other employability skills, career coaching, retirement planning, career/life-role integration counseling, spousal relocation, training, program evaluation, work adjustment counseling, and vocational appraisal services. Because marketing is a critical part of a successful private practice, practitioners must realistically determine whether they have the skills to offer a service and whether that service has a market. The following are potential clients for each of the aforementioned services:

Service	Potential Clients
Individual and group career counseling	The general public; may target specialized groups, such as transitional workers, women, or retirees
Testing/assessment	The general public; may target high school students doing career planning or other groups
Outplacement	Business and industry involved in reducing their workforce and seeking placement services; often specialize in white-collar workers
Job placement	The general public; some agencies specialize in clerical, technical, or other types of workers
Headhunters	A specialized form of job placement; often involves recruiting and placing corporate executives, school superintendents, scientists
Résumé and employability skills development	General public; often targets young workers (e.g., college students), workers in transition, and those who have lost their jobs
Retirement planning	Workers preparing for retirement; may target military or other people from a specific industry
Career coaching	Individuals who wish to make career decisions or improve performance at work; assist clients in developing plans and supporting their efforts to implement those plans
Career/life-role Integration	General public; may target workers at midlife or new entrants to labor force
Training	Other professionals who want to upgrade their skills in various areas; may target those interested in setting up a private practice
Consultation	Businesses, governmental agencies, schools, colleges and universities, federal programs (e.g., Job Training Partnership Act)
Career development program evaluation	Businesses, governmental agencies, schools, colleges and universities, federal programs with career development programs
Work adjustment	The general public; on a contract basis to businesses counseling

Service	Potential Clients
Spousal relocation	Businesses; primarily those businesses interested in transferring executives who have employed spouses who are seeking careers
Vocational appraisal	Social Security Administration; insurance companies; others interested in establishing extent of vocational disability
Career information	Develop customized information packets for clients who do not wish to pursue information independently

In addition to determining what services they have to offer and whether a client group is available in their area, practitioners must assess the degree of competition. For example, outplacement has become highly competitive, and large outplacement firms, such as Drake Beam Marin, not only have well-developed outplacement programs but also have a national network of offices that can be called on to assist workers in finding jobs in a wide variety of job markets. These same firms often offer a spousal relocation service that is not only lucrative but also helps them establish corporate contacts. Only a few individuals can compete with the large outplacement firms. However, a number of career counselors have developed outplacement services for small companies in areas where relocation does not entail extensive geographic moves.

Location of the Office

Many private practitioners find it convenient and less expensive to use portions of their residences for their offices. Obviously, this eliminates commuting, rental fees, janitorial services, and so on. Some parking must be provided for clients, and this may become a major issue in some areas, particularly if group counseling is provided for 8 to 12 clients at a time. Using one's residence as a business office is impossible in some residential areas because of zoning restrictions.

Many counselors locate offices in settings that cater to professionals because of accessibility; the availability of parking; opportunities to share services, such as receptionist, telephone answering, and perhaps billing services with other professionals; as well as opportunities to increase the likelihood of referrals.

Image

An office located in a professional office building also helps project the professional image that many career counselors desire, particularly if they are involved with consultation in business and industry. The exact location and nature of the office depends on the types of services to be offered, costs, desire for professional image, and convenience. As already noted, career counselors may offer a variety of services to the public. The backbone of most private practices is career counseling, but many practitioners are engaged in other services. Although it is probably true that many private practitioners simply begin their businesses and let them evolve, a careful plan should be developed to offer services and market them to the public.

In deciding what services to offer, several questions should be asked (Ridgewood Financial Institute, 1995). The first is, Am I really in business? It is certainly the case that many private practitioners hedge on this question simply because their private practice is a part-time practice.

Before deciding what type of services are to be offered, the response to this question must be in the affirmative and must be followed by some other obvious questions: If I am in business, what business am I in? Will I specialize in career counseling? If yes, which services will I offer? Are any underserved groups present in my community? Are career development services being offered that could be offered more effectively? At less cost? Once private practitioners decide that they are really in business, that their private practice is really more than a hobby, and that they can offer effective services, it is time to ask a series of other questions.

Chief among the other questions to be answered is, Am I projecting the right image? (Ridgewood Financial Institute, 1995). It is certainly possible to build a successful private practice that specializes in career counseling operating out of an office in the home. It is less likely that a private practitioner can build a highly successful consultation or outplacement service from a home office, primarily because of the need to establish an image that will attract potential business clients. In real estate, there are three rules for selecting property: location, location, location. In private practice, particularly if there is an expectation of competing with well-established outplacement and corporate counseling firms, the three rules may well be image, image, image. Credentials, office space, stationery, business cards, personal dress and demeanor, and written and verbal presentations are all part of one's business image and must be attended to in building a practice.

To assess image, compare facilities, equipment, stationery, dress, and so on, to those of the competition and ask, Which would I choose? Some potential private practitioners, after making this comparison, decide to join group practices so that they can learn to project the "right" image. Others elect not to compete for business in certain arenas.

In the following section, marketing a private practice is discussed. However, in assessing whether to start or expand a current practice, the question arises: Do I know how to market my current services, or if I elect, to expand a new service? (Ridgewood Financial Institute, 1995). There are literally dozens of ways to market services. Private practitioners must be aware of these and, perhaps more importantly, be apprised of which ones are actually cost effective. If knowledge of marketing strategies and their effectiveness is not developed, marketing consultants may be contacted.

Ultimately a business plan must be developed with specific objectives. Marketing, selection of office space, image, and a host of other decisions and activities grow out of the objectives that are established.

STUDENT LEARNING EXERCISE 14.2

Imagine that you are developing a marketing plan for your soon to open private practice, Make a list of the strategies that you might employ.

1.
2.
3.
4.
5.
6.

Marketing the Service

Most career counselors working in public institutions are aware of the need to market their programs, but because they are paid regularly by a public or private institution, the immediate need to market is less pressing. Private practitioners are paid by their clients, thus no clients—no income. This is precisely the reason why many private practitioners start working in institutional settings, initiate part-time private practices, gradually expand their practices, and once a client base is built, sever their relationships with their employers. These successful private practitioners have learned to market their services successfully.

Many strategies can be employed to market career development services. But before any strategy is employed, the first step is to get comfortable with the idea of advertising. Many counselors who have worked in public institutions have an aversion to advertising because it almost seems unprofessional (Ridgewood Financial Institute, 1995). Advertising is legal, it is professional, and it is essential to the establishment and maintenance of your private practice. Obviously, advertisements should be tastefully done, but there are no limitations on where they can be placed. Web sites on the Internet with links to other Web sites, newspapers, newsletters, magazine ads, billboards, television and radio spots, and posters are a few of the potential ways to advertise a service. Another way to advertise a private practice is a tasteful brochure that outlines your services and solicits business (see Figure 14.1).

One of the best types of advertisements is the non-ad. One psychologist in private practice writes regularly for an airlines magazine. Because of the exposure he has received, he is invited to conduct more than 100 workshops per year. Another prepares a weekly column for a local newspaper. Still others serve in high-visibility volunteer positions where their names are frequently mentioned in local news media. Making appearances at several clubs, parent groups,

Is Career Counseling or Planning for You?	**About New Directions**
• I would like to examine my career options.	• Career Planning and Decision Making
• I would like to assess my abilities and interests.	• Preretirement
• I am not satisfied with my present position.	• Midcareer Change
• I cannot decide on a career.	• Job Market Reentry
• I am uncertain how to change my career after the age of 35.	• Employment Search Skills
• I am registered with 15 employment agencies and not one has contacted me for an interview.	• Job Campaign Strategy
• I don't know how to set up a complete employment search campaign.	• Complete Résumé Writing Service
• I feel nervous and uncomfortable in an interview.	• Interview Skills
• I want to return to school but cannot decide on a course of study.	• Aptitude, Achievement, and Interest Testing
	• Advanced Educational Planning

Additional bullets under "About New Directions": • Preretirement • Midcareer Change • Job Market Reentry • Employment Search Skills • Job Campaign Strategy • Complete Résumé Writing Service • Interview Skills • Aptitude, Achievement, and Interest Testing • Advanced Educational Planning

FIGURE 14.1 Portions of a Brochure for Career Directions, Hackensack, New Jersey

and professional associations to discuss career counseling and development is another non-ad marketing strategy employed by many practitioners. To use this strategy effectively, the private practitioner must have good public speaking skills and must be able to project a professional image. Name recognition is an important part of marketing any service, and depending on the non-ad activity, the service provided can help build the desired image.

A marketing campaign may begin with non-ads, but soon a target group must be developed, a list of the marketing strategies to be employed must be compiled, an advertising budget must be developed, and an advertising calendar must be laid out. This campaign can be tied to the services being offered. For example, a private practitioner might decide to run weekly advertisements in the local newspaper to publicize a résumé development service in January through May, because many high school and college students are beginning the job hunt at this time. These advertisements might be supplemented with posters placed in dormitories and on high school bulletin boards. The following are tips from successful practitioners about marketing a private practice.

> Private career counseling demands flexibility on the part of the owner/counselor along with creativity since private practice income fluctuates. Career counseling expertise needs to be marketed to several sectors other than private clients. Seminars, consulting, writing newspaper columns, teaching, and outreach counseling for nonprofit groups are necessary in order to advertise the practice, "grow the business," and make an adequate income.
>
> JOAN F. YOUNGBLOOD,
> *Creative Career Counseling*

> In order to make a private career counseling practice thrive, you need to attract clients. Advertising and publicity are two ways of attracting clients. Know the difference between advertising and publicity. Advertising costs you money. Publicity makes you money.
>
> To get your private career counseling practice going (i.e., making money), you will need to spend up to 50 percent of your time in marketing and sales activities. Marketing and sales are not like counseling activities. If marketing and sales are not activities that you enjoy, you should think long and hard about spending so much time in an activity that you don't like. Think about this—Would you advise a client to spend 50 percent of his or her time in an activity that the client dislikes?
>
> RICHARD L. KNOWDELL,
> *National Certified Career Counselor*

> Networking and visibility within the communities you are planning to serve is essential Because counselors are often uncomfortable doing marketing, they often do too little to promote themselves. Referrals come from a broad marketing campaign, encompassing contact development with friends, colleagues, and other professionals who potentially serve your client profile in other capacities. Initially, 50 percent of your time should be spent in marketing activities to generate referrals and a client base. Advertising, workshops, and community service are other techniques that are essential in your marketing plan to increase credibility and visibility as an expert in your field.
>
> BARBARA TARTAGLIONE,
> *Career Connection*

Networking is a process by which counselors interact with other professionals for the purpose of gaining access to business opportunities and/or referrals. Career counselors often attend local, regional, and statewide professional meetings for counselors to develop and reinforce their own expertise and to enhance the likelihood that clients will be referred to them by other professionals. Career counselors who offer consultation to business and industry should probably extend their networking to organizations such as the American Society for Training and Development along with local meetings of counselors and psychologists because people employed in local businesses belong to this association.

Direct solicitation of services via mail, telephone, or personal contact is also a method of gaining clients, particularly if consultation services are offered. These types of contacts can also be used to extend networks and perhaps gain referrals for other services offered, such as career counseling. Some career counselors believe that the best contacts are made in informal meetings, such as over lunch. Although no data supports this supposition, the business lunch seems to be widely employed as a marketing strategy.

All forms of advertisement should adhere to the ethical guidelines of the practitioner's profession (see Chapter 4). Generally speaking, advertisements may contain a listing of the person's highest relevant degree, licenses and certifications, and professional services offered. Advertisements may not include endorsements for past clients and may not make claims of likely success, even if these statements do represent facts (NBCC, 1996). Sample advertisements are shown in Figure 14.2.

It is also worth noting that networking strategies, advertisements, public appearances, direct solicitations, and other marketing strategies, although they do yield immediate results, do not necessarily result in great numbers of clients or multiple offers to engage in lucrative counseling jobs. The marketing of a private practice can take months and perhaps years. Moreover, marketing *never* stops. Clients terminate and consultation contracts end. In order for a practitioner to continue to earn an income, clients must be found and new contracts negotiated. Marketing may become easier, but it always remains an essential task for private practitioners.

BUDGETING

A private practice is a for-profit business that requires a great deal of planning, including the development of a careful budget. Table 14.2 shows a budget planning sheet utilized by Frank Karpati of Career Directions. However, most private practitioners use a software package to budget expenses and maintain their records.

It is also imperative that careful logs be kept for income tax purposes; many commercially developed log books are available. Any type of record, including ordinary date books, will suffice as long as the records are backed up by receipts for all expenses. In determining whether a deduction is legitimate, the IRS expects the taxpayer to establish a clear relationship between the expense and the business. An emergency room physician successfully argued that a garage door opener allowed him to get to emergencies sooner. A noted speaker who gives 100 to 150 speeches per year also argued that a Jacuzzi was essential to help him deal with the stresses of travel. However, both cases are on the "fringes of acceptability" and might have been disallowed by another auditor. Entertainment, travel, meals, equipment purchases, furniture, malpractice insurance, and continuing education are all legitimate expenses if records are kept properly. However, a consultation with a knowledgeable accountant may be the first step to take in setting up a private practice, and continuing consultation regarding the legitimacy of expenses may be the best means of avoiding problems with the IRS.

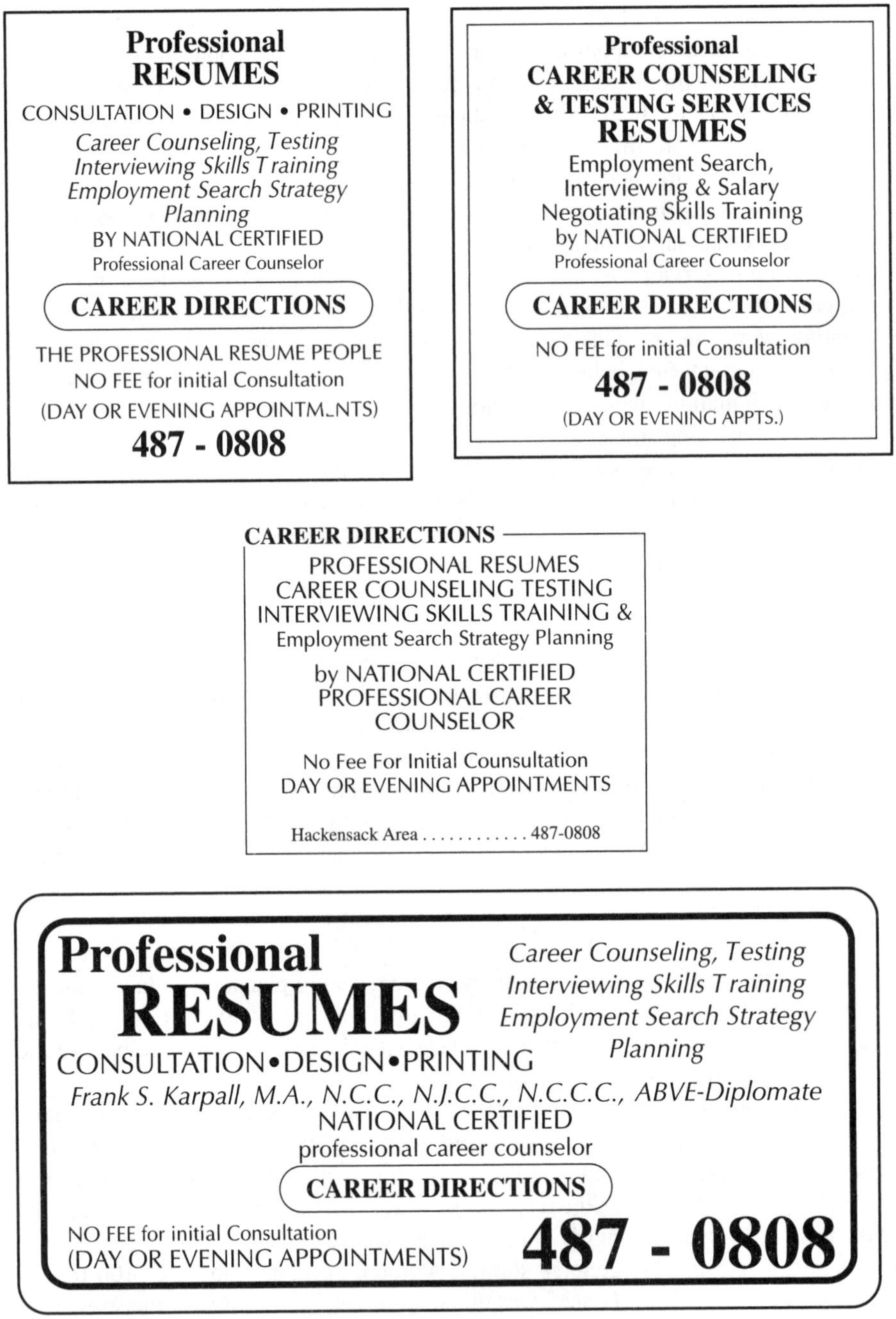

**Professional
RESUMES**

CONSULTATION • DESIGN • PRINTING

*Career Counseling, Testing
Interviewing Skills Training
Employment Search Strategy
Planning*
BY NATIONAL CERTIFIED
Professional Career Counselor

CAREER DIRECTIONS

THE PROFESSIONAL RESUME PEOPLE
NO FEE for initial Consultation
(DAY OR EVENING APPOINTM_NTS)
487 - 0808

**Professional
CAREER COUNSELING
& TESTING SERVICES
RESUMES**

Employment Search,
Interviewing & Salary
Negotiating Skills Training
by NATIONAL CERTIFIED
Professional Career Counselor

CAREER DIRECTIONS

NO FEE for initial Consultation
487 - 0808
(DAY OR EVENING APPTS.)

CAREER DIRECTIONS

PROFESSIONAL RESUMES
CAREER COUNSELING TESTING
INTERVIEWING SKILLS TRAINING &
Employment Search Strategy Planning

by NATIONAL CERTIFIED
PROFESSIONAL CAREER
COUNSELOR

No Fee For Initial Counsultation
DAY OR EVENING APPOINTMENTS

Hackensack Area 487-0808

Professional

RESUMES

CONSULTATION•DESIGN•PRINTING

*Career Counseling, Testing
Interviewing Skills Training
Employment Search Strategy
Planning*

Frank S. Karpall, M.A., N.C.C., N.J.C.C., N.C.C.C., ABVE-Diplomate
NATIONAL CERTIFIED
professional career counselor

CAREER DIRECTIONS

NO FEE for initial Consultation
(DAY OR EVENING APPOINTMENTS)
487 - 0808

FIGURE 14.2 Sample Telephone Directory Advertisements for Career Directions,
Hackensack, New Jersey

TABLE 14.2   Annual Budget Planning/Expenses Sheet

Advertising			**Outside Contractors**	
Yellow Pages	____		Administrative Service	____
Other Printed Material	____		Consultants & Training	____
Mailing/Postage	____		Total	$____
Total	$____		**Rent**	
Automobile			Total	$____
Purchase	____		**Office Equipment**	
Depreciation	____		Service Contracts	____
Insurance/Registration	____		Computer	____
Repairs/Maintenance	____		Depreciation	____
Fuel	____		HP Laser	____
Total	$____		Depreciation	____
Professional Membership and Dues			Copier	____
			Depreciation	____
Total	$____		Total	$____
Publications			**Office Furniture**	
Library	____		Desks	____
Depreciation	____		Depreciation	____
Total	$____		Chairs	____
Professional Liability Insurance			Depreciation	____
			Filing Cabinets	____
Total	$____		Depreciation	____
Computerized Services			Other	____
Software	____		Total	$____
Supplies	____		**Telephone**	
Printing	____		Office	____
Business Travel			Home	____
Air Transportation	____		Cellular	____
Ground Transportation	____		Total	$____
Lodging	____		**Public Relations/Entertainment**	
Meals	____		Total	$____
Miscellaneous	____			
Total	$____			

Fees

It is generally acknowledged that the financial status of the client should be taken into consideration in fee setting. However, assuming that the client has adequate financial resources, that does not answer the question, "How much should I charge?". There are several possible answers to this question. One of the most common ways of setting fees in career counseling is to look at the fees of competitors and establish a commensurate fee schedule (Ridgewood Financial Institute, 1995). Another is to set fees in accordance with those being charged for psychotherapy, apparently based on the assumption that the practitioner's time and services are as valuable as those of the psychotherapist. A common fee-setting strategy is to charge less for group counseling than for individual counseling. Unfortunately, no data provides definitive answers to the question, What are career counselors charging for various services?

Fees ranging from $75 to $200 per hour and beyond are charged by various mental health practitioners for psychotherapy. As suggested earlier, some practitioners gear their fee structure to that of those charged by psychotherapists in their geographic region. Clients are probably paying $80 to $100 per hour for career counseling, which is considerably less than clients pay for psychotherapy. However, many career counselors also charge assessment fees for interest inventories, personality assessments, and aptitude tests, and these can exceed $300 in some instances.

If the data about the fees for career counseling are unclear, those regarding career development consultation are simply unavailable. Some consultants who work with business and industry to set up career development programs, to design performance appraisal systems, and to improve employee–employer relations charge $1,000 to $2,500 per day based on private feedback to the author. However, it is likely that the range of fees for consultation services is much broader—perhaps ranging from $500 to $5,000 per day, depending on the problem and the reputation of the consultant.

In addition, relatively little information about fees is available in the area of outplacement work. Outplacement firms and individual practitioners have demanded and received a fee based on the employee's salary for three months (see Chapter 11). Therefore, if the employee is paid $5,000 per month, the outplacement fee would be $15,000. However, these fees have been charged for outplacement of middle- and upper-management personnel. When businesses hire outplacement firms to work with blue-collar workers, the fee is typically much lower, although the number of employees is usually larger.

The fee schedule should be established at the time the service is initiated along with the method of payment. The following statement appears in the contract signed by each client of Career Directions.

FEE SCHEDULE

The fee for a 70–120 minute consultation is $180.00 payable at the time of the conference. This fee also includes counselor research, preparation and testing services. Therefore, for the fee the client should expect to receive 2½ to 3 hours of professional services. Although the exact number of sessions cannot be initially determined, counseling is usually completed within four to six sessions.

In order for the counseling service to maintain its ability to function and provide the services you need, it is necessary to require of all clients that they be responsible for the time set aside for their consultation. This is particularly essential since a counselor's time is allotted to you alone for the duration of your session, and cannot be used in any other way. In the event that illness or emergency prevents your coming for counseling, you must notify the agency at least 24 hours in advance. The counselor will be happy to discuss this matter with you at length if you deem it appropriate.

One factor that plays a major role in the establishment of fees for psychotherapy that cannot be counted on in providing reimbursement for career counseling is health insurance. Many clients who come for psychotherapy have health insurance that pays some or all of the expense of the treatment. In those instances where insurance pays a portion (80 percent) of an established fee (perhaps $70 per hour), psychotherapists often charge more for the service because the out-of-pocket cost to the client is not great. However, unless the client also has a mental health problem that can be treated simultaneously with the career problem, health insurance does not pay for the service. This fact alone may dictate that fees for career counseling be lower than those for psychotherapy.

Billing

One inevitable aspect of all forms of private practice is the need to collect fees. Many practitioners request that payment by check or credit card be made at the time the counseling is provided. However, whenever bills are unpaid, regardless of the circumstances, billing agencies and even collection agencies are often utilized to collect overdue accounts. The amount of money spent on collection and lost as a result of unpaid bills varies with the situation. However, bad debts are a realistic part of all business and reduce expected income.

The Ridgewood Financial Institute (1995) suggests several ways to increase payment for services. For example, collect complete information on every client, including name, address, telephone number, and Social Security number so that collection can be expedited. Perhaps more importantly, when clients fill out information forms about themselves they should also be informed of their financial obligation, how payment is expected (cash, check, or credit card), and what will happen on past-due accounts. Some practitioners charge late fee penalties, sometimes labeled business costs. Payment at time of service delivery is a means of reducing unpaid bills. This does not prevent receipt of bad checks, but it probably reduces the number of outstanding bills to be collected.

Many practitioners have a series of "collection letters," with the message ranging from a friendly reminder that payment is past due to a warning that the bill is about to be turned over to a collection agency. The use of a collection agency is a last resort because their fees often run to 50 percent of the debt and, ultimately, many of these agencies rely on threats to credit ratings as a basic collection strategy. Finally, some practitioners bring suit in small claims courts, have office assistants telephone people in arrears, and even accept in-kind services (such as repairs to home or office) as payments. Whereas none of these methods is particularly desirable, they all result in increased income and should be considered alternative methods for increasing the profitability of the practice.

Other Business Details

The establishment of a private practice involves dealing with a host of other details including establishing a recordkeeping system, considering the possibility of using an answering service (versus an answering machine), hiring assistants and/or clerical workers, choosing an appropriate liability insurance policy, and selecting an accountant. Some of these decisions are relatively simple. For example, most practitioners purchase liability insurance from companies that offer group rates through professional associations such as the American Counseling Association and the American Psychological Association. Other decisions depend on costs, the image that is being projected, and the personal preference of the practitioner.

DEVELOPING A TESTING FILE   One detail that deserves special consideration is the establishment of a testing file. All private practitioners are faced with identifying and securing a set of tests and inventories that can be used to facilitate their clients' career development. The first consideration in this process is to "qualify" to purchase tests. Publishing companies that produce, distribute, and in many instances score the results require that people who order tests provide proof that they are qualified by virtue of training, licensing, and/or certification to administer and interpret the tests they wish to purchase. Professional ethics also dictate that competence be considered of primary importance when using tests and inventories. Finally, the potential for malpractice suits against people who carelessly use tests and inventories is considerable.

ESTABLISHING A CAREER RESOURCE CENTER   In Chapter 9 the importance of a career information center was discussed as well as some guidelines for establishing a center. Schutt's *How to Plan and Develop a Career Center* (2008) can also be helpful. However, an objective for the private practitioner must be to minimize costs while providing an adequate information source to meet client needs. Answering the questions, "Who are (or will be) my clients?" and, "What will their informational needs be?" is the starting place for establishing the center. The next step is probably to determine what information can be obtained inexpensively through state and federal Web sites. *The Occupational Outlook Handbook* and the occupational information database contained in O*NET are two free and potentially very useful sources of information for private practitioners. Each state also publishes lists of job openings and there are a number of Web sites that provide salary information. Another important consideration is that the use of these Web sites cuts down the space requirements for the office.

Summary

Career counseling in private practice offers a rewarding if challenging career option. However, it also requires a set of skills in addition to those taught in most graduate programs. Career counseling in private practice requires that counselors be able to conceptualize and market a business operation, which involves everything from selecting an office to designing a marketing comparison. Individuals considering this option must carefully consider whether they are equipped personally and professionally to take on such an enterprise. The professional and economic rewards are probably substantial for those who successfully develop a private practice, although, as is the case with most small businesses, the risk of failure measured in economic terms is high.

Chapter Quiz

T F   **1.** Career coaching, which was once conducted by a variety of professionals, is primarily offered by counselors licensed as private practitioners.

T F   **2.** Most state licensing boards have established private practice standards for career counselors.

T F   **3.** The private practitioner's office is of relatively little importance if it is pleasant and comfortable, and it affords a high level of privacy.

T F   **4.** The National Career Development Association has been at the forefront of providing advice to consumers about the choice of a career counselor.

T F   **5.** Counselors and psychologists in private practice generally follow the ethical standards set forth in the NCDA code of ethics.

T F   **6.** Liability insurance is as important for career counselors as it is for others in private practice.

T F   **7.** It is recommended that at least 50 percent of a private practitioner's time be spent in marketing,

T F   **8.** Recessions or upticks in the business cycle have little impact on the flow of clients into private practitioners' offices.

T F   **9.** Private practices in career counseling are generally difficult to establish, but the "good news" about this statement is that there is typically very little competition for clients in most markets.

T F **10.** The Latin phrase *caveat emptor*, or "let the buyer beware," is till sound advice when selecting a private practitioner.

(1) F (2) F (3) F (4) T (5) F (6) T (7) T (8) F (9) F (10) T

References

Bench, M. (2003). *Career coaching: An insider's guide.* Palo Alto, CA: Davies Black.

Hoyt, K. B., & Lester, J. L. (1995). *Learning to work: The NCDA Gallup survey.* Alexandria, VA: National Career Development Association.

Knowdell, R. L. (1996). *Building a Career Development Program,* Mountainview, CA: Davies-Black.

National Career Development Association. (1988). *The professional practice of career counseling and consultation: A resource document.* Alexandria, VA: Author.

National Career Development Association. (1999). Retrieved from http://www.ncda.org,

National Career Development Association. (2010). Consumer guidelines for selecting a career counselor. Retrieved from http://www.ncda.org,

Practice Pointer (n.d.). Marketing strategies for private practice therapists. Vol. 1, Issue 3. Retrieved from http://www.buildimage.com/MarketingStrategies.pdf.

Ridgewood Financial Institute. (1995). *Guide to private practice* (2nd ed.). Hawthorne, NJ: Author.

Schutt, D. (2008). *How to plan and develop a career Center* (2nd ed). Chicago: Ferguson.

15

Career Development Programming in Business Organizations

Things to Remember

- The differences in perspective between career development specialists in business and those in most other institutions
- The types of interventions used in business and industry

- The process of planning a career services program in business
- The role managers and HRD professionals play in the delivery of career development services in business

The term *career development* takes on a circumscribed meaning in a business context. Thus far, career development has been discussed as a lifelong process that results in the choice, entrance, and adjustment to a series of occupations that together can be characterized as a person's career. Hall (1990) pointed out the fundamental difference between the vocational psychologists, such as Donald Super, and organizational psychologists, such as himself, who are concerned with business and industry. Vocational psychologists are more concerned with the individual processes of development, whereas industrial psychologists focus more on the situational variables associated with adjustment in the business setting. Job performance, commitment to the organization, job mobility, family-work interactions, and other similar variables are of greatest concern to career development specialists in business and industry (Hall, 1990). Hall's point will be elaborated on later in this introduction

The recession that began in late 2007 and ended technically in 2010 will have lingering implications for business generally and human resources specifically, of which career development programs are a part, for several years in the future. In some instances these programs were the first to be cut as profits sank. This was also true during the downturn in the business cycle in the 2000–2002. However, both the recessions and the accompanying layoffs sometimes refocused business leaders on the need to provide career services to their employees. A notable example is the United Auto Workers–Ford (UAW-Ford; now UAW-Ford Visteon) which was initiated in 1987 as a life-work planning program and renegotiated in 2005 and 2007 (UAW-Ford, 2010a). One of the focal points of the current UAW-Ford (2010b) program is helping workers qualify for apprenticeship programs that, when completed, allow them to advance in the corporation. To date, over 17,000 workers have graduated from these apprenticeships, half of which are minorities and women (UAW-Ford, 2010b). The UAW-Ford agreement also includes scholarship programs for the dependent children of current employees, former employees, and deceased employees.

The UAW-Ford agreement is not unique, but it has led the way for this type of collaboration. One-hundred and seven joint labor-business career development programs in Canada and the United States were listed on the **Nationwide Canadian Organized Labour and Union Website Links** (XPDNC) Web site (http://www.xpdnc.com/links/crrdjlm.html) in April 2010. Approximately one-third of these programs are the results of the UAW-Ford Visteon collaboration. Some of the collaborative efforts between unions and business leaders are focused on the family, others on easing the stresses of layoffs, and still others on retraining and advancement. For the most part these programs are administered by the unions. Other programs are the result of corporate efforts and are managed by the corporate staff.

GlaxoSmithKline (GSK) is a major pharmaceutical company that is headquartered in the United Kingdom and has major operations in the United States. Its career development program is administered internally by career specialists in conjunction with human resource development and management personnel. GSK's (2010) career development Web site is instructive, about the services offered in the program as well as the program objectives. The program is clearly aimed at current and prospective workers in that it focuses on the services offered to help employees advance in the corporation. For example, the Web site lists the availability of the following career development services:

- *Performance and Development Planning (PDP)* Aimed at helping the employee establish personal goals within the corporate framework; delivered by the employees' managers.
- *Career Innovation Zone* Offers tools and tips to employees to help them establish career direction; delivered online and includes inventories and suggestions for enhancing employability skills.
- *myLearning* Catalogs educational opportunities listed online. Suggests employees work with managers to develop a plan to take advantage of professionally led and e-learning experiences. Workshops and e-learning materials may focus on topics ranging from internal résumés to leadership development that are "delivered to employees through self-directed activities, managers, and career specialists.
- *Coaching and Mentoring* Work performance and personal feedback program; delivered by managers, mentors, and external career coaches.
- *On-the-job Development* Work assignments designed to enhance employee potential in the corporate structure; delivered my managers.
- *Job Postings* Employees have access to job openings across the corporation; delivered online by HRD personnel.

It is interesting to compare GlaxoSmith Klines's (GSK) offerings to a list of services enumerated by Osipow (1982) almost 30 years ago. His list includes (1) helping employees assess their work styles and helping them change those aspects of their styles that may be ineffective

(SK's PDP); (2) helping managers identify the negative effects of repetitive work, forced relocation, and job loss (GSK not included); (3) identifying the strains associated with two-career families and presumably helping ameliorate the stresses growing out of those relationships (GSK may include in workshops); (4) helping managers identify the hazards associated with stress and work (not included in GSK list); (5) preparing people for retirement (retirement planning probably included in myLearning workshops); (6) improving the process of performance appraisal (GSK PDP); and (7) identifying the special concerns of professionals, such as scientists (GSK coaching and feedback).

Although there are communalities between the GSK list of services and the supposed services listed by Osipow (1982), one major difference becomes obvious. The GSK list focuses on increasing the effectiveness of workers and making them more valuable to the company, which is in keeping with Hall's (1990) explanation presented at the outset. Osipow's list focuses more on the overall well-being of the worker (e.g., by reducing stress).

What are the implications of the GSK list of services offered by that corporation and Osipow's proposals? In another article also written 30 years ago, Wilbur and Vermilyea (1982) suggested that career development specialists must take on the identity of businesspeople first and counselors or psychologists second. This requires them to recognize the importance of the profit motive, emphasize enhancing the functioning of the business, and perhaps change their ideas about the level of evidence deemed acceptable to guide decision making.

In individual counseling, the only concerns are client satisfaction and change. As a career counselor in business and industry engaged in designing and selling services, "operational quality, and efficiency, customer satisfaction, market penetration, resource allocation, and demonstration of impact" (pp. 31–32) become concerns because every business is dedicated first to making a profit. Counselors who are accustomed to putting individual growth first, as Osipow seemed to do, will somehow have to reconcile these two goals. This is not to suggest that these two areas are incompatible, but if one must be emphasized, individual development will typically be given a lower priority. Also, counselors and psychologists are systematically trained to look for scientific proof that an intervention works. Business decisions are usually not based on hard evidence, and managers are much more likely to rely on their intuition and experience to make decisions (Wilbur & Vermilyea, 1982), something that may be frustrating to the person trained to think more scientifically. As has been shown from time to time throughout this book, business decisions such as outsourcing and "offshoring" are more often than not driven by the profit motive and not the welfare of the worker, which may also be disturbing to career counselors and vocational psychologists.

PROGRAMMING FOR CAREER DEVELOPMENT

A Brief History

Knowdell (1982, 1984) traced the origins of career development programs in business to the early 1970s, when governmental regulation placed pressure on businesses to provide equal employment opportunity. Although Knowdell is undoubtedly correct about the development of comprehensive career development programs for all employees, specialized programs aimed at orienting, socializing, and enhancing the careers of managers probably began much earlier (Hall, 1990).

Citicorp, General Electric, AT&T, and NASA were among the first corporations to implement comprehensive programs. Ford Motor Company, American Airlines, GlaxoSmithKline, Pfizer, and numerous other companies have initiated programs in the past few years. Some of these programs have been reduced in scope to include new hire orientation, corporate job postings, and manager led coaching/feedbacks to save money.

THE CORPORATION'S VALUES Many corporations still provide extensive educational programs aimed at assisting their employees to function more effectively in their current positions and to acquire new job skills that will enhance their opportunities for advancement. It is possible for employees in a few corporations to earn baccalaureate and advanced college degrees with the assistance and support of their businesses.

What distinguishes these rudimentary career development programs from those that are more highly developed is that comprehensive programs are systematic and focused. A career development system within a business is "an organized, formalized, planned effort to achieve a balance between the individuals' career needs and the organizations' workforce requirements" (Leibowitz, Farren, & Kaye, 1986, p. 4). The remainder of this chapter focuses on the rationale for design and implementation of comprehensive career development systems. This discussion is based on the assumption that the career development program is an internal entity. However, some consulting firms, such as BDI (2010), offer outsourced career development programs to businesses in the Chicago area. Other consulting firms, such as CareerTrainer in San Jose, California, offer consulting and outsourcing services as well.

Rationale

Knowdell (1982, 1984) suggested that one of the primary forces behind the emergence of career development programs in business and industry has been external pressure to provide equality of employment opportunity. Many businesses have been pressured to demonstrate fairness in their recruitment, retention, and promotion procedures. Career development programs that make employees aware not only of their own potential but also of job openings within the company have been seen as one means of enhancing equal employment.

London and Stumpf (1986) noted that the impetus for career development programs may be primarily internal to the business. They suggest that such programs are needed to develop career motivation that they believe is based in career resilience, career insight, and career identity. Career resilience reflects workers' abilities to keep positive perspectives even when their careers are not going as well as they would like. Career insight has to do with personal realism about one's own career potential and requires feedback about performance to develop. Career identity is the extent to which workers' personal identities are related to their careers and are reflected in their career directions and goals.

Leibowitz, Farren, and Kaye (1986) also suggested that the current rationale for developing a career development program grows out of meeting internal needs rather than succumbing to external pressure. Career development programs allow businesses to make better use of their employees' skills; to increase the loyalty of employees; to enhance communication; to increase employee retention; to contribute to the effectiveness of personnel systems, such as performance appraisal and promotion; and to help classify organizational goals. These organizational benefits accrue because managers and employees learn how to manage their own careers and increase their understanding of the organization and its policies. They are also better able to give and receive feedback about their performances, establish realistic goals about their careers, and increase the sense of personal responsibility for themselves.

Reports from business organizations such as the National Alliance of Business (1986) and programs such as the UAW-Ford program (1987, 2005, 2010a), have made corporate executives aware that it will become increasingly important for corporations to develop and enhance their current employees' work-related capabilities if they are to remain competitive. The labor force of most businesses will be in place for the next 10 to 15 years, and well-conceived corporate strategies designed to orient, train, and promote current workers will enhance organizational functioning. In short, many corporate executives are concluding that career development programs are good business.

INITIATING THE PROGRAM

Early Steps

Initiating a successful career development program requires certain prerequisites. Among the more important of these are sanctions from top-level executives. Career development programs require various types of organizational changes, and without support from the power structure these changes are unlikely to occur. One CEO sent a memorandum to all managers that "career development will be our number one priority." Not surprisingly, that corporation has one of the finest career development programs in existence.

Establishing a budget to support the program is also an important early step. Choosing a manager who can develop the program is also an important prerequisite to change. The credentials of the manager and the amount budgeted for the development of the program depend on the type of program to be developed. The manager should be knowledgeable about career development, testing, and career counseling. Moreover, a successful manager needs a basic understanding of organizational functioning, management principles and practices, as well as of the general area of human resource planning and development. Specialized knowledge of management information systems, performance appraisal systems, personnel selection and development practices, instructional technology, and a host of other skills would of course be useful to the manager of a career development program.

Budgeting for the career development program requires setting forth a developmental budget as well as an operating budget. The initiation of a program in a major corporation can easily cost $300,000 to $400,000, again depending on the nature of the program. A budget for the development of a career development program should include the following lines:

- Manager's salary
- Support personnel salaries
- Consultant's fees/expenses
- Travel expenses to model programs
- Materials acquisition
- Furnishings—desks, bookcases
- Equipment, including computers and printers
- Web site development
- Printing in-house materials, brochures, and so forth
- Training expenses (orienting managers, training workshop leaders)

The actual cost of operating the program may in fact be quite modest depending on the size of the corporation and the type of programs to be delivered. The budget for the program will contain many of the aforementioned budgetary lines, although the amounts for consultants' fees, travel, materials acquisition, equipment procurement, furnishings, printing, and training should be reduced greatly. However, an additional line—evaluation costs—should be added to the operating cost budget.

One additional step should be taken at the outset of the program: determining an organizational niche for the career development program. Typically, these programs are placed under the umbrella of the vice president or director of human resource development (HRD). Leibowitz, Farren, and Kaye (1986) note the importance of the current HRD effort in most corporations, which involves activities such as training new hires and veteran employees, posting job vacancies, evaluating the compensation plan, enhancing employee performance appraisal, and designing a career development program that enhances all these efforts. For example, one of the jobs assigned to an HRD manager is inventorying the available labor supply (i.e., determining the skills available to focus on the mission of the organization). The career development program can be designed in a manner that enhances the assessment of employees' skills and thus improves this effort. The career development program can also be instrumental in identifying which employees are engaged in acquiring various types of new skills, thus making the forecasts of needs to recruit employees outside the corporation more accurate.

Needs Assessment

Accurately assessing employee needs is another important early step in the design of a career development program. The needs assessment should be designed in a manner that answers several key questions, including What is the extent of our need for career development programming? and, What type of program should we have? However, several questions must be answered prior to embarking on a needs assessment: What data collection procedure should be employed? What domains of employee concerns should be sampled? How will the needs of special groups of employees be identified?

DATA COLLECTION PROCEDURES   Some corporations have used employee interviews to determine their need for a career development program. This may be satisfactory as a means of ascertaining top-level management's perceptions of needs, but the process is generally too time consuming and expensive to use with all employees. A questionnaire should be sent either to a random sample or to all employees, depending on tradition and preference. Obviously, sampling reduces the cost, but if the corporation routinely surveys all employees in its data-gathering efforts, a census should be conducted.

The extent to which follow-up procedures are employed to increase return rates depends on factors such as the availability of funds and representatives of return rates. Every effort should be made to ensure that returns are both representative of the employees and accurate in their portrayal of employee attitudes. With regard to the latter, every effort should be made to guarantee employee anonymity if the returns are accurately to reflect employee career development needs. Some corporations use outside firms for data collection as one means of ensuring confidentiality. If this is not possible, questionnaires can be posted on the company's Intranet and returned to a secure server.

DOMAINS TO BE SAMPLED   The needs assessment questionnaire should be designed to collect information in the following domains: (1) desire for assistance with career planning; (2) preferred source of assistance with career development (e.g., manager, career counselor); (3) preferences for types of career development activities; (4) aversions, if any, to career development activities; and (5) evaluation of current career development activities (if they exist).

Desire for Assistance.   If you build it, will they (the employees) come? An early study showed that as many as 77 percent of employees may participate in some aspects of the career development program (Wowk, Williams, & Halstead, 1983). My guess is that, given the current employment situation, the percentages of people who would participate would be higher. However, it is important for program design purposes to know how many people expect to participate and to be able to estimate when they might participate if various types of career development activities are made available. Thus, direct questions regarding employees' interest in participating in the career development program should be included in the instrument. So should indirect indicators of interest, such as degree of satisfaction with current position. Workers who are dissatisfied with their current jobs may very well be the first to volunteer to participate in the program. Typical questions might ask the following:

1. Rate your interest in exploring other career opportunities within the company.
2. Indicate the extent to which you are satisfied in your current position.

Source of Assistance. It is possible to deliver career development services through managers, career counselors employed by the corporation, external consultants, computerized programs, and so forth. Employees should be queried with regard to the people and/or delivery services they think would be best in providing career development services. If an outside firm is being considered, reactions to this option should be explored. All possible options considered feasible by the managers in charge of program development can be presented on a questionnaire such as the following for reaction:

1. Indicate the extent to which you would find each of the following people acceptable as sources of assistance with your own career planning:
   a. Your immediate supervisor
   b. A professional career counselor employed by the corporation
   c. A career counselor outside the corporation who would be brought in to provide assistance to employees
   d. Other—please specify

Preferences and Aversions to Career Development Activities. Recently, at a meeting of representatives from a corporation considering the implementation of a career development program, a debate arose about the wisdom of using a particular personality inventory as part of a career development program. This debate highlighted that some individuals are uncomfortable with values and personality inventories, and perhaps other activities, that are often included in career development programs. It is therefore important to ascertain how employees feel about activities such as discussions of interests, values, personality, decision-making style, and career change. If widespread aversion exists to activities such as taking and discussing work values inventories, either among managers or employees, these should either not be included in the program or should be designated as optional activities. If employees feel uncomfortable with an activity, it is unlikely that their responses to questions or their participation in the activity will reflect their true values or attitudes. Items for sampling attitudes in this domain might include a variety of options:

1. The following is a list of activities that are often included in career development programs. Please rate the extent to which you would feel comfortable participating in each:
   a. Completing an interest inventory
   b. Completing a personality inventory
   c. Discussing your work values
   d. Discussing long- and short-term career goals

    e. Discussing your ideal work setting

    f. And so forth

Evaluation of Existing Efforts.   Most companies have some aspects of a career development program, usually in the form of job-related feedback during performance evaluation. All aspects of a program currently in place should be evaluated in the needs assessment process so decisions can be made about their retention and/or modification. It is also useful to ascertain whether employees are aware of the new opportunities being offered by the corporation, such as paid educational experiences, in-house staff-development sabbatical programs, and so forth. These activities become more important as the career development program evolves and people take active roles in managing their own careers. The needs assessment may point to an increased need for information about these programs or even to modifications that need to be made in them. Sample items might include the following:

    1. To what extent has your performance appraisal been useful to you in your career planning?

    2. Rate the degree to which the corporate educational leave policy is useful to you.

IDENTIFYING SPECIAL NEEDS   The design of the career development program can be enhanced by sampling the aforementioned five domains. However, the needs assessment is not complete unless it focuses on the special needs of various subgroups of employees, such as women, minorities, and new hires. Federal legislation such as the American with Disabilities Act, the Equal Employment Opportunities Act and state level legislation in some states that prohibits discriminations against gays and lesbians has sharpened this focus and increased the need for a careful needs assessment for all groups.

    The purpose of a career development program is to benefit both the company and the employee by helping to develop employee potential. As noted earlier, corporations that fail to develop talent from within find themselves hard-pressed to compete (e.g., National Alliance of Business, 1986). The career development program must be designed not only to identify talent but also to help develop that talent.

    The needs assessment questionnaire should be designed to determine the extent to which new hires and others understand the corporate occupational structure and the degree to which it offers them opportunities for advancement. These data may be useful in designing employee recruitment and orientation programs as well as in providing information to employees who have considerable tenure with the company.

    The career development needs assessment should also be structured so that it identifies barriers to career mobility. Women may have child care problems; minorities and poor whites may have had few educational opportunities or may have attended substandard schools. Both groups may have observed or experienced discrimination. For example, a 1988 Gallup survey revealed that 62 percent of the African Americans surveyed had observed discrimination in the workplace, either directed toward themselves or others (NCDA, 1988). In 1999 the NCDA reported that 73 percent of the adult workers surveyed responded that there was no discrimination in their workplaces, whereas 8 percent indicated that both women and minorities were discriminated against. Seven percent of those surveyed believed that white people were discriminated against in their workplaces.

    Many corporate executives are extremely sensitive about asking questions on the employee survey about emotionally laden issues such as discrimination. Although this is understandable, if a decision is reached not to ask these questions on the needs assessment questionnaire, other means of ascertaining this information should be devised, such as hiring external consultants to conduct interviews with various groups of employees.

The special needs of subgroups of employees can be determined if employees are asked to provide certain types of demographic data (e.g., gender, race, employment status, type of job held, and years of employment) and if questions are included in the data collection process that highlight potential problems. Literature reviews of the career development programs encountered by various subgroups can be a useful way of identifying needs that should be addressed.

It would not be unexpected to determine not only that male and female employees have different career development needs but also that employees working in different departments or units have differing concerns. For example, it is literally impossible for the sales staff of many corporations to attend career development workshops, but they can use DVD players and workbooks that address career development issues.

It is also likely that the desire for career development activities varies across departments and units and that the types and levels of activities desired are markedly different. These and the other factors mentioned affect the design of the career development program and should, therefore, be anticipated in the development of a needs assessment questionnaire.

A WORD ABOUT MECHANICS AND PLANNING   As noted earlier, the needs assessment survey may be embedded in a routine employee questionnaire or administered separately. Such typical issues as concerns about confidentiality must be attended to if results are to accurately reflect employee opinions. One atypical concern that arises in the assessment of career development needs is that some managers are concerned that the data collection process itself raises false expectations about career development programming (Leibowitz et al., 1986). This can be avoided in two ways: through a disclaimer or through item selection.

If the career development needs assessment survey is conducted as an exploratory step to provide data for the planning of a career development program, this should be stated in the introduction to the questionnaire. If time lines have been established for the initiation of a program, then these should be stated as well. By telling employees that the company is soliciting employee input as one way of informing the decision-making process regarding the implementation of a career development program, raising false expectations can be avoided. Similarly, if the company plans to implement a career development program two years hence, indicating this on the questionnaire leads to realistic expectations about when the program will be implemented. Also, no questions should be placed on the career development needs assessment questionnaire that are not realistic alternatives for inclusion in the program. For example, if no consideration is being given to the development of a computerized career development system, this should not be posed as an option for delivering the program.

DESIGNING THE PROGRAM

The California Lawrence Livermore National Laboratory program has served as the prototype for many career development programs in other organizations (Knowdell, 1982). The "Livermore Labs" program focuses on career and life planning and has three major components. The first of these is the career resource center (CRC), which contains college catalogs, career information, self-help books, and other information. CRC personnel also assist employees in developing internal or external résumés. The internal résumé is developed for use in pursuing job changes within the organization, whereas the external résumé is used in pursuing a new job outside the corporation. Understandably, many corporations have not included an external résumé development service as a part of their programs.

The second component of the Livermore Labs program is individual career counseling. However, the counselors who provide this service also provide assistance with financial planning, preparation for retirement, family problems, and a host of other concerns (Knowdell, 1982).

Career assessment workshops constitute the third component of the Livermore Labs program. These consist of 40 hours of intensive career exploration. The actual content of individual seminars may vary to some degree. For example, résumés may be developed, interviewing skills may be practiced, and organizational needs may be discussed. Recently, one subdivision of the program, the Management Skills Assessment Program, was soliciting applications from employees who wished to improve their management skills.

One type of information that can be used in developing a career plan is through career paths—a process that identifies sequential lines of career progression in an organization (Leibowitz et al., 1986). As can be seen in Figure 15.1, the entry job for administrative support personnel may be as an office assistant, and the corporate accountant (see Figure 15.2) typically enters the system as a financial systems analyst. These and other career paths are developed on the actual experience of employees who have moved to supervisory and managerial levels and thus reflect the promotion practices of the corporation.

The GlaxoSmithKline pharmaceutical company's program, which was discussed earlier, is parallel in many ways to the Livermore Labs program. However, GSK, as a part of its occupational information program, provides employees with career path information for many of the top supervisory and management positions.

Ford Motor Company, in conjunction with the United Auto Workers (UAW-Ford, 1987, 2005, 2010b), has developed what it terms an employee development and training program. This program uses a series of life/education advisers who conduct one-on-one advising sessions with employees to assist them with educational and personal development planning and goal setting. These advisors also conduct life/education planning workshops; provide information to employees regarding educational, career, and personal growth needs; and collect material about training opportunities.

One of the expected outcomes of the UAW-Ford program is personal growth. A second is educational and career development. However, it is relatively clear that in this program less emphasis is placed on career exploration, interests, and decision making and more emphasis is placed on educational planning than in the other programs discussed.

The Essential Components

Gutteridge (1986) lists five general types of organizational tools: (1) self-assessment tools, (2) individual counseling, (3) internal labor market information/placement exchanges, (4) organizational potential assessment processes, and (5) developmental programs. The Livermore Labs program uses workshops as its essential self-assessment tool. GlaxoSmithKline offers workshops in which assessment devices are administered, scored, and interpreted. It also provides workbooks that assist in self-assessment tools. The UAW-Ford program relies on workshop activities for assessment.

Many corporations provide no individual career counseling with credentialed career counselors. Frequently, supervisors or managers provide "career counseling," coaching, or advice as a part of their performance appraisal meetings. As Gutteridge (1986) noted, this is one of the more controversial aspects of the program. According to Brooks (1984), "Despite claims that

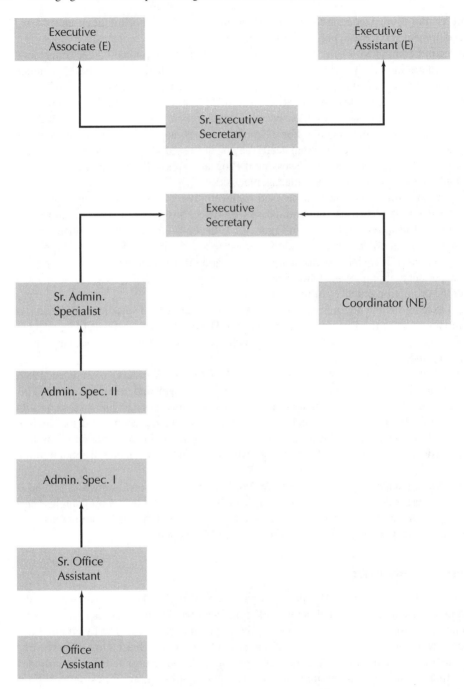

FIGURE 15.1 Career Path for Administrative Support Personnel

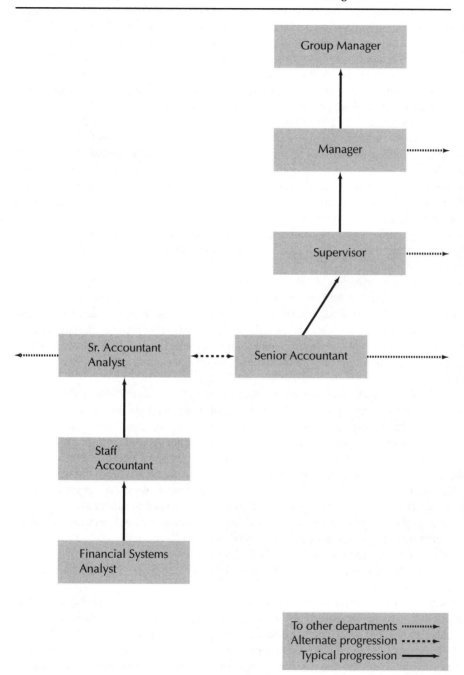

FIGURE 15.2   Career Path for Corporate Accounting

managers can or should provide career counseling for employees, managers seldom have either the skill or the inclination to provide these services" (p. 397). The concept of managers acting as career coaches has a fairly long history and seems to be increasingly popular (Doyle, 1999). The objective of managerial career coaching is performance enhancement. It is typically a one-on-one process that is often initiated during performance appraisal feedback sessions. The keys to the success of career coaching are the manager's ability to (1) identify organizational needs, (2) identify people with the potential to meet those needs, and (3) engage in an employer-employee relationship that will support positive and negative feedback and growth.

Effective career development programs must have adequate descriptions of the duties performed by the workers in their organizations and the minimum requirements (education and skills) for performing those duties. It is also important that information about career ladders/paths be provided and that all information be readily accessible to employees. For those companies that are prepared to assist workers to seek employment outside the corporation, information about careers in the local area, state, and region must be made available. Educational information, like occupational information, may be of two types: internal and external. Most corporations offer ongoing training to employees. Many also offer the opportunities to explore additional education and training outside the corporate structure. Information about these opportunities must also be readily available.

Communicating information about job openings via job postings, usually on the company Intranet, is one aspect of helping employees identify and pursue career opportunities. Helping employees develop internal résumés and job interviewing skills is another important aspect of this function. Often a CRC is established and staffed to provide these services. However, some companies rely on employee newsletters, bulletins posted in employee lounges and other places, and computerized systems to help employees identify job opportunities and to pursue them.

Every successful organization has an ongoing program to assess the potential of its employees to fill key roles in the organization. In the case of upper-level management, succession planning is engaged in making sure that organizational leadership has continuity. Promotability forecasts are also developed, partially on the basis of performance appraisal information. In some instances, promotability forecasts are developed on the basis of performance in assessment centers, although these centers are primarily used to assess potential for supervisory and managerial positions (Gutteridge, 1986). When assessment centers are used, corporate assessors design a variety of individual and group exercises that are related to functioning as a manager. These assessors then form a panel, usually made up of managers who observe and evaluate employees' performance. As Gutteridge (1986) noted, the panel's recommendation is typically in the form of a "go–no go" recommendation. Skills inventories, which are detailed descriptions of the employee's work history, training, and accomplishments, may also be used in making a final decision.

Of the developmental programs that are offered in various organizations, perhaps none has received more attention than mentoring. Kram (1986) suggested that mentoring, which she defines as "relationships between junior and senior colleagues that contribute to career development" (p. 161), serves two functions: psychosocial and career. Career functions are those that help the junior members of the relationships prepare for advancement in their organizations, whereas psychosocial functions enhance their feelings of competency and clarify their identities.

To fulfill the career function, mentors "sponsor" junior members by helping them make interpersonal connections, give feedback about relevant job performance, provide support, create opportunities to demonstrate competence, and provide challenging work opportunities. The psychosocial function is fulfilled by role modeling of appropriate organizational behaviors of personal and professional concern, providing ongoing support and reinforcement, and acting as a friend (Kram, 1986).

Although the obvious beneficiary of the mentoring relationship is the junior member, Kram (1985, 1986) suggests that the senior member benefits as well. Feelings of involvement, making a contribution to the organization, the reciprocal support from the junior member of the dyad, and reliving earlier trials and successes are all benefits of being a mentor.

Mentoring is not without its pitfalls, particularly in cross-gender situations. Martin, Harrison, and DiNitto (1983) reported that cross-gender mentoring can reduce performance as well as feelings of competence and well-being. Kram (1985, 1986) identified five reasons for these outcomes:

1. Anxiety about the boundaries of the relationships develops, particularly concerns about intimacy and sexual attraction.
2. Reliance on traditional sex roles results in a protective attitude by the male and a failure to establish independent roles.
3. Ineffective role modeling is conducted by males because of different expectations for females in male-dominated organizations.
4. Cross-gender mentoring relations are often viewed suspiciously by managers and employees, with the result that the public image of the relationship becomes the primary concern rather than the well-being of the female
5. When a woman working in a male-dominated organization is given special attention, peer resentment results because of concern about "unfair" competition; the result is that the woman is forced to choose between her mentor and her peers, with either choice being detrimental to her development.

Bowen (1985) also reiterated many of Kram's (1985, 1986) concerns about cross-gender mentoring. He concluded from his study that gender-related problems may not be as great as some might anticipate although envy, jealousy by spouses and others, and snide remarks by colleagues can all result from cross-gender mentoring relationships.

Almost everyone agrees that some form of mentoring occurs within most organizations and that it generally facilitates career development, a point that has been substantiated in a number of research studies that examined the careers of managers (e.g., Reich, 1985). Formal mentoring programs where junior hires are linked to senior mentors are increasingly popular, but it seems that the process of assigning mentors to protégés is tantamount to program failure (Kram, 1986). Instead of involuntary assignment, which often leads to resentment and role confusion, it seems best to screen potential mentors carefully, to enlist their voluntary participation in the program, to prepare them to become mentors through formal training about the role of the mentor, to develop mentoring skills, to orient them to the relationship between the mentoring program and the organization and acquaint them with the potential problems associated with cross-gender and cross-cultural mentoring processes, and to allow the mentoring process to occur normally instead of forcing it (Kram, 1985, 1986).

The actual design of each program depends to some degree on employees' needs. It is also related to the resources available, the culture and goals of the organization, and the extent to which the program has been integrated with the other HRD functions. For example, the UAW-Ford (2005) program has turned much of its attention to helping people who have been laid off make the transition to other jobs.

Integration with HRD

The career development program should be designed in a manner that enhances the overall function of the human resources development program. The following are examples of how this may be accomplished.

PERFORMANCE APPRAISAL   This HRD function can be enhanced by designing activities that prepare employees to ask specific questions of their supervisors at the time of the performance appraisal. For example, employees may want to ask the following questions:

- How does my current performance affect my promotability?
- What are my deficiencies and how can I remediate them?
- Based on your knowledge of the company, how can I best prepare myself for advancement?
- What are the strategies that I can employ that will most enhance my current job performance?

Many employees report that their managers are uncomfortable in their performance appraisal sessions, with the result that the sessions are brief and the feedback terse. Of course, managers can also be trained to be more specific in their feedback and in discussing the implications of the employee's performance, and to provide "advice" regarding the directions the employee should take.

TRAINING   Materials about the company's training policies should be included in the CRC and distributed in career counseling sessions as well as in workshops.

JOB POSTING   Employees who participate in the program should be made aware of the job posting procedure as well as general hiring practices.

SKILLS INVENTORIES/PROMOTABILITY FORECASTS   The results of skills profiles developed in workshops can be placed in employees' records and thus help managers gain a more complete picture of the availability of talent and the potential promotability of various employees.

COMPENSATION SYSTEMS   Information gained in workshops regarding employees' perceptions of the fairness and adequacy of the compensation system can be communicated to managers.

PROGRAM IMPLEMENTATION

Leibowitz, Farren, and Kaye (1986) recommend that a career development program be built on existing programs and practices. As already stated, for maximum effectiveness the program should not only be built on existing programs but also be carefully integrated with them (Gutteridge, 1986; Mirabile, 1986). Mirabile (1986) also pointed out that although methodology and program design are important, unless managerial and employee ownership of the program are gained, the program is likely to struggle. Leibowitz, Farren, and Kaye (1985, 1986) suggested that advisory groups made up of managers and employees may be an effective way of gaining the support that is needed to make the career development program viable. Mirabile (1986) provided even more specific suggestions, such as meeting with the executive vice president of the organization to clarify the organization commitment, to solicit input regarding the program's content, and to clarify the goals of the program as they relate to the organization's goal. He also suggested similar meetings with divisional vice presidents, a cross-section of employees, and other key personnel in the HRD organization.

After the program has been designed, a small pilot program should be implemented and evaluated (Gutteridge, 1986; Leibowitz, Farren, & Kaye, 1985, 1986; Mirabile, 1986; Sampson, 2008). The evaluation of the pilot must necessarily have a focus on employee and organizational needs. Early research (Wowk et al., 1983) suggested that when formal career development programs are offered, well over 60 percent of the employees participate in some aspect of the program, with the heaviest participation being in accessing career information. They also report that managers' perceptions of the benefits of the programs include reduced turnover and increased productivity and profitability. However, it has been suggested repeatedly (e.g., Brooks, 1984; Hall, 1990) that we need better-designed evaluation studies that produce information relating to both managerial and employee needs.

The needs assessment discussed at the outset should be one of the reference points in designing the evaluation of the pilot programs. If the program has not met the needs of the participants, it cannot be deemed effective. It is also true that records of attendance, turnover, performance, productivity, and profitability are regularly kept by all organizations, and all existing data sources can be monitored as sources of evaluative data.

Finally, with regard to evaluation, these studies need not always be elaborate. Moravec (1982) reported that a career counseling program saved one bank nearly $2 million in one year by reducing employee turnover, increasing productivity, and enhancing promotability. It seems likely that both managers and employees would be quite satisfied with a program of this type.

Once evaluative data of the pilot program are collected, the program needs to be fine-tuned and offered to employees throughout the organization (Sampson, 2008). Perhaps the only cautionary word that should be added at this juncture is that widespread participation can be expected and that programming for full implementation should take this into account. To reintegrate and expand on the earlier report by Wowk and colleagues (1983), 77 percent of the employees in organizations that offered formalized career counseling programs participated by accessing career information, 74 percent participated in human resource planning, 70 percent took advantage of training and workshops, 61 percent were involved in career evaluation, 60 percent engaged in career counseling, and 47 percent participated in special groups. Although Wowk and her colleagues did not specify the time period in which the participation occurred, 71 percent of the programs surveyed were implemented in the five years prior to their survey, and most of the participation in the programs occurred within a relatively short period of time.

BENEFITS

Even though career counselors in business and industry may need to concern themselves more with corporate profit, they should still be concerned with the impact on individuals of the programs they design. Knowdell (1982) reported that the results of the follow-up of managers and supervisors in Livermore Labs revealed that 66 percent of both groups believed that employee morale had improved, 88 percent of the supervisors felt that the company would recoup the costs associated with the program, and 73 percent of the employees reported making significant changes in their careers or lives as a result of the program.

Schmidt (1990) summarized the evaluation results from a number of programs in her review of the literature on the effectiveness of career development programs in business and industry. For example, in evaluations of the IBM career development program in San Jose,

California, employees reported improvement in their ability to engage in self-assessment and planning. They also reported higher acceptance of responsibility and ownership of their career plan and increased awareness of career opportunities within the company. Schmidt also reported on the successes of programs located in two banks. The managers of the Third National Corporate program reported that the career development program was worthwhile but time consuming (Goodstein, 1987), whereas employees of the National Bank of Washington seemed to have experienced major improvements in their attitudes as a result of the program. Managers in both banks also reported a dramatic improvement in customer deposits, return on assets, and stock returns, all of which were reasons for promoting career development (Johnson & Bell, 1987). The Dow Jones & Company employees and managers reported that communication had improved and that job changes were now viewed more positively by employees as a result of their program (Brozeit, 1986). None of these reports is as dramatic as the one-year saving of $2 million that resulted from the implementation of a career development program in a bank reported by Moravec (1982). However, the reports generally support the idea that both organizational and individual goals are enhanced.

Summary

Although evidence suggests that both employees and employers benefit from career development programs in business and industry, the future of these programs is uncertain because of business cycles, mergers, and the cost of the programs. Increasingly, it is incumbent on career development professionals to be accountable—that is, to show that these programs contribute to the profitability of the company. When programs are developed, they must be tailored specifically to the corporation in which they are lodged, based on the needs and resources of the business. Some programs will be minimal, whereas others will be exemplary. However, the central elements in all programs are accurate information about the jobs in the business; mechanisms to communicate this information; and a system that allows employees to traverse organizational boundaries to pursue, train for, and enter new careers within the organization. Some organizations undoubtedly rely on the technology of computerized systems to deliver these components, whereas others depend more on people-oriented approaches. It is probably the case that both technology and people are needed to deliver high-quality career development programs in business and industry.

Chapter Quiz

T F   1. Career development programs within business organizations are often the result of collaborative efforts between labor and management.

T F   2. The coordinator of the business career development program has many responsibilities, not the least of which is being primarily responsible for the delivery of the content of the program.

T F   3. Hall and others stress that the career development specialist within business organizations must adopt a corporate perspective that is essentially based on profits and is less concerned about the welfare of the employee.

T F   4. One aspect of the GlaxoSmithKline career development program that is unlikely to be found in programs located in educational institutions is feedback about personal characteristics.

T F   5. Career development programs such as the one developed by GalaxoSmithKline are a relatively new phenomenon, probably dating back to the 1980s.

T F   **6.** A major impetus for development of career services programs in business was EEO legislation.

T F   **7.** The evaluation of career development programs in business and industry is based on only one question: Did it add to the bottom line of the business?

T F   **8.** It is fairly easy to predict what will happen to career development programs during recessions: The number of programs will diminish.

T F   **9.** Internal job postings are a typical part of a business career development program.

T F   **10.** Career development programs are typically internal to the organization, but some businesses outsource them to consulting firms.

T (10) T (9) F (8) F (7) T (6) F (5) F (4) F (3) F (2) T (1)

References

BDI. (2010). Business decisions incorporated. Retrieved from http://www.businessdecisions.com/partners.asp.

Bowen, D. D. (1985). Were men meant to mentor women? *Training and Development Journal, 44,* 30–34.

Brooks, L. (1984). Career planning in the work place. In D. Brown, L. Brooks, et al. (Eds.), *Career choice and development: Applying contemporary theories to practice* (pp. 386– 405). San Francisco: Jossey-Bass.

Brozeit, R. K. (1986). If I had my druthers. *Personnel Journal, 65,* 84–90.

Doyle, J. (1999). *The business coach: A game plan for the new work environment.* New York: Wiley.

GlaxoSmithKline. (2010). Career development. Retrieved from http://www.gsk.com/careers/career-development.htm.

Goodstein, H. (1987). Career planning. *The Bunker's Magazine, 170,* 58–64.

Gutteridge, T. G. (1986). Organizational career development systems: The state of the practice. In D. T. Hall et al. (Eds.), *Career development in organizations* (pp. 50–94). San Francisco: Jossey-Bass.

Hall, D. T. (1990). Career development theory in organizations. In D. Brown, L. Brooks, et al. (Eds.), *Career choice and development* (2nd ed., pp. 422–454). San Francisco: Jossey-Bass.

Johnson, P., & Bell, D. (1987). Focused vision for focused performance. *Training and Development Journal, 45,* 56–59.

Knowdell, R. L. (1982). Comprehensive career guidance programs in the workplace. *Vocational Guidance Quarterly, 30,* 323–326.

Knowdell, R. L. (1984). Career planning and development programs in the workplace. In N. C. Gysbers et al. (Eds.), *Designing careers* (pp. 482–507). San Francisco: Jossey-Bass.

Kram, K. E. (1985). *Mentoring at work.* Glenview, IL: Scott, Foresman.

Kram, K. E. (1986). *Mentoring in the workplace.* In D. T. Hall et al. (Eds.), *Career development in organizations* (pp. 160–201). San Francisco: Jossey-Bass.

Leibowitz, Z. B., Farren, C., & Kaye, B. L. (1985). The 12-fold path to CD enlightenment. *Training and Development Journal, 43,* 29–32.

Leibowitz, Z. B., Farren, C., & Kaye, B. L. (1986). *Designing career development systems.* San Francisco: Jossey-Bass.

London, M., & Stumpf, S. A. (1986). Individual and organizational career development in changing times. In D. T. Hall et al. (Eds.), *Career development in organizations* (pp. 21–49). San Francisco: Jossey-Bass.

Martin, P. Y., Harrison, D., & DiNitto, D. (1983). Advancement for women to hierarchical organization: Analysis of problems and prospects. *Journal of Applied Behavioral Science, 19,* 18–33.

Mirabile, R. J. (1986). Designing CD programs the OD way. *Training and Development Journal, 44,* 38–41.

Moravec, M. (1982). A cost effective career planning program requires a strategy. *Personnel Administration, 27,* 28–32.

National Alliance of Business. (1986). *Employment policies: Looking to the year 2000.* Washington, DC: Author.

National Career Development Association. (1988). *Planning for and working in America: Report of a national survey.* Alexandria, VA: Author.

National Career Development Association. (1999). National survey of working America. Available at www.ncda.org, accessed 11/29/01.

Osipow, S. H. (1982). Counseling psychology: Applications in the world of work. *Counseling Psychologist, 10,* 19–25.

Reich, M. H. (1985). Executive views from both sides of mentoring. *Personnel, 62,* 42–46.

Sampson, J. P., Jr. (2008). *Designing and implementing career programs: A handook for effective practice.* Broken Arrow, OK: National Career Development Association.

Schmidt, S. (1990). Career development programs in business and industry. *Journal of Employment Counseling, 27,* 76–83.

UAW. (2010). About the UAW. Retrieved from http://www.uaw.org/about/barg.cfm.

UAW-Ford. (2010). The Ford-UAW apprenticeship program. Retrieved from http://www.uawford.com/jac_frameset.html.

UAW–Ford. (1987). *Life education planning program.* A status report in the UAW–Ford program. Dearborn, MI: UAW–Ford National Development and Training Center.

UAW–Ford. (2005). UAW–Ford report. Retrieved from www.uaw.org/contracts/03/ford/ford15.cfm

Wilbur, C. S., & Vermilyea, C. J. (1982). Some business advice for counseling psychologists. *Counseling Psychologist, 10,* 29–30.

Wowk, R., Williams, D., & Halstead, G. (1983). Do formal career development programs really increase employee participation? *Training and Development Journal, 44,* 82–83.

16

Program Evaluation and Evidence-Based Practice

Things to Remember

- The difference between research and evaluation
- The role of research and evaluation in promoting evidence-based practice

- Two models of program evaluation and how they are applied
- The difference between formative and summative evaluation

Chapter 12 dealt with career development programming in public schools. It drew on the ASCA National Model (2005) for its rationale for a number of reasons, not the least of which was the model's emphasis on results reports and accountability. However, the need for program evaluation goes far beyond K–12 institutions. Every institution or agency that fields a career development program should regularly evaluate the processes, outcomes, and contributions of the components to the impact of the program in order to generate accountability data and provide information that can be used to improve the program.

Accountability is the presentation of data and other information to stakeholders regarding the outcomes of a program. These reports should demonstrate why a program should be retained, areas where the program requires strengthening, and in some instances why the program should be discarded. It is perhaps unfortunate, but the termination of programs is relatively rare. However, a few years ago programs aimed at preventing drug use by children and adolescents were instituted in many public schools as a result the funding provided by the Drug Free Schools Act. Evaluations of these programs in a number of schools consistently suggested that the programs were not effective in attaining their primary objective and as a result they were terminated.

Generally speaking evaluation is the process by which the needs to be addressed by the program, the nature of the program processes (formative evaluation), and the worth or outcomes (summative evaluation) of a program are determined. A corporate board may ask, "Is the career development program worth the money that is being invested in it? Does it positively affect our bottom line?" Boards of education faced with decreasing budgets may wonder if the career development program is as worthwhile as a reading program or some other academic program? Community and four-year colleges may ask similar questions. An individual in private practice may ask two types of questions: "Does the income from the business justify the effort and investment in the practice?" and "How effective are the services that I offer?" It should be clear that one of the purposes of evaluation is to inform decision-makers who may alter, promote, or terminate the program. The second and related purpose is to answer questions about the effectiveness of the program and its components so that it can be improved by eliminatiing ineffective practices and replacing them with new, more efficacious practices. As was pointed out in Chapter 12, there is increasing interest in what are termed evidence-based practices.

Well-designed programs rely on evidence-based practices if they are available. Such practices are rooted in the results stemming from rigorous research. Carey, Dimmitt, Hatch, Lapan, and Whiston (2008) suggested that the "gold standard" for this research is the traditional experimental model, although they agreed that other models such as quasi-experimental ones may be used as well to produce strong or promising evidence. It is not clear whether these authors intended to omit qualitative designs from their list of research designs that could be used to produce evidence-based products, but it is my view and the view shared by many (e.g., Brantlinger, Jimenez, Klinger, Pugach, & Richardson, in press) that carefully conducted qualitative research has a place in the process.

When Carey and his colleagues (2008) speak of evidence-based practice, they are referring to strategies that can be applied across settings or interventions that have ecological validity. Although such validity is an important prerequisite to recommending that a program or intervention be endorsed as evidence-based, it need not be a concern for program evaluators. One of the major distinguishing factors between research and evaluation is concern about contextual or ecological validity. Program evaluators are focused on the worth of a technique, strategy, or program in the setting in which it was implemented. In a limited sense program evaluation has the same goal as research, to produce evidence that a technique, intervention, or program has the desired outcome in a more circumscribed setting. Therefore program evaluators must select reliable, valid measures of the "what" (program outcomes), use randomly assigned treatment and comparison groups, use appropriate statistical analysis, and conduct follow-up studies to determine if positive outcomes are maintained over time. They will also wish to replicate the use of the technique or program in their own agency or institutions.

Program evaluation begins at the point that the program is designed and the objectives written. The objectives are the roadmap for the evaluation process, and the more carefully crafted they are, the simpler the design of the evaluation becomes. Well-written program objectives indicate who will be affected, when the intervention will be completed, and what the outcome will be. The "where" issue may also be included in the objective if the settings are a concern. For example, some interventions may be delivered in the career resource center while others may be offered in classroom settings and still others in the counselors' offices. The setting or place of the intervention is often implied. Career counseling is offered in counselors' offices. One-credit career classes will be offered to group of students in classroom settings.

LEVELS OF QUESTIONS

Program objectives and thus outcome measures may be simple or complex and may include the measures that are to be used to determine outcomes (e.g., ability self-ratings). An example of a simple objective has to do with the numbers or percentages that may use the career development program within a specified period of time. The evaluation of this objective may involve the career resource center's secretary keeping a record of the names of people who come to the center. The number of people plus the number of visits can be counted and a report of the results written and disseminated. This type of objective says nothing about the expected impact of the visits on the clients, and thus the evaluation ignores possible outcomes. This is not to suggest that simple numbers may not indicate outcomes that have occurred as a result of client participation. A high school counselor may wish to know if individual educational planning sessions with second semester juniors produced higher numbers of college applications during the subsequent fall than was the case during the previous fall. Because many college admissions offices require applications for admissions to be signed by one of the counselors in the student's school, the counseling staff could make a notation on their calendars for each application signed. Later tallies can be made and a comparison between the baseline and post leave post intervention as is intervention period be made. The results would be a rough estimate of the outcomes of the individual planning sessions, but it might be sufficient for local purposes. However, the data produced with this relatively weak evaluation design would not allow counselors to conclude that they had in fact developed an evidence-based approach to increasing college admissions. In the next section types of evaluation designs will be considered, some of which can be used to establish evidence-based practices in a local setting.

EVALUATION DESIGNS

In 2005 Brown and Trusty, drawing on the work of Firestone (1987), Patton (1980, 1997), and others, set forth the following taxonomy of evaluation models:

  I. Quantitative models (approaches that paint a numerical picture)
    A. Pre-experimental designs
    B. Experimental and quasi-experimental models
    C. Descriptive designs
    D. Observational designs
    E. Correlational designs
  II. Qualitative designs (approaches that paint a word picture)
    A. Case studies
    B. Ethnography
    C. Focus groups
  III. Mixed evaluation models (includes strategies from both I and II)

Before proceeding, it is important to note that the quantitative and qualitative evaluation models grow out of logical positivism and constructiveness philosophies (see Chapter 2) respectively and should generally be used to evaluate interventions and programs anchored in these philosophies. However, there are times when the approaches used together provide complementary information that better answer the questions being asked than either one used separately.

Pre-Experimental Designs

Let's return to the example given earlier of the school counseling staff that wants to determine the effectiveness of a college advising program. They collected baseline data in the fall of 2008, involved all students in one-on-one post–high school planning sessions with an emphasis of going to college in the spring of 2009, and counted the number of students who made college applications in the fall of 2009. They found that the number of college applications increased by 20 percent. Was the program effective? It is impossible to tell because of external threats to the validity of the design and for a variety of other reasons.

External validity has to do with things outside the program that may influence the outcomes. Several factors may have increased the number of college applicants. Teachers may have become aware that the counselors were intent on increasing college applications and "helped" by identifying and advising students to consider college attendance. Parents might have acted in a similar fashion. A local bank may have increased the amount of money available for student loans. Many factors outside of the experimental design may have skewed the results. Similarly, "internal variables" my have influenced the outcome. The class of 2009 may have been more intelligent and scored higher on college admissions tests than the class of 2008. The counselors themselves may have inadvertently paid more attention to the class of 2009 as well. The bottom line is that it is probably wise to avoid using pre-experimental designs in program evaluations. The U.S. Department of Education Institute for Education Sciences (2003) concluded that pre-experimental designs yield faulty information.

Quasi-Experimental and Experimental Evaluation Designs

Experimental designs are nearly impossible to use in applied settings because a number of variables must be manipulated, not the least of which is random assignment of clients to treatment and control groups. An example illustrates this point: A college counselor wishes to determine the efficacy of a small group approach in the development of job interviewing skills. She advertises the group sessions and assigns 20 volunteers to treatment and wait-list control groups using a random number generator. Students in both groups are asked to participate in a job interview session with a trained interviewer who is instructed to follow a set interview protocol with all 20 students. After samples of interview behavior are obtained the wait-list control groups is told that their training will have to be postponed for five weeks because one trainer is no longer available. The treatment is administered by a person who is unaware of the specific objectives of the study. After five weeks both groups are once again asked to provide a videotaped sample of their interview behavior using the same interviewer, and a reliable rating protocol is used to rate the pretreatment and posttreatment interview behavior. After five weeks both groups are once again asked to provide a sample of their interview behavior and their behavior is once again rated by trained raters.

According to the counselor, the evaluation design outlined in the foregoing paragraph has many advantages. We in each case listed below pertains to the evaluators

1. We have a check on the equivalency of the groups because we have collected and rated interview behavior prior to the interventions and ruled out the possibility that it is the pre-interview test not the intervention that accounted for observed outcomes.
2. We have control for "history"—that is, the impact of some historical event such as a popular magazine or newspaper publishing a series on interview behavior. If that had occurred, it seems likely that it would have impacted both groups equally.
3. Because we have a follow-up data collection point for the first experimental group, we have an opportunity to determine if the first experimental group maintains the skills that were identified at the first posttest

There are some advantages and a few disadvantages to the experimental study outlined here, but the major disadvantages of this design if used in an applied setting are lack of randomization of treatment and control group assignment, training a colleague to administer the treatment to minimize experimenter bias, and postponing treatment for some students. Because of the complexities of experimental designs, career counselors in applied settings often use quasi-experimental designs.

Why are these designs called quasi-experimental designs? The most frequent answer has to do with the control groups used in applied settings; it is rarely possible to randomly assign clients to treatment and control groups. Typically the evaluator uses one of two approaches to deal with this problem. The first is to look for a control group that by most estimates is *similar* in as many aspects (e.g., age, race, gender, SES) as possible to the experimental group. The second approach to dealing with a nonrandomized sample is to apply a statistical technique called analysis of covariance to minimize the effects of differences. Often both matching and statistical control are utilized to minimize the possibility that the design will yield erroneous results. There are no totally satisfactory approaches to eliminating the bias introduced as a result of using a nonrandomized approach, but these evaluation designs are often used by program evaluators faced with the impossibility of using fully randomized designs.

It comes as a surprise to some professionals that N = 1 or single-subject designs are included under the general rubric of experimental designs, or more specifically quasi-experimental deigns. Single-subject designs have been used for more than 70 years to establish causal relations at the individual subject level (Horner et al., in press). However, these designs are rarely used by evaluators who are examining the outcomes of career development interventions, perhaps because most career development interventions are delivered in groups. It is also the case that single-subject designs are typically utilized when the interventions target relatively simple behaviors, such as visits to the career resource center. It is also the case that while it is possible to document what is termed experimental control by using reversal designs such as ABAB designs, these techniques require that the intervention be withdrawn and then reinstituted after the problem or issue returns, which most professionals view as unethical. Moreover, threats to external validity can only be established through extensive replication.

Descriptive Designs

It is likely that descriptive designs are the techniques most frequently used by evaluators of career development programs. Four designs fall into this category: (1) survey, (2) correlational, (3) observational, and (4) causal comparative (Brown & Trusty, 2005). Only survey designs will be discussed here because the others have limited utility in program evaluation.

Experimental and quasi-experimental designs are used to answer causal questions, such as, Did the career development interventions "cause" changes in certain behavior (e.g., job search skills), self-perceptions (e.g., self-efficacy, self-concept) or other psychological variables (e.g., attitudes). As the title (experimental/quasi-experimental) implies, descriptive designs are primarily used when the evaluator wishes to describe what occurred often on the basis of self-reports. For example, descriptive designs might be used to determine the following:

1. How many times client groups visit the career resource center
2. How many clients found jobs after visiting the center
3. How many students had entered their stated occupational five years after graduation
4. Clients' perceptions of the worth, value, or quality of the services they received from career counselors
5. The demographic characteristics of students who use the service
6. The perceptions of the career development program by nonusers of the service, such as parents and supervisors
7. How clients rank-order the influence of persons who had an effect on their career choices
8. Clients perceptions of the degree to which they achieved their goals as a result of career counseling.

THE PROCESS OF SURVEY RESEARCH

When designing a survey evaluation, several questions must be addressed. The most important of these has to do with the data needed to inform stakeholders about the effectiveness of the program. Once this is determined other questions can be addressed. Another question that must be answered pertains to the financial and other resources available to support the evaluation project. The answer to the resources question will influence the issue of the approach used to collect the data. Mailed surveys are expensive. Consider that duplication, postage, stationery, scoring, and collating the data may cost as much as five dollars per person. Costs can be reduced by using questionnaires that can be scored and the data collated by computer. Using e-mailed questionnaires with encrypted responses is an increasingly popular strategy for collecting survey responses, but a certain amount of technological competency is required to use this approach, particularly if the responses are to be collated as they are returned. Telephone surveys can also be utilized under certain circumstances, but they are labor intensive at the point of data collection and later in data collation. The data collection vehicle will provide some of the cues to the design of the questionnaire as will the target group to be surveyed. Regardless of the survey methodology employed, every consideration must be given to maintaining the confidentiality of the responses and motivating person to respond. One motivational technique that is probably underutilized is entering all respondents who wish to furnish their names and telephones numbers in a lottery and awarding a cash prize to the winner.

I was employed to evaluate the quality of the advising program in a North Carolina community college. There had been many complaints about the program, particularly the availability of advisors and the accuracy of the information they provided. The focus of the evaluation was clear and I decided that since the survey instrument was brief to conduct a series of telephone interviews with samples drawn from the college transfer program and the vocational programs. Programs such as nursing were omitted from the study because students who entered the program were required to follow a well-advertised, lock-step curriculum. The questions that were designed dealt with the availability of the advisors and the accuracy of the information they provided. Institutional policy required advisors to post a schedule of advising hours and to be in their offices during those hours. Advisors were also required to provide their advisees with a schedule of when they would be available for telephone advising sessions to accommodate students who were not on campus during scheduled in-office advising times.

As I drafted questions, an administrative issue arose: "Should I have students identify their advisors and thus evaluate individual behavior?" The decision, which was out of my hands, was no. The interview protocol began with the collection of some demographic data—whether the student was full-time or part-time, their major or curriculum, and how far they commuted to attend classes. At the beginning of the conversation with students, they were told that names were not being entered on the response sheet, that the information would be reported as group data, and the purpose of the interview was to collect data that would be used to improve the community college. Students were asked to respond *yes* or *no* to the following questions that were posed about the advising system:

1. Do you know your advisor's name? _____

2. Do you know his or her location on the campus? _____

3. Are you aware of your advisor's in-office advising schedule? _____

4. Are you aware of his or her telephone advising schedule? _____

5. In the past three months have you tried to see your advisor in his or her office during posted advising hours? _____

6. Was he or she available when you went to the office? _____

7. During the last three months have you tried to contact your advisor by telephone during the hours when he or she was supposed to be available for telephone advising? _____

8. If yes, was the advisor available when you called? _____

9. Have you ever tried to schedule an in-office appointment for advising? _____

10. Were you able to schedule the appointment? _____

11. Has your advisor ever contacted you regarding your program of studies, schedule, or a related matter? _____

Students were then asked to answer the following questions by providing the type of information specified:

12. During the past few months, how many times have you tried to contact your advisor? _____

13. How many times were you able to contact your advisor? _____

14. If you have been able to contact your advisor during the past three months, please rate the helpfulness of your contact(s). Check as many as apply.

_____ **a.** Advisor was knowledgeable and provided the information I needed

_____ **b.** Advisor was unable to provide the information I needed but got back to me promptly with the necessary information.

_____ **c.** Advisor was unable to provide the information I needed and did not get back to me.

_____ **d.** Advisor gave me incorrect information

_____ **e.** Other _____

Overall I would rate my experiences with my advisor as

_____ **a.** Very satisfactory

_____ **b.** Satisfactory

_____ **c.** Neither satisfactory nor unsatisfactory

_____ **d.** Unsatisfactory

_____ **e.** Very unsatisfactory

Do you have any final remarks you wish to make regarding the advising system?.

QUALITATIVE EVALUATION STRATEGIES

Three qualitative approaches to program evaluation were identified in the outline presented earlier: case studies, ethnography, and focus groups. Each of these approaches, like the quantitative approaches presented in the foregoing section, are time-consuming and require a great deal of knowledge and substantial resources to use. For example, ethnography is an observational strategy that was developed by anthropologists and sociologists attempting to identify patterns of human behavior. Two of these qualitative approaches lend themselves to program evaluation: case studies and focus groups. I have elected to emphasize only focus groups because of its utility in evaluation of both program process (formative) and outcomes (summative). It also provides information that might not be provided by surveys alone and thus has has the advantage of being a mixed model approach to evaluation. Also, it is my belief that the typical practitioner can learn to use focus groups more easily than the other qualitative strategies listed.

Focus groups, like other qualitative evaluation approaches, can be used to identify attitudes, beliefs, and perspectives within a particular context, which in our case is the career development program. Rennekamp and Neil (n.d.) define a focus group as a grouping together of 6 to 12 people who are similar in one or more ways, are guided through a 60- to 90-minute facilitated discussion on a clearly defined topic with the purpose of collecting information regarding the perceptions of the group members on the topic at hand. They suggest that focus groups can be used in numerous ways, including identifying program needs, program design, program improvement and outcome evaluation. Although it is possible to conduct a focus group by telephone, via an electronic chat room, or through the use of conferencing software, the emphasis here will be on traditional face-to-face focus groups.

In the discussion of quantitative designs, the importance of randomly selected clients was emphasized. Participant selection for focus group is determined by the purpose (questions to be answered) of the group. For example, if the evaluator is interested in the perceptions of people who used the career development program to gain employability skills, the group would be drawn from among clients who were involved in employability skills training. If the evaluator is interested in why certain groups did not use the service, the focus group would be comprised of nonparticipants. Qualitative evaluation shares one of the concerns raised by quantitative evaluators, which is that it is probably best if the evaluation process is left to a person not affiliated with the program itself.

The process for planning and leading focus groups has been discussed in many studies (American Association of Community Colleges, 2009; Mcconnell, 2000; Rennekamp & Neil, n.d.). The following steps have been identified:

1. Identify the major objectives of the meeting. Is the group being formed to identify needs and to examine program processes or program outcomes?
2. Write down five or six specific questions to be answered by the group. Four types of questions are needed:
   A. Opening questions that may focus on the group members' experiences with the program: How many times have you used the services of the CRC? What services have you used?
   B. Questions that begin to focus the attention of the group on the purpose that the group should follow: How did you learn about the CRC? What prompted you to use the CRC? Were there any surprises when you came to the CRC?
   C. Key questions that focus on the primary objective of the group: What have you learned as a result of your experiences? What are you disappointments with your experiences? What else would you like to have learned? How could that have been accomplished?

D. Ending or wrap up questions that bring the group to a close: Have we exhausted the topic of what you learned and your disappointments with your experience? Would anyone like to sum up our conversation today?

The next steps are to decide who will facilitate the group, recruit group members, plan to videotape or make an audio recording of the group if possible, and schedule the meeting in a comfortable setting. The facilitator should be a skilled group leader who is able to involve all of the focus group members in the process, which would hopefully include all graduates of counselor education, counseling psychology, and social work programs.

One departure from typical leadership behavior is note taking if the group conversation is not going to be recorded. As the group moves along certain key ideas, attitudes and judgments will be disclosed by the group members and notations should be made during the group and immediately after the group ends. The facilitator's notes and the notes that arise from the replay of the recording of the group (if available) are the primary basis for the analysis of the data. If possible, more than one person familiar with the objectives of the focus group should review the facilitator's notes and recordings, and their observations should be compared to those of the facilitator. If the purpose of the focus group was to collect summative (outcome) data, the analysis will focus on the statements that pertain to this objective. The rule for the analysis is that it is driven by the objective(s) of the study.

If a transcript of the session is available, Rennekamp and Neil (n.d.) suggest that a process known as indexing may be useful. Indexing involves reading a transcript of the focus group conversation and "coding" critical statements in the margins. For example, if the primary purpose of the focus group is to collect data about outcomes of the group, all comments relevant to that objective might be coded as O1, O2, O3. Redundant outcome comments would be coded in a similar manner (e.g., O1) and other useful information such as process data would be coded using another notation such as P1. If the transcript is prepared on a word processor, the comments coded O1 could be "cut and pasted" into a new document for interpretation. Evaluators could then present summary statements that reflect the opinions, attitudes, and reports of behavior change discussed in the group. This procedure would be repeated with comments coded O2, O3, P1, and so forth. These summary statements then serve as the basis for the evaluator's report.

Audiotapes and videotapes of the focus groups open up other analytic possibilities. Two individuals familiar with the objective of the evaluation could code statements in a manner similar to the one used with transcripts. They could then get together to review these tapes, compare observations, and draw conclusions that would be inserted into the report.

Which Approach to Evaluation?

Generally speaking, programs or interventions based on postmodern philosophy should be evaluated using qualitative designs and programs or interventions rooted in logical positivism should be evaluated using methods rooted in this philosophy. However, using a mixed model of evaluation that includes both approaches may provide information about the program or intervention not yielded by using a single evaluation model. To illustrate this latter point, consider the example of an evaluator in a community college career resource center who wishes to determine the impact of a one credit hour course focused on choosing an occupation. She uses a quasi-experimental design because the comparison group is enrolled in a one hour study skills class. One of the outcomes is that students in the career development class make career choices that are most often aligned with

STUDENT LEARNING EXERCISE 16.1

Are You Ready to Lead a Focus Group?

Experts stress that focus group success depends on careful planning and skilled group leadership. Please rate your group leader's skill using a 1 to 3 scale: 1— needs work; 2— uncertain; and 3— has this skill.

_____ **1.** Can explain the purpose of the group.

_____ **2.** Can move the group from early chitchat to the main purpose of the group.

_____ **3.** Can identify similar ideas from two or more group members and verbalize them for the group.

_____ **4.** Can identify, interpret, and respond to nonverbal communication by group members.

_____ **5.** Can encourage shy group members to participate.

_____ **6.** Can cut off group members who want to dominate the group's time.

_____ **7.** Can recognize cultural differences in verbal and nonverbal ways and respond appropriately.

_____ **8.** Can involve the group in summarizing and terminating the group.

their Holland (1997) interest profile, which suggests that the class is effective. A follow-up focus group that examines the class process might be able to identify critical aspects of the class that were at least partially responsible for the outcome and some observations suggesting that certain aspects of the course were superfluous. This information could be helpful in redesigning the class. Not every evaluation requires the use of both quantitative and qualitative designs, but to reiterate, there are times when the mixed evaluation model is preferred.

Summary

Accountability is increasingly important in an age where shrinking budgets force administrators to make choices about the relative worth of various programs. Although evaluators examining the value of career development programs in business may use different criteria than those working in educational institutions, the need for carefully designed evaluation strategies is critical in all settings. Three models—quantitative, qualitative, and mixed—have been discussed in this chapter. The approaches that have been emphasized—quasi-experimental, survey, and focus groups—are those that seem to have the greatest utility in field or applied settings. The gold standard of evaluation, experimental designs, has much to recommend it, but it is nearly impossible to apply in field or applied settings.

Chapter Quiz

T F **1.** The distinguishing aspect of quasi-experimental designs is that both the experimental and control group are assigned randomly.

T F **2.** Qualitative designs are used to paint a word picture of the program being evaluated.

T F **3.** Qualitative designs are primarily useful as a tool to look at program process.

T F **4.** Single-subject designs are classified as quasi-experimental designs.

T F **5.** It is a truism that program evaluation begins when program objectives are written.

T F **6.** Chat rooms can be used to conduct focus groups.

T F **7.** Indexing is a process used in the analysis of focus group data to identity themes in the comments.

T F **8.** Mailed follow-up surveys have proved to be a relatively inexpensive way to collect evaluation data.

T F **9.** After the purpose of the evaluation is established, focus group facilitators should draw up a list of program participants and group members should be chosen at random from this list.

T F **10.** Every effort should be made to select focus group members who have as little in common as possible in order to achieve diversity in the group.

(1) F (2) T (3) F (4) T (5) T (6) T (7) T (8) F (9) F (10) F

References

American Association of Community Colleges. (2009). Focus group guidelines: Bow to plan and facilitate a focus group. Retrieved from http://plus50.aacc.nche.edu/docs/pubs/TOC/7_ConductingFocusGroupsAndUsingFocusGroupData.pdf

Brantlinger, E., Jimenez, R., Klinger, E., Pugach, M., & Richardson, V. (in press). Qualitative studies in special education. *Exceptional Children.*

Brown, D., & Trusty, J. (2005). *Designing and Leading Comprehensive \School Counseling Programs.* Belmont, CA: Brooks/Cole.

Carey, J. C., Dimmit, C., Hatch, T. A., Lapan, R. T., & Whiston, S. (2008). Report of the National Panel for Evidenced-based school counseling outcome research coding protocol and evaluation of student success skills and second step. *Professional School Counseling, 11*, 197–206.

Firestone, W. A. (1987). Meaning in method: The rhetoric of quantitative and qualitative research. *Educational Researcher, 16,* 16–21.

Holland, J. L. (1997). *Making vocational choices* (3rd ed.). Englewood Cliffs, NJ: Prentice-Hall.

Horner, R. H., Carr, E. C., Halle, J., McGee, G., Odom, S., & Wolery, M. (in press). The use of single-subject research to identify evidence-based practice in special education. *Exceptional Children Journal.*

McConnell, E. A. (September/October 1999). Practical advice for planning and conducting focus groups–Brief article. *AORN Journal, 48*, 280–283.

Patton, M. Q. (1980). *Qualitative Evaluation Methods.* Thousand Oaks, CA: Sage.

Patton, M. Q. (1997). *Utilization-Focused Evaluation* (3rd ed). Thousand Oaks, CA: Sage.

U. S. Department of Education Institute for Education Sciences. (2003). Identifying and Implementing Educational Practices Supported by Rigorous Evidence: A User Friendly Guide. Retrieved from http://www2.ed.gov/rschstat/research/pubs/rigorousevid/rigorousevid.pdf

Trends and Issues: Looking Ahead

17

Trends in the Labor Market and the Factors That Shape Them

Things to Remember

- The major occupational shifts that are occurring in the U.S. workforce
- The factors that contribute to these shifts and will continue to do so in the decade ahead

- The increasing role of minorities in the labor market
- The problems that confront the government and American workers in the years ahead

The workplace in this country has always been in a state of flux, primarily because of technological advances and changing economic conditions. The first industry to experience rapid and dramatic job change was agriculture and that change continues to this day. Millions of people were displaced as tractors and combines replaced horses and hand labor. Technology will continue to change the nature and type of work that people do, but today the impact of the global economy is reshaping the occupational structure as well. However, this chapter is not about understanding the global economy or the nuances of how technology influences job growth and decline. It is about understanding that change in the labor market is inevitable. As a career development professional, you will need to help your clients understand that, during their working lives, they need to monitor their jobs and anticipate changes that may occur. Survival in the modern workplace requires a certain degree of prescience. Unless workers in many industries develop a sense of the changes that are to come, they will be out of work as surely as the coal miners in West Virginia were in the middle of the twentieth century and the textile workers are today.

Some of the changes that are occurring today and will occur in the future have been quite sudden and dramatic, which was the case in 2001 when terrorists crashed two Boeing 767s into the World Trade Center and when hurricane Katrina hit New Orleans in 2005. The jobs of tens of thousands of people were temporarily displaced because of disrupted communications systems, people's reluctance to travel, and reduction in oil consumption that resulted from a sharp decrease in travel. Most change occurs far more gradually as a result of economic cycles, the impact of wage differentials in the United States and the rest of the world on business decisions, the impact of technology, and business consolidations. For example, in 2007 the unemployment rate in the United States hovered at near 4 percent and as a result of a series of economic events rose steadily to nearly 10 percent in 2010 where it stands now.

STUDENT LEARNING EXERCISE 17.1

The matter of jobs in the future has been touched on from time to time throughout this book. Before reading this chapter, test your skill as a futurist and identify three to five trends in the occupational structure of this country as we move toward 2018.

Even given the likelihood that many of the changes that occur within the occupational structure cannot be anticipated even by the savviest prognosticator, predictions about the future of jobs in the U.S. workforce abound. One set of these predictions is considered in this chapter. Predicting the future is hazardous business, and even the best estimates often leave many factors unaccounted for. The risk of error increases with the need for precision and the distance projected into the future. Even though we cannot build a formula that weights all factors accurately, we can usually identify those factors that are most likely to be influential. We can then either proceed on the basis of all other things being equal or, as the Bureau of Labor Statistics does, with a best-case and worst-case approach that identifies the range within which real change is likely to occur. In this chapter, four broad topics that relate to anticipated change and the present structure in the world of work are discussed:

Causes of long-term trends

Causes of short-term trends

The occupational world through 2018

Sources of information on change and structure

The issue of sources of occupational information was addressed in Chapter 8. That leaves three of these issues to be addressed in this chapter. Perhaps the most important of these is what types of jobs will be available both now and in the future. Generally speaking occupational groups can be divided into two sectors: service providing and manufacturing. Alcoa produces aluminum by converting raw materials into finished products. The construction industry converts raw materials into houses, buildings, roads, and so forth. Service-providing groups produce no products. Rather, they offer medical, educational, financial, and custodial services, to name a few. For the most part job growth in this country is occurring in the service sectors and this is expected to continue through 2018 (BLS, 2009a). The second issue addressed is the matter of the specific jobs that are available now and will be in the future. It is this second issue that is of greatest concern to career counselors and other career development professionals. The third issue taken up in this chapter is the *who* of the labor force—that is, the people who fill the jobs that are available in the economy.

CAUSES OF LONG-TERM TRENDS

Technology

In the introduction to this chapter, the impact of technology on agriculture was mentioned. The result of mechanization in farming changed the landscape of America forever as people left the farm to find jobs in cities. Technology continues to have an impact. Just as technology has eliminated jobs in the past, it is currently eliminating jobs and changing the face of others. Table 17.1 presents a list of occupations that are expected to decline in the next eight years (BLS, 209b). By looking at this list, can you tell which occupations are declining because of advances in technology? Offshoring? Other factors? The services of telemarketers are being enhanced by automatic dialers that call the number, wait for a response, deliver a message if an answering machine is reached, and switch to a live telemarketer if a potential client answers. Clerical jobs of all types are another group of occupations that is being impacted by technology, as is shown in Table 17.1. Voice-activated computers, user-friendly software packages that allow workers to do much of their own clerical work, and high-speed scanners are only a few of the reasons these jobs are declining in numbers. Machine operators are being eliminated because computers can be programmed to operate the machines and because old and new operations that require machine operator are being placed in other countries.

TABLE 17.1   Sixteen Occupations with the Projected Greatest Percentage Decline in 2008–2018 Period

Occupation	Projected decline in percentages
Textile winding twisting and drawing out	40.7
Sewing machine operators	33.7
Postal services; clerical	30.3
Lathe and turning machine tool setters	26.7
Order clerks	26.1
Photographic procession machine operations	24.3
File clerks	23.4
Machine feeders and offbearers	22.2
Paper machine setters and operators	21.5
Computer operators	18.6
Postal service clerks	18.0
Multiple machine operators	14.7
Door to door sales	14.8
Electronic equipment assemblers	14.7
Office and administrative support personnel	11.6
Telemarketers	11.1

Source: BLS (2010–2011).Occupational Outlook Handbook, author http://www.bls.gov/oco/

The Global Economy

Fifty years ago the goods and services produced in the United States were consumed in this country. This is no longer true, particularly as it relates to manufactured products. For example, the U.S. trade deficit with China exceeded 226 billion dollars in 2009 (U.S. Census Bureau, 2010), The overall U.S. trade deficit is not entirely due to the importing manufactured goods; most of the oil consumed in the United States is imported from Saudi Arabia, Venezuela, Mexico, and elsewhere. Although the U.S. tends to import more than it exports agricultural products, manufactured goods, and other goods and services produced in this country are sold abroad.

The nature of the global economy goes far beyond exports and imports. Most corporations in this country are multinational, which means not only do they do business with other countries, but they have investments and operations abroad as well. Companies have relocated their customer service operations offshore, and software development and production operations for U.S. companies can be found in places such as Ireland and India. For example, it is likely that the production of this book occurred in India.

For the most part the decision to place production and other aspects of a business is partially an economic one. As can be seen in Table 17.1, the number of sewing machine operators, a major group of employees in the textile industry, is expected to decrease by nearly 34 percent by 2018. Why? In 2007 the average hourly compensation of textile workers in the United States was $21.17 as compared to those of textile workers in Mexico ($3.04), the Philippines ($1.12), and Taiwan ($6.66). In addition, environmental regulations in many countries are far less stringent than those in this country and the cost of commodities such as electricity is lower. The prices of labor and electricity are two reasons that the manufacturing giant Alcoa is exploring building production plants in China.

The United States has also been the beneficiary of foreign leaders' business decisions to locate a portion of their businesses in this country. These decisions have largely been driven by the fact that the United States has the world's largest and most robust economy and that we use the money that we earn to buy products such as automobiles, electronics, and furniture. Toyota, Hyundai, BMW, Mercedes Benz, Sony, and Hitachi have all located major manufacturing and assembly facilities in this country, which have produced thousands of jobs. The location of manufacturing and assembly facilities in the United States is due in some instances to the fact that American labor is not necessarily more expensive than it is in other countries. For example, the labor costs in the auto-producing industries in Germany in 2007 were 16 percent higher than they were in the United States (WikiInvest, 2008). The BLS (2010b) reported that average production labor costs in Germany are generally higher than they are in this country, but labor costs in Japan are about 33 percent less than they are in this country; hourly wages in the Republic of Korea are nearly 50 percent less. Transportation costs, political considerations such as fear of tariffs, and the availability of skilled labor also influence business decisions.

The future portends the continuation of fierce rivalries among both companies and countries to create climates that will attract business investments. These crosscurrents impact the type of work available and the geographic location of that work. Moreover, it impacts the wages paid to workers, the fringe benefits available to them, and the quality of their workplaces.

Finally, to reiterate, the economies of the world are linked. A weak economy in a country that purchases goods and services from the United States hurts businesses and, thus, workers. Similarly, because of the sheer magnitude of our economy, a recession in this country reverberates through the economies and, thus, the labor markets of the world.

OTHER ECONOMIC FACTORS

The global economy is an economic factor that is shaping the labor force in the United States in the future and may be the major one at this juncture. However, there are other economic factors that have profound impacts on the availability of work. For example, we are now in a long-term housing market decline. The housing boom that characterized the early part of the 2010 decade came crashing down as people overestimated their ability to pay for larger, more expensive houses, credit card debt skyrocketed, and banks foolishly extended low interest credit to people with incomes that would not warrant the size of the loans provided. The demand for houses created a great demand for construction workers and businesses that produced building supplies, appliances, furniture, and similar products profited. When the demand for new homes "crashed," people could not sell existing houses and the demand for construction labor and related goods and services diminished precipitously.

Low interest rates generally stimulate growth in the business sector, which in turn influences the number of jobs available. If a business borrows $50 million at 4 percent to expand an existing operation, the annual cost in interest is approximately $2 million per year. If the rate is 8 percent, the cost is $4 million per year. In order to pay off the debt, the business must earn $2 million more and that in itself makes the expansion riskier. The downside of low interest rates is that it makes it harder for the U.S. government to finance its considerable debt because foreign investors may find more lucrative investments elsewhere.

The national debt, which is likely to pass $15 trillion mark within the next few years and translate into over $ 30,400 for every man, woman, and child in the country, will also have an impact on the labor force in direct and indirect ways. In order to pay off the national debt, the government must either stimulate the economy and increase the number and quality of jobs, which increases personal income and thus tax revenue, or raise the tax rate. Increasing taxes to pay down the debt or to fund the government diminishes the amount of money that people have to save or spend on goods and services. When debt increases the ability of the government to provide services is limited because money must be diverted to pay the interest on the national debt. Therefore, a high level of national debt is typically a drag on the economy and reduces economic growth and job creation. The debate in this area is what constitutes a high level of debt? Almost everyone agrees for the first time that the current debt is unsustainable without having a dramatic negative impact on job creation.

The value of the dollar in the currency exchange market is another economic factor that influences job growth. For example, when the value of the dollar is low versus the Japanese yen, businesses in this country that compete with the Japanese have an advantage. Japanese businesses sell goods in the United States and get dollars in return. They then must use the dollars they receive, which are worth relatively less than the yen, to buy yen to pay for goods and services in Japan. Because this exchange buys fewer yen than would be the case if the dollar were worth more than the yen, costs in Japan are driven up and this increases the competitive advantage of U.S. businesses.

Population Factors

In earlier editions of this book, population factors, such as the baby boomers, birth rates, and the influx of minority workers into the labor market, were at the center of the discussion. The BLS (2009a) reports that trends of the past are expected to continue into the future with increases in labor force participation by Hispanics, African Americans, and others. What is not certain is whether these projections account for the 700,000 to 900,000 legal immigrants who enter this country each year (Center for Legal Immigration Studies, n.d.). Also, what is not accounted for by BLS projections is the impact of the approximately 11 million illegal workers who work at a variety of jobs. An illegal worker is someone who did not enter this country in accordaqnce with laws that govern U.S. immigration and thus does not possess a work permit, often referred to as a green card because of its color. The "coyotes" who are involved in arranging illegal passage to this country through Mexico often provide directions for securing illegal work permits. The types of jobs held by illegal workers are typically low-paying jobs in agriculture and construction. Others find jobs as domestic workers, maids and custodians, wait staff workers, retail salespeople, and other similar types of jobs.

The **issues** involving illegal workers are varied. Some Americans want to close the borders and deport all illegal workers. Others wish to establish a procedure by which these workers can become legitimate. It seems unlikely that this country will be able to mount a program to deport 11 million people, although it seems certain that some illegal aliens will be expelled from this country. It is more likely that some type of program will be put into place that allows workers to legitimize their standing in this country. Although they are illegal entrants to this country, they fill a legitimate need for workers in a segment of our labor force. Once they become legitimate parts of the labor force, workers who are now illegal will be in a better position to demand appropriate pay and working conditions, which they rarely receive at this time.

The presence of illegal workers' children in schools has created other issues for school counselors and career development professionals generally. Some of these children wish to continue their education after high school and the matter of in-state versus out-of-state tuition fees for these students has been debated by state legislators across the country. Children born in this country are citizens, but most of the children of illegal immigrant were born in other countries and are not citizens. Other children of illegal workers do not pursue postsecondary education because they are afraid that their parents' status will be jeopardized. The future of the children as workers is also tentative because they are not citizens.

Birth rate, legal and illegal immigration, longevity, and retirement rates are but a few of the long-term population trends that influence the availability of workers in the labor market. The demographics of the labor force are projected to shift in a few categories (BLS, 2009a). For example the percentage of the labor force of Latino heritage is expected to reach 17.6 percent of the workforce by 2018, up from approximately 14 percent in 2008. The percentage of Asian Americans in the workforce is expected to reach 5.6 percent in 2018; African Americans are projected to make up 12.1 percent of the labor force by 2018, which is only a slight increase. White workers are expected to make up less than two-thirds of the labor force in the United States by 2018.

The projections regarding the percent of 16- to 24-year-old workers in the labor force in the coming years is expected to remain relatively stable at 12.7 percent. However, the percentage of the labor force in the 55 and over age category is expected grow and reach 25 percent of the labor force by 2018 as baby boomers age. Workers in their so-called prime working age of 25–55 will account for slightly more than 63 percent of the labor force.

The overall implications of these statistics are difficult to assess. However, given the increase in the oldest group of workers, it can be expected that retirements will influence the availability of jobs for younger workers. But, as has been noted from time to time throughout this book, older workers are electing to continue their careers on a full- or part-time basis in order to maintain their incomes and because the enjoy their work. These decisions may make it more difficult for younger workers to move up in their occupations. Certainly, the workplace will be increasingly diverse. The increase of minorities in the workplace heightens the need to develop an appreciation for cultural differences among the current labor force and among future workers. This may well be the major challenge confronting career development professionals in public schools, postsecondary educational institutions, and in the workplace itself as we look ahead. Advocacy on behalf of minority workers, women, and illegal workers is also needed as we look ahead. Also, it seems likely that workers who speak a second language will be at an advantage because of the nature of the labor force, the presence of a global economy, and the diversity of the clientele served by most businesses.

The Size of Government

Local, state, and national government agencies employ millions of people. Arguments for and against downsizing government at all levels abound. Generally speaking, conservatives favor smaller government and liberals or as they are sometimes termed progressives favor larger government, but these lines have been blurred in recent years. Government agencies are operated at taxpayers' expense and are seen as a burden on the economy by some for that reason. This issue is likely to be debated at length for some time, but should there be a decision to downsize government at all levels, the result would be dramatic.

CAUSES OF SHORT-TERM TRENDS

Several examples of factors producing short-term trends can be identified. Viewed objectively, these usually have less effect than do long-term trends. Nevertheless, to individuals who are caught in the crunch produced by transitory factors, the impact can be devastating. Some influences have a generalized effect across almost the entire economy; others may be more specific.

One of the most obvious causes of short-term trends is various types of calamities, either those caused by humans or by natural disasters. Earthquakes, hurricanes, floods, and volcanic eruptions can disrupt and change occupational patterns in the area for extended periods of time. Unexpected freezes in citrus-growing areas may not only destroy the current crop but also, if trees are seriously damaged, require new plantings that need several years to become productive.

Human disasters can be just as disruptive. War or the threat of war diverts large numbers of workers from civilian occupations to military assignments. It further affects others by switching manufacturing and other sectors to the production of military goods. It may create serious shortages of workers in fields that are considered less essential to the national welfare.

New directions in fashion, recreation, and other activities can also alter the occupational structure by creating new demands or reducing old ones. For example, unisex salons have largely replaced barbershops. Similarly, changes in lapel width and hemline height can make clothing obsolete long before it wears out. Imitation of movie idols, popular athletes, or television stars can create demands where none previously existed. Some technological developments occasionally start as fads (e.g., iPods) and quickly become the basis for large-scale job creation.

Seasonal variations are also influential. Summers tend to increase demand for goods and services in mountain and seaside resorts; winters have the same effect on resorts located in warm areas. The back-to-school season includes buying in retail stores, for which manufacturers have been preparing. Planting time and harvest time change typical patterns in agricultural areas. The annual holiday shopping season creates demand for temporary sales workers, letter carriers, transportation workers, and other workers.

Short-term economic factors also exert an influence. Although the general business trend over long periods is either upward or downward, small segments of that larger trend show considerable variation. Factors that create these short-term zigzags include strikes, unexpected surpluses or shortages of raw materials or processed goods, temporary market disruptions, fluctuations in access to short-term capital caused by changes in interest rates, inflationary pressures, changing tax laws, and sometimes even the anticipation of possible events.

THE OCCUPATIONAL WORLD THROUGH 2018

Having identified some of the factors most likely to create occupational change, the world of work as it is today and as it may be in the near future is examined briefly. The previous discussion pointed out the sudden changes that can occur. Major changes usually take some time to transpire; thus, a projection based on recent trends is usually the safest estimate of what the near future is likely to hold. Most of the attention in this discussion focuses on the period between 2008 and 2018, for which Bureau of Labor Statistics estimates are available.

Projections for the Future

The Bureau of Labor Statistics (2009a, 2009b, 2009c) regularly issues forecasts regarding the various aspects of the labor force. Table 17.2 contains three types of information: a list of the fastest-growing occupations based on numbers and corresponding increase in the percentage of increase in those same jobs as well as information about the education needed to enter the occupations listed.

What do the data in Table 17.2 tell you? The most obvious answer can be found in the column that shows the total number of job openings due to the combination of growth plus openings resulting from workers retiring or leaving the occupation for some other reasons. The second column shows information about the percentage of vacancies expected by 2018 resulting from growth of the occupation. The higher the percentage, the faster the growth, but as can be seen rapid growth does not necessarily translate directly into job openings. The third column presents an estimate of the length and type of training needed for the job. The estimate is a minimum and does not take into consideration the distinct likelihood that factors such as education and experience may be needed for employment.

It is also important to note that many of the jobs with the greatest number of openings in the decade ahead require very little in the way of formal training. However, as has been shown from time to time, the jobs that pay the most require some postsecondary education. Also, there will continue to be jobs for people with relatively little education, albeit low-paying jobs, in spite of the often-stated myth that the jobs for the marginally educated are disappearing.

It is interesting to note that many of the occupations listed in Tables 17.2 in the health care arena. This is related to the fact that people are living longer, but as they age, people require higher levels and more intensive health care. Also, only a very limited number of occupations listed in Table 17.2 deal primarily with technology, which will also be a surprise to many. In a sense, jobs in the future will be where they were in the past with the exception of manufacturing jobs. Many of the jobs listed in Table 17.1, which highlighted the jobs in decline, were in the manufacturing sector.

TABLE 17.2   The 2008–2018 Projections of 20 Occupations with the Largest Number of Job Openings Based on Growth and Replacement, the Percent of Increase Due to Growth, and an Estimate of the Education/Training Needed to Enter the Jobs.

Job Title	Projected openings (in thousands)	Percent/due to growth	Training Required
Cashiers	1720	3.5	Brief OJT
Retail sales	1627	8.4	Brief OJT
Wait staff	1466	6.4	Brief OJT
Customer service reps	1108	17.7	Moderate Term
Registered nurses	1039	22.2	Associate's degree
Fast food workers	967	14.6	Brief OJT
Office clerks	771	11.9	Brief OJT
Laborers, freight movers	746	−.08	Brief OJT
Teachers, elementary	597	15.8	Bachelor's degree
Stock clerks/order fillers	563	1.8	Brief OJT
Truck drivers, heavy	555	13.0	Brief OJT
Janitor/maids/housekeepers	553	4.3	Brief OJT
Teachers, postsecondary	553	15,1	Doctorate
Home health aides	553	50.0	Brief OJT
Child care workers	523	10.9	Brief OJT
General managers	502	−.01	Bachelor's degree + exp
Accountants/auditors	498	21.7	Bachelor's degree
Supervisors	489	111.9	Work experience
Receptionists	480	15.2	Brief OJT
Home care aids	478	46.0	Brief OJT

Source: BLS 2010–2011). Occupational Outlook Handbook. Author. http://www.bls.gov/oco/

Practical Implications

Career development professionals must understand the implications of the changes in the labor market if they are to provide accurate career information to their clients. In Chapter 1, the need to encourage a variety of job choices for ethnic and racial minorities and marginalized groups in general was discussed. With the exceptions of Asian Americans, these groups are overrepresented in the low-paying occupations. At the point they are making occupational decisions, students need to be aware of the long-term economic implications of their choices. Moreover, because of the relationship between education and the availability of high-paying jobs, great effort must be expended to ensure that there is equity in the educational arena as well.

Finally, people who are actively considering a manufacturing occupation need to be aware of its declining status in the U.S. labor force. Currently there is much discussion of green jobs—that is, jobs that will decrease reliance on fossil fuels, replacing them with jobs that produce lower levels of so called greenhouse gases, which some argue is accelerating global warming and climate change However, U.S. workers will still be competing with workers from other countries that earn less money, accept fewer fringe benefits, and, in many instances, try to be more productive than their U.S. counterparts. However, it is worth noting that the lazy American myth that some people have accepted is just that—a myth. The American worker is the most productive worker in the global economy (AP, 2007). In 2007 the average American worker produced $63,885 in wealth compared to Ireland ($55,986) and France ($54,609). A part of this difference can be attributed to the number of hours spent working: U.S. 1,804 hours; French 1,564. However, the number of workers in at least seven Asian countries worked more than 2,200 hours in the same period and produced far less (e.g., China's industrial worker produced $12,642).

Sources of Information on Change and Structure

Whether one is assisting sixth graders to become more familiar with occupations generally, high school graduates to initiate job searches, workers with disabilities to move to compatible jobs, or structurally unemployed workers to find new directions, both helper and client need information about the present and future structure of the world of work as well as about likely change in the near and distant future. Current, useful information is available in a variety of publications.

Information about the current and projected national occupational structure is as close as the Internet. The Bureau of Labor Statistics Web site (http://www.bls.gov) provides up-to-date information on a regular basis.

Summary

One objective in this chapter was to make readers aware that the occupational structure and labor force are dynamic in nature. Some of the major forces that have far-reaching consequences for the occupational structure, including technological, economic, and population variables, were identified. A brief discussion of the factors that have short-term effects on the labor market was also presented. Familiarity with the current and future status of the labor market can be of great value to practitioners who hope to maximize their client's potential in the world of work.

Chapter Quiz

T F   **1.** The business decision to move a part or all of a company to another country is almost totally based on the wages that the company will have to pay its workers.

T F   **2.** It is possible for an occupation to be one of the fastest growing but still have relatively few job openings.

T F   **3.** American workers produce greater amounts of wealth than workers in other countries primarily because they are better trained for their jobs.

T F   **4.** Predictions about job growth get less precise as the timeline for the prediction lengthens.

T F   **5.** The first industry impacted by job decline resulting from technology was agriculture.

T F   **6.** The list of jobs that are declining clearly shows the impact of technology and "offshoring."

T F   **7.** Educators have long worried about the job market for dropouts and other undereducated workers. Based on our best current estimate there will be few job openings for this group, and thus their fears are well founded.

T F   **8.** A weak American dollar—that is, a dollar that is worth relatively less than foreign currency—is most likely to hurt U.S. exports and thus American jobs.

T F   **9.** Productivity is defined as the amount of wealth created by the average worker.

T F   **10.** The ethnic group of workers that is expected to increase the fastest in the next eight years is Asian Americans.

(1) F (2) T (3) F (4) T (5) T (6) T (7) F (8) T (9) T (10) F

References

AP. (2007). U.S. workers are world's most productive. Retrieved from http://www.msnbc.msn.com/id/20572828/

BLS. (2009a). The 30 occupations with the largest employment decrease, 2008–2018. Retrieved from http://www.bls.gov/new.release/ecopro.t08.htm

BLS. (2009b). The 30 occupations with the largest number of total job openings due to growth and replacements, 2008–2018. Retrieved from http://www.bls.gov/news.release/ecopro.t10.htm.

BLS. (2009c). The 30 occupations with the largest number of total job openings due to growth. Retrieved from http://www.bls.gov/new.release/ecopro.t10.htm

BLS. (2010a). Employment projections: 2008–2018 Summary. Retrieved from http://bls.gov/news.release/ecopro.nr0.htm

BLS. (2010b). International comparisons of hourly compensation: Cost of manufacturing , 2007. Retrieved from http://www.bls.gov/ilc/chartbook.htm#section3.

Center for Legal Immigration Studies. (n.d.). Retrieved from www.cis.org/topics/legalimmigration.html

U.S. Census Bureau. (2010). Trade in goods with China. Retrieved from http://www.census.gov/foreign-trade/balance/c5700.html#2009

WikiInvest. (2008). Auto Industry. Retrieved from. http://www.wikinvest.com/industry/Auto_Makers

Trends and Issues in Career Information, the Job Search, Career Development, and Career Development Programming

Things to Remember

- The predictions about the trends associated with career information, career assessment, and career counseling

- The issues associated with career information, career assessment, and career counseling

Predicting the future is difficult even under the best of circumstances. However, it is important to look ahead, consider what might occur, and prepare for the eventualities that seem most likely. Career counselors cannot become complacent if they are to serve their clients well. Technology will continue to drive much of the innovation in career development, but there will be changes in the way we think as theories change and as the labor market continues to shift. My goal is to summarize what I think will be the changes that are likely to occur so that you can, if you wish, be ahead of the curve as you deliver career development services. Because expected changes in the labor market have already been discussed, the focus here will be on career counseling, career information, and the manner in which career development programs are conceptualized and delivered.

This chapter attempts to identify the trends and issues that will affect career development theory, research, and practice in the next 20 to 25 years. Of course, predicting the future can be risky as well as rewarding. For example, Herr (1974), writing in the National Vocational

Guidance Association's decennial volume *Vocational Guidance and Human Development,* made the following predictions for the decade following the publication of the volume: (1) There will be increased specificity in the objectives of vocational guidance programs; (2) the counselor will increasingly act as an agent of change, and "he or she will proffer his (or her) skills indirectly rather than directly in behalf of those he (or she) serves" (p. 564); and (3) the emphasis of vocational guidance in the next decade will be on prevention rather than remediation. History has documented the accuracy of Herr's prediction that career development programs are designed to produce specific results such as the competencies spelled out in the 2003 American School Counselor Association (ASCA) model, and they are currently more likely to be evaluated on their ability to produce specific outcomes. However, the predicted shift in counselors' roles from working with individuals to functioning as environmental agents of change has never materialized.

We saw a rise in the number of preventive career development programs in the career education movement of the 1970s, but by 1981 when Ronald Reagan assumed the presidency, the back-to-basics educational movement had all but eliminated these programs in most of our country's schools. Preventive career development programs have remained in place, but in 1989, 1995, and 1999 only about 40 percent of U.S. adults were in their current positions because of planning (Brown & Minor, 1989, 1992; Hoyt & Lester, 1995; National Career Development Association, 1999), which suggests that large numbers of people are not being affected by any type of program. These same Gallup surveys suggest that 10 million to 12 million adults each year need assistance in finding jobs, again indicating that preventive programs are either not in place or are not working.

Ten years after Herr's (1974) projections, Gysbers (1984) took on a similar task, again writing for the National Vocational Guidance Association (NCDA). He made the following projections regarding career development theory and practice:

1. The meanings given to career and career development continue to evolve from simply new words for vocation (occupation) and vocational development (occupational development) to words that describe human careers in terms of life roles, life settings, and life events that develop over the life span.
2. Substantial changes have taken place and will continue to occur in the economic, occupational, industrial, and social environments and structure in which the human career develops and interacts and in which career guidance and counseling take place.
3. The number, diversity, and quality of career development programs, tools, and techniques will continue to increase in almost geometric progression.
4. The population served by career development programming and the settings where career development programs and services take place have increased and will continue to do so. (p. 619)

Gysbers's (1984) predictions are somewhat more general than those set forth by Herr (1974) and as such had a higher probability of being accurate when they were cast. However, it is still unclear whether the meaning of career development is actually going to broaden, as Gysbers (1984) suggested. Some, like McDaniels (1989), certainly seem to be pushing in that direction by defining *career* as something other than the occupations held over the life span. Others, like Holland (1997), seem to be more in favor of the traditional idea of career. However, economic, social, and industrial changes have been accelerated; the number and diversity of career development tools (although *not* the quality) have increased rapidly; and the populations and settings served by career development specialists certainly have increased since 1984.

Both Herr (1974) and Gysbers (1984) made relatively few predictions about the future of career development and, as has already been noted, took somewhat different approaches (general versus specific) to doing so. In 1990 Zunker made nearly two dozen projections, focusing primarily on the issues that will confront workers in the future. For example, he projected that the future would provide alternative work patterns, such as job sharing and telecommuting (working in the home on a computer), trends that are well documented as coming to fruition by McDaniels (1989). However, he also predicted that the job market of the future would make some dramatic shifts, a prediction that is clearly contradicted by the data presented earlier in this volume. Similarly, Zunkers's (1990) projection that workers would place less value on financial rewards does not seem to be well founded, probably because the "data" that he used seem to be drawn from armchair philosophy rather than empirical sources.

For the most part, Herr (1974), Gysbers (1984), and Zunker (1990) were on target with their projections. When they became quite specific in their projections or relied on "faulty" databases, predictions appeared to be less accurate.

The sixth edition of this book (Isaacson & Brown, 1997) contained 15 predictions about the future of career information, career counseling, and career development. With two exceptions, these predictions have been supported by the events that occurred between the sixth edition and the writing of this one. The most notable of these exceptions had to do with the prediction of a convergence in thinking and practice about providing counseling services to cultural minorities. The fact is that ideas about and recommendations for practices regarding career counseling for cultural minorities have diverged quite sharply since 1997, primarily because of the increasing popularity of postmodernism. This divergence has been so dramatic that the prediction has been dropped from the current edition. The second of our predictions not supported by events was a convergence in recommendations regarding career counseling for men and women. Differences in recommendations between career counseling for men and women have persisted because of the continuing need to address equity, role participation, and initial career choice issues when dealing with women (Melamed, 1995). Some of the predictions included in the earlier editions are retained and others discarded. A few new predictions are added as well.

TRENDS: CAREER INFORMATION

1. There will be a continuing effort to improve the delivery of occupational information. Throughout this book, numerous innovations regarding the delivery of occupational information have been illustrated. Events such as placing O*NET and the *Occupational Outlook Handbook* on the Internet are but two of these innovations. The development of CareerOneStop (www. careeronestop.org) is another important step in the improvement of occupational information at the national level, and there are parallel moves in many states.

Efforts to improve the quality and delivery of occupational information will continue and perhaps accelerate as the nation attempts to deal with high levels of unemployment and underemployment. The use of the Internet to improve the delivery of occupational information will certainly accelerate and as it does the use of print materials will decline.

2. There will be an increased sensitivity to, as well as increased efforts to meet, the occupational information needs of adults. Two national surveys (Hoyt & Lester, 1995; NCDA, 1999) suggested that large numbers of adults have never used any type of occupational information. The problem is most acute among those adults who failed to finish high school (40 percent reported using no source) and Hispanics (35 percent reported using no source), but even one-fifth of college graduates reported using no source of occupational information. When these data are paired with other information (e.g., only 41 percent of the employed respondents reported being in their current jobs because they followed a definite plan, and 27 percent believed they needed assistance finding occupational information), the problem of helping adults access and use career information seems acute. The current economic downturn and the human misery it has created will, at least in the short-term, prompt people to engage in information-based decision making.

3. The number of online sources of occupational information has literally exploded in the past five years. This trend seems likely to intensify to the point that these sources will almost totally replace print resources. Niles and Harris-Bowlsbey (2005) list several informational functions that can be filled by computers, including database searches; crosswalking, defined as linking two databases, such as occupational and educational information; simply delivering information; and linking sources of information to provide expanded, more comprehensive information. Print sources of information cannot match these capabilities.

4. Graduate school courses dealing with development career information will continue to decrease their emphasis on career information. A 20-year-old survey of counselor education programs (Sampson & Liberty, 1989) suggested that the textbooks used in the preparation of counselors in the area of career development increasingly emphasize career counseling and focus less on occupational information. This trend continues today. At the time when members of our society need more career information, training programs appear to be placing less emphasis on orienting counselors and psychologists to identifying, evaluating, and using information.

The reduction in time spent on career information is partially because of the recognition of the need to pay more attention to career counseling, which is a healthy sign. However, because most counselors and counseling psychologists are required to take only one course that deals with the various aspects of career development, career counseling coverage is replacing time spent on career information. The result of all this is that career counselors and career development specialists will increasingly have to rely on their own study and in-service training for their knowledge of career information.

5. Our basic understanding of how to select and use occupational information will continue to receive a low priority by researchers. Except for 45-year-old studies by Krumboltz and colleagues (e.g., Krumboltz & Schroeder, 1965; Krumboltz & Thoreson, 1964), few researchers have made attempts to identify factors that lead to the effective uses of occupational information, and with a few exceptions (e.g., Brown, 1990) the entire area has received little comment. Perhaps researchers assume that career development specialists understand how to select, evaluate, and use career information. Regardless of the reasons for omission, it is expected that career development specialists will continue to ignore the general topic of career information.

6. Career counselors and members of the general public will have increasing access to free career information through systems like O*NET and state systems such as Virginia Career View. Most of the databases in these systems are now available online, and their number will undoubtedly increase. The result of these and other developments is that occupational information is available in the homes of millions as well as in public agencies.

Issue: **Will career counselors rely on free online information issued by the gvernment at the expense of commercially produced materials?**

TRENDS: THE JOB HUNT

1. Information about job openings, salary, and job hunting tips will increasingly be made available online through the One-Stop Career Center Web sites functioning at the state level.

2. The complexity of the job search coupled with a dynamic labor market will increasingly require job hunters to seek assistance from career development experts. Job hunters are confronted with an amazing array of information and resources ranging from the traditional to newly developed online databases. On the surface new online database Web sites such as Monster.com will simplify the job search process, but as Simmons (2001) notes, job hunting requires much more than placing a résumé in a computer database. Keyword searches can help identify job vacancies as can Web sites that provide links to newspaper advertisements of job openings. Other Web sites can provide comparative salary information by geographic location. Links to databases such as O*NET can provide data about job requirements, whereas others such as the online version of the *Occupational Outlook Handbook* provide job descriptions and predictions about the future of the occupation. Simply put, workers will be forced to identify and assimilate more information about jobs than ever before. On the surface this would appear to make the job search simpler, but the prediction here is that the wealth of information will result in job hunters seeking help with interpreting the information available to them.

Issue: **Will online job hunts and other strategies such as virtual job interviews replace traditional search techniques for most jobs?**

TRENDS: CAREER ASSESSMENT

1. It seems likely that Internet-based career assessment will grow dramatically in the immediate future. What is more difficult to predict is the likely impact of the availability of free online assessment devices, beginning with the Interest Profilers that were integrated into the O*NET program this year. It seems likely that the other tools in the O*NET package will also be integrated into the system at some level. Accessing this system will allow agencies that provide career counseling and assessment services to reduce their assessment and information cost while using psychometrically sound instruments.

2. Postmodern theories are increasing in popularity and as they do the discussion of qualitative assessment in career counseling increases as well. Amundson and his colleagues (2009) discuss using the employment roadblock map as a way to visually represent the career problem, the use of metaphors, questioning and storytelling, and what they term structured assessment strategies, which are traditional inventories. It seems highly unlikely that these traditional strategies will be supplanted by qualitative assessment techniques. It seems far more likely that qualitative and traditional assessment techniques will be used together in the future, as has always been the case.

Issue: **Will the growing emphasis on empirically based strategies limit the use of qualitative assessment techniques that heretofore have been largely unsupported by research?**

TRENDS: CAREER COUNSELING

1. Career counseling will be increasingly recognized as a counseling specialty that requires expertise in both personal and career counseling as well as related assessment strategies. Crites (1981) was one of the early advocates of this position. Numerous books (e.g., Amundsen, Harris-Bowlsbey, & Niles, 2009; Anderson & Vandehey, 2006) and articles (e.g., Brown, 1995; Krumboltz, 1993; Subich, 1993) have taken a similar position by emphasizing the interrelationship of personal and career concerns and asserting that counselors and psychologists need to be prepared to deal with both.

2. Certification of career counselors will become an increasing concern among counselors and psychologists. To date, most psychological licensure laws provide licensees with a generic license to practice, and for the most part the psychology profession has not been concerned about the credentials of career counselors. However, the first licensing law passed for counselors (in Virginia) contained a provision for recognizing career counseling specialists. Although not much progress has been made toward realizing this prediction since it was first made in 2000, it still seems viable.

3. There will be a continued divergence of thinking about the career counseling practices for men and women. Most current career counseling books contain sections on the special career counseling needs of women (e.g., Andersen & Vandehey, 2006; Gysbers, Heppner, & Johnston, 2003). A few (e.g., Zunker, 2002) also contain chapters on the special needs of men, whereas others consider the topic of gender simultaneously (e.g., Brown & Brooks, 1991).

The biological fact that women bear children and men do not must be a consideration in career counseling. So must the socialization of gender roles and the impact this makes on career development and career choice. Continuing realities regarding initial career choice, role participation, and discrimination in the workplace must be addressed when counseling women faced with career issues.

4. Increasing attention will be given to the issues involved in counseling cultural minorities. One result of this focus will be the adoption of different strategies at each stage of the process when providing career counseling for minorities. For example, there is well-founded speculation that Native Americans are more likely to be visual than auditory learners (Okun, Fried, & Okun, 1999). This has profound implications for the presentation of occupational information and test interpretation. Leong's (1993) finding that some Asian Americans prefer a dependent decision-making style also has tremendous implications for providing counseling services to this group because much career development literature is predicated on the idea that clients prefer independent decision-making styles. Other factors that will require changes in career counseling practices for ethnic minorities are differences in time perspective, in the display of emotions, and in nonverbal and verbal styles (Okun et al., 1999).

As noted throughout this book and others, career counselors need to be sensitive to the values of cultural and ethnic minorities and sexual orientation (e.g., Andersen & Vandehey, 2006; Gelberg & Chojnacki, 1995), as well as other differentiating factors in the career counseling process. An attempt has been made to focus attention on factors such as communications and decision-making styles as well as other variables that will undoubtedly influence both the processes and outcomes of career counseling. As Betz (1993) suggested, information from the multicultural counseling literature should be incorporated into the career counseling literature. This includes the recommendations advanced by Arrendondo and colleagues (1996).

5. John Holland's theory (1997) will continue to dominate the assessment of interests and research on variables such as occupational satisfaction. However, the social cognitive theory of Lent, Brown, and Hackett (2002) and Gottfredson's (2002) developmental theory of circumscription and compromise are likely to receive increasing attention. Thus far the interest in Gottfredson's theory has been primarily of interest to researchers, and it seems unlikely to have a major impact on practice in the future (cf. Schultheiss' 2008 review). Conversely, as the authors of social cognitive theory have shown (Lent et al., 2002), there is an upsurge of interest by researchers in social cognitive theory, and this has translated into an increase in the use of the theory by practitioners. In their review of the 2008 career development research and practice literature, Patton and McIlveen (2009) identified seven research articles based on social cognitive career theory, four related to Holland's theory, and two related to Gottfredson's ideas. No other traditional theory stimulated more than one article, including Super's theory.

Super's (1990) developmental theory seems likely to receive less attention from practitioners and researchers alike because its segmental construction makes it hard to generate testable hypotheses and its complexity makes it difficult to translate into practice. Krumboltz's (Mitchell & Krumboltz, 1996) social learning theory may also receive less attention, perhaps because Lent and his colleagues (2002), were truer to the ideas advanced by Bandura's (1986), which is a popular learning theory and one that is easier to research. Lent and associates placed great emphasis of Bandura's self-efficacy construct and cognitions generally in their theory, whereas Krumboltz emphasized other variables such as self-observed generalizations which were learned primarily through classical and operant conditioning.

However, it iis worth noting that Krumboltz (Mitchell & Krumboltz, 1996) articulated an approach to career counseling based on his theory that is highly meritorious and should gain acceptance by practitioners. The future influence of the other theories of career development discussed in Chapters 2 and 3 is harder to forecast, although it seems likely that all of them will have some impact on both research and practice. The theory of work adjustment has been in the professional literature since the late 1960s, was fully articulated almost two decades ago (Dawis & Lofquist, 1984), and has still not drawn widespread support from practitioners. Perhaps it never will, even though it has much to offer.

Postmodern theories (Amundson et al., 2009; Bloch, 2005; Bright & Pryor, 2005; Young, Valach, & Collin, 2002) will increasingly gain attention. Numerous forces are driving this interest, not the least of which is widespread acceptance of postmodern philosophy. The multicultural movement and recommendations (e.g., Arrendondo et al., 1996) growing out of that movement support this trend as well.

6. Postmodern thought has already made a tremendous impact on the way many career counselors work with their clients. Books by Amundson and colleagues (2009) and articles by Neimeyer (1988, 1992), Savickas (1997), and Bloch (2005) provide clear guidelines for various aspects of career assessment and career counseling. More traditional research, such as the book by Gysbers and his colleagues (2003), also incorporate many postmodern ideas into their recommendations about practice. The result is that postmodern ideas will have a greater impact on the future, although it seems unlikely they will supplant traditional approaches altogether. Career development practice is still largely based on the modern philosophical base that holds that tests and inventories are useful tools, and some of the postmodernists, such as Amundson, recognize their value as well.

Issue: **Will the three-sessions-and-a-cloud-of-dust approach to career counseling (Crites, 1981) that has characterized much of career counseling give way in the future to a more holistic approach, as been suggested by Super and others for several decades?**

TRENDS: CAREER DEVELOPMENT PROGRAMMING

1. Career counseling and career development programming will continue to operate without a solid empirical basis. Herr and Cramer (1996) identified a number of areas within the career development domain that need empirical investigation. In many ways, it would be easier to identify the areas that do not warrant additional research: none. However, the career development literature abounds with support for many of the ideas presented throughout this book (e.g., Chope, 2008; Gottfredson & Johnston, 2009; Patton & McIlveen, 2009). However, we have not even begun to answer the classic question, What types of intervention are most useful with which types of clients? We have also not yet answered basic questions about the types of counselors or counseling that are most effective, nor have we begun to understand fully the interaction of human and computerized systems (Sampson, 1990). As Herr and Cramer (1996) suggest, much research still needs to be conducted.

2. Although career development programming will continue to be important, it will be secondary to the school reform movement that grips many of this country's public schools. The result is that comprehensive, district-wide career development programs such as those discussed in Chapter 12 will be difficult to implement. This is not to suggest that individual schools cannot have outstanding career development programs, or that comprehensive programs are impossible to develop.

ASCA's (2003, 2005) *National Model for School Counseling Programs* offers school counselors a rationale for the development of comprehensive career development programs that are integrated into the entire school counseling program. Authoritative books aimed at supporting the application of the ASCA model (e.g., Brown & Trusty, 2005) are rapidly adding to the material available to program builders. The result is that many school districts are already engaged in the implementation of this model, although the exact number is impossible to ascertain.

3. Career development programming internal to business and industry will decline as services are outsourced to consulting firms. Now more than ever businesses have adopted a "bottom-line" philosophy—that is, expenditures for programs such as career development must add to the profits of the organization if they are to be retained. The costs of outsourced services are easier to control, and their downsizing and elimination is less painful. Because it is difficult to establish the relationship between cost and income, the number of new programs is likely to be small and the number of existing program is likely to be reduced. The counterforce to the pressure to reduce or eliminate career services in business is likely to come from unions.

Issue: **Will the emphasis on career development programs grow or contract in response to the 2007–2010 recession?**

STUDENT LEARNING EXERCISE 18.1

Select any of the issues presented in this chapter and make a list of the arguments for and against the possible outcomes. For example, why might career development programs grow or contract between 2010 and 2018?

Summary

The future is difficult to assess, although the track record of authorities in the field has been respectable. The predictions in this chapter are based on my best judgment after making a careful review of the field. However, career counselors need to be constantly vigilant for shifts in thinking and practice, particularly those rooted in research. Unfortunately, we are many years away from a time when career development practice will be driven by research. In the absence of research, theory becomes even more important because it provides a rationale for systematic practice.

Chapter Quiz

T F **1.** Some postmodern career counselors seem unwilling to discard traditional assessment strategies, which is a contradiction to postmodern theory.

T F **2.** Perhaps the most easily identifiable trend in the general area of career development is increased reliance on the Internet.

T F **3.** According to the information presented in this book, the career development theory that will definitely increase in importance in actual practice is Super's theory.

T F **4.** The career development theory that is demonstrably impacting career development research is social cognitive career theory.

T F **5.** Most researchers who have made predictions about the future of career development have been largely on target.

T F **6.** The prediction that seemed the least likely to be on target when it was made 20 years ago that people would turn away from money as the major concern in career choice making to self-growth and satisfaction is in fact accurate based on current research.

T F **7.** Interest inventories grew out of the postmodern assessment tradition.

T F **8.** John Holland's theory, which has been highly influential up to the present, is in all likelihood in decline.

T F **9.** The major barrier to placing government-developed assessments online has been their failure to meet psychometric standards.

T F **10.** The author predicts that virtual strategies including interviews will replace face-to-face approaches.

(1) T (2) T (3) F (4) T (5) T (6) F (7) F (8) F (9) F (10) F

References

American School Counselor Association. (2003). *ASCA National Model for school counseling programs.* Alexandria, VA: Author.

American School Counselor Association. (2005). *ASCA National Model for school counseling Program* (Rev. ed.). Alexandria, VA: Author.

Amundson, N. E. (2003). *Active engagement: Enhancing the career counseling process* (2nd ed.). Richmond, BC: Ergon Communications.

Amundson, N. E., Harris-Bowlesbey, J., & Niles, S. G. (2009). *Essentials of Career Counseling: Processes and Techniques* (2nd ed.) Columbus, OH: Pearson.

Andersen, P., & Vandehey, M. (2006). *Career Counseling and Development in a Global Economy.* Boston: Houghton Mifflin

Arrendondo, P., Toporek, R., Brown, S. P., Jones, J., Locke, D., Sanchez, J., & Sadler, H. (1996). Operationalization of the multicultural counseling competencies. *Journal of Multicultural Counseling and Development, 24,* 42–78.

Bandura, A. (1977). *Social learning theory.* Englewood Cliffs, NJ: Prentice-Hall.

Bandura, A. (1986). *Social foundation of thought and action: A social–cognitive theory.* Englewood Cliffs, NJ: Prentice-Hall.

Betz, N. E. (1993). Toward the integration of multicultural and career psychology. *Career Development Quarterly, 42,* 53–55.

Bloch, D. P. (2005). Complexity, chaos, and nonlinear dynamics: A new perspective on career development theory. *Career Development Quarterly, 53,* 194–207.

Bright, J. E., & Pryor, R. G. L. (2005). The chaos theory of careers: A user's guide. *Career Development Quarterly, 53,* 291–305.

Brown, D. (1990). Summary, comparison, and critique of the major theories. In D. Brown, L. Brooks et al. (Eds.), *Career choice and development* (pp. 338–363). San Francisco: Jossey-Bass.

Brown, D. (1995). A values-based approach to facilitating career transitions. *Career Development Quarterly, 44,* 4–11.

Brown, D., & Brooks, L. (1991). *Career counseling techniques.* Boston: Allyn & Bacon.

Brown, D., & Brooks, L. (1996). Introduction to career development. In D. Brown, L. Brooks, et al. (Eds.), *Career choice and development* (3rd ed., pp. 1–11). San Francisco: Jossey-Bass.

Brown, D., & Minor, C. W. (1989). *Working in America.* Alexandria, VA: National Career Development Association.

Brown, D., & Minor, C. W. (1992). *Career needs in a diverse work force: Implications of NCDA Gallup survey.* Alexandria, VA: National Career Development Association.

Brown, D., & Trusty, J. (2005). *Designing and leading comprehensive school counseling programs.* Pacific Grove, CA: Brooks/Cole.

Chope, R. C. (2008). Practice and research in career counseling and development 2007. *Career Development Quarterly, 57,* 98–173.

Crites, J. O. (1981). *Career counseling: Models, methods, and materials.* New York: McGraw- Hill.

Dawis, R. V., & Lofquist, L. (1984). *A psychological theory of work adjustment.* Minneapolis: University of Minnesota Press.

Gelberg, S., & Chojnacki, J. T. (1995). Developmental transitions of gay/lesbian/bisexual affirmative, heterosexual counselors. *Career Development Quarterly, 43,* 267–273.

Gottfredson, G. D., & Johtsun, M. I. (2009). John Holland's contributions: A theory-ridden approach to career assistance. *Career Development Quarterly, 58,* 99–107.

Gottfredson, L. (2002). Circumscription and compromise: A revision. In D. Brown, L. Brooks, et al., *Career choice and development* (4th ed., pp. 85–148). San Francisco: Jossey-Bass.

Gysbers, N. C. (1984). Major trends in career development theory and practice. In N. C. Gysbers et al., (Eds.), *Designing careers: Counseling to enhance education, work, and leisure* (pp. 618–632). San Francisco: Jossey-Bass.

Gysbers, N. C., Heppner, M. J., & Johnston, J. A. (2003). *Career counseling: Process, issues, and techniques* (2nd ed.). Boston: Allyn & Bacon.

Herr, E. L. (1974). The decade in prospect: Some implications for vocational guidance. In E. L. Herr (Ed.), *Vocational guidance and human development* (pp. 551–574). Boston: Houghton Mifflin.

Herr, E. L., & Cramer, S. H. (1996). *Career guidance and counseling through the life span: Systematic approaches* (5th ed.). Glenview, IL: Scott, Foresman.

Holland, J. L. (1997). *Making vocational choices: A theory of vocational personalities and work environment* (3rd ed.). Englewood Cliffs, NJ: Prentice Hall.

Hoyt, K. B., & Lester, J. N. (1995). *Learning to work: The NCDA Gallup survey.* Alexandria, VA: National Career Development Association.

Isaacson, L. E., & Brown, D. (1997). *Career information, career counseling, and career development* (6th ed.). Boston: Allyn & Bacon.

Krumboltz, J. D. (1993). Integrating career and personal counseling. *Career Development Quarterly, 42,* 143–148.

Krumboltz, J. D., & Schroeder, D. (1965). Promoting career guidance through reinforcement and modeling. *Personnel and Guidance Journal, 44,* 19–26.

Krumboltz, J. D., & Thoreson, C. E. (1964). The effects of behavioral counseling on group and individual settings on information-seeking behavior. *Journal of Counseling Psychology, 11,* 323–333.

Lent, R. W., Brown, S. D., & Hackett, G. (2002). Career development from a social cognitive perspective. In D. Brown, L. Brooks, et al. (Eds.), *Career choice and development* (4th ed., pp. 225–311). San Francisco: Jossey-Bass.

Leong, F. T. L. (1993). The career counseling process for racial-ethnic minorities: The case of Asian Americans. The *Career Development Quarterly, 42,* 26–40.

McDaniels, C. (1989). *The changing workplace: Career counseling strategies for the 1990s and beyond.* San Francisco: Jossey-Bass.

Melamed, T. (1995). Career success: The moderating effects of gender. *Journal of Vocational Behavior, 47,* 295–314.

Mitchell, L. K., & Krumboltz, J. D. (1996). Social learning approach to career decision making: Krumboltz's theory. In D. Brown, L. Brooks, et al. (Eds.), *Career choice and development* (3rd ed., pp. 223–281). San Francisco: Jossey-Bass.

National Career Development Association. (1999). National survey of working America. Retrieved from www. ncda.org

Neimeyer, G. J. (1988). Cognitive integration and differentiation in vocational behavior. *Counseling Psychologist, 16,* 440–475.

Neimeyer, G. J. (1992). Personal constructs in career counseling and development. *Journal of Career Development, 18,* 163–174.

Niles, S. G., & Harris-Bowlsbey, J. (2005). *Career development interventions in the 21st century* (2nd ed). Columbus, OH: Merrill.

Okun, B. F., Fried, J., & Okun, M. L. (1999). *Understanding diversity.* Pacific Grove, CA: Brooks/Cole.

Patton, W., & McIlveen, P. (2009). Practice and research in career counseling and development—2008. The *Career Development Quarterly, 58,* 118–161.

Sampson, J. P., Jr. (1990). Computer-assisted testing and the goals of counseling psychology. *Counseling Psychologist, 18,* 227– 239.

Sampson, D. E., & Liberty, L. H. (1989). Textbooks used in counselor education programs. *Counselor Education and Supervision, 29,* 111–121.

Savickas, M. L. (1997). Constructivist career counseling: Models and methods. *Advances in Personal Construct Psychology, 4,*149–182.

Schultheiss, D. E. P. (2008). Current status and future agenda for the theory, research, and practice of childhood career development, *Career Development Quarterly, 57,* 7–24.

Simmons, J. (2001, December). Searching for work will now be a full-time job, experts say. *Counseling Today, 1,* 21–22.

Spokane, A. (1991). *Career interventions.* Englewood Cliffs, NJ: Prentice Hall.

Subich, L. M. (1993). How personal is career counseling? *Career Development Quarterly, 42,* 129–131.

Super, D. E. (1990). A life-span, life-space approach to career development. In D. Brown, L. Brooks, et al. (Eds.), *Career choice and development* (pp. 197–261). San Francisco: Jossey-Bass.

Young, R. A., Valach, L., & Collin, A. (2002). A contextualist explanation of career. In D. Brown et al., *Career choice and development* (4th ed., pp. 206–254). San Francisco: Jossey- Bass.

Zunker, V. G. (1990). *Career counseling: Applied concepts of life planning* (3rd ed.). Monterey, CA: Brooks/Cole.

Zunker, V. G. (2002). *Career counseling: Applied concepts of life planning* (6th ed.). Pacific Grove, CA: Brooks/Cole.

NAME INDEX

A

Aburdene, P., 18
Adelman, C., 274
Allyn, D. P., 303
Amatea, E. S., 285
Amundson, N. E., 71, 72, 97, 104, 106, 107
Anastasi, A., 164, 169, 170
Andersen, P., 143, 171
Arbona, C., 39, 109, 110
Argyropoulou, K, 33
Arnold, J., 34
Arrendondo, P., 85
Astin, H. S., 27, 28
Atkins, C. P., 240, 241
Azrin, N. H., 236, 238

B

Baker, H. E., 205
Baker, S. B., 280
Bandura, A., 38, 60, 62, 64, 151
Basso, K. H., 100, 102
Beck, A, 37
Belz, J. R., 294
Bench, M., 16, 315, 316, 317
Bendick, M., Jr., 135
Berry, J. W., 39
Betz, N. E., 15, 16, 27, 28, 63, 125, 151, 152, 378
Biller, E. F., 287
Bingham, R. P., 99
Bjorkquist, P. M., 305
Blan, F. W., 294
Blau, P. M., 26, 27, 28, 39
Blazini, A. P., 39
Bloch, D. P., 26, 28, 67, 68, 69, 71, 236
Blocher, D. H., 156
Blustein, D. L., 7, 8, 9, 13, 28, 29, 97, 128
Bordin, E. S., 26
Borgen, F., 63
Borgen, W. A., 104
Borman, G., 288
Borow, H., 27, 37, 39, 73, 74
Brammer, L. M., 252
Brantlinger, E., 350
Bremer, C. D., 121
Brenner, O. C., 39

Brewington, J. O., 235
Bright, J. E, 68, 69
Bright, J. E., 29
Brooks, L., 339, 345
Brott, P. E., 148, 149
Brown, D., 8, 16, 27, 28, 37, 40–41, 62, 63, 64, 66, 82, 85, 97, 99, 101, 102, 109, 113, 124, 125, 132, 134, 135–136, 144, 147, 150, 151, 152, 156, 162, 198, 213, 264, 265, 266, 272, 274, 278, 279, 282, 283, 284, 295, 301, 351, 353, 374, 376, 377, 378, 380
Brown, M., 39
Brown, S. P., 125
Brozeit, R. K., 346
Buescher, K. L., 301
Bullock, E. F., 65
Burck, H., 44, 132
Burns, R. W., 266
Butcher, E., 306
Butterfield, L. D., 252
Byars-Winston, A. M., 106

C

Cahill, M., 135
Cai, D., 102
Cameto, R., 287
Campbell, C. A., 258, 260, 282
Campbell, R. B., 199
Caporoso, R. A., 122, 237
Carey, J. C., 260, 350
Carter, R. T., 28, 37, 38, 39, 101, 111
Casas, J. M., 109, 110
Casserly, M., 39
Cataldi, E. F., 109, 110
Chan, K. S., 39
Chope, R. C., 160
Chung, Y. B., 128, 129
Cochran, L., 156
Collin, A., 27, 66, 68, 70
Colquhoun, H., 123
Conway, M. A., 287
Corning, A. F., 16
Crace, R. K., 104
Crites, J. D., 48
Crites, J. O., 145, 282
Crouse, J., 37

D

D'Andrea, M., 98
Dailey, M. J., 302
Davenport, D. W., 132
Dawis, R. V., 27, 28, 34, 36
Day, S. X., 34
de Shazer, S., 71, 72, 77
deBlois, C. S., 294
Deming, A. L., 131
Dewey, C. R., 150
Diamont, M, 120
Dilley, J. S., 74
Dolliver, R., 70
Dolliver, R. H., 150
Donnay, D. A., 152
Downing, N. E., 124
Doyle, J., 342
Duggan, M. H., 124
Duncan, O. D., 28
Dvorak, P., 251, 252

E

Eck, A., 235
Eden, D., 235
Egan, G., 100
Eisenstadt, S., 239
Elliot, E. S., 303
Elliot, J. E., 128
Elmore, R., 132
England, G. W., 36
Ettinger, J., 192, 194
Evans, N. J., 298

F

Farr, J. M., 236
Fassinger, R. E., 128
Feather, N. T., 39
Feller, R. W., 142, 144, 147, 167
Fiedler, C. R., 85, 107
Finnegan, R., 132
Firestone, W. A., 351
Fitzgerald, L. F., 15, 28, 125
Forrest, L., 305
Fouad, N. A., 37, 106, 171
Fretz, B. R., 133
Fukuyama, M. A., 110, 202
Fuqua, D. R., 166

G

Galassi, M. D., 160
Garis, J. W., 199, 202
Garrett, M. T., 100

Gassin, E. A., 288
Gault, F. M., 161
Ghiselli, E. E., 165
Gibson, D. M., 150
Gilmartin, D., 118
Gim-Chung, R. H., 38
Ginzberg, E., 257
Goldman, L., 145, 146, 147
Gonzalez, R. C., 7, 17, 18, 28
Goodson, W. D., 301
Goodstein, H., 346
Goodyear, R. K., 171
Gottfredson, G. D., 161
Gottfredson, L. S., 27, 28, 30, 33, 37, 40, 41, 49–52
Gould, R., 44
Grayson, T. E., 286
Greene, J. P., 111
Greenhaus, J. H., 39
Gregory, R. J., 146
Griff, N., 294
Grover, L., 287
Guidubaldi, J., 120
Gupta, S., 161
Gutteridge, T. G., 339, 342, 344, 345
Gysbers, N. C., 97, 106, 107, 123, 259

H

Haberstroh, S., 206
Hackett, G., 26, 27, 28, 39, 62, 63, 64
Hall, D. T., 330, 332, 345
Hall, J. P., 237
Haller, A. O.
Hammer, T., 133
Hansen, J. C., 160, 161
Hansen, K., 236
Hanson, W. E., 171
Harmon, L. W., 128
Harris-Bowlsbey, J., 199, 200
Hartman, B. W., 166
Hartung, P. G., 28
Harvill, R. L., 98
Healy, C. C., 145, 146, 293, 294
Helwig, A. A., 239, 240, 241
Heppner, M. J., 97, 123
Herr, E. L., 186, 282
Ho, D. F., 98, 99, 109
Ho, D. Y. F., 38, 39
Ho, M. K., 38, 39, 101
Hogan, R., 165
Holland, J. L., 27, 28, 30–34, 36, 76, 127, 144, 148, 152, 155, 157, 158, 160, 161, 162, 165, 169, 171, 183, 185, 264, 269, 278, 358

Holly, K. A., 307
Horner, R. H., 353
Hotchkiss, L., 27, 37, 39, 73, 74
Howard, A., 133
Hoyt, K. B., 232, 257, 292, 293, 294, 306, 314
Humes, C. W., 287

I

Ibrahim, F. A., 38
Imhoff, A. R., 37
Ivey, A. E., 98, 99, 101, 102, 107, 145
Ivey, M. B., 98

J

Jackson, C. W., 135
Jacobs, E. E., 98
Jacobs, S. J., 128
Janis, I. L., 75, 106
Jencks, C., 37
Jepsen, D. A., 74
Jessell, J., 283
Johnson, C. A., 296, 308
Johnson, D.C., 303
Johnson, M. K., 73, 74
Johnson, P., 346
Johnson, R. W., 160
Johnson, S., 272, 287
Johnston, J. A., 97, 123
Jones, G. B., 76
Jones, L., 76
Jones, L. K., 160, 161
Jones, M. L, 237
Jurgens, J. C., 124

K

Kahnweiler, J. B., 304
Kanchier, C., 132, 237
Kanzaki, G. A., 50
Kapes, J. T., 147, 199
Karunanayake, D., 287
Katz, M. R., 202
Keith-Speigel, P., 82
Kelly, F. D., 65
Kim, M., 102
Kiselica, M. S., 122
Kivlighan, K. M., 307
Kluckhorn, F. R., 37, 38, 101
Knapp, R. R., 156, 157
Knowdell, R. L., 150, 315, 316, 322, 332, 333, 338, 339, 345
Kobylarz, L., 258, 266, 282, 287
Koocher, G. P., 82

Kosciulek, J. F., 121
Kram, K. E., 342, 343
Kraus, L., 118
Krumboltz, B. L., 63, 64, 77
Krumboltz, J. D., 25, 26, 27, 60, 61, 62, 63, 64, 77

L

LaFromboise, T. D., 39
Laird, J., 109
Lam, C. S., 237
Lanning, W., 294
Larsen, L. M., 166
Lee, K. C., 38
Leibowitz, Z., 133, 333, 335, 338, 339, 344, 345
Lent, R. W., 62, 63, 64, 77, 303
Lenz, J. G., 27, 64, 65
Leong, F. T. L., 15, 28, 37, 38, 39, 54, 109, 144, 161, 162, 171, 294
Lerman, R. L., 222
Leung, S. A., 161
Levinson, D. J., 44, 133
Lilley, W., 248
Lim, L., 3
Lofquist, L. H., 26, 27, 34
London, M., 333
Lonner, W. J., 169, 171
Lucas, J. L., 152
Lunneborg, P. W., 27
Luzzo, D. A., 152, 284, 294
Luzzo, D. A.15

M

Ma, P. W. W., 106, 110
Mackelprang, R. W., 118
Magoon, T. M., 306
Mallinckrodt, B., 133
Malott, K. M., 150
Mann, L., 75, 106
Maples, M. R., 202
Maranelli, R. P., 112
Marin, G., 38
Marin, P. A., 199
Marin, V. M., 38
Marland, S. P., Jr., 257
Martin, P. Y., 343
Masson, R. L., 98
Mather, J., 121
Mau, W. C. L., 110
Mazel, M., 204
McDaniels, C., 14
McDivitt, P. J., 48
McGoldrick, M., 150

McWhirter, E. H., 7, 8, 9, 13, 97
McWhirter, J. J., 39
Mehrens, W. A., 169
Meichenbaum, M., 64
Melamed, T., 6, 37, 39, 123
Messing, J. K., 112
Miles, J. H., 126
Miller, M. J., 185
Mirabile, R. J., 344, 345
Mitchell, A. M., 60, 61, 63, 64, 77
Mitchell, L. K., 60
Mitchell, W. D., 74
Mohatt, G. V., 39
Monrad, M., 213
Moore, K. A., 126, 127, 128
Moravec, M., 345, 346
Morin, W. J., 251, 252
Morris, L. L., 266
Mortimer, J. J., 73, 74
Mueser, P., 37
Murphy, P., 44, 132
Murray, N., 236
Myers, I. B., 144, 162
Mylonas, K., 33

N

Naisbitt, J.
Neimeyer, G. J., 70, 71
Newman, J. L., 113
Niles, S., 199, 202
Niles, S. G., 306, 307
Noeth, R. J., 161

O

Okiishi, R. W., 150
Oliver, L., 170, 306
Osipow, S. H., 331, 332
Ostheimer, B., 39

P

Padula, M. A., 294
Paivandy, S., 65
Parsons, F., 25, 53, 143
Pask-McCartney, C., 287
Patton, M. Q., 351
Patton, W., 160
Pedersen, P. B., 28
Perosa, L. M., 132
Perosa, S. L., 132
Perry, J. C., 7, 8, 9, 13, 97
Perry, J. D., 120
Peterson, G. W., 26, 27, 28, 64, 65, 66, 67, 298, 299, 308

Peterson, N., 7, 17, 18, 145, 146, 147, 166, 169, 171
Petrie, T. A., 294
Phillips, S. D., 37
Pichette. E. F., 100
Pickering, J. W., 301, 304
Pietromonaco, J. G., 39
Platt, J. J., 235
Podmostko, M., 121
Poehnell, G., 104, 106
Pope, M., 128, 129
Portes, A., 8
Ports, M. H., 238, 246
Post-Kammer, P., 288
Posthuma, B. W., 306
Prediger, D. J., 82, 145, 146, 161
Prilleltensky, I., 7, 8, 98
Prince, J. P., 170, 172
Pryor, R. G., 29, 68, 69, 156
Pyle, K. R., 306, 307

Q

Quinn, M. T., 303

R

Reardon, R., 27, 64, 65, 66, 296–299, 308–309
Reed, C. A., 308
Reich, M. H., 343
Reskin, B. F., 73
Restle, F., 74
Rife, J. C., 235
Riggio, R. E., 240, 241
Robbins, S. B., 304
Robinson, N. K., 170
Rock, K. S., 39
Roe, A., 26, 27
Roessler, R. T., 287
Rokeach, M., 37, 38, 39, 101, 144, 152, 154, 155
Romero, J. H., 135
Roselle, B. E., 202
Rotberg, H. L., 152, 153
Rottinghaus, R. J., 160
Rounds, J., 34, 161
Rush, K. L., 124
Ryan, C. A., 39
Ryland, E. K., 241, 243

S

Salomone, P. R., 135
Salsgiver, R. O., 118
Sampson, J. P., 27, 64, 65, 66, 147, 166, 186, 198, 199, 205, 297–299, 301, 303, 306, 308, 345
Sandler, S. B., 185

Saunders, D., 65, 73
Savickas, M. L., 48, 67, 71, 109, 111, 303, 379
Schenck, S. J., 121
Schlossberg, N. K., 132, 133
Schmidt, S., 345, 346
Schnell, A., 195
Schultheiss, D. E. P., 378
Schutt, D. A., Jr., 192, 194, 195, 197
Schwiebert, V. L., 168
Sears, S., 14
Sharf, R. S., 36, 49, 63
Shartle, C. L., 14
Shin, H., 102
Sidiropoulou-Dimakakou, D., 33
Silliker, S. A., 238
Simek-Morgan, L., 98
Simmons, J., 377
Skinner, M. E., 121
Slaney, R. B., 161
Smart, D. W., 39
Smart, J. F., 39
Snyder, R., 133
Soh, S., 162, 171
Spokane, A. R., 282, 305, 306
Srebalus, D. J., 82, 144, 301
Stark, S., 132
Stephens, D. B., 241
Stephens, W. R., 10
Stern, L., 136
Stiglitz, J. 2, 5
Stoddard, S., 118
Stone, G. L., 306
Strodtbeck, F. L., 37, 38, 101
Strohmer, D. C., 113
Subich, L. M., 235, 377
Sue, D. W., 28, 38, 101, 102, 109
Sundberg, N. D., 169
Super, D. E., 12, 13, 14, 16, 26, 27, 28, 37, 42–49, 132, 143, 144, 155, 257, 379
Susskind, J., 52
Swaney, K., 34

T

Tang, M., 162
Taylor, K. M., 152, 156
Taylor, S., 237
Thomas, K. R., 133
Thomason, T. C., 100
Thompson, M. N., 237
Thorgren, J. M., 148
Tieg, S., 52

Timmons, J., 121
Tinsley, H. E. A., 171, 172
Tittle, C. K., 169
Toffler, A., 18
Tomlinson, E., 186
Trimble, J. E., 39
Trusty, J., 85, 265, 266, 272, 274, 278, 282
Tversky, A., 74
Tyler, L. E., 150

U

Unruh, W. R., 132

V

Vaitenas, R., 134
Valach, L., 27, 66, 68, 70
VanHoose, W. H., 82
Vondracek, F. W., 166
Vroom, V. H., 75

W

Walker, M., 120
Ward, C. M., 99
Waters, L. E., 126, 127, 128
Wegman, L., 236
Weinrach, S. G., 145
Westerfeld, J., 132
Westwood, M., 104
Whiston, S. C., 260
Whitcomb, S. B., 236
Whitfield, E. A., 142, 144, 147
Whitney, D. R., 144
Wholeben, B. E., 163
Wiener, Y., 134
Wilbur, C. S., 332
Wilkes, S. B., 294
Williamson, E. G., 147
Willis, C. G., 163
Wowk, R., 335, 345
Wright, G., 74

Y

Yates, C. J., 239
Yeh, C. J., 106, 110
Young, R. A., 26, 27, 53, 67, 68, 70, 148, 285, 379

Z

Zunker, V. G., 120, 238, 375, 378
Zytowski, D. G., 132, 152, 160, 169

SUBJECT INDEX

A

AARP. *See* American Association of Retired Persons (AARP)
Ability Profiler, O*NET, 164
Absolute constraints, 74
Academies, 217
Accreditation of colleges and universities, 231
Acculturation, 39
ACES. *See* Association of Counselor Education and Supervision (ACES)
Achievement Pattern Profiler (APP), 107
Achievement profiling, 104
Actions, 61
Activity, 38
Adolescents, occupational and educational information for, 179
Adults
  competencies and indicators, 296, 297
  occupational and educational information for, 179
Adults, occupational and educational information for, 179
Advertising of private practice, 321–323
Advising, 302–303
Advocacy
  for clients in need, 85
  in VBMCC, 107–108
AFQT. *See* Armed Forces Qualification Test (AFQT) score
African Americans, 109
Age Discrimination in Employment Act, 108, 134
Agencies, 288–289
Allocentrism, 38
American Airlines, 332
American Association of Retired Persons (AARP), 135, 136
American Counseling Association (ACA), 81
  Code of Ethics, 82–85
American Indians, 110–111
The American Occupational Structure, 73
American Psychological Association (APA), 15, 81
American School Counselor Association (ASCA), 10, 15
Americans with Disabilities Act, 119, 279
APP. *See* Achievement Pattern Profiler (APP)
Apprenticeship
  getting information on, 189
  programs, 220–222
Aptitudes, 143
Armed Forces Qualification Test (AFQT) score, 205

Armed Services Vocational Aptitude Battery (ASVAB), 164
  Career Exploration Program, 205
Army Alpha, 11
Artistic environment, 32
Artistic individuals, 31
ASCA National Model: A Framework for School Counseling Programs, 258
ASCA National Model, career development program, within framework of, 256–289
Ashland Interest Assessment (AIA), 159
Asian Americans, 110
Assessment
  individual student planning (ISP), 277–278
  needs. *See* Needs assessment, career development program
  qualitative, 148–151
  quantitative, 146–147, 151–168
  selecting devices for, 168–171
  technical qualities in selecting devices for, 168–169
  trends in, 377
Association of Counselor Education and Supervision (ACES), 15, 195
Association of Training and Development (ASTD), 17
Associative learning experiences, 61
ASVAB. *See* Armed Services Vocational Aptitude Battery (ASVAB)
Asynchronous chat rooms, 206
ATM. *See* Automatic teller machines (ATM)
AT&T, 332
Automatic teller machines (ATM), 18

B

Balance sheet, 75, 76
BAT. *See* Bureau of Apprenticeship and Training (BAT)
BDI, 333
Behavioral objectives, 266, 267–268
Behavioral rehearsal intervention, 107
Bias
  cultural, 169–171
  gender, 169–171
  language, 170–171
  norming, 170
Biculturalism, 38
Bienculturation, 38
Boston Civic Service House, 10
Boston Guidance Bureau, 11

Breadwinners' Institute and the Vocation Bureau, 10
Brief interventions, 301
Bureau of Apprenticeship and Training (BAT), 220
The Butterfly Effect, 68

C

CACREP. *See* Council for the Accreditation of Counseling
    and Related Programs (CACREP)
CAI. *See* Career Assessment Inventory (CAI)
California Department of Corrections and Rehabilitation,
    131
California Lawrence Livermore National Laboratory
    program, 338
Campbell Interest and Skill Survey (CISS), 159
Card sorts, 149–150
Career, defined, 14
Career, impact of, on occupational attainment and
    earnings, 73
Career aspirations, 50
Career assessment, trends in, 377
Career Assessment Inventory (CAI), 160
Career assessment workshops, 339
Career Beliefs Inventory, 166
Career choice, 14
    variables influencing, 37–39
Career classes, in middle schools, 285
Career coaching, 16, 315–317
Career conferences, 187
Career counseling, 305–307
    defined, 97–98
    for displaced workers, 125
    for former military personnel, 130–131
    for GLBT clients, 129
    for individuals with disabilities, 120–122
    for individuals with mental illness, 122
    legal issues and, 86
    in postsecondary educational institutions, 305–307
    suggestions, 306–307
    trends in, 377–379
    for women in workforce, 123–124
Career counseling competencies and performance
    indicators
    career development theory, 87
    coaching, consultation, and performance
        improvement, 89
    diverse populations, 89–90
    ethical/legal issues, 90
    individual and group counseling skills, 87–88
    individual/group assessment, 88
    information/resources, 88
    program management and implementation, 89

research/evaluation, 90–91
supervision, 90
technology, 91
Career counselors
    in private practice, 313–328
    billing, 327
    budgeting, 324–327
    developing testing file, 327
    establishing career information center, 328
    establishing private practice, 317–329
    fees, 325–326
    guidelines for consumers, 314–317
    location of office, 319
    marketing service, 321–323
    qualifications for, 314
    types of services, 318–319
Career days, 186–187
Career Decision–Making (CDM) System, 157–158
Career Decision–Making Self-Efficacy Scale, 152
Career Decision Scale (CDS), 165
Career development
    ASCA model and, 258–264
    defined, 15
    history of, 9–13
    language of, 13–16
    need for services in, 13
    in postsecondary educational institutions,
        292–309
    standards for, 258
*Career Development and Vocational Behavior of Ethnic
    Minorities,* 109
Career Development Facilitators (CDF), 92
Career Development Inventory (CDI), 48
Career development program, in business organizations,
    330–346
    benefits, 345–346
    designing, 338–344
    early steps, 334–335
    history of, 332–333
    HRD and, 344
    implementation, 344–345
    initiating, 334–338
    needs assessment, 335–338
    rationale for, 333–334
    trends in, 379–380
Career development program, within framework of ASCA
    National Model, 256–289
    administrative support for, 264
    budgeting, 271
    designing, 269–271
    implementation of, 271–274

needs assessment, 265–266
process of, 264–271
Career Development Quarterly, 14, 17, 160
Career education, 10, 15–16, 257–258
Career education programs, 16
Career exploration, 48
Career exploration centers (CEC)
    basic criteria for locating and designing, 194–195
    criteria for collecting material, 196–197
    establishing, 193–195
    initiating collection, 197
    renovating, 195
    technological competencies, 195–197
Career Exploration Program, ASVAB, 205
Career fairs, 188
Career guidance, 15, 16
Career information, 15, 16
    trends in, 375–376
Career information–processing model (CIP), 64–66
Career intervention, 15–16
Career issues, identification of, 103–106
Career Key, 76
CareerLine, 305
Career maturity, 45
Career Maturity Inventory (CMI), 48
Career Occupational Preference System (COPS), 157
Career-O-Gram, 148–149
Career orientation (COT), 48
Career Orientations Placement and Evaluation Survey (COPES), 156
CareerPath, 239
Career pattern, 44
Career planning, 48
Career program activities, 301–308
    advising, 302–303
    career counseling, 305–307
    career courses, 303
    consultation, 305
    information dispensation, 305
    internships, 305
    major fairs, 303
    peer program, 307–308
    self-directed activities, 304
    Web sites, 301–302
    workshops and seminars, 304
Career resource centers (CRC), 192, 296. *See also* Career exploration centers (CEC)
Career theories
    assumptions underpining, 29–30
    chaos, 67–68
    contextualist, 66–67
    of decision making, 74–76
    developmental, 41–52
    dual labor market, 73
    Gottredson's theory of circumscription and compromise, 49–52
    Holland's theory of vocational choice, 30–34
    learning, 60–66
    life span, life space theory, 42–49
    purpose and evaluation of, 25–29
    social cognitive, 62–64
    status attainment, 73
    theory of work adjustment (TWA), 34–37
    trait-and-factor, 30–37
    values-based, 37–41
Career Thoughts Inventory (CTI), 65, 166, 308
CDF. *See* Career Development Facilitators (CDF)
CDI. *See* Career Development Inventory (CDI)
CD-ROM technology, 184, 185
CDS. *See* Career Decision Scale (CDS)
Celerity, 35
CETA, Comprehensive Employment and Training Act (CETA)
Chaos theories, 67–68
Chat rooms
    asynchronous, 206
    synchronous, 206
Children
    materials for, 188
    occupational and educational information for, 178–179
Choosing a Vocation, 11
Choosing Your Vocation, 25
Chronically poor, 126
Circumscription and compromise, Gottfredson's theory of, 49–52
Cisco Systems, academy, 217
CISS. *See* Campbell Interest and Skill Survey (CISS)
Citicorp, 332
Civic Service House, in Boston, 10
C-LECT. *See* Computer-Linked Exploration of Careers and Training (C-LECT)
Clients
    GLBT, 129
    in need, advocacy for, 85
    right of, to choose, 83
    with special needs, 117–136
CMI. *See* Career Maturity Inventory (CMI)
Collateral, 38
Colleges and universities, 227–232
    accreditation, 231
    admissions requirements, 227–229
    continuing education, 231–232

Colleges and universities (*Continued*)
  factors to consider in choosing a, 230
  financial aid, 229
  gaining admission to, 230–231
Community colleges, 226–227
Community psychology, 8
Community resources, 288–289
Compensation system, 344
Competence, 82–83
Comprehensive Employment and Training Act (CETA), 218
Comprehensive K-12 career development programs,
  designing and implementing, within framework of
  ASCA National Model, 256–289
Computer-assisted career guidance systems (CACGS), 184
  benefits from, 198–199
  effectiveness of, 199
  present status of, 204–205
Computerized Heuristic Occupational Information and
  Career Exploration System (CHOICES), 204
Computerized Vocational Information System (CVIS), 10
Computer-Linked Exploration of Careers and Training
  (C-LECT), 204
Conflict model, 75
Congruence, 36
Constructivist theories, 27
Constructivist theory, 148–151
Consultation, 305
Conventional environment, 33
Conventional people, 31
COPES. *See* Career Orientations Placement and Evaluation
  Survey (COPES)
COPS. *See* Career Occupational Preference System
  (COPS)
Correspondence, 36
COT. *See* Career orientation (COT)
Council for the Accreditation of Counseling and Related
  Programs (CACREP), 231
CRC. *See* Career resource centers (CRC)
Crisis career counseling, 103
Crowley Independent School District of Crowley, Texas, 217
CTI. *See* Career Thoughts Inventory (CTI)
Cultural bias, in selecting assessment devices, 169–171
Cultural generalizations, 98
Cultural group membership, 39
Culturally appropriate goals, establishment of, 106–107
Culture, internalized, 39
Currency exchange market, value of dollar in, 366

D

DAT. *See* Differential Aptitude Test (DAT)
Debt, 366

Decision making
  facilitating, 103
  theories of, 74–76
Delayed entrants, 117
Department of Labor Employment and Training Agency
  (DOLETA), 183, 192
Descriptive designs, of program evaluation, 353
Descriptive models, 74
Designs, program evaluation, 351–353
  descriptive, 353
  experimental, 352–353
  pre-experimental, 351–352
  quasi-experimental, 352–353
Developmental theories, 41–52
Diagnostic inventories, 165–167
  support for, 166–167
Dictionary of Holland Occupational Codes, 33
Dictionary of Occupational Titles (DOT), 10, 180
Differential Aptitude Test (DAT), 163
Differential prediction, 170
Direct contact, 186
Direct solicitation of services, 323
Disadvantaged people, career development programs
  for, 126–127
Discouraged workers, 13
Displaced workers, 124–125
  career counseling for, 125
Distributive philosophy, 7
Diversified cooperative education, 215
DOLETA. *See* Department of Labor Employment and
  Training Agency (DOLETA)
Do-no-harm principle, 82
DOT. *See Dictionary of Occupational Titles (DOT)*
Dropout prevention groups, 284
Dual labor market theory, 73

E

Economically disadvantaged, 125–128
  career counseling for, 127–128
Economic Classification Policy Committee (ECPC), 4
Economic factors, as labor market trend, 366
Education
  career, 10, 15–16, 257–258
  continuing, 231–232
  general, 213
  information on, 189–190
  vocational, 214–215
Educational and Career Exploration System (ECES), 13
Educational institutions, 189
Educational Testing Service, 202
Education for All Handicapped Children Act, 119

EEOC. *See* Equal Employment Opportunity Commission (EEOC)

Elementary school, program planning tips for, 282–283

Elimination by aspects approach, 74–75

E-mailed questionnaires, for surveys, 354

Employability skills, 235–237

    developing, 239–245

Employment agencies

    private, 247–248

    public, 246–247

Employment Management Association (EMA), 10

Employment networks (EN), 122

Empowerment model, 7

EN. *See* Employment networks (EN)

Enabling option, 133

Enculturation, 38–39, 98

Endurance, 36

Enterprising environment, 33

Enterprising people, 31

Environment

    artistic, 32

    conventional, 33

    enterprising, 33

    investigative, 32

    realistic, 32

    social, 32–33

    work, 31–33

Environmental conditions and events, 60

Equal Employment Opportunity Commission (EEOC), 124

Equal Opportunity Act, 219

Ethical Standards for Internet Online Counseling, 82

Ethnic identity development, 98

Ethnic minorities, 108–111

Ethnography, 356

Eurocentric values, 28, 37

Evaluation and accountability, planning and implementing, 280–286

Ex-offenders, 131–132

    career counseling for, 131–132

Expectancies, 75

Expectancy model, 75

Experiential deficits, 121

Experimental designs, of program evaluation, 352–353

Expressed interests, 143

F

FAFSA, Free Application for Federal Student Aid (FAFSA)

Family Educational Rights and Privacy Act (FERPA), 86

Family Financial Statement (FFS), 229

FastWEB, 229

FERPA. *See* Family Educational Rights and Privacy Act (FERPA)

FFS. *See* Family Financial Statement (FFS)

Field trips, 282

Financial aid, 229

Financial Aid Form, 229

Finding Your Interests (FYI), 205

Fitzgerald Act, 220

Focus groups, 356–357

Ford Motor Company, 331, 339

Free Application for Federal Student Aid (FAFSA), 229

Free market system, 4

FYI. *See* Finding Your Interests (FYI)

G

G20, 5

Games, 185

GATB. *See* General Aptitude Test Battery (GATB)

Gay, lesbian, bisexual, and transgender (GLBT), 128–129

    career counseling for, 129

GCDF. *See* Global Career Development Facilitator (GCDF)

Gender, 40

    impact of, on occupational attainment and earnings, 73

Gender bias in selecting assessment devices, 169–171

General Aptitude Test Battery (GATB), 36

General cultural dimension, 98

General education, 213

General Electric, 332

General related instruction, 216

Genetic endowment and special abilities, 60

Genograms, 150–151

Georgia, University of, 227

GlaxoSmithKline (GSK), 331–332, 339

GLBT. *See* Gay, lesbian, bisexual, and transgender (GLBT)

Global Career Development Facilitator (GCDF), 92

Global economy as labor market trend, 365

Globalization

    benefits of, 5

    factors leading to, 4

Goal-oriented change, 7

Goals 2000: Educate America Act, 214

Goal-setting process, 39, 106

Goal statements, 266

Goodwill Industries, 116

Government agencies, 368

Government Printing Office, U.S., 182

Government size, as labor market trend, 368

Group counseling skills, 87–88

Guidance curriculum, planning and implementing, 272–274

Guide for Occupational Information, 180
*Guidelines for the Preparation and Evaluation of Career
    Information Literature,* 197

H

Harrington–O'Shea Career Decision-Making
    System, 34, 160
Harvard College, 227
Headhunting, 248
Health science academies, 217
Hidden job market, 239
High school, program planning tips for, 286–288
High school students
    preparation for work and, 214–217
    targeting, with special needs, 286–288
Hispanic Americans, 109–110
Holland code, 31, 183
Homework assignments, 107, 206
How to Counsel Students, 11
How to Plan and Develop a Career Center, 328
Human disasters, 368
Human nature, 38
Human resource development (HRD), 335
    career development program and, 344

I

IBCES. *See* Internet-based career exploration systems
    (IBCES)
IBM, 13
    career development program, 345–346
IHispano, 239
Illegal workers, 367
Immigration, and labor market, 366–367
Indexing, 357
Individual career counseling, 306, 339
Individualized career plan (ICP), 274, 275
Individualized case-managed activities
    internships, 305
Individualized education programs, 108, 214, 278
Individual student planning (ISP), 274–278
    assessment, 277–278
Individuals with disabilities, 118–122
    career counseling for, 120–122
Individuals with Disabilities Education Act (IDEA), 108,
    236, 260
Individuals with Disabilities Education Improvement Act,
    8, 214
Industrial psychologists, 330
Information
    career, 16, 375–376
    dispensation, 305

educational, 189–190
    labor market, 179–180
    occupational, 178–190
    source of, 180–184
        on change and structure, 371
    world-of-work, 48
Information System for Vocational
    Decisions (ISVD), 13
Insourcing, 4
Instrumental learning experiences, 61
Intake interviews, 306
Interest Finder (IF), 170, 205
Interest inventories, 156–162
    support for, 160–162
Interest Profiler, O*NET, 160
Interest rates, 366, 369
Interests, 143–144
Internalized culture, 39
International Monetary Fund (IMF), 5
Internet, 4
    career counseling and assessment on, 205–207
Internet-based career exploration systems
    (IBCES), 106–107
Internships, 305
Interviews, 239–241
    with experts, 185
Inventoried interests, 143
Investigative environment, 32
Investigative people, 30–31

J

Jewish Vocational Service, 119
Job, defined, 14
Job Accommodation Network, 108
Job Corps, 219
Job hunt, 239
    trends in, 376–377
Job market, investigating, 238–239
Job placement services, 245–252
    online centers, 250–251
    outplacement, 251–252
    private employment agencies, 247–248
    public employment services, 246–247
    secondary and postsecondary school
        placement, 248–250
    for workers with disabilities, 121
Job posting, 344
Jobs, 14
    executing searches, 237–245
Job-search process, 234–235

Job seekers
   with criminal records, 237
   with disabilities, 237
Job shadowing, 186
Job Training Partnership Act (JTPA), 128, 218–219
Job tryouts, 120
Journal of Career Development, 17
Journal of Counseling Psychology, 17
Journal of Vocational Behavior, 14
JTPA. *See* Job Training Partnership Act (JTPA)
Judeo-Protestant position role, 18
Judeo-Protestant work ethic, 18
Junior colleges, 226–227
Junior high school students, CACGS for, 200

K

Keyword searches, 207, 377
Knowledge of preferred occupations, 48
Kuder Occupational Interest Survey (KOIS), 160
   Form DD, 158
Kuder Task Self-Efficacy Scale, 152

L

Labor cost differences, 3
Labor market information, 179–180
Labor market trends, 362–371
   economic factors, 366
   government size, 368
   long-term, 364–368
   occupational world through, 369–371
   population factors, 366–368
   short-term, 368–369
   sources of information on change and structure, 371
Laissez-faire liberalism, 17
Language bias, 170–171
Learning experiences, 60–61
Learning theories, 60–66
Liability suits, 86
Life-career rainbow, 46, 48
Lifeline, 104–106
Life satisfactions, 47
Life span, life space theory, 42–49
Life stages, 43–44
Lifestyle planning, 284
Life Values Inventory (LVI), 155–156
Lineal–collateral social relationship, 102
Lineal social values, 110
Livermore Labs program, 338–339, 345
Local service clubs, 288
Logical positivism, 98, 148, 157, 351, 357
Lost-outs, 217
LVI. *See* Life Values Inventory (LVI)

M

Mailed surveys, 354
Major fairs, 303
Manifest interests, 143
Manpower Defense Training Act, 218
Manpower Development and Training Act (MDTA), 218
Marketing campaign, 322
Master Career Counselor (MCC), 91, 92
Master Career Development Professional (MCDP), 91–92
MBTI. *See* Myers–Briggs Type Indicator (MBTI)
MCC. *See* Master Career Counselor (MCC)
McCarron–Dial System (MDS), 167
MCDP. *See* Master Career Development Professional (MCDP)
MDS. *See* McCarron–Dial System (MDS)
MDTA. *See* Manpower Development and Training Act (MDTA)
Mental illness, career counseling for individuals with, 122
Middle school, program planning tips for, 283–285
Midlife job changers, 132–133
Military Career Guide, 184
Military Education Online, 184
Military personnel, former, 129–131
   career counseling for, 130–131
Military training, 222, 223–224
Minnesota Ability Test Battery, 36
Minnesota Importance Questionnaire, 36
Minnesota Satisfaction Questionnaire, 36
Minnesota Satisfactoriness Scales, 36
Minority groups, 108–111
Minority students, 287
Monoculturalism, 38
Monocultural theories, 28
Multicultural Assessment Standards, 82
Multienculturation, 38
Multiple aptitude test batteries, 163–165
   support for, 164–165
Multipotentialed students, 287–288
Multipurpose tests and inventories, 167–168
   support for, 168
Myers–Briggs Type Indicator (MBTI), 162
Myers-Briggs Type Inventory, 207
My Vocational Situation, 165

N

NASA, 332
NASP. *See* National Association of School Psychologists (NASP)
National Alliance of Business, 333
National Apprenticeship Program, 220
National Association of Guidance Supervisors, 11

National Association of School Psychologists (NASP), 15

National Bank of Washington, 346

National Board of Certified Counselors (NBCC), 12, 81, 91, 206

National Career Counseling and Guidance Guidelines, 282

National Career Development Association (NCDA), 12, 17, 81, 91, 97, 197, 315

The National Career Development Guidelines: Local Handbook for Postsecondary Institutions, 296

National Center on Secondary Education and Transition, 287

National Certified Career Counselor Certification, 12, 91

National debt, 366

National Defense Education Act, 12

National Educational Assessment Program, 212

National Education Association, 10

National Occupational Information Coordinating Committee (NOICC), 12, 258

National Skills Standards Act, 214

National Society for the Promotion of Industrial Education (NSPIE), 9, 10

The National Standards for School Counseling Programs, 258

National Vocational Guidance Association (NVGA), 9, 10, 11, 17, 373–374

National Vocational Guidance Bulletin, 11

Natural disasters, 368

NBCC. *See* National Board of Certified Counselors (NBCC)

NCDA Guidelines for the Use of the Internet for the Provision of Information and Planning Services, 82

Needs assessment, career development program
in business organizations, 335–338
within framework of ASCA National Model, 265–266

Negative characteristics, 74

Networking, 323

Neutral characteristics, 74

No Child Left Behind, 146, 215, 260

NOICC. *See* National Occupational Information Coordinating Committee (NOICC)

Non-ad, 322, 323

Non-Sexist Vocational Card Sort (NSVCS), 160

Norming (standardization) bias, 170

North American Free Trade Agreement (NAFTA), 4

North American Industry Classification System (NAICS), 4

North Carolina, University of (Chapel Hill), 227

North Carolina Career Resource Network, 236

North Central Association of Colleges and Secondary Schools, 231

NSVCS. *See* Non-Sexist Vocational Card Sort (NSVCS)

O

OASIS. *See* Occupational Aptitude Survey and Interest Schedule (OASIS)

Objective assessment devices, 151

Occu-Find, 205

Occupation, defined, 14

Occupational Aptitude Survey and Interest Schedule (OASIS), 167

Occupational change (world through 2018), 369–371
future projections, 369–370
implications of, 370–371
information sources, 371

Occupational Choice: An Approach to a General Theory, 11

Occupational choice, values-based theory of, 27, 37–41
propositions of, 40–41
status and use of, 41

Occupational classification system
Holland's, 33
NAFTA, 4
O*NET. *See* Occupational Information Network (O*NET)
U.S. Department of Labor and, 12

Occupational information, 178–190
types of, 184–190

Occupational Information Network (O*NET), 10, 180–183
Ability Profiler, 164
definitions, 181–182
Interest Profiler, 160
using, 182–183

Occupational Outlook Handbook (OOH), 16, 119, 180, 183–184, 271, 328, 375, 377

Occupational Self-Efficacy Scale, 152

Occupations: The Vocational Guidance Journal, 11

Offshoring, 3. *See also* Outsourcing

Older workers, 134–136
career counseling for, 135–136

One-Stop Career Centers, 192–193

O*NET Interest Profiler, 160

Online job placement centers, 250–251

On-the-job training, 218

OOH. *See* *Occupational Outlook Handbook* (OOH)

Organizational development and change theory, 8

Organizational psychologists, 330

Outplacement services, 251–252

Outsourcing, 3, 4

P

Pace, 36

Paraprofessionals, 20

Parents, involving, 285–286

A Parents' Guide to Career Development, 286
Pattern identification, 104
Peer counseling programs, 307–308
Pencom, 238–239
Performance appraisal, 344
Personal dimension, 98
Personality, 144
Personality inventories, 162–163
  support for, 163
Personal-psychological characteristics, 143–145
  aptitudes, 143
  interests, 143–144
  personality, 144
  values, 144–145
Person-nature relationship, 38
PESCO 2001/Online, 168
Pfizer, 332
Placement services. *See* Job placement services
Planning committee, forming, 265
Planning for Life, 274
Population factor as Labor market trends, 366–368
Position, defined, 14
Positive characteristics, 74
Post–high school opportunity programs, 189–190
Postmodern career counseling, 69–71
Postmodern theories, 66–72
Postsecondary educational institutions, career development
    in, 292–309
  activities, 301–308
    advising, 302–303
    career counseling, 305–307
    career courses, 303
    consultation, 305
    information dispensation, 305
    internships, 305
    major fairs, 303
    peer program, 307–308
    self-directed activities, 304
    Web sites, 301–302
    workshops and seminars, 304
  career resource center, 296
  developing program, 297–301
  institutions, 295–296
  program evaluation, 308–309
  students, 294–295
Poverty, 9, 85
Practice Pointer, 317
Preconditions, establishing, in program development,
    264–265
Predictive validity, 160, 161, 164–165
Pre-experimental designs, of program evaluation, 351–352

Prescriptive models, 74
Preventive career development programs, 374
Principles for Diversity Competent Group Workers, 111
Print materials, 188
Private employment agencies, 247–248
Private Industry Council, 218
Private job placement agencies, 288
Program evaluation, 308–309, 349–350
  designs, 351–353
    descriptive, 353
    experimental, 352–353
    pre-experimental, 351–352
    quasi-experimental, 352–353
  objectives, 350–351
  qualitative approaches to, 356–358
Program planning tips
  for elementary school, 282–283
  for high schools, 286–288
  for middle school, 283–285
Protestant movement, 17
Protestant work ethic, 17–18
Proven practices, 24
Psychodynamic theory, 27
Psychology
  community, 8
  industrial, 330
  organizational, 330
  vocational, 330
The Psychology of Occupations, 12
Psychometric instruments, 10
Psychosociological model of career choice and work
    behavior, 28
Public employment services, 246–247
Public job placement agencies, 288
Pushouts, 217

Q

QSC. *See* QuantumShift! Coaching (QSC)
Qualitative approaches to program evaluation, 356–358
Qualitative assessment, 148–151
Quantitative assessment, 146–147, 151–168
  support for, 151
QuantumShift! Coaching (QSC), 316
Quasi-experimental designs, of program evaluation,
    352–353

R

Race, impact of, on occupational attainment and
    earnings, 73
Racial/ethnic identity development, 98
Reading-Free Vocational Interest Inventory, revised
    (RFVII), 159

Realistic environment, 32
Realistic people, 30
RecruitAbility, 239
Recursive thinking, 7
Rehabilitation
  defined, 119
  services in, 119, 120
  vocational, 119
Rehabilitation, Comprehensive Services, and
    Developmental Disabilities Amendments of
    1978, 119
Rehabilitation Act Amendments of 1998, 122
Rehabilitation Act of 1973, 119
Rehabilitation counselors, 85, 108, 119, 279
Relativism, 7
Researched-based interventions, 15
Reserve Officer Training Corps (ROTC) program, 222
Responsibilities, honoring your, 83–84
Responsive services, planning and implementing,
    278–280
Résumés, 241–245
  chronological format, 243
  functional format, 242
  sample plain text, 244
Retirees, occupational and educational information for, 179
RFVII. *See* Reading-Free Vocational Interest Inventory,
    revised (RFVII)
Rhythm, 36
Riley's Guide, 239
Role play, 149
Rust Belt, 124

S

SAT. *See* Scholastic Aptitude Test (SAT)
SCANS. *See* Secretary's Commission on Achieving
    Necessary Skills (SCANS)
SCCT. *See* Social cognitive career theory (SCCT)
Scholastic Aptitude Test (SAT), 146, 170, 228
School-based placement activities, 249
School-to-Work Opportunities Act (STWOA), 214,
    219, 258
School to work (STW) activities, 214
Seasonal variations, impact on labor market, 368–369
Secondary and postsecondary school placement services,
    248–250
Second-order questions, 71, 72
Secretary's Commission on Achieving Necessary Skills
    (SCANS), 19
Self-concept, 43, 44, 46, 47
Self-control, 38
Self-directed activities, 304

Self-Directed Search (SDS-R), 157
Self-efficacy, 40, 60, 63
  career decision–making, 202
  measurements, 151–152
    support for, 152
Self-esteem
  development of, 18
  unemployed, economically deprived people, 126
Self-observation generalization, 61
Seminars, 304
SES. *See* Socioeconomic status (SES)
SESA. *See* State employment security agency (SESA)
SFBCC. *See* Solution-focused brief career counseling
    (SFBCC)
Sheltered workshops, 237
SIGI, 202
SIGI PLUS, 13, 202, 203, 204
SII. *See* Strong Interest Inventory Assessment Tool (SII)
SIMCITY, 185
Sixteen P. F. Personal Career Development Profile
    (16PFQ), 163
Skills Confidence Inventory, 152
Skills inventories/promotability forecasts, 344
Smith–Hughes act, 10
Social cognitive career theory (SCCT), 62–64
  social learning, 60–62
  socioeconomic, 73–74
  status attainment, 73
Social Darwinism, 17
Social environment, 32–33
Social justice, advocacy for, 5–7
Social learning theory, 60–62
Social people, 31
Social-psychological processes, 73
Social relationships, 38
Social Security Administration (SSA), 122
Socioeconomic status (SES), 29, 37, 73
Socioeconomic theories, 73–74
SOICC. *See* State Occupational Information Coordinating
    Committee (SOICC)
SOLER approach in counseling, 100
Solution-focused brief career counseling (SFBCC), 71–72
Special groups, theories for, 27–28
SSA. *See* Social Security Administration (SSA)
Standards for the Ethical Practice of
    Web-counseling, 82
State employment security agency (SESA), 246–247
State Occupational Information Coordinating Committee
    (SOICC), 184
Status attainment theory, 73
STOWA. *See* School-to-Work Opportunities Act (STWOA)

Strong Interest Inventory Assessment Tool (SII), 158, 160–161
Student Personnel Association for Teacher Education, 11
Students, postsecondary educational institutions, 294–295
Students with disabilities, 286–287
STW. *See* School to work (STW) activities
Super's Work Values Inventory—Revised SWI-R, 155
Supported work programs, 237
Survey research process, 354–355
Synchronous chat, 206

T

Task approach skills, 61
Technical qualities in selecting devices for assessment, 168–169
Technical schools, 224, 226
Technical–terminal programs, 226–227
Technology as labor market trend, 364
Telephone surveys, 354
Terminal programs, 226–227
Tested interests, 143
Testing and assessment in career development, 142–173.
    See also Assessment
  background, 145–146
  clinical, quantitative, and qualitative approaches to assessment, 146–168
  interpreting results, 171–173
  personal-psychological characteristics, 143–145
  selecting devices, 168–171
Texas Workforce: Youth Information and Services, 236
Theory of work adjustment (TWA), 34–37
  status and use of, 36–37
Ticket to Work and Work Incentives Improvement Act, 108
Ticket to Work Program, 122
Time orientation, 38
Today's Military, 184
Trade agreements, 4
Trade schools, 224, 226
Traditional model, 7
Training, 344
Training time, 213–214
Trait-and-factor theory, 29, 30–37
Transitional activities, 236
Transition plan, 278
Tripartite model, 25
TWA. *See* Theory of work adjustment (TWA)
Two-year transfer programs, 226

U

UAW-Ford agreement, 331, 339
Underemployed individual, 126
Unemployed individual, 126

Unemployment rate
  in China, 3
  in European Union (EU), 3
  in Japan, 3
  for minorities, 6
  in Russia, 3
  in United States, 2
United Auto Workers (UAW), 331, 339
Universal dimension, 98
Universities. *See* Colleges and universities
University of Georgia, 227
University of North Carolina at Chapel Hill, 227
Up-to-date portfolio, 278
U.S. Employment Service (USES), 246
U.S. News, 231
USES. *See* U.S. Employment Service (USES)

V

Vacophy, 11
Valence, 75
  negative, 154
  positive, 154
Values, 37–39, 144–145
  development of, 38–39
Values-based multicultural career counseling
  advocacy in, 107–108
  application to group career counseling, 111–112
  assessing cultural variables in, 99–100
  communication style in, 100–103
  establishment of culturally appropriate goals, 106–107
  facilitating decision-making process in, 103
  identification of career issues, 103–106
  implementation and evaluation of interventions, 107
Values-based theory of occupational choice, 27, 37–41
  propositions of, 40–41
  status and use of, 41
VCS. *See* Vocational Card Sort (VCS)
Veterans Affairs, U.S. Department of, 119, 131
Virtual career exploration centers, 193
Visual images, 107
Vocation, 14
Vocational Card Sort (VCS), 161
Vocational choice, Holland's theory of, 26, 30–34
Vocational education, 214–215
Vocational Education Act, 12
Vocational Education Research Center, 12
Vocational guidance, history of, 9–13
Vocational Guidance and Human Development, 374
Vocational Preference Inventory, 31
Vocational preferences and competencies, 43
Vocational preparation, 213, 214–215

Vocational psychologists, 330
Vocational rehabilitation, 119
Vocational schools, 224, 226
Vocation Bureau, 10
Voluntary changers, 133–134

W

Wages, 3–4
Wall Street Journal, 251
Web-counseling, 205–207
  establishing Web sites as, 207
Web sites, 301–302
Wide Range Interest and Occupation Test, 34
Women in workforce, 123
  career counseling for, 123–124
Work
  future of, 18–20
  meaning of, 17–20
  reasons for, 17–18
Work adjustment, theory of. *See* Theory of work
    adjustment (TWA)
Work environment, 31–33

Work experience programs, 187–188, 215–217
Work hazards, 32
Work Importance Locator (WIL), 155
Work Importance Profiler, 155
Working poor, 9
Work samples, 120
Work satisfactions, 47
Workshops, 304
  sheltered, 237
Work values, 37, 38, 40
Work values inventories, 152–156
  support for, 156
World Bank, 5
World-of-work information (WWI), 48
World-of-Work Map, 201, 202
World Report, 231
WWI. *See* World-of-work information (WWI)

Y

Yahoo! Directory, 189